owned mostly
by Jones family
for 100 yrs
DOW
JONES
(owns Wall Street Journal)

Industrials
track Fortune 50
How we're doing
100 stocks

Standard
&
Poors(?)
tracks
500 stocks

Moody

Morningstar
rates
mutual
funds

(Frank)
RUSSELL
2000
TACOMA
TRACK
small
companies
most
high
tech

What's difference
What does

MW00332563

M&ONEY BANKING

David H. Friedman

AMERICAN
BANKERS
ASSOCIATION™

This publication is designed to provide accurate and authoritative information in regard to the subject matter covered. It is sold with the understanding that the publisher is not engaged in rendering legal, accounting, or other professional service. If legal advice or other expert assistance is required, the services of a competent professional person should be sought.

From a Declaration of Principles jointly adopted by a Committee of the American Bar Association and a Committee of Publishers and Associations.

Library of Congress Cataloging-in-Publication Data
Friedman, David H., 1942-
    Money & banking / David H. Friedman.—3rd ed.
        p. cm.
    Includes index.
    ISBN 0-89982-316-5:
        1. Banks and banking.   2. Money.   3. Money and banking.
    I. Title
    HG1601.F75   1993
    332. 1--dc20   93-10975
                                                                              CIP

© 1985, 1989, 1993, by the American Bankers Association
Third Edition, 1993
1995 Printing
All rights reserved. No part of this publication may be reproduced, stored in a retrieval system, or transmitted in any form or by any means—electronic, mechanical, photo-copying, recording, or otherwise—without prior written permission from the American Bankers Association.

Printed in the United States of America

Contents

List of Exhibits

CHAPTER 6

CHAPTER 7

CHAPTER 8

About the Author

David H. Friedman is an economist, author, and banking instructor who has held several major positions at the Federal Reserve Bank of New York.

Mr. Friedman designed the Essentials of Banking seminar for the American Institute of Banking and the General Banking Curriculum for the Professional Development Program of the American Bankers Association. He is the author of the ABA textbook *Deposit Operations*, the ABA's "A Preface To Banking" and "The Bank Book," four booklets on economics and banking subjects, and several segments of *The Money Encyclopedia*.

Mr. Friedman has been on the faculty of the American Institute of Banking in New York since 1974. He is an assistant professor of economics at Brooklyn College, where he has been a member of the college faculty since 1965. Mr. Friedman has conducted seminars and training programs on banking operations, the U.S. payments mechanism, and a broad range of economics and management subjects for the American Institute of Banking, the Bank Administration Institute, and ABA's Business of Banking School.

Mr. Friedman has a BA and an MA in economics from Brooklyn College and has completed course work and examinations for a PhD in economics at the New School for Social Research. He lives in East Brunswick, New Jersey. His wife Alice, daughter Lynne, and son Paul, provided the collective support and encouragement that were essential in the writing of *Money and Banking*.

Preface

This third edition of *Money and Banking* updates the text written in 1988. The revisions reflect the dramatic changes that have occurred in the bank regulatory, operational and competitive environment in the past five years. Some restructuring of the text was also undertaken. In particular, the chapters on the Federal Reserve and the monetary and fiscal policy tools have been introduced earlier in the text, and the more advanced material in most chapters is now presented as a series of extended studies at the end of the text. These can either be used or not, depending on the level of the class and the time constraints facing each class.

I hope this new edition will prove to be a more flexible teaching tool for American Institute of Banking (AIB) instructors, as well as an effective learning vehicle for both introductory-level and advanced AIB students. The primary focus of the text—to present basic concepts and principles relating to money and banking—remains unchanged. *Money and Banking* serves as an introductory text for new bankers and as a refresher text for experienced bankers who are preparing for advanced course work. To meet the needs of both these groups, each chapter builds on the preceding chapters to establish an increasingly more comprehensive and integrated view of the role of money and banking in the U.S. and world economies.

As an aid to instructors and students alike, each chapter of *Money and Banking* begins with a list of learning objectives and an overview of the chapter content, and ends with a summary of key concepts, a series of questions suitable for students' self-test or classroom discussion, and student exercises (where appropriate) designed to enhance the learning experience. Answers to these discussion questions and the exercises can be found in the appendix.

Bankers' needs were kept in mind in establishing the following objectives:

- ❐ to expose bankers to the key concepts, theories, processes, and interrelationships that link money and banking to the workings of the U.S. economy

- ❐ to generate insights into the role of money in the economy and the roles of banks as creators of money and as participants in the nation's payments mechanism

- ❐ to provide an understanding of how banks work, the regulatory environment in which banks operate, and the way in which banks serve as a conduit for the implementation of monetary policy

- ❐ to acquaint bankers with the major banking issues and trends likely to affect banks in the 1990s

- ❐ to examine the structure, functions, and powers of the Federal Reserve and the impact that Federal Reserve monetary policy tools and regulations have on banks and the economy

□   to acquaint bankers with the debate between monetarists and Keynesians over the role of money and interest rates in the economy and how monetary policy control should be implemented

□   to examine the relationship of banks to the international financial system, the U.S. balance of payments, and the workings of the foreign exchange markets

The text is divided into 15 chapters, which are grouped in 6 parts. Part 1 provides a broad overview of money and the U.S. economy. The evolution of money, the basic functions of money, and the principal payment devices used today are examined. The text then discusses the key role of savings and lending in the economy and examines the various measures of U.S. economic activity. The role of commercial banks is compared with that of other financial intermediaries, and the many types of deposit accounts in existence today are examined. The creation of money through the lending process is then thoroughly explained in order to illustrate why and how commercial banks serve as a major conduit for implementing monetary policy. Part 2 focuses on the Federal Reserve and its role as the nation's central bank. The functions, history, and unique quasi-governmental structure of the Fed are examined, as are its principal monetary policy tools—the discount rate, reserve requirements, and open-market operations. The fiscal policy tools of taxation and government spending, which are not in the purview of the Federal Reserve, are also discussed.

Part 3 presents a broad overview of the business of banking. Bank operations and the key role of banks in the nation's payments mechanism are discussed. The text then looks at banks as business firms—examining the key sources of bank earnings, types of bank loans, and banks' funds management strategies. Bank regulation is then introduced, with a look at the principal bank regulatory agencies, as well as the major banking laws and regulations that have helped shape the current competitive environment. The final chapter in this section focuses on current trends and issues in banking, including the debate over what bank-related businesses banks should be allowed to engage in.

Part 4 focuses on the Federal Reserve's strategies for implementing its monetary policy objectives. The key tenets of monetarist and Keynesian theory also are presented, and we see how these opposing theoretical underpinnings affect policymakers' approaches to monetary policy. The author then examines the nation's policy goals of full employment, price stability, and economic growth—and the trade-off between inflation and unemployment that confronts economic policymakers. Factors affecting U.S. productivity also are examined.

Part 5 shifts the focus to the world of international banking, with an emphasis on the role banks play in facilitating world trade and payments through foreign exchange markets. Balance-of-payments measures and the U.S. trade deficit are examined, as is the special role of the U.S. dollar in the international financial system. In addition, U.S. policies toward foreign banks operating in the United States are compared with the treatment afforded U.S. banks abroad.

Part 6 presents more in-depth discussions of many of the topics presented in the preceding chapters—including, in some cases, a broader historical perspective. This material is included for the benefit of students wishing to delve more deeply into these subjects.

I would like to express my gratitude to the members of my review committee. They provided invaluable help in revising the text and in critically reviewing initial drafts. These highly capable and dedicated people are:

Earl F. Smith
Department Head for Financial and Credit Management
Central College, Houston Community College System
Houston, Texas

Wendy Kirkpatrick
Director of Microcomputer Applications
Washington State Community College
Marietta, Ohio

I would also like to give special recognition to the innovative contributions of Lisa Underwood, project manager of this third edition of *Money and Banking*.

David H. Friedman

PART I Money and the U.S. Economy

1

Money

Objectives

After successfully completing this chapter, you will be able to

- ☐ list the basic functions of money,
- ☐ trace the three-stage evolution of money,
- ☐ summarize how the value of money has been determined from the past to the present, and
- ☐ describe the nature and importance of the types of money and payment devices used in the United States today.

Introduction

In ancient Egypt, money was sacred: only mystical items issued by pharaohs and blessed by the gods served as money. Modern money is commercial rather than sacred, and mystical only in the article of faith that has always supported money's value—our willingness to accept money in exchange for goods and services.

Money is an accepted means of making and receiving payments, a common frame of reference for determining value or comparing worth, and an efficient method of storing purchasing power and accumulating wealth.

In this opening chapter, we explore the concept of money and its functions, the evolution of money, changes in the way the value of modern money is determined, and what constitutes money in the United States today.

To expand your understanding of money, you are encouraged to read Extended Study 1, "The Money Supply," which explores how the nation's supply of money is measured and controlled.

The Functions of Money   (3) Basic functions

Economists commonly define money in terms of its three basic functions. Its importance lies in what it does, not in what it is made of or what it looks like. Clearly, one basic function of money is to serve as a *medium of exchange*, but money has two other important functions: to serve as a *unit of account* and to serve as a *store of value*.

A Medium of Exchange

Throughout the ages, people have used countless items as mediums of exchange. The ancient Greeks and Romans, for example, used longhorn cattle as money. In fact, the Latin word *pecus*, meaning cattle, is the root of *pecunia*, or money, from which our word *pecuniary* is derived. If people are willing to accept an item in exchange for goods, services, or settlement of debt—whether it be the brass rings used as money by the pharaohs of ancient Egypt or the shark's-tooth money used by the people of Micronesia early in this century—that item serves as money.

A nation's money consists of those items generally accepted in exchange for goods and services or in settlement of debt. In the simplest sense, then, money is nothing more than a nation's generally accepted medium of exchange.

A Unit of Account

Any item generally accepted as a nation's medium of exchange also will serve as that nation's unit of account. In this capacity, money serves as a standard for measuring the relative value, or worth, of goods and services.

In the United States, the dollar sets a standard of value: it acts as a unit of account. As a consumer, you know that a $500 television set is twice as expensive as a $250 suit. If your after-tax income is $2,000 per month, you know that buying the television set will cost the equivalent of one week of labor.

Money also defines the value of items in a company's balance sheet. When a loan officer examines the inventories, fixed assets, and raw materials listed in the balance sheet of a company that has applied for a loan, the officer is examining a set of values based on a single unit of account—the dollar.

A Store of Value

The third function of money is to serve as a store of value—a means to hold and accumulate purchasing power for future use. In its function as a store of value, money allows us to buy goods and services without having to exchange other goods and services. This characteristic distinguishes a money economy from a barter economy.

One drawback of a barter economy (one in which trading goods and services is the medium of exchange) is the lack of assurance that any given item in your immediate possession will be accepted in trade for a different item that you might want from someone else. The need to preserve the quality and physical condition of goods held in storage for future exchange is another drawback of a barter economy. A cow, for example, may sicken and die, leaving its owner with nothing to barter. In contrast, dollars can be efficiently stored and accumulated.

Money is best understood as a medium of exchange that also serves as a standard unit of account and as a store of value. Not every item selected as a medium of exchange functions well as a standard and as a store of value. In the seventeenth century, settlers in Virginia used tobacco leaves as money. In some ways, tobacco was a practical choice as a medium of exchange: it was the key crop upon which the colonial economy was based, and the settlers lacked sufficient supplies of any other acceptable money. However, because tobacco leaves vary greatly in size, texture, and shape, they were ill-suited as a standard of value. No uniform price could be established for like goods and services because the money itself was not uniform, and making exact change was a physical impossibility. Tobacco leaves also proved to be a poor store of value. The accumulation of purchasing power was both costly and risky, given the large amount of space needed for storage and the vulnerability of stored crops to damage caused by changes in the weather. Ultimately, tobacco leaves were abandoned as a medium of exchange because they failed to accommodate all three functions of money.

The Evolution of Money

From ancient times to the present, many diverse items have served as money for the peoples of the world. Some, such as cattle, furs, bark, cloth, and tea, have been useful commodities in themselves; some, such as the paper money used in fifteenth-century Europe, have been exchanged as representations of value; and some, such as the currency issued periodically in seventh-century China and the paper money that constitutes our modern national currencies, have had the backing of state powers. The use of these various types of money—called *commodity money*, *representative money*, and *fiat money*—traces the evolution of money from earliest times to the present.

Commodity Money   *usually not uniform*

Romans Salt

The world's earliest monies were mediums of exchange that also were useful commodities. The inherent value of the commodity itself supported its use as an exchange medium for goods and services. The ancient Romans, for example, used salt as money because of its desirability as a food additive. In fact, salt has held universal appeal as a valued medium of exchange. In parts of Africa, salt bricks were used as money from the fourteenth century to the 1920s.

Left, wampum, a native American money, fashioned into a belt. Below, salt-brick money used by the people of Ethiopia from the fourteenth century to the 1920s.

Photos courtesy of the Smithsonian Institution, National Numismatic Collection.

While ancient Romans were exchanging bricks of salt, the Chinese were purchasing goods and services with gold—the world's oldest commodity money. The scarcity and luster of gold and the mystical properties attributed to it made this commodity money universally accepted throughout the ancient world.

Commodity monies are acceptable to people who share little except an awareness of the intrinsic worth of the commodity. Unfortunately, most commodity monies lack the physical characteristics necessary to ensure their performance as uniform standards of account and good stores of value. Even gold lacks the easy divisibility and portability necessary for a truly efficient and practical exchange medium.

Although gold coins still circulate as a medium of exchange in a few countries, gold today functions primarily as a store of value. Commodity monies still play an important role, however, in countries where recurring economic and political upheaval have eroded confidence in government-issued paper money and bank deposits.

Two-Tier Gold System

Although gold bullion (gold in the form of ingots) is held today by many governments of the world as a store of internationally accepted value, virtually all use of gold as a medium of exchange between governments ended between 1968 and 1972. This was the result of a successful effort by the United States to wean the major industrial nations away from using gold as a basis for determining the relative values of national monies (foreign exchange rates). During this period, the industrial nations agreed to a two-tier gold system under which supply and demand would determine the market price of gold (about $340 an ounce in mid-1992), while the United States would fix the government-to-government exchange price for gold (set at $42.22 an ounce in 1972). The major industrial powers also agreed not to buy or sell gold in the private market. As a result of these agreements, the gold reserves held by governments have become frozen assets: few governments are willing to pay other governments in gold—since gold is exchangeable at $42.22 an ounce—whereas the actual value of gold is about eight times that in the world's private markets.

Representative Money

The impracticality of using commodity money for widespread commercial transactions first became apparent in Europe in the fifteenth century. As trade and economic activity began to expand, the need for more efficient money became pressing.

European tradesmen and merchants began to deposit their precious-metal money with goldsmiths, who were the earliest bankers. The goldsmiths, with gold inventories of their own, had the vault space and security necessary to safeguard the money. The goldsmiths gave receipts for these precious-metal deposits, and tradesmen and merchants began exchanging the receipts, which was a more practical, rapid, and safe method of payment than exchanging the precious metal itself. These receipts, the precursors of modern currency, were representative money; they represented claims on items of value held at a central depository. Since the holder of representative money could redeem the receipt at the depository for commodity money or bullion, people were willing to accept the receipt as money. Therefore, this representative money functioned as an effective medium of exchange.

Fiat Money

today's

Fiat money represents the third major stage in the evolution of money. It began to take hold in sixteenth- and seventeenth-century Europe with the emergence of strong nation-states and central governments. Fiat money is money by decree—a medium of exchange mandated by a government and backed by the law and power of the state. Virtually all the coin and currency used today is fiat money issued by the governments and central banks of the nations of the world. With rare exceptions, modern coinage is minted with metal that has a commodity value by weight less than the face value stamped on the coin. Modern paper currency can no longer be exchanged or redeemed for commodity money or precious-metal bullion. Thus, both coin and currency function as money by government decree. The ease of divisibility, the portability, and the relative difficulty of counterfeiting modern-day coin and currency enable them to function effectively for the myriad small, personal and commercial transactions that take place daily in the marketplaces of the world.

It would be wrong to conclude, however, that our willingness to accept fiat money is rooted in law or in the power of the state. No body of law or power of state can guarantee or force acceptance of a medium of exchange—in any form—unless it assures that the exchange medium will be a good standard and store of value.

Twentieth-century monetary history is replete with episodes of citizens repudiating their governments' fiat money because of its diminishing purchasing power. The economic and financial problems of Germany in the 1920s and of Hungary and China in the late 1940s resulted in severe inflation because the governments of those countries simply issued more money in an attempt to remedy the situation. As a result, their fiat money became virtually without value.

Large firms drew the weekly payroll from the Reichsbank in Berlin (1923).

Photo courtesy of AP/Wide World.

Thus, modern economies need no longer search for items to serve as effective mediums of exchange, but rather must be concerned with the ability of governments to maintain the purchasing power of the world's monies.

German note for 500 million marks, circa 1919-1923.

Photo courtesy of the Library of Congress.

The Value of Money

The value of modern money is based on what it can buy in the marketplace—that is, its purchasing power. The value of one U.S. dollar is the same whether that dollar takes the form of a metal coin, a currency note, or a bookkeeping entry in a bank account. This was not always the case. For much of America's early history the intrinsic worth of money was a paramount measure of its value.

Today, money's purchasing power relates directly to the prices of the goods and services on which that money is spent. As prices rise, the purchasing power of a given amount of money declines. As prices fall, the purchasing power of this money increases. From 1990 to 1991, the prices for U.S. goods and services increased by 3 percent, resulting in a small reduction in the dollar's purchasing power. However, the dollar's value declined by about 3.5 percent each year from the early 1980s to the early 1990s because prices rose during the 1980s (and the purchasing power of the dollar fell) by nearly 40 percent. In 1992 Americans had to pay nearly $1.40 for goods and services that cost $1 in 1982. Thus, the purchasing power of a dollar in 1992 was about 60 percent of what it was in 1982.

Government efforts to regulate money in a modern economy are an attempt to maintain and enhance the purchasing power of money. This involves controlling the quantity of money in the economy as a means of stabilizing prices. When there is too much money in an economy, the prices of goods and services generally rise. This is because consumers, businesses, and governments with excess money all compete for available goods and services. This competition drives up prices and, in turn, reduces money's purchasing power, generating the phenomenon known as inflation.

In essence, then, the value of money is inversely related to its availability. The greater the quantity of money in circulation, the smaller the purchasing power of each unit of money. The smaller the quantity of money in circulation, the greater the purchasing power of each monetary unit.

In the eighteenth century and the early decades of the nineteenth century, gold and silver coins were used as the predominant form of money. Governments were generally unable to issue more of this money than the amount of precious metal that they held in their treasuries, that they could dig out of the ground, or that they could obtain in exchange for goods sold to other nations. Not faced with similar restrictions on paper currency, however, governments and banks could (and did) overissue paper currency, thereby rapidly increasing the supply of money and reducing the value of each currency note. During periods when there was an overissuance of paper currency and bank-created money, the ensuing inflationary increase in the prices of all goods and services eroded the value of money and weakened the acceptability of paper currency in many countries. Today, with checkbook money used as the predominant money in most countries, governments attempt to control the quantity of money, and thus its value, through the monetary policy powers of their central banks.

Gold Standards and Bimetallic Standards

During the nineteenth century, many industrial nations, including the United States, attempted to regulate the value of their national money by operating first under a gold standard and later under a bimetallic (gold and silver) standard.

Under a gold standard, a nation defined the value of its money not in terms of its purchasing power but in terms of a fixed weight of gold. The United States, for example, allowed its paper money to be converted into gold at a predetermined rate of exchange. A gold standard worked well as long as gold supplies kept pace with national production and income. In the late 1800s, however, gold production slowed with the end of the California and Australia gold rushes, and prices of goods and services fell throughout the world.

In many countries, declining prices and wages caused by the gold shortages led to economic unrest, which resulted in strikes, rising unemployment, and political instability. In the United States, falling prices prompted farmers and unions to press aggressively for the use of silver as well as gold as a monetary standard. As a result, the government adopted a bimetallic standard.

Under the bimetallic standard, the U.S. Treasury agreed to exchange U.S. currency for either gold or silver at a predetermined weight ratio—for example, currency could be exchanged for 16 ounces of silver or one ounce of gold. However, this dual standard worked even less efficiently than the gold standard in maintaining the value of U.S. money because other countries did not agree to maintain the same ratio of exchange. As a result, different value systems existed throughout the world for the same commodity monies.

Changes in the relative supply and demand for either gold or silver in any part of the world led to a rapid disappearance of the more expensive money from circulation. As changes in supply and demand drove up the price of gold, the cheaper silver was circulated while the more expensive gold was hoarded, melted down, or sold abroad, causing it to disappear from circulation. This principle that "cheap money" tends to drive "dear money" from circulation is known as Gresham's Law, so named for Britain's sixteenth-century master of the mint, Sir Thomas Gresham, who first identified this economic phenomenon.

U.S. Money Today

In the United States today, coin, paper currency, and checkable deposits—deposits from which payments can be made by check or electronic funds transfers (EFTs)—are the accepted mediums of exchange (although only U.S. coin and currency are designated as legal tender). Credit cards, a commonly used payment device, do not qualify as a medium of exchange. By extending credit to the bearer, credit cards simply delay the moment of payment. Exhibit 1.1 compares the use of these various payment devices. It shows that about four out of five payment transactions involve coin and currency, but they constitute only about 1 percent of the total dollar volume of all payment transactions.

EXHIBIT 1.1 **Personal, Commercial, and Financial Payment Transactions**

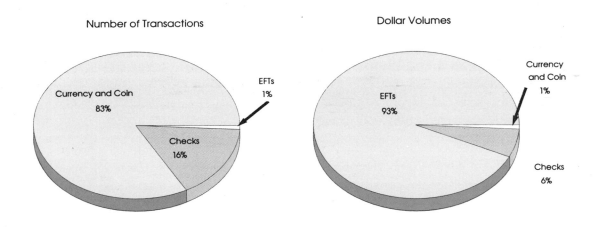

Source: Federal Reserve Bank of Kansas City, *Economic Review*, September/October 1989.

Coin

Coin is indispensable to innumberable daily purchasing transactions, yet it represents a small percentage of the total dollar volume of transactions. About $30 billion in coin was in circulation in 1992—about 3 percent of all U.S. money.

Modern American coin, like most of the world's contemporary "small change," is made of various base metals whose intrinsic value is worth less than the amount stamped on the face of the coin. U.S. coin is minted by the Treasury and distributed by the nation's 12 Federal Reserve banks. Coin is carried as a liability on the Treasury's books and as an asset on the books of all other institutions that hold coin.

Currency

Like coin, currency is widely used, but primarily by individuals for relatively small transactions. About $300 billion in currency was in circulation in 1992 (constituting about 30 percent of all U.S. money). Today's currency consists almost entirely of Federal Reserve notes, printed by the Treasury and issued by the nation's 12 Federal Reserve banks. Unlike coin, U.S. currency is not a direct responsibility of the Treasury but of the Federal Reserve, the central bank of the United States. When issued, it is carried as a liability on the Federal Reserve's books and as an asset on the books of all other institutions that hold currency, including the Treasury.

From 1914 to 1968, Federal Reserve notes were partially backed (collateralized) by gold because that was seen as a means of tying U.S. currency into the gold standard. It ensured that Federal Reserve banks would not overissue paper money, and thereby generated public acceptance of the currency.

In 1914, Federal Reserve notes were required to be backed by 40 percent gold and 100 percent eligible paper (reduced to 60 percent eligible paper in 1917). Eligible paper consisted of the short-term loan agreements of businesses and farmers that commercial banks presented to the Federal Reserve banks as collateral for loans they obtained from the Federal Reserve. The Federal Reserve banks obtained the gold they needed from the U.S. Treasury through a bookkeeping purchase arrangement. The Treasury issued gold certificates (claims on the U.S. gold stock) to the Reserve banks in return for credit to the Treasury's checking account at the Federal Reserve in the amount of the gold certificates issued.

The gold and eligible-paper backing requirements initially were designed to automatically regulate the issuance of currency to match the pace of economic growth. Economists believed that the backing requirements would ensure that currency would not be overissued because only short-term bank loans (those made to expand manufacturing or farm output) were designated as eligible collateral by the Federal Reserve. Thus, only increased business activity, as evidenced by increased bank lending, could generate the collateral necessary for the issuance of additional currency.

In the 1930s, the idea that currency could be automatically regulated gave way as new insights were developed into the workings of the economy and new theories were proposed for the regulation of money. Requirements for backing paper money were liberalized and reduced. Congress allowed Federal Reserve banks to use assets other than eligible paper, such as U.S. government securities, to back currency. By the 1940s, Congress had reduced the gold-backing requirement to 25 percent, and in 1968 it eliminated gold backing entirely. Today, Federal Reserve notes are backed by the assets of Federal Reserve banks. About 80 percent of these assets consist of government securities owned by the Federal Reserve—more than $275 billion in 1992. Less than 5 percent of the assets of Federal Reserve banks consist of the gold certificates purchased from the Treasury in the 1914 to 1968 gold-backing era.

Checkable Deposits

Most of us rely on checking accounts as our predominant means of buying goods and services and paying bills. In fact, checks are used to effect more than 90 percent (by dollar value) of all commercial and personal payments in the United States by consumers, businesses, and governments.

Checkable deposits—the total amount of account balances on the books of banks and other financial institutions against which checks can be drawn—constituted about 70 percent of the nation's money in 1992 (about $625 billion). About half of all checks written in the United States are drawn by individuals—approximately 30 billion checks were written by individuals in 1991. More than half of these checks are for amounts less than $50. Payroll checks from businesses are the source of most of the money against which Americans write personal checks. In fact, about two-thirds of the checks written by businesses are payroll checks. In 1992, Americans wrote about 57 billion checks totaling more than $40 trillion against some 125 million checking accounts. The extensive reliance on checks by American consumers, businesses, and government entities is reflected in the growth of check volume in recent decades. From the early 1950s to the early 1990s, the total number of checks written more than quadrupled, representing a growth rate of about 5 percent annually.

The traditional checkable deposit in the U.S. banking system is the demand deposit (checking account), which pays no interest but allows the holder to withdraw funds on demand and to transfer funds by check. Because demand deposits are the core component of the nation's money supply and because they are created in the commercial lending process, mainly by the nation's 12,000 commercial banks, the Federal Reserve's attempts to control the money supply focus on regulating the ability of banks to create demand deposits.

Only since the late 1970s have commercial banks and thrift institutions—savings banks, savings and loan associations, and credit unions—been allowed to offer checkable deposits that pay interest. In mid-1992, Americans held about $350 billion in these interest-earning checkable deposits—primarily negotiable order of withdrawal (NOW) accounts and credit union share drafts—compared with about $300 billion held in traditional demand deposits at commercial banks and thrifts. Americans held an additional $600 billion in money market deposit accounts which, although they pay interest and allow limited check-writing privileges, are legally classified as savings deposits rather than as checkable deposits. (Extended Study 1 discusses the various definitions of the nation's money supply, in which checkable deposits, but not time and savings deposits, are included in the narrowest definition of money supply—known as M1.)

Legal Tender and Checkbook Money

Although checks are the preferred means of payment in the United States today, they carry no status as legal tender. The term *legal tender* refers to money items designated by the government and the courts as acceptable payment for goods and services or settlement of debt. In effect, the designation of certain items as legal tender leaves sellers of goods and services and creditors with no legal recourse to demand any other form of payment.

In the United States, only U.S.-minted coin and Federal Reserve-issued paper currency are designated as legal tender. Coin has always been so designated, whereas government-issued paper currency was first elevated to this status during the Civil War, in an attempt to win public confidence in paper money. In 1933, Congress made all U.S. coin and currency legal tender for all public and private debts.

Americans prefer using checkbook money, despite its lack of legal tender status, because it serves as a more efficient medium of exchange than coin or currency for many transactions. This preference is not new; bank deposits have been the dominant component of America's circulating money since the 1860s.

The Advantages of Checkbook Money

A check offers consumers numerous advantages:

- ❑ the ability to spend small or large amounts with the same instrument
- ❑ deterrence to theft or counterfeiting because of the signature requirement
- ❑ the ability to stop payment after a transaction has been made
- ❑ written proof of payment in the form of a canceled check
- ❑ a clear audit trail through the check collection process, which allows for the identification of errors or improper transactions
- ❑ extended use of account funds (consumer float) due to the time required for check collection by recipients and their banks

In today's economy, the reliance on legal tender status has been supplanted by public confidence in the strength, safety, and soundness of the American banking system. This confidence has been bolstered by ongoing government supervision and inspection of banks as well as by deposit insurance by the Federal Deposit Insurance Corporation (FDIC). The check-clearing and collection system of the Federal Reserve also has helped to make checkbook money highly acceptable by promptly crediting banks with payment for checks drawn on other banks and by speeding up the check collection process nationwide.

Electronic Funds Transfers (Wire Transfers)

A relatively small but important proportion of payments in the United States (about 1 percent) is made by means other than coin, currency, or check. These payments are made electronically by computer or terminal between banks, between banks and the Federal Reserve, and between banks and large corporations. As exhibit 1.1 shows, the dollar value of these electronic funds transfers is so great that it represents more than 90 percent of the total dollar volume of personal, commercial, and financial payment transactions in the United States today.

Electronic funds transfers (EFTs) are also gaining in popularity among consumers, businesses, and the government as a means of effecting payment transactions. Today, nearly 20 percent of American workers (about 20 million) receive their pay in the form of electronic transfers of funds from their employers to their bank accounts and approximately half of America's 30 million senior citizens receive their Social Security benefits electronically. The federal government has been the leading force behind the development of EFTs in an attempt to cut costs associated with the use of paper checks and to utilize the increased efficiency that EFTs allow. Since 1976, most Americans who receive federal payments such as payroll checks, Social Security benefits, or tax refunds have had the option of receiving these payments electronically. In 1988, the federal government's Vendor Express program began paying all government contractors electronically. This program is expected to greatly expand the use of corporate trade payments (CTPs), the electronic payment for goods and services between corporations.

Electronic funds transfer is a payment device that is already used extensively by European consumers and businesses. Known as *giro* (pronounced Jye-ro) these payments typically are made through a computer terminal at a bank or post office against funds held in the payer's giro account or against cash presented by the payer to the bank or post office.

While there are some private, bank-run giro systems in Europe, the government-run postal giros provide the competitive standard for this type of service. These systems, established as adjuncts to the post office, use the existing postal infrastructure. Germany has an extensive postal giro system, as does Britain, which established a national postal giro in 1968. Sweden's sophisticated postal giro provides consumers with account statements after each transaction (in most other countries, giro systems provide account statements monthly).

The European giro systems are often cited as potential models for providing a payment system to low-income Americans who typically do not maintain checking accounts.

Credit Cards

Credit cards are extremely popular payment devices, used by 80 percent of all American families. About 15 percent of all consumer spending in the United States is done with credit cards. As noted previously, credit cards are not a medium of exchange, but a deferred-payment device that allows consumers to acquire goods and services immediately while making payment (usually by check) at a later time. In effect, the use of a credit card is similar to accepting a prearranged loan.

In 1992, Americans held more than 300 million credit cards. Many of these cards reflect bilateral (two-party) arrangements made with consumers by department stores and gasoline companies. They allow the credit card user to buy goods and services on credit from the institution, merchant, or chain that issues the card.

The most popular form of credit card, however, reflects a multilateral (three-party) arrangement entered into by consumers, banks that issue the cards, and participating merchants. VISA and MasterCard are examples of this type of credit arrangement, which allows consumers to buy goods and services on credit from thousands of participating merchants. Most multilateral credit cards also allow the user to draw cash on credit from participating banks. In the late 1980s, competition for credit card customers intensified with the entry of Sears (Discover card) and American Express (Optima Card) as major credit card issuers. In 1990, credit card competition became even more intense when the American Telephone and Telegraph Co. issued its AT&T universal card.

Credit card use increased dramatically in the 1980s, primarily among those two-thirds of credit card users who opt to use the revolving credit feature of the cards (paying off charges in monthly installments). Outstanding credit card balances grew from a 19 percent share of all consumer credit in 1981 to a 30 percent share in 1991. Average outstanding credit card balances also increased—by about 10 percent per year during the 1980s—and stood at about $1,300 per credit card in 1991.

The popularity of bank cards in the 1980s and 1990s has been matched by their profitability for banks. On average, banks earn a higher return on credit cards than on most other bank loans because credit cards are unsecured loans (no collateral backs the loan). As such, they carry a higher risk to a bank than do other kinds of loans, which banks seek to cover by charging high interest rates. Also, credit card interest rates are slow to change when other interest rates rise or fall. In a period of declining rates, such as the early 1990s, banks pay lower interest on deposits, which reduces their costs of obtaining funds. At the same time, banks continue to receive high interest from credit card users who are paying off charges monthly. The result is a wider profit spread for banks between their costs and their income.

The Circulation of Money

In the United States today, the Federal Reserve determines how much money should circulate to maintain a growing, noninflationary economy. The Federal Reserve attempts to control the nation's money supply with its monetary policy tools. The public, however, freely determines the form in which that money is held—principally through its use of the banking system.

When people or businesses want more coin or currency, they typically cash checks at their local banks. That is, they exchange one form of money (checkbook money) for another form of money (cash). Banks, in turn, do the same thing. When banks need more coin or currency than they have on hand to meet growing public demand, they "buy" the cash with the deposit balances they maintain at a Federal Reserve bank. That is, they exchange an equal amount of deposit money for cash money. Banks that do not have an account at a Federal Reserve bank typically rely on a correspondent bank, exchanging part of their deposit balance at the correspondent bank for cash.

As people and businesses spend their newly obtained cash, it flows back into the banking system in the form of other business and individual deposits. As banks accumulate more cash than they need for their day-to-day transactions, they deposit the cash for credit to their own accounts at Federal Reserve banks or at correspondent banks where the funds can be more effectively used for business, check-clearing, or investment purposes.

When cash deposits are received at Federal Reserve banks, currency that is too worn for further circulation is culled from these deposits, destroyed, and replaced. Unfit coin is returned to the Treasury for melting and recasting. As additional coin and currency are needed by the Federal Reserve banks, either to replace unfit cash or to meet expanding demand, orders are placed with separate Treasury divisions—the Bureau of the Mint for coin and the Bureau of Engraving and Printing for currency.

The total amount of money available in the economy remains the same whether people and businesses convert their checkable deposits into cash or deposit cash for credit to their checking accounts. However, as will be explained in later chapters, the form in which money is held—whether as cash, as savings, or as checkable deposits—has important implications that affect the ability of banks to make loans and the ability of the government to control the money supply.

Summary

Money has three basic functions: It serves as a medium of exchange, allowing goods and services to be sold at different times and in different places; it is a unit of account, enabling comparable values to be placed on diverse goods and services; and it is a store of value, enabling purchasing power to be stored for future use.

Money has evolved over the years from commodity money, which was a medium of exchange having inherent value (such as salt); to representative money, which was redeemable for something of value (for example, goldsmiths' receipts); to fiat money, which is money by government decree (for example, U.S. currency).

Although only coin and currency are designated as legal tender in the United States, the vast majority of payments (by dollar volume) are made by checks and electronic funds transfers drawn against checkable deposits in banks.

In the modern era, the acceptability and value of money are rooted not in money's intrinsic worth, but in its purchasing power. Governments attempt to maintain the purchasing power of money by controlling the quantity of money in circulation. In the eighteenth and nineteenth centuries, governments relied on gold and bimetallic standards to ensure control. In the twentieth century, government control over money is maintained through the monetary policy powers of nations' central banks (the Federal Reserve System in the United States).

Questions

1.   Briefly describe the three functions of money and explain which function, if any, holds the greatest importance.

2.   Why is fiat money a preferable alternative to commodity money?

3.   What is the difference between barter and the use of commodity money?

4.   "Gold as a commodity money would be a poor medium of exchange in today's American economy." Do you agree or disagree? Explain.

5.   Must fiat money be designated as legal tender by a government in order for it to be generally accepted as a nation's money? Does legal tender status ensure the general acceptability of money? Does government insurance for deposit money affect its acceptability as money? Explain your answers.

2

Money and Economic Activity

Objectives

After successfully completing this chapter, you will be able to

☐ define gross domestic product and other measures of U.S. economic activity,

☐ explain how saving and lending are important to our economy,

☐ compare the role of banks, other financial intermediaries, and brokers and dealers in our economy,

☐ explain how the Federal Reserve uses its monetary policy to achieve economic balance, and

☐ give reasons why the impact of monetary policy differs among various borrowers in the credit markets.

Introduction

Without money, economic activity as we know it would not exist. With no accepted medium of exchange and no standard or store of value, the practical administration of our country's material resources would be impossible. A money economy expedites the production, distribution, and consumption of goods and services.

Consider the American economy and your place in it. Without the capital formation process made possible by a money economy, industrialization, mass production, and economic growth would not have taken root in the eighteenth century. Specialized jobs and geographic mobility would not be common today, and spending, saving, and lending relationships would not be accepted facts of modern life.

In this chapter we will explore the relationship of money to economic activity and to the economic functions of production, income, spending, saving, and lending. We look first at the various measures of economic activity—gross (and net) domestic product, national income, personal income, and disposable personal income. We will examine the important roles that banks and other financial intermediaries play in the economic process, and will analyze how the Federal Reserve's monetary policy affects the nation's economic balance.

For additional study of a related topic, you are encouraged to read Extended Study 2, "Business Cycles," which examines the cyclical nature of business activity in our economy.

The Circular Flow of Economic Activity

The most basic measure of an economy's size and performance is its gross domestic product (GDP)—a measure of the total value of all new goods and services produced within a country in a given period, typically one year. In 1992, the United States generated a GDP (mainly in the form of services) of more than $5.8 trillion.

The nation's GDP reflects the interaction of the consumer, business, and government spending sectors in our economy. As exhibit 2.1 illustrates, these economic sectors supply each other with factors of production in the form of land, labor, capital, and entrepreneurial talent. In return, the various sectors receive money income in the form of wages, rent, interest, profits, and (in the case of government) taxes. They then spend this income to buy goods and services they have helped produce. Without income, consumers, businesses, and governments could not generate a demand for goods and services.

EXHIBIT 2.1   **The Circular Flow of Economic Activity**

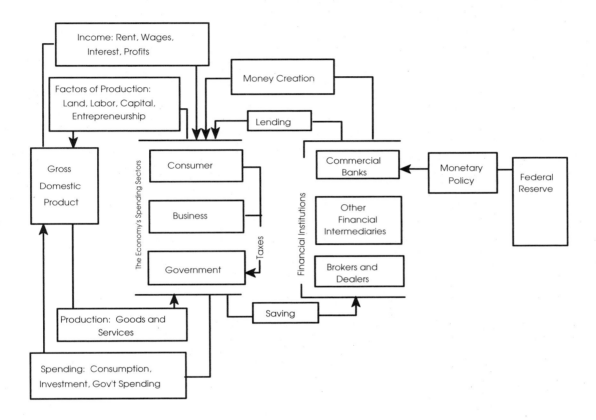

Motivations for Spending

Economists divide the economy into consumer, business, and government sectors because each group's motives to spend, save, and borrow differ. Consumer spending is motivated by people's wants and needs. The U.S. economy is a consumer-oriented economy, with consumption spending on food, clothing, medical care, and recreation accounting for approximately 60 percent to 65 percent of the GDP.

Business spending is motivated by profit. Business decisions to spend—to invest in new factories and equipment, to hire new workers, to replace old machines, or to build inventories of raw materials—are based essentially on the desire for financial gain. Although business spending, or investment, represents only about 10 percent to 15 percent of the GDP, this spending is profoundly important to the economy's well-being because it typically creates new jobs.

Government spending is motivated by the desire to achieve various social and public objectives. The tax-collecting ability of the approximately 80,000 state and local governments in the United States is a key factor in their spending plans. But for the federal government, tax collection is less of a constraint in spending. Since the 1930s, the federal government has used spending and taxation as major tools for achieving economic objectives. Government spending accounts for about 20 percent to 25 percent of the GDP.

The Role of Savings and Lending

Not all consumer, business, and government income is spent—some of it is saved. Economists define savings as income not used to buy goods and services. Using this definition, consumers typically save 5 percent to 6 percent of their disposable (after-tax) incomes and most businesses retain a portion of their earnings as savings. Some state and local governments end their fiscal years with budget surpluses. As exhibit 2.1 illustrates, savings represent a "leakage" from the economy's circular flow of income and spending—money that is saved might otherwise be used to buy goods and services and to generate income.

If savings were literally hoarded—kept out of circulation by being stuffed into mattresses or cookie jars—the economic consequences could be devastating. Without an infusion of new money, some goods and services might remain unsold because there would not be enough money in circulation to buy them. Given this situation, producers faced with declining sales might cut back production and lay off workers. In turn, the unemployed would spend less, worsening the economic slump and generating even bigger layoffs. Eventually, the entire economic system would spiral down into a recession—a prolonged period of falling production and rising unemployment—until those consumers, businesses, and governments that had hoarded their savings began to use that money to sustain themselves. Only then would the downward spiral begin to reverse.

In another scenario, producers faced with declining sales caused by a shortage of money might cut prices. With lower prices, a smaller supply of money could absorb all available goods and services and maintain the economic balance. The problem here is that wages, rents, and interest constitute prices also. Yet even in a deflationary period of falling prices, workers, landlords, and creditors are reluctant to accept cuts in their incomes. Moreover, it is uncertain whether a deflationary contraction would be any less devastating to the economy than a recession.

In reality, of course, most of the money saved by consumers, businesses, and governments is not hoarded, but is deposited in a vast assortment of financial institutions and invested in various financial instruments. Commercial banks and other financial intermediaries then pump the money back into the economy's spending stream by lending it to consumers, businesses, and governments that want to spend more than they currently have. Again, exhibit 2.1 illustrates this flow. Without savings and the resultant lending, businesses would be unable to undertake large capital projects requiring long-term financing. The economy will maintain its balance as long as the money flowing out of the spending stream as savings is offset by money pumped back in by the lending of commercial banks and other financial institutions.

Credit Availability and Economic Growth

The money saved by consumers, businesses, and governments, combined with the money created by commercial banks, provides the U.S. economy with a vast pool of loanable funds. Loans enable the various economic sectors to spend more than their current incomes would allow. Without credit, our economy and other modern industrial economies would slow and stagnate. Fewer consumers would be able to buy cars, houses, and vacation trips if these purchases had to be financed solely with savings or current income. Businesses might be unable to replace obsolete machinery or buy the raw materials required for production. If current taxes had to match current spending, governments would have to reduce the scale of their public works and social programs, including payments to Social Security recipients, the unemployed, and those on welfare. Thus, the ability of the economic sectors to obtain substantial amounts of credit has been a key factor in the growth of the U.S. economy.

During the course of any given year, U.S. consumers, businesses, and governments borrow funds and repay loans. On balance, however, more new credit is extended by the nation's financial institutions each year than is repaid. As a result, the total amount of credit outstanding in the United States has increased annually. In the 1960s, about $200 billion a year was added to the credit total; in the 1970s, about $250 billion to $300 billion a year was added; and in the 1980s, largely because of greatly increased borrowing by the federal government, total credit increased by about $500 billion to $600 billion a year. In 1992, the total of all outstanding consumer, business, and government debt stood at more than $11.4 trillion.

Measures of Economic Activity

The U.S. Department of Commerce uses statistical records called national income and product accounts to track the economy's performance. These measures of U.S. economic activity include real GDP, net domestic product, national income, personal income, and disposable personal income. The relationships between these accounts are illustrated in exhibit 2.2, which shows how money links production and consumption in a complex, circular flow of economic activity. A brief discussion of each of these measures of economic activity follows.

SS 2010

US Dept of Commerce tracks GDP

MOST Important Chart

Consumer 7 suppliers & spenders of money
Business money for T-Bill Savings Bond
Gov. makes money

Balance Budget to pay off Take surplus 2002 Mp

EXHIBIT 2.2   **National Income and Product Accounts**

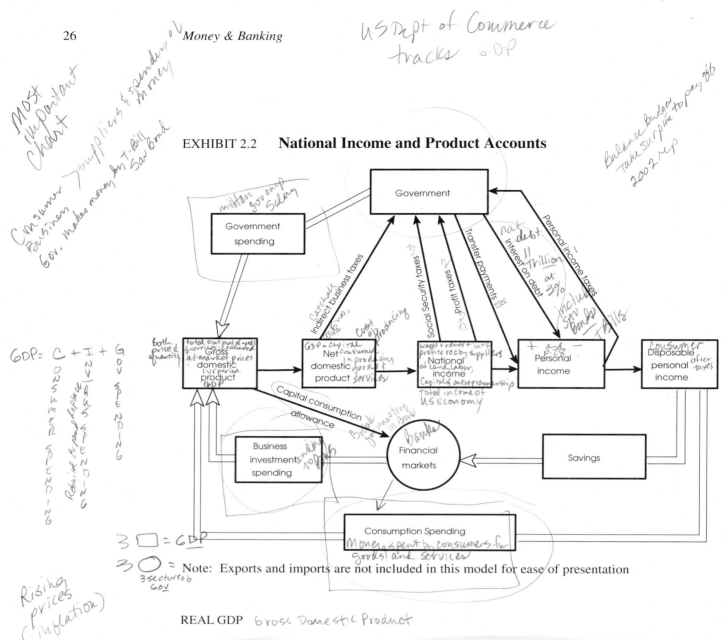

GDP = C + I + Gov

CONSUMER SPENDING
INVEST BUS SPENDING (Retire old & replace)
GOV SPENDING

3 □ = GDP
3 ○ =
3 sectors of Gov

Rising prices (inflation)

current (nominal)

Note: Exports and imports are not included in this model for ease of presentation

REAL GDP   Gross Domestic Product

The gross domestic product represents a country's total output of goods and services measured at market prices over a one-year period. Because the GDP measure reflects both the price and quantity of goods and services, an increase in prices can generate a measure of apparent growth that does not reflect an actual increase in production or national living standards. For this reason, the *nominal* GDP (the measure of total output using current prices) is adjusted for rising prices (inflation), and the resulting figure is called *real* GDP. The calculation of real GDP is made by selecting a base year (at present, 1987) against which prices for the current year are compared; a price index number is then developed that reflects the percentage change in prices between the two years. Then, real GDP is determined using this formula:

$$\frac{\text{Nominal GDP}}{\text{Price Index Number}} \times 100 = \text{Real GDP}$$

(Base yr & current year prices compared. PIN reflects % change in prices between yrs)

In 1992, the price index number (the GDP deflator) was 119, meaning that 1992 prices were 19 percent higher than 1987 prices. As noted previously, the nation's GDP in

1992 totaled $5.8 trillion. This nominal GDP translates into a real GDP in 1992 of $4.9 trillion, as calculated here:

$$\frac{\text{Nominal GDP } \$5.8 \text{ trillion}}{\text{Price Index Number } 119} \times 100 = \$4.9 \text{ trillion}$$

Exhibit 2.3 shows the nation's GDP in both nominal (current) dollars and 1987 dollars (real GDP).

EXHIBIT 2.3   **Gross Domestic Product**
(seasonally adjusted)

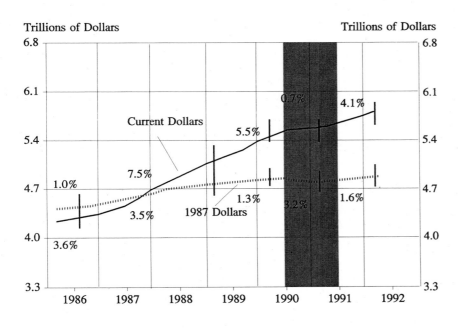

Shaded area represents a period of business recession.

Percentages are annual rates of change for periods indicated.

NET DOMESTIC PRODUCT

Each year, while producing new goods and services, an economy consumes some portion of its existing capital goods (buildings, machinery, and equipment) through wear and tear and obsolescence. The amount of capital consumed in producing goods and services is subtracted from the gross domestic product to obtain the net domestic product (NDP).

product. In 1992, U.S. producers consumed more than $625 billion worth of capital goods—measured in terms of loss of value in real property caused by age, deterioration, or obsolescence—in generating the year's production. This consumption of capital, or depreciation, equaled about 11 percent of total (nominal) GDP in 1992. This economic cost of production is subtracted from the GDP to obtain the net domestic product, which reflects more accurately the dollar value of all goods and services produced during the year. For 1992, the nation's net domestic product totaled about $5.2 trillion.

NATIONAL INCOME

Manufacturers often incur additional production costs in the form of sales, excise, real estate, and other indirect taxes. Typically, the prices of manufactured goods reflect these added costs. By subtracting indirect business taxes from the net domestic product measure, we obtain a measure not only of the cost of resources used in production, but the income received by the sellers of these resources. This measure is called *national income*.

The national income is the sum of all wages, rents, interest, and profits received by the suppliers of land, labor, capital, and entrepreneurship—the total income of the U.S. economy. In 1992, U.S. national income amounted to about $4.7 trillion.

PERSONAL INCOME

Not all income received by the suppliers of resources is available for their personal use or disposition. A portion of the income received by businesses must go to the federal government to pay employees' Social Security taxes and taxes on corporate profits. These two outflows of money are subtracted from the national income measure when calculating personal income. On the other hand, people and businesses also receive income from government sources that must be added to the national income measure when calculating personal income. The two sources of government payments that must be considered are transfer payments—monies that the government transfers directly to people, such as Social Security payments, veterans' payments, and unemployment insurance payments—and the interest paid by the government on its outstanding debt. Personal income—the net result of these two subtractions and two additions to national income—totaled about $4.9 trillion in 1992.

DISPOSABLE PERSONAL INCOME

Disposable personal income is a measure of the amount of income that people have available for spending and saving after they pay taxes. Most of this after-tax income—about 95 percent—is spent on goods and services (consumption). The remainder is saved, with the monies going into a broad range of time and savings deposits at commercial banks and other financial intermediaries and into financial instruments having different degrees of liquidity, risk, and return. In 1992, disposable personal income totaled about $4.3 trillion.

GDP AS A MEASURE OF SPENDING

The gross domestic product is both a measure of production (the total dollar value of all newly produced goods and services) and a measure of income (the total income received by consumers, businesses, and governments). It also can be seen as a measure of spending—the sum of all the monies spent by consumers on goods and services (consumption, or **C**); plus the monies spent by businesses from retained earnings and borrowings to rebuild inventories, expand factories, and replace deteriorated equipment (investment, or **I**); plus the tax monies and borrowings spent by federal, state, and local governments (government spending, or **G**).

An additional component of GDP as a measure of spending is the net flow of money reflecting imports and exports. Total expenditures on domestic goods are reduced when Americans spend part of their incomes on imports, and are increased when foreigners spend part of their incomes on American exports. The net effect of these international transactions on GDP spending is the difference between the value of our imports and exports. If exports exceed imports, the GDP will be slightly greater than the sum of **C+I+G**; if imports exceed exports, as they did in 1992 (by about $30 billion), the GDP will be lower.

[handwritten annotation:] GDP = Consumption (total monies spent) + Investment (money spent by Bus) + Government Spending (tax monies spent by fed, state & local gov)

Changing from Gross National Product to Gross Domestic Product

[handwritten annotation: excluded overseas earnings of Am co.]

In 1991, the U.S. Commerce Department, Bureau of Economic Analysis, which collects and publishes America's national income and product accounts data, changed the key measure used to determine the economy's production and spending levels from gross national product (GNP) to gross domestic product (GDP).

GNP had been used by the U.S. government and American economists for more than 50 years as a measure of the total value of all newly produced goods and services (and the sum of all consumer, business and government spending). However, GNP had not been used in most other countries because it was seen as an inaccurate measure of a nation's production and spending.

Technically, the GNP counts goods and services produced (and money spent) by *residents*, whether or not those residents—workers and business firms—are actually in the country whose economy is being measured. In the United States, the GNP counted goods and services produced by American companies operating in other countries. The U.S. GNP also excluded from the count all the goods and services produced in the United States by foreign workers and foreign companies.

(Continued from previous page)

GDP, however, focuses only on *where* goods and services (and income and spending) have been produced. Goods and services produced in the United States, whether by American or foreign-owned companies, are counted in the United States GDP total; goods and services produced by American companies abroad are not.

The Commerce Department changed from GNP to GDP because the GDP measures only production, income, and spending that takes place in the United States. Thus, the GDP gives economists and government officials a more accurate picture of the linkages between these activities and other important internal U.S. performance measures, such as employment, productivity, and investment in factories and equipment. It also enables the United States to more readily compare its overall economic performance with that of other countries.

Surprisingly, in the United States, total GNP and total GDP differ very little; only about one percentage point or less separates the two. In other countries, however, the differences can be substantial. For example, because so many American companies manufacture goods in Canada, Canadian GNP is almost 4 percent smaller than its GDP. By contrast, because Kuwait has made enormous investments in other countries (on which it earns interest, rents, and profits), its GNP is one-third larger than its GDP.

Debtors and Creditors in Our Economy

In recent decades, consumers, businesses, and governments have borrowed funds equal to about one-sixth of the GDP each year from the nation's banks, other financial intermediaries, and credit markets. In any given year, consumers borrow nearly 40 percent of this total, businesses absorb about 30 percent, the federal government takes from 15 percent to 20 percent, and foreign borrowers and state and local governments borrow the remainder.

The consumer sector, through its savings, provides about two-thirds of the funds supplied to all borrowers. Most of the remaining funds supplied to borrowers are provided by the business sector.

As noted previously, the total of all outstanding consumer, business, and government debt in the United States in 1992 exceeded $11.4 trillion. The composition of this debt is shown in exhibit 2.4.

EXHIBIT 2.4   **Outstanding Debt of the U.S. Government, Consumer, and Business Sectors in 1992**

Sector		Amount (billions of dollars)		
Federal government		$3,873		*Rank*
Federal debt held by federal agencies and trusts		961		
Net federal debt			$2,912	3
State and local governments			883	4
Consumers	Mortgages	$3,056		
	Other Loans	845	3,901	1
Business	Mortgages	988		
	Bonds	1,052		
	Bank loans	724		
	Other market Instruments	970	3,734	2
	Total		$11,430	

Sources: Federal Reserve Bank of St. Louis, *National Economic Trends*, July 1992, and Federal Reserve *Bulletin*, August 1992.

CONSUMERS

We as consumers, through our savings, supply most of the funds available for lending and investment in the United States. About 80 percent of consumer savings is placed with banks and other financial intermediaries, while the other 20 percent is invested directly in credit market instruments. Consumers also borrow, as shown in exhibit 2.4 by the $3.9 trillion in outstanding consumer debt in 1992. As shown, three-fourths of this debt is mortgage debt that has been assumed in the purchase of residential housing; only one-fourth represents funds borrowed for installment buying and other short-term personal reasons.

The consumer sector has total financial assets of about $6.5 trillion; this includes holdings of money, liquid near-money instruments, such as savings and time deposits at banks and thrifts, and stocks and bonds. However, the consumer sector's actual wealth, or net worth, far exceeds the difference between its financial assets and its financial liabilities (outstanding debt) because consumer net worth includes not only financial assets but nonfinancial assets such as real estate and household goods. Economists estimate that the consumer sector's net worth is about $12 trillion.

BUSINESSES

As shown in exhibit 2.4, the business sector is the second largest net debtor in the U.S. economy, with total outstanding debt of more than $3.7 trillion in 1992. The cash flow from retained earnings of business firms provides only part of the funds the business sector needs for annual capital spending; the remainder must be borrowed or raised by selling stock (new equity capital). Nearly half the total business debt represents funds borrowed to finance inventories and to replace and modernize plants and equipment. More than one-quarter of all business debt is mortgage debt.

GOVERNMENTS

Government debt accounts for about one-third of the nation's outstanding debt. Governments, like businesses, owe more than the sum of their own financial assets. As shown in exhibit 2.4, about three-fourths of the government sector debt is federal debt (about $2.9 trillion in 1992 after federal debt held by federal agencies and trusts is subtracted from the total); the remainder is state and local government debt.

As exhibit 2.5 shows, most of the federal debt is held by commercial banks and other financial intermediaries. In addition, state and local governments, and the Federal Reserve hold more than one-quarter of the federal debt. About 16 percent of the federal debt is held by foreign investors, essentially foreign governments who hold U.S. government securities as part of their international reserve assets.

EXHIBIT 2.5   **Holders of the Federal Debt in 1992**

	Amount (billions of dollars)	Percent of Total
Net Federal Debt	$2,912	
Held by:		
Federal Reserve banks	288	10
State and local governments	490	17
Commercial banks	252	9
Other financial intermediaries [1]	1,009	34
Business firms	151	5
Individuals	264	9
Foreign investors	458	16
	$2,912	100%

Source: Federal Reserve *Bulletin*, August 1992

---

[1]   Includes insurance companies, money market funds, savings banks, savings and loan associations, credit unions, pension funds, and government securities dealer firms.

Our Growing Federal Debt

Most of the federal government's debt was incurred during the 1980s when the government made substantial cuts in both federal income taxes and corporate profit taxes. These tax cuts, designed to stimulate economic growth, caused a massive shortfall in tax revenue. At the same time, the government increased defense spending while transfer payments to Social Security recipients and others were also rising.

Prior to the 1980s, growth in the federal debt largely reflected rapid borrowings to meet war needs. The government incurred substantial debt during World War II (1941-1945) when it borrowed massive amounts of money to mobilize an army quickly and buy war materiel. Additional debt was incurred in the 1950s, to fund the Korean War, and in the 1960s, during the Vietnam War. A tax cut in the 1960s, coupled with increased spending on social programs, also drove up the government's debt level.

The explosion of federal debt in recent decades (coupled with high interest rates in the 1980s) generated soaring growth in the interest payments that the federal government must make to debt holders. In 1975, the federal debt totalled less than $400 billion. By 1990, the debt had grown to $2.4 trillion. As shown in exhibit 2.6, during this 15-year-period, interest on the debt grew from 7.5 percent of federal outlays ($25 billion) to 16.1 percent of federal outlays ($202.4 billion). Today, the government's interest payments exceed every component of government spending except defense and Social Security. Economists have projected that net federal debt will grow to $4 trillion by 1995 based on anticipated federal borrowings in the 1990s. If that projection holds, interest payments on the debt would absorb 16.5 percent of projected federal spending.

EXHIBIT 2.6   **Interest on the Federal Debt**

	Amount (in billions of dollars)	Percent of Total Federal Spending
1975	25.0	7.5
1980	62.8	10.6
1985	152.9	16.2
1990	202.4	16.1
1995 est.	257.4	16.5

Source: Budget of the United States Government, fiscal year 1993.

Borrowing and Lending Relationships

To a borrower, a loan represents a debt; to a lender, it represents an asset. When a commercial bank or other financial intermediary makes a loan, it obtains a financial asset—a promissory note or loan agreement from the borrower stipulating the terms and conditions of repayment. Similarly, when a bank or other financial intermediary buys a corporate or government note or bond (in effect, making a loan to the corporation or government unit), it also obtains a financial asset. The note or bond is itself a promise to repay the holder under terms and conditions usually stipulated on the instrument. Thus the $11.4 trillion in outstanding debt owed by U.S. consumers, businesses, and governments in 1992 represents $11.4 trillion in assets or financial wealth to the holders of the loan agreements, notes, bonds, and other financial instruments that constitute the total debt.

Sources of Credit

About 75 percent of all funds borrowed in the nation's credit markets represents loans of financial intermediaries, including commercial banks, to consumers and businesses. The remaining funds are obtained by businesses and governments directly from the nation's credit market—from the people and the institutions that buy the debt instruments of businesses and governments seeking to borrow funds.

As consumers, we rely almost exclusively on loans from banks and other financial intermediaries as our source of credit. The nation's savings banks and savings and loan associations have long been an important source of mortgage credit. Commercial banks, finance companies, and credit unions are primary sources of short-term and intermediate-term credit for personal spending, ranging from automobile loans and education loans to loans to finance the purchase of stocks and bonds.

Bank officer conferring with client.

Photo by Robert Rathe, courtesy of the National Bank of Washington.

Most business debt is owed to commercial banks and other financial institutions. Businesses rely on two major sources of credit—loans from commercial banks and funds obtained directly from the credit market itself through the sale of short-term and long-term debt instruments ranging from commercial paper to bonds. Businesses typically sell new bond issues to raise money for long-term building and capital investment programs.

Most businesses also have a third key source of funds—the equity market—but this source does not involve borrowing or lending. When a corporation seeks to raise capital by issuing new shares (equity) in the corporation, it is, in effect, selling a segment of the corporation itself. The purchaser of the newly issued corporate stock is not lending the company money, but is buying an asset that may increase or diminish in value depending on whether the corporation prospers. Stockholders typically share proportionally in the company's earnings, through dividends and a higher market price for their stock. If the corporation does poorly, stockholders may see the value of their stock decline. Because stockholders are not creditors but owners, they rank low in terms of the legal priority of their claims against the assets of a corporation that is unable to repay its debts.

Rather than rely on bank loans, governments rely almost exclusively on selling their own debt instruments in the credit market. These debt instruments include notes and tax warrants issued by states and localities, as well as Treasury bills, notes, certificates, and bonds issued by the federal government. Most of these government securities are purchased by commercial banks and other financial intermediaries and become part of their investment portfolios. U.S. government securities are attractive investments because of their liquidity, their high quality, and their worldwide acceptability as a store of value.

Financial Intermediaries

Financial intermediaries take in funds from consumers who choose to save and lend the funds principally to consumers who choose to borrow. These loans, together with the business and consumer loans of commercial banks, provide the economy with the bulk of its investment funds. Not only are commercial banks and thrift institutions (savings and loan associations, savings banks, and credit unions) considered to be financial intermediaries, but so too are life insurance companies, pension plans, and money market funds, because their investment activities provide loan funds to the issuers of the notes and bonds they purchase.

The nation's commercial banks, thrift institutions, and insurance companies provide about half the funds borrowed by consumers, businesses, and governments. Exhibit 2.7 shows the relative asset size of these financial intermediaries over the decades. Commercial banks have long been the largest single source of credit. However, that dominance is being increasingly challenged. In the 1970s, thrift institution assets grew

EXHIBIT 2.7   **Assets of Selected Financial Intermediaries, 1950-1992**

(billions of dollars)

	Commercial Banks	Savings and Loans	Savings Banks	Credit Unions	Life Insurance Companies
1950	69	17	22	1	64
1960	258	72	40	6	120
1970	576	176	79	18	207
1980	1,537	631	172	72	479
1985	2,329	1,072	219	137	880
1992	3,519	900	500	200	1,580

Sources: Federal Reserve *Bulletin*, U.S. League of Savings Associations.

faster than commercial bank assets, largely because thrift institutions were able to provide consumers with new types of accounts and services that commercial banks were unable to match because of regulatory restraints.

In the 1980s, commercial banks saw an even larger erosion of their market share of credit. Major nonbank companies, such as Sears, American Express, General Electric, and Westinghouse, began to expand their businesses to include financial services and loans to consumers and other companies. In 1970, nonbank companies, such as General Motors Acceptance Corporation (GMAC), were providing only 5 percent of total consumer and business credit. By 1990, nonbank companies, propelled by the gains of the firms that expanded into financial services in the 1980s, were providing 13 percent of the nation's credit.

In the late 1980s, the nation's large corporations also began to increase their use of direct financing as a means of obtaining funds. Instead of borrowing from banks, these companies borrowed funds by selling their own commercial paper (short-term, uncollateralized promissory notes) directly to the public. In 1970, commercial paper provided businesses with only 2 percent of their borrowed funds; commercial bank loans provided nearly 30 percent. By 1990, commercial paper was providing corporations with 6 percent of their credit while commercial bank loans had declined to 25 percent. Exhibit 2.8 shows the sharp growth of commercial paper in the late 1980s. From 1987 to 1992, the amount of commercial paper outstanding increased by 70 percent.

The two decade-long effect on commercial banks of regulatory restraints, competition from major nonbank lenders, and corporations' increased use of commercial paper sales to obtain borrowed funds has been profound. In 1970, commercial banks were providing nearly 30 percent of all borrowed funds; by 1990, commercial banks' share had fallen to 20 percent.

EXHIBIT 2.8 **Nonfinancial Commercial Paper Outstanding**
(seasonally adjusted)

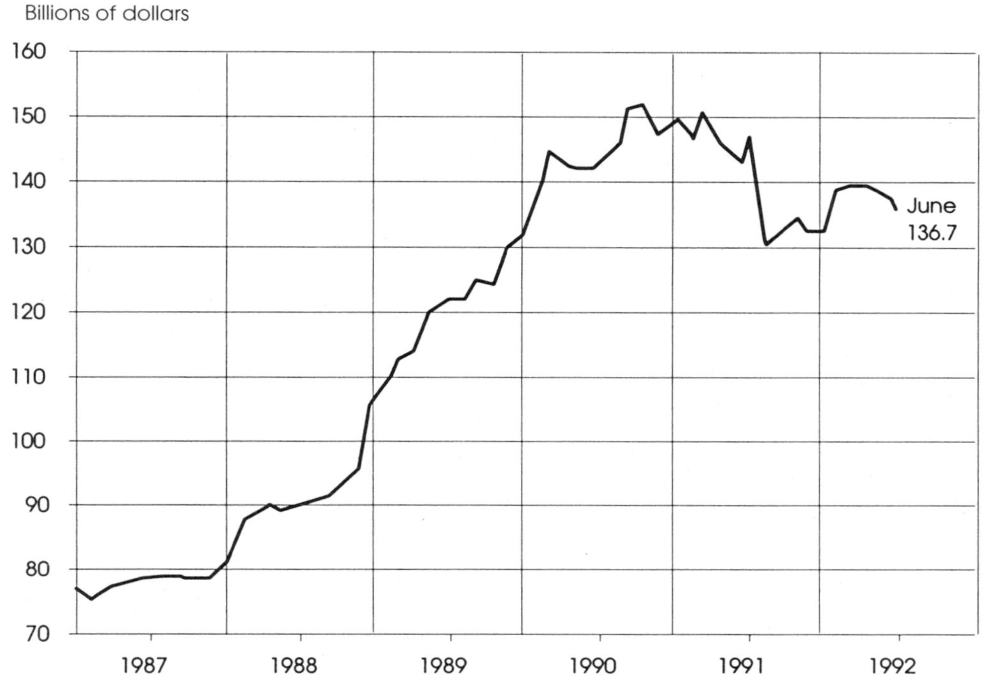

Billions of dollars

Source: Federal Reserve Bank of New York

Commercial Banks and Money Creation

Commercial banks have traditionally differed from other financial intermediaries in that only they could create money (in the form of new demand deposit balances) by making loans. Because demand deposits (checking accounts) represent the core medium of exchange in the U.S. economy and because commercial banks still create most of the demand deposit dollars that circulate in the U.S. economy, the Federal Reserve primarily uses the nation's 12,000 commercial banks to implement its monetary policy. (This relationship is illustrated in exhibit 2.1.)

A bank that makes a loan monetizes a private debt by accepting as an asset the debt obligation of the borrower—the borrower's promise to repay. The bank simultaneously creates a liability on its books in the form of a demand deposit balance in the amount of the loan.

To create money, a bank must have reserves—funds on deposit at a Federal Reserve bank or vault cash—at least equal to the amount of money to be created. The more reserves a bank has, the greater its potential for expanding earnings because it can continue to make new loans and investments. The fewer reserves a bank has (or the closer its reserves are to its own liquidity margin or to the reserve requirements of the Federal Reserve), the smaller its potential for expanding earnings.

Commercial bank lending creates an increasing amount of demand deposits throughout the economy. The creation of these deposits by the banking system is constantly modified by such factors as the flow of money between banks and other financial intermediaries, the movement of funds from checking to savings accounts, and the cashing of checks; however, the changing level of reserves available to banks is the chief factor determining how much money can be created by the commercial lending process. How banks create money through the lending process is discussed in greater detail in chapter 4, "Commercial Banks and Money Creation."

Brokers and Dealers

The interaction between borrowers and lenders in the U.S. economy is made more efficient through the work of a relatively small group of securities dealer firms and several thousand brokerage firms. Brokers and dealers serve as key middlemen between borrowers and lenders seeking to make a match in the credit markets. These firms maintain markets for trading both new and outstanding issues of notes, bonds, and other debt instruments.

Brokerage firms, which are typically associated with the stock market, sell their services for a fee. Dealer firms, which are typically associated with the bond markets, assume risk on their own behalf by buying the new debt issues of a corporation or government agency. They then seek to make a profit by reselling the debt instruments at a higher price to commercial banks, savings and loan associations, life insurance companies, pension plans, and other financial intermediaries.

Brokers and dealers help facilitate a rapid and efficient flow of credit from lenders to borrowers in the U.S. economy. The nation's major government-securities dealer firms serve as a primary market through which the Federal Reserve implements the nation's monetary policy through open-market operations (the Federal Reserve's daily buying and selling of outstanding U.S. government securities). About half the nation's 40 to 50 major government-securities dealer firms operate as virtually autonomous departments of major banks.

Monetary Policy, Credit Markets, and Interest Rates

Monetary policy affects the cost and availability of credit to consumers, businesses, governments, and in particular, the nation's depository institutions. When monetary policy is expansive, credit usually is available at relatively low interest rates. But when monetary policy becomes restrictive and interest rates begin to rise, competition in the marketplace determines how demand for credit will be matched with a limited supply of loanable funds.

The Federal Reserve and Monetary Policy

The Federal Reserve, which is the nation's central bank, seeks to control the money creation of commercial banks so that the economy does not get too much money, which can lead to inflation, or too little money, which can lead to recession. By controlling bank reserves, it can change both the cost of money (interest rates) and the availability of money (the growth rate of the money supply). The control of reserves also effectively determines the profit potential in bank lending and investing.

If the economy is experiencing inflation, the Federal Reserve will try to restrain bank lending (money creation) by pursuing a tight or restrictive monetary policy characterized by high interest rates and a relatively slow rate of money supply growth. If the economy is in a recession, the Federal Reserve will try to stimulate lending by pursuing an easy or expansive monetary policy characterized by low interest rates and a relatively fast rate of money supply growth. The objective is to keep the economy's money flows (income, spending, savings, lending, and bank-created money) in balance—that is, to promote yearly increases in real GDP (economic growth) without sporadic periods of recession or inflation.

A tightening of monetary policy is implemented slowly, as the Federal Reserve reduces the growth rate at which it supplies reserves to banks. As the rate of growth begins to slow against strong demand for reserves by banks that want to increase loans (earning assets), the cost of reserves begins to rise. If banks have to pay more for reserves, they will generally charge more for loans and seek to earn more on investments to make an expansion in earning assets profitable. Some banks, however, will be induced to cut back on lending, either in response to the rising cost of reserves or to a falloff in loan demand from customers unwilling to pay higher loan rates.

Banks that respond to rising costs by retrenching typically allow loans to be repaid without extending new loans and may sell some securities to convert assets into reserves. These types of adjustments reduce the amount of demand deposits in the nation's banking system and hence the level of reserves needed to support those deposits. However, not all borrowers of bank funds are affected in the same way by this retrenchment. As we have seen, consumer, business, and government borrowers rely on different institutions and markets for credit. Thus some borrowers may actually get a larger share of available credit at the expense of others.

A further discussion of business cycles and how they affect various segments of the economy is included as Extended Study 2.

Credit Markets and Interest Rates

Banks typically post higher interest rates when they find that they cannot satisfy all the credit demands of potential borrowers. As a result, some corporations may borrow less, and thus spend less, in periods of tight credit. However, smaller and newer business firms may find they cannot afford the higher interest rates on loans or may find that, even at higher rates, banks simply do not have enough funds available to meet their needs. Large corporations tend to be less concerned about rising interest rates for bank loans. They often bypass the banking system entirely—by raising funds directly in the credit market through the sale of commercial paper or bonds or by financing their capital spending through retained earnings.

Bank Loan Charge Practices

Traditionally, banks have charged a preferential interest rate on loans to their most creditworthy corporate customers. This lower rate for valued business customers is called the bank's *prime rate*. The availability of prime rate loans generally is based on the length and scope of a bank's relationship with a corporate borrower, the level of compensating deposit balances maintained by the borrower at the bank, and the corporation's loan and repayment history.

The prime rate of large money center and regional banks frequently is reported in the business media as the interest rate that all banks charge for business loans. However, many banks today base their loan charges on a cost-of-money rate plus a spread to cover their operating costs. Other banks use a cost index to develop a multiple-rate structure for their business loans. Changing practices with respect to banks' loan charges have resulted in accusations of banks misleading the public and unfairly discriminating by using a multiple loan-rate structure. In fact, some banks have been sued on these grounds.

Banks also are often criticized for implicitly discriminating against small and new businesses during periods of tight money and rising interest rates by channeling their scarce credit primarily to prime-rate borrowers. Although many banks today specifically allocate a portion of their lending to small and new businesses, this controversy tends to resurface whenever bank credit becomes scarce.

Before the 1980s, when banks and thrifts were subject to interest rate ceilings on time and savings deposits, the thrift industry and the mortgage market typically felt the impact of tight money most strongly because high market interest rates made the lower, regulated interest rates paid by thrifts on deposits less attractive. As thrifts lost funds to higher-paying Treasury bills and money market funds, the thrifts had less available to lend. They often found that they were unable to make mortgages, which represent the single largest borrowing need of the consumer sector. Today, higher market interest rates generally compel thrifts to increase the rates they pay on deposits to remain competitive but also to charge more for mortgages. As a result, economists estimate that a one percentage point rise in mortgage rates results in 200,000 fewer new housing starts (houses in process of construction).

In some states consumers find that, as interest rates rise, automobile loans and other installment credit also become harder to find because maximum consumer loan rates, set by state usury laws, crowd these loans out of the market. If market interest rates and business loan rates, which are not covered by usury laws, are higher than the usury ceilings, banks channel funds from potential consumer borrowers to higher-paying business borrowers or to higher-return investments. As a result, sales of big-ticket consumer items tend to decline. In fact, a one-percentage-point rise in interest rates typically results in 500,000 fewer automobile sales.

To finance government spending, governments borrow money directly from credit markets, not from banks. The federal government is not bound by statute or policy to a maximum interest rate that the Treasury may pay to sell its new bills, notes, certificates, or bonds. However, most states and localities are limited to some maximum rate. Thus, when interest rates rise, they often get a smaller share of the money available in the credit markets. Even so, the federal government is not immune to rising interest costs because about one-third of the federal government's debt has to be refinanced each year at prevailing interest rates.

Interest Rates and Bank Loan Charges

Bankers assess a broad range of factors in determining loan charges. The interest rate a bank charges for its loans generally reflects the bank's assessment of its credit risk, its cost of funds, administrative costs and profit margin, and the possible effects of inflation.

A primary concern in determining loan charges is the bank's perception of the credit risk involved in the loan—the risk that the borrower will not repay the loan when it is due. Accurately assessing and charging for the credit risk associated with a loan is one of the most difficult tasks that banks face.

In the early 1980s, many of the nation's large banks assessed too favorably the credit risks involved in lending money to foreign countries whose major source of export earnings was oil. A subsequent reduction in oil prices and a glut in world oil supplies sharply reduced the export earnings of oil-producing countries and caught many of them without sufficient funds to repay outstanding loans. In the late 1980s, banks that made extensive commercial real estate loans also failed to adequately assess credit risks. These banks experienced substantial loan losses when real estate developers, hurt by slumping markets, could not meet their loan repayment terms.

In determining loan charges, banks also must consider their general cost of funds—what they have to pay to depositors or to other banks to obtain funds. The cost of funds may differ, even for banks of like asset size in the same region of the country, because different banks typically rely on different sources of funds and have different investment opportunities.

For most banks, the cost of funds grew significantly in the 1980s with the introduction of NOW accounts and money market deposit accounts. Banks saw a sharp increase in their interest costs as the public transferred funds from non-interest-bearing demand deposit accounts and low-interest-paying time accounts to the newly authorized accounts that paid market rates.

In the early 1990s, however, banks saw their cost of funds decline. The Federal Reserve initiated an easy money policy in 1990 to stimulate the economy. While this policy succeeded in driving down market interest rates through 1992, banks found little consumer or business demand for new loans and little need to continue to attract or retain high-interest-paying time and savings deposits. Most banks lowered interest rates paid on these deposits, which triggered substantial transfers of deposits into government securities and money market funds from consumers and business firms seeking higher returns. Banks' interest costs declined from the combined effect of substantially lower interest rates paid on deposits and, for most banks, a smaller base of interest-bearing deposits.

Bank loan charges also reflect an assessment of the rate of inflation over the term of a loan, or the probable decline in the purchasing power of money during the time the loan is outstanding. This assessment is important because banks want to be repaid in dollars equal in value to those loaned.

Finally, bank loan charges reflect the administrative costs incurred in maintaining and servicing loans, as well as the margin of profit that banks want to achieve on loans. Banks often express their profit margin as a percentage "spread" over the costs they incur in obtaining reserves to support loans, plus an allowance for administrative costs and their assumption of risk.

Summary

When consumers, businesses, and governments spend money, they generate demand for the production of goods and services. In turn, the income that consumers, businesses, and governments receive for producing those goods and services is used to satisfy that demand and to generate saving, investment, and further spending. Money links these processes in a complex circular flow of economic activity. Important measures of the nation's economic performance include real GDP, net domestic product, national income, personal income, and personal disposable income.

Financial intermediaries take in funds from consumers, businesses, and governments that choose to save some of their income and then lend those funds to consumers, businesses, and governments that choose to borrow. These loans provide the economy with the bulk of its investment funds and are a key factor in its long-term growth.

Because commercial banks create new money (in the form of demand deposit balances) when they make loans, the Federal Reserve's monetary policy attempts to control commercial bank lending. It does this by changing the cost of money (interest rates) or the availability of money (growth of the money supply). If the amount of bank-created money adds too much to the existing supply, inflation can result; if it adds too little, recession can result. The objective of monetary policy is to prevent or to counter such economic imbalances.

Questions

1. How does the economy benefit when consumers place their savings in banks and other financial intermediaries instead of holding savings as cash?

2. What functions do financial intermediaries, brokers, and dealers perform that lenders and borrowers could not perform for themselves?

3. What would be the economic and financial consequences if the U.S. government announced it was nullifying the federal debt and that in the future the government would spend only the taxes that it collected?

4. Why does the Federal Reserve focus primarily on controlling commercial bank lending as opposed to other financial intermediary lending?

5. Why do rising interest rates affect consumer, business, and government borrowers differently?

3

Financial Intermediaries

Objectives

After successfully completing this chapter, you will be able to

☐ describe the principal financial intermediaries in the United States today,

☐ summarize how increased competition in the 1980s changed the business orientation of banks, thrifts, and other intermediaries,

☐ distinguish between demand deposit accounts, savings and time deposit accounts, NOW accounts, and money market deposit accounts,

☐ compare the relative importance of the major deposit liabilities of commercial banks, and

☐ identify recent changes in banking laws and regulations that have significantly affected the nature of bank deposits.

Introduction

Financial intermediaries link savers with borrowers, accepting money from those who want to save it and lending it in turn to consumers, businesses, and governments who choose to borrow funds. These institutions are all but essential in our modern economy. As we engage in the many financial transactions of day-to-day living, financial intermediaries enable us to manage our money with great efficiency, safety, and convenience.

In this chapter, we take a broad look at the key financial intermediaries, including depository institutions—commercial banks and thrifts—and nondepository institutions—money market funds and finance companies. We also will discuss the major types of deposit instruments—transaction accounts and various types of time and savings accounts—as well as the competitive relationships that form the basis of our nation's financial system. We will consider how changes in banking laws, regulations, and management in the 1980s affected these relationships.

For additional study of related topics, you are encouraged to read Extended Study 3, "Interest Rate Regulation," which explains the origins and the consequences of regulations governing interest paid on deposits, and Extended Study 4, "Overview of the Financial Institutions Reform, Recovery and Enforcement Act of 1989," which reviews measures taken by Congress to address problems that emerged in the U.S. financial system in the 1980s.

The Changing Competitive Environment

Commercial banks are the key financial intermediaries in the economy's saving and lending process. As exhibit 3.1 shows, the nation's 12,000 commercial banks hold $3.5 trillion ($3,500 billion) in assets, equal to about 45 percent of the $7.8 trillion in assets held by all the other major financial intermediaries cited.

In recent decades, however, the importance of other financial intermediaries in the saving and lending process has grown and these institutions have become more competitive with commercial banks. In the 1970s, thrift institutions—savings and loan associations (S&Ls), savings banks, and credit unions—began offering checking account services that previously had been provided only by commercial banks. Today, thrifts compete directly with commercial banks by providing similar services and engaging in similar lending activities.

The competition facing commercial banks was further increased in the 1980s by the rapid growth of such nondepository intermediaries as money market funds, pension funds, and finance companies. Banks also had to contend with emerging competition from such nonfinancial intermediaries as brokerage firms and retailers that in the 1980s began offering banking-type services, including deposits. These changes have had a significant impact on the nation's financial structure as well as on competitive relationships among intermediaries.

In the late 1980s and early 1990s, commercial banks regained some of the business they had lost to thrift institutions in the previous decade. The nation's thrifts were hit hard with serious liquidity and earnings problems. Many thrifts became increasingly unprofitable as interest rate ceilings were gradually raised after 1980 and then eliminated in 1986. There were a spate of thrift insolvencies and mergers during the 1980s, which considerably reduced the number of thrift institutions in the industry. For example, between 1982 and 1992, more than half the nation's 5,000 S&Ls were merged, acquired by other institutions, or closed.

EXHIBIT 3.1   **Financial Intermediaries**

Type of Financial Intermediary	Number of Institutions	1992 Asset Size (billions of dollars)
Commerical Banks	12,000	$3,500 *billion = 3.5 trillion*
Thrift Institutions		
Savings and Loan Associations *WA Mut Savings*	2,100	900
Savings Banks	400	500
Credit Unions	13,000	200
Nondepository Financial Institutions		
Insurance Companies	5,000	1,600
Money Market Funds	875	600
Finance Companies	3,000	550

Major Depository Intermediaries

Commercial banks and thrift institutions are our nation's principal depository intermediaries. Not many years ago, each type of depository had characteristic products, services, and customer markets—largely determined by government regulation. Today, these distinguishing characteristics have largely disappeared. (Major changes in the regulation of banks and thrifts brought about by legislation in the 1980s and 1990s are discussed in more detail in chapter 9.)

Commercial Banks

A commercial bank is a private corporation, chartered by a state or the federal government, that accepts demand deposits and makes commercial loans. Accepting demand deposits and making loans to businesses were traditionally the only activities associated with commercial banking. Since the 1960s, however, most commercial banks have expanded to become full-service "financial department stores" serving both consumer and business markets, and deriving their earnings not only from loans, but also from financial investments and the sale of financial services.

Most of the nation's 12,000 commercial banks now offer time and savings deposit accounts, rent out safe deposit boxes, exchange foreign currency, maintain automated teller machines (ATMs), issue credit and debit cards, and sell traveler's checks. They perform these services in addition to their more traditional functions of accepting demand deposits and providing corporations with short-term loans. Some of the nation's largest banks also operate trust departments and deal in government securities.

Most commercial banks are small, state-chartered, privately owned institutions. As exhibit 3.2 shows, more than half of all U.S. banks have assets of $50 million or less and typically employ fewer than 50 people. Only about 2,800 banks (less than 25 percent) have assets of more than $100 million. A few commercial banks are global corporations with hundreds of branches and thousands of employees. These banks are concentrated in the nation's money centers—New York, Chicago, and San Francisco—and they hold a relatively large share of the banking system's total deposits.

EXHIBIT 3.2   **Commercial Bank Size (as of December 31, 1991)**

Bank Asset Size	Number of Banks	Percentage of Banks	Percentage of Assets
Less than $25 million	2,846	24.7	1.3
$25-50 million	3,092	26.8	3.3
$50-100 million	2,750	23.9	5.7
$100-500 million	2,209	19.2	13.5
$500-1,000 million	257	2.2	5.3
More than $1 billion	365	3.2	70.9
Total	11,519[1]	100.0	100.0

[1]   Excludes banks that were not in operation for the full year and banks not covered by FDIC insurance (mainly foreign banks in the U.S. that do not engage in retail banking).

Source: Federal Reserve Bank of Atlanta, *Economic Review*, May/June 1992.

The primary role of a commercial bank is to make loans. That activity creates the demand deposit dollars that serve as the nation's principal form of money. About 30 percent of commercial bank loans, by dollar volume, are made to business firms; about 20 percent of the total amount of loans are made to consumers; and another 40 percent of commercial bank loans are for mortgages, many on residential properties, but most on commercial properties.

As recently as the 1960s, demand deposits (non-interest-bearing checking accounts) dominated the deposit structures of commercial banks. Today, as exhibit 3.3 shows, money market deposit accounts (MMDAs) and small-denomination time deposits (interest-earning accounts that technically cannot be withdrawn on demand) are the predominant type of commercial bank deposit. In 1992, commercial banks held nearly $1 trillion in MMDAs and small-denomination time deposits, and about $600 billion in consumer savings deposits and large-denomination time deposits held principally by businesses. Commercial banks held only $500 billion in demand and other checkable deposits—including negotiable order of withdrawal (NOW) and automatic transfer service (ATS) accounts. The ownership of demand deposits at commercial banks is weighted heavily toward the business sector. More than 65 percent, by dollar volume, of bank demand deposits are owned by businesses; only one-third or so of bank time deposits are large-denomination certificates of deposit owned by corporations.

EXHIBIT 3.3   **Business and Consumer Deposits in 1992**
(billions of dollars)

Type of Deposit	Commercial Banks	Thrift Institutions	Total
Passbook savings deposits	$279	$241	$520
Small-denomination time deposits	544	396	940
Large-denomination time deposits	319	70	389
Demand deposits	248	67	315
Other checkable deposits	261	98	359
Money market deposits	434	176	610
IRA and Keogh deposits	148	126	274

Source: Federal Reserve Board, Statistical Release H.6 (508), August 1992.

BANK HOLDING COMPANIES

Approximately 6,000 bank holding companies nationwide own or control a total of 9,000 banks, which hold about 90 percent of the commercial bank deposits. (A bank holding company is a corporation that owns or controls one or more banks.) The corporate structure of bank holding companies allows them to

- ☐ engage in financial activities and offer new services through their nonbank subsidiaries, which banks are not allowed to do. Such activities range from selling economic information and data-processing services to brokering gold bullion, providing investment advice, and underwriting many forms of insurance.

- ☐ provide banks with a structural device to expand their geographic markets. Both state and federal banking regulations severely restrict branching. But prohibitions against branching do not apply to the activities of bank holding companies. Thus a bank holding company can enter markets that a bank cannot. In fact, the growth of bank holding companies since the 1960s has been greatest in those states with the most restrictive branching laws.

- ☐ own and control any number of commercial banks within a state. If the holding company's bank subsidiaries adopt similar marketing strategies, common logos, and nearly identical names, the public may come to view them as branches of a single bank, rather than as separate entities.

- ☐ expand nationally. Today, 55 multistate bank holding companies have subsidiaries in 36 states. Altogether, bank holding companies operate about 1,500 banking offices outside their home states, as well as thousands of nonbanking offices ranging from computer sites and loan production offices to credit card centers.

(A more detailed discussion of the activities and regulation of bank holding companies can be found in Extended Study 5.)

Thrifts

In 1992, thrift institutions numbered about 400 savings banks, 2,100 savings and loan associations, and 13,000 credit unions.

Traditionally, the role of savings banks and S&Ls was to lend depositors' savings to individuals who wanted to buy homes; the role of credit unions to lend savings for major purchases. However, new payment- and deposit-related powers granted to thrift institutions in the 1970s and 1980s effectively eliminated most of the differences in the deposits taken and loans made by banks and thrifts. In the 1980s, many thrifts found that their expanded powers did not guarantee increased business or profits. The end of the decade saw a collapse of the savings and loan industry and growing public concerns over the safety of the deposit insurance programs for thrift institutions.

SAVINGS AND LOAN ASSOCIATIONS

Savings and loan associations (S&Ls) are depositories that specialize in residential mortgage lending. Most S&Ls are small; some are owned by their members—that is, the savers and borrowers—but most are owned by stockholders. Savings and loan associations may be chartered by either a state or the federal government.

Savings and loan associations held about $900 billion in assets in 1992. More than 60 percent of those assets were residential mortgage loans and mortgage securities. S&Ls' mortgage holdings represent about 25 percent of all outstanding residential mortgages held by all lending institutions. Commercial mortgage loans made up another 10 percent or so of the assets of S&Ls. In some states, consumer installment loans and commercial loans have become another important segment of S&Ls' lending activity, but for the industry as a whole, consumer and commercial loans accounted for only 5 percent of total assets in the early 1990s. Offsetting these assets were time and savings deposits, which accounted for more than 80 percent of the total liabilities of S&Ls.

Today, the business activities and products of many S&Ls and commercial banks overlap in significant ways. In 1980, Congress enacted legislation (the Monetary Control Act of 1980) that equalized the residential real estate lending powers of federally chartered savings and loan associations with those of federally chartered commercial banks. Geographic restrictions and maximum loan limitations on S&Ls were removed, and S&Ls' authority to make acquisition, development, and construction loans was extended. The Monetary Control Act also significantly broadened the investment powers of federally chartered savings and loan associations and gave them the same powers as commercial banks—to issue credit cards, offer NOW accounts, and engage in trust and fiduciary activities. Two years later, Congress gave S&Ls commercial lending and still broader investment powers in the Thrift Institutions Restructuring Act of 1982.

Origins of S&L Problems. In the early 1980s, the new interest-earning transaction accounts authorized for banks and thrifts introduced a degree of instability to the operations of savings and loan associations. S&Ls saw their traditional source of funds shift from stable, low-cost, long-term passbook deposits to volatile short-term accounts sensitive to market interest rates, which were rising at that time. More important, S&Ls' income—mainly from fixed-rate mortgages—failed to keep pace with their rising cost of funds. The result was a substantial squeeze on profits.

To expand their earnings, many S&Ls drew on recently granted powers, and switched from making low-yielding residential mortgages to high-yielding—but riskier— consumer loans, business loans, and commercial real estate loans. However, a large number of S&Ls overextended themselves and suffered substantial losses when economic conditions soured and commercial real estate and business borrowers could not repay.

In 1982, about 85 percent of all S&Ls lost money and two-thirds found themselves with liabilities that exceeded the total market value of their assets. Although interest rates declined sharply in the mid-1980s, many S&Ls continued to lose money because of bad loans, excessive operating costs—including very high interest rates paid on deposits—and fraud.

Strains on the S&L Deposit Insurance Fund. By 1985, the Federal Savings and Loan Insurance Corporation (FSLIC), the federal agency that insured S&L depositors, had only about $2 billion available to protect an industry whose assets at that time exceeded $1 trillion. That same year, the government established a program to protect the limited funds of the FSLIC by keeping insolvent institutions open temporarily, under government management, until they could be merged with healthy thrifts or commercial banks. It was thought that these mergers would eliminate the need for FSLIC payouts to depositors at insolvent institutions. (An insolvent institution is one with liabilities that exceed the accounting value of its assets.)

Over the next two years, 60 insolvent S&Ls came under the FSLIC's management. These S&Ls had a combined negative net worth of nearly $6 billion, which would have had to be paid to depositors and creditors if those institutions had been closed and their assets liquidated. To further strengthen the FSLIC's ability to deal with S&L insolvencies, Congress in 1987 approved a financing arrangement to provide the FSLIC with nearly $11 billion in additional funds. This infusion of new funds, however, was not sufficient to meet the FSLIC's needs; more S&Ls were found to be insolvent and some had to be closed, necessitating a substantial FSLIC payout of funds to insured depositors. Growing strains on the underfinanced FSLIC raised public concerns about the overall health of the industry and the thrift deposit insurance program.

Legislation to End the S&L Crisis. Congress moved to address these concerns in 1989 by enacting the Financial Institutions Reform, Recovery and Enforcement Act (FIRREA), which is discussed in detail in Extended Study 4. The act created an Office of Thrift Supervision to oversee S&Ls, disbanded the FSLIC, and established the Savings Association Insurance Fund (SAIF). It also created a new agency—the Resolution Trust Corporation (RTC)—to take over the insolvent S&Ls and find buyers for them or liquidate their assets and pay off insured depositors.

From 1989 to 1992, about 650 S&Ls, with total assets of about $250 billion, were taken over by the RTC and either sold to healthy banks or thrifts, or liquidated. Another 350 S&Ls, with total assets of nearly $250 billion, were also identified as potential RTC takeovers in the mid-1990s. However, the RTC's takeover ability has been questioned because of problems the agency has encountered in liquidating the assets of failed S&Ls. In 1992, the RTC held more than $100 billion in hard-to-sell assets and was receiving only 55 cents on the dollar for those S&L assets that could be sold. Industry analysts estimate that the federal government may ultimately have to provide the RTC with $150 billion to make up the difference between revenue received from liquidating S&L assets and funds paid out to insured depositors.

The collapse of the savings and loan industry in the 1980s wiped out the gains of 30 years of S&L deposit and loan growth. It also threatened to cripple S&Ls as major depository institution competitors in the 1990s. In 1992, only half the S&Ls that had been operating in 1980 were in existence and anxious depositors were continuing to withdraw funds—even from soundly managed associations. Commercial banks were making nearly 40 percent of all U.S. residential mortgage loans while savings and loan associations accounted for only 30 percent. Industry analysts project that if this trend continues, commercial banks will become the nation's primary providers and holders of residential mortgages by the end of the decade.

Factors in the Collapse of the S&L Industry

The collapse of the S&L industry in the late 1980s had its origins in the deregulation of interest rates that Congress set in motion in the Monetary Control Act of 1980. However, other contributing factors were:

❑ the 1980 increase in FDIC insurance coverage from $40,000 to $100,000 per account,

❑ the low capital requirements and liberal accounting rules that were accorded S&Ls in the 1980s, and

❑ the inability of the Federal Home Loan Bank Board (FHLBB), the agency that regulated S&Ls in the 1980s, to attract and retain enough examiners to monitor and prevent risky and unsound S&L practices.

Brokered CDs. The 1980 increase in FDIC insurance coverage brought large denomination ($100,000 or more) certificates of deposit (CDs) under deposit insurance for the first time. Owners of these large CDs could place these funds in any bank or thrift—no matter how weak its earnings or how poorly managed—without fear of loss. In the 1980s, many S&Ls relied extensively on *brokered CDs* to obtain funds when they were nearly insolvent. Working through nationwide brokerage firms, S&Ls offered large CDs to individuals and business firms in areas of the country where the S&Ls could not reach on their own. S&Ls paid high interest rates on these CDs and used the funds to expand unsound lending and investments.

In some instances, brokerage firms placed these CDs with groups of investors, with each group member owning part of a $100,000 deposit. For such individuals, the joint ownership provided a higher interest return than the return available on smaller savings certificates while providing the same degree of deposit insurance protection.

In 1991, Congress placed a limit on insurance coverage for brokered CDs. Today, only banks and thrifts that significantly exceed all capital requirements can accept brokered CDs.

Capital Requirements and Accounting Rules. A capital requirement specifies how much of its owner's money (as a percent of the bank's assets) a bank must set aside as a cushion for possible losses that it may take on upaid loans or on poor investments. Because bank owners are required to invest a substantial amount from their own funds, they are more likely to restrain their managers from making risky or speculative loans and investments. In the case of S&Ls, capital requirements were set low. In 1980, the FHLBB reduced those requirements from 5 percent to 4 percent and in 1981, reduced them to the legal minimum of 3 percent—half the requirement for commercial banks.

In the early 1980s, the FHLBB also liberalized accounting rules for S&Ls. The new rules had the effect of enabling insolvent S&Ls to record the value of their assets, liabilities, and capital in such a way that they appeared to be solvent (the value of assets equaled the value of liabilities plus capital). For example, S&Ls were allowed to mark up capital funds by adding substantial amounts for goodwill—estimates of how much money a potential buyer might pay for the S&L if it were sold.

In 1986, the U.S. General Accounting Office reported to Congress that more than 450 S&Ls were insolvent—on the basis of generally accepted accounting principles (GAAP). The S&Ls in question held assets of $113 billion, or 11 percent of the total assets of the S&L industry in 1986. In 1987, Congress ordered the FHLBB to reinstitute generally accepted accounting principles in evaluating the financial condition of S&Ls. However, the requirement was to be phased in through 1993 in an effort to allow financially troubled thrifts to meet the stricter solvency requirements.

S&L Examiners. The number of examiners available to the FHLBB in the early 1980s was insufficient to monitor and prevent risky and unsound S&L practices. The number of field examiners employed by the FHLBB declined every year from 1981 to 1984. The FHLBB lost examiners because its pay scale—unlike those of other examining agencies—was subject to federal civil service limitations. In 1985, those limitations were removed and the salaries of S&L examiners were raised to those of bank examiners. The number of S&L examiners grew sharply after 1984, from about 1,300 to 3,400 by 1989. However, by the late 1980s the problems of S&Ls could no longer be contained through the examinations process.

SAVINGS BANKS

Savings banks are the smallest category of thrift institutions in terms of numbers. There were only about 400 such banks in 1992, but they held $500 billion in assets (see exhibit 3.1). Like savings and loans, the traditional role of savings banks has been to accept savings deposits and to channel these deposits into mortgages.

Savings banks are located primarily in New England and the Mid-Atlantic states. They were first organized in the early 1800s, before commercial banks started accepting individual savings deposits, to encourage thrift and provide a safe repository for public savings.

Until the 1980s, most savings banks were state-chartered, state-supervised, nonstockholder institutions operated by boards of trustees for the benefit of depositors. The depositors owned these banks and received profits in the form of interest on deposits. In the 1980s, Congress gave mutual savings banks new powers to offer interest-bearing checking accounts, make local business loans (up to 5 percent of the bank's assets), and to offer demand deposit accounts to business loan customers as well as to consumers. Congress also broadened savings banks' overall lending and investment powers and gave mutuals the option of converting to federal charter and becoming stockholder institutions. By issuing stock, savings banks could more readily obtain capital to expand and compete more effectively. Most mutuals converted to stock ownership.

Savings banks have traditionally obtained most of their funds from small individual deposits, with passbook deposits typically supplying about 90 percent of savings banks' funds. Upon presenting a passbook, the depositor can have savings deposits converted to cash, although savings banks can require the depositor to provide written notice at least seven days before withdrawal. About 60 percent of savings bank assets are in the form of mortgages; most of the remainder is invested in U.S. government and corporate bonds.

CREDIT UNIONS

Credit unions make up the largest category of thrift in terms of numbers—about 13,000 in 1992—but the smallest category in terms of assets—about $200 billion in 1992. Credit unions are cooperative associations of depositors with a common interest or affiliation, who pool their savings by buying shares and then borrowing from the pool. Share ownership in turn allows members to borrow from the pool of all credit union shares. Members are paid dividends (interest) on their shares using the income from the credit union's loans and other investments.

Most of the nation's credit unions are very small, with few, if any, full-time paid employees. Many credit unions operate on the corporate premises where employees work, with members working at the credit union on a voluntary, part-time basis. Rent-free space provided by the sponsoring employer and no labor costs keep overhead low and often give small credit unions a competitive edge in lending rates over other thrifts. However, some credit unions have assets that exceed those of many S&Ls and savings banks. About one-third of the nation's adult population (60 million) are credit union members.

Member's savings—share accounts—represent about 85 percent of the total liabilities of credit unions. Loans to members account for more than 75 percent of total assets. Traditionally, credit union loans have been short-term loans repaid in installments. But changes in banking law and regulation in the 1970s and 1980s drastically altered the scope of credit union activities.

Credit unions now make mortgage loans of up to 30 years, offer checking account services through share draft accounts, and offer certificates of deposit through variable-rate share certificates. The Monetary Control Act of 1980 permitted credit unions to make overdraft loans on share draft accounts and to make real estate cooperative loans.

New services in the early 1980s increased the operating costs of credit unions but also spurred their growth. By the end of the decade, the share of the thrift deposit market held by credit unions grew by more than 30 percent, outpacing asset growth at savings banks and savings and loan associations, as well as commercial banks (see exhibit 3.4).

EXHIBIT 3.4   **Comparative Growth of Credit Unions, Other Thrift Institutions, and Commercial Banks 1960-1985**

| | Average Annual Asset Growth | | |
	Credit Unions	S&Ls and Savings Banks	Commercial Banks
1960-1970	12.5%	7.9%	9.0%
1970-1980	15.0%	11.0%	10.3%
1980-1985	13.7%	8.1%	8.7%

Sources: Federal Reserve *Bulletin*, FDIC Annual Reports, CUNA Yearbook and Statistical Report.

Federal regulations governing credit unions give them many competitive advantages over other types of thrift institutions and commercial banks, and in the view of many bankers, these advantages have been largely responsible for helping credit unions register the rapid asset growth seen in exhibit 3.4.

For example, until the 1980s, federally chartered (and some state-chartered) credit unions were subject to a 12 percent ceiling on loan rates, which made their loans very appealing to borrowers. At the same time, interest rates on credit union savings accounts were not subject to the low rate ceilings that were then applicable to savings deposits at banks and other thrifts.

As cooperatives, credit unions are considered nonprofit entities and are not subject to taxes. Also, credit unions are subject to fewer regulations than banks. These advantages have raised issues about the fairness of competition between credit unions and other depository institutions.

Broader issues related to the safety and soundness of credit unions became a concern of Congress and the public in the 1990s. About 10 percent of the nation's credit unions do not have federal deposit insurance. Rather, these credit unions—more than

1,400 with $18.6 billion in deposits—are insured by one of nine private insurance funds.

The 1991 insolvency of the private insurance fund that covered credit unions in Rhode Island necessitated a temporary state-mandated closing of Rhode Island's credit unions and triggered national concern over the safety of all credit union deposits. Most of the 20 states that permit private deposit insurance for credit unions moved quickly to bolster public confidence by requiring credit unions covered by private funds to obtain federal coverage. At the same time, legislation was introduced in Congress to impose federal insurance on all credit unions. However, no action was taken on these bills in 1992.

Nondepository Intermediaries

In the last decade, nondepository financial intermediaries have emerged as significant competitors of banks and thrifts. Nondepository intermediaries include money market funds, life insurance companies, pension funds, and finance companies, as well as nonfinancial intermediaries—businesses that do not provide financial products and services as a primary activity.

Money Market Funds

Although money market funds behave in some ways like depository institutions, they are technically considered to be open-end investment companies that purchase securities on behalf of individual or institutional investors. In 1992, there were 875 money market funds; of these, one-third held only tax-free investments. Not all these funds are open to individuals—many are for the exclusive use of institutional investors; others are sponsored by brokerage firms. Money market funds should not be confused with money market deposit accounts, a type of account that commercial banks and thrifts were authorized in December 1982 to offer in competition with money market funds (discussed in more detail later in this chapter).

Typically, money market funds offer a checking account option that enables shareholders to write checks of $500 or more against their shares. Shares also can be redeemed by electronic transfers (wire transfers) sent by the fund to an investor's bank account. Most general-purpose funds require minimum initial investments—as low as $500— while some require no minimum. By contrast, institutional investor funds may require minimum investments of $50,000 or more.

Most money market funds invest in short-term certificates of deposit, commercial paper, and U.S. Treasury bills. On occasion, they also purchase other high-grade money market instruments. Some money market funds limit their investments to U.S. government securities in order to attract investors who are averse to credit risk. Other funds invest exclusively in Eurodollar certificates of deposit, tax-exempt municipal bonds (for tax-conscious investors), or shares of other funds.

The first money market funds began operations in 1972, and by 1978, these funds held about $10 billion in assets. Today, the funds have more than 10 million shareholders with assets of $600 billion. The phenomenal growth of the funds in the early 1980s—before banks could offer money market deposit accounts—was sparked by interest-rate-conscious individuals and institutions that increasingly shifted money from bank and thrift accounts into higher-yielding money market funds. The continued growth of the funds into the 1990s, however, has confounded many bankers.

In December 1982, banks and thrifts were authorized to offer a new type of account—a money market deposit account (MMDA)—that would enable them to compete directly with money market funds. Money market deposit accounts, like the balances held in money market funds, are checkable and pay a market interest rate, but have the added advantage of being covered by government deposit insurance. Most banking analysts thought that the availability of the new money market deposit accounts would attract interest-sensitive depositors back to banks and thrifts and that the uninsured money market funds would lose their competitiveness. Instead, money market funds continued to grow, increasing their deposits to $600 billion in 1992.

Money market funds have been able to attract and retain deposits because they generally offer higher interest rates than those offered by banks and thrifts on their money market deposit accounts. This interest rate edge reflects the broader scope in which money market funds can invest and trade in riskier, higher-paying financial instruments. In addition, because accounts held at money market funds and the money market deposits held at banks and thrifts have slightly different characteristics, they appeal to different types of investors.

Life Insurance Companies

Life insurance companies are another type of financial intermediary that compete with banks and thrifts for individuals' savings. By selling risk protection, primarily to individuals, they receive savings in the form of contractual premium payments paid by policyholders. Although holders of insurance policies typically do not use their policies as savings accounts, the accumulated cash value of a life insurance policy can be readily drawn on to provide the policyholder with liquidity. Life insurance companies are thus considered to be financial intermediaries because they accumulate the funds they receive from premiums and place them in relatively risk-free, long-term investments such as corporate bonds and multifamily and commercial mortgages.

Until the 1940s, life insurance companies were the single largest holder of the nation's consumer savings funds. In the last 40 years, however, the deposit growth of thrifts and banks has dwarfed the growth of the nation's 5,000 life insurance companies. In 1992, life insurance companies (see exhibit 3.1) held about $1.6 trillion in assets, compared with $1.6 trillion in assets held by thrifts and $1.5 trillion in consumer time and savings deposits (including MMDAs) held by commercial banks.

Pension Funds

Another important category of financial intermediary is pension funds, which administer savings that have been set aside by employers and employees for retirement income. The nation's 7,800 pension funds held more than $2 trillion of retirement savings in 1992. About 40 percent of that amount was held in funds administered by federal, state, and local governments; 40 percent was held in funds managed by private trustees, including bank trust departments; and 20 percent was held in funds administered by insurance companies. Federal government funds invest most of their assets in U.S. Treasury securities, while other pension funds invest most of the funds they receive in corporate stocks and bonds.

Finance Companies

The nation's 3,000 finance companies also are classified as financial intermediaries. They provide two types of credit—wholesale and retail. Wholesale credit is provided to merchants so that inventories of merchandise can be carried until they are purchased by consumers. Retail credit is provided to consumers so that big-ticket items, automobiles in particular, can be bought on installment. Finance companies obtain their funds by borrowing from commercial banks and insurance companies, as well as by selling their own promissory notes—either secured (collateralized) or unsecured—directly in the credit market.

Wholesale credit involves advancing funds to merchants, primarily auto dealers, usually on the merchant's promissory note. These notes are ordinarily secured by warehouse or trust receipts covering the merchandise to be financed. Retail credit involves direct lending to consumers evidenced by a personal promissory note. A lien is placed on the article purchased so that the article can be recovered if the borrower defaults on the loan; in the case of a car, insurance policies covering fire, theft, and accident also are required.

In the 1980s, finance companies gained an increasingly larger share of the auto loan and general consumer installment loan market from banks and other providers of consumer credit. These gains are reflected in the $550 billion in total assets held by finance companies in 1992.

Major automobile finance companies such as General Motors Acceptance Corporation and Chrysler accounted for almost three-quarters of all new auto loans in the 1980s. As a result, in 1992 finance companies held about 30 percent of the $260 billion in auto loans outstanding in the United States. Finance companies have used below-market financing rates—from 2.9 percent down to zero—in lieu of price tag reductions to boost sluggish car sales, making it difficult for commercial banks to compete for auto loans. In addition, banks were hindered by their high cost of funds in the early 1980s, coupled with interest rate ceilings in many states that prevented them from charging enough on consumer loans to meet their costs.

Many major finance companies that are not involved in the auto loan market, such as General Electric, Westinghouse, and Borg-Warner Acceptance Corporation, originally were set up to finance the products of their parent manufacturing companies, but increasingly they finance the products of other companies as well.

Nonfinancial Intermediaries

In the 1980s, nonbank businesses, such as retailers and brokerage firms, found a way to acquire "consumer banks", which gave them the ability to provide consumers with banking services and deposits. Exhibit 3.5 contains a list of the major nonbank businesses that acquired consumer banks in the 1980s. These businesses are sometimes referred to as nonfinancial intermediaries because providing financial services and accepting deposits are not their primary activities.

EXHIBIT 3.5   Major Nonbank Corporations that Operate Consumer Banks

Name of Holding Company	Primary Business	Name of Subsidiary Consumer Bank
Advest Group, Inc. Hartford, CT	Brokerage/Mutual Funds	Advest Bank Hartford, CT
Aetna Life and Casualty Hartford, CT	Insurance	Liberty Bank & Trust Gibbsboro, NJ
American Express Co.	Travel and entertainment card	Boston Safe Deposit and Trust Co. Advisory Bank & Trust Minneapolis, MN American Express Centurion Bank, Newark, DE
Bear Stearns Co. New York	Brokerage	Custodial Trust Co. Trenton, NJ
Chrysler Corp. Highland Park, MI	Manufacturing/ Finance Co.	Automotive Financial Services, Inc., Highland Park, MI
Dreyfus Corp. New York	Brokerage/Mutual Funds	Dreyfus Consumer Bank Orange, NJ
General Electric Co. Stamford, CT	Manufacturing/ Finance Co.	Monogram Bank Blue Ash, OH
Home Group Inc. New York	Insurance	Premium Bank Oceanside, CA

14o6/170

(Exhibit 3.5 continued)

J.C. Penney Co. Inc. New York	Retail Chain	J.C. Penney National Bank Harrington, DE
John Hancock Sub- sidiaries, Inc. Boston, MA	Insurance	First Signature Bank & Trust Co., Boston, MA
Merrill Lynch & Co. New York, NY	Brokerage	Merrill Lynch Bank & Trust Co., Plainsboro, NJ
Montgomery Ward & Co. Chicago, IL	Retail Chain	Clayton Bank & Trust Co. Clayton, DE
Sears, Roebuck and Co. Chicago, IL	Retail Chain	Greenwood Trust Co. New Castle, DE Hurley State Bank Hurley, SD
Travelers Corp. Hartford, CT	Insurance	Massachusetts Co. Boston, MA

A consumer bank does not make or hold business loans. Nonbank businesses found a loophole in the Bank Holding Company Act of 1956 that enabled them to purchase commercial banks and, by divesting the banks' business lending activities, retain ownership and control of the banks. This bank ownership practice was prohibited by federal law in 1987. However, Congress permitted the nonbank firms that had entered the banking business before the prohibition to retain ownership of their consumer banks—170 in all. (See Extended Study 5 for a more extensive discussion of consumer banks.)

In the 1960s, only two nonfinancial intermediaries—the Sears department store chain and General Motors—provided significant financial services. At that time, their combined income from financial services was under $100 million. In the 1980s, the top 10 nonfinancial intermediaries—mainly brokerage firms and Sears—earned a total of more than $2 billion annually from sales of financial services. The foremost nonfinancial intermediaries today include Sears, Merrill Lynch, American Express, and the financial subsidiaries of other major corporations as shown in exhibit 3.5.

In 1982, Sears, the nation's largest retail chain, broadened its role as an intermediary by establishing financial service centers in some of its stores. These centers offer insurance, real estate, and brokerage services and are staffed by representatives from the insurance, banking, and brokerage businesses that Sears is affiliated with or owns. (Sears owns two consumer banks, a savings and loan association, an insurance company, the nation's largest real estate brokerage firm, and the fifth-largest securities brokerage house in the United States.) Sears also offers consumer credit to more than

35 million credit card holders. If the Sears Financial Network had bank status, it would be the largest interstate bank in the United States.

Merrill Lynch, another of the major nonfinancial intermediaries, is the world's largest securities brokerage firm; it also owns a consumer bank, a real estate financing company, and an insurance company. In addition to services associated with banking, brokerage, real estate, and insurance, Merrill Lynch maintains a money market fund that allows account holders to draw checks against their investment in the fund. Other brokerage firms offer similar money market fund services to their customers.

A customer that establishes such an account must maintain a minimum balance (typically $15,000) in funds or securities for investment purposes. The customer obtains unlimited check-writing privileges against the account and receives other specialized services from the brokerage firm, such as a reconcilement service for outstanding checks. Funds in excess of the base amount are "swept" daily into one of several money market funds controlled by the brokerage firm.

The American Express Company, another major nonfinancial intermediary, acquired a major securities brokerage firm and three consumer banks in the 1980s. It now offers credit card payment and installment credit to millions of households and business firms (in addition to its traditional travel and entertainment card) and is one of the most popular names in traveler's checks.

Other major nonfinancial intermediaries that compete with banks and thrifts include the financial subsidiaries of large corporations, such as General Electric Credit Corporation and General Motors Acceptance Corporation (whose role as finance companies has already been discussed). GMAC is the fourth-largest financial institution in the United States. It has more than 8 million customers, including 400,000 residential mortgage holders in two mortgage companies that it purchased in 1985. Finance companies that own banks (Beneficial Finance, for example, owns a savings and loan association) and communications conglomerates that own financial subsidiaries (RCA owns both NBC and CIT Financial) will also likely offer an increasingly broad range of bank services in the 1990s.

Many commercial banks and thrifts have attempted to meet the challenge of the nonfinancial intermediaries by offering new products and services that have long been the exclusive province of nonbank firms. For example, some banks now offer their own discount brokerage services—through brokerage firms that they have acquired, by establishing discount brokerage subsidiaries, or by contracting services through independent brokerage firms. Other banks have focused on generating entirely new areas of business and income—such as trading in the financial futures market for their customers and expanding into nonfinancial fields such as data processing and telecommunications.

Major Types of Deposits

Bank liabilities have changed markedly in the past 10 years. Innovations in banking and changes in banking laws and regulations have created new types of deposits and have altered the definitions and characteristics of existing deposits, thereby shifting the deposit-taking focus of the banking industry. Basically, deposits can be categorized as transaction (checkable) accounts or as savings accounts—although the distinction is increasingly hazy. (Exhibit 3.3 compares the total amounts of various types of business and consumer deposits held by banks and thrifts in 1992.)

Transaction Accounts

Transaction accounts are deposits from which payments can be made using checks, drafts, payment orders of withdrawal, or telephone transfers drawn against funds on deposit. Demand deposits and NOW accounts are the two principal types of transaction accounts. Automatic transfer service (ATS) accounts and credit union share drafts also are checkable deposits. In 1992, commercial banks held about $250 billion in noninterest-earning demand deposits and about $260 billion in other (interest-earning) transaction accounts. By comparison, thrift institutions held $67 billion in demand deposits and $98 billion in other transaction accounts (as seen in exhibit 3.3).

With the Monetary Control Act of 1980, Congress mandated that depository institutions must maintain reserves against all "transaction accounts," which it defined as all deposits (including interest-earning deposits) on which checks may be drawn. This represented a significant change in the government's regulation of interest-earning deposits. These deposits had previously been treated as savings deposits, which carried lower reserve requirements than demand deposit accounts. (At the same time, the Monetary Control Act also exempted personal time and savings deposits from the Federal Reserve's reserve requirements.)

DEMAND DEPOSIT ACCOUNTS

Demand deposit accounts are traditional checking accounts that allow the holder to make payments by writing checks and to withdraw cash on demand. Interest on demand deposits has been prohibited by the federal government since 1933. However, when negotiable order of withdrawal (NOW) accounts, automatic transfers from savings to checking accounts, phone transfers from savings accounts to third parties, and money market deposit accounts appeared in the late 1970s and early 1980s, the characteristics that differentiated demand deposits from time deposits all but disappeared. Today, a demand deposit is specifically defined as a deposit that is payable on demand—that is, a customer may withdraw funds from the account with no advance notice, usually by writing checks or using an automated teller machine.

Most demand deposit balances held in banks are for commercial accounts. Personal checking account balances represent only about one-quarter of total demand deposit balances. However, personal accounts constitute 90 percent of the total number of demand deposit accounts at most banks.

Demand deposit accounts were traditionally the exclusive preserve of commercial banks, but since 1980 these accounts have been offered by savings banks, savings and loan associations, and credit unions as well. Moreover, with the increased competition from interest-bearing transaction accounts, most bankers expect little growth in demand deposit accounts—either in total balances or in numbers of accounts.

Although the traditional checking account appears to have little potential for growth, banks have continued to innovate in their demand deposit offerings. For example, many banks have actively promoted flat fee checking accounts to consumers, which carry fixed monthly charges rather than imposing a variable fee based on balance levels and number of checks written. Many banks also have introduced streamlined checking accounts with very low service charges to provide a "lifeline" service to low-income individuals and senior citizens.

NOW ACCOUNTS

Negotiable order of withdrawal (NOW) accounts—the other major category of transaction accounts—are, in effect, interest-earning checking accounts.

NOW accounts were created by savings banks in New England in the 1970s and achieved national prominence when state courts in Massachusetts and New Hampshire ruled that such accounts were in compliance with banking law despite the 1933 federal prohibition against the payment of interest on checking accounts. To enable commercial banks in those states to compete with the savings banks, Congress in 1974 authorized all depositories in Massachusetts and New Hampshire to offer NOW accounts. Congress later extended this authority to all depositories in the other four New England states (1976), to New York (1978), and to New Jersey (1979). The Monetary Control Act of 1980 brought regulatory equity to banks and thrifts in other parts of the country by authorizing NOW accounts for depositories in all states beginning in 1981. As noted previously, the Monetary Control Act also classified NOW accounts as transaction accounts subject to reserve requirements.

Time and Savings Accounts

Besides transaction (checkable) accounts, the other broad category of deposit accounts consists of various types of time and savings accounts (interest-earning deposits that technically cannot be withdrawn on demand). In the past, depositors held their savings funds in passbook savings accounts and in a limited range of other time deposits because demand deposits (checking accounts) did not pay interest. Today, banks and thrifts, in their efforts to compete for depositors' savings, offer a broad range of time and savings accounts as well as checkable accounts that pay interest.

TIME AND SAVINGS DEPOSITS

Time deposits are defined as any deposit in a bank account that cannot be withdrawn before a specified date or without advance notice. Time certificates of deposit are offered in various denominations and varying maturities. Large-denomination certificates of deposit (in amounts of $100,000 or more) offered to corporations are a major source of time deposits for commercial banks (see exhibit 3.3). Banks and thrifts held a total of more than $1.3 trillion in time deposits in 1992.

A time deposit cannot be withdrawn for at least seven days after it is made. If it is withdrawn before that or prior to the maturity of the time deposit contract, an interest penalty will be charged. If a time deposit is withdrawn within the first six days after it is made, the penalty is loss of at least seven days' interest. For business time deposits with maturities of 18 months or longer, the penalty is loss of one month's interest. If interest on a time deposit is paid monthly (as is requested by many elderly customers) and the funds are withdrawn, the bank may look to the principal of the time deposit to satisfy the penalty. A savings deposit contract gives the depository the option of requiring seven days' prior written notice of intent to withdraw, but funds can be withdrawn without loss of interest.

The Monetary Control Act of 1980 exempted both personal time and savings deposits, as well as business time deposits having maturities of one and a half years or more, from the Federal Reserve's reserve requirements. In 1990, the Federal Reserve exempted all business time deposits from reserve requirements.

PASSBOOK SAVINGS ACCOUNTS

Passbook savings accounts were traditionally the staple deposit of savings banks and savings and loan associations. Today, however, funds in passbook accounts represent about one-third of all consumer-oriented time deposits in commercial banks and about 15 percent of the total deposits of all banks and thrifts. Until 1975, passbook savings accounts could be held only by individuals and certain nonprofit organizations. Beginning in 1975, partnerships and corporations were permitted to hold savings deposits of up to $150,000; this limitation was removed in March 1986 when interest rate ceilings on savings accounts were abolished.

The introduction of NOW accounts in the 1980s, other interest-earning transaction accounts, and savings certificates (small-denomination fixed-maturity time deposits) whose interest rate could track with market rates, had a corrosive effect on passbook savings balances. The effect, however, was not as substantial as many industry analysts expected. In December 1982, when money market deposit accounts were introduced, savings deposits at banks and thrifts totaled almost $360 billion. Passbook savings balances declined in the mid-1980s and in the early 1990s, but by mid-1992 savings deposits stood at $520 billion.

Despite the relatively low interest return on passbook accounts and the greater convenience and higher returns available on the newer kinds of savings accounts, most consumers continue to hold on to their passbooks. Many consumers like the passbook itself—they like to "hold" their money and watch it grow. They also like to be able to deposit or withdraw small amounts at will, with no maturity or penalty constraints. Long-standing public familiarity with passbook accounts also may be a factor in their continued popularity.

With the removal of interest rate ceilings in 1986, banks were no longer limited to paying 5 1/4 percent interest on passbook accounts. However, the general decline in market interest rates in the late 1980s and early 1990s prompted most banks to lower, rather than raise, the passbook rate. Some banks also converted their passbook accounts from fixed-rate to variable-rate accounts. Nonetheless, most bankers do not expect the public's favorable attitudes toward passbook savings to change.

MONEY MARKET DEPOSIT ACCOUNTS

Money market deposit accounts (MMDAs) are savings deposits on which a limited number of checks can be written each month.

As noted previously, the Garn-St Germain Act of 1982 authorized depositories to offer this new type of account so that banks and thrifts could provide depositors with an account that was competitive with those offered by money market funds. The new account was not subjected to any interest rate ceilings, which were then still in effect, and holders were permitted limited check-writing privileges. Moveover, unlike the money market funds, MMDAs are insured by the government.

A money market deposit account carries no minimum maturity, but banks may require seven days' notice of withdrawal. Depositors may make six transfers per month from the account, only three of which may be by third-party check and three by pre-authorized transfer. However, depositors are permitted unlimited withdrawals of cash or transfers to another account within the same bank, either by mail or in person.

Since March 1986, money market deposit accounts have not been subject by law to minimum balance requirements. Nevertheless, most banks and thrifts continue to require a $1,000 or $2,500 account balance minimum as a matter of management discretion.

There are no interest rate ceilings on MMDAs—banks can pay any interest rate they choose. In 1992, many banks paid split interest rates on MMDA funds, paying a lower rate if account balances dropped below a stated minimum.

Although money market deposit accounts offer limited check-writing privileges, Congress has classified them as savings accounts rather than as transaction accounts for reserve requirement purposes. Because time and savings deposits are not subject to costly reserve requirements, this classification makes MMDAs more competitive with the accounts offered by the money market funds (which also are not subject to reserve requirements).

The MMDA became a major deposit at banks and thrifts soon after it was authorized in 1982. By 1992, approximately $610 billion had been deposited in MMDAs at banks and thrifts—far more than the total amount of either demand deposits or other check-able deposits (exhibit 3.3). Most of these MMDA funds, however, were not shifted from the money market funds, as many bankers had originally expected, but were redeposited from more traditional (and lower-paying) demand, time, and savings accounts.

SAVINGS CERTIFICATES

Savings certificates are time deposits with fixed maturities and fixed interest rates and are offered in small denominations, primarily to individuals. These certificates are usually nonnegotiable; that is, they must be presented to the bank by the original depositor for redemption. Although they can be issued in any denomination, most banks require a minimum deposit of $500 to $2,500 for their certificates, depending on maturity. Once issued, no funds may be added to or withdrawn from the certificate until it matures. In 1992, banks held about $185 billion in certificates with 6 to 12 months maturity, and more than $160 billion in certificates with 30 months or longer maturity. These maturity ranges were the two most popular savings certificates on banks' books.

LARGE DENOMINATION CERTIFICATES OF DEPOSIT (CDS)

Large denomination CDs ($100,000 or more) are offered by banks primarily to corporations. CDs have fixed interest rates and are payable at maturity, which can be any date seven days or longer after deposit of the funds. Although CDs can be issued in nonnegotiable bearer form (payable only to the deposit-holder by the issuing bank) the most popular CDs among big corporations are those that are negotiable (salable in the secondary market).

Most of the nation's large banks offer their CDs through nationwide brokerage firms as well as through their own local or regional offices. By using a brokerage firm to sell its CDs—particularly a firm with an extensive network of nationwide offices—a bank can reach a broader market than it could reach on its own. Banks generally have to pay a higher interest rate on their brokered CDs than on those issued locally. However, banks have found that these higher interest rates tend to be less than the rates they would otherwise have to pay to borrow funds in the nation's money or capital markets. In 1992, banks held more than $300 billion in large denomination CDs.

IRAS AND OTHER RETIREMENT ACCOUNTS

Self-employed workers and workers not covered by an employer's pension plan are able to open interest-earning retirement accounts, some of which are tax-deduct-ible. For the self-employed, these accounts are known as Keogh accounts or SEP accounts (simplified employee pension). For others the accounts are called IRA accounts (individual retirement accounts).

Most banks offer IRA accounts as trust or custodial time accounts. IRAs may carry a fixed or a variable interest rate over the life of the account, with withdrawals not allowed (without a 10 percent IRS tax penalty) until the depositor reaches age 59 1/2. Individuals not covered by a pension plan can deposit up to $2,000 a year in a tax-deferred IRA account. That is, funds deposited can be subtracted from total income on which taxes are paid. Individuals covered by a pension plan also can open IRA accounts on which interest is not subject to taxation until withdrawal. However, in most instances the funds deposited cannot be deducted for tax purposes.

In 1981, IRAs were available to all employees as part of broader tax reform measures enacted by Congress. With this liberalization of eligibility, IRA deposits soared. Banks, thrifts, brokerage firms, and other financial institutions held about $26 billion in IRA deposits in 1981. By 1986, when Congress rescinded the liberalization, more than $350 billion in IRA deposits were being held for 20 million account holders, with commercial banks holding about one-quarter of this total.

Since 1987, IRAs have been subject to income thresholds that prevent all but low-income earners from deducting IRA deposits from current taxes. Among the factors that influenced Congress to change the rules was a sense that the tax deduction was being used primarily by upper-income individuals as a tax shelter and that the Treasury would lose about $26 billion in income tax revenue from 1987 to 1991 if the deduction continued.

Some bankers contend that without broad tax deductibility IRAs will fade as a meaningful deposit product of the 1990s. Other bankers feel that IRAs will continue to attract substantial funds, based on the fact that one-third of IRA holders who opened accounts between 1981 and 1986 continue to qualify for the annual $2,000 maximum tax-free deduction. They also note that interest earned on all IRA accounts is tax deferred until withdrawal and that all IRA funds are protected by FDIC insurance. In 1992, banks held about $150 billion in IRA and Keogh deposits.

Summary

Commercial banks and thrift institutions (savings banks, savings and loan associations, and credit unions) are among the nation's key financial intermediaries. Changes in banking law and regulation in the early 1980s eliminated most of the legal differences between commercial banks and thrift institutions, and today the business activities and products of banks and thrifts overlap significantly. At the same time, nondepository financial intermediaries (life insurance companies, pension funds, finance companies, and money market funds) and nonfinancial intermediaries (retail firms and brokerage firms)—none of which are covered by the laws that govern banks and thrifts—have emerged as growing sources of competition.

Major changes in banking law embodied in the Monetary Control Act of 1980 greatly affected the composition and cost of bank and thrift liabilities (deposits) in the 1980s. Funds increasingly moved from noninterest-bearing demand deposit accounts and low-earning passbook savings accounts into new transaction accounts that pay money market rates. Competitive relationships among financial intermediaries also changed as funds moved from banks to nonbank intermediaries.

The traditional differences between demand deposits and time deposits were largely erased by changes in banking law and practice in the 1980s. The emergence of interest-earning checkable deposits (such as NOW accounts and money market deposit accounts) and IRAs significantly altered the public's savings practices, and caused demand deposits to lose much of their appeal. The public's use of the new types of time deposits and interest-bearing transaction accounts—accentuated by escalating interest rates in the early 1980s—had a devastating impact on the nation's savings and loan associations.

Questions

1. What are the major differences between a commercial bank, a savings and loan association, a credit union, and a money market fund?

2. What competitive advantages, if any, do nonfinancial intermediaries such as Merrill Lynch and Sears have over commercial banks?

3. What are the major types of time deposits offered by commercial banks?

4. Explain how a money market deposit account operates.

5. Cite three changes in the deposit structure or operations of financial intermediaries that were brought about by the Monetary Control Act of 1980.

4

Commercial Banks and Money Creation

Objectives

After successfully completing this chapter, you will be able to

☐   contrast the lending process of a commercial bank with that of other financial intermediaries,

☐   explain how the banking system creates money through the process of multiple deposit creation,

☐   describe how banks gain and lose reserves, and how these reserve changes affect bank lending and economic activity, and

☐   evaluate the role of banks in the implementation of monetary policy.

Introduction

In the 1800s, commercial banks in the United States created money by issuing their own bank notes. The federal government ended this practice among state-chartered banks when it passed the National Banking Act in 1863, and among nationally chartered banks in 1913 when it gave the newly established Federal Reserve banks the exclusive franchise to issue U.S. currency. Today, commercial banks no longer issue currency, but they still create money on their books through the lending process.

In this chapter we will examine how the lending process of a commercial bank differs from that of other financial institutions that do not have money-creating power. We also will examine the Federal Reserve's use of banks and bank reserves to implement monetary policy, and the impact of this practice on the lending process and on economic activity.

Nineteenth century bank note backed by the Treasury of New York.

Photo courtesy of the Library of Congress.

Overview of Bank Lending and Money Creation

Financial intermediaries help maintain a balanced economy and stimulate growth in production, employment, and income. They do this by transferring savings from consumers, businesses, and governments that have excess funds to consumers, businesses, and governments that need additional funds.

A financial intermediary lends out the funds it takes in from depositors—either directly, or indirectly by buying an interest-earning asset, such as a government security or a corporate bond. In buying (investing in) an earning asset, the intermediary is in effect lending funds to the government or corporation that issues the security.

Until recent years, commercial banks were unique among financial intermediaries in that they alone had the power to create demand deposit money through the lending process. This money-creating power, a power held exclusively by commercial banks until 1980, historically distinguished the lending process of commercial banks from that of other financial intermediaries. This also explains why the federal government's monetary policy has traditionally been directed primarily at commercial banks.

The pace at which a bank can create demand deposits (and hence make loans) depends on the size of its reserves (that is, the amount of cash it holds in its vaults and the amount of funds it holds on deposit at its district Federal Reserve bank). A bank's ability to create demand deposits is based on the underlying principle that only part of its assets must be held in liquid form (as vault cash or near-money assets) to meet the claims of other banks presenting depositors' checks for collection or of depositors withdrawing cash.

This principle of *fractional reserves* is the basis for the modern practice of central banks establishing reserve requirements as a tool of monetary policy. In the United States, reserve requirements are set by the Federal Reserve. Reserve requirements are stated percentages of liquid assets that depositories must hold by law against their outstanding demand liabilities. In recent years, the Federal Reserve's reserve requirements have been extended to cover all depository institutions, where previously they applied only to commercial banks that were members of the Federal Reserve. Even without established reserve requirements, however, a bank or thrift would need to hold some fraction of its assets in liquid form—as cash or as deposit balances with other banks—to maintain its day-to-day viability as a depository institution.

A bank's reserves are the raw material it uses for making new loans and investments. The Federal Reserve in turn maintains control over lending and investing through its regulation of bank reserves. Bank lending and investing are tightly controlled activities because the banking system can create amounts of money that are several times larger than the original reserves. This process of multiple deposit creation can profoundly affect the economy. Thus the regulation of reserves controls the growth of the money supply and also influences the cost of funds in the banking system and the profit potential of bank lending and investing.

The Lending Process of a Thrift Institution

When a thrift institution, such as a savings bank or a savings and loan association, takes in funds and then lends them out, it exchanges one form of asset for another—a cash asset for a loan asset. (Although thrifts now have the power traditionally reserved to banks to create money through the commercial loan process, most thrift lending still takes the form described here.) We can trace the normal lending process of a thrift making a loan—in effect, redistributing its assets—by using T-accounts, which are abstracts of an institution's balance sheet that show only those changes in assets and liabilities that are being examined.

Assume that the First Intermediary Savings and Loan Association receives $100,000 in cash deposits from a number of different depositors for credit to their savings and time accounts. Further, assume that First Intermediary's management feels that it should hold liquid assets (cash assets or reserves) equal to 10 percent of its deposits at all times to meet customers' demands for cash and to pay other banks for check collection. (Although banks and thrifts are not required to hold reserves against personal time and savings deposits, their liquidity needs serve as a de facto reserve requirement.)

If First Intermediary decides to hold $10,000 in cash assets against its new $100,000 in deposits, it then has $90,000 in funds available for lending. Let's assume that First Intermediary chooses to redistribute its assets by making a mortgage loan of $90,000 with these funds.

In granting the mortgage, the borrower receives a $90,000 check drawn on First Intermediary or on its account at a correspondent bank. In exchange for relinquishing $90,000 of its cash assets to the borrower, the savings and loan obtains a new earning asset in the form of the mortgage loan. This redistribution of First Intermediary's assets increases its earnings and profit prospects because cash assets, as purely liquid assets, do not earn a return, whereas earning assets do. The loan has not increased the amount of money in the economy, however. Before the loan, $100,000 in cash was deposited in First Intermediary by various depositors. After the loan, the mortgagee holds $90,000 of those funds, and First Intermediary holds the remaining $10,000 as necessary liquidity against the claims of its depositors.

T-accounts can be used to show how First Intermediary's balance sheet is affected, first by the cash deposits, and then by the loan.

First Intermediary Savings and Loan
(Before the Loan)

Assets		Liabilities	
Cash assets	+ $100,000	Savings deposits	+ $100,000

First Intermediary Savings and Loan
(After the Loan/Redistribution of Assets)

Assets		Liabilities	
Cash assets	+ $10,000	Savings deposits	+ $100,000
New mortgage loan	+ $90,000		

Note that the T-accounts show only the asset and liability accounts affected by the transaction, with a plus or minus sign to indicate an increase or decrease for each account. Since a T-account is a microcosm of a full balance sheet, it must balance—that is, the change in assets and liabilities must match (equal pluses and minuses on each side or offsetting plus-minus entries on one side).

The Lending Process of a Commercial Bank

The lending process of a commercial bank is similar to that of a thrift in that the cash receipts from depositors increases both its assets and its deposit liabilities, which enables it to make additional loans and investments. However, cash received by banks is rarely loaned out in the same form. Instead, it is normally deposited in the bank's account at its district Federal Reserve bank as additional reserves. These reserves in turn enable the bank to create new money through the lending process, as shown in the following example.

Assume that First Commercial Bank takes in $100,000 in cash deposits from businesses and individuals for credit to their checking accounts. Further assume, for the sake of simplicity, that the Federal Reserve requires the bank to meet a 10 percent reserve requirement, which in this case means that the bank must hold $10,000 in reserves against these new deposits. (Actual reserve requirements vary depending on the amount of total transaction deposits a bank holds.)

Given these assumptions, First Commercial Bank now has $100,000 in cash assets (held either as vault cash or as a deposit balance at its Reserve bank), giving it $90,000 in excess reserves against which it can create $90,000 in new demand deposits by making a commercial loan. A bank's *total reserves* are those cash assets it holds or owns that are eligible for meeting the reserve requirement. (Only vault cash and deposit balances held at the Reserve Bank are eligible.) *Excess reserves* are those reserve assets held that are in excess of *required reserves*—the amount required to meet the reserve requirement. An easy way to remember these terms and relationships is through the following equations:

1. Total reserves = required reserves + excess reserves

2. Excess reserves = total reserves - required reserves

Now assume that First Commercial agrees to lend $90,000 to a local merchant.

When a commercial bank makes a business loan, it accepts as an asset the borrower's debt obligation (the promise to repay), and creates a liability on its books in the form of a demand deposit balance in the amount of the loan. The deposits that banks create when they make loans are backed by financial or physical assets that collateralize the promissory note or loan agreement. Again, the loan transaction can be shown using T-accounts:

First Commercial Bank
(Before the Loan)

Assets		Liabilities	
Cash assets	+ $100,000*	Demand deposits	+ $100,000
* Required reserves	$10,000		
Excess reserves	$90,000		

First Commercial Bank
(After the Loan)

Assets		Liabilities	
Cash assets	$100,000*	Demand deposits	$100,000
New business loan	+ $90,000	Demand deposit created for business borrower	+ $90,000
* Required reserves	$10,000		
Excess reserves	$90,000		

First Commercial Bank's loan created a sum of money ($90,000) that did not exist before—in the form of a demand deposit balance for the merchant who received the loan. This act of money creation increased the bank's assets and liabilities by $90,000 each. Thus the loan did not simply bring about a redistribution of assets as occurred when First Intermediary Savings and Loan made its loan.

In the case of First Commercial Bank, the new $90,000 in demand deposit money does not disappear when the merchant uses the loan proceeds to buy inventory. The supplier of the merchandise in turn deposits the $90,000 check in its own bank. This bank forwards the check for collection to First Commercial, which pays the check by transferring $90,000 of its cash assets to the supplier's bank. Having paid the check, First Commercial also strikes from its books the $90,000 deposit liability previously carried for the merchant borrower. After the check collection process is completed, its books look like this:

First Commercial Bank
(After Check Collection)

Assets		Liabilities	
Cash assets	$10,000*	Demand deposits	$100,000
New business loan	+ $90,000		
* Required reserves	$10,000		
Excess reserves	0		

The $90,000 that First Commercial created as a demand deposit balance still exists, but now it is entered on the books of another bank in the account of the supplier that sold the merchandise to the merchant borrower.

Reserve Requirements and Liquidity Constraints

A bank's ability to create additional money depends on its excess reserves. When a bank has no excess reserves, it cannot create any more demand deposits. To do so would result in a reserve requirement deficiency—and a financial penalty—as soon as the newly created funds were spent. In our example, First Commercial bank no longer has any excess reserves. The effects of an attempt by First Commercial to increase its earning assets by making a $5,000 loan would be as follows:

First Commercial Bank
(After Second Loan)

Assets		Liabilities	
Cash assets	$10,000*	Demand deposits	$100,000
Initial business loan	$90,000	Demand deposit created for new business borrower	+ $ 5,000
New business loan	+ $ 5,000		
* Required reserves	$10,000		
Excess reserves	$ 0		

After the check collection process was completed, First Commercial's books would look like this:

First Commercial Bank
(After Check Collection)

Assets		Liabilities	
Cash assets	$5,000*	Demand deposits	$100,000
Initial business loan	$90,000		
New business loan	+ $5,000		

* Required reserves (deficiency) - $5,000

First Commercial Bank would now have only $5,000 in cash assets (in the form of vault cash and/or a deposit balance at the Federal Reserve). However, it is required to hold an amount equal to 10 percent of its demand deposits—$10,000. In essence, the $5,000 loan has generated a reserve deficiency of $5,000. To meet the 10 percent reserve requirement, First Commercial must hold $10,000 in reserve assets against its $100,000 in demand deposits. In payment for the new business borrower's check, however, it had to transfer $5,000 of its reserves to another bank. As a result, even though its books continue to balance (assets equal liabilities), it has a reserve deficiency. In fact, even in the absence of legal reserve requirements, the senior management of First Commercial might feel that $5,000 in cash assets would represent too little liquidity to protect the bank against the cash demands of its depositors.

This illustrates a key principle of money creation: a bank cannot create an amount of money greater than its excess reserves (or excess liquidity). This is because it will lose a dollar in reserves (cash assets) for every dollar it creates when the proceeds of its new loans are disbursed and the loan funds are transferred through the check collection process. This limitation applies to individual banks, but not to the banking system as a whole which, in its totality, is capable of multiple money creation.

Multiple Deposit Creation

Multiple deposit creation describes the ability of the banking system to create an amount of deposits many times greater than its initial amount of reserves. Again, we can illustrate this concept by using T-accounts to trace a commercial bank loan. This time, however, the effect of the loan on other banks will be followed, as newly created deposits move from bank to bank. For simplicity, we will assume that all the bank-created deposits stay in the banking system, that all the newly created funds are held as demand deposits, and that each bank creates loans equal to every available (excess) reserve dollar. Although these assumptions are unrealistic, they do not distort the fundamental process by which banks collectively create multiple deposits.

Assume Bank One receives a cash deposit of $100,000 from a corporate customer for credit to the customer's checking account. Assume, too, that the Federal Reserve's reserve requirement on transaction accounts is 10 percent. Thus, Bank One must hold $10,000 in required reserves against its new $100,000 deposit, leaving $90,000 in excess reserves against which it can create $90,000 in additional funds through the act of lending.

Bank One
(After Initial Loan)

Assets		Liabilities	
Cash assets	$100,000*	Demand deposits	$100,000
New commercial loan	+ $90,000	Demand deposit created for borrower	+ $90,000

* Required reserves	$10,000
Excess reserves	$90,000

When Bank One makes the loan, both its assets and its liabilities temporarily increase to $190,000, reflecting the addition of the loan to its earning assets portfolio and the addition of the newly created demand deposit to its total liabilities. As soon as the borrower uses the newly created funds, however, Bank One's assets and liabilities will decline to their pre-loan level.

Assume that the borrower, a small business firm, uses the loan proceeds to buy new computer equipment and pays with a check drawn on Bank One. The computer manufacturing company deposits the check in its account at Bank Two. When the borrower's $90,000 check clears, Bank One will strike from its books the $90,000 demand deposit liability carried for the borrower. Thus, after check clearance, Bank One again has $100,000 in assets and $100,000 in liabilities. Note, however, that the composition of its assets has changed (as shown in the following T-account). Before the loan, Bank One held $100,000 in cash assets. Now it holds $10,000 in cash assets and $90,000 in loan assets. The $10,000 in cash assets meets the bank's 10 percent reserve requirement.

Takes from cash assets to pay check thus reducing excess res and add demand deposit

Bank One
(After Check Collection)

Assets		Liabilities	
Cash assets	$10,000	Demand deposits	$100,000
Loan	$90,000		

The $90,000 in deposit dollars created by Bank One now appears as a deposit by the computer manufacturing company on the books of Bank Two, increasing that bank's liabilities. Bank Two's cash assets also increase by $90,000 when it receives payment for the check drawn on Bank One. Bank Two, subject to the same 10 percent reserve requirement, must keep $9,000 against that new deposit, but can lend out an amount equal to the remaining $81,000 in reserves.

Bank Two
(After Check Collection)

Assets		Liabilities	
Cash assets	$90,000*	Demand deposits	$90,000

* Required reserves	$ 9,000
Excess reserves	$81,000

When Bank Two makes a loan, its assets and liabilities will increase temporarily, but will return to their pre-loan level when the amount of the borrower's check is collected by yet another bank. Assume that Bank Two makes an $81,000 loan to a borrower who uses the loan proceeds to pay for data processing services. When the service corporation deposits the check in its account at Bank Three, Bank Two's newly created $81,000 in demand deposits will then move to Bank Three, together with $81,000 in cash assets transferred by Bank Two in payment for the check.

Cash assets and demand deposit liabilities move from one to other bank

Bank Two
(After Loan and Check Collection)

Assets		Liabilities	
Cash assets	$ 9,000*	Demand deposit	$90,000
Loan	$81,000		

* Required reserves	$ 9,000
Excess reserves	$ 0

Bank Three is now in a position to create demand deposits equal to $72,900, or 90 percent of its new reserve assets. When it does so, it will give still another bank the ability to create new deposits.

Bank Three
(After Check Collection)

Assets		Liabilities	
Cash assets	$81,000*	Demand deposit	$81,000

* Required reserves	$ 8,100
Excess reserves	$72,900

In theory, this process of bank deposit creation could continue through many banks and generate, in our example, a total amount of deposits 10 times greater than the $100,000 in cash deposits that initially started the process. Exhibit 4.1 illustrates this multiple expansion of bank deposits.

EXHIBIT 4.1   **Multiple Expansion of Bank Deposits**

Position of Bank	New Deposits	New Loans and Investments	Required Reserves
Bank One	$100,000	$90,000	$10,000
Bank Two	90,000	81,000	9,000
Bank Three	81,000	72,900	8,100
Bank Four	72,900	65,610	7,290
Bank Five	65,610	59,050	6,560
Bank Six	59,050	53,140	5,910
Bank Seven	53,140	47,830	5,310
Bank Eight	47,830	43,050	4,780
Bank Nine	43,050	38,740	4,310
Bank Ten	38,740	34,870	3,870
Sum of first 10 banks' deposit expansion	651,320	586,190	65,130
Sum of remaining banks' deposit expansion	348,680	313,810	34,870
Total for banking system	$1,000,000 (Multiple expansion)	$900,000 (Net creation)	$100,000 (Original deposit)

Note: Reserve requirement = 10%

Multiple expansion equation:

$$\frac{1}{\text{Reserve Requirement}} \times \text{Initial deposit} = \text{Total deposits}$$

Multiple expansion in above example:

$$\frac{1}{.10} \times \$100,000 = 10 \times \$100,000 = \$1,000,000$$

The multiplier, or expansion coefficient, is the reciprocal of the reserve requirement ratio. That is, if the reserve requirement ratio is 10 percent, or 1/10, the multiplier is 10. This means that the banking system could theoretically generate $1 million in total deposits using the $100,000 initial cash deposit as a base. Of this $1 million, $900,000 would be newly created money. If the reserve requirement were 20 percent, the expansion coefficient would be 5 (the reciprocal of 20 percent, or 1/5), and the $100,000 initial cash deposit could increase to only $500,000.

Loan Repayment and Deposit Contraction

Just as the lending process affects a bank's balance sheet, so do loan repayments. But whereas the lending process creates money through the multiple expansion of bank deposits, the net repayment of loans reduces the banking system's assets and liabilities and effectively contracts the multiple expansion of deposits. These effects are often difficult for individual banks to perceive because their receipts of loan repayments and new lending typically blend together in an ongoing process. However, the effects of a loan repayment can be examined through the use of T-accounts.

Assume that First Commercial Bank is fully loaned and is subject to a 10 percent reserve requirement on demand deposits. Its books look like this:

First Commercial Bank

Assets		Liabilities	
Cash assets	$10,000*	Total demand deposits	$100,000
Loan A	$25,000		
Loan B	$50,000		
Loan C	$15,000		

* Required reserves	$10,000
Excess reserves	$ 0

Now assume that Borrower B repays Loan B to First Commercial with a $50,000 check drawn against an account at another bank. When First Commercial collects the check, its books will look like this:

*paid off loans:
goto excess reserves
and adds to cash assets*

First Commercial Bank
(After External Loan Repayment)

Assets		Liabilities	
Cash assets	$60,000*	Total demand deposits	$100,000
Loan A	$25,000		
Loan C	$15,000		

* Required reserves	$10,000
Excess reserves	$50,000

Note that the loan repayment did not result in an increase in First Commercial's total assets or total liabilities, but did change the composition of its assets. First Commercial now has $60,000 in cash assets (reserves) and is in a $50,000 excess reserve position. In effect, First Commercial could make another $50,000 loan, creating $50,000 in new demand deposits.

The repayment of Loan B added to First Commercial's reserves and expanded its lending capacity. However, the reserves it acquired came from another bank, whose reserves and lending capacity were reduced. Without a net addition to reserves for all banks, a loan repayment at one bank will not lead to a further multiple expansion of deposits or loans in the banking system.

Assume, though, that Borrower B repays its loan to First Commercial with a check drawn against funds it has in an account at First Commercial. After the check is posted internally by First Commercial, its books will reflect a reduction in assets and liabilities of $50,000.

First Commercial Bank
(After Internal Loan Repayment)

Assets		Liabilities	
Cash assets	$10,000*	Total demand deposits	$50,000
Loan A	$25,000		
Loan C	$15,000		

-50,000 (Loan A)   -50,000.00 (Total demand deposits)

* Required reserves	$ 5,000
Excess reserves	$ 5,000

Note that although First Commercial has not gained or lost any reserve assets (its cash assets remain unchanged at $10,000), its lending capacity has increased. Because its deposit base has been reduced (contracted), First Commercial can now meet its 10 percent reserve requirement with only $5,000 in reserve assets. This puts it in a position of having $5,000 in excess reserves. If we assume that First Commercial will fully utilize this $5,000 gain in excess reserves to expand its loans, the banking system would be capable of again generating $50,000 in additional deposits. It would then have the same $100,000 total deposit base it had before Loan B was repaid.

Influences on Multiple Deposit Creation

The multiple expansion illustrated in exhibit 4.1 is based on a simplistic set of assumptions that do not reflect the real world of banking. In reality, some deposits created by banks "leak" out of the banking system into nonbank financial institutions and into money market instruments such as U.S. Treasury bills. Also, consumers and businesses typically convert some of their newly acquired demand deposits into cash and time deposits.

Another fact that adds to the complexity of multiple deposit expansion is that reserve requirements vary depending on the amount of deposits a bank holds. Moreover, they change every year. In 1993, for example, banks and other depositories were subject to the following reserve requirements:

- ❏ 3 percent on the first $46.8 million of transaction deposits (checkable deposits), and

- ❏ 10 percent on any transaction deposits above this level.

In addition, all depository institutions were allowed to subtract $3.8 million from their transaction deposits before applying the reserve requirement percentages.

A further complication is the fact that banks do not usually create money equal to every available excess reserve dollar. This is because each day's check collections are subject to next-day corrections (adjustments) that can increase or decrease the previous day's deposit balance and reserve totals. Also, the pace of deposits flowing in and out of a bank on any given day is often so rapid and the volume so large that it is only at the end of a day, or perhaps a day or two later, that the bank knows precisely how much in reserves it has available to support new loans. Thus, there are almost always excess reserves in the banking system, even when loan demand is very strong.

Because cash held by banks as vault cash is an asset that can be counted to meet reserve requirements, depositors' cash needs also can affect the mathematical progression of new money creation. Every request for cash requires the bank, in essence, to dip into its reserves. Thus, as depositors cash checks against their own deposits, a bank loses reserves in an amount equal to the cash drain. With a smaller reserve base, or with no excess reserves at all, a bank's lending (money creation) ability is blunted.

The public holds about $300 billion in cash and $700 billion in checkable deposits. Thus, it is reasonable to assume that for every new checkable deposit dollar created by the banking system, the public will take some of it in the form of cash. Conversely, every time cash is deposited for credit to a checking or savings account, banks' reserves increase on a dollar-for-dollar basis. During the course of any given week, the cash position of most banks fluctuates on a fairly predictable basis. Most banks take in

more cash than they pay out on Mondays and Tuesdays, largely reflecting the accumulated weekend cash receipts deposited by merchants; on Thursdays and Fridays, on the
other hand, most banks pay out more cash than they take in, because of business and
consumer demands for increased weekend liquidity and pocket money.

The movement of funds from checkable deposits into time and savings deposits also
affects the money expansion process by changing the amount of required and excess
reserves held by banks. Banks are required to maintain reserves against transaction
accounts but not against time and savings deposits. Thus whenever consumers transfer
funds from their checking accounts into savings instruments, banks' required reserves
decline and their excess reserves increase.

For example, take the case of an individual with $10,000 in a checking account. If the
reserve requirement is 10 percent on transaction accounts, the bank holding this
account would be required to hold $1,000 in reserves in the form of vault cash or a
deposit balance at its district Federal Reserve bank. If that individual transfers the
$10,000 into a certificate of deposit at the same bank, the bank's required reserves
would decrease by $1,000 because banks are not required to keep reserves against
certificates of deposit. As a result, the bank would have $1,000 in excess reserves and
$1,000 in new lending or investing capacity.

Reserve requirements represent a "cost" to banks because reserves are assets that have
to be set aside in noninterest-earning form. Thus banks take reserve requirement costs
into consideration when they determine their loan charges and the interest rates they
pay on deposits. Because a bank can increase its earnings by investing funds that do
not need to be held as reserves, a bank typically pays one-eighth or one-quarter of a
percent higher interest on certificates of deposit than it would if it had to hold reserves
against certificates of deposit.

When Congress authorized banks and thrifts to offer money market deposit accounts in
December 1982, many bankers argued that unless these accounts were exempted from
reserve requirements, banks would be unable to match the interest rates paid by the
money market funds, which are not subject to any reserve requirements. Congress
concurred, and in a technical amendment to the initial authorization, money market
deposit accounts were classified as savings deposits rather than as transaction accounts, thereby exempting them from reserve requirements.

The Reality of Multiple Deposit Creation

If we examine the money creation process using more realistic assumptions, we get
a more accurate picture of the multiple expansion process in the banking system.
Assume there is a 10 percent reserve requirement against checkable deposits and a 5
percent reserve requirement against time deposits. (From 1980 to 1991, banks were
subject to a 3 percent reserve requirement on business time deposits with maturities of
less than 1 1/2 years.) Further assume that for every new demand deposit dollar held
by depositors, they choose to hold $0.50 in cash and $1.00 in time deposits. Finally,

assume that Bank One has $100,000 in excess reserves, which enables it to create $100,000 in new demand deposit money by making a loan.

Bank One

Assets		Liabilities	
Loan	+ $100,000	Demand deposit created for borrower	+ $100,000

The borrower of Bank One's $100,000 uses the loan proceeds to pay, by check, various outstanding bills. The check recipients deposit these checks in Bank Two, but prefer to hold $0.50 in cash and $1.00 in time deposits for every dollar of demand deposits held. Thus the recipients of the $100,000 in checks wind up with $20,000 in cash, $40,000 in time deposit accounts, and $40,000 in demand deposits.

Bank Two

Assets		Liabilities	
Reserve account	+ $100,000*	Demand deposits	+ $40,000
Cash	- $20,000	Time deposits	+ $40,000

* Required reserves	$6,000
Excess reserves	$74,000

Bank Two must now hold an additional $6,000 in required reserves—$4,000 against its new demand deposits (10 percent of $40,000) and $2,000 against its new time deposits (5 percent of $40,000). Bank Two's total reserve gain is $80,000, reflecting the $100,000 reserve account credit it received in the check collection process, partially offset by the $20,000 paid out in cash. By subtracting the $6,000 in required reserves from the bank's $80,000 in total reserves, we see that the bank's excess reserve position is $74,000. It now has the capacity to create $74,000 in new demand deposits by making loans. Assume that it does so, and that the borrowers deposit the loan proceeds at Bank Three.

Assume that the recipients of these loan proceeds also prefer to hold a portion of their newly acquired funds in cash and savings accounts. Using the same ratio as before, the $74,000 in loan receipts takes the following form: $14,800 is held as cash, $29,600 is held in time deposit accounts, and $29,600 is held as demand deposits. This is reflected on Bank Three's books as follows:

Bank Three

Assets		Liabilities	
Reserve account	+ $74,000*	Demand deposits	+ $29,600
Cash	- $14,800	Time deposits	+ $29,600

* Required reserves	$4,440
Excess reserves	$54,760

Bank Three must hold $4,440 in required reserves—$2,960 against its demand deposits (10 percent of $29,600) and $1,480 against its time deposits (5 percent of $29,600). Because the bank's total reserve position is $59,200, its excess reserves equal $54,760. This sum represents Bank Three's maximum potential contribution to the money creation process of the banking system—assuming it too will make loans in the amount of its excess reserves.

We can now compare the results of the three banks' experience in this example with that of the banks in the simplified version summarized in exhibit 4.1. Under the more realistic assumptions of this example, each bank has less in excess reserves because some reserves are used in paying out cash. This is true despite the fact that the banks in our more realistic example had lower reserve requirements for the amounts held in time deposits. It is readily apparent, then, that both reserve requirements and the public's daily choices as to what form their money shall take are equally powerful constraints on multiple expansion in the banking system. Under the more realistic assumptions used in this example, the banking system would be capable of generating new demand deposits equal to only about 1.5 times the initial amount of excess reserves (rather than 10 times, as seen in exhibit 4.1). The T-account balance sheet for the banking system after full multiple expansion in our example is as follows:

Banking System

Assets		Liabilities	
Cash paid out	- $ 76,500	Demand deposits	+ $153,000
Loans	+ $382,500	Time deposits	+ $153,000
Total	+ $306,000	Total	+ $306,000

In our more realistic example, banks would be able to create $382,500 in new money (the amount of all loans) while generating $153,000 in demand deposits and time deposits and paying out $76,500 in cash.

In reality, it is difficult to calculate a precise multiplier or coefficient of expansion. Reserve requirements differ for different sizes of deposits. Also, bank customers freely move funds from cash to demand and time deposits and back. A single multiplier, such as the 10 used in our earlier example, is valid only in theory. The concept of multiple expansion of bank deposits, however, is valid in both theory and in practice.

In 1992, the banking system's reserves, totaling about $50 billion, were supporting nearly 15 times that amount in transaction deposits (about $700 billion) and about $1,700 billion ($1.7 trillion) of time and savings deposits. As noted previously, reserve requirements against transaction accounts in 1992 ranged from 3 percent to 10 percent depending on how much of these deposits a bank held. There were no reserve requirements against time or savings deposits.

The Implementation of Monetary Policy

The Federal Reserve attempts to ensure that the amount of deposits created by the nation's banking system is appropriate for the needs of the economy—neither too much nor too little. The central bank does this by controlling the amount and cost of reserves available in the banking system. In implementing monetary policy, however, the Federal Reserve does not involve itself with the decisions that an individual bank's management may make on a daily, weekly, or monthly basis to achieve its overall earnings goals in conformity with its lending or investing policies. Banks are free to compete against each other, against other financial intermediaries, and in other markets, for a customer's deposit and loan business and, most important, for the reserves that help them achieve their earnings goals. The Federal Reserve's focus is on the total amount of reserves available in the banking system, not the amount available to any individual bank.

In a recession, the Federal Reserve typically seeks to stimulate bank lending in order to spark needed business and consumer spending. To this end, it wants to provide additional reserves to the banking system for expanding loans. With demand for loans low—a characteristic of recession—banks often find interest rates declining as these new reserves expand the base of available reserves. Banks tend to see this monetary policy as consistent with their own goals because an expansion of excess reserves increases banks' earnings potential. Indeed, declining interest rates themselves increase the value of the securities held in banks' portfolios—a major component of most banks' earning assets.

In a period of inflation, on the other hand, the Federal Reserve's monetary policy goals may directly conflict with banks' lending goals, as the Federal Reserve seeks to restrain bank lending to hold down credit-induced buying. To counter inflation, the Federal Reserve will typically attempt to hold back reserves, and with demand for bank loans strong, interest rates often rise. Banks thus tend to see anti-inflationary monetary policy as reducing their earnings prospects. It cuts them off from the reserves they need to meet their customers' loan demands and raises their cost of doing business. Moreover, rising interest rates generate paper losses on the securities held in bank portfolios that were purchased when rates were lower.

The Federal Reserve boardroom in Washington, D.C.

Photo courtesy of the Federal Reserve Board.

Control of Bank Reserves

The Federal Reserve can control bank lending by altering the quantity of reserves available in the banking system. To do so, it uses one or more of its monetary policy tools: reserve requirements, the discount rate, and open-market operations.

RESERVE REQUIREMENTS

Change % required

The Federal Reserve can control bank lending by changing the rules concerning reserve requirements. For example, it can change the percentages of reserves required to be held against designated liabilities. If it raises reserve requirements, the amount of excess reserves in the banking system is immediately reduced as banks earmark some or all of those reserves to meet the higher requirements.

Change which on which assets constitute reserve

The Federal Reserve also can change the rules as to which bank assets constitute legal reserves. Currently, only vault cash and deposits at a Federal Reserve bank are acceptable. (Depository institutions that are not members of the Federal Reserve System can maintain a reserve deposit at a Reserve bank by means of a pass-through deposit made at a correspondent bank, which is then redeposited at the Federal Reserve.) If the Federal Reserve allowed other assets—such as government securities—to be used as reserves, the total amount of reserves available in the banking system would expand immediately.

Change what is the base

The Federal Reserve also can change the base against which banks must keep reserves by including (or excluding) certain types of liabilities from its list of bank liabilities against which reserves must be maintained.

THE DISCOUNT RATE

Another way the Federal Reserve can alter the quantity of reserves in the banking system is by changing the discount rate—that is, the interest rate it charges depositories that borrow from it. By raising the discount rate, it can discourage banks from borrowing reserves, while lowering the discount rate has the opposite effect. Often, a change in the discount rate can have as much psychological impact on the economy as the actual monetary effect. It is seen as a signal of the Fed's intentions for monetary policy in coming months.

The Federal Reserve also can control bank lending by explicitly or implicitly changing the ground rules under which banks can obtain loans of reserves. By changing its lending practices, the Federal Reserve can increase or decrease the amount of borrowable reserves available to banks.

OPEN-MARKET OPERATIONS

The Federal Reserve also can regulate the amount of reserves in the banking system by buying or selling government securities in the open market. When the Federal Reserve buys securities, bank reserves (and the nation's money supply) increase because the Federal Reserve pays with checks drawn on itself. When those checks are collected, banks' reserve accounts are increased, as are the demand deposit accounts of the securities sellers. Since the checks are not collected against any commercial banks, the Federal Reserve's purchase of securities does not simply redistribute reserves and money but actually creates new reserves and demand deposits.

When the Federal Reserve sells securities from its $290 billion portfolio, bank reserves and money supply decline accordingly. Private purchasers—firms dealing in government securities—pay with checks drawn on their banks. When the Federal Reserve collects these checks, it reduces the reserve accounts of the banks on which the checks were drawn just as the banks reduce the demand deposit balances of their dealer depositors. Since these reserves and deposits are not transferred into other commercial banks, as would occur in a private transaction, but are retained by the central bank, the effect is a reduction in bank reserves and money supply.

Thus when the Federal Reserve buys T-bills, the money supply increases because the Federal Reserve pays for its purchases with an infusion of "new" money. Conversely, when the Federal Reserve sells T-bills, the money supply decreases because the T-bills are paid for with money transferred from the nation's banks to the Federal Reserve.

Effects of Monetary Policy Controls

An increase in the quantity of reserves available to banks is expected to spur bank lending. Assume, for example, that a bank obtains additional reserves through the Federal Reserve's open-market purchase of a U.S. Treasury security. Although the bank then must keep more required reserves against the new deposit of the securities seller, it has a significant margin of excess reserves against which new loans can be made (new demand deposits created).

A bank will seek to turn its excess reserves into income-generating assets by making loans or investments. As the recipients of these bank loans or investments spend their money in the economy, the funds are deposited in other banks throughout the country. Total deposits in the banking system increase, resulting in still more money creation for the economy and increased earning assets for banks. As we have seen, the multiple creation of bank deposits expands the nation's money supply by an amount up to several times greater than the initial expansion generated by the first loan.

"Easy" Monetary Policy in the Early 1990s

An "easy" monetary policy is supposed to reduce interest rates, stimulate bank lending, and increase both consumer and business borrowing and spending. In the early 1990s, the Federal Reserve made monetary policy progressively easier—reserve requirements were reduced, the discount rate was lowered, and open market operations were used to expand bank reserves. However, despite a steady decline in interest rates paid on deposits and charged on loans, there was no appreciable increase in bank lending or

(Continued from previous page)

consumer or business borrowing and spending. Economists theorize that three factors may explain why easy monetary policy in the early 1990s did not work.

❑ American consumers and corporations borrowed so extensively in the 1980s that they could not afford to take on any additional debt in the early 1990s, despite low interest rates.

❑ Banks were reluctant to lend to business borrowers, despite having an ample supply of excess reserves. New risk-based capital requirements meant that banks had to set aside more capital against loans than against investments. Limited capital caused most banks to pump excess reserves into securities investments instead of loans. Pressure on banks from the regulatory agencies to make less risky loans also had an impact on making banks more cautious in their lending. That caution was understandable; for the two years 1990-1991, banks had to write off $62 billion for bad loans—loans that will probably not be repaid—made in the 1980s.

❑ Long-term interest rates, such as those on 5-year U.S. government bonds and 10-year corporate bonds, did not decline very much—despite the steady decline in banks' interest rates. The smaller decline of long-term rates reflected deep-seated doubts in U.S. financial markets that inflation in the 1990s would be kept under control. High long-term interest rates deterred businesses from borrowing in the financial markets to finance plant expansions or other long-term needs. Consumers tend to save less and spend more when interest rates are low. However, in the face of little income growth and the high long-term rates available on financial instruments in 1991 and 1992, consumers maintained a slow spending pace.

In a similar fashion, reserve losses may depress bank lending. If a bank loses reserves as the result of the Federal Reserve's open-market sales of securities, the bank's assets and liabilities usually must be adjusted. If the bank has no excess reserves, it will face a temporary reserve deficiency. It must then seek to obtain the reserves it needs to meet reserve requirements by selling its secondary reserve assets (government securities held in the bank's investment portfolio), borrowing federal funds from other banks, borrowing from the central bank, calling in loans, or making some other balance sheet adjustment.

A bank that loses excess reserves may not have to make such extensive adjustments immediately. However, banks with numerous loan commitments outstanding may well have to respond quickly. If reserves do not materialize, these banks must adjust their assets and liabilities so that they can honor their commitments.

An individual bank can meet a reserve deficiency by borrowing from another bank or selling securities to a private dealer firm. However, the banking system as a whole can meet a reserve deficiency only with an infusion of reserves from outside the system. No amount of asset and liability adjustments by banks will create new reserves. At best, a given bank can transfer its reserve deficiency to another bank, or a group of smaller banks can redistribute their reserve deficiencies to one or two large money market banks. But, on balance, the banking system itself will still hold the same amount of reserves.

The Federal Reserve could, as a matter of policy, cause (or allow) a reserve deficiency in the banking system to develop as a means of reducing the money supply. Within days, the money supply would decline as banks' loans were repaid and no new loans were made (demand deposits created). Only when the total deposit base of the banking system declined sufficiently would the amount of available reserves—which would remain unchanged—again meet reserve requirements.

Bank Response to Monetary Control

When the Federal Reserve wants to restrain bank lending and money supply growth, it generally implements restraint by gradually reducing the growth rate at which it supplies reserves to the banking system. As the expansion of reserves begins to slow against strong demand for reserves by banks wanting to make loans and increase their earning assets, the cost of reserves begins to rise. Almost immediately, the increased cost of reserves is reflected in an increased cost of federal funds—the reserves that banks sell (lend) to one another.

Federal funds transactions are the primary reserve adjustment device used by the nation's biggest banks. The cost of federal funds, known as the federal funds rate, increases as banks compete for reserves to expand their individual loan and investment portfolios. Note that the trading of reserves between banks is known as the federal funds market because banks, in effect, buy or sell their Federal Reserve account balances to one another.

Fed Funds Market

When the cost of reserves increases, banks must charge more on loans and command more on investments to make any expansion in earning assets profitable. Some banks will be induced to cut back on loans, as their management responds to rising costs, or to a decline in loan demand from customers who are unwilling to pay higher loan rates for borrowed funds. Banks that respond in this way typically will allow loans to be repaid without extending new ones (and may sell some securities to convert assets into reserves); this reduces their deposit base and their need to maintain a high level of reserves. These adjustments invariably reduce the amount of demand deposits in the nation's banking system and the amount of required reserves needed to support those deposits. (The Federal Reserve's use of its monetary policy tools and the relationship between the Fed's policy goals and the banking system are explored in greater detail in later chapters.)

Summary

Commercial banks create new money (demand deposits) when they make commercial loans; in contrast, other financial intermediaries primarily lend out existing funds that have been taken in from depositors—a process that does not create money. The ability of banks to create new demand deposits depends on their level of reserves—the amount of vault cash they hold and the amount of funds they have on deposit at the district Federal Reserve bank.

When new reserves enter the banking system, banks can expand demand deposits by a multiple of those reserves. When reserves are withdrawn from the banking system, deposits must contract by a multiple of the lost reserves. The deposit multiplier shows how much demand deposits can change when reserves change. Simply stated, the multiplier is the reciprocal of the reserve requirement ratio. The mathematics of new money creation, however, is actually affected by a number of complex factors such as the public's ongoing shifts of funds between cash and time deposits, and the varying reserve requirement percentages applied to banks of different deposit size.

In implementing monetary policy, the Federal Reserve does not involve itself with the specific management decisions of individual banks, but rather focuses on the total amount of reserves available in the banking system to support all loans. To implement policy, the Federal Reserve relies on three general control devices—reserve requirements, the discount rate, and open-market operations. Its attempts to restrain or spur bank lending and money supply growth influence the federal funds rate—the cost of reserves that banks buy and sell to one another.

Questions

1. Explain the use of T-accounts in analyzing the lending process of banks.

2. Evaluate the following statement: "As my bank's commercial loan officer, I do not create money; I simply lend out the money that depositors have placed in the bank."

3. If there were no reserve requirements, could banks create an infinite amount of demand deposits? Would they?

4. How can a bank that finds itself with a reserve deficiency obtain new reserves? Would these options work if the entire banking system needed additional reserves? Explain.

5. How are federal funds transactions used by banks to adjust their reserves?

PART II *The Role of the Central Bank*

5

The Federal Reserve

Objectives

After successfully completing this chapter, you will be able to

- ☐ discuss the major problems with the nation's money and banking system that led Congress to establish the Federal Reserve,

- ☐ describe the structural characteristics of the quasi-governmental Federal Reserve System,

- ☐ explain how members of the Board of Governors, members of the Federal Open Market Committee, and directors of the 12 Federal Reserve banks are selected,

- ☐ cite the major functions of the district Federal Reserve banks, and

- ☐ explain the special functions of the Federal Reserve Bank of New York.

Introduction

The Federal Reserve is one of the most important and powerful institutions in the United States. It implements the nation's monetary policy in an attempt to control the cost of money (interest rates) and the availability of money (money supply). But unlike the central banks of most other industrialized nations, it is only quasi-governmental.

In this chapter, we will explore the problems in the money and banking system that led Congress to establish a central monetary authority in 1913. Then we will examine the structure of the Federal Reserve System, including the Board of Governors (which operates as a federal government entity), the 12 Federal Reserve banks (which are private and largely autonomous), and the commercial banks that are members of the Federal Reserve. We also will look at the varied functions of the Federal Reserve, which include providing payment services for depositories and serving as the bank for the government, in addition to its pivotal function of setting the nation's monetary policy.

Extended Study 6, "The Federal Reserve's Statement of Condition," provides a financial profile of the Federal Reserve and a more detailed look at the activities that contribute to its special role in the banking system and the economy.

A Unique Central Bank

Every nation in the world has a central bank. A central bank, like a central government, distinguishes a nation as a political entity. The nations of Europe had central banks even before the industrial revolution. The Bank of Sweden and the Bank of England, two of the world's oldest central banks, were founded in the late 1600s. Thus, the concept of a central bank is not new.

*The Bank of England,
one of the world's oldest
central banks.*

*Photo courtesy of the
British Embassy.*

Although central banks may differ to some extent in their structure, function, and economic role, they all share certain common characteristics. A central bank has the sole power to issue a nation's paper currency. It serves as a lender of last resort (a source of guaranteed liquidity) to banks and other institutions. It acts as the government's bank, marketing the government's debt and acting on behalf of the government to safeguard the value of the nation's money in international trade (usually by buying and selling the nation's money in foreign exchange markets). A central bank also seeks to control the growth of a nation's money supply to achieve national economic objectives.

The Federal Reserve meets the definition of a central bank, but has a fundamentally different structure than most other central banks. Most central banks are more closely tied to the executive branch of their government than is the Federal Reserve. Most also are directly responsible to their government's treasury or finance minister.

The Federal Reserve, in contrast, has a quasi-governmental and decentralized structure that enables it to establish the nation's monetary policy separate from and independent of the fiscal policies (taxation and government spending policies) of the president and the Congress. Exhibit 5.1 illustrates the separate derivation of monetary and fiscal policies in the United States.

EXHIBIT 5.1   **Independent Derivation of U.S. Monetary and Fiscal Policy**

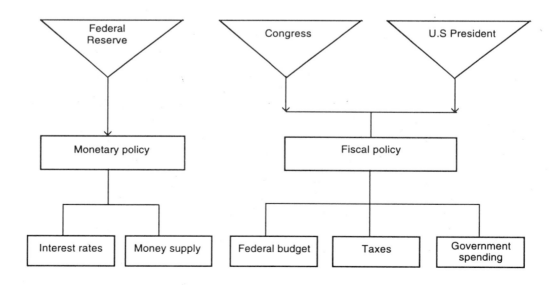

Est 1913

Bankers Bank

Origins of the Federal Reserve

The Federal Reserve is a product of the early historical experiences that shaped U.S. attitudes and practices toward money, banking, and government power. Its structure also reflects the government's attempts to correct specific defects in the U.S. banking system that had developed toward the end of the nineteenth century. Established in 1913, the Federal Reserve was not initially intended to direct the economy toward the attainment of economic goals.

U.S. economists and government officials in the early 1900s believed that the government should not intervene in the natural interaction of competitive market forces. They also believed that it was unnecessary to have a central bank manage the economy to achieve balance in the market, even during periods of economic disturbance—they saw the economy and its flows of money as self-balancing entities.

The preamble to the Federal Reserve Act passed by Congress in December 1913 gives four reasons for establishing a new U.S. central bank:

"To provide for the establishment of Federal Reserve banks, to furnish an elastic currency, to afford means of rediscounting commercial paper, to establish a more effective supervision of banking in the United States, and for other purposes."

Defects in the U.S. Banking System

Congress, in creating the Federal Reserve System, was attempting to deal with structural defects in the nation's money and banking system that were causing increasing instability in the nation's economy. These defects included an inelastic currency, the pyramiding of bank reserves, a lack of central supervision of banks, and an inefficient national payments mechanism. Each of these defects bears closer study.

AN INELASTIC CURRENCY

First, the nation lacked a mechanism to make the supply of paper currency responsive to the changing demands of businesses and consumers. The inelasticity of the nation's currency was rooted in the nation's early experiences with the issuance and control of paper currency. The United States emerged from the Revolutionary War politically independent but virtually bankrupt. The Continental Congress had financed the revolution by issuing paper currency far in excess of the capacity of the colonies to produce goods and services. The result was massive inflation. By the war's end, Continental currency had become almost worthless; in 1790, Continental paper was redeemed by the new United States at one U.S. cent to the Continental dollar.

5 elements of Supply & Demand

Close substitute (if you can - elastic) (product)

Elastic Supply

VCR cost 500.00 raise price to 600.00 demand go down Luxury item Elastic product consumer demand goes up or down with the price

Inelastic toilet paper milk Keep on buy no matter what price

The bitter experiences of Colonial merchants, soldiers, tradesmen, and farmers with nearly worthless government-issued paper currency had a profound impact on the course of U.S. monetary history. (This historical context is discussed in more detail in Extended Study 11, "The Evolution of Bank Regulation.") Delegates to the Constitutional Convention voted to prohibit the states from issuing paper money and granted to Congress the exclusive power "to coin money and regulate [its] value" (article 1, section 8). Congress, however, sensitive to the nation's disastrous experience with government-issued paper money, did not use its power to issue currency until the financial emergency generated by the Civil War, more than 70 years later.

Most of the money that circulated in the United States in the late 1700s was foreign coinage, primarily Spanish and British coins, which Americans either hoarded or used to buy imported goods. The small quantity of U.S. currency that circulated in the fledgling U.S. economy consisted of the notes issued by the First (1791) and later the Second (1816) Banks of the United States. After the Second Bank of the United States closed in 1836, the dominant form of currency became private bank notes issued by state-chartered commercial banks (redeemable on demand for gold or silver).

As state-chartered banks proliferated, so did currency issued by state banks. Only then did paper currency become a significant factor in the U.S. economy. By the 1860s, before the federal government took away the power to issue notes from state-chartered banks, as many as 8,000 different issues of state bank notes circulated in the United States. There was no uniform national currency, and the state-bank-note currency system was confusing and inefficient. Banks rarely accepted at face value notes from depositors issued by unknown banks. Books the size of telephone directories were circulated to help bank managers identify bogus issues and determine the credit-worthiness and ability of issuing banks to redeem their paper for gold or silver.

From the mid-1860s (when the National Banking Act of 1864 was passed) until the establishment of the Federal Reserve in 1913, the nation's paper currency consisted mainly of national bank notes. This currency was given by the government to nationally chartered banks, which then issued the notes as their own. Because national bank notes had to be fully collateralized by government securities, however, the nation's supply of paper currency depended on the government's debt. The supply of currency expanded and contracted in direct response to changes in the value of government securities in the nation's bond markets rather than in response to the economy's needs. When the government began repaying its Civil War debt by redeeming and retiring securities issued in earlier years, the supply of collateral available for note issuance shrank. And with it shrank the size of the money supply. This inelasticity meant that the U.S. economy could not adjust to the changing monetary needs and demands of the public.

PYRAMIDING OF BANK RESERVES

Another defect in the nation's early banking system was the pyramiding of local banks' reserves into a few of the nation's money center banks, which left local banks with insufficient liquidity in times of stress. This was a result of the nation's system of unit (no-branch) banking and dual regulatory control of banks. (These concepts are discussed in later chapters.) The National Banking Act of 1864 specified a three-tier structure of reserve requirements for nationally chartered banks. Smaller "country" banks could keep some of their reserves in vault cash but were required to deposit most of their reserves with larger "reserve city" banks. Reserve city banks (those in the nation's major cities) in turn had to deposit most of their own reserves in still larger central reserve city banks (those in the nation's money centers of New York, Chicago, and St. Louis). The central reserve city banks had to keep all their reserves in vault cash.

Because the banking system's reserves were dispersed throughout the country, they could not be transferred quickly to banks in regions that might be under liquidity pressure. And since the central reserve city banks were the ultimate repositories of the banking system's reserves, they were particularly susceptible to cumulative pressures that often led to bank panics.

A bank panic typically would begin in the Midwest when small, farmer-oriented banks found that they did not have enough currency on hand to pay out to farmers. This phenomenon occurred with seasonal regularity when farmers sold their crops. The small banks would call on their reserve city correspondents for their reserves. The reserve city correspondents, having insufficient cash for their own needs, would in turn call on the central reserve city banks for their own reserves. As a result, these central reserve city banks often encountered liquidity problems when they were hit all at once with the cumulative cash needs of thousands of country banks.

The severe Bank Panic of 1907 precipitated the establishment of the Federal Reserve. It was a typical bank panic in all but its severity. When New York City banks did not have enough funds to honor reserve claims immediately, they quickly called in loans made to brokers and dealers. Broker and dealer firms, in turn, sold stocks and bonds to raise money to repay their loans. The ensuing selling frenzy on Wall Street drove down the prices of securities, making it impossible for some firms to make repayment. The defaulting brokers and dealers in turn brought down a number of banks with them. Moreover, as New Yorkers learned of the plight of brokers and banks, many panicked and withdrew their funds from sound banks, thereby adding to the illiquidity of the banking system. During the 1907 panic, currency and coin became so scarce in New York City that banks, merchants, and tradesmen began issuing and exchanging personal IOUs to stay in business.

The fundamental problem, however, was not so much the pyramiding of reserves as it was the lack of a lender of last resort for the banking system. What was required was a source of guaranteed liquidity that all banks could tap when they needed money.

LACK OF CENTRAL SUPERVISION OF BANKS

Another problem that led to the formation of the Federal Reserve was the lack of uniform protection of the public's bank deposits. The nation's banking system, which had allowed banking laws and regulations to develop along separate federal and state lines, resulted in the decentralized supervision of banks. As a result, there was no mechanism for uniformly protecting the public's bank deposits on a nationwide basis.

National bank notes of the 1860s decorate a song sheet.

Photo courtesy of the Library of Congress.

AN INEFFICIENT NATIONAL PAYMENTS MECHANISM

The lack of an efficient national payments mechanism was the final problem that needed to be resolved. Checkbook money could not be transferred quickly or easily from one part of the country to another because no nationwide system existed for clearing and collecting checks. Banks typically had correspondent accounts and clearing arrangements with larger banks in their localities or regions, but there were few direct cross-country relationships. In the absence of a central bank having account relationships with most banks across the country, and with the number of banks growing rapidly (in excess of 10,000 banks by 1913), the clearing and collection of interregional checks was far from efficient. Some of the inefficient practices that needed to be corrected involved exchange charges, circuitous routing, non-par checking, use of uncollected funds as reserves, and the maintenance of compensating balances with many correspondent banks.

Exchange Charges. Some banks imposed an exchange charge on checks presented for payment by out-of-town banks. This charge covered the costs incurred in shipping gold or cash to pay for checks, the normal banking practice before the Federal Reserve was created.

Circuitous Routing. To avoid exchange charges, banks frequently sent checks on long, circuitous collection routes across the country. This magnified the risks banks incurred in collecting checks since checks might not be properly forwarded or could be lost in transit. Final payment took an excessively long time, and there was no direct way for banks to return dishonored items. The cross-country collection process was costly to the banking system as well as to the public.

Non-par Checking. Exchange charges for out-of-town checks meant that checks were credited to depositors' accounts at less than par (face) value. Because of this practice, out-of-town checks often were not accepted in commercial dealings. Business firms typically required payment of bills either in currency or with a local check.

Uncollected Funds as Reserves. Correspondent banks receiving checks deposited by respondent banks for collection developed the practice of crediting their respondents' accounts immediately, even though the checks could not be collected for several days. Since these accounts made up a substantial portion of the legal reserves of the nation's country banks, the practice resulted in reserves, which were designed to assure bank safety and liquidity, being held in uncollected funds.

Compensating Balances to Collect Checks at Par. In attempting to receive full face value for deposited checks, banks often fragmented their reserve deposits, maintaining many different correspondent account balances in banks in different banking regions. The practice of maintaining compensating balances to collect checks at par damaged bank liquidity and grew exceedingly costly as check usage proliferated.

THE CENTRAL BANKING SOLUTION

The Bank Panic of 1907 motivated Congress to establish a national monetary commission to study the defects in the U.S. money and banking system and to propose a solution. The Aldrich Commission (named for the senator who chaired the body) heard testimony and evaluated different options for more than three years. The commission finally recommended that a central bank controlled by bankers be established to solve the nation's interrelated money and banking problems.

The plan was immediately attacked by the Progressives, particularly William Jennings Bryan, who feared it would increase the power of the nation's money center banks without sufficiently protecting national interests. The Aldrich Commission's recommendations received little political support and generally were ignored by the media and the public.

In 1912, Representative Carter Glass of Virginia (chairman of the House Committee on Banking and Finance) and H. Parker Willis (the committee's advisor) prepared an alternative central banking plan for newly elected President Woodrow Wilson. Their plan sought to address the concerns of the Progressives. With some key modifications made by President Wilson, most notably the addition of a government-appointed Board of Governors that would have supervisory and administrative oversight of the central bank, this plan was to become the Federal Reserve Act of 1913.

The act that Congress approved in December 1913 was a masterpiece of political engineering, a grand political compromise that some historians contend was Woodrow Wilson's greatest single achievement as president of the United States. The structure of the Federal Reserve reflects this compromise between competing political and economic interests.

The Structure of the Federal Reserve

The Federal Reserve is a quasi-governmental entity that combines governmental and private features and mandatory and voluntary features in an integrated three-tier pyramidal structure, as exhibit 5.2 illustrates.

EXHIBIT 5.2   **The Quasi-Governmental Structure of the Federal Reserve**

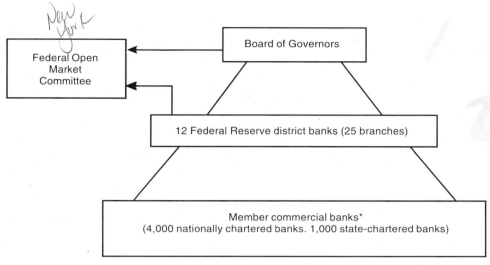

New York

| Federal Open Market Committee |
| Board of Governors |
| 12 Federal Reserve district banks (25 branches) |
| Member commercial banks* (4,000 nationally chartered banks. 1,000 state-chartered banks) |

*All depository institutions, not only member banks, are subject to the Fed's reserve requirements.

The top of the pyramid consists of the Board of Governors, which is an entity of the federal government. This seven-member governing body is primarily responsible for monetary policy, supervision and regulation of banks, and broad oversight of the operations of the Federal Reserve banks.

The middle of the pyramid consists of 12 regional Federal Reserve banks, one in each of the nation's 12 Federal Reserve districts. These are private corporate entities that together serve as the nation's central bank.

Off to the side of the pyramid is the 12-member Federal Open Market Committee (FOMC), which sets the nation's monetary policy. It consists of the seven governors and five Federal Reserve bank presidents.

At the base of the pyramid are the 5,000 commercial banks that are members of the Federal Reserve. All nationally chartered banks are required to be members, whereas state-chartered banks can choose whether or not to become members. Monetary policy traditionally has been channeled through these member banks. However, since 1980 all the nation's depository institutions have been subject to the Federal Reserve's reserve requirements. This change, which Congress made in the Monetary Control Act of 1980, effectively broadened the channel through which monetary policy flows.

Congress has not significantly modified the Federal Reserve System since its inception in 1913. Prior to the Monetary Control Act of 1980, the most notable modifications were in the Banking Acts of 1933 and 1935, which more tightly centralized monetary policy power at the Board of Governors level. In nearly 80 years, however, there have been no fundamental changes in the Federal Reserve's structure.

The Board of Governors

The Board of Governors is the governmental component of the Federal Reserve System. The seven governors who compose the board are appointed by the president of the United States for 14-year nonrenewable terms of office. Appointments must be confirmed by the Senate. Like Supreme Court justices, Federal Reserve governors cannot be removed from office at the will of the president, a policy designed to insulate the board from political pressure. Once in office, the governors are expected to make decisions in accordance with the broad national interest, not the partisan interest of the administration that appointed them. The 14-year terms are staggered so that one governor's term expires and one new governor is appointed every two years. This feature ensures that no president can "stack" the board.

The president also designates which of the seven governors will serve as the chairman of the Board of Governors. However, the four-year term of the chairman does not coincide with the president's term of office. Thus a newly elected president must wait two years before designating a new chairman. Moreover, in practice, the existing chairman is invariably redesignated to serve as chairman for another four years. It would be politically and managerially awkward for a president not to do so, since a chairman who is not redesignated could still serve as one of the seven governors. This awkward situation has occurred only once since 1913. In 1948, President Truman was involved in a bitter dispute with the Federal Reserve over whether or not to allow interest rates to change in the post-World War II economy and did not reappoint Mariner Eccles as chairman. Eccles continued to serve as a governor, however, until his term expired in 1951.

The Federal Reserve Act stipulates that only one member of the Board of Governors may be selected from each of the 12 Federal Reserve districts, and that the president must, in selecting appointees, give "fair representation" to the "financial, agricultural, industrial, and commercial interests and geographic divisions of the country." Congress wanted to ensure that all regional and economic interest groups would be represented in the monetary policy decision-making process.

The Board of Governors resides in Washington, D.C., and meets formally several times each week to transact its business. It makes decisions on matters related to the course of monetary policy, as well as on the regulation of banks, including applications of bank holding companies for new service powers.

DECIDING MONETARY POLICY

The seven members of the Board of Governors constitute a majority of the 12-member Federal Open Market Committee, which is the key monetary policy decision-making body within the Federal Reserve. At monthly FOMC meetings, the course of monetary policy is reviewed, evaluated, and if appropriate, changed.

The Board of Governors has the sole power to determine reserve requirements for the nation's depository institutions. It also determines the procedures and conditions under which the 12 Federal Reserve banks can make discount window loans to depository institutions in their role as lenders of last resort. The board has veto power over discount rates (interest rates for discount window loans) set by the Reserve banks. The board also can set stock market margin requirements on the use of credit in securities transactions.

REGULATING THE BANKING SYSTEM

The Board of Governors also supervises and regulates the activities of the Federal Reserve banks, regulates bank holding companies, and issues regulations that lending institutions must follow to comply with the major federal consumer credit protection laws.

Despite its autonomy, the Board of Governors is accountable to Congress. In accordance with the Full Employment and Balanced Growth Act of 1978, it must report twice a year to Congress on the condition of the economy and the stance of monetary policy. Although the board often has to defend its actions against congressional criticism, there is no direct means short of legislation that Congress or the president can employ to change board decisions.

The chairman of the Board of Governors, considered by many to be the nation's second most powerful government official, meets frequently with the president and the secretary of the treasury and is involved in all key domestic and international economic policy decisions. On an operational level, board members and staff maintain close working ties with officials and staff of the Treasury Department, the Office of Management and Budget, the Council of Economic Advisors, and other agencies. Congress frequently asks the board for its evaluation of economic issues, and board members frequently testify before congressional committees on pending legislation related to money, banking, or the economy.

Federal Reserve Districts

The Federal Reserve Act of 1913 specified that the U.S. central bank would consist of as many as 12 regional central banks. The nation was to be divided into Reserve districts, with each district having its own Reserve bank. In this way, power would be decentralized and fragmented to ensure against the new central bank becoming too powerful and dominating the nation's economic affairs. Also, because the U.S. economy of 1913 was far more regionally disparate than it is today, the Reserve district concept addressed regional development needs and economic interests.

Exhibit 5.3 shows the 12 Federal Reserve districts and the cities where the Reserve banks have headquarters, as well as the locations of the branch banks. The districts vary greatly in size, reflecting the attempt to counterbalance banking power with size of territory. The Midwest and Far West, where few large banks are located, are divided into massive territorial blocks. The Northeast, where much of the nation's banking is concentrated, is segmented into five relatively small districts. The second Federal Reserve district, which is one of the smallest, encompasses only New York state,

Fairfield County in Connecticut, and the 12 northern counties of New Jersey. Yet the Federal Reserve Bank of New York holds 25 percent of the total assets of the 12 Federal Reserve banks—a reflection of the disproportionate size of banks in the New York district compared with those in other districts.

EXHIBIT 5.3   Federal Reserve Districts and Their Branch Territories

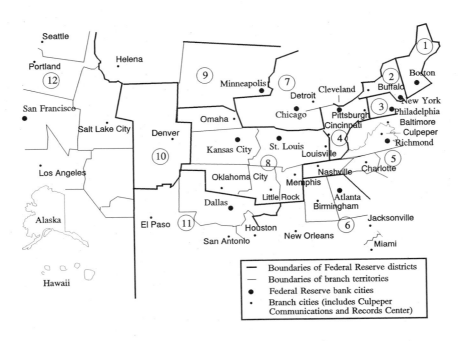

Congress did not itself establish the precise geographic structure of the Federal Reserve districts. Rather, section 2 of the Federal Reserve Act established a three-member committee (the secretary of the treasury, the secretary of agriculture, and the comptroller of the currency) to designate "not less than 8 nor more than 12 districts." The act also stipulated that districts created by the committee could be readjusted, and that new districts, not to exceed 12 in all, could be created by the Board of Governors. Nevertheless, the selection committee quickly became embroiled in a public relations war between cities vying for the elite status that designation as a Reserve city (and hence Reserve district) entailed.

In an effort to accommodate the national banks, many of whom the committee feared would change to state charters to avoid mandatory Federal Reserve membership, the committee initiated a preference poll for district affiliation. The results of this poll guided the committee's ultimate designation of the 12 districts and the 12 cities that to this day remain the headquarters for Reserve banks.

In the early years of the Federal Reserve, some board members favored a district consolidation to four or six districts. They feared that the smaller Reserve banks might be unable to attract qualified leaders or achieve high operating efficiency. Other board members opposed consolidation on the grounds that the greater number of Reserve banks made it harder for any single sectional group or special interest to gain control of the system.

Today the Board of Governors cannot alter the number of districts unless authorized to do so by legislation amending the Federal Reserve Act. It can, however, change district boundaries, which it has done on a minor scale on several occasions. It also can eliminate or relocate Reserve bank branches and Federal Reserve regional check-processing centers.

Adjusting district lines to accommodate banks or natural markets or to improve the Federal Reserve's operating efficiency does not generally cause controversy. However, any attempt to consolidate Reserve districts or eliminate Reserve bank branches would likely be aggressively opposed by regional and local interests and congressional representatives who would see such a move as leading to a loss of regional prestige. This may explain why the original selections of Reserve bank cities have remained unchanged since 1914.

Federal Reserve Banks

The 12 Federal Reserve banks are private corporate entities rather than entities of the federal government. Their general operations are broadly supervised by the Board of Governors, but their day-to-day central banking activities are largely independent of board involvement. Relative to each other, they function as autonomous institutions.

The 12 Reserve banks and their 25 branches are the banking service arms of the central bank and the locus of the nation's payments mechanism. As exhibit 5.4 shows, the Federal Reserve banks hold the banking system's reserves, lend funds to depositories, issue the nation's currency and coin, clear and collect about 35 percent of the nation's checks, provide banking services to depository institutions and to the government, and examine state-chartered member banks. The Reserve banks also participate in the monetary policy-making process through the involvement of the five Reserve bank presidents who serve on the FOMC. The Federal Reserve Bank of New York has additional functions in implementing the Fed's open-market operations and in dealing with the central banks of other nations.

EXHIBIT 5.4   **Functions of the Federal Reserve Banks**

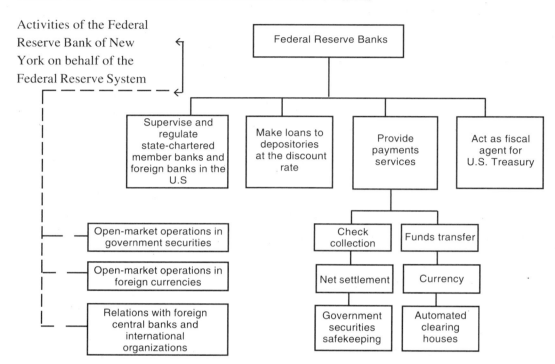

THE SELECTION OF DIRECTORS

The organization of the Reserve banks reflects the attempt by Congress in 1913 to ensure that central banking power would not rest completely in the hands of bankers, and that regional interests would be considered in central bank decision making.

As exhibit 5.5 illustrates, each Reserve bank is managed by a nine-member board of directors (six of whom must be nonbankers). Directors of the Reserve bank boards are selected in three different ways. Each board consists of three classes of directors (designated A, B, and C), each consisting of three directors who each serve three-year terms.

Class C directors are appointed by the Board of Governors. These appointments give the board some nominal supervisory oversight of the operations of the Reserve banks. Class C directors cannot be bankers or have any relationship with, or financial interest in, a bank. They typically are educators, lawyers, retired business executives, and leaders of community groups. The chairman and deputy chairman of each Reserve bank's board, who each serve one-year terms, are selected by the board from the Class C directors.

The six Class A and Class B directors are elected by member commercial banks. Class A directors can be bankers, and they usually represent the interests of the district's member banks. Class B directors, however, cannot be bankers or have any relationship with, or financial interest in, a bank. Thus, while member banks elect the majority of each Reserve bank's nine-member board of directors, no more than three directors may represent banking interests. To further diffuse the power of large commercial banks over the central bank, member banks are grouped by the amount of capital they hold into three size categories—small, medium, and large—and the banks in a given category select one of the Class A and one of the Class B directors. This ensures that small rural member banks in any given district cannot be dominated by large, urban banks, since large banks in any district can capture only one of the banker seats

EXHIBIT 5.5   **Selection of the Federal Reserve Banks' Boards of Directors**

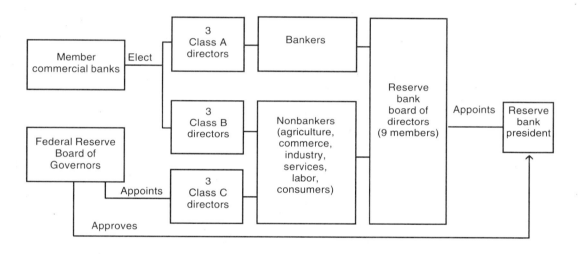

Note: Each of the 12 Federal Reserve banks has its own bank president and nine-member board of directors.

The complexity of the director selection process reflects the deep-seated sensitivities to banking power that concerned Congress in 1913. In the 1970s, concern over whether Reserve bank directors were appropriate representatives of their districts' interests caused Congress to modify the selection process. The Federal Reserve Act initially specified that in selecting Class B and Class C directors, the Board of Governors and the district member banks should give due attention to the interests of agriculture, commerce, and industry. Congress felt that the changing nature of the U.S. economy, its labor force, and its economic interests should be reflected in the selection process. There also was some concern that Reserve bank directors were not, and had never been, truly representative of the American people (virtually all directors were white males).

In 1977, to expand representation on the Reserve bank's boards, the Federal Reserve Act was amended to require that due consideration be given to "services, labor, and consumers," and that selections of directors be made "without discrimination on the basis of race, creed, color, sex, or national origin."

THE POWER OF DIRECTORS

The directors of the Reserve banks do not truly run the Reserve banks since most of the Reserve banks' functions are statutory or governmental in nature. The directors today primarily serve as information channels between regional business, banking, and other interests and the Washington-based Board of Governors. However, because the Reserve banks' directors appoint the banks' presidents and first vice presidents (subject to the Board of Governors' approval), they indirectly influence the monetary policy-making process. In addition, directors typically provide information on regional business and credit conditions and give advice to their Reserve bank presidents for use at FOMC meetings.

The Federal Reserve Act requires each Reserve bank's board of directors to set the discount rate for their district every two weeks. They either reconfirm, raise, or lower the existing rate. The Board of Governors has veto power over any rate change it feels is inconsistent with the needs of the national economy. In recent years, the Board of Governors has generally conveyed its sentiments on the need for rate changes to the Reserve bank presidents in advance of the bank boards' regular meetings. In effect, the Board of Governors asks the directors for, and typically gets, the discount rate it wants. The rate-setting power of the Reserve banks' directors, therefore, has become more ceremonial than real.

The Split Discount Rate—Dissent or Delay?

On rare occasions, a strong-willed Reserve bank board of directors has registered its dissent with the Board of Governors' monetary policy direction by failing to vote a discount rate change for their district that has already been set by the other Reserve banks, accepted by the Board of Governors, and publicly announced. When this occurs, a split discount rate prevails—that is, one district's rate is higher or lower than that of the other districts throughout the country.

When the discount rate remains split for a prolonged period, it can be economically disruptive. Since other interest rates often are pegged to the discount rate, a split rate may serve as an artificial incentive for banks and businesses to transfer funds and loan demands from one region of the country to another.

However, most split-rate situations are temporary and do not reflect dissent within the Federal Reserve. Because Reserve bank boards of directors do not all meet on the same day or even in the same week, a split rate usually reflects a lag in meeting times. A discount rate that remains split for two weeks or more, however, would likely represent dissent.

(Continued from previous page)

To eliminate the appearance of dissent resulting from administrative lag, the Board of Governors sometimes holds the votes of Reserve bank directors for several days until all are in, then publicly announces a nationwide rate change. Announcement of a discount rate change by the Board of Governors, rather than separately by each Reserve bank, gives more authority to the monetary policy-making power of the Federal Reserve.

RESERVE BANK EARNINGS

The 12 Federal Reserve district banks are profit-making entities, although they are not motivated by profit and do not keep most of their profits. Reserve banks generate profit mainly from the interest they earn on the nearly $300 billion in government securities that constitute the Federal Reserve's open market portfolio. These securities have been purchased by the Reserve banks over the decades in implementing monetary policy. Other earnings are derived from the fees the Federal Reserve charges for clearing checks and electronically transferring funds and from interest on discount window loans to depositories. In the 1980s, the gross earnings of the Reserve banks averaged approximately $20 billion a year. The Reserve banks, however, keep only about 5 percent of these funds. Annual earnings in excess of what the Reserve banks and the Board of Governors need to cover their operating expenses, plus what they need to pay a statutory 6 percent dividend on Federal Reserve bank stock owned by member banks, are returned to the Treasury.

The considerable earnings of the Federal Reserve have long given it the capacity to fund itself. This freedom from the congressional appropriations process has, on occasion, raised some concern in Congress that the central bank may be too independent and not as accountable to Congress as would be the case if Federal Reserve expenses were part of the federal budget. Without the "power of the purse," it has been argued, Congress has no true power to control the Federal Reserve. This concern, however, has never been widely shared by members of Congress.

THE FEDERAL RESERVE BANK OF NEW YORK

Not all Reserve banks are equal in asset size, market power, or influence. Their dissimilarities can be traced to the initial unequal division of Reserve bank districts, the concentration of banking power in key cities, and the changing nature of the economy in different regions of the United States.

The Federal Reserve Bank of New York is the premier bank in the nation's central banking system and has a unique role, as illustrated again in exhibit 5.4. In fact, to many foreign central banks and governments, it *is* the central bank. The influence of the Federal Reserve Bank of New York is primarily a result of its location in the banking and financial center of the world.

The New York Reserve bank alone implements open-market operations, the Federal Reserve System's primary policy tool. Its trading desk buys and sells government securities in accordance with the general directives of the FOMC on behalf of the entire system. In addition, the president of the New York Reserve bank is the only Reserve bank president who is a permanent member of the FOMC, traditionally serving as vice chairman of the committee.

The Federal Reserve Bank of New York also has a unique international role. It acts as the government's and the FOMC's operating arm in the foreign exchange market. It buys and sells foreign currencies in New York to stabilize disorderly exchange market conditions, and it buys and sells U.S. government securities on behalf of foreign central banks. In 1992, the New York Reserve bank held more than $275 billion in government securities in custody for foreign and international accounts. Since 1924, the bank also has acted as the repository for the world's gold bullion reserves; today, it stores gold for about 75 foreign countries, central banks, and international financial organizations.

The Federal Open Market Committee

The 12-member Federal Open Market Committee is the monetary policy decision-making center of the Federal Reserve. Its open-market operations (the buying and selling of U.S. government securities) determine the cost and availability of money and credit in the U.S. economy. Exhibit 5.6 illustrates the structure of the FOMC and its relationship to the Board of Governors and the 12 Reserve banks in implementing monetary policy directives.

EXHIBIT 5.6   **Composition of the Federal Open Market Committee**

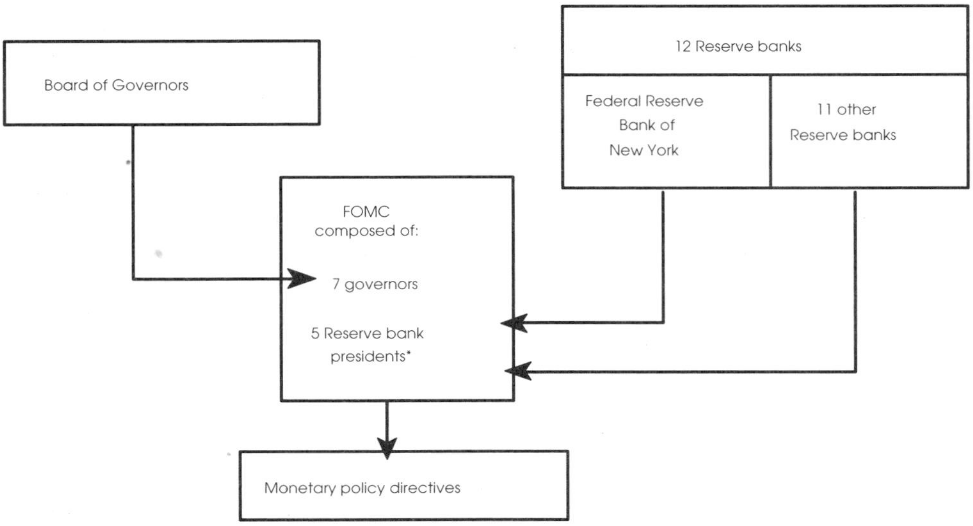

*Includes the presidents of FRBNY and four other Reserve banks.

The FOMC consists of the seven members of the Board of Governors and five Reserve bank presidents—including the president of the Federal Reserve Bank of New York, who is a permanent member. The four other Reserve bank presidents, who serve one-year terms, are selected in rotation from four regional clusters of the other 11 Reserve banks: 1) Boston, Philadelphia, and Richmond; 2) Cleveland and Chicago; 3) Atlanta, St. Louis, and Dallas; and 4) Minneapolis, Kansas City, and San Francisco.

No statutory rules govern the FOMC's organization. By tradition, however, the chairman of the Board of Governors also serves as chairman of the FOMC, and the president of the New York Reserve bank serves as vice chairman.

The committee formally meets in Washington, D.C. every six weeks or so. Committee members routinely communicate with each other almost daily, however, and if economic or financial conditions warrant action between regular meetings, additional meetings or telephone conferences are held.

At every formal meeting, the committee must vote on a course of action for monetary policy—to tighten, to ease, or to maintain the status quo. This vote governs policy until the next meeting. Several times each year, the committee also votes on long-range policy objectives and operational targets. Committee decisions are incorporated into a policy directive that is forwarded to the Federal Reserve Bank of New York for implementation through its open-market operations.

The FOMC was created by the Banking Acts of 1933 and 1935, which amended the original Federal Reserve Act of 1913. It was not until the 1950s, however, that open-market operations became the dominant mechanism for implementing the nation's monetary policy.

RESERVE BANK PRESIDENTS AND THE FOMC

The participation of Reserve bank presidents as members of the FOMC became a point of litigation in the 1980s, when several members of the House and Senate initiated suits in federal court to remove the five Reserve bank presidents from the FOMC. These suits contended that it is improper for five private citizens, who are neither appointed by the president nor confirmed by the Senate, to set the government's monetary policy. The suits were dismissed by the court on the grounds that the congressional litigants had no legal standing to bring such suits.

In 1984, however, a federal court agreed to rule on the merits of a suit brought by Senator John Melcher (D-Montana) to remove the Reserve bank presidents from the FOMC. In a 1986 ruling, the federal court held that the composition of the FOMC, while "unusual," was not unconstitutional. The court noted that the structure of the Federal Reserve had been carefully crafted by Congress in 1913 to blend both public and private interests in order to ensure a balanced approach in addressing the nation's money and banking problems. Moreover, Congress had actively debated the composition of the FOMC in 1935 when it established the committee's current membership. The court further maintained that the Constitution does not bar private citizens from carrying out government functions. In 1987, a federal appeals court again rejected

Senator Melcher's suit. The appeals court ruled that the merits of his argument about the appropriateness of the FOMC's membership were not judicially relevant. It further held that only Congress can change the membership of the FOMC.

The issue of whether the decision-making power of the central bank should be shared between the private sector and the government and between regional and national interests may well be addressed by Congress in the 1990s; a number of bills to change the composition or the role of the FOMC were introduced in Congress in 1991 and 1992.

Legal Challenges to FOMC Structure

Legal challenges to the structure of the FOMC appear to be motivated by several factors. Some members of Congress contend that the monetary policy views of Reserve bank presidents too closely follow the views of commercial bankers in their districts. Thus, by implication, the participation of Reserve bank presidents in the monetary policy decision-making process gives commercial banking interests too great an influence. However, the contention that Reserve bank presidents dominate the FOMC has never been supported by evidence. To the contrary, a majority of the Board of Governors has never been outvoted on the FOMC by the votes of the five Reserve bank presidents.

A second point of contention is the notion that the president needs more control over monetary policy decision making. At various times during the last two decades, members of Congress have disagreed with the policy decisions of the FOMC, particularly the committee's unwillingness in the 1980s to accommodate the fiscal policies of the president. Removing the Reserve bank presidents from the FOMC would give the president, who appoints members of the Board of Governors, more control over monetary policy decision making. In addition, if the seven Washington-based governors were alone in deciding monetary policy, greater weight would be given to national rather than regional considerations. The fact that this contention is not widely shared in the House or Senate may explain why some members of Congress have followed a judicial approach, rather than a legislative approach, to a challenge of the FOMC.

Member Banks

At the base of the Federal Reserve's pyramidal structure are 5,000 member banks. As exhibit 5.7 shows, current membership in the Federal Reserve includes all 4,000 federally chartered commercial banks, as well as about 1,000 state-chartered commercial banks.

EXHIBIT 5.7   **Mandatory and Voluntary Membership in the Federal Reserve System**

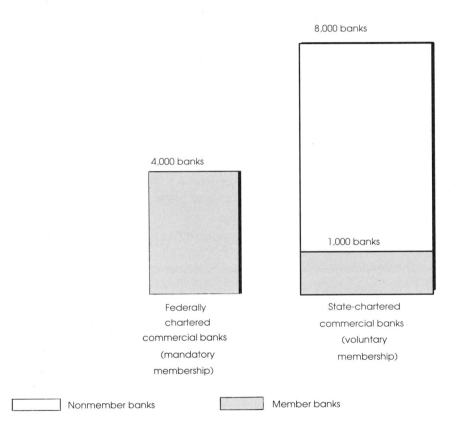

The Federal Reserve Act of 1913 stipulates that all nationally chartered banks must be Federal Reserve members, whereas state-chartered banks have the option to become members. The membership option for state-chartered banks reflects still another aspect of the political compromise embodied in the Federal Reserve Act. Congress was reluctant to impose federal law over state-chartered banks, an action some feared would destroy the nation's dual banking system.

Banks that are members of the Federal Reserve must subscribe to stock in their district Federal Reserve bank in an amount equal to 6 percent of their own capital stock and surplus. Of this amount, half (3 percent) must be bought and half must remain subject to call for purchase. Member banks receive a cumulative 6 percent dividend on their stock each year. Stock subscriptions were intended to provide the Reserve banks with their initial working capital. While the Federal Reserve is self-funding today, stock ownership remains a unique part of the structure of the U.S. central bank.

Membership in the Federal Reserve traditionally provided certain benefits to members but also imposed certain costs. The principal benefits were access to the discount window and to Reserve bank services. The principal costs were the "tax" that member banks incurred by being required to hold noninterest-earning reserves, and supervision and regulation by the Federal Reserve (or the Comptroller of the Currency, in the case of national banks) rather than a state government. The requirement that member banks purchase Reserve bank stock also became a cost in recent decades when market rates on alternative investment opportunities began to exceed the 6 percent dividend the Federal Reserve pays on that stock.

The Monetary Control Act of 1980 made membership in the Federal Reserve less relevant since it required both member and nonmember banks to hold reserves. The Federal Reserve also now provides access to its discount window to all depository institutions that are subject to its reserve requirements and makes Reserve bank services available to all depositories for the same explicit fees. In effect, the principal benefits of membership are now available to both member and nonmember depositories on an almost equal basis.

The Federal Advisory Council

The Federal Advisory Council is a private advisory group that serves as an information channel for the Federal Reserve. The council consists of 12 members, one appointed by each of the Federal Reserve banks. Members are usually leading bankers in their Reserve district. Each member serves for one year. At least four council meetings are held annually at the Federal Reserve Board in Washington, D.C. Additional meetings may be called by the Board of Governors or by the council itself.

The Federal Advisory Council reviews and discusses Federal Reserve operational matters and monetary policy, but does not exert any overt influence on the operations of the Reserve banks or on monetary policy. Rather, its primary role is to transmit bankers' views directly to the Board of Governors and to provide the board with grassroots information and views on the impact of its actions.

Functions of the Federal Reserve

The many significant functions of the Federal Reserve can be grouped into three broad categories: setting and implementing monetary policy, providing payment services for depositories, and serving as the bank for the government. Exhibit 5.8 presents a listing of Federal Reserve functions within these categories. Because its role in setting and implementing monetary policy is discussed in considerable detail in subsequent chapters, let us look first at the Federal Reserve as a provider of payment services for depositories and as a bank for the government.

EXHIBIT 5.8   **Functions of the Federal Reserve**

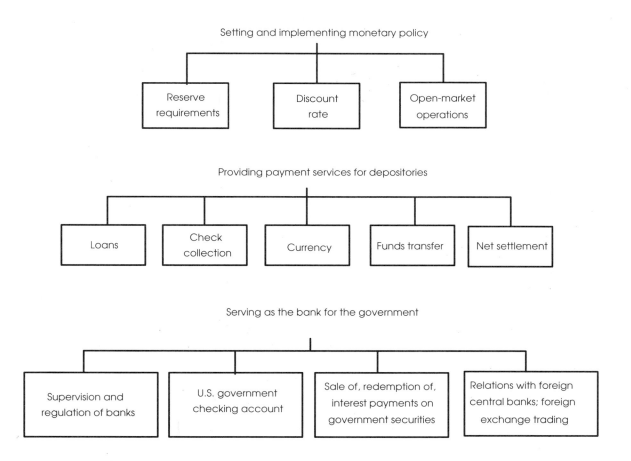

Providing Payment Services for Depositories

Federal Reserve banks play a major operational role in the nation's payments mechanism. Virtually all of the nation's circulating paper currency consists of Federal Reserve notes issued by the 12 Federal Reserve banks. Approximately one-third of the nation's checks move through the Federal Reserve's nationwide check collection system. The Federal Reserve also operates an extensive network of regional check-processing centers and automated clearing houses. An electronic funds transfer system, called Fedwire, moves money and government securities among banks having reserve accounts at the Federal Reserve and aids banks in the efficient adjustment of their reserve balances.

Reserve banks also provide safekeeping facilities for paper securities held by depositories, collect interest payments on these securities, and credit payment of matured securities to depositories' reserve accounts.

Serving as Bank for the Government

The Federal Reserve's hands-on supervisory responsibilities for state-chartered member banks, bank holding companies, and foreign banks operating in the U.S. are delegated by the Board of Governors to the Reserve banks. The 12 Federal Reserve banks maintain staffs of bank examiners that conduct the field examinations of state-chartered member banks, foreign bank branches and agencies, and nonbank subsidiaries of bank holding companies in their districts. Reserve banks also must approve certain types of bank and bank holding company applications. They maintain staffs of banking analysts and economists that review applications and analyze the potential anticompetitive effects of bank proposals.

Federal Reserve banks also act as fiscal agents for the U.S. government. As the government's banker, Reserve banks hold and issue new Treasury securities and savings bonds sold by the Treasury to dealers and the public. They effect payment for these securities through transfers of funds over Fedwire. Reserve banks also make periodic interest payments on behalf of the government on outstanding Treasury and federal agency debts.

Reserve banks maintain the government's disbursement checking accounts, from which virtually all federal spending and transfer payments are made, and they effect transfers of funds between the U.S. government and foreign governments. Although Federal Reserve notes (currency) are liabilities of the Federal Reserve, the issuance of currency (which includes the storage of new currency and the removal from circulation of unfit coins and notes) is, effectively, also a fiscal agent service provided by the central bank for the government.

HISTORY OF FISCAL AGENCY FUNCTIONS

From 1789 to 1916, the government's banking needs were handled primarily through the nation's private banking system. With the exception of a 17-year period

(1846-1863) when the Treasury performed all its banking functions directly, private banks served as fiscal agents for the Treasury. They assisted in making interest payments on government debt and, from time to time, in receiving subscriptions to new debt offerings. In 1846, a subtreasury system was established to provide services to the Treasury. Under this system, nine subtreasuries performed government functions related to coin, paper currency, payment of maturing debt, cashing of Treasury checks, and holding and transfering government deposits.

The Federal Reserve's role as provider of fiscal services began in 1916 when the Treasury transferred its fiscal agency operations from the existing national banks to the newly established Federal Reserve banks. By 1919, most of the services formerly provided to the Treasury through the subtreasury system also had been assumed by the Federal Reserve.

Initially the Federal Reserve's fiscal agency functions consisted almost entirely of the payment of coupons (interest due) on the Treasury's debt, the receipt of Treasury funds for transfer to other banks, and the receipt of government securities for redemption. When the United States entered into World War I in 1916, Reserve banks involved themselves extensively in marketing the government's debt.

In the 1920s, the Treasury authorized the Federal Reserve banks, as fiscal agents, to cancel and reissue securities by telegraph wire from one Federal Reserve district to another as a means of providing support for the marketing of Treasury securities. This telegraph transfer procedure was the precursor of the book-entry securities transfer service that the Reserve banks introduced to the nation's payments mechanism in the late 1960s.

Setting and Implementing Monetary Policy

Notwithstanding its important functions in the U.S. payments mechanism and as the bank of the U.S. government, the primary function of the Federal Reserve is to control the nation's supply of money and credit in an attempt to achieve balanced economic growth. Responsibility for formulating monetary policy is shared by the Board of Governors and the Federal Reserve banks; members of the Board of Governors and Reserve bank presidents jointly control the discount rate and, through their participation on the FOMC, control open-market operations.

Exhibit 5.9 presents an overview of the Federal Reserve System. In the following chapter we will see how the Federal Reserve attempts to implement monetary policy through three basic monetary tools—reserve requirements, the discount rate, and open-market operations. These tools enable the Fed to influence the nation's economic activity—income, employment, output, and prices.

EXHIBIT 5.9   **Overview of the Federal Reserve System**

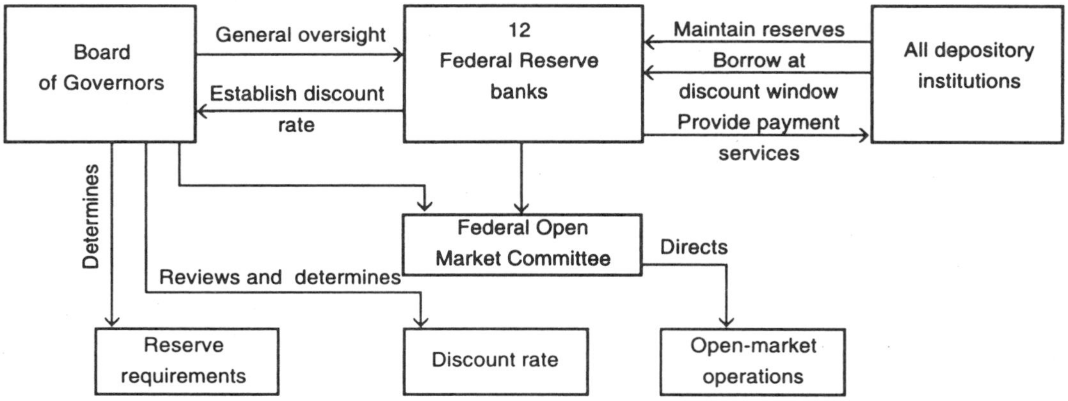

Board of Governors: 7 members: appointed by president and con-
                                             firmed by Senate for 14-year terms with one
                                             new member appointed every 2 years

Federal Reserve banks: 12 banks, each with 9-member board of direc-
                                             tors: 3 appointed by the Board of Governors to
                                             represent the general public, the other 6 elected
                                             by member banks (3 of whom can be bankers)

Federal Open Market Committee: 12 members: 7 members of the Board of
                                             Governors, 5 Reserve bank presidents

Summary

The Federal Reserve is responsible for formulating and implementing the nation's monetary policy. It was established by Congress in 1913 to provide the nation with an elastic (responsive) paper currency; to act as a lender of last resort to prevent bank illiquidity; to improve the efficiency of the nation's check collection system; and to provide a degree of federal supervision over banking. Over the decades its objectives were expanded to include control of the cost and availability of money and credit to achieve the national goals of price stability, full employment, and economic growth.

The Federal Reserve is a unique quasi-governmental central bank. It consists of 12 regional Reserve banks, which are private corporations nominally owned by member banks and run by boards of directors. The Reserve banks are supervised by a Board of Governors (seven presidentially appointed officials). The key monetary policy decision-making entity within the Federal Reserve System is the 12-member Federal Open Market Committee (FOMC). The committee's operating arm in implementing monetary policy is the Federal Reserve Bank of New York. About 5,000 commercial banks are members of the Federal Reserve.

The Federal Reserve's major nonpolicy functions are to provide payment services to depositories at explicit charges, to act as the banker and fiscal agent of the U.S. Treasury, and to supervise and regulate the banks under its jurisdiction.

Questions

1. Why was the nation's check collection system in the nineteenth century inefficient?

2. What four major problems did the Federal Reserve Act of 1913 try to solve?

3. Based on the structure of the Federal Reserve, what objectives do you think Congress had when it created the central bank?

4. How independent is the Federal Reserve? Would the country be better served if both monetary and fiscal policy were responsibilities of the administration? Why or why not?

5. What characteristics do the 12 Federal Reserve district banks and the Federal Reserve member banks have in common? How do they differ?

6

The Tools of Monetary and Fiscal Policy

Objectives

After successfully completing this chapter, you will be able to

- ☐ distinguish between general and selective monetary policy tools,
- ☐ describe how the discount rate is used as a monetary tool,
- ☐ cite the three ways that reserve requirements can be used to control the creation of money,
- ☐ explain how open-market operations work, including how the dealer market is used in implementing monetary policy,
- ☐ differentiate between monetary and fiscal policy, and
- ☐ describe the blend of monetary and fiscal policy that best counters inflation and recession.

Introduction

Monetary policy involves the management of a nation's money supply to ensure the availability of money and credit in quantities and at interest rates consistent with specific economic objectives. Fiscal policy involves the use of a government's spending and revenue-producing activities (taxation) to achieve specific economic goals. In the United States, monetary policy is the province of the Federal Reserve while fiscal policy is the responsibility of Congress and the president.

The basic monetary policy tools wielded by the Federal Reserve are the discount rate, reserve requirements, and open-market operations. The primary fiscal policy tools are federal spending and taxation. Each monetary and fiscal policy instrument affects the economy in a different way. Monetary tools change the amount or composition of bank reserves, the money supply, and the level of interest rates. These changes directly affect banks through their lending activities and through the spending patterns of businesses. Fiscal tools affect after-tax income and consumer spending for goods and services.

In this chapter, we examine how the nation's monetary and fiscal policy tools work, examine their strengths and weaknesses, and discuss key factors that affect their use in fighting recession or inflation.

The Federal Reserve's policies on discount window lending (loans of reserves to banks), its use of the discount rate as a monetary policy tool, and its use of reserve requirements have undergone profound changes since 1913. To gain a historical perspective on the evolution of the discount window, you are encouraged to read Extended Study 7, "Evolution of the Discount Window and the Discount Rate." To learn more about the economic and financial environment of the 1970s and the issues that led Congress to restructure reserve requirements and expand the Federal Reserve's policy powers, you are encouraged to read Extended Study 8, "Uniform Reserve Requirements."

Monetary Policy Tools

Monetary policy tools are classified as either general or selective in their application and impact on the economy. *General* policy tools seek to control the total quantity, availability, or cost of money throughout the economy without regard to the purpose of the funds. These policy instruments typically work by increasing or decreasing bank reserves. *Selective* policy tools focus on a specific financial market or component of total credit, such as stock market lending, consumer credit, or real estate. They attempt to control the cost or flow of funds only in selected sectors of the economy.

The Federal Reserve's administration of monetary policy and its use of monetary policy tools are essentially general, rather than specific, in nature. U.S. monetary policy is oriented toward the total economy and toward broad national economic goals. Under this general approach, decisions on who gets money and credit and at what price (interest rate) are decided in the marketplace rather than by the central bank.

Central banks in other countries use selective policy tools far more than the Federal Reserve does. Many foreign countries direct their monetary policy toward specific sectors or industries to promote social objectives and industrial growth. In some countries, central banks lend money to government units for public projects, invest central bank funds in private companies, and make loans to favored industries at below-market rates.

For example, the central bank of Mexico uses its reserve requirement powers over commercial banks to direct loans to specific industries and into low-income housing. The central bank of Japan lends money to specific companies to help achieve broad national growth objectives. And the central bank of Italy uses its monetary policy powers to prevent banks from lending money for reasons that are inconsistent with the nation's development efforts.

In contrast, the Federal Reserve relies primarily on one general monetary policy tool to achieve U.S. economic goals: open-market operations. The Federal Reserve buys and sells U.S. government securities, thereby increasing or decreasing bank reserves and the nation's money supply. In this way, the Federal Reserve seeks to move the economy in an appropriate direction at an appropriate speed. The Federal Reserve's general approach to monetary policy, its extensive use of open-market operations, and its reliance on the marketplace to allocate money and credit set it apart from most of the world's central banks.

Before we examine the Federal Reserve's open-market operations, let us look at the two lesser general monetary policy tools used by the Federal Reserve—the discount rate and reserve requirements.

The Discount Rate

   The discount rate is the interest rate that Federal Reserve banks charge commercial banks and other depository institutions that borrow reserves. An increase (or decrease) in this basic cost-of-reserves rate is meant to act as a powerful depressant (or stimulant) to depositories' borrowings from the Federal Reserve and their subsequent loans to private borrowers. In theory, by raising or lowering the discount rate, the Federal Reserve can reduce or expand business lending and investment spending in the economy. A change in the discount rate also can serve as an announcement to the banking community and the public that a change in monetary policy is being made.

However, the Federal Reserve no longer uses the discount rate in this manner. In practice, discount rate changes lag well behind changes in other key short-term interest rates, such as the federal funds rate. Discount rate changes typically are made to support monetary policy changes that have been implemented weeks or months earlier through open-market operations.

To understand the modern-day role of the discount rate as a monetary policy tool, we must first examine the workings of the Federal Reserve's discount window and the central bank's role as a lender of reserves to depositories.

CRITERIA FOR FEDERAL RESERVE LENDING

The Federal Reserve has established three sets of criteria for lending reserves to depositories: short-term adjustment credit, seasonal credit, and extended credit.

Short-term Adjustment Credit. The Federal Reserve lends reserves to depositories so that banks can meet their reserve requirements, to cover a sudden drain of liquidity, or to allow the borrowing banks time to adjust their assets and liabilities to cope with tight money pressures that the Federal Reserve itself may be generating with its open-market operations. Most of the Federal Reserve's lending falls into this category.

The nation's large city banks do most of the borrowing from the Federal Reserve's discount window, but they borrow only for a day or two at a time. Small country banks tend to borrow less frequently, but when they do, it is typically for a week or longer.

The way in which Federal Reserve short-term adjustment loans affect bank reserves can be illustrated using a T-account. Assume that First Commercial Bank borrows $1 million from its district Federal Reserve bank.

First Commercial Bank		Federal Reserve Bank	
Assets	Liabilities	Assets	Liabilities
Reserve account	Borrowings from Federal Reserve	Discount loans	Reserve account of First Commercial
+ $1 million	+ $1 million	+ $1 million	+ $1 million

First Commercial receives a direct credit to its reserve account at the Federal Reserve bank. Thus, the discount window loan does not merely redistribute bank reserves within the banking system, but generates a net increase of $1 million in bank reserves. When the loan is repaid, bank reserves will decline by $1 million. On any given day, the total amount of outstanding borrowings from the Federal Reserve by all depositories represents the increase in bank reserves supplied to the banking system through the discount window.

Seasonal Credit. The Federal Reserve also lends reserves to small and medium-sized depositories that experience strong seasonal disturbances in their deposit and loan flows and that lack access to national money markets to adjust to these disturbances. Many banks in agricultural and resort communities are subject to wide seasonal variations in their banking business that affect their reserve positions for 90 days or more at a time. A two- or three-day loan from the Federal Reserve would not address the needs of these banks. Thus, the Federal Reserve developed a seasonal borrowing criterion in the early 1970s to help banks in these circumstances. Very few banks qualify for these loans; of those that do, few use the seasonal borrowing option. The discount rate charged for seasonal loans is an adjustable rate that takes prevailing market rates into account; however, the rate charged for seasonal credit can never be set lower than the rate applicable to short-term adjustment credit.

Extended Credit. The Federal Reserve also lends reserves to depositories in its capacity as lender of last resort when exceptional circumstances or practices threaten an individual depository with failure because of illiquidity. Extended credit (emergency lending) is very rare, and when it is used by the Federal Reserve it usually makes nationwide headlines.

In 1988, for example, the Federal Reserve Bank of Dallas used extended credit lending to maintain the liquidity of the First Republic Bank until the FDIC could put an emergency relief plan in place for this bank, the thirteenth largest in the United States. Four years earlier, the Federal Reserve Bank of Chicago used extended credit to assist the Continental Illinois National Bank and Trust Company of Chicago, the eighth largest bank in the country.

In the 1970s, Congress amended the Federal Reserve Act to establish a penalty rate (an interest charge in excess of the short-term adjustment discount rate) on extended credit lending of long duration. The penalty rate concept is reflected in the Federal Reserve's rules for extended credit discount window loans. Under those rules, one rate pertains to the first 30 days of extended credit borrowing. A higher adjustable rate, somewhat above market rates, is imposed if borrowings extend beyond 30 days, but the higher rate can never be less than the discount rate applicable to short-term adjustment credit plus one-half percentage point.

A penalty rate also may be charged if a bank is forced to borrow an exceptionally large amount from the Federal Reserve for overnight use because of an operational or computer problem. Under the Federal Reserve's rules, the highest seasonal or extended credit rate being charged at the time can be applied to such loans. The Federal Reserve adopted the penalty rate for short-term operating problem loans in 1986 to encourage banks to strengthen their internal processing and computer systems so they could avoid major operational problems that would have to be covered with Federal Reserve loans.

In October 1992, the discount rate for short-term adjustment credit was 3.0 percent. The seasonal credit discount rate was 3.3 percent; extended credit carried a discount rate of 3.8 percent.

THE DISCOUNT WINDOW "SAFETY VALVE"

The Federal Reserve primarily uses the discount rate and discount window loans of reserves as a safety valve for individual banks under reserve pressure. The safety valve enables banks to obtain reserves for one or two days until they can make broader adjustments in their assets and liabilities to bring their reserves in balance with their deposits.

Under the safety valve approach, small banks are generally granted easier access to adjustment credit than large banks, which typically have access to a broad range of alternative funding sources. Also, as exhibit 6.1 shows, the discount rate is set below other short-term money rates, such as the federal funds rate. The goal is not to encourage banks to borrow more, but to ease the cost burden on borrowing banks that are experiencing stress from insufficient reserves and need additional liquidity.

EXHIBIT 6.1   The Discount Rate and the Federal Funds Rate

As seen in exhibit 6.2, the Federal Reserve tries to maintain a spread of no more than two percentage points between its discount rate and the generally higher federal funds rate. Such a spread ensures that if market rates rise, the Federal Reserve will not see the discount window abused by banks that are not under pressure, but simply in search of a source of cheap reserves. A narrow spread also ensures that if market rates fall, the role of the safety valve will be maintained. Thus, most changes in the discount rate in recent years have been initiated to align the discount rate with changes that have occurred in other short-term interest rates.

EXHIBIT 6.2   **Spread between Federal Funds Rate and Discount Rate**
(Weekly)

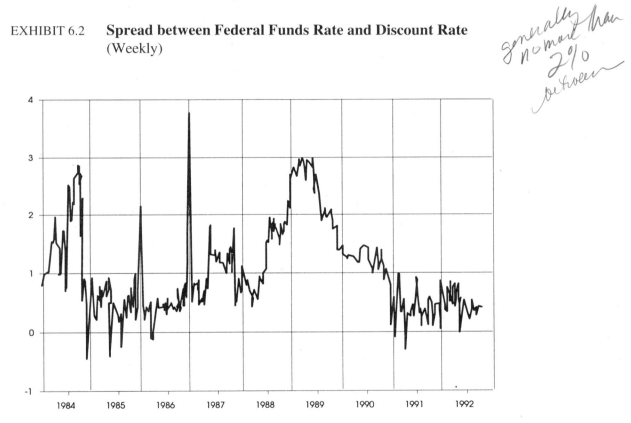

Source: Federal Reserve Bank of New York.

The Federal Reserve banks administer discount window lending to ensure that borrowed reserves are used in a manner consistent with the safety valve approach. Reserve banks ask borrowing institutions the reason for each discount window loan request and they review changes in the institution's weekly financial statement as well as the overall record of the institution's past discount window use. The Reserve banks use the following criteria to evaluate whether borrowed reserves are being misused:

- ❏ frequency of discount window borrowing
- ❏ the number of consecutive weeks an institution has borrowed

(handwritten margin notes: Rate of Res Req varies based on the type of liabilities and assets)

- [ ] the borrower's pattern of discount window use over successive periods of 13 weeks or longer
- [ ] the amount borrowed as a percentage of total deposits
- [ ] the amount borrowed as a percentage of required reserves
- [ ] repetitive patterns of borrowing, such as continuous weekend or every-other-week borrowings. (Such patterns are considered a misuse of the safety valve, and Reserve banks do not allow these borrowings to continue.)

Reserve Requirements *(handwritten: used sparingly)*

(handwritten margin note: Short term & long term effect)

Changing reserve requirements is the single most powerful monetary policy tool that any central bank can use to control its nation's money supply. The power of reserve requirement changes lies in their double impact—they have both a short-term and long-term effect. A change in reserve requirements does not increase or decrease total reserves immediately. Initially, it alters only the composition or allocation of required and excess reserves in the banking system. Over time, however, a change in reserve requirements results in greater or smaller demand deposit expansion in the banking system and consequently affects the growth of money supply in the economy.

Because of the strong impact of reserve requirement changes on the financial markets, the Fed uses its powers to change reserve requirements sparingly. The effect of changed reserve requirements can be demonstrated using T-accounts. Assume there is a 15 percent reserve requirement against demand deposits and that Bank A has $50,000 in excess reserves:

Bank A
(With a 15 Percent Reserve Requirement)

Assets		Liabilities	
Total reserves	$200,000*	Demand deposits	$1,000,000
Loans	$800,000		
*Required reserves	$150,000		
Excess reserves	$ 50,000		

(handwritten margin note: Increase Reserves → anti-inflation policy, less to loan, less to buy down, prices come down)

Bank A is currently capable of creating $50,000 in new money. The banking system as a whole is theoretically capable of creating almost $350,000 in demand deposits through the multiple expansion process (a 15 percent reserve requirement would produce a coefficient of expansion of about 7). Assume that the Federal Reserve increases its reserve requirement from 15 percent to 20 percent as part of a bold new anti-inflation monetary policy program. Bank A's total reserves do not change, but Bank A must now allocate its excess reserves to meet the higher reserve requirement.

Bank A
(With a 20 Percent Reserve Requirement)

Assets		Liabilities	
Total reserves	$200,000*	Demand deposits	$1,000,000
Loans	$800,000		

* Required reserves	$200,000
Excess reserves	$ 0

As a result of the reserve requirement change, Bank A's immediate lending capability has been reduced. Moreover, the banking system's ability to create money over time has been blunted as well.

If the Federal Reserve had reduced reserve requirements from 15 percent to 10 percent as a stimulative measure, the impact on Bank A and on the banking system would have been equally profound. Again, Bank A's total reserves would not be affected immediately. However, with an additional $50,000 in excess reserves, Bank A would now be capable of creating $100,000 in new money by making a $100,000 loan. The banking system's theoretical coefficient for multiple money creation would now be 10 instead of 7, and in theory, the banking system could create $1,000,000 in new money instead of the $350,000 possible under the 15 percent reserve requirement assumption.

Bank A
(With a 10 Percent Reserve Requirement)

Assets		Liabilities	
Total reserves	$200,000*	Demand deposits	$1,000,000
Loans	$800,000		

* Required reserves	$100,000
Excess reserves	$100,000

THE POWER TO CHANGE RESERVE REQUIREMENTS

The Federal Reserve Board was given the power to change reserve requirement percentages in the 1930s, but only within ranges established by Congress. The Monetary Control Act of 1980 established a new system of reserve requirements; the percentages in effect in 1993 are shown in exhibit 6.3. The act gave the Federal Reserve authority to change requirements on transaction accounts above the large bank *breakpoint* ($46.8 million in 1993) within an 8 percent to 14 percent range. The board also can change reserve requirements on business time deposits within a 0 percent to 9 percent range. (Congress exempted from reserve requirements all personal time and savings deposits in 1980; the Federal Reserve reduced reserve requirements on business time deposits to 0 in 1990.)

EXHIBIT 6.3   **Reserve Requirements, 1993**

The Federal Reserve's reserve requirements apply to all commercial banks, savings banks, savings and loan associations, credit unions, Edge Act corporations, and U.S. branches and agencies of foreign banks in the United States, whether or not they are members of the Federal Reserve.

Deposits subject to reserve requirements *	Reserve requirement ratio
Transaction accounts **	3% on the first $46.8 million
	10% on amounts over $46.8 million ***

*   In 1992, there were no reserve requirements against time and savings deposits or other non-transaction account liabilities. From 1980 to 1990, however, there were 3 percent reserve requirements on both short-term (less than 18 months) business time deposits and Eurodollar borrowings (borrowings by U.S. banks from banking offices in other countries). From 1980 to 1983, there had also been a 3 percent reserve requirement on long-term (more than 18 months) business time deposits; that requirement was reduced to 0 in 1983.

 ** Transaction accounts consist of demand deposits, NOW accounts, share draft accounts, automatic transfer service accounts, and any other accounts or deposits from which payments or transfers may be made. (Money market deposit accounts, however, are not classified as transaction accounts.) In calculating required reserves, banks can subtract from their total of transaction accounts the amount of cash items in the process of collection and deposits of other banks on their books. Banks can also subtract $3.8 million from their reservable liabilities.

*** The breakpoint between the 3 percent and 10 percent reserve requirement on transaction accounts is indexed. Each year the Board of Governors is required to increase the breakpoint by 80 percent of the growth in transaction accounts during the prior year. The Monetary Control Act of 1980 established a $25 million baseline. In 1993, the breakpoint was set at $46.8 million.

Supplemental Reserve Requirements. The Federal Reserve Board also has the power to impose a supplemental reserve requirement of up to 4 percent on transaction accounts. If the board were to use this power, these supplemental reserves would earn a market interest rate. To impose the supplemental reserve requirement, the board must have the consent of at least five of its members and must consult with other bank and thrift regulators. In addition, the Federal Reserve must submit a report to Congress explaining why the supplemental requirement is being imposed. The only acceptable reason for imposing it is to increase the amount of required reserves to a level essential for the conduct of monetary policy. The supplemental requirement cannot be used to generate interest income for depositories. To date the Board of Governors has never used this power.

Extraordinary Reserve Requirements. If the Federal Reserve determines that extraordinary circumstances exist, the Board of Governors also has the power to impose reserve requirements on any liability and in any ratio for six months. To impose such extraordinary reserve requirements, however, the board must have the consent of at least five of its members, must consult with appropriate congressional committees, and must submit a report to Congress explaining why these requirements are being imposed. The board must review with Congress its reasons to continue the requirements beyond six months.

CHANGING RESERVE REQUIREMENTS AS A POLICY TOOL

The Federal Reserve has never used changes in reserve requirement percentages as a primary monetary policy tool for fighting short-term inflation or recession. In large part, this has been because reserve requirement changes are too blunt, powerful, and long-lasting in their effect. Before 1980, a change in reserve requirements against demand deposits of no more than one-quarter of a percentage point was capable of increasing or decreasing the banking system's required reserves by about $1 billion. Reserve requirement changes were also seen as causing excessive administrative difficulties and high implementation costs for smaller banks.

In the 1970s, the Federal Reserve's reluctance to raise reserve requirements to fight inflation was heightened by concerns that member banks would leave the Federal Reserve System to avoid the impairment to profitability that reserve requirements impose. This was one of the problems that the Monetary Control Act of 1980 solved by subjecting all depository institutions to the Fed's reserve requirements. However, the new reserve requirements established by the Monetary Control Act were not put in place fully until 1987. Thus, for most of the 1980s, banks and thrifts were subject to varying elements of both the old and the new reserve requirements. Changing reserve requirements under these conditions would have been difficult and costly.

It was not until 1992 that the Federal Reserve made its first significant change in the new reserve requirements. The Fed reduced reserve requirements on transaction accounts above the $42.2 million level (the breakpoint in effect in 1992) from 12 percent to 10 percent, and in so doing converted more than $8 billion in required reserves to excess reserves. The reduction was made to reduce banks' funding costs, thereby strengthening banks' balance sheets and positioning them to make more loans. (Assuming a coefficient of money expansion of 10, an $8 billion increase in excess reserves could, in theory, generate $80 billion in new loans and demand deposits in the banking system.)

DETERMINING RESERVE ASSETS AND RESERVABLE LIABILITIES

The Federal Reserve uses reserve requirements to implement monetary policy in two other ways. These involve the Federal Reserve's authority to determine the kind of assets that depository institutions can use to meet reserve requirements and the kind of liabilities that are subject to reserve requirements.

At present, only vault cash and reserve account balances can be used to meet reserve requirements. If the Federal Reserve were to classify government securities held by banks or correspondent account balances as additional eligible or "legal" reserve assets, total reserves would increase immediately. If the Federal Reserve were to remove vault cash from its list of legal reserve assets, as was the case before 1962, total reserves would immediately diminish.

The Federal Reserve also can redefine what liabilities are subject to reserve requirements. This would not increase or decrease total reserves, but would significantly change the amount of required and excess reserves in the banking system. For example, if the Federal Reserve added federal funds borrowings to the list of reservable liabilities, banks would have to come up with more required reserves to cover their federal funds liabilities.

The Federal Reserve actively used its ability to specify which liabilities were subject to reserve requirements in the 1960s and 1970s. For example, it classified Eurodollar borrowings and the proceeds of commercial paper sales of bank affiliates as *reservable* liabilities. In October 1979, as part of a broad program to restrain inflation and hold down credit expansion, the Federal Reserve imposed special marginal reserve requirements on a wide range of member banks' managed liabilities. Liabilities that were made subject to the marginal reserve requirements included large, short-term certificates of deposit, Eurodollar borrowings, repurchase agreements, and federal funds borrowings from nonmember banks. These reserve requirements were removed in July 1980.

In 1992, the Federal Reserve again used its definitional ability in an effort to close loopholes in the reserve requirement rules that some banks had used in the 1980s to avoid reserve requirements, thus weakening monetary policy control. The Federal Reserve tightened its definition of *transaction accounts* to include such liabilities as *time deposit sweep accounts* from which banks transfer idle balances in corporate transaction accounts into seven-day CDs at the end of each day, and *multiple money market deposit accounts* that enable holders to make funds transfers in excess of the limits applicable to individual money market accounts. The Federal Reserve also classified *tellers checks*, as reservable liabilities. Tellers checks are checks drawn by a bank on an account it holds at another bank. (*Cashiers checks*, which are drawn by a bank on itself, had long been classified as reservable.) In defining liabilities such as those cited above as *transaction accounts*, the Federal Reserve made them subject to 1992's applicable 3 percent or 10 percent reserve requirement.

Uniform Reserve Requirements for All Depositories

Monetary Control Act of 1980

Congress restructured reserve requirements in the Monetary Control Act of 1980 to strengthen monetary policy control and to bring uniformity between the Federal Reserve's reserve requirements on member banks and the reserve requirements that had been imposed by the states on nonmember banks.

Until 1980, banks that were not members of the Federal Reserve were subject only to the reserve requirements imposed by the states. Because the states imposed reserve requirements for liquidity and safety reasons rather than for the monetary policy control reasons that motivated the Federal Reserve, the state requirements were far more liberal than those of the Federal Reserve. For example, many states allowed nonmember banks to hold a substantial part of their required reserves in the form of earning assets, such as U.S. government securities, or in the form of correspondent balances that would have been held anyway in the routine course of banking business.

State-chartered banks that were not members of the Federal Reserve had a competitive advantage over member banks because they did not incur any costs in meeting reserve requirements. Some studies indicated that nonmember banks were as much as 10 percent more profitable than member banks of like size because of reserve requirement disparities. The Monetary Control Act of 1980 established uniform reserve requirements for all the nation's depository institutions, thereby eliminating this competitive disparity and at the same time broadening the Federal Reserve's monetary policy power.

CALCULATING REQUIRED RESERVES

The Federal Reserve also sets the rules governing how banks calculate their reserve requirements. Under the Federal Reserve's 1993 rules, depository institutions with transaction deposits of $44.8 million or more must compute their required reserves once every two weeks, based on their daily average deposit balances beginning Thursday of the first week and ending Wednesday of the third week. As exhibit 6.4 illustrates, reserves held in a two-week *maintenance period* are based on deposits that were held in a two-week *computation period* that lags the maintenance period by two days. Depositories with total deposits of less than $3.8 million are exempt from maintaining and reporting reserves. Depositories with total transaction deposits of less than $44.8 million have only to compute and report their required reserves to the Federal Reserve once every quarter for a one-week period during the quarter. The small depositories' exemption and the quarterly computation for mid-sized depositories were efforts to reduce the reporting and management burden on small banks and thrifts and to relieve the processing burden on Federal Reserve banks.

EXHIBIT 6.4   **Contemporaneous Reserve Requirements**

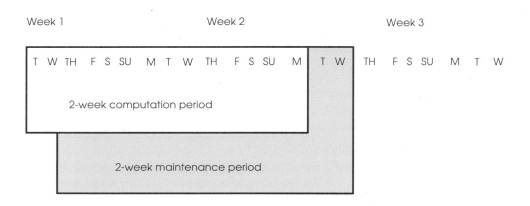

The Federal Reserve's rules mean that a bank can be in a deep reserve deficit on any given day during the two-week maintenance period as long as it balances those deficits with reserve surpluses of like amounts on other days. Depositories are allowed to carry a reserve deficit (or surplus) of at least $50,000 or 4 percent of required reserves, whichever is the larger amount, into the next maintenance period. However, banks must cover a reserve deficit with a surplus of like amount in the following period. That is, a bank with a 4 percent deficit in a given two-week period must generate a 4 percent surplus in the following two-week period to avoid a costly reserve penalty. Similarly, a bank with a 4 percent surplus in a given period can generate a 4 percent deficit in the next period without being penalized. In fact, it is advantageous for the bank to do so, since reserve carryovers can be transferred for one maintenance period only.

Shifting from "lagged" to "contemporaneous" reserve requirements. In 1984, the Federal Reserve instituted its present reserve rules, known as *contemporaneous reserve requirements.* These rules changed the procedures that had been used since 1968, which were known as *lagged reserve requirements.* Under lagged reserve requirements, all banks could hold reserves in the present week based on deposits that were held two weeks earlier, as seen in exhibit 6.5. The shift from lagged to contemporaneous reserve requirements was intended to give the Federal Reserve better control over the growth of bank reserves.

EXHIBIT 6.5   **Lagged Reserve Requirements**

	Week 1	Week 2	Week 3
	TH F S SU M T W	TH F S SU M T W	TH F S SU M T W

T W

1-week computation period

1-week maintenance period

Under lagged reserve requirements, banks knew at the beginning of each banking week (Thursday) what their required reserves had to average for that week. By tracking their actual daily reserve balances against the average daily amount of reserves they were required to hold, banks could determine the exact amount of reserves they would need at the end of the week and the exact amount of excess reserves they had available to support new loans. By using every available dollar of excess reserves, banks' lending provided a base for strong money supply growth that supported inflationary trends. Contemporaneous reserve requirements enable the Federal Reserve to better control monetary policy. Banks are forced to be moderate in their lending because they do not know the exact amount of required reserves they will need for the current banking week.

Open-Market Operations   *Used most monetary policy tool*

The Federal Reserve's open-market operations involve the purchase and sale of government securities. These operations are the principal and most important policy tool used by the Federal Reserve to change the cost and availability of money and credit in the economy. Purchases of government securities in the open market by the Federal Reserve add reserves to the banking system, enabling banks to expand their loans and investments. Sales of securities by the Federal Reserve from its System Open Market Account portfolio take reserves out of the banking system, thereby restricting the ability of banks to make loans and investments.   *purchases from dealer firms & sales*

Again, T-accounts can be used to demonstrate the effect of an open-market purchase of securities by the Federal Reserve. When the Federal Reserve buys $1 million of securities in the open market from dealer firms, it pays for them with checks drawn on itself. The result of the check collection process, shown in the following T-accounts, is an increase in bank reserves of $1 million (held temporarily at First Commercial) reflecting credit for the account of the selling dealer firm at First Commercial. The check collection process also generates a $1 million increase in the money supply (the addition to the dealer firm's checking account).

Purchase Increased bank reserves and therefore money supply [handwritten]

Seller dealer's account is at [handwritten]

Federal Reserve Bank of New York

Assets	Liabilities
System Open Market Account	Reserve Account of First Commercial
+ $1 million	+ $1 million

First Commercial Bank

Assets	Liabilities
Reserve account	Demand deposit of dealer firm
+ $1 million	+ $1 million

Government Securities Dealer Firm

Assets	Liabilities
Checking account at First Commercial + $1 million	
Securities held - $1 million	

First Commercial must hold some of its new reserves as required reserves against the dealer's new $1 million deposit. However, the bulk of the reserves can be used to fund new loans and create new money. If a 10 percent reserve requirement is assumed, then the banking system, through the multiple expansion process, could in theory generate $9 million in new deposits from a base of $1 million in total deposits (and $900,000 in excess reserves).

The following T-accounts demonstrate the effect of an open-market sale of securities by the Federal Reserve:

Sale Reduces Bank reserves and money supply [handwritten]

Federal Reserve Bank of New York

Assets	Liabilities
System Open Market Account	Reserve Account of First Commercial
- $1 million	- $1 million

First Commercial Bank

Assets	Liabilities
Reserve account	Demand deposit of dealer firm
- $1 million	- $1 million

Government Securities Dealer Firm

Assets		Liabilities
Checking account at First Commercial	- $1 million	
Securities held	+ $1 million	

A sale of securities by the Federal Reserve Bank of New York from the System Open Market Account reduces bank reserves and the money supply. The Federal Reserve bank collects the dealer firm's check by reducing First Commercial's reserve account by $1 million. First Commercial, in turn, reduces the dealer firm's checking account to reflect the check payment.

If First Commercial had $1 million in excess reserves before the Federal Reserve's open-market sale, it now would find that it had temporarily lost its lending capability. If First Commercial had no excess reserves, it would be plunged into a temporary reserve deficiency. Either circumstance would likely cause First Commercial to borrow reserves in the federal funds market, sell securities from its investment portfolio, or make some other asset or liability adjustment to enable the bank to achieve reserve requirement balance or to continue to make loans. However, since the total amount of reserves in the banking system would be reduced by the Federal Reserve's open-market sale, First Commercial's success in obtaining reserves could only result from the willingness of some other bank, or group of banks, to part with reserves (assuming no discount window borrowing). The ability of the banking system to create money would remain restricted. It should be emphasized, however, that the Fed's use of open-market operations can be thwarted by other factors that influence the money supply.

SECONDARY EFFECTS OF OPEN-MARKET OPERATIONS

When the Federal Reserve buys government securities in the open market, it increases demand for these financial assets. An increase in demand for securities, whose supply is momentarily fixed, drives up the price of securities. Because securities prices and their investment yields (interest rates) are inversely related, an increase in securities prices drives down interest rates. At the same time, the Federal Reserve's open-market purchase adds to bank reserves. If this increase in the supply of reserves is not offset by an increase in demand for reserves by banks, it also should help drive down interest rates. As interest rates fall and securities prices rise, the market value of securities in banks' investment portfolios increases as well.

When the Federal Reserve sells securities from the System Open Market Account portfolio, it effectively increases the market supply of those financial assets. An increase in the supply of securities, in the context of stable market demand, drives down the price of securities. Because of the inverse relationship between securities prices and interest rates, a reduction in securities prices drives up interest rates. The objective of the Federal Reserve's open-market sale of securities is to reduce the level of bank reserves—and thereby the money supply. If the decrease in reserves is not offset by a decreased demand for bank reserves by banks, the open-market sale also will drive up interest rates. As interest rates rise and securities prices fall, the market value of securities in banks' portfolios declines as well.

THE DEALER MARKET

The Federal Reserve conducts its open-market operations with a vast portfolio of U.S. securities and some federal agency securities that it has acquired over the decades in implementing monetary policy. In mid-1992 this portfolio stood at about $275 billion.

In conducting open-market operations, the Federal Reserve, working exclusively through the trading desk of the Federal Reserve Bank of New York, transacts business with a select group of about 40 dealer firms. The firms with whom the Federal Reserve conducted business in the early 1990s, most of whom are headquartered in New York City, are listed in exhibit 6.6. These dealers in government securities constitute the open market.

EXHIBIT 6.6　**Open-Market Dealer Firms**

Bank of America NT & SA
Barclays de Zoete Wedd Securities Inc.
Bear, Stearns & Co., Inc.
BT Securities Corporation
Carroll McEntee & McGinley Incorporated
Chase Securities, Inc.
Chemical Securities, Inc.
Citicorp Securities Markets, Inc.
CRT Government Securities, Ltd.
Daiwa Securities America Inc.
Dean Witter Reynolds Inc.
Deutsche Bank Government Securities, Inc.
Dillion, Read & Co. Inc.
Discount Corporation of New York
Donaldson, Lufkin & Jenrette Securities Corporation
The First Boston Corporation
First Chicago Capital Markets, Inc.
Fuji Securities Inc.
Goldman, Sachs & Co.
Greenwich Capital Markets, Inc.
Harris Government Securities Inc.
Kidder, Peabody & Co., Incorporated
Aubrey G. Lanston & Co., Inc.
Lehman Government Securities Inc.
Merrill Lynch Goverrment securities Inc.
J. P. Morgan Securities, Inc.
Morgan Stanley & Co., Incorporated
The Nikko Securities Co. International, Inc.

(Continued from previous page)

Nomura Securities International, Inc.
Paine Webber Incorporated
Prudential Securities Incorporated
Solomon Brothers Inc.
Sanwa-BGK Securities Co., L.P.
Security Pacific National Bank
Smith Barney, Harris Upham & Co., Inc.
SBC Government Securities Inc.
UBS Securities Inc.
S. G. Warburg & Co., Inc.
Yamaichi International (America), Inc.

Source: Federal Reserve Bank of New York, January 1992

Some of the open-market dealer firms are the autonomous dealer departments of the nation's large money center banks. Most, however, are not associated with banks. To become a participant in the open market (that is, to do business with the Federal Reserve), a dealer firm must first demonstrate that it has adequate capital and that it has handled substantial business volume over a long time period. It must then be prepared to submit reports of its trading activities and positions to the Federal Reserve Bank of New York. If the New York Reserve bank determines that the dealer's capabilities and business volumes are substantial, that the firm has sizable markets in government securities, and the firm is willing to provide the New York Reserve Bank with useful market information and analysis for implementing monetary policy, an open-market trading relationship is generally established.

In 1992, the Federal Reserve Bank of New York made several technical changes in the criteria it uses for establishing and maintaining open market trading relationships with dealer firms. The New York Reserve Bank ended its requirement that primary dealer firms must maintain a 1 percent share of total government securities trading volume in the open market to continue to do business with the New York trading desk. In place of this requirement, the New York Reserve Bank instituted a capital (owner's equity) adequacy standard. The minimum requirements in 1992 were $100 million in owner's equity for commercial bank-related dealer firms and $50 million in owner's equity for dealer firms not affiliated with banks. Changes such as these were aimed at expanding the number of dealers in the open market in the interest of more competitive trading.

A trading relationship does not mean that the New York trading desk deals with every single dealer firm in the open market on any given day. To maintain its operating efficiency, the New York Reserve bank operates through a constantly changing daily nucleus of seven or eight open-market dealer firms.

The dealer market is critical to the efficient implementation of open-market operations. By working through dealers, the Federal Reserve ensures that its purchases and sales of government securities will increase or decrease bank reserves and money supply, regardless of the business or reserve strategies that banks may be following. For example, in an environment of rising interest rates and growing business loan demand, banks typically would be reluctant to part with reserves needed to fund high-earning loans by purchasing securities from the Federal Reserve. However, banks have no control over the actions of their dealer firm depositors, so that dealers who are eager to buy securities from the Federal Reserve will expedite the reduction in reserves that banks themselves may have been unprepared to accept.

Since dealer firms are motivated by profit, which they generally make through their secondary market purchases and sales, their willingness to buy from or sell to the Federal Reserve is not generally based on concerns over the availability of reserves, but rather depends solely on price and marketability. The Federal Reserve's trading desk, on the other hand, is not motivated by profit. Its motivation is to increase or reduce bank reserves and money supply in accordance with policy directives and targets established by the FOMC to achieve national economic goals. If necessary, the Federal Reserve will take a loss on an open-market transaction to achieve its monetary policy goals. The Federal Reserve can sell securities from its portfolio (to reduce bank reserves) at a price low enough to entice the most reluctant of dealer buyers. It can buy securities at a price high enough to obtain securities inventories of the most reluctant dealer sellers (to increase bank reserves).

The Open Market and Foreign-Owned Dealer Firms

The open market has taken on a decidedly international character since the mid-1980s. For example, 16 of the 41 primary dealer firms that constituted the open market in 1990 were owned by foreign organizations. These firms accounted for about one-third of open-market trading volume.

This change in the open market reflects the increasing importance and volume of investments by foreigners in U.S. government securities. It did not occur, however, without controversy. In 1986 and 1987, the Federal Reserve accepted four Japanese firms as primary dealers in the open market in the face of strong congressional sentiment favoring restrictions. In 1987, in fact, both the House and Senate passed bills to deny Japanese companies status as primary dealers until Japan reciprocated for U.S. firms.

The Federal Reserve, however, contended that the Japanese dealer firms, like other domestic and foreign dealers in the open market, had met all Federal Reserve standards for trading as primary dealers. Thus, their participation was consistent with the long-established policy of equal regulatory treatment for domestic and foreign institutions competing in the United States. The Federal Reserve also contended that Japan had increased access for U.S. firms to the Japanese securities markets and stock exchange in 1987 and was actively

(Continued from previous page)

considering further measures to open Japanese financial markets to U.S. companies. In so doing, Japan was attempting to comply with the intent of the proposed legislative restrictions.

In 1988, however, Congress enacted legislation (the Primary Dealers Act) based on the principle of reciprocal regulatory treatment for foreign dealer firms competing in the U.S. government securities market. Since then, the Federal Reserve has adopted a policy consistent with that legislation. The Fed will not designate, or continue to bestow, primary dealer status on any foreign-owned dealer firm that is based in a country that does not provide the same competitive opportunities to U.S. companies as it does to its domestic firms in the underwriting and secondary market trading of government securities.

The Primary Dealers Act provides that the Federal Reserve determine, on a case-by-case basis, that a foreign government accords to U.S. firms the same competitive opportunities in its securities market as its national firms enjoy. In 1992, for example, a French insurance company acquired a controlling interest in the U.S. primary dealer firm, Donaldson, Lufkin & Jenrette. The Federal Reserve found that competitive opportunities in the French government securities market were the same for French and U.S. dealer firms. Thus, Donaldson, Lufkin & Jenrette was granted continuing primary dealer firm status.

THE IMPACT OF OPEN-MARKET OPERATIONS

Although open-market operations are conducted in New York (mainly through dealer firms that are headquartered in New York), the impact of open-market operations on bank reserves, money supply, and interest rates is nationwide. This is because banks throughout the country are linked to each other through extensive correspondent relationships and through the highly efficient nationwide federal funds market.

When the Federal Reserve sells securities to open-market dealer firms, the dealers usually pay with borrowed funds. Dealers typically finance their daily activities and inventories with funds borrowed each day from the nation's large money center banks (located in New York, Chicago, and San Francisco). These banks, in turn, generally purchase federal funds daily, in part to accommodate their dealer customers.

These federal funds come from banks all over the country. Suppose, for example, that a bank in Montana with $1 million in excess reserves and no borrowers sells those reserves in the federal funds market. A New York money market bank buys the reserves to fund a loan to an open-market dealer customer. After the dealer purchases the Federal Reserve's securities, the dealer's checking account will decrease, as will the reserves held by the New York money market bank. Yet, in effect, those reserves came from Montana.

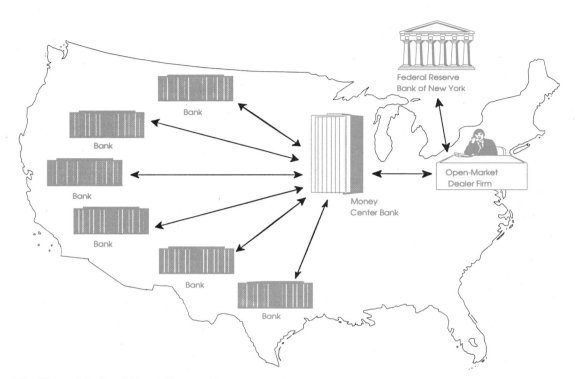

The Flow of Federal Funds Borrowings

When the Federal Reserve buys securities from open-market dealers, the dealers' checking accounts increase, as do the reserves held by the dealers' banks. But both the dealers and their banks have to repay yesterday's loans, and as those loans are repaid, banks in all parts of the country (such as the Montana bank just cited) experience increases in their reserve accounts.

The lending-borrowing relationship between banks and dealers and the lending-borrowing relationship between small banks and big banks in the federal funds market transmit the impact of open-market operations to bank reserves, money supply, and interest rates in all corners of the banking system.

THE USE OF OPEN-MARKET OPERATIONS

The power to buy and sell government securities was granted to Reserve banks by the Federal Reserve Act of 1913. It was not until the 1920s, however, that the monetary policy impact of changes in the Federal Reserve's portfolio became generally understood, and it was not until the Banking Act of 1935 that the present structure of the FOMC was established. General reliance on open-market operations as the primary monetary policy tool did not begin until 1951, when the Federal Reserve and the Treasury agreed that monetary policy would no longer have to be directed toward maintaining rigidly stable interest rates on Treasury securities. This agreement, known as the Accord of 1951, ended the fixed interest rate policy that the Federal Reserve had introduced in 1941 to enable the Treasury to finance World War II borrowings at low cost.

With the Federal Reserve no longer bound to maintain fixed interest rates, it could use open-market operations to expand or contract bank reserves and bank lending (and thereby decrease or increase interest rates) as a means to counter recessionary or inflationary movements in the economy. It also began to use open-market operations on a day-to-day basis to offset or nullify undesired changes in bank reserves and money supply resulting from nonpolicy factors. These changes are caused by factors unrelated to monetary policy, such as the Treasury Department's borrowing activities, and changes in the public's relative holdings of cash, demand deposits, and time deposits. The use of open-market operations, both as a tool to effect change in the economy and as a defensive instrument to ensure stable daily markets, is discussed in greater detail in chapter 11.

Moving toward a more open market. The primary dealer firms that constitute the open market play an important role in meeting the government's borrowing needs. They do this by purchasing massive amounts of newly-issued Treasury securities, which they ultimately resell to others. To purchase large amounts of new securities, however, dealers have to participate in Treasury auctions.

Until 1992, the Treasury relied on *multiple price auctions* for selling new securities to dealer firms. Under auction rules, each primary dealer would submit a bid indicating the price it would pay for a specific amount of the securities being auctioned. The Treasury would accept the highest bid first, then move progressively down to lower bids until it had sold all the new securities subject to the auction. The result was that some primary dealers would invariably pay more than others for the same securities.

In 1991, the open market was shaken by a scandal involving one of the market's major primary dealer firms—Salomon Brothers. The firm admitted that it had engaged in illegal bidding practices in several auctions, using customers' names to submit multiple bids to obtain a price and supply advantage over other dealer firms.

The scandal prompted congressional hearings and demands that the Treasury, the Securities and Exchange Commission (SEC), and the Federal Reserve reform Treasury auction and open-market trading practices. Strong concerns were raised that the multiple price auction was susceptible to dealer manipulation; that the market was vulnerable to price-fixing collusion among dealers; and that primary dealer firms had an unfair advantage in buying new Treasury securities. Those concerns, however, were tempered by recognition of the key role that primary dealer firms play in both the implementation of monetary policy and the government financing process. To strike a balance and to open the market to more dealers, the Treasury, the SEC, and the Federal Reserve agreed to leave the primary dealer system intact, but to change the Treasury auction and the criteria used for granting firms primary dealer status.

In 1992, the Treasury changed its auction from multiple price to *single price*. Under the single price auction, the Treasury sells all the securities being auctioned at one price—not necessarily at the high price bid, but at the price that will ensure that all the new securities being auctioned will be sold. Dealers who bid on varying amounts of securities all pay the same price for the securities they buy. However, under the single price auction dealers who bid low prices face a greater risk that they will be shut out of purchases. This risk is expected to increase if the number of market participants expands in the 1990s. The Treasury expects that primary dealers will have to raise their auction bids to cover this risk, which will lead to more aggressive pricing and competition in the open market—and increased revenues for the government.

Changes made by the Federal Reserve Bank of New York in the criteria it uses for establishing and maintaining open market trading relationships with dealer firms were part of the coordinated effort by the regulators to open the primary dealer market to a broader range of participants.

Selective Controls

Although the Federal Reserve's use of monetary policy tools is essentially general in nature, it has occasionally used selective controls to influence the cost or flow of funds in selected sectors of the economy. As noted previously, central banks in many other countries use selective controls routinely. Selective monetary policy controls in the United States have usually involved a tightening or relaxing of required down payment or maturity terms for a particular class of loans. The purpose of such controls is to alter the amount of funds being loaned for a particular purpose without changing the level of bank reserves or the availability of bank credit in the economy as a whole.

In the past, the Federal Reserve has used selective policy tools to control stock market credit, consumer credit, and real estate credit. Stock market credit is the only selective monetary policy power the Federal Reserve Board still holds. Other selective controls were authorized to meet particular emergencies and were removed when the emergency ended. During World War II (1941-1945) and again during the Korean War (1950-1952), the Federal Reserve was given power to limit credit extended for purchasing consumer durable goods. Authority to limit real estate credit also was granted to the Federal Reserve as a Korean wartime measure. These selective controls, designed to prevent an inflationary surge in critical markets, took the form of minimum down payment requirements with maximum repayment periods for amounts borrowed.

MARGIN REQUIREMENTS

The Securities Exchange Act of 1934 gave the Federal Reserve Board power to establish margins on loans made for the purpose of purchasing or carrying securities. Margin requirements are implemented through Federal Reserve regulations G, T, U, and X. A margin is the difference, or spread, between the market value of securities used as collateral for a loan and the amount of the loan granted; a margin requirement sets the maximum spread in percentage terms.

Margin requirements were established to prevent excessive stock market speculation through the control of credit used for stock purchases. A margin requirement set at 100 percent would effectively prohibit the use of any credit to buy stocks. A margin requirement of 75 percent means that only 25 percent of the value of the securities used as collateral can be borrowed. A margin requirement of 50 percent (the margin that was in effect in 1992) means that only 50 percent of the value of the collateral securities can be borrowed. In effect, the margin requirement represents the percentage of the loan down payment that the borrower has to have in cash.

Since the 1930s, economists have been unable to find any evidence of a relationship between stock market margin requirements and the level of prices, employment, or output in the economy—the ultimate goals of monetary policy. Moreover, there is some question whether margin requirements, by themselves, can effectively control stock market speculation since some lenders are not subject to margin requirements. Also, borrowers interested in speculation can deny intent, pledge other assets as collateral for loans, and buy stocks anyway.

Fiscal Policy Tools

Whereas monetary policy tools are the province of the Federal Reserve, fiscal policy tools are wielded by Congress and the president. Federal spending and taxation are the two fiscal policy tools the federal government relies on to change the pace and direction of the economy. In theory, if the economy is slipping into a recession, the federal government can increase its spending and reduce taxes. If the economy is expanding rapidly and inflationary pressures are building, the federal government can reduce its spending and increase taxes. In practice, however, the ability of the government to use fiscal policy in this way, to deal with recession and inflation, is extremely limited. These limitations stem from the lengthy political process involved in changing federal spending programs or tax laws and the nondiscretionary or automatic nature of much of the government's spending and taxation. Primarily for these reasons, the record of U.S. fiscal policy in countering inflation has been poor.

All government spending must be funded from either tax receipts or borrowings. If the government increases its spending and raises taxes to finance the increased spending, money is merely transferred from the private sector to the public sector, and total spending typically does not increase. (In essence, the decrease in consumer spending is offset by the increase in government spending.) Likewise, if the government reduces its spending while reducing taxes, consumer spending is likely to increase, with the result that total spending remains unchanged.

If, however, the government increases its spending by borrowing, total spending will increase. In fact, if the economy is operating at or near its full resource (labor and capital) potential, an increase in government spending can force an expansion of bank reserves and money supply that can overstimulate the economy into inflation. This occurs because federal spending in excess of tax receipts requires substantial federal borrowings. These borrowings, in turn, put pressure on the Federal Reserve to provide ample reserves (and money supply growth) to ensure that banks have sufficient funds to lend to dealer purchasers of the government's increasing debt issues. This interrelationship between fiscal and monetary processes contributed significantly to the inflation that plagued the U.S. economy in the 1970s and the early 1980s.

The Federal Budget

Any imbalance between the amount the federal government spends and the amount it collects in tax revenues appears as either a federal budget surplus (an excess of tax revenues) or a federal budget deficit (an excess of government spending). A budget deficit represents the amount of money the federal government has to borrow by selling new Treasury securities to fund its current spending.

In a recession, the application of fiscal policy requires the government to spend more to boost total spending in the economy. Since tax revenues typically fall during a recession, increased government spending to counter a recession generates a budget deficit. During inflationary times, fiscal policy calls for a reduction in government spending to restrain overall demand for goods and services in the economy. Since tax revenues generally increase (reflecting the growth in nominal incomes) in periods of inflation, a decrease in government spending normally generates a budgetary surplus.

Since the 1930s, when fiscal policy was introduced as a means to stimulate total spending, the federal budget has been increasingly structured to automatically stabilize the economy against severe downturns in the business cycle. One way has been through built-in spending programs designed to provide people with a base level of income (and subsequent spending). Many of these programs, such as unemployment insurance, are triggered by the downturn itself. As recession begins to worsen and worker layoffs mount, the number of people collecting unemployment insurance increases. So does the total dollar amount spent by the government to support the states' unemployment insurance bills.

The federal income tax is also designed to stabilize the economy. The federal tax structure automatically counters inflation and recession by taking in more tax dollars when incomes rise (inflation) and taking in fewer dollars when incomes decline (recession). Under both the progressive tax structure in effect before 1986, and under the modified proportional tax structure in effect since then, tax rates increase with increases in income, as exhibit 6.7 shows.

Typically, in times of inflation, individual nominal incomes rise rapidly (although real incomes may not increase at all). These nominal income gains put people into higher tax brackets. Before Congress changed the tax law in 1986, this phenomenon, known as bracket creep, yielded the government about 1 1/2 percent more tax revenue for every 1 percent gain in the nation's personal income.

EXHIBIT 6.7   **Federal Income Tax Structures**

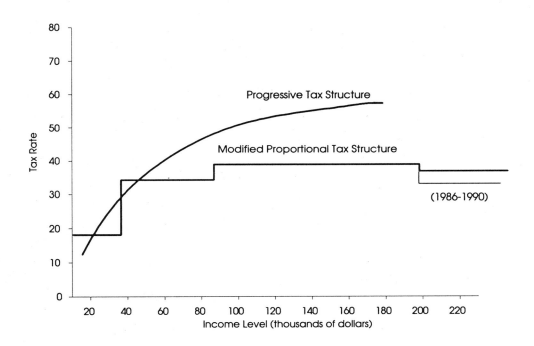

Note: Congress adopted the modified proportional tax structure in lieu of the progressive tax structure in 1986. In 1990, Congress raised the top margin tax rate to 31 percent from 28 percent on top income earners.

The concept of automatic stabilization has, on occasion, also been tried in federal budgeting. Under a budgetary approach known as *full-employment budgeting*, an estimate is made of the total amount of tax revenues the government would receive if the economy were operating at full productive capacity and full employment. Government spending is then pegged to this estimated full-employment tax revenue level. In theory, any deficit created by the pegged spending level provides the appropriate degree of stimulus necessary to propel the economy toward its full employment level. (If the economy is at full employment, government spending and tax revenues will balance and no deficit will be created.)

Since they were introduced in the 1930s, the nation's automatic stabilizers have tended to blunt the severity of the economy's business cycle downturns. Some studies indicate that, on average, the stabilizers have reduced the severity of U.S. recessions by about one-third. Automatic stabilizers, however, have proved less successful in countering inflation.

COUNTERING INFLATION

One way to counter inflation is to raise taxes, but raising taxes has rarely been used as an anti-inflation policy tool in the United States. There have been only two broad increases in individual income taxes since World War II, and both were designed as temporary measures to finance wars (the Korean and Vietnam wars). The only other large tax increases since the 1950s were taxes imposed mainly on businesses or special-purpose taxes, such as the gasoline tax (to support highway construction) and the windfall-profits tax on oil (to offset the enormous profits of oil companies resulting from the decontrol of oil prices).

Social Security taxes were raised substantially from the late 1970s to the early 1990s, not as an anti-inflationary measure, but to fund the rapid growth in Social Security outlays. Increases in the Social Security tax rate and tax base raised the maximum Social Security tax (plus medicare) paid by wage earners to $5,328.90 in 1992, more than six times the maximum tax paid in 1976.

One reason that Congress tends not to raise income taxes to fight inflation is that most members of Congress do not care to be identified with implementing a measure that is likely to be unpopular with most voters. A related problem in the 1970s and early 1980s was the public perception that the federal income tax structure was unfair and that any increase would be disproportionately borne by middle-income earners. The change from a progressive tax structure to a modified proportional tax structure was instituted by Congress in 1986 largely in response to this sentiment.

Deficit Spending. Another method for countering inflation is to reduce government spending. But in addition to the political problems associated with cutting federal spending programs, a large proportion of that spending is nondiscretionary—Congress and the president have no real short-term control over it. Nondiscretionary spending includes social programs, transfer payments (sometimes called *entitlements*), and interest on the federal debt that represent, at least in the short run, contractual obligations of the government that must be paid. In 1992, about 65 percent of total federal spending was for social programs and entitlements—such as Social Security, medicare and medicaid, federal and military pensions, welfare, veterans' benefits, and unemployment compensation—and interest on the federal debt.

The Federal Debt. Before the government began to use fiscal policy (in the 1930s) to achieve economic goals, the government ran few budgetary deficits. In the nation's early history, several deficits were incurred to finance wars, but surpluses in later years offset most of these. In 1916, when the United States entered World War I, the federal debt stood at only $1.2 billion.

During the three years of World War I, the government borrowed $25 billion, and despite annual budget surpluses throughout the 1920s, the federal debt was only reduced to $17 billion by 1929 (equal to about 17 percent of the GDP at that time). The Great Depression of the 1930s and the introduction of fiscal policy to stimulate total spending resulted in 10 consecutive annual deficits. These boosted the federal debt to nearly $50 billion by 1941 and the beginning of World War II. However, the government borrowed more than $200 billion during World War II and, as exhibit 6.8 shows, by 1945 the federal debt equaled about 115 percent of the GDP.

During the 1950s and 1960s, the government ran small but persistent annual budget deficits, and the national debt slowly began to grow. But because the economy grew faster, the ratio of federal debt to GDP steadily declined. (A declining ratio of federal debt to GDP is a favorable bellwether of the economy's capacity to absorb debt.)

An explosion of new social programs in the late 1960s and early 1970s and the Vietnam War saw government spending more than double from 1966 to 1973. By 1981, the federal debt had tripled, surpassing the $1 trillion level and, as seen in exhibit 6.8, for the first time since the 1940s the ratio of federal debt to GDP began to steadily increase.

A recession in 1981, coupled with a substantial tax cut, caused a massive decline in tax revenues while government spending continued to soar. By 1989, when the economy's growth began to slow, the debt had nearly tripled, to almost $3 trillion. From 1989 to 1992, the federal debt grew to nearly $4 trillion—as tax revenue growth slowed and government spending increased in response to recession and the economy's sluggish recovery—and no signs of a decline in the debt to GDP ratio were in evidence.

EXHIBIT 6.8   **Federal Debt Held by the Public as a Percent of GDP**

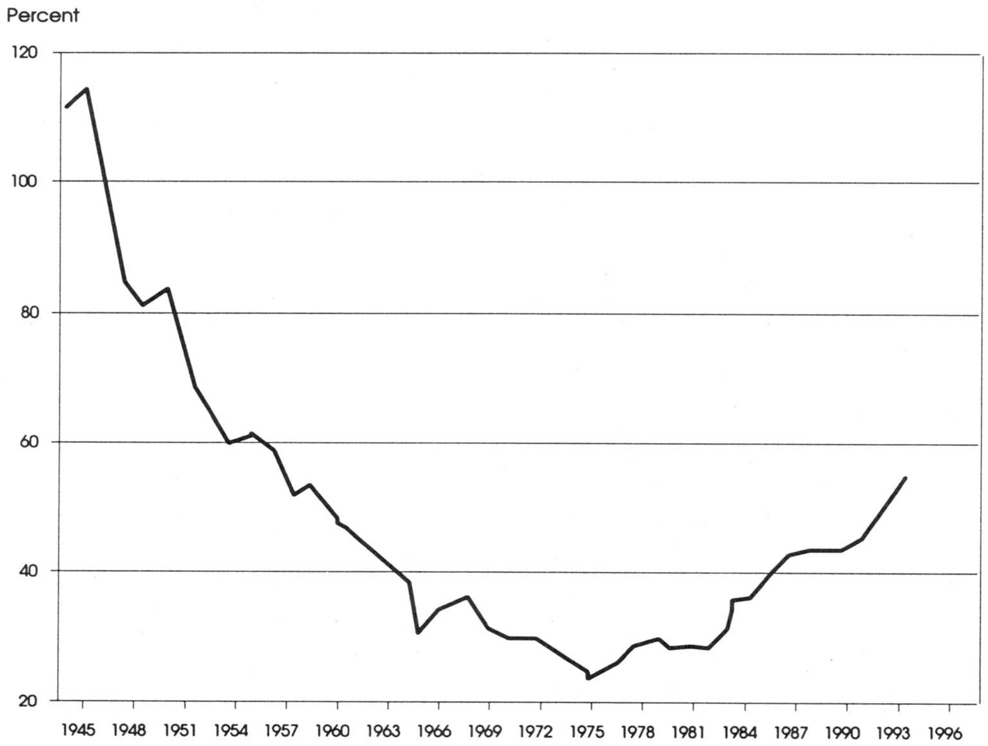

Percent

Monetary and Fiscal Policy Balance

No single tool of monetary or fiscal policy is strong enough to control the economy. Containing inflation and countering recession are best accomplished when monetary and fiscal policy are working in the same direction. The need for monetary and fiscal policy balance is rooted in the different ways that monetary and fiscal policy tools work in the economy. The monetary tools affect interest rates, bank reserves, and money supply growth; the fiscal tools affect income, spending, and savings. Exhibit 6.9 shows how the various fiscal and monetary policy instruments can be used to counter inflation and recession.

Since the 1980s, a key policy dilemma has been how to rein in the government's deficit spending without tripping the economy into recession or fueling inflation. The Federal Reserve has contended that open-market operations, discount rate changes, and reserve requirement rules in themselves cannot maintain a balanced economy without a reduction in the federal deficit. Through 1992, fiscal policymakers, however, have been unable to develop a broad public and political consensus on specific spending reductions or tax increases necessary to reduce the deficit.

EXHIBIT 6.9   **Use of Monetary and Fiscal Policy Instruments**

Fed   *Pres & congress*

Monetary Policy	**Fiscal Policy**

To counter inflation   *Reduces money supply*

Increase discount rate	Increase taxes
Raise reserve requirements	Reduce government spending
Sell government securities from the open-market portfolio	

To counter recession   *Increases money supply*

Reduce discount rate	Reduce taxes
Lower reserve requirements	Increase government spending
Buy government securities in the open market	

Summary

The Federal Reserve relies on three general policy instruments in implementing monetary policy: the discount rate, reserve requirements, and open-market operations. Changing the discount rate can, in theory, depress or stimulate bank borrowings from the Federal Reserve and banks' subsequent lending. Changing reserve requirements, which is the most powerful monetary tool, alters the composition of required and excess reserves in the banking system and changes banking's coefficient of demand deposit expansion for the future. Open-market operations—the Federal Reserve's buying and selling of government securities—are the central bank's principal policy tool. Federal Reserve purchases of government securities in the open market add reserves to the banking system, while sales from the Federal Reserve's portfolio reduce reserves.

The federal government also relies on two fiscal policy instruments—government spending and taxing powers—to change the pace and direction of the economy. An increase in government spending and a reduction in federal taxes can act as a strong anti-recessionary stimulus to the economy; a reduction in government spending and an increase in federal taxes can act as a powerful anti-inflationary restraint. However, the ability of the government to use fiscal policy has become increasingly limited because of the political difficulties involved in changing federal spending programs or tax laws and the nondiscretionary nature of much of the government's spending and tax receipts.

Questions

1. Discuss the validity of this statement: "The 1980 Monetary Control Act's imposition of universal reserve requirements strengthened the Federal Reserve's ability to conduct monetary policy."

2. How is the discount rate (and discount window lending) used today as a monetary policy tool?

3. Whenever the Federal Reserve buys or sells anything, bank reserves and the money supply change. Why, then, does the Federal Reserve limit its buying and selling to government securities in the open market?

4. Changing reserve requirement percentages is one way that reserve requirements can be used as a monetary policy tool. What are two other ways?

5. Outline an appropriate anti-inflationary economic policy that uses the three monetary and two fiscal policy tools in a complementary way.

6. Why is an anti-inflationary fiscal policy more difficult to implement than an anti-inflationary monetary policy? Would the nation's economic policy be more effective if the Federal Reserve determined both monetary and fiscal policy?

PART III The Business of Banking

7

Bank Operations and the Payments Mechanism

Objectives

After successfully completing this chapter, you will be able to

☐ explain how the U.S. payments mechanism differs from that of most other industrialized nations,

☐ identify three ways that interbank checks are collected in the U.S. banking system,

☐ interpret MICR instructions and other informational check data,

☐ explain how banks process and manage check data,

☐ distinguish between Federal Reserve float and bank float, and

☐ list and describe the major wholesale and retail electronic funds transfer systems and services.

Introduction

The role of banks in lending money often overshadows their equally important role in the nation's payments mechanism. The operations of banks in meeting the public's need for cash, in clearing and collecting checks, and in transferring funds electronically provide the power that drives our nation's $5.8 trillion economy.

The primary activity of most bank employees is operations. The majority of bank jobs involve check collection and electronic funds transfers—either directly or by providing the numerous administrative, accounting, computer, marketing, and security-related support services necessary to carry out banks' payment activities.

In this chapter, we will examine bank operations within the context of the U.S. payments mechanism, focusing on the key internal processes and activities of banks that relate to payment devices and practices. We will look at the basic features of the U.S. payments mechanism, the importance to banks of cash and cash assets, the check collection process and creation of float, and the major electronic funds transfer systems in use today.

The U.S. Payments Mechanism

The term *payments mechanism* denotes the instruments and systems used in an economy to transfer money, make payments, and settle debts among individuals, businesses, governments, and financial institutions. The U.S. payments mechanism is based primarily on the use of checks and electronic funds transfers, and to a lesser extent on cash. It also depends on the relationships between and among commercial banks, other financial institutions, and the Federal Reserve in transferring, processing, and settling money balances.

The U.S. payments mechanism differs in some important ways from the payments mechanism in most other industrialized countries. The three features that most distinguish the U.S. payments mechanism are:

- ❏ the extensive role of the central bank,
- ❏ the number of depository institutions involved, and
- ❏ the number and dollar volume of transactions.

The Federal Reserve, the nation's central bank, plays an extensive operational role in the U.S. payments mechanism. The Federal Reserve is often referred to as a "bank for banks" because it does for banks what banks do for their depositors. The 12 Federal Reserve banks and their 25 branches provide a range of payments services—from the collection of checks and the electronic transfer of funds to the safekeeping of securities and the provision of coin and currency. They also are the nation's centers for the distribution of currency and coin within the banking system. More than one-third of all checks written in the United States are cleared through the Federal Reserve's banks, branches, and regional check processing centers (RCPCs). The Federal Reserve also operates a funds transfer (wire transfer) system over which money and government securities can be transferred instantaneously. Known as Fedwire, the system is the primary mechanism through which the nation's major banks do most of their interbank business.

The U.S. payments mechanism is different from that of most other nations because it is composed of such a large number of separate depository institutions. Historically, state and federal laws have prevented U.S. banks and thrift institutions from offering deposit and payment services outside small geographic areas or, at times, outside a single state. As a result, there are about 30,000 independent financial institutions that receive deposits and make payments for themselves and their depositors primarily through bookkeeping transfer—that is, by check.

Because the nation's depositories are fragmented into many small, self-contained units, the U.S. payments mechanism is characterized by the vast number and dollar volume of money and payment-related transactions that occur among financial institutions. For example, a check deposited in the U.S. banking system is typically handled by two or three different banks in the collection process.

The Federal Reserve building.

Photo courtesy of the Federal Reserve Board.

Cash

Even in our modern world of credit cards and point-of-sale terminals, coin and currency play an important role as convenient monies for small, day-to-day transactions. Meeting the public's demand for coin and currency is a primary responsibility of banks. A bank's cash activities include the cashing of personal or payroll checks—converting deposits into currency—and serving as a depository for the public's excess cash (which is credited to depositors' demand and time accounts). The Federal Reserve serves as the source of the nation's coin and currency, providing cash to depositories as they respond to the cash demands of the public.

Monetary policy does not determine the nation's supply of currency. The public freely decides in what form and in what proportions it wishes to hold its money balances. In 1992, the public held about $275 billion in cash, but used only a small part of that cash for transaction purposes. Cash holdings have expanded at a rate of almost 10 percent per year for the past two decades. The soaring growth rate of currency in circulation has confounded many economists and bankers because it seems inconsistent with the public's increasing use of credit cards, checks, and electronic funds transfer payments.

Economists have two theories to explain this phenomenon. One holds that inflation and rising taxes in the 1970s and early 1980s gave life to a burgeoning underground economy in the United States. In this underground economy, cash is used as a medium of exchange and as a savings (hoarding) instrument to avoid income and sales taxes and to mask illicit drug and other criminal activities.

The other theory, which is more widely accepted, is that much of the nation's currency has been shipped overseas and is being used by foreigners who would rather deal in U.S. currency than in their own inflationary or unstable currencies.

The changing denominations of currency in circulation lend support to both theories. In 1992, about 50 percent of all cash outstanding consisted of $100 bills, a denomination consumers and businesses do not typically use in day-to-day transactions.

The Federal Reserve and Currency Issuance

Exhibit 7.1 illustrates the U.S. cash distribution system. The U.S. Treasury mints new coins and prints currency, which the Federal Reserve distributes to the nation's banks. Federal Reserve banks sort and count the millions of Federal Reserve notes they receive each day from depositing banks, withdrawing from circulation worn or mutilated notes, which they destroy and replace with newly issued currency. In the 1990s, the U.S. Treasury's Bureau of Engraving and Printing produced about 8 billion new Federal Reserve notes each year, which were used to replace destroyed notes and to meet the demand from banks for additional currency.

EXHIBIT 7.1   **U.S. Cash Distribution System**

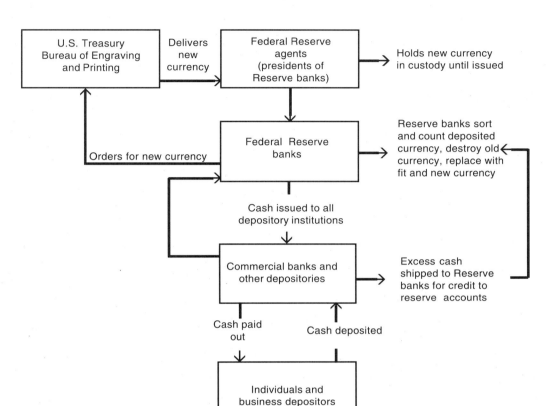

Banks that want more currency pay for it from the reserve account balances they hold at Federal Reserve banks. When a Reserve bank fills a bank's order for additional cash, it charges the amount ordered against the bank's reserve account. Similarly, banks may ship their excess cash to a Federal Reserve bank, which credits it to their reserve account. In either case, the result is simply a redistribution of assets on the bank's books.

For example, a commercial bank that orders $1 million in $10 and $20 bills from its district Federal Reserve bank is charged against its reserve account as this T-account shows:

Commercial Bank

Assets		Liabilities
Reserve account	- $1 million	
Vault cash	+ $1 million	

Similarly, a commercial bank that ships $1 million in excess vault cash to its district Federal Reserve bank increases its reserve account by that amount.

Commercial Bank

Assets		Liabilities
Reserve account	+ $1 million	
Vault cash	- $1 million	

New Currency for the 1990s

In 1991, the Treasury changed the way it prints Federal Reserve notes. To improve detection of counterfeit bills—particularly those made by using high-quality photocopy technology—the Treasury began printing all new $50 and $100 bills with a plastic-like security thread stripe vertically embedded in each note. The thread is imprinted with the bill's denomination and the letters *USA* visible only under certain light. An added line around the portrait on each bill reads *The United States of America* but in type so small that the line appears as a solid line except when magnified.

To hold down annual printing costs, new, smaller denomination currency will be introduced gradually in the 1990s. Thus, for a time, new security thread currency and older currency will circulate together. As the older notes become worn the Federal Reserve will replace them with the new security thread currency and put them into the cash distribution system as illustrated in Exhibit 7.1.

Cash Assets

A bank's cash assets, also called its *primary reserves*, include cash held in the bank's vault or at tellers' stations, deposit balances at correspondent banks and at the district Federal Reserve bank, and cash items in the process of collection (funds about to be credited to the bank through the check collection process). Managing these cash assets is another important area of bank operations.

Primary reserves are the assets that a bank relies on as its first source of liquidity to meet depositors' demand claims. A bank's primary reserves generally exceed those required to meet the Fed's reserve requirements because only vault cash and a bank's deposits at a Federal Reserve bank can meet reserve requirements.

Effective management of cash assets can have an important impact on bank profitability. Excess vault cash held in each branch of a multibranch, retail-oriented bank can be exceedingly costly in terms of lost opportunities for revenue since idle cash is not an earning asset. Excess cash balances also can present day-to-day management problems due to lack of appropriate storage space and adequate security. When cash is deposited in a correspondent account or in an account at a Reserve bank, however, it becomes a working asset. It can be used to earn a return, if invested, or to settle other transactions, such as check collection or electronic funds transfers.

Too little cash, on the other hand, also can prove costly to a bank. Frequent special deliveries of cash from correspondents or the district Federal Reserve bank are expensive in terms of transportation costs. Also, customer relations may deteriorate if depositors are denied the exact currency mix they request in transactions at tellers' windows.

Check Collection

Checks are used to effect more than 90 percent (by dollar value) of all personal and commercial payments in the United States today. It is estimated that Americans wrote about 57 billion checks totaling more than $40 trillion in 1992. With this volume it is easy to see why the check collection process is the largest operational activity of banks.

A check is legally a promise to pay, but operationally it is an instruction form that tells the bank on which it is drawn to transfer money from one account on its books to cash or to another account on its books. Or, the check can be used to collect funds from an account at another bank for credit to an account on its books. The check collection process—the procedures and practices that banks use to follow a check's instructions—is illustrated in exhibit 7.2.

The check-processing operations of all banks are structured to conform to the following practices:

❑   Payment by check cannot be made without the physical transfer of the paper instrument. Presentment of the check itself, not just the information on the check, is essential to collection.

❑   Check processing requires the gathering of different elements of payment information, acting in accordance with this information, and transporting checks among depositing and paying banks.

EXHIBIT 7.2   **Check Collection Process**

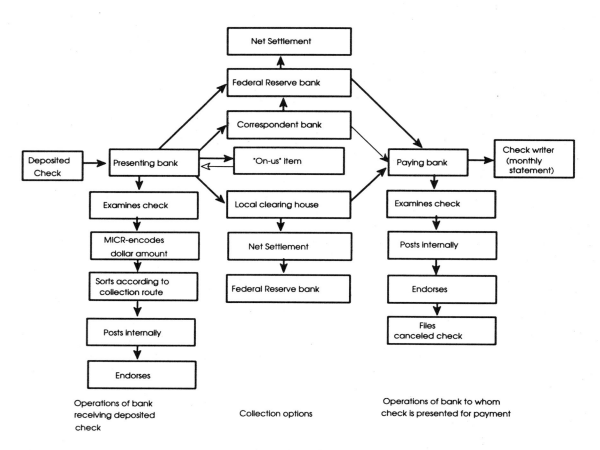

Source: David Friedman, *Deposit Operations, 3rd.* (Washington, D.C.: American Bankers Association, 1992), p. 127.

❒ The transfer of funds by check is provisional (not final) and is subject to both the presenting and paying banks' verification of the legitimacy of the check, its endorsements, and the availability of funds in the check writer's account.

❒ The check collection process can be reversed to correct for errors or for checks that a paying bank refuses to honor.

Check Information Processing

A check includes several instructions, represented by pieces of information, that a bank must follow to collect funds for its customers. Today, virtually all checks are processed by machines; thus the most important instructions on checks are those that allow high-speed check-sorting machines to read and sort properly the tens of thousands of checks that banks receive from their depositors each day. These instructions appear as magnetic ink character recognition (MICR) symbols across the bottom of all checks. Exhibit 7.3 explains the function of the MICR check-encoding symbols, which are basically for check-routing and identification purposes.

EXHIBIT 7.3 **MICR Encoding**

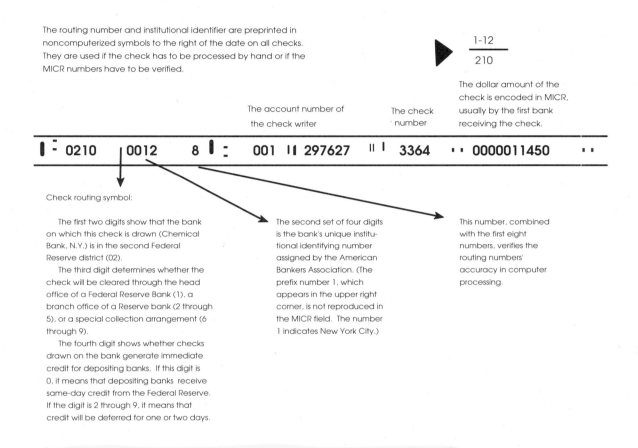

The routing number and institutional identifier are preprinted in noncomputerized symbols to the right of the date on all checks. They are used if the check has to be processed by hand or if the MICR numbers have to be verified.

The account number of the check writer

The check number

The dollar amount of the check is encoded in MICR, usually by the first bank receiving the check.

Check routing symbol:

The first two digits show that the bank on which this check is drawn (Chemical Bank, N.Y.) is in the second Federal Reserve district (02).

The third digit determines whether the check will be cleared through the head office of a Federal Reserve Bank (1), a branch office of a Reserve bank (2 through 5), or a special collection arrangement (6 through 9).

The fourth digit shows whether checks drawn on the bank generate immediate credit for depositing banks. If this digit is 0, it means that depositing banks receive same-day credit from the Federal Reserve. If the digit is 2 through 9, it means that credit will be deferred for one or two days.

The second set of four digits is the bank's unique institutional identifying number assigned by the American Bankers Association. (The prefix number 1, which appears in the upper right corner, is not reproduced in the MICR field. The number 1 indicates New York City.)

This number, combined with the first eight numbers, verifies the routing numbers' accuracy in computer processing.

MICR encoding of all checks was made an industry standard in 1956. Since then, computerized reader-sorters have enabled banks to handle an enormous volume of checks rapidly. The reader-sorters also have allowed banks to automate their accounting systems so that data recording and credit and debit postings to individual accounts can be done quickly and efficiently.

In computerized systems, reader-sorters register the MICR data on checks, sort them, and produce a magnetic tape that records each transaction. The tape maintains a sequential list of each account number affected, the dollar amount of every transaction to be posted to each account, and a code to indicate whether the posting is a debit or a credit. Some banks produce one tape at the end of each banking day; others run separate tapes as soon as checks are received from a clearing house or from in-house pickups. The number and frequency of tape runs depend on the bank's size and its volume of check transactions. Banks with multiple branches usually wait until late in the day to prepare a final tape that integrates all of the day's debit and credit transactions from its various offices.

Once a final tape has been prepared, the bank enters the data on the tape into its master files. The computer updates the file for each account to reflect the current day's debits and credits as registered on the tape. A new closing balance is computed for each account. The sum of these balances becomes the demand deposit total that appears in the bank's daily statement. In addition, a new master file for the next day's transaction activity is generated.

The computerization of deposit accounting has allowed banks to cope with a growing volume of checks while reducing costs and improving back-office operating efficiency.

A reader-sorter machine.

Photo courtesy of International Business Machines Corporation

Check Collection Options

Once the information on a check is registered and interpreted, bank personnel must select the quickest and least expensive option for collecting each check. In theory, a bank that receives a check drawn on any other bank could present it directly to that bank for payment. Such *direct send* collection might work, for example, if only two banks existed in a given region and nearly all checks received by either bank were written by people or businesses that had accounts at one of those banks. Such direct send collection does occur to a limited extent in the U.S. banking system, but given the number of U.S. banks and the small size of most banks' local and regional markets, this is not an efficient industry-wide collection practice.

To obtain relatively quick payment, banks would have to establish clearing accounts at thousands of other banks, resulting in a costly use of bank assets. Because it is far too costly and time-consuming for banks to present checks separately to numerous other banks, local clearing houses and correspondent banking relationships have developed in the United States. Smaller banks clear checks through larger regional banks which, in turn, rely on Federal Reserve banks and local clearing houses to collect much of their deposited check volume. The various check collection routes in the U.S. banking system—including *on-us* collection and use of local clearing houses, correspondent banks, and Federal Reserve banks—are shown in exhibit 7.4.

EXHIBIT 7.4   **Check Collection Routes in the U.S. Banking System**

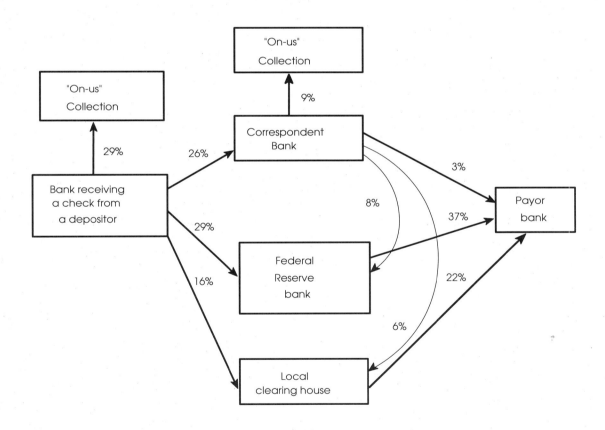

Note: Numbers represent the percentage of checks routed in this manner.

ON-US ITEMS

About 30 percent of all checks received by banks are cleared internally—that is, they are deposited in the same bank on which they are drawn and are collected through internal adjustments to the bank's books. These checks, called *on-us* items, are presented by depositors who want to cash checks drawn on their own accounts or who want to deposit checks drawn on other account holders at the bank (not an unusual situation in small towns or rural areas where one bank may serve a large geographic area). Banks typically run all checks received from depositors through their reader-sorter processing machines to segregate on-us checks. These checks are then handled as internal credit and debit adjustments. The check writer's account is reduced by the amount of the check, and the depositor's account is credited with a like amount.

LOCAL CLEARING HOUSES

Approximately 15 percent of all checks are cleared through local clearing houses or clearing arrangements. A clearing arrangement involves banks in a given area that regularly receive large numbers of deposited checks drawn on each other. Representatives of these banks meet at a central site—either a separate facility or one of the banks in the arrangement—to exchange and collect payment for local checks. There are about 1,500 such clearing arrangements throughout the country. Collection is made by *netting* the amounts presented by the banks against one another. That is, banks pay or receive only the difference between amounts presented to and from all other participants. Settlement for the transactions of major regional clearing houses is made against accounts that the participating banks maintain at Federal Reserve banks.

By using clearing houses, banks are spared the expense of transporting and presenting checks individually to numerous other banks. More important, only one low-balance clearing account must be maintained since collection in a clearing house arrangement is made by netting. This represents a more efficient use of a bank's cash assets than maintaining separate accounts at many banks. Exhibit 7.5 illustrates the check collection process for three banks using a local clearing house; the net difference between the dollar amount of checks presented by a bank and those checks drawn on it is settled against the bank's reserve account at the district Federal Reserve bank.

COLLECTION THROUGH A CORRESPONDENT BANK

About 25 percent of checks received by banks from depositors are forwarded to correspondent banks for check collection. Typically, smaller banks that do not own reader-sorters and those banks that do not have direct account relationships with the Federal Reserve maintain accounts with correspondents for check collection and other services.

When a correspondent bank receives a batch of checks from a respondent bank, the check collection process can take several different routes. If the check is drawn on another bank that maintains an account with the same correspondent, the correspondent simply transfers the deposit credit from one account to another account on its books. If the presented check is drawn on a bank that does not have an account relationship with the correspondent, the respondent's account is credited for the amount of the check and the check is sent either to a local clearing house or to a Federal Reserve bank.

EXHIBIT 7.5   **Check Collection Process through a Local Clearing House**

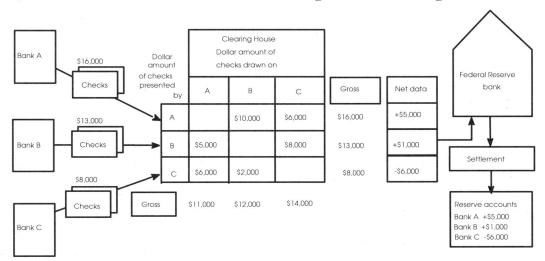

COLLECTION THROUGH THE FEDERAL RESERVE

About 30 percent of all checks are cleared directly through Federal Reserve banks. Correspondent banks also rely extensively on the Federal Reserve for inter-regional collection. The Federal Reserve collects checks by transferring credit balances from one reserve account to another in much the same way that individual banks collect on-us checks. Exhibit 7.6 illustrates the check collection process through a Federal Reserve bank.

For banks that have reserve accounts at different Federal Reserve banks, an extra step is involved. Each Federal Reserve bank has an interdistrict settlement account that it maintains on the books of the Interdistrict Settlement Fund in Washington, D.C., which handles settlements among Federal Reserve banks. A check presented to a Reserve bank that is drawn on a bank in another Reserve district results in a transfer of interdistrict settlement account balances from one Reserve bank to another.

Banks' Demand Deposit Accounting Units

Checks taken in by tellers or presented for payment by another bank, a clearing house, or a Federal Reserve bank all contain important data that affect a bank's assets and liabilities. Most banks have a demand deposit accounting (DDA) unit that processes and collects this data.

A bank's DDA unit typically examines all checks to see if account numbers and dollar amounts are correct and to determine whether any checks should be dishonored (returned unpaid). The DDA unit also posts all debits and credits to the appropriate customer accounts. Posting is the process by which a bank internally pays for a check (debiting a check writer's account) or makes a payment (crediting a depositor's

EXHIBIT 7.6   **Check Collection Process through a Federal Reserve Bank**

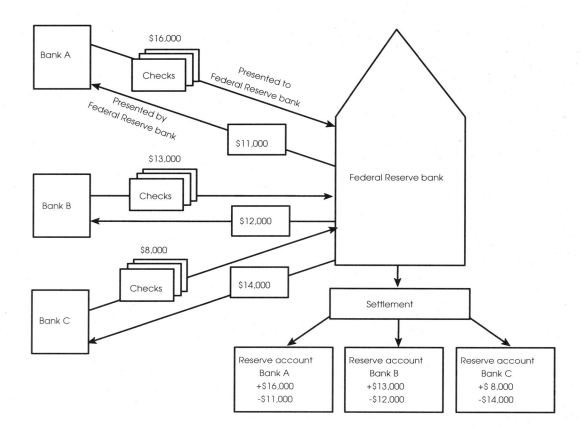

account). This information is used to calculate the bank's end-of-day demand deposit position.

The DDA unit also prepares insufficient funds reports that indicate, for each account involved, the dollar amount of checks paid and the overdraft that would result if all postings were allowed to stand. The unit also prepares uncollected funds reports that show, for each account, any deposited funds for which credit is being deferred. Bank management uses both insufficient funds reports and uncollected funds reports to decide whether to pay or return checks.

A bank's DDA unit also reports on all newly opened and closed accounts in which there have been particularly large increases or decreases in balances. The DDA unit also prepares reports of stop payment orders and hold orders.

Another function of the DDA unit is to prepare monthly statements of each account's activity. Banks issue monthly statements to account holders not only to accommodate their customers' recordkeeping, but also to protect the bank's own legal interests.

Customers are legally obligated to examine their statements and to notify the bank if any error is found. Under the Uniform Commercial Code (UCC), the body of commercial law that governs check practices, depositors have up to one year from the date of a statement (and receipt of the accompanying canceled checks) to notify the bank of a forged or unauthorized endorsement (the signature on the back of the check that authorizes the transfer). All states have laws that parallel these provisions of the UCC.

The major function of most banks' internal reporting systems, of which DDA reporting is a part, is to record inflows and outflows of funds as quickly as possible and thereby determine the net funds available to the bank for lending or investing. Time is critical because of opportunity cost. At an interest rate of 10 percent, a bank that leaves $1 million idle overnight loses approximately $275 in revenue that it would have earned had it loaned or invested the funds for one day.

Float

Float is commonly thought of as the "extra money" that is created because of the time interval between payment by check and the time funds are actually debited from a check writer's account. However, float is also created among banks when funds are credited to a deposit account before checks have been collected. An examination of this kind of float—called *Federal Reserve float*—follows.

Federal Reserve Float

The Federal Reserve routinely credits banks for checks they present for payment before the checks are collected from the banks on which they are drawn. This practice results in extra reserves, known as Federal Reserve float, being created in the banking system.

Federal Reserve banks credit checks presented for payment by depositing banks in accordance with a set schedule. The accounts of depositing banks are credited on the day checks are presented (for checks drawn on banks located in the same city as the Reserve Bank or on the U.S. Treasury, for instance), the next business day (for checks drawn on banks in nearby cities but not located near a Federal Reserve office), or a maximum of two business days later (for checks drawn on banks in distant cities). A depositing bank receives credit in accordance with this schedule regardless of whether the presented checks have actually been processed by the Federal Reserve bank or shipped to the paying bank. As soon as the depositing bank receives credit (even if the checks are later returned for cause), the funds can be used to meet reserve requirements, to support new loans, or to make investments. Until the paying bank's account at the Reserve bank is debited, extra reserves—or float—exist on the books of the banking system.

The Federal Reserve's policy of quickly crediting checks presented for payment provides the nation with a more efficient, speedier check collection system than if Federal Reserve banks credited banks in accordance with actual collection times. Immediate check credit eliminates any uncertainty about a depositing bank's usable funds (reserves) and enhances the efficiency of checks as business and consumer payment devices. However, because float adds extra reserves to the banking system, it makes monetary policy objectives more difficult to achieve.

Although float has always affected monetary policy control, a sharp increase in float in the 1970s (from about $3 billion per day early in the decade to $6 billion per day in 1979) focused increased congressional and banking industry attention on the Federal Reserve's quick crediting practice. Congress saw float as an interest-free loan to the banking system from the central bank. Congressional disapproval was reflected in the Monetary Control Act of 1980, which required the Federal Reserve to eliminate Federal Reserve float or to charge banks for float credit at prevailing interest rates. In response to the act, the Federal Reserve significantly reduced float in the 1980s. It established an air-carrier transportation system to speed up cross-country check collection and modified some of its presentment deadlines and availability schedules. Since the mid-1980s Federal Reserve float has averaged only about $500 million a day.

TYPES OF FEDERAL RESERVE FLOAT

Federal Reserve float is created whenever credit is granted to banks depositing checks for collection before Reserve banks have received payment for the checks. Depending on the cause, three types of float may occur:

- ❏ transportation float
- ❏ holdover float
- ❏ rejected-items float

Transportation float results from delays in the transport and physical presentment of checks for payment. Bad weather or equipment breakdowns can interfere with carriers' delivery schedules and prevent timely presentment of checks from Reserve banks to paying banks. Holdover float results from processing delays at Federal Reserve banks. For example, computer breakdowns or unexpected surges in check volume sometimes prevent the Federal Reserve from meeting its own delivery deadlines. Rejected-items float can occur if the Reserve banks' sorting machines reject a large number of damaged checks. Because rejected checks must be processed manually, some of those checks may not be processed in time to meet the normal transportation schedules.

Float could be eliminated entirely if the Federal Reserve abandoned its deferred availability schedule and granted credit for deposited checks only after checks had been collected. To do so, however, would severely hamper the efficiency of the nation's check collection system. Improved check-processing technology and speedier transportation have over the decades speeded up the check collection process and shortened the deferred availability schedule. For example, in the 1920s and 1930s, the Federal Reserve's deferred availability schedule ranged up to eight days. In 1940, the maximum deferment was reduced to three days; and in 1951, it was shortened to the current two-day maximum.

THE CREATION OF FEDERAL RESERVE FLOAT

We can trace the creation of Federal Reserve float using T-accounts as we did in the previous chapter to trace multiple deposit creation. In the following example, we look at how float is reflected on the books of a Federal Reserve bank and how two commercial banks that clear their checks through this Federal Reserve bank are affected.

Assume that on Monday, First Commercial Bank presents the Federal Reserve bank with $10 million in checks drawn on Second Commercial Bank. According to the Reserve bank's deferred availability schedule, credit for these checks is posted to First Commercial's account on Tuesday, the day after presentment. The Reserve bank's posting on Monday will show an asset increase of $10 million (cash items in the process of collection) offset by a $10 million liability increase (deferred availability items). In effect, the Reserve bank records on its books that it has received $10 million in checks for credit to another bank, is in the process of collecting those checks, and is deferring credit for the checks for one day.

Federal Reserve Bank

Assets	Liabilities

Cash items in process
   of collection   + $10 million
	Account of First Commercial Bank
	
	Account of Second Commercial Bank
	
	Deferred availability items
	
	                 + $10 million

If the Federal Reserve can sort the $10 million in checks presented by First Commercial Bank and deliver them to Second Commercial Bank by the following day (Tuesday), then no float will be created. The Reserve bank's books will look like this on Tuesday:

Federal Reserve Bank

Assets	Liabilities
Cash items in process of collection + $10 million (Monday) - $10 million (Tuesday)	Account of First Commercial Bank + $10 million (Tuesday) Account of Second Commercial Bank - $10 million (Tuesday) Deferred availability items + $10 million (Monday) - $10 million (Tuesday)

If, however, the Reserve bank cannot sort and deliver the checks to Second Commercial by Tuesday, this will create float. Suppose a snowstorm prevents carriers from delivering the processed checks to Second Commercial until Wednesday. In this case, the books of the Reserve bank will look like this on Tuesday:

Federal Reserve Bank

Assets	Liabilities
Cash items in process of collection + $10 million (Monday)	Account of First Commercial Bank + $10 million (Tuesday) Account of Second Commercial Bank Deferred availability items + $10 million (Monday) - $10 million (Tuesday)

First Commercial's account has been credited with $10 million in usable reserve assets in accordance with the Reserve bank's deferred availability schedule. The reduction in the deferred availability items account reflects the end of credit deferment. However, because the checks have not yet been received by Second Commercial, they are not collected and must still be carried as cash items in the process of collection on the Reserve bank's books. There now exists $10 million in float (or excess reserves) in the banking system that has been created by the Federal Reserve. In accounting terms, float reflects the difference between the Federal Reserve's cash items in the process of collection (assets) and its deferred availability items (liabilities).

If the checks are presented to Second Commercial on Wednesday, the $10 million in float will be eliminated because the Reserve bank then will debit Second Commercial's account by $10 million and debit its own cash items account by $10 million. Federal Reserve float is continually being created and eliminated in the banking system in this manner.

Now let's look at how this float affects the other banks involved. First Commercial had to wait only one day before it received credit in fully collected funds from the Federal

Reserve bank. Thus on Monday its books showed a $10 million increase in cash items in the process of collection, which offset the $10 million in credit postings it made to depositors' accounts.

First Commercial Bank

Assets	Liabilities

Cash items in process of
   collection   + $10 million
	Demand deposit accounts
	   + $10 million

Second Commercial Bank and its check-writing depositors are the beneficiaries of the $10 million in Federal Reserve float created by the Federal Reserve bank. Because Second Commercial's books carried no debits to its account at the Reserve bank or to its depositors' accounts on Tuesday, it had the use of $10 million in reserves for one day longer than scheduled, and its depositors had the use of their checkbook funds for one day longer than they should have. Had there been no delay in the check collection process, Second Commercial would have paid $10 million to First Commercial through an account transfer on the books of the Reserve bank on Tuesday. Instead, because of the delay in its receipt of the $10 million in checks from the Federal Reserve, Second Commercial's account balance at the Reserve bank is debited by $10 million on Wednesday. Second Commercial then sorts the checks and makes the necessary internal debits to its depositors' (check writers') accounts.

Bank Float and Delayed Availability

Because the check collection process takes time, checks received from depositors are initially recorded on a bank's books as uncollected (unavailable) funds. This liability posting is offset by an asset posting of an equal dollar amount of cash items in process of collection. The initial posting by a bank of a $1,000 deposited check and the subsequent posting after receipt of payment for this check is shown here:

Initial Posting for a Deposited Check

Assets	Liabilities

Cash items in process of
   collection
   + $1,000
	Demand deposit
	   (unavailable funds)
	   + $1,000

Posting after Collection of a Deposited Check

Assets	Liabilities
Reserve account at Federal Reserve + $1,000	Demand deposit (unavailable funds) - $1,000
Cash items in process of collection - $1,000	Demand deposit (usable collected funds) + $1,000

Banks traditionally gave depositors usable funds credit for deposited checks in accordance with their own delayed availability schedules. While these schedules varied, depositors generally were not allowed to use check funds until several days after a check had been deposited, regardless of the speed with which checks were actually processed and credited by the Federal Reserve.

Until 1988, when Congress imposed limits on the delays that banks could place on deposited checks, there was no nationwide policy that governed when depositors received credit for deposited checks. Only California, New York, and seven other states had laws that specified maximum check holding periods. Most banks used complex availability schedules based on the Federal Reserve's estimates of how long it should take to transport a check between various regions of the country. These schedules generated wide disparities. For example, before 1984, when New York's delayed availability law went into effect, some New York banks granted credit on deposited checks drawn on out-of-state banks within four to six business days, while other banks held back credit for as long as 22 business days.

Banks also adopted different policies for different customers. Some banks allowed customers of long standing and selected business accounts that deposited and wrote a large number of checks, to draw cash against newly deposited checks but required other customers to wait in accordance with a delayed availability schedule, ostensibly until their deposited funds became "good."

If the sum of checks presented for payment against the account of a given depositor exceeds the amount of available funds registered to the depositor's account that day, the paying bank has the option of honoring or dishonoring (refusing to pay) the checks. In some cases, a bank will honor the checks if the account has a combined total of uncollected and available funds in excess of the total of presented items. The paying bank in this case assumes the risk that checks being collected for the depositor could be returned unpaid. Banks are most apt to assume this risk for business accounts with which they have long-standing relationships.

Bank policies and their delayed availability schedules became a source of increasing controversy in the 1980s. Consumer groups complained that it was unfair for banks and thrifts to impose lengthy delays on the granting of usable funds credit for deposited checks since the collection of a check takes no more than a few days between banks anywhere in the United States. They argued that banks presenting checks typically receive credit to their own accounts from paying banks within two days. However, every day that a bank holds back credit to a depositor beyond the day it has been paid, it can profit by investing the funds itself. Consumer groups argued that this practice represented a misuse of customers' funds.

Delayed availability of funds presented special problems for new bank customers who had moved from another state and wanted to draw funds against checks written on their former banks. Delays for these customers were particularly long and irksome. Consumer groups also complained that few banks told customers up front of their delayed availability policies. Most customers learned of their bank's policy only when checks drawn on uncollected funds were returned unpaid.

Bankers contended that the delays in crediting checks to depositors were justified, given the imperfections in the nation's check collection system and the law's clear delineation of rights and liabilities in the collection process. Bankers maintained that every check must be treated, in principle, as a potentially "bad" check—even though in practice less than 1 percent of all checks are returned unpaid.

DELAYED AVAILABILITY STANDARDS

Consumer displeasure with banks' delayed availability practices prompted Congress to establish national standards in 1988. The federal law—known as the Expedited Funds Availability Act—preempts the eight state availability laws that had been in force before 1988 unless the laws require shorter holds for a category of checks other than those mandated by the act. The federal law also requires banks to disclose to customers their availability practices and procedures.

Under the federal standards (implemented through the Federal Reserve's Regulation CC), banks must make funds available within two business days of deposit for local checks and within five business days of deposit for other checks. Banks also must grant next-day availability on all government checks, certified checks, and bank checks. In addition, the first $100 of any deposited check must be made available on the next day.

Some bankers argued that the short time delays imposed by the federal rules would increase check fraud and bad-check losses for banks because customers would be able to withdraw funds against deposited checks before banks received notification that a check was bad. To minimize these risks under the new rules, Congress exempted from coverage all new accounts, check deposits over $5,000, customers that repeatedly overdraw their checking accounts, and checks that a bank reasonably believes will not be paid. In these cases, a bank need not follow the deferred availability schedule, but must provide the consumer with a notice of hold stating the reason for the hold, its date of expiration, and specific identification of the items in the deposit that are being held.

NEW RETURN-ITEMS PROCEDURE

The Expedited Funds Availability Act also addressed a fundamental problem that banks faced in the check collection process. If a check was returned unpaid—for insufficient funds or other cause—it was routed back the way it came. The depositor's bank often did not know that a check had been dishonored until it was received from the dishonoring bank, sometimes as long as 10 days to two weeks after the day of presentment.

The slow process by which dishonored checks have traditionally been returned to presenting banks is related to three factors. First, checks that are being returned must be processed by hand because the information needed to reroute the check does not appear in MICR form on the check. Second, banks were not required to inform presenting banks immediately that a check was being returned, nor was there any incentive to return the item quickly. Thus, most banks used the mail as the least expensive—and slowest—method of returning dishonored checks. Third, checks had to be returned in the reverse order in which they were presented, including any intermediary steps through a correspondent bank or a Federal Reserve bank.

To address this problem, Congress mandated that the Federal Reserve speed up the return-items process and gave the Federal Reserve broad authority to change the banking system's check collection rules to accomplish that objective. The Federal Reserve's Regulation CC was formulated in 1988 with this objective in mind. The regulation allows banks to return dishonored checks directly to the bank of first deposit, bypassing all intermediaries. It also designates the Reserve banks as central notification sites for banks returning checks so that they can immediately inform depositing banks of any checks that have been dishonored and are in the process of being returned. A depositing bank can then immediately block the withdrawal of funds against the dishonored check.

Electronic Funds Transfer Systems and Services

No discussion of the U.S. payments mechanism would be complete today without including electronic funds transfer (EFT) systems and services, which have become indispensable to modern-day banking. Banks increasingly use EFT to borrow funds from each other, to invest daily surplus funds, to settle clearing balances in the check collection process, and to provide instantaneous transfer services for depositors. Nevertheless, there is no uniform, nationwide EFT system in America. Rather, there are several *wholesale* systems that move hundreds of billions of dollars of interbank funds each day and several *retail* systems that provide consumer electronic banking services in selected regions of the country. There are also tens of thousands of bank and thrift EFT terminals located in depositories and elsewhere.

Wholesale Electronic Funds Transfer Systems

Banks use two major wholesale EFT systems—Fedwire and CHIPS. The Federal Reserve's funds transfer network, known as Fedwire, is the main domestic system that large banks use to adjust their reserve balances. About half of the $2 trillion in interbank electronic transfers made each day are over Fedwire.

The Fedwire provides direct electronic transfer services to about 7,000 banks that have access to the system through in-bank terminal or computer links. Thousands of other depositories—mainly small banks and thrifts—have access to the Fedwire through telephone links.

Fedwire is used to transfer reserve account balances (federal funds) from one bank to another, to transfer U.S. government and federal agency securities (in book-entry form), and to transfer funds on behalf of bank customers. Transfers on behalf of customers (third-party payments) most often involve payments or receipts for the purchase or sale of such financial assets as commercial paper, corporate bonds, and U.S. Treasury securities, or the overnight investment or transfer of account balances as part of the cash management operations of major corporations.

CHIPS, the Clearing House Interbank Payments System, is the focal point for payments in the international dollar market. Each day, about 90 percent of all international interbank dollar transfers—about 200,000 daily transfers valued at $1 trillion a day in 1992—are moved through CHIPS. The New York Clearing House Association operates the system, which consists of about 400 sending and receiving devices, ranging from simple terminals to large-scale computers. The system links 130 financial institutions—mostly the branches of foreign banks in New York City and New York's large money center banks—to a central computer.

Daylight Overdrafts through EFTs

Bankers and regulators have become increasingly concerned over risks in wholesale electronic banking. During the course of a day, so much electronic money flows in and out of the nation's large money center banks so rapidly that some banks on occasion pay out more electronic funds than they have on their books. These *daylight overdrafts* typically last for several minutes until incoming electronic funds from other banks provide coverage. It is virtually impossible for sending and receiving banks to know with any certainty at any given moment of the day whether a given bank has a positive or a negative balance on its books. This is particularly true of large Fedwire users that have direct computer-to-computer access to the Federal Reserve bank. Bankers and regulators are concerned with the size and concentration of these overdrafts

(Continued from previous page)

because one bank's inability to make good on its daylight overdrafts could lead not only to its own failure, but also to the failure of other banks receiving the overdrafted electronic funds. Although only a small number of banks incur daylight overdrafts on Fedwire and CHIPS, the overdrafts exceed more than $140 billion per day. For individual banks, the dollar value of overdrafts can routinely top the value of their total assets.

In 1986, the Federal Reserve introduced requirements designed to reduce the risks involved in using wholesale electronic systems. Banks that use Fedwire and CHIPS must establish a dollar limit on the daylight overdrafts they will accept on behalf of banks or companies for whom they transfer funds. They also must set a limit on the combined total daylight overdrafts they will accept over both EFT systems. These limits are based on a multiple of a bank's capital as determined by the bank's own rating of its creditworthiness, credit policies, and operational controls and procedures. Banks with excellent ratings can incur daylight overdrafts up to the largest allowable multiple of capital—2.25 in 1992. Banks with poor self-appraisals and banks that do not rate themselves are not allowed to incur overdrafts.

Banks that use CHIPS established additional rules in 1990 to reduce risks in dealing with international interbank transfers. Under these rules, each CHIPS participant must enter into a loss-sharing agreement with the New York Clearing House Association under which it pledges to provide a portion of the funds necessary to make good on all CHIPS transfers if one or more CHIPS participants fail. Each bank also is required to place U.S. Treasury securities in a collateral account at the Federal Reserve Bank of New York that would be used to cover CHIPS losses if any bank failed to honor its pledge. In 1992, CHIPS participants had deposited more than $3 billion in the collateral account.

The Federal Reserve's risk-reduction measures have blunted the growth of daylight overdrafts and have focused bankers' attention on the risks in electronic banking. Nevertheless, the magnitude of daylight overdrafts remains sizable and the Federal Reserve intends to take additional measures in the 1990s to reduce or eliminate this risk. These measures may include reductions in bank overdraft limits, pricing overdrafts, and changes in the wholesale EFT systems themselves. One proposal has been made that banks net electronic payments to one another, transferring only the difference between payments that otherwise would be sent separately between any two banks on the same day.

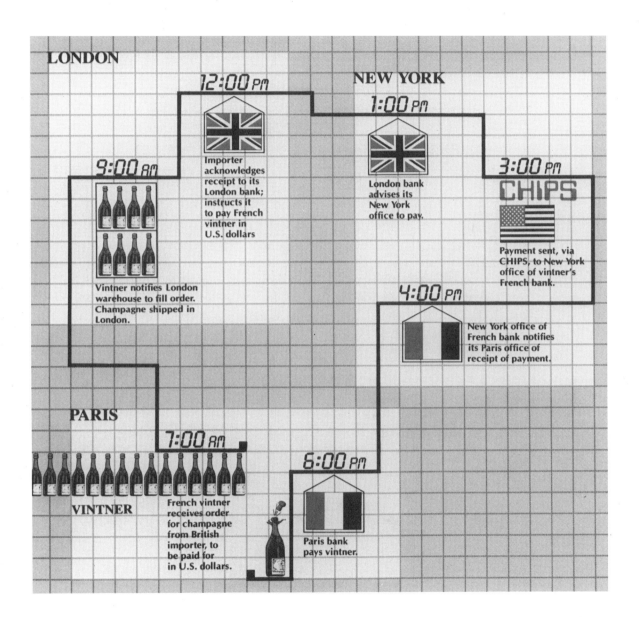

A sample CHIPS transaction.

Courtesy of the New York Clearing House Association.

Retail Electronic Funds Transfer Services

Retail-oriented electronic funds transfer systems are increasingly changing the way banks provide services. The major EFT systems and services in the 1990s are

- ❑ automated teller machines (ATMs)
- ❑ point-of-sale (POS) terminals
- ❑ automated clearing house (ACH) services
- ❑ telephone bill-paying services
- ❑ home banking services

AUTOMATED TELLER MACHINES (ATMS)

The most widely used retail EFT services offered by banks today are those provided by automated teller machines. About 85,000 ATMs were being used in 1992. These minicomputers, which operate 24 hours a day, are placed in the outside walls or lobby entrances of banks or at freestanding locations. Typically, ATMs are accessed by the customer inserting an encoded plastic card and pressing a numerical keyboard to enter a personal identification number (PIN). In the 1980s, increasing numbers of banks linked their ATMs to those of other banks to form regional networks to provide services to customers from more locations, including some from out of state. By 1992, about 30 percent of all ATM transactions were being made at other banks' ATMs.

The most widely used ATM service allows a depositor to withdraw cash against a checking or savings account. At some banks, depositors also can make cash withdrawals against preauthorized lines of credit, national credit cards, or an overdraft account. ATMs also allow customers to make deposits to checking and savings accounts and, in some instances, to pay utility bills or repay installment loans. Some ATMs will allow a split deposit (in which part of the total is paid out in cash) up to a maximum dollar amount without verifying the deposit.

About one-third of all transactions handled by ATMs are account balance inquiries. These often are initiated by customers before and after a cash withdrawal or deposit transaction to assure themselves of the accuracy of the machine. Most ATMs also allow users to transfer funds between checking and savings accounts. A few ATMs can transfer funds to a third-party account maintained on the bank's books (for example, a utility company's account).

POINT-OF-SALE TERMINALS AND DEBIT CARDS

Some banks offer EFT services that involve the use of point-of-sale (POS) terminals and debit cards. A POS terminal is a minicomputer placed by a bank at a retail site. Customers pay for goods or services through a direct debit to their bank account with simultaneous credit to the merchant's account. POS terminals also allow shoppers to obtain an authorization or a guarantee from the bank that personal checks drawn on their accounts at the bank are covered by available funds in those accounts. Bank customers use a plastic debit card issued by the bank to activate a POS terminal for payment. Funds are immediately transferred from the depositor's account at the bank to the merchant's account (in the case of a retail purchase) or to the account of a company participating in an EFT program, such as a utility or mortgage company (in the case of a monthly bill).

Electronic payments take different forms.

Photos courtesy of International Business Machines Corporation.

Most POS systems have several major drawbacks. They eliminate the float associated with payment by check or credit card, they tie merchants into only one bank, and they can be used only by customers with accounts at the POS-deploying bank. In some states, however, POS systems are shared by several banks, a feature that broadens the potential number of POS users for participating merchants. Although most POS terminals deployed today are used by merchants and consumers to authorize or guarantee checks, many bankers see this as an interim step toward the broader acceptance and use of the direct-debit features of POS systems (for automatic bill-paying, for example) in the 1990s.

AUTOMATED CLEARING HOUSE (ACH) SERVICES

Automated clearing house services offer an electronic alternative to writing, clearing, and collecting paper checks. ACH services enable corporations and the government to put payment information, such as payroll data, on a magnetic tape or computer disk. Banks process these tapes through their own computers to obtain the appropriate credit and debit information; they then forward the tapes to the ACH where, in the case of corporate payroll data, computers debit the account of the corporation's bank and credit the accounts of the banks where the corporation's employees have their accounts. Additional tapes with credit information are delivered to these receiving banks.

TELEPHONE BILL-PAYING SERVICES

Some banks offer a service that allows customers to make electronic funds transfers over the telephone, through direct touchtone telephone hookup to their bank's computer. Payments are sorted by the computer and are either credited directly to a merchant's account at the bank or, if the merchant does not have an account there, remitted by mail to the merchant in the form of a banker's check. The overall public response to telephone bill-paying has been mixed. In 1992, only about 500 banks and thrifts offered this service.

HOME BANKING SERVICES

Home banking enables consumers to transmit payment instructions to their banks from a personal computer or terminal in the home. In fully automated systems, the bank acts on these payment instructions by transferring funds electronically between accounts or to other banks. In a number of partially automated systems, banks forward bankers' checks to merchants and other banks to fulfill payment instructions. In the 1980s, large banks invested heavily in developing home banking systems, but customer response was disappointing. In 1992, fewer than 50 banks were offering home banking services and only 100,000 households nationwide were using these services. Most banking industry analysts maintain that home banking has proven unpopular to date because banks have not made their computer payment services more attractive or less costly to consumers than paying by check, credit card, or debit card.

The Future of Retail EFT Systems and Services

Many bankers believe that EFT technology will soon revolutionize the way individuals and businesses make payments and use banks in this country. Other bankers contend that changes in banking law and regulation—and, even more important, changes in the attitudes of bank customers—must occur before any of the EFT systems and services now available significantly alter the payment practices and patterns of American consumers and businesses. These changes are not likely for three or four decades.

Most bankers see in EFT systems the key to reducing costs associated with check clearing and collection. The cost to banks of maintaining checking accounts and processing checks increased significantly in the 1980s. Rising wages, postal rates, transportation costs, equipment costs, and Federal Reserve service charges drove up banks' operating expenses. Banks' interest expenses also rose due to the popularity of interest-earning checking accounts, such as NOW accounts and money market deposit accounts. The application of EFT technology to check processing—to reduce or eliminate the costly physical handling of paper checks and to replace most of the routine functions performed by bank tellers—is in the forefront of change in the 1990s. However, myriad legal, economic, and attitudinal factors over which banks have little control deter more widespread use of electronic payments and transfer systems on the retail level.

Summary

Banks play a major role in the nation's payments mechanism—that is in meeting the public's need for cash and in processing checks and electronic funds transfers. The largest single operational activity of banks is clearing and collecting the 57 billion checks written annually in the United States. Check collection involves interpreting the various elements of information contained on checks, acting on this information, and transporting checks to other banks for payment.

MICR coding has enabled the processing and interpreting of check information to be computerized. However, banker judgment is still required to select the least expensive and quickest collection option—a local clearing house, a correspondent bank, or the Federal Reserve—for those checks that are not drawn on the bank itself.

The Federal Reserve follows a fixed schedule for crediting banks for checks they present for payment. Because checks are often credited before they are actually collected, extra reserves are created in the form of Federal Reserve float. Since 1980, when the Monetary Control Act required the Federal Reserve to charge explicit fees for all its payment services, including float, the Federal Reserve has significantly reduced float through speedier cross-country collections and modifications to some of its availability schedules. The long delays practiced by some banks in giving depositors usable funds credit for checks drawn on out-of-town banks prompted Congress in 1987 to legislate maximum nationwide delayed availability limits.

Banks rely on two major electronic funds transfer systems—Fedwire and CHIPS—to perform much of their interbank business as well as to provide instantaneous money transfer services for depositors. Although there are no nationwide retail electronic funds transfer systems, banks today have deployed more than 85,000 ATMs (automated teller machines), and a growing number of banks have linked their ATMs by establishing local and regional EFT networks. In addition to point-of-sale terminals, automated clearing house services, and telephone bill-paying and other home banking services that are already available, other electronic banking services are likely to be offered to consumers in the 1990s.

Questions

1. Inasmuch as cash can be counted toward meeting reserve requirements, is it advantageous for a bank to have cash on hand in excess of its daily needs?

2. What are the three basic ways that interbank checks are collected in the United States? What factors determine a bank's choice of collection option?

3. Explain how a local clearing house operates and the advantages it offers for clearing checks.

4. What are MICR instructions, what is their significance, and how do banks manage MICR data flow?

5. What is Federal Reserve float, how does it occur, and how does it differ from bank float? In your answer, explain how uncollected funds differ from available funds.

6. Why have retail electronic funds transfer systems and services been slow to develop in the United States? Is the electronic payments revolution in U.S. banking inevitable? Justify your answer.

8

The Bank as a Business Firm

Objectives

After successfully completing this chapter, you will be able to

- ☐ name the key sources of bank earnings and principal types of investments,

- ☐ describe the major classifications of bank loans,

- ☐ define loan commitment fees, compensating balances, loan participations, and loan loss reserves,

- ☐ differentiate between U.S. government securities, federal agency securities, and municipal obligations,

- ☐ trace changes in funds management strategies over the last three decades, including factors considered in developing asset/liability management strategies today, and

- ☐ explain the purpose and use of various funds management strategies such as asset allocation, liability management, and spread management.

Introduction

As recently as the turn of the century, commercial banks focused primarily on meeting the credit needs of businesses. They made short-term loans to businesses to finance traded goods, to manufacturers to buy raw materials, and to merchants to carry inventories. Even then the term *commercial bank* was not entirely apt, because by the year 1900 banks were taking in more than one-fifth of their total earnings from investments rather than from commercial loans.

Today, the business of most banks includes both short- and long-term business and consumer loans; residential and commercial mortgages; and investments in federal, state, and local government securities. Many banks also sell a variety of other financial services to corporate and consumer customers.

One important way of learning about a business is to examine its balance sheet—its statement of assets, liabilities, and net worth. In this chapter we will examine the balance sheet of the banking system, particularly its earning assets (loans and investments). We also will examine the banking system's income statement to learn more about the various income and expense items that do not appear on a balance sheet, yet which absorb considerable bank resources and yield substantial revenues.

We also will explore the principles and practices of asset/liability management. With few exceptions, banks are corporations owned by stockholders who are interested in earning dividends. As such, profitability is clearly a major concern of bank management. Bank earnings are determined both by economic forces and by management proficiency in continually adjusting the bank's assets and liabilities (its sources and uses of funds). As we will see, the management of bank funds has adapted to economic, competitive, and technological changes that turn-of-the-century bankers could not have imagined.

New *risk-based* capital requirements have become a significant factor in the 1990s in the way banks conduct their lending and investment. You are encouraged to read Extended Study 9, "Capital Adequacy Standards" for a review of these requirements. Banks also have begun to adopt new strategies to supplement their management of sources and uses of funds. For further study, read Extended Study 10, "New Strategies for the 1990s". It examines the securitization of assets, hedging in the futures market, and other strategies banks are employing to generate additional revenues and to reduce expenses.

Balance Sheet Analysis

A balance sheet is a statement of a company's financial condition at a specific time. It lists the company's assets on one side and its liabilities and net worth (or capital) on the other side—and as its name suggests, both sides must balance. Exhibit 8.1 shows a balance sheet for the U.S. commercial banking system in 1992 based on total amounts of assets, liabilities, and capital of 11,700 domestically chartered commercial banks;

EXHIBIT 8.1   Balance Sheet for the Commercial Banking System

Assets		Liabilities and Capital	
Cash Assets	7%	Transaction deposits	22%
Currency and coin	16%	Savings deposits	23%
Reserves with Federal Reserve	14%	Time deposits	31%
Deposits at banks	27%		
Cash items in process of collection	43%	Borrowings	4%
	100%	Other liabilities	12%
Federal funds sold	5%		
Securities (investment account)	22%	Capital account	7%
U.S. government	80%		
Municipal and Federal agency	20%		
	100%		
Securities (Trading Account)	1%		
Loans	60%		
Business	25%		
Real estate	45%		
Consumer	18%		
Other (including agricultural)	12%		
	100%		
Other Assets	5%		
Total Assets	100%	Total liabilities and Capital	100%

Note: Percentages are based on total assets/total liabilities and capital for 11,700 domestically chartered commercial banks—$3.1 trillion in mid-1992.

Source: Federal Reserve *Bulletin*, August 1992.

but rather than showing total dollar amounts, each asset account is shown as a percentage of total assets, while each liability account is shown as a percentage of total liabilities plus net worth. In this way, it provides industry norms against which individual bank comparisons can be made. This systemwide balance sheet also suggests the relative importance of various types of bank assets and liabilities.

Bank assets are listed on a balance sheet in descending order from the most liquid, such as cash, to the least liquid, such as the bank's building and equipment. (An asset's liquidity refers to how quickly it can be turned into money.) Analysts typically group bank assets into four categories—cash assets, securities (or investments), loans, and other assets. A bank's investments and loans are its earning assets, the assets on which the bank earns a return. An examination of the banking system's earning assets can provide insight into the earning strengths of banks and the sources of most bank income. For an effective analysis, bank earnings must be evaluated against the costs banks incur to raise funds to produce or acquire earning assets.

Bank liabilities also are listed on a balance sheet in descending order of liquidity. (The liquidity of a liability refers to how quickly it can be withdrawn.) Bank liabilities and capital are grouped into six categories—transaction deposits, savings deposits, time deposits, borrowed funds, other liabilities, and capital account. As exhibit 8.1 shows, savings and time deposits constitute more than half of banks' total liabilities. By examining the various items found on the balance sheet of a typical bank, we gain a good understanding of the basic business of banking. We will look first at bank assets and then at bank liabilities.

Cash Assets

A bank's cash assets provide it with primary liquidity—that is, immediately available funds that can be used to honor the demands of depositors for coin and currency (check cashing), or to honor requests for payment by other banks in the check collection process. A bank's cash assets consist of cash held in its vault and at teller stations, its reserve balance at the district Federal Reserve bank, deposits with correspondent banks, and cash items in the process of collection. These assets generally do not earn an interest or investment return for the bank but may entitle it to some services. For example, many small banks pay for the check-clearing services provided to them by their correspondent banks by maintaining an agreed-upon daily compensating deposit balance with their correspondents. On average, banks hold about 7 percent of their assets as cash assets.

Federal Funds Sold

Banks frequently sell reserve balances (federal funds) to one another for one day use. (The term *federal funds* derives from the reserve account balances that banks maintain at Federal Reserve banks.) Indeed, money market banks routinely use federal funds purchases and sales as a mechanism for adjusting their reserve positions on a daily basis so that they neither hold excess reserves, which represent a lost opportunity to earn a return, nor incur costly reserve deficiencies. Small community-based banks that may have excess reserves but no market for overnight loans typically sell their reserves to larger money market banks. Banks throughout the country use Fedwire, the Federal Reserve's funds transfer network, to make instantaneous transfers of reserve account balances.

Securities [Asset considered secondary reserves]

The second major category of assets on a bank's balance sheet—comprising about 20 percent of the banking system's total assets—is its investment securities. A bank's securities portfolio consists primarily of debt obligations of federal, state, and local governments. These assets constitute a secondary source of liquidity for banks (after cash assets). Securities are considered secondary reserves because they are more readily salable than loans and thus are more liquid. Liquidity, however, is no longer the primary reason banks invest in securities.

Banks invest in securities primarily because they provide interest income. However, securities also can result in capital gains or losses. Banks carry the value of the securities they own on their books at cost rather than at market value. If interest rates rise, bond prices fall and banks face capital losses if they sell securities. If interest rates fall, bond prices rise and banks generate capital gains when they sell securities.

Securities investments also allow banks to diversify the risks they take in lending funds and can forge strong account and deposit relationships with local governments by purchasing their newly issued securities. In addition, securities allow banks to meet pledging requirements against trust operations, and they serve as collateral for government deposits. Until 1980, securities also could be used to meet state reserve requirements. For all these reasons, many banks traditionally viewed their investment portfolios as earning assets that were not subject to complete management control. Today, however, banks increasingly manage their investments as a profit-making activity, just as they do their lending activities.

U.S GOVERNMENT OBLIGATIONS

More than three-quarters of all bank investments are made in U.S. government obligations (Treasury bills, notes, and bonds). Treasury bills (T-bills) are the shortest-term debt obligations of the U.S. government, with original maturities typically of three or six months. Treasury notes and bonds are long-term debt obligations, with original maturities of one to four years in the case of notes and five or more years in the case of bonds.

U.S. Treasury securities offer banks an investment free of credit risk (risk of default); a large, accessible secondary market; and income exempt from state and local taxes. For this reason, banks use Treasury securities, primarily T-bills, as their major short-term investment vehicle and as their backup source of liquidity for meeting seasonal demands for funds and unexpected drains of primary liquidity.

Most banks hold their Treasury securities in book-entry form at Federal Reserve banks. In this form they can be transferred instantaneously over Fedwire to buyers throughout the country. The Federal Reserve also buys and sells Treasury securities, primarily T-bills, in implementing monetary policy through open-market operations. The government securities market has so many potential buyers and sellers that the Federal Reserve can easily buy or sell huge dollar amounts of Treasury bills on a moment's notice.

MUNICIPAL OBLIGATIONS AND FEDERAL AGENCY SECURITIES

Municipal obligations (securities issued by states and localities) and federal agency securities are the other significant investment outlet for most banks; they make up about 20 percent of the banking system's investment portfolio. Municipal securities are issued by states and cities and consist of short-term (one year or less) tax anticipation notes and tax warrants and long-term (one year or more) bonds.

Federal agency securities are issued by U.S. government-owned or government-sponsored corporations and agencies. These include the Federal Home Loan Mortgage Corporation (FHLMC), Federal National Mortgage Association (FNMA), Federal Housing Administration (FHA), Tennessee Valley Authority (TVA), Government National Mortgage Association (GNMA), Banks for Cooperatives, Federal Intermediate Credit Banks (FICB), and Federal Home Loan Banks (FHLB). Banks hold certificates that represent participation in a portfolio of loans held by the agencies; however, these certificates are classified as investments rather than loans.

Many of the nation's 80,000 state and local governments finance their short-term revenue needs by selling tax anticipation notes that mature within one year. These notes may be issued not only by the governments themselves, but also by various state and local agencies—including local housing authorities, school districts, and drainage and sewer authorities. As their name suggests, these notes are issued in anticipation of taxes, other revenues, or the proceeds from the sale of long-term bonds pledged to retire the notes.

Many banks purchase the tax warrants and notes of their local municipality directly from the municipality on a negotiated basis. Large regional and money center banks often buy state and local obligations through competitive bidding. Several hundred commercial banks and investment bankers may competitively bid for the new issues of key states or large cities throughout the country; many banks, however, bid only on issues of cities or states in their region.

The large money center banks that bid on municipal securities typically rely on either a private rating service to classify the credit risk of the issues they are purchasing or on the credit evaluation of local banks that closely follow the affairs of the issuing government. Most state and local governments provide banks with detailed information about their financial affairs to facilitate the sale of their issues even though municipal securities are exempt from registration under federal securities laws.

Because income earned on all state and local obligations is exempt from federal income tax, municipal bonds pay lower interest returns than other investment instruments. For several decades, commercial banks were able to reduce their effective tax rates below those of other corporations by investing in municipal securities. A bank's ability to take advantage of tax-exempt sources of income is limited, however, by the amount of its taxable income. In the 1980s, many banks experienced declines in earnings with the result that heavy investments in tax-exempt obligations, which pay lower returns, were no longer attractive.

In the early 1980s banks purchased fewer municipal securities because they had less profit to shelter with tax-exempt investments. In addition, a change in federal tax regulations in 1982 disallowed part of the interest deductions for municipal bond carrying costs. As a result, many banks shifted to tax-sheltered leasing to minimize taxes. Another factor that dissuaded banks from holding municipal securities was the increased credit risk prospects (risk of default) of some issuers of state and local government securities in the 1980s.

Loans

Economists see bank lending as a means of creating money that profoundly affects the nation's economic well-being. To a commercial banker, lending is the basic business of banking. Commercial banks held more than $2 trillion in loan assets in 1992, about 65 percent of their total assets. Bank loans vary widely in terms of type of borrower, loan size, length of maturity, use of borrowed funds, repayment schedule, and degree of risk. Most banks maintain a diversified loan portfolio encompassing business and consumer loans and mortgages.

In making loans, banks do not operate on a first-come, first-served basis, nor do they wait for new deposits and make a single loan equal to their excess reserves, as in the T-account examples discussed in chapter 4. Rather, banks lend funds in accordance with predetermined loan policies designed to maximize their return on loan assets while minimizing their exposure to risk.

Large banks generally operate under formal loan policies that allow loan officers to make loans within prescribed dollar limits without clearance from higher levels of authority. A bank's loan policy is usually set by its senior management (with the approval of the board of directors) based on the bank's long-range plan for achieving business goals and objectives. Each potential loan is evaluated within the context of this loan policy as well as on its own merits. Adhering to a bankwide loan policy is not an easy task, however, because loan demand is typically uneven among a bank's broad range of business and consumer borrowers. Also, a bank may not have enough excess reserves at any given time to meet an increased demand for loans.

An examination of the major types of bank loans—business, real estate, consumer, and other—illustrates both the diversity of bank lending and some of the factors that affect this basic business of banking.

BUSINESS LOANS

Loans to businesses have traditionally been the single largest loan category on the books of most commercial banks. Today, however, they constitute about 25 percent of all commercial bank loan assets. That small proportion reflects changing business borrowing practices and, as exhibit 8.2 shows, a decline in business lending since 1989.

EXHIBIT 8.2   **Business Loans: All Commercial Banks**
(seasonally adjusted)

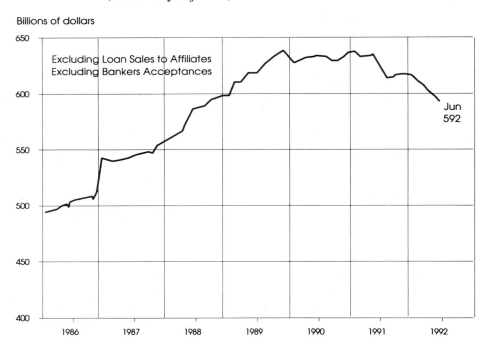

Source: Federal Reserve Bank of New York

A business loan is any loan made to an individual, partnership, or corporation (other than a financial institution or a farmer) for business or professional purposes. These loans can be single-payment or installment loans and can be either secured by collateral or unsecured. Most business loans made by banks are short-term loans, typically with a maturity of three months to one year.

Business loans usually carry low processing costs in relation to the generally large size of the loans and relatively low risk (that is, their loss incidence is low compared with losses incurred in other loan categories). In most states, business loans are not subject to usury limits (maximum interest rates that lenders can charge borrowers), and bank management has considerable flexibility in pricing them. Commercial and industrial loans are some of the lowest-yielding bank loans. To increase the profitability of these loans, many banks charge loan commitment fees or require compensating balances.

Loan Commitment Fees. A loan commitment fee is a separate service charge that a bank levies on a corporate borrower in exchange for preauthorizing a loan that will actually be made weeks or months in the future. In the 1980s, banks increasingly relied on loan commitment fees to increase their income on commercial and industrial loans. These fees eventually became a significant component of many banks' noninterest earnings.

Loan commitments, however, reduce a bank's flexibility in managing its loan portfolio. A bank can increase or decrease the dollar amount of the loans it makes by changing the interest rates it charges on loans and the noninterest terms it imposes on credit lines; loan commitments, however, may lock the bank into future loan expansion.

In making loan commitments to corporate customers, banks may not know exactly how much the corporation will be borrowing or exactly when the funds will be borrowed. Moreover, repayments of short-term business loans often are tied to the corporation's cash flow, which may vary seasonally. Although most banks carefully monitor the dollar amounts of their loan commitments, a bank that relies heavily on loan commitment fees can never be sure that on any given day it will have sufficient reserves to honor all commitments that could be exercised on that day. If banks have to borrow reserves to honor their prepaid commitments, they may find themselves paying more for funds than they are charging for the prearranged loan.

Compensating Balances. Many banks increase the profitability of their business loans by requiring compensating balances. When they do so, borrowers are required by the loan agreement to maintain deposit balances equal to a fixed percentage of the loan value. Some banks require a minimum daily balance, while others require an average daily balance during the term of the loan.

The additional income a bank can generate by investing compensating balances increases the bank's return on the loan. Compensating balances also provide a bank with added protection because the bank has priority over all other creditors with respect to the balances on deposit. If the borrower defaults on the loan, the bank can use any existing deposit balance to offset the outstanding loan balance.

The practice of requiring compensating balances, however, is far from universal. In the 1980s, banks and corporate borrowers increasingly opted for explicit fee charges to cover loan costs rather than relying on compensating balances. Corporations often find it difficult to maintain compensating balances because they must meet daily cash flow requirements.

CONSUMER LOANS   *include credit cards*

A consumer loan is a loan made to an individual (other than a farmer) for a personal expenditure other than the purchase of real estate or securities. Today, consumer loans constitute about 20 percent of commercial banks' loan assets. Most consumer loans are short-term installment loans that require partial repayments at predetermined time intervals—monthly payments, for example. A considerable portion of bank consumer lending is in the form of credit extended on bank credit cards. Because repayment of principal and interest is typically made on a scheduled basis, most consumer loans generate a predictable cash flow return to the lending bank.

Some banks book consumer installment loans as *discount loans* to provide an immediate cash flow return. In a discount loan, the bank deducts the interest due on the loan from the proceeds given the borrower at the time the loan is made.

Processing costs for consumer loans tend to be high in relation to their small size. Also, because consumer loan rates are subject to usury ceilings in many states, consumer loans become increasingly less profitable for banks whenever market interest rates rise above these ceilings. In addition, consumer loans carry relatively greater credit risk than other loans and are subject to numerous consumer protection regulations, some of which require extensive and costly recordkeeping. The Federal Reserve's Regulation B, for example, prohibits a bank from discriminating in its lending policies on the basis of age, race, color, national origin, religion, sex, marital status, or receipt of income from welfare programs. Regulation Z requires banks to meet certain standards in advertising their credit services, to make full disclosures of the actual cost of each loan, and to answer customer complaints within a specified period.

REAL ESTATE LOANS

Any loan secured by a mortgage, a deed of trust, or some other recorded lien on real estate (in which the bank can take title to the property if the terms of the loan are not met) is classified as a real estate loan. Whereas most bank loans are classified according to their intended purpose (such as commercial and industrial, consumer, and agricultural loans), mortgage loans are an exception in that they are classified by the type of collateral involved (real estate).

Real estate loans, like consumer loans, generate a predictable cash flow to lending banks, but earnings yields on real estate loans are typically lower than yields on most other loans. In the past, real estate loans were the lowest-risk loans a bank could make because they were fully collateralized by property that appreciated while the principal was repaid, thus reducing the bank's credit risk exposure. Banks' experience with commercial real estate loans in the 1980s, however, has raised doubts about the validity of this long-standing banking premise. Many banks took losses on commercial real estate loans when borrowers defaulted and banks found that the market values of the properties collateralizing the loans were less than the amount of the outstanding loans.

State usury ceilings made real estate loans unattractive to banks in the late 1970s and early 1980s because high market interest rates exceeded the maximum rates banks could charge on residential mortgages. However, the sharp decline in market interest rates in the mid-1980s helped bring down residential mortgage rates to their lowest levels in a decade and triggered a spate of home buying and mortgage refinancing. In the late 1980s and early 1990s, banks' mortgage lending soared as mortgage rates declined again and banks increasingly filled the mortgage market void created by the closing of large numbers of insolvent S&Ls and the flight of anxious depositors from sound S&Ls. By 1992, real estate loans accounted for 45 percent of bank lending.

Since the late 1970s, the residential mortgage policies of all banks have had to conform to the Community Reinvestment Act of 1977. This federal legislation (which is discussed in more detail in chapter 9) sought to address allegations that some banks in the nation's major cities were redlining—that is, excluding certain areas of the city from eligibility for mortgage loans without regard to the merits or creditworthiness of each mortgage applicant.

OTHER LOANS

Depending upon a bank's location and its size, other types of loans may play a significant part in a bank's business. These loans may include

- ❑ agricultural loans
- ❑ loans to securities brokers and dealers
- ❑ loans to individuals for the purchase of stocks and bonds
- ❑ loan participations

For banks in the Midwest and the South, agricultural loans provide a significant source of income. Any loan made to a farmer or rancher for any purpose associated with operating a farm or ranch is considered an agricultural loan.

For large banks in New York, Chicago, and San Francisco, loans to securities brokers and dealers and to other financial institutions are more common. Those loans are generally made to enable brokers and dealers to buy securities for their own account or for their customers. High-grade securities typically secure these very short-term loans, which bear relatively low interest rates.

Some banks make loans to enable individuals to purchase stocks and bonds. Banks that make loans of that type must obtain a statement from borrowers as to the purpose of the loan proceeds in order to determine whether the loan is subject to the Federal Reserve's Regulation U (which limits the amount of credit that a bank can extend to an individual to purchase corporate stock when the stock serves as collateral for the loan).

Banks often participate in loans that are too large for them to absorb individually. A loan participation is the sharing of a loan by two or more banks. By spreading the loan among several banks, each bank commits less of its reserves and also reduces its own risk. Banks also participate in loans that may be too large for them to assume legally on their own. The lending limit for a single loan for nationally chartered banks, for example, is an amount no greater than 15 percent of the bank's capital and surplus

(25 percent if the loan is fully secured). This limit was raised from 10 percent by the Garn-St Germain Act of 1982. Correspondent banks also typically participate in large business loans made by their respondents to diversify their portfolios and to share in good loans (if they have excess reserves) as part of their correspondent banking relationships.

OTHER ASSETS

The last category of assets on the banking system's balance sheet is *other assets*. Other bank assets include

- ☐ small holdings of non-government-related debt obligations, primarily corporate bonds and stock. Under the Banking Act of 1933, banks are not permitted to purchase corporate stock and most corporate bonds for their own accounts. There are, however, some corporate obligations that banks are permitted by law to hold. In addition, banks may legally own stocks and bonds, for a limited time, which are acquired as a result of a defaulted loan secured by stocks and bonds. Moreover, banks may still own corporate stocks and bonds purchased before enactment of the Banking Act of 1933. Some banks also have minor investments in foreign securities.
- ☐ banks that are members of the Federal Reserve own Federal Reserve bank stock. Member banks must purchase stock in their district Federal Reserve bank in an amount equal to 3 percent of their own capital and surplus (with an additional 3 percent subject to call by the Federal Reserve). Banks that hold Federal Reserve bank stock receive a statutory 6 percent annual dividend on these securities.
- ☐ fixed assets (a bank's buildings and equipment).
- ☐ accrued income receivable (interest earned on loans and investments but not yet collected).

Liabilities and Capital

We turn now from the asset side of the banking system's balance sheet to the liabilities and capital side (refer again to exhibit 8.1). We see that deposits make up about 75 percent of banks' liabilities. The capital account represents a bank's liabilities to its owners.

TRANSACTION DEPOSITS

The first category of deposits on the banking system's balance sheet is transaction deposits. This includes both demand deposits, the traditional transaction deposits of banks, and newer types of checkable deposits such as NOW accounts. Together they account for about 20 percent of banks' liabilities.

Demand deposits have long been considered the most stable and least expensive source of bank funds. They are stable because checking account holders typically do not switch accounts from one bank to another, and they are inexpensive because, since

1933, banks have not been allowed to pay interest on checking accounts. For these reasons, bankers refer to checking account deposits as *relationship deposits*. Funds flow to a bank because a customer chooses to maintain a relationship with that bank (often because the bank is conveniently located) and wants a checking account to make payments.

Demand deposits began to decline as an important source of bank funds in the 1970s because, for one reason, banks began marketing sophisticated cash management services to corporations that held large demand deposit balances. With a cash management service, banks invest end-of-day demand deposit balances overnight to generate investment returns for corporate accounts. These investment vehicles include repurchase agreements, commercial paper, and Eurodollars.

In the late 1970s and 1980s, demand deposit totals at banks also declined as consumers began to switch funds from non-interest-earning demand accounts into interest-earning checkable accounts such as NOW accounts, automatic transfer service accounts, and money market deposit accounts. In 1992, demand deposits accounted for less than 10 percent of total bank liabilities.

The total amount of demand deposits outstanding on a bank's books is only a gross measure of the investment funds available to the bank from demand deposits. Some portion of a bank's demand deposit balance is always unavailable funds; that is, some funds deposited by check are always in the process of collection from the banks on which the funds are drawn. Banks also maintain deposits with other banks to facilitate transactions from customers, to compensate for services obtained from correspondents, and to serve as reserve deposits. When these bank-owned deposits, plus cash items in the process of collection (which are carried on a bank's books as assets), are subtracted from a bank's demand deposits total, the resulting figure is termed *net demand deposits*. That figure more closely approximates the investable portion of funds obtained through demand deposits.

TIME AND SAVINGS DEPOSITS   50% liabilities

A bank's balance sheet usually groups major types of time and savings deposits. We see from exhibit 8.1 that time and savings deposits constitute more than half the banking system's total liabilities. In chapter 3 we examined the various types of time and savings deposits offered by banks, including passbook savings accounts, money market deposit accounts, savings certificates, and IRAs and other retirement accounts (all of which attract consumer deposits), and large-denomination certificates of deposit (which are primarily used by businesses).

Like demand deposits, consumer time and savings deposits at commercial banks have traditionally been viewed as relationship deposits—that is, they were seen as a relatively stable source of bank funds. Until 1984, consumers who maintained savings and time accounts at commercial banks gave up the opportunity to earn more on their funds at a savings bank or savings and loan association that could pay higher interest rates under Regulation Q. Apparently, these consumers were motivated by factors other than rate of return—the convenience, for example, of having both a savings and a checking account at the same bank.

The phaseout of Regulation Q ceilings between 1980 and 1986 permitted banks to offer new types and maturities of consumer-oriented time deposits and to pay market interest rates on the funds. However, the elimination of interest rate ceilings also introduced a degree of instability in time and savings deposits as a source of bank funds. In the 1980s, most banks were forced to compete aggressively with other banks, thrifts, and other financial intermediaries for new types of deposits, especially savings certificates and money market deposit accounts.

Consumers responded with remarkable sensitivity to interest rate differences and changing rates of return. They demonstrated not only a willingness to move funds from traditional time and savings accounts into higher-yielding savings certificates at their banks, but also a willingness to transfer savings funds out of banks into higher-paying Treasury bills and money market funds. Then, as market conditions continued to change, banks saw many consumers transfer monies from maturing money market instruments back into money market deposit accounts at banks.

BORROWINGS

Another category of liabilities on a bank's balance sheet is borrowings. As exhibit 8.1 shows, borrowed funds constituted less than 5 percent of the banking system's total liabilities in 1992. The major sources of borrowings for banks are federal funds, repurchase agreements, and funds borrowed from a Federal Reserve bank.

Banks typically buy federal funds from one another to meet reserve requirements, honor loan commitments, or offset unexpected reserve drains. Immediately available funds that are obtained for more than one day are referred to as *term federal funds*. A repurchase agreement allows a bank to sell securities and then repurchase them, generally a day or two later, at a predetermined price. Banks also can borrow funds from Federal Reserve banks—a practice known as discount window borrowing.

Other Liabilities

Bank liabilities other than deposits and borrowed funds include various payables and contingency reserves. Payables are funds set aside to pay taxes, interest on deposits, and such other expenses as salaries and dividends. Banks also carry reserves to cover loan losses and unearned loan income as liabilities.

Loan Loss Reserves. Reserves that banks carry to cover expected but undetermined losses from borrowers who are likely to default on their loans are included as *other liabilities* on their books. These reserves are variously referred to as charge-offs, valuation reserves, or reserves for bad-debt losses. The bank regulatory agencies require banks to set aside funds for possible loan

(Continued from previous page)

losses, and state and federal bank examiners routinely review each bank's loss reserves in light of each outstanding loan. If examiners consider a loan to be uncollectible, the examiners can require the bank to charge off the loan to the loan loss reserve.

Banks routinely evaluate their loans, classifying them in the same manner as examiners do (categorizing bad loans as *watch list*, *substandard*, *doubtful*, and *loss*). Many banks reserve for possible losses against these bad loans by setting aside each month a portion of operating profits in anticipation of the actual charge-off. These banks often will charge off bad debts prior to examination since this is a sign to regulators of a well-managed institution.

Unearned Income. Banks also register on their books as *other liabilities* a separate posting of all unearned income—that is, any prepaid interest received on loans. Because unearned income is routinely recorded on a bank's books in each loan category as well, the separate unearned income posting, like loan loss reserves, must be subtracted from a bank's total loans to obtain a net measure of a bank's loan portfolio.

CAPITAL ACCOUNT

The last item on a bank's balance sheet, again as seen in exhibit 8.1, is its capital account. A bank's capital account consists of equity (stock) issued by the bank, its surplus (capital funds not yet allocated), and undistributed profits. Capital provides a bank with a protective cushion against bad loans and bad investments. Thus, a bank with adequate capital is capable of handling riskier transactions than a bank with inadequate capital. The more capital a bank has, the greater the protection the bank provides to its stockholders and creditors. Under federal banking regulations, a bank's capital account also determines the maximum-size loan that can be made to any one borrower.

Like any other business, a bank must earn an adequate return on its capital in order to encourage future stockholder investment. Banks, however, typically have less capital in relation to assets than most other businesses. In 1992, the capital of all U.S. banks totaled only 7 percent of the banking system's total assets. As seen in exhibit 8.3, however, the amount of capital held by banks varies by size, with smaller banks typically holding higher percentages of capital than larger banks.

To improve capital adequacy, many banks issue subordinated capital notes and debentures (types of debt instruments) instead of new voting stock. By relying on debt capital, the issuing bank avoids diluting its earnings or management's current control over the bank. In addition, banks can deduct interest paid on capital notes and debentures from pre-tax earnings, which provides a considerable tax advantage. In contrast, dividends on preferred and common stock are paid from after-tax earnings.

EXHIBIT 8.3   **Capital-to-Asset Ratios**

		For Commercial Banks with Assets of:					
Year	All Banks	$20-$25 million	$25-$50 million	$50-$100 million	$100-$500 million	$500 million-$1 billion	$1 billion +
1987	6.06	9.37	8.59	8.21	7.39	6.77	5.27
1988	6.17	9.41	8.82	8.44	7.56	6.72	5.43
1989	6.34	9.71	8.98	8.66	7.68	6.94	6.65
1990	6.36	9.95	9.06	8.73	7.80	7.39	5.64
1991	6.68	9.95	9.20	8.83	7.92	7.17	6.04

Source: Federal Reserve Bank of Atlanta, *Economic Review,* May/June 1992.

Income Statement Analysis

Unlike a balance sheet, which tallies a bank's assets and liabilities at a point in time, an income statement shows a bank's profit or loss over a period of time, usually a quarter or a year. An analysis of a bank's income statement can provide insight into how well a bank is performing as a business firm. Exhibit 8.4 is an income statement for the commercial banking system, showing the various sources of bank earnings and expenses. A bank's income is categorized as interest income and non-interest income, while its expenses are either interest-related expenses or operating expenses.

EXHIBIT 8.4   Income Statement for the Commercial Banking System

	Amount (billions)	Percentage of Total
Interest Income		
Interest on loans	$207	61
Interest on securities	56	16
Interest on deposits with other banks	9	3
Federal funds sold	9	3
Noninterest Income		
Service charges on deposits	13	4
Other operating income	44	13
Total income	$338	100%
Interest Expenses		
Interest on time and savings deposits	135	48
Federal funds bought	14	5
Other borrowed funds	14	5
Noninterest Expenses		
Salaries and benefits	52	18
Occupancy expenses	17	6
Other operating expenses (includes deposit insurance premiums)	52	18
Total expenses	$284	100%
Loan loss provisions	$32	
Securities gains	$3	
Income before taxes and after securities gains and losses	$25	
Net income	$18	

Note: The figures shown are based on 1991 data.

Net Interest Income

Interest received from loans is the largest source of bank revenue. Lesser amounts of interest revenue derive from investment income, interest on federal funds, and interest on deposits maintained in other banks. Net interest income is a bank's gross interest revenue minus its interest expense (primarily interest paid on deposits).

Since interest income can be either taxable or tax exempt, the income total is adjusted for analytical purposes so that revenue from tax-exempt securities is reflected in taxable form. In this way, each dollar of interest revenue is made equal on a pretax basis.

Interest revenue is attributable to a bank's earning assets, while interest expense is attributable to its interest-bearing liabilities (primarily time and savings deposits). A bank's net interest income reflects both the size of the bank's earning assets and the bank's interest rate spread. A bank's interest rate spread can be calculated by taking the bank's net interest income as a percentage of its earning assets during a given time period.

Noninterest Income

A bank's noninterest income—consisting primarily of bank fees and commissions—is small compared to its interest income. Principal sources of noninterest income include service charges on demand deposit accounts, trading account profits and commissions (as distinct from interest earned on trading account securities), trust department fees, foreign exchange trading profits, and fees for loan commitments and standby letters of credit.

Noninterest Expenses

Banks categorize their noninterest expenses separately from their interest expenses. Noninterest expenses include salaries and other personnel expenses, occupancy and equipment expenses, and other operating expenses, such as deposit insurance premiums that must be paid to the Federal Deposit Insurance Corporation (FDIC).

As exhibit 8.5 shows, banks' interest and noninterest income growth surged in the late 1980s and then slowed dramatically in the early 1990s, while noninterest expenses continued to increase steadily by about 7 percent per year. The sharp slowdown in income growth largely reflects smaller interest income from declining commercial bank lending to business firms. The steadiness of expense growth primarily reflects continuing increases in employee benefits costs and deposit insurance premiums. In the 1990s, bankers were looking increasingly to fee income as a way to boost revenues, and to aggressive cutting of support and overhead costs as ways to slow operating expense growth.

EXHIBIT 8.5   Annual Growth of Commercial Bank Revenue and Operating Expenses

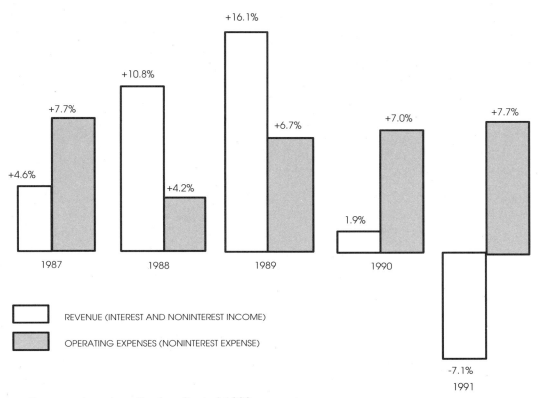

REVENUE (INTEREST AND NONINTEREST INCOME)

OPERATING EXPENSES (NONINTEREST EXPENSE)

Source: American Banker, Sept. 4, 1992.

Net Income

Net income is the so-called bottom line of any income statement. For banks, net income is calculated by first adding all interest and noninterest income and then subtracting all interest expenses, noninterest expenses, and loan loss provisions (funds set aside to cover likely losses on defaulted loans). It also takes into account income taxes and any securities losses or gains (after-tax capital gains or losses arising from a bank's sale of investment securities). Because the timing of securities sales is discretionary, securities profits or losses can provide an important clue to a bank's performance. Securities losses, for example, can be a significant drain on capital, and the existence of such losses may lead a financial analyst to question the quality of a bank's asset/liability management.

PROFITABILITY

Bank profitability is generally assessed in terms of a bank's *return on assets* (ROA)—a measure of net income as a percentage of total assets—and a bank's *return on equity* (ROE)—a measure of net income as a percentage of equity.

In the 1980s, profitability for most banks declined. Bank interest costs increased disproportionately to income as banks paid interest on an increasingly large share of their total deposits. Many banks also incurred losses on their securities holdings in the early 1980s and on their loans throughout the decade. Increased amounts of loan loss reserves were set aside to cover probable but undetermined losses on loans, particularly by banks with large portfolios of agricultural loans, energy loans, commercial real estate loans, and loans to less-developed countries (LDC loans).

The nation's largest banks experienced the sharpest rise in interest costs because of their heavy reliance on rate-sensitive purchased funds. They also experienced the largest loan losses because of the size of their LDC loans (and the need for increased loan loss provisions). Small banks saw interest costs rise because holders of checking accounts increasingly shifted their demand deposits into interest-bearing transaction accounts and because holders of time deposits increasingly transferred their fixed-rate time deposits into higher-yielding money market deposit accounts. Many small banks in farming states saw profits plummet as increasing numbers of agricultural borrowers defaulted on their loans.

The early 1990s brought some improvement in banks' profitability. Interest expenses declined substantially as banks reduced interest rates paid on time and savings deposits in response to weak loan demand and the general decline in short-term interest rates. Banks also took substantial capital gains on securities purchased earlier and sold in 1991 and 1992. However, banks also saw a surge in noninterest expenses. Sharp increases in FDIC insurance premiums imposed on banks were one source of the surge. Banks saw premiums increase from $0.12 per $100 of insured deposits in 1990 to $0.23 in 1992. Another source—particularly for large banks in the Northeast and Middle Atlantic states—were increases in loan loss reserves that banks had to set aside because of borrowers' deteriorating loan repayment prospects in the wake of the economy's sluggish recovery from the 1990-1991 recession.

Key Performance Ratios

Bank analysts consider an ROA of 1 percent and an ROE of 15 percent to be the standards for good bank profitability performance. As seen in exhibits 8.6 and 8.7, in 1991 the nation's banks registered an average ROA of 0.55 percent and an average ROE of 8.2 percent. However, in assessing a bank's performance, analysts and bankers generally rely on peer group comparison of ROA and ROE as well as other key performance measures. Some of these other measures are

- ❏ net interest margin (interest revenue minus interest expense)
- ❏ rate of return on securities and loans
- ❏ capital account as a percentage of total assets

❏ time and savings deposits as a percentage of total deposits

❏ average interest rate paid on total time and savings deposits

In making a peer group comparison, performance measures for a bank are compared with the averages for banks of like asset size and like customer base to assess relative performance. This analysis is more meaningful than a comparison of one bank against the banking system as a whole. Business markets and competitive forces differ too significantly for banks of widely disparate size to make relevant comparisons. For example, comparing the performance of a community-based bank with less than $25 million in assets against the performance of a money center bank with $1 billion in assets and several foreign branches would not prove meaningful. Exhibits 8.6 and 8.7 show banks' ROA and ROE within their relevant size peer group.

Income statement analysis is a useful tool for assessing bank performance, but because banking is a management-intensive industry, it is often the strength of management and not operating ratios that determines long-term bank performance. Analysts usually supplement statistical comparisons with qualitative assessments of bank management before making judgments concerning a bank's asset/liability management strategy or financial condition.

EXHIBIT 8.6   **Return on Assets (ROA)**

Avg .55 percent

Year	All Banks Average	$0-$25 million	$25-$50 million	$50-$100 million	$100-$500 $1 million	$500 million- $1 billion	$1 billion+
		For Commercial Banks with Assets of:					
1987	0.09	0.26	0.46	0.66	0.73	0.51	-0.15
1988	0.83	0.36	0.61	0.77	0.80	0.58	0.89
1989	0.50	0.60	0.73	0.88	0.91	0.88	0.35
1990	0.50	0.60	0.71	0.81	0.79	0.77	0.39
1991	0.55	0.64	0.75	0.86	0.85	0.56	0.45

Source: Federal Reserve Bank of Atlanta, *Economic Review*, May/June 1992.

EXHIBIT 8.7   **Return on Equity (ROE)**

Year	All Banks Average	For Commercial Banks with Assets of:					
		$0-$25 million	$25-$50 million	$50-$100 million	$100-$500 million	$500 million- $1 billion	$1 billion+
1987	1.49	2.75	5.39	8.02	9.93	7.51	-2.80
1988	13.51	3.79	6.96	9.15	10.53	8.67	16.40
1989	7.85	6.15	8.14	10.12	11.81	12.72	6.21
1990	7.81	6.02	7.81	9.29	10.14	10.37	6.86
1991	8.21	6.46	8.10	9.68	10.78	7.85	7.49

Source: Federal Reserve Bank of Atlanta, *Economic Review*, May/June 1992.

Asset/Liability Management

In recent years banks have become much more aggressive in their pursuit of profits through the active management of bank funds. Increasingly, bank earnings are determined by management proficiency in continually adjusting the bank's assets and liabilities (its sources and uses of funds).

Until the 1960s, bank funds management was largely passive. Bankers operated under the assumption that a bank's earning assets (its loans and investments) had to be financed with demand deposits of corporations and time deposits of individuals. They assumed that only by taking in additional deposits could reserves be acquired that would allow for more loans and investments. Since banks had little control over the level of their deposits—their primary source of funds—sound bank management dictated that banks had to maintain substantial liquidity in the form of primary reserves (cash assets) and secondary reserves (highly liquid, short-term securities). To the extent that excess funds were available, business loans were the primary use of these funds. Bank profits then equaled the difference between the stable interest rates banks paid on core deposits (maximum rates were fixed by law and regulation), and the slightly higher but equally stable interest rates banks charged to borrowers.

In the 1960s and 1970s, the management of bank funds was revolutionized when bankers began focusing on liabilities—meeting demands for new loans by buying or borrowing needed funds. This approach, called liability management, requires bankers to carefully evaluate and use a balanced blend of sources of funds over which they have complete control, such as federal funds, large-denomination corporate certificates of deposit, repurchase agreements, and Eurodollar borrowings. These types of liabilities are also called *managed liabilities.*

The approach to managing bank funds changed focus again in the 1980s. The Monetary Control Act restructured and simplified reserve requirements early in the decade, and Regulation Q ceilings were eliminated in 1986. At the same time, interest-bearing transaction accounts were introduced, which significantly altered the public's deposit practices. As a result, banks no longer rely on stable demand deposits and consumer time and savings deposits as guaranteed sources of funds.

Banks developed new funds management strategies in the 1980s as the spread narrowed between the interest rates banks paid for funds and the interest rates they earned on loans and investments. These strategies included attempts to match assets and liabilities by maturity and duration, and attempts to maintain balanced or favorable repricing gaps in the timing of maturing assets and liabilities.

Many factors influence the precise strategy a bank follows to obtain and use funds. These factors include the bank's size, business orientation, market, and number of branches. Underlying any funds management strategy, however, is a bank's need for excess reserves to expand loans and investments. And whatever strategy is adopted, bankers must abide by the constraints of the bank's liquidity needs and reserve requirements, as well as the general impact of monetary policy on the cost and availability of reserves. In addition, all banks must contend with the strategies of competitors as they manage their own assets and liabilities and pursue their own business goals. Ultimately, however, a bank's funds strategy is determined by the judgment of bank management. We will look briefly at the funds management options most often chosen by banks.

Asset Allocation Strategy

With an asset allocation strategy, a bank seeks to expand earnings by continually reallocating funds between loan and investment assets. Before any funds are allocated, however, the bank must meet its operating expenses and provide for those fixed assets (buildings and equipment) necessary to conduct the bank's business. Thereafter, funds are allocated into the following four categories in descending order of priority:

- ☐ primary reserves
- ☐ secondary reserves
- ☐ income account
- ☐ residual account

The first allocation of funds is to primary reserves—vault cash and account balances with the district Federal Reserve bank and correspondent banks—to meet reserve requirements and the bank's day-to-day liquidity needs.

The next allocation, to secondary reserves, is based on the bank's forecasted loan and deposit growth over the coming year. Funds are invested in secondary reserve assets of differing maturities—primarily Treasury securities—based on this forecast. Ideally, the bank's secondary reserve assets will mature just as the bank needs funds to meet loan demand or to cover deposit outflows.

After allocations have been made to primary and secondary reserves, any remaining funds are used to meet loan demand. The bank's loan portfolio is, effectively, its income account. If, after all loan demand has been met, there are residual funds, they are invested in long-term Treasury, federal agency, and state and local securities. These securities holdings comprise the bank's residual account.

Under an asset allocation strategy, banks buy securities when loan demand is soft and interest rates are low. When loan demand builds, banks sell securities to raise funds to meet loan demand. However, rising interest rates usually accompany strong loan demand, and when interest rates rise, banks take capital losses as they sell securities. Taking capital losses makes sense as long as the bank can more than offset its losses with interest earnings on loans made using the funds obtained through the sale of the securities. (Taking capital losses may also make sense if they can be used as a tax offset to shelter other income.)

Liability Management Strategy

Another widely used funds management strategy is based not on a bank's assets but on its liabilities. Banks that use a liability management strategy fund loan and investment growth by borrowing or buying money. In order to accommodate desired increases in earning assets, banks try to manage increases in their liabilities by drawing on financial instruments and utilizing market practices that they can control. Liability management typically entails borrowing federal funds, issuing negotiable certificates of deposit, borrowing Eurodollars, using the proceeds of commercial paper sold by affiliates, and engaging in repurchase agreements. A brief discussion of the major types of managed liabilities (funds that are subject to management discretion) follows.

FEDERAL FUNDS

Borrowing federal funds is part of the liability management strategy of many banks. As noted previously, federal funds are immediately available funds that banks borrow (buy) from and lend (sell) to each other for one business day. Most money market banks prepare early-morning estimates of their expected reserve positions for that day and, on the basis of those estimates, adjust their reserves with daily purchases or sales of federal funds. The money market banks in New York City typically are at the vortex of the federal funds market, buying reserves from regional and small community-based banks and channeling those funds to their own broker, dealer, or multinational customers.

Because banks use the federal funds market so extensively as a source of funds for adjusting reserve positions, market conditions are generally a key barometer of monetary policy. Indeed, because the cost of federal funds—the federal funds rate—is so keenly sensitive to shifts in the demand for and supply of reserves in the banking system, the Federal Reserve uses the federal funds rate as an operational target for its open-market operations.

The Federal Funds Market

The use of federal funds as a key component of bank liability management strategy began in the 1960s when the Federal Reserve changed its reserve requirement rules and allowed banks to count vault cash as part of their reserves. This increased the amount of reserves available for purchase or sale. In addition, the Federal Reserve refused to open its discount window routinely to supply banks with additional reserves. Then, in 1963, the Comptroller of the Currency ruled that nationally chartered banks could post federal funds transactions as purchases and sales, not as borrowings and loans—a ruling that removed federal funds transactions from federal restrictions governing how much money a bank could lend to a single borrower.

Throughout the 1960s, banks became increasingly sophisticated in reducing the level of their excess reserve balances. In 1960, commercial banks that were members of the Federal Reserve held, on daily average, an amount of excess reserves equal to 4 percent of their required reserves; by 1970, the daily average had fallen to less than 1 percent. During the 1960s, strong competition emerged among the money market banks for correspondent banking business. To improve their competitiveness, these banks began to develop trading positions in federal funds in order to provide a new service to their respondent banks—the buying and selling of immediately available funds.

NEGOTIABLE CERTIFICATES OF DEPOSIT (CDS)

Another part of the liability management strategy of most large banks is issuing negotiable CDs. As discussed in chapter 4, a negotiable certificate of deposit is an instrument that represents an interest-paying deposit balance of at least $100,000, payable to whoever holds the instrument at maturity (the initial depositor can sell the certificate in the secondary market).

Large-denomination negotiable CDs dominate the liability structure of most of the nation's large commercial banks. In 1992, the largest U.S. banks (those with assets in excess of $1.4 billion) held about $150 billion in these CDs.

Large banks use CDs as an integral part of their liability management strategy. When loan demand begins to build, these banks aggressively bid for CD depositors. The bidding continues as long as banks can earn more on loans than they have to pay to attract CD deposits. When loan demand begins to slow, banks allow existing CDs to mature and be withdrawn, and they reduce their marketing efforts among corporations. Banks typically will lower their CD rates as loan demand and loan charges (interest rates) begin to fall.

The Origin of the Negotiable CD

The negotiable CD was invented in 1961 by Citibank (then First National City Bank of New York) as a way to enable corporations to obtain an interest return on their demand deposits. At that time, Regulation Q not only prohibited banks from paying interest on demand deposits but also specified that interest-earning time deposits (CDs) had to have minimum maturities of 30 days. The negotiable CD offered banks a way to convert high reserve requirement demand deposits into lower reserve requirement time deposits while providing an interest return to holders.

Citibank developed a secondary market for CDs by gaining the support of a major government securities dealer firm that agreed to buy or sell existing CDs to enable corporations to get their money back without having to wait 30 days. A corporation that had to meet a multimillion dollar payroll on the 15th of the month, for example, could buy a CD on the 1st of the month, then sell it in the secondary market on the 14th, in time to cover its payroll checks. The corporation would receive the equivalent of 14 days' worth of interest on its money, reflected in the sale price of the CD; the purchaser, perhaps another corporation seeking a return on two-week money, would receive 16 days' worth of interest when the CD matured on day 30.

EURODOLLAR BORROWINGS

Borrowing Eurodollars is another part of the liability management strategy of many large banks. Eurodollars are dollar-denominated deposits on the books of banking offices outside the United States that large U.S. banks with overseas branches often draw upon to obtain reserves. When the head office of a U.S. bank wants to borrow funds from its overseas branch, it typically instructs the branch to bid for Eurodollar deposits. Since overseas deposits are not subject to reserve requirements and FDIC insurance premiums, an overseas branch office can usually afford to pay a slightly higher rate to attract funds than its U.S. head office. Generally, Eurodollar depositors are corporations with accounts at U.S. banks.

When the overseas branch buys the Eurodollar funds, it instructs the sellers to have their banks in the United States pay the dollars directly to the buying branch's head office in the United States. When the head office receives the transferred funds, they are recorded on the books as assets *due from* the bank's own foreign branch. The head office records the corresponding liabilities as liabilities *due to* its own foreign branch and not as deposits.

Until 1969, *due to* Eurodollar liabilities were not subject to reserve requirements. Thus, a bank borrowing Eurodollar funds to increase its reserve accounts could make full use of the funds without having to hold a fraction of them as required reserves against outstanding deposit liabilities. The overall level of Eurodollar borrowings diminished in the 1970s and 1980s because new regulations required banks to maintain a 3 percent reserve requirement against their Eurodollar borrowings. The Federal Reserve eliminated the requirement in 1990 in an effort to stimulate bank lending by increasing excess reserves and making Eurodollar borrowings attractive again as a ready—and less expensive—source of additional reserves.

Because a bank has to have access to an overseas bank in order to borrow Eurodollars, competition for Eurodollars is generally not as strong as for domestic sources of funds. Nevertheless, large money center banks that have ready access to the Eurodollar market frequently use Eurodollar borrowings for overnight and weekend funding arrangements. Unlike the CD market, the Eurodollar market is essentially an overnight market with interest rates that are subject to larger and more frequent changes.

COMMERCIAL PAPER SALES OF BANK AFFILIATES

Another part of the liability management strategy of some banks involves using the proceeds of commercial paper issued by a bank's affiliates. Commercial paper consists of short-term unsecured (uncollateralized) promissory notes issued by corporations—generally those with very solid credit ratings—as a means of borrowing funds for a limited period from purchasers of the paper.

Although banks are not permitted to issue commercial paper, many banks are owned by holding companies that can. The issuance of commercial paper by a bank holding company can benefit the bank in one of two ways. The holding company can deposit the proceeds from its commercial paper sales in the bank, thereby increasing the bank's funds. Since these funds are classified as borrowed funds rather than deposits, they are not insured and are not subject to FDIC insurance premiums or reserve requirements. Thus, every dollar received by the bank from sales of commercial paper can be used to support an additional dollar of new loans. The holding company also can use the proceeds from the commercial paper offering to purchase loans or investments from the bank, thereby improving the bank's overall earning asset position.

Since the bank subsidiary is usually a bank holding company's major investment or asset, commercial paper issued by a bank holding company is generally considered by investors to be of high quality and is perceived to be secured by the implicit backing (assets) of the bank itself. Because commercial paper is unsecured and is subject to greater market risk, the interest rates offered on commercial paper generally exceed the interest rates that banks themselves pay on time deposits of equivalent maturity. For some bank holding companies, the combination of a strong bank implicitly backing the paper plus a high interest rate makes their commercial paper easily salable. Although it is not an available source of funds for all banks, commercial paper has become an important source of short-term money for many banks.

REPURCHASE AGREEMENTS

Another part of many banks' liability management strategy involves the use of repurchase agreements. Under a repurchase agreement (also known as an RP or repo), a bank sells government securities from its own portfolio with a promise to buy the securities back at a higher price after a short time, usually a few days. The repurchase agreement usually is posted on the bank's books as an uninsured liability of the bank to the purchaser.

Because repos are not subject to reserve requirements, banks can pay an attractive interest return on them and still profit because they can convert all their newly freed reserves into earning assets. Repos are an integral part of modern liability management strategy. They also have become essential to the cash management programs that many banks market to corporations, state and local governments, and some individual accounts. Under these programs, corporations, municipalities, and individuals that typically have daily idle funds enter into continuing or long-term repo contracts with their banks. Repos are by far the most popular overnight investment vehicle offered by banks because of the ease with which they may be accessed by cash management bank customers.

OTHER SOURCES OF PURCHASED FUNDS

Some banks use purchases of term federal funds and loans sold under repurchase agreements as part of their liability management strategy. However, use of these two sources of funds has never really emerged as a significant and widespread bank liability management tactic.

Term federal funds are federal funds that have a maturity of more than one day—typically two days to one year. In 1978, the Comptroller of the Currency ruled that these funds, because their maturity exceeded one day, were subject to the lending limit for any one borrower that nationally chartered banks must adhere to—at that time, 10 percent (since raised to 15 percent) of a bank's capital stock and surplus. That ruling substantially dampened banks' broader use of this source of funds.

Banks first began to sell loans under repurchase agreements in 1969. However, unlike other repos, loan repos are not exempt from reserve requirements because the Federal Reserve classifies them as reservable deposits. Loans sold under repos also are subject to the lending limits for any one borrower that apply to nationally chartered banks.

Borrowing funds from the Federal Reserve is another source of funds available to banks. Most banks, however, do not use that source of funds routinely as part of their liability management strategy. Over the decades the Federal Reserve has come to see its lending as a safety valve—a way of easing pressure on banks least able to cope with short-term asset or liability adjustments during tight money periods. Thus, the Fed discourages banks from using the discount window as a source of low-cost funds to expand their earning assets.

Spread Management Strategy

Besides asset allocation and liability management strategies, another approach to funds management used by many banks focuses on interest rate spread. Because banks typically take in deposits and make loans at different times, increases or decreases in interest rates can place a bank in a position of paying higher interest on deposits than the interest it is earning on loans and investments. Banks that practice spread management strategy attempt to protect themselves from falling into such a position by maintaining a constant difference (or margin) between the average interest rate they pay for funds and the average interest rate they receive on funds loaned and invested.

The premise of spread management is that banks cannot consistently and accurately forecast interest rate changes and cannot restructure their balance sheets quickly enough to match interest-rate changes. Recognizing these limitations, spread management strategy requires banks to hedge against fluctuations in interest rates. That is, banks must maintain a close balance between what they pay for funds and what they charge for funds. If they achieve balance, the bank's spread will be stable. As market interest rates rise, both the bank's cost of funds and its return on invested and loaned funds will increase proportionally. As market rates decline, both costs and returns will fall in tandem.

Achieving balance is not easy, however, because a bank's interest-rate-sensitive assets, such as commercial and industrial loans, and its interest-rate-sensitive liabilities, such as corporate certificates of deposit and federal funds borrowed, are seldom equally and proportionally responsive to changes in interest rates. For example, in a market of rising interest rates, a bank may have to pay more for borrowed funds. If it cannot readily increase the return on its interest-sensitive assets to offset the increased cost of those borrowings, the bank's spread will decline.

If a bank's balance sheet were perfectly matched—that is, if the timing and amount of its deposits and loan repayments perfectly matched its withdrawals and new loans— there would be no concern about changes in interest rates. It could simply raise or lower the rates it charged to reflect the rates it paid.

Such perfect matching of funds flows, however, is not feasible. Borrowers' scheduled repayments tend not to match the withdrawal patterns of depositors. If banks tried to force borrowers to tailor their loan requests to the payment patterns of depositors, banks would lose business. Nonetheless, tactics to implement spread management emerged in the 1980s when bankers sought to more effectively match or balance their bank's assets and liabilities. These tactics include maturity matching, duration matching, and variable rate pricing of loans and deposits.

MATURITY MATCHING

Some bankers try to match the maturities of specific loan and investment assets with the maturities of specific deposit liabilities.

For example, if a bank makes $1 million in new mortgage loans, it might seek to take in $1 million in passbook savings and IRA deposits because mortgage assets and passbook savings and IRA account liabilities are all likely to remain on the bank's books for a long time. On the other hand, if the bank takes in $500,000 of funds from 30-day corporate CDs, it might seek to match these funds with an equal investment in a 30-day Treasury bill. If interest rates have increased by the time the CDs mature and the bank has to pay more to retain the funds, it can reinvest or lend at a higher rate the funds that are available from the maturing Treasury bill. Also, if the corporation withdraws its CD funds, the maturing Treasury bill assures that the bank has ready funds available to meet this withdrawal.

A matching strategy is not easy to implement, however, because demand for loans within specific maturity categories, such as one-year business loans, and the availability of high-return money market investments may not always match the maturities of new deposits coming into the bank. Also, economic conditions may justify holding back on making new loans or investments at the very time that deposits flowing into the bank would require a matching of these new funds with new loans or investments.

DURATION MATCHING

Some bankers try to match their assets and liabilities on the basis of duration—the average length of time that assets and liabilities are expected to remain on the balance sheet.

For example, the average duration of a 30-year mortgage is known to be about five to six years. This is because many mortgage holders sell their homes after a few years, while others prepay their mortgages and still others default on their mortgage loans. Thus, 30-year mortgages carried in a bank's loan portfolio need only be matched against five- to six-year deposits.

An effective duration matching strategy is not easy to achieve. It requires continual monitoring of a bank's duration positions and constant realignments of the duration of assets to the bank's liabilities. For most bank managers, this can be tedious, demanding, and costly.

VARIABLE RATE PRICING ON LOANS AND DEPOSITS

Many banks try to maintain their interest-rate spreads by making new loans and new deposits subject to variable interest rates—rates that change every month (or every year in the case of mortgages)—to reflect changes in the bank's cost of and return on funds.

GAP MANAGEMENT

Gap management involves selectively mismatching assets and liabilities to capitalize on expected interest-rate change. This strategy involves grouping bank assets and liabilities into specific time periods according to when these assets and liabilities will have to be repriced. That is, the bank's balance sheet is divided into time periods—

three months, six months, one year—and the *gap* is identified between the amount of assets and the amount of liabilities that will have to be repriced in any given period.

For example, if a bank has more assets than liabilities subject to repricing in the next 90 days, it is considered to be *asset sensitive*—which suggests a vulnerability to falling interest rates. If interest rates fall, the bank will obtain a lower return on the assets that are being repriced. However, the bank is still locked into paying higher interest on those liabilities that have not yet matured. If, on the other hand, the bank has more liabilities than assets maturing in a given time period, it is considered to be *liability sensitive* for that period—and vulnerable to rising interest rates. If interest rates rise, the bank will have to pay a higher rate on those liabilities that are being repriced. However, the bank is still locked into the lower rates it is receiving on assets that have not yet matured.

Some banks try to capitalize on an expected interest rate change by selectively mismatching assets and liabilities. A bank that believes interest rates will fall over the next six months, for example, may try to make its balance sheet liability sensitive for that time period. If rates fall, the bank will benefit because it reprices its liabilities at lower rates while it still receives higher rates on assets that have not yet matured.

A fixed-rate, long-term loan locks a bank into an interest return that cannot be changed if short-term conditions increase bank costs. For this reason, interest rates on long-term loans tend to be higher than those imposed on short-term loans. On the other hand, a loan portfolio weighted toward fixed-rate, long-term maturities can generate substantial earnings if interest rates decline for a protracted period after the loans are made. In fact, as interest rates declined and then stabilized in the mid-1980s, most banks shifted toward more fixed-rate, longer-term loans and longer-term investments.

Increased Regulatory Attention to Asset/Liability Management

Asset/liability management has become an increasingly important aspect of the regulatory examinations of banks. Regulators now require that banks of all sizes have written policies not only on their investment strategies, but also on their asset/liability (or gap) management strategies. When examining a bank, regulators investigate whether the bank's funds management policies are being followed; if not, the examiner will set an agreed-upon time by which the bank is expected to be back to its targeted asset/liability positions.

In previous years, regulators had found that managers of many smaller banks were unaware of the requirements for proper management of assets and liabilities; in consequence, some banks were not giving sufficient attention to liquidity and earnings. Today, with the assistance of innovative computer software programs, most bankers are able to manage their banks' assets and liabilities with considerable accuracy and efficiency.

Summary

The business of banking is no longer limited to making commercial loans. Increasingly, banks also make consumer loans and residential and commercial mortgages, invest in government securities, and sell a variety of financial services to businesses and consumers.

A bank's financial statements provide important information about its financial condition. Similarly, the balance sheet and income statement of the commercial banking system as a whole provide valuable insights into the business of banks. The balance sheet shows the relative importance of various categories of assets (loans still rank first) and liabilities (time and savings deposits represent the largest share). A similar review of the banking system's income statement facilitates a comparison of banks' interest income (primarily from loans and investments) and interest expenses (primarily interest paid on time and savings deposits), as well as the relative importance of fee income and rising operating expenses to bank profitability.

Faced with intense competition in recent years, banks have increasingly turned to aggressive funds management techniques to beef up profits. In the 1960s and 1970s, banks found ways to increase their liabilities (and thus expand their earning assets) at their own discretion, rather than passively waiting for deposits. Funds management strategies can be broadly categorized as asset allocation, liability management (in which banks fund their asset growth by buying or borrowing federal funds, large certificates of deposit, and Eurodollars), spread management (which focuses on the spread between the interest rates that banks pay for deposits and the rates they earn on loans and investments), and gap management (in which banks selectively mismatch the maturities of their assets and liabilities to capitalize on expected interest rate changes).

Questions

1. Discuss the constraints commercial banks face in their pursuit of profits.

2. Cite the three largest loan categories on commercial banks' books and two characteristics that differentiate each loan category.

3. Why would a business firm pay a loan commitment fee? Why would a bank impose a compensating balance on a loan? Why would a bank participate in a loan with another bank?

4. Why do banks buy securities? Explain the difference between U.S. Treasury securities, federal agency securities, and municipal obligations.

5. What are the objectives of an asset allocation strategy?

6. What is liability management? If you were in charge of liability management at your bank, what sources of managed liabilities would you rely on and why?

7. What tactics can be used to implement a spread management strategy?

9

Bank Regulation

Objectives

After successfully completing this chapter, you will be able to

☐   explain the major goals of bank regulation,

☐   define unit banking and dual banking and discuss the merits of each,

☐   identify the key responsibilities of the federal bank regulatory agencies—the Federal Reserve, the Comptroller of the Currency, and the Federal Deposit Insurance Corporation,

☐   name the significant changes in banking brought about by federal legislation in the 1980s and early 1990s, and

☐   list the major consumer regulations and the procedures generally followed by bank examiners to determine regulatory compliance with the Community Reinvestment Act.

Introduction

Banking regulation has been shaped by many factors—the economic function that banks fulfill as creators of money, the nation's historical experiences with money and its control, public attitudes toward banks, and the long-standing national debate over the power and rights of the federal government relative to those of the states. These factors have resulted in a unique system in the United States in which regulatory power over banks is shared by both federal and state agencies (a dual regulatory system), and bank branching is tightly restricted (a unit banking system).

In this chapter we will examine our nation's bank regulatory structure and the major principles, laws, and regulations that set the boundaries for the business of banking. We will look first at the public policy goals of bank regulation and briefly profile the principal regulatory agencies and their responsibilities. We will then look at five laws that significantly reshaped banking in the 1980s and 1990s: the Monetary Control Act of 1980; the Garn-St Germain Act of 1982; the Competitive Equality Banking Act of 1987; the Financial Institutions Reform, Recovery and Enforcement Act of 1989; and the Federal Deposit Insurance Corporation Improvement Act of 1991. Finally, we will look at the major banking regulations and the role of bank examinations in effecting regulatory compliance.

Extended Study 11, "The Evolution of Bank Regulation," looks at the major historical developments that have shaped government regulation of U.S. banks and the current examinations and rating process. Extended Study 12, "Current Banking Regulations," briefly summarizes each of the 30 Federal Reserve regulations that govern U.S. banking today.

Regulatory Goals and the Structure of Banking

Banks are subject to numerous laws and regulations that govern most aspects of their operations and their business activities. The federal government's major goal in regulating banks is to protect banks, their depositors, and the communities in which they operate from bank failures. Banks must operate prudently and have sufficient liquidity (or access to it) to prevent a loss of public confidence in the safety and soundness of the banking system. The assets and liabilities of banks also must be managed so that there is minimum risk of failure and monetary loss for depositors.

Promoting competition in banking is another regulatory goal of the federal government. Regulation is intended to ensure that banks adhere to uniform rules in advertising, marketing, and offering new deposits, and that banks do not become so large that a few dominate the industry. Because banks have the power to create money, the government also sees in bank activities the potential for anticompetitive abuse in other markets. In an unregulated environment, for example, it is thought that banks could acquire manufacturing subsidiaries and drive out competition in those industries by supplying their subsidiaries with low-cost money and credit. That specter has led the government to see banks in a narrow business context—as extenders of credit primarily to businesses and, until 1980, as exclusive acceptors of demand deposits. That narrow regulatory perception places banks more in the category of public utilities than of private manufacturing and service firms.

The federal government also seeks to use regulation to protect bank owners from management fraud and from management's placing depositors' funds in unsafe loans and investments, and to ensure bank owners a reasonable rate of return on capital invested. Protecting consumers of bank credit and bank services from discrimination, deception, and violation of their rights is the final goal of federal regulation.

These goals have been pursued and achieved since the 1930s primarily through a system of shared regulation and supervision among different federal agencies, as shown in exhibit 9.1. Bank regulation is the implementation of banking laws through government-issued rules and directives; bank supervision is the enforcement of those rules and directives through bank examinations, off-site monitoring, and analysis of data and information on banking performance and practice.

To achieve its public policy goals, bank regulation in the United States has focused on preventive measures. For example, until recently, bank regulations prohibited the payment of interest on demand deposits and set maximum interest rates on time and savings deposits to reduce destructive competition between banks. Today, bank merger and acquisition activities continue to be restricted to prevent banks from becoming so large that they inhibit competition. The federal government controls the terms and conditions under which banks can obtain and use assets and liabilities. It also insures bank depositors against loss; fixes capital requirements; establishes liquidity, solvency, and profitability guidelines; outlines a code of rights for consumers; and prohibits banks from engaging in unfair or discriminatory practices. These preventive measures have resulted in a complex banking structure that encompasses dual banking, unit banking, and correspondent banking.

Dual Banking   *chartered by fed gov or state*

Dual banking refers to the system of dual regulation in U.S. banking under which a bank may be chartered by the federal government or by the state in which it is domiciled. Banks not only can choose whether they want to be chartered (and thus regulated) under federal or state law, but also can alter their choice at will. Regulatory control and the examination of banks is shared by the federal government and the state in which the bank is located.

Bankers, regulators, and economists have been debating the public benefits and costs of this unique dual banking system since it became a reality in 1863. Opponents of dual

EXHIBIT 9.1   **Types of Federal Bank Regulation**

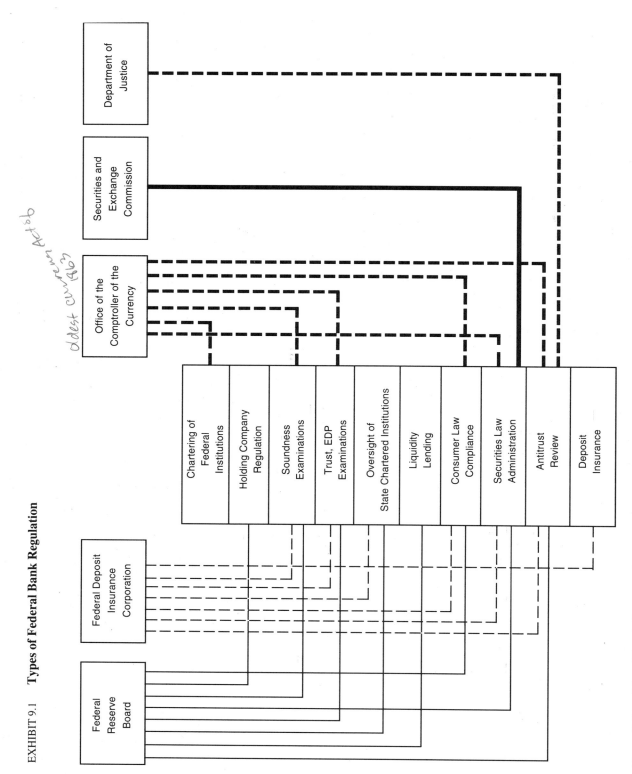

Note: Solid and dotted lines indicate each federal agency's area of regulatory responsibility.

banking argue that it does not benefit the public. They argue that the states, by perpetuating a system of small, unit-scale banks, have denied the nation's rural and suburban communities the benefits of large, full-service money center banks. Certainly the lack of uniformity among state banking laws is disruptive in today's banking environment, which is increasingly interstate in nature. Opponents of dual banking also contend that because bankers can shop around for a charter from state to state, decisions on who receives a charter can involve pressure and political favor. This can result in undeserving groups receiving charters, which in turn may cause services to depositors to fail to meet reasonable standards.

Opponents of dual banking further contend that only the resources of the federal government can ensure highly paid and well-trained bank examiners. They see dual federal and state examinations as wasting time and money, as well as failing to clearly delineate regulatory responsibility. Moreover, they claim, the dual banking system enables the banking industry to play off federal regulators against state regulators. Regulators may compete to attract new bank charters or to retain existing ones by offering loose regulation that is not in the public interest.

Proponents of dual banking argue that dual regulation embodies the same principle of checks and balances that underlies our nation's structure of government. Because a bank can choose a state or federal charter and change its charter at any time, the potential for abusive actions or poor performance by either the federal or state regulatory agencies is checked.

Proponents further contend that the dual banking system enables state governments to apply banking rules and regulations that more closely relate to the needs and concerns of local communities and their depositors. They also feel that healthy competition among chartering authorities stimulates banking innovation and allows for experimentation at the state level without national disruption of the banking system. Proponents of dual banking point, for example, to the introduction of NOW accounts in Massachusetts in the late 1970s, and the innovative maximum-delay provisions on the crediting of deposited checks that were introduced in New York and California in the 1980s. New services and consumer protection that prove beneficial to the public can be expanded to the national level if they prove useful in selected states. Exclusive federal control of bank chartering, they argue, would neither guarantee better banking regulation nor the automatic correction of defects in the bank regulatory structure.

Unit Banking

Unit banking is the term used to characterize the prevailing composition of the U.S. banking industry—thousands of small, single-office (unit) banks with no branches. The U.S. has a unit banking industry because state and federal laws and regulations have severely limited banks' ability to branch, merge, or expand business activities interstate.

Until the 1980s, most states tightly restricted bank branching, permitting branching only within a limited geographic area surrounding a bank's head office or prohibiting branching within the state. During the 1980s, however, most states began to liberalize their branching laws. As shown in exhibit 9.2, by 1990 only 2 states still prohibited branching while 36 states had changed their laws to allow statewide branching on an unrestricted basis. (Twelve states still limit statewide branching by preventing banks from opening branches in all areas of their states.)

EXHIBIT 9.2   **State Branching in the 1990s**

Branching Allowed Statewide	Branching Limited Geographically Within the State
Alaska	Alabama
Arizona	Arkansas
California	Georgia
Connecticut	Illinois
Delaware	Indiana
Florida	Iowa
Hawaii	Kentucky
Idaho	Minnesota
Kansas	Montana
Louisiana	Nebraska
Maine	New Mexico
Maryland	Wisconsin
Massachusetts	
Michigan	Branching Prohibited
Mississippi	(Unit Banking State)
Nevada	
New Hampshire	Colorado
New Jersey	Missouri
New York	
North Carolina	
North Dakota	
Ohio	
Oklahoma	
Oregon	
Pennsylvania	
Rhode Island	
South Carolina	
South Dakota	
Tennessee	
Texas	
Utah	
Vermont	
Virginia	
Washington	
West Virginia	
Wyoming	

Federal law continues to prohibit interstate branching, but defers to state laws as the final authority. For example, the 1927 McFadden Act instructs all nationally chartered banks to follow the various branching laws of each state, and the Douglas Amendment of the 1956 Bank Holding Company Act prohibits a bank holding company (BHC) from acquiring a bank in any but the BHC's home state unless authorized by state law.

Just as most states liberalized their own statewide branching laws in the 1980s, so too did they liberalize their laws on interstate banking. Forty-six states enacted reciprocal banking agreements with one another. Under a reciprocal banking agreement, a state agrees to allow banks in other states—usually only those within its region—to open banks within its state provided those states reciprocate. About half of these agreements allow for states outside the region to be included in the early 1990s.

Most of these laws, however, pertain to bank holding companies, allowing BHCs to expand interstate by acquiring an existing bank and operating it as a new subsidiary. Only seven states—Montana, Nevada, New York, Oregon, Rhode Island, Utah, and Virginia—also permit out-of-state banks to acquire banks within their states and turn them into branches. Operating a newly acquired bank as a subsidiary, rather than as a branch, is more costly. As self-contained banks, subsidiaries are subject to reserve requirements, capital requirements and examinations, and the requirement to maintain separate management structures, computers, and accounting systems.

The structure of banking is expected to change in the 1990s as a result of states' liberalized banking laws. However, many bankers and industry analysts see the need for a federal interstate branching law to ensure that change leads to a more efficient and stronger banking system. An interstate branching law, it is contended, would establish uniform interstate branching rules in all regions and speed up the pace of change by reducing the costs associated with operating out-of-state banks. (A further discussion of the movement toward interstate banking is included in chapter 10, "Trends and Issues in Banking.")

Because of long-standing prohibitions on branching and limitations on mergers, the U.S. banking industry has not followed the historical pattern of other U.S. industries. The consolidation of small firms into a few industrial giants and the development of mass-marketing strategies for selling nationally available products and services have characterized many U.S. industries, but not banking. Bank failures caused a sharp reduction in the number of banks in the United States in the 1920s and 1930s. However, from the 1940s to the mid-1980s the number remained at about 14,000. Since then, bank failures and mergers have pruned the industry to about 12,000 banks.

Correspondent Banking

Because the size and scope of bank markets have historically been restricted in the United States, banks in this country have developed extensive correspondent banking relationships. A correspondent bank holds account balances of other banks and provides various services, such as check collection, to respondent banks through these accounts.

Before the establishment of the Federal Reserve banks in 1914, small banks relied exclusively on larger correspondents as depositories for their reserve funds and as providers of check collection services, particularly for deposited checks drawn on banks in other regions. Even after 1914, most small banks continued to rely on correspondents for check collection services because, until 1980, only commercial banks that were members of the Federal Reserve System had direct access to the Federal Reserve's check collection service. Membership in the Federal Reserve meant adhering to the Federal Reserve's reserve requirements, which were more costly than those the states imposed on nonmember banks (because the Federal Reserve required member banks to keep their reserves in non-interest-earning deposits at Reserve banks). Thus, most of the nation's smaller state-chartered banks (of which there were about 8,000 in 1992) never became members of the Federal Reserve System.

Today, correspondent banks typically provide their respondent banks with the following banking and payments services:

- ☐ check collection services
- ☐ loan participations
- ☐ backup lines of customer credit
- ☐ issuance of dividend checks to respondents' stockholders
- ☐ maintenance of dividend reinvestment programs for respondents' stockholders
- ☐ investment advice
- ☐ analysis of respondents' operating problems
- ☐ third-party cash management services (which make optimal use of available cash)

Respondent banks pay for correspondent services either directly (through a fee) or indirectly (by maintaining a required minimum account balance with the correspondent).

Bank Regulatory Structure

Today's bank regulatory structure is the result of many solutions—and compromises—to money and banking issues and problems that have confronted the nation throughout its history. Exhibit 9.3 illustrates the role of the three major federal bank regulatory agencies—the Comptroller of the Currency, the Federal Reserve, and the Federal Deposit Insurance Corporation—and that of the state banking authorities. It also shows the various regulatory classifications of banks: national banks and three categories of state-chartered banks—those that are members of the Federal Reserve, those that are not members but are insured by the FDIC, and those that are neither members of the Federal Reserve nor federally insured.

Thus, not all commercial banks fall under the jurisdiction of the same regulator, and most are regulated by more than one government agency. The choice of charter (state or federal) determines whether a bank's primary regulator will be a state or a federal agency. Most federal regulation of state-chartered banks is optional. For example, state-chartered banks may join the FDIC and the Federal Reserve. (Federal Reserve members must be FDIC-insured, but state-chartered banks that choose to be FDIC members need not be members of the Federal Reserve.) In practice, essentially all the nation's 8,000 state-chartered commercial banks are FDIC members. Thus, virtually all state-chartered banks are jointly regulated by federal and state authorities. These banks are subject to the examinations and administrative rules and regulations of more than one regulatory agency.

State Banking Departments

All states charter commercial banks, and some states charter savings banks, savings and loan associations, and credit unions as well. Two-thirds, or approximately 8,000, of the nation's 12,000 commercial banks are state chartered. A state charter is granted upon investigation of the applicant's background and a finding that the bank meets the state's capital requirements. States examine the institutions they charter, rule on their acquisitions and branching applications, and issue advisory opinions on acquisition applications received from bank holding companies. States also examine the branches and agencies of foreign banks operating in their state.

Federal Reserve

Although the Federal Reserve is the central monetary authority for the United States, it does not play an exclusive role in the supervision of the nation's banks. The Federal Reserve shares its regulatory power with other federal agencies and with state governments.

The Federal Reserve examines state-chartered member banks, bank holding companies and their domestic nonbank subsidiaries, the overseas activities of banks and bank holding companies, and the U.S. banking and nonbanking operations of foreign banks. It rules on merger and branching applications of state-chartered members banks and issues advisory opinions on merger applications submitted by national banks and FDIC-insured, state-chartered nonmember banks. The Federal Reserve also rules on permissible activities for bank holding companies.

Comptroller of the Currency

National banks are chartered by the Office of the Comptroller of the Currency, which is a unit of the U.S. Treasury Department. All national banks, except those in U.S. overseas territories, are required to be members of the Federal Reserve System. The Comptroller's office also examines national banks and rules on their merger and branching applications.

EXHIBIT 9.3   **Bank Regulatory Structure**

TYPE OF BANK	CHARTERED BY	EXAMINED BY	SUBJECT TO RESERVE REQUIREMENTS IMPOSED BY	DEPOSITS INSURED BY	SUBJECT TO REGULATIONS OF	BANK HOLDING COMPANIES REGULATED BY
National banks	Office of the Comptroller of the Currency (OCC)	State OCC	Fed Reserve	FDIC	OCC Fed Reserve FDIC	Fed Reserve
State banks that are members of the Federal Reserve	State	State Fed Reserve	Fed Reserve	FDIC	State Fed Reserve FDIC	Fed Reserve State
State banks that are not members of the Federal Reserve but are insured by the FDIC	State	State FDIC	Fed Reserve	FDIC	State Fed Reserve FDIC	Fed Reserve State
State banks that are not members of the Federal Reserve and are not insured by the FDIC	State	State	Fed Reserve		State	Fed Reserve State

The Federal Deposit Insurance Corporation

The Federal Deposit Insurance Corporation (FDIC) provides insurance coverage through its Bank Insurance Fund (BIF) for national banks and for those state-chartered commercial and savings banks that elect to be insured. Insurance is mandatory for national banks and those state-chartered banks that opt for Federal Reserve membership or are subsidiaries of bank holding companies. The FDIC also provides insurance coverage through its Savings Association Insurance Fund (SAIF) for federally chartered savings banks and for savings and loan associations that had been insured by the Federal Savings and Loan Insurance Corporation (FSLIC) until that agency's dissolution by Congress in 1989.

The FDIC examines state-chartered banks that are FDIC-insured but are not members of the Federal Reserve; it rules on merger and branching applications of state-chartered banks that are not members of the Federal Reserve; and it issues advisory opinions on merger applications of Federal Reserve member banks and FDIC-insured, state-chartered nonmember banks. The FDIC also manages and liquidates assets of failed banks, and since 1989 has had administrative responsibility for the operations of the Resolution Trust Corporation (RTC). The FDIC's major responsibilities are outlined in exhibit 9.4.

Deposit Insurance Reform

The FDIC insures depositors at banks and thrifts up to $100,000 per person. The current insurance ceiling was instituted in 1980 by the Monetary Control Act, which raised coverage from a $40,000 limit that had been established in 1974. The FDIC was created in 1933 following the failures of more than 9,100 banks from 1930 to 1933. Its major functions were to protect depositors—especially small depositors—against loss, to bolster public confidence in banks, and to prevent bank runs.

The FDIC was immediately successful; bank runs stopped and bank failures rapidly declined. As exhibit 9.5 shows, bank failures remained low for almost 50 years. From the 1930s through the 1970s banks frequently received FDIC-insurance premium rebates as a result of the low level of payouts from the insurance fund to depositors at failed banks, which was one measure of the FDIC's success. Also, the annual number of problem banks (banks in danger of failing) on the FDIC's examinations watch list never exceeded 200 out of an industry total of more than 14,000 banks.

EXHIBIT 9.4   **FDIC Responsibilities**

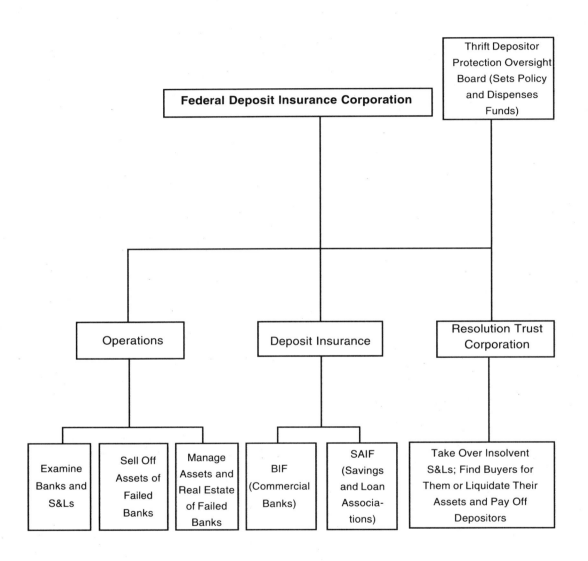

EXHIBIT 9.5   **Failures of FDIC-Insured Banks, 1934-1993**

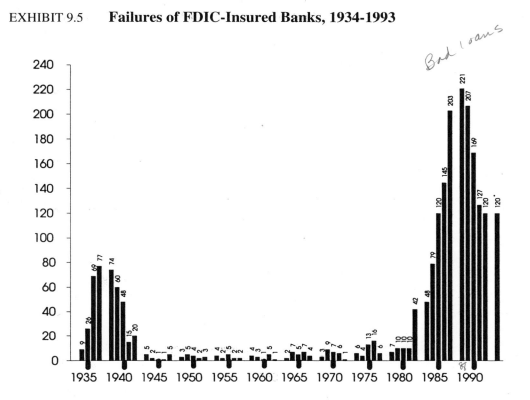

*Estimated by the FDIC

Sources: Federal Deposit Insurance Corporation; Congressional Budget Office;
American Banker, January 4, 1993; *New York Times*, August 19, 1992.

In the 1980s, the number of bank failures soared as banks saw the quality of their assets deteriorate and their capital levels plummet from bad loans. The FDIC, for the first time in its history, suffered major losses as it paid out funds to insured depositors at closed banks and provided financial assistance to banks purchasing the assets and liabilities of failing banks.

Approximately 1,100 banks failed from 1985 to 1992. But these failures did not impair public confidence in banking or trigger widespread deposit withdrawals, in part because of federal deposit insurance protection. However, the bank failures of the late 1980s did impair the solvency of the Federal Deposit Insurance Fund. By 1990, the FDIC had paid out $23 billion from its reserves, reducing its pool of reserve funds to $8.5 billion. In 1991, the Congressional Budget Office reported to Congress a strong likelihood that the FDIC would not have sufficient funds to cover expected bank failures over the following 18 months and by 1992 the reserves could be totally depleted.

The need to fund the FDIC and hold down insurance payouts became a major priority for government and the banking industry and led to enactment, in December 1991, of the Federal Deposit Insurance Corporation Improvement Act (FDICIA).

The act provided new funding to the FDIC and changed the way deposit insurance premiums will be assessed in the 1990s, but it did not make any fundamental changes in deposit insurance coverage.

Deposit Insurance Premiums

The 1989 Financial Institutions Reform, Recovery and Enforcement Act (FIRREA) requires the FDIC to hold reserve funds equal to 1.25 percent of the total deposits it insures. FIRREA also established a schedule for banks' premiums to ensure that the FDIC's reserve ratio would be maintained. The act set bank premiums for 1990 at $0.12 for every $100 of insured deposits. In 1991, premiums were increased to $0.23 per $100 of insured deposits to replenish reserve funds and the FDIC indicated that premiums might have to be increased to as much as $0.30 per $100 of insured deposits to provide needed additional reserves. FDICIA, however, instructed the FDIC to change the way it assesses banks for deposit insurance from fixed premiums based on each bank's total deposits to fees linked to risk. Many bankers (and the FDIC) had long contended that assessing deposit insurance premiums on the basis of a bank's or thrift's size was inconsistent with the principle that insurance premiums should be related to risk and was unfair to fiscally healthy institutions. The new 1993 premium system, as seen in exhibit 9.6, maintains the $0.23 per $100 premium for three-quarters of the nation's banks and more than half the nation's thrifts.

While the new premium system is more equitable, some industry analysts remain unconvinced that this approach will provide an incentive for banks to avoid excessive risk taking or will hold down fiscally sound banks' premium costs. They point to FDICIA's authorization to the FDIC to borrow up to $30 billion from the Treasury to bolster the insurance fund's reserves. The act requires the FDIC to repay its borrowings, with interest, over the next 15 years from premiums assessed on banks.

Other industry analysts maintain that continuing increases in deposit insurance premiums in the 1990s could impose a cost burden large enough to impair many banks' profitability, which could weaken the banking system and thus increase the long-term vulnerability of the deposit insurance fund. It is estimated that 1993's risk-based premiums will cost banks about $600 million and thrifts about $180 million.

Deposit Insurance Coverage

Deposits at banks and thrifts are insured up to $100,000 per person at each bank or thrift where an individual has an account. Under FDIC rules, all accounts associated with the same Social Security number (or taxpayer identification number) at a given bank are added together in determining the $100,000 limit for deposit insurance

EXHIBIT 9.6   **The Risk-Based Deposit Insurance Fee Structure, 1993**

(cents per $100 of insured deposits)   FIRREA

Supervisory groups

Capital Category	Healthy	Supervisory Concern	Substantial Supervisory Concern
Well Capitalized	$0.23 9,115 banks 1,428 thrifts	$0.26 1,766 banks 266 thrifts	$0.29 363 banks 33 thrifts
Adequately Capitalized	$0.26 192 banks 136 thrifts	$0.29 164 banks 157 thrifts	$0.30 174 banks 79 thrifts
Under Capitalized	$0.29 18 banks 7 thrifts	$0.30 26 banks 38 thrifts	$0.31 222 banks 162 thrifts

Note: The risk-based fee structure for deposit insurance went into effect in January 1993. In 1992, all banks paid a flat fee of $0.23 per $100 of deposits.

Source: Federal Deposit Insurance Corporation, *New York Times*, September 16, 1992.

coverage. These rules provide total coverage for most bank and thrift depositors, although it is estimated that about one million households have some deposits that are uninsured. These depositors, half of whom are retirees, hold more than the $100,000 limit in accounts at individual banks.

Insurance coverage can be increased at a single bank for account holders who establish an IRA or Keogh account. Retirement accounts are insured separately. Accounts — single established by depositors in the name and Social Security number of their spouse or children also are covered separately, as are joint accounts among family members or business partners.

In 1991 the Treasury proposed to reduce banks' excessive risk taking by limiting deposit insurance coverage to $100,000 of insurance across all depository institutions. The FDIC had argued that the 1980 increase in deposit insurance coverage from $40,000 to $100,000 encouraged some bankers to take excessive risks in their lending and investing, because of the near-total insurance coverage the 1980 increase provided to most corporate depositors. The FDIC maintained that a reduction in account coverage might induce bankers to take less risk because their actions would be open to the scrutiny of corporate depositors, most of whom would no longer be insured. Such an approach had little support in Congress or among bankers during the debate over deposit insurance reform in 1991. However, FDICIA did limit the scope of some FDIC insurance coverage. The act limits insurance coverage on brokered deposits and accounts established for employee pension plans to those offered only by banks with the highest capital rating.

THE FDIC AND BANK FAILURES

The FDIC can respond to a failed bank in one of four ways:

- ❐ It can pay out insurance to the bank's depositors (outright payoff);
- ❐ It can allow a sound bank to buy selected assets and assume the liabilities of the failed bank (purchase and assumption);
- ❐ It can sell all the bank's assets and its insured liabilities to a sound bank (whole bank purchase); or
- ❐ It can take over the bank and operate it in an attempt to nurse it back to fiscal health (open bank assistance).

In an outright payoff, the FDIC closes the failed bank and pays off the insured depositors. It then liquidates the assets of the bank, distributing the proceeds to the failed bank's creditors and to uninsured depositors. If any funds remain, an unlikely occurrence in most bank failures, they are distributed to the bank's stockholders. In the event of a shortfall, if the bank's failure is due to proven fraud or mismanagement, the FDIC pursues legal means to collect its losses from the failed bank's officers, directors, and major stockholders.

In a purchase and assumption procedure, the FDIC solicits bids for the failed bank. Banks making such bids are permitted to designate to the FDIC those assets of the failed bank that they are willing to buy. Assets not selected, (principally loans) are retained by the FDIC. The purchasing bank assumes all liabilities of the failed bank, effectively keeping the failed bank open. However, because the liabilities of the failed bank exceed the value of the assets selected by the purchasing bank, the FDIC makes up the difference with a cash payment to the purchasing bank.

In the 1980s, the FDIC relied extensively on the purchase and assumption approach for dealing with failed banks—especially larger banks. This approach assured continued banking and credit services to the depositors of the failed banks and avoided the financial and economic disruption that usually follows losses incurred by uninsured depositors and creditors. In addition, this approach was less costly to the FDIC than paying off insured depositors. (Cash payments made to purchasing banks for unselected assets were substantially less than the amounts that would have had to be paid to insured depositors.)

As bank failures began to increase in the late 1980s, the FDIC's purchase and assumption approach came under strong criticism from many bankers and members of Congress. They argued that by not allowing banks to fail (to go out of business), the FDIC had effectively provided de facto insurance for all depositors, creditors, and stockholders of banks. They also argued that the purchase and assumption approach eliminates the market discipline that uninsured depositors—mainly large corporations—would otherwise exert on bank owners and managers to limit risk. If uninsured depositors felt vulnerable, they would likely withdraw their funds or threaten to do so if they sensed that their bank's lending or investment actions were becoming too risky. Such action would tend to restrain overexuberant bank management. However, because the FDIC's purchase and assumption policy effectively protects uninsured depositors, bankers may be encouraged to take greater competitive and business risks in an effort to maximize their bank's market shares and profits.

In response to this criticism, the FDIC adopted two additional approaches in the late 1980s for dealing with failed banks.

Under the whole bank purchase approach, sound banks are asked to bid for all the assets and the insured deposits of the failed bank. Banks making such bids cannot select only the desirable assets of the failed bank—they must factor into their bids possible losses on bad loans and collection costs. Moreover, the purchasing bank assumes only insured liabilities, effectively keeping the failed bank open, but shifting potential FDIC losses to uninsured depositors.

Under certain circumstances the FDIC may actually take over a failing bank and operate it until it can be nursed back to fiscal health. This approach may be used if sound banks are unwilling or unable to bid for the failing bank, and if the bank's closing would require too large a payout from the insurance fund. It will also likely be used in the early 1990s for those banks that fall below minimum capital requirements (about 50 in late 1992). Congress mandated such harsh sanctions in the 1991 deposit insurance legislation. (Capital requirements and the regulatory sanctions applicable to weakly capitalized banks were discussed in chapter 8.)

Office of Thrift Supervision   *created 1989*   *FIRREA*

The Office of Thrift Supervision (OTS) was created by Congress in 1989 to assume most of the regulatory and supervisory powers of the Federal Home Loan Bank Board, which Congress disbanded that year. The OTS charters federal savings and loan associations and federal savings banks. However, these institutions are examined by the FDIC, which administers the insurance fund for S&Ls. The OTS is responsible for issuing regulations that govern the activities of S&Ls and S&L holding companies.

Federal Housing Finance Board

The Federal Housing Finance Board oversees the activities of the 12 regional Federal Home Loan Banks. These banks provide subsidized loans to members of the Federal Home Loan Bank system, which was previously administered by the Federal Home Loan Bank Board. Membership in that system is mandatory for S&Ls, and since 1989 optional for commercial banks and credit unions that have more than 10 percent of their loans in residential housing.

National Credit Union Administration

The National Credit Union Administration (NCUA) charters federal credit unions, provides insurance coverage for federal credit unions and for state-chartered credit unions that elect insurance, and examines all credit unions that it insures. The NCUA also acts as the lender of last resort for credit unions.

The Justice Department

The antitrust division of the Justice Department (part of the executive branch of the U.S. government) also has a role in bank regulation. It is responsible for enforcing antitrust laws in connection with bank mergers and bank holding company acquisitions. The Justice Department also renders advisory opinions on merger proposals of both state-chartered and nationally chartered banks.

Federal Financial Institutions Examination Council

Congress established the Federal Financial Institutions Examination Council in 1978, as part of the Financial Institutions Regulatory and Interest Rate Control Act, to coordinate and standardize activities among the federal regulators of financial institutions. Since 1978, the council has developed a uniform examinations process and a uniform financial institutions rating system. The five agencies comprising the council in 1992 were the FDIC, OTS, Federal Reserve Board, OCC, and the NCUA.

Every commercial bank is supposed to be examined once a year by its primary federal or state regulators. The regulatory agencies also review the condition of overseas branches of U.S. banks in conjunction with domestic examinations. These reviews are conducted either on-site or by examining the records of overseas offices maintained at each bank's domestic head office. In the 1980s, the various federal regulatory agencies and a number of states began a program of alternate-year examinations. Under this program, federal and state regulators take turns examining state-chartered banks, each examining a given bank every other year. Extended Study 11 includes a discussion of the uniform examinations process and rating system.

Recent Banking Legislation

In the 1980s, U.S. banking was profoundly affected by several major pieces of legislation—particularly the Monetary Control Act of 1980, the Garn-St Germain Act of 1982, the Competitive Equality Banking Act of 1987, and the Financial Institutions

Reform, Recovery and Enforcement Act of 1989. Banking in the 1990s has already felt the impact of further legislation—the Federal Deposit Insurance Corporation Improvement Act of 1991. In addition, the U.S. Supreme Court has been forced to reassess the long-standing Glass-Steagall Act of 1933. An overview of each of these laws follows.

The Monetary Control Act of 1980

In passing the Depository Institutions Deregulation and Monetary Control Act of 1980 (called the Monetary Control Act of 1980 throughout this text), Congress made the most significant changes in U.S. banking regulations, the powers of the Federal Reserve, and the Federal Reserve's control of monetary policy since the 1930s. The Monetary Control Act profoundly altered the competitive relationship between banks and thrift institutions, strengthened the ability of consumers to obtain higher interest rates on time deposits, and gave depositories across the country the power to offer new types of interest-earning transaction accounts (such as NOW accounts).

The act gradually phased out interest rate ceilings on time and savings deposits at banks and thrifts (Regulation Q) from 1981 to 1986. The act also increased FDIC insurance coverage on all deposits to $100,000 for each account. Mutual savings banks were authorized to obtain a new federal charter that allowed them broader powers to provide more services and to compete with commercial banks. Savings and loan associations and credit unions also were given more powers. Previously, these thrift institutions had been limited primarily to mortgage and mortgage-related lending.

Most significant to banks, the Monetary Control Act extended the Federal Reserve's reserve requirements to all depository institutions—both member and nonmember commercial banks, savings banks, savings and loan associations, credit unions, Edge Act and agreement corporations, and, under the terms of the 1978 International Banking Act, the branches and agencies of foreign banks in the United States. In one stroke, the Federal Reserve gained control over the money-creating and lending capacity of almost all the nation's depositories. At the same time, by imposing uniform reserve requirements on all depositories, it made competition fairer between member and nonmember commercial banks and between banks and thrifts.

In addition to requiring all depositories to maintain reserves, Congress also provided a new way for nonmember banks and thrifts to maintain reserves. Under a pass-through arrangement, reserves may be deposited at Federal Reserve banks indirectly through the commingled reserve deposits of major correspondent banks, the Federal Home Loan banks, or NCUA's Credit Union Central Liquidity Facility, which serves as the lender of last resort for credit unions. The pass-through arrangement gave nonmember depositories that had long-standing account relationships with correspondent banks (and thrifts that had relationships with other federal regulatory authorities) the ability to meet the Federal Reserve's reserve requirements within the context of these existing account relationships.

The Monetary Control Act simultaneously reduced reserve requirements for commercial banks that were members of the Federal Reserve and raised requirements for nonmembers. Member banks' required reserves were phased down over a three-year period (1980-1983) while nonmembers' reserve requirements were phased up over an eight-year period (1980-1987). The net effect of the reduction in member banks' reserves and the increase in nonmembers' reserves was an overall decline in total reserves. Monetary policy control was improved, however, because the reserve requirements covered a greater number of financial institutions.

The major impetus behind the passage of the Monetary Control Act was concern over the Federal Reserve's declining membership. During the 1970s, more than 500 banks left the Federal Reserve. As banks dropped out of the Federal Reserve, they withdrew their reserves, thereby weakening the Federal Reserve's control over the nation's supply of money and credit. In fact, the Fed's control of the nation's bank deposits was declining by about 1 percent each year.

With passage of the Monetary Control Act, Congress not only addressed the problem of declining Federal Reserve membership, but also resolved other major banking issues that had emerged during the 1970s. For example, it addressed the questions of whether banks should be permitted to offer interest-earning checking accounts (yes), whether rates paid on consumer savings should be limited by interest rate ceilings (no), and whether banks and thrifts should continue to be regulated differently (no). The act also reflected changes in the nation's regulatory approach.

Concern for regulatory and competitive equity between domestic banks and the branches and agencies of foreign banks in the United States had led Congress to enact the International Banking Act of 1978. This act subjected the U.S. branches and agencies of foreign banks to the Federal Reserve's reserve requirements and gave them access to Federal Reserve services. By subjecting all the nation's financial institutions to uniform reserve requirements, the Monetary Control Act was consistent with this new regulatory approach.

The Monetary Control Act of 1980 also granted open access to Federal Reserve loans, as well as access to all Federal Reserve payments services, and to all depository institutions holding transaction accounts. Congress also required the Federal Reserve to price its services explicitly and to make them available to all depository institutions at a uniform price and under uniform terms. The act specified that the Federal Reserve, in setting its fees, had to take into consideration all its direct and indirect costs. For example, Congress mandated that banks either be charged for Federal Reserve float at the current federal funds rate or that such float be eliminated. The Federal Reserve also had to start charging for overhead, as well as for the imputed costs for taxes that would have been paid and return on capital that would have been earned had the services it provided been furnished by a private business firm.

The Garn-St Germain Act of 1982

The Depository Institutions Act of 1982, widely known as the Garn-St Germain Act, substantially extended the powers of banks and thrifts and the activities of bank regulatory agencies beyond those established by the Monetary Control Act of 1980.

One of its provisions enabled banks to offer money market deposit accounts in competition with existing money market funds. The act also provided for additional assistance to the struggling thrift industry. Specifically, it allowed for merger-related assistance from the FDIC to prevent savings banks and savings and loan associations from failing, provided for emergency acquisition allowances to banks seeking to buy a failing thrift institution, authorized thrift institutions to issue net worth certificates to maintain their capital bases, and authorized banks to make due-on-sale (nonassumable) mortgages in those states that had prohibited them. The lending and investing powers of thrift institutions also were expanded.

The Garn-St Germain Act also increased the limit on the maximum amount that commercial banks could lend to any one borrower to 15 percent of capital and surplus (up from 10 percent, with an additional 10 percent allowed if the loan is fully secured).

The act also exempted the first $2 million in transaction accounts and other reservable liabilities of every depository in the nation from reserve requirements. (The exemption level is indexed to take account of annual deposit growth; in 1993 the level was the first $3.8 million.) This provision released most of the nation's credit unions from reserve requirements. A technical amendment to the act in 1983 also exempted the new money market deposit accounts from reserve requirements.

The Competitive Equality Banking Act of 1987

Another important 1980s banking law, the Competitive Equality Banking Act of 1987, was prompted by a number of troublesome issues that emerged during that decade. The most prominent of those issues was the insolvency of the FSLIC. The act not only recapitalized the FSLIC, but also provided safeguards for the FSLIC's insurance premium base. FSLIC-insured S&Ls were forbidden from switching to FDIC insurance for one year. Thereafter, institutions switching insurers were to be assessed a costly exit fee designed to discourage switching.

Congress also expanded the FDIC's power to arrange interstate acquisitions of troubled banks. It gave the FDIC authority to operate "bridge" banks for as long as three years. Bridge banks take over the assets and liabilities of a failed bank (and thus avoid costly insurance payouts to depositors) until a merger can be effected with a sound bank.

The act also closed the *consumer bank* or *nonbank* bank loophole in the Bank Holding Company Act, which had inadvertently allowed nonfinancial corporations to own and operate banks. The 1987 act redefined a bank as any institution insured by the FDIC. However, Congress grandfathered those nonbank banks in operation before 1987.

Another section of the Competitive Equality Banking Act, known as the Expedited Funds Availability Act, established maximum check-hold periods for banks and required the Federal Reserve to change check collection procedures to speed up the return of dishonored checks to a depositor's bank. As discussed in more detail in chapter 7, new delayed availability rules went into effect in September 1990.

The 1987 law also requires that all adjustable rate mortgages made by banks and thrifts include a maximum life-of-the-loan interest rate.

The Financial Institutions Reform, Recovery and Enforcement Act of 1989 (FIRREA)

The Financial Institutions Reform, Recovery and Enforcement Act was passed primarily to address problems that had emerged in the 1980s in the S&L industry and the S&L insurance system. Extended Study 4 discusses in detail the major provisions of FIRREA.

The act provided funds for the sale or closing of insolvent S&Ls and established a new agency under the management of the FDIC to do so—the Resolution Trust Corporation. FIRREA also restructured and strengthened the deposit insurance funds of both banks and S&Ls, creating a separate Bank Insurance Fund (BIF) and a separate Savings Association Insurance Fund (SAIF) under the FDIC's control.

Congress established a new Office of Thrift Supervision (OTS) within the Treasury to regulate and charter federal S&Ls, tightened restrictions on S&L activities, and raised S&L capital requirements to increase safety and soundness within the S&L industry. In addition, FIRREA sought to redirect S&Ls to their traditional role as residential mortgage lenders by offering loan inducements from Federal Home Loan Banks to S&Ls that keep 70 percent or more of their assets in mortgages, home-equity loans, or mortgage-backed securities investments.

FIRREA also required the regulatory agencies to make public their evaluations of banks' and thrifts' compliance with the Community Reinvestment Act. In a further effort to root out discrimination in lending, a section of FIRREA known as the Home Mortgage Disclosure Act requires all mortgage lenders with assets exceeding $10 million to provide periodic data to their regulators on the mortgage applications they have received—accepted and rejected—categorized by the income, race, and sex of the applicants. Federal Home Loan Banks were also required to lend low interest funds to S&Ls that use the money for mortgages in low- and moderate-income areas or for other community-based activities.

The Federal Deposit Insurance Corporation Improvement Act of 1991 (FDICIA)

In 1991, Congress provided new funding for the depleted federal deposit insurance fund by passing the Federal Deposit Insurance Corporation Improvement Act (FDICIA). However, the act also made profound changes in America's bank regulatory structure by limiting the scope of federal deposit insurance, giving the Federal Reserve new authority to regulate foreign banks in the U.S., and requiring federal regulators to issue new rules and restrictions aimed at reducing banking risks.

Congress gave the FDIC $70 billion in new borrowing authority. The act increased the amount the FDIC could borrow from the Treasury to cover payouts to depositors at failed banks from $5 billion to $30 billion. However, the FDIC has to repay those borrowings, with interest, within 15 years from premiums assessed on banks. The act further allows the FDIC to borrow up to $45 billion for working-capital needs. Those borrowings, with interest, also must be repaid but the FDIC can use funds it receives from the sale of assets of failed banks.

The scope of federal deposit insurance was limited by FDICIA because the act restricted the FDIC's application of its *too big to fail* policy. Under this policy, the FDIC had pledged to back all deposits at large banks, regardless of the amounts in any given account. The policy was designed to protect financial markets and the economy from the destablization that massive losses by uninsured depositors would cause if a large bank failed.

Many bankers had long maintained that liberal use of the *too-big-to-fail* policy encouraged risk-averse depositors to maintain accounts only at large banks and did not reduce these banks' risk taking. Bankers noted too that the cost to the FDIC of paying off all depositors at large banks was invariably borne by both small and large banks through higher insurance premiums. Congress concurred in this assessment.

Beginning in 1995, the FDIC can invoke the too-big-to-fail policy only if a large bank failure would directly threaten the stability of the financial system and only if the Federal Reserve, the Treasury, and the president approve. If such an exception is made, and the FDIC pays off both insured and uninsured depositors at the failed bank, the costs of the payout must be recovered by a special premium assessed on all banks.

Other changes made by FDICIA in the federal deposit insurance program included limiting brokered deposits and altering the way in which deposit insurance premiums are assessed on banks. FDICIA limited insurance coverage on brokered deposits and accounts established for employee pension plans only to those offered by banks with the highest capital rating. To give banks an incentive to attain this rating, FDICIA also required the FDIC to change the way it assesses banks for deposit insurance, moving from a fixed premium approach to fees linked to risk.

The act gave the Federal Reserve new authority to examine the branches, agencies, and nonbank operations of foreign banks in the United States, a measure designed to raise the level of foreign bank supervision in the U.S. to the level of federal supervision of domestic banks. (Technically, under FDICIA, the Federal Reserve is required to examine foreign banks only if the OCC and the FDIC cannot. Given the number of domestic examinations in the early 1990s, most industry analysts expect that the Federal Reserve will examine most of the foreign banks operating in the U.S.)

Congress also tightened domestic banking supervision by requiring regulators to build into their bank examination and rating systems specific regulatory restrictions linked to deficiencies in bank capital. Regulators must place banks and thrifts in one of five capital categories, based on their capital-to-asset ratios. These categories range from *well capitalized* (best) to *critically undercapitalized* (worst). Progressively stricter regulatory sanctions must be applied to any bank or thrift whose capital ratio declines from one category to another.

FDICIA also required regulators to establish new measures of bank safety, such as minimum earning levels; placed limits on banks' real estate lending; tightened bank auditing requirements; and mandated uniform disclosure of banks' and thrifts' deposit interest rates, fees, and other conditions applicable to their time and savings accounts. This latter mandate was embodied in a section of FDICIA called the Truth in Savings Act.

Other Banking Laws

The rapidly changing competitive and regulatory environment of the 1980s prompted federal and state regulators to reassess the applicability of several long-standing banking laws, most notably the Glass-Steagall Act. That legislation, a portion of the Federal Banking Act of 1933, separated commercial banking from investment banking so that commercial banks could no longer underwrite securities or act as securities brokers. Banks were permitted to pool assets in trusts (commingled funds), act as managing agents for customers, and purchase stock through dealers for customers' accounts; however, under the prohibitive "wall" of Glass-Steagall, banks could not provide these services to the general public. In the 1980s, banks and brokerage firms increasingly breached the Glass-Steagall wall with the assistance of liberal rulings from federal regulators and the Supreme Court.

In the early 1980s, the Federal Reserve authorized bank holding companies to serve as investment advisers to closed-end investment companies; reluctantly allowed an industrial conglomerate to establish the first nonbank bank; and permitted one of the nation's largest bank holding companies—Bank America Corporation—to acquire Charles Schwab, the nation's largest discount brokerage firm. The Comptroller of the Currency authorized national banks to acquire or establish brokerage subsidiaries, and the FDIC authorized its members to form securities service subsidiaries. The Supreme Court, in separate rulings, upheld each of these regulatory authorizations.

In the mid-1980s, the separation between banking and the securities business became increasingly hazy. The OCC allowed banks to underwrite collateralized mortgage obligations, and the Federal Reserve authorized bank holding companies to sell shares of mutual funds through subsidiaries. The Federal Reserve also allowed Bank America's brokerage unit to participate in a public stock offering. Even more important, a federal appeals court ruled that Bankers Trust, one of the nation's largest wholesale banks, could legally issue corporate commercial paper without violating the Glass-Steagall Act. Following that ruling, the Federal Reserve authorized bank holding companies to engage in modest levels of underwriting. New York State, which had enacted its own version of the Glass-Steagall Act, also authorized state-chartered banks in New York to participate in underwriting activities.

New York Stock Exchange. Banks increasingly partici- pate in brokerage activities.

Photo courtesy of the New York Stock Exchange, Inc. 1988.

In the late 1980s, the Federal Reserve broadened its underwriting authorization and approved applications by the holding companies of three large money center banks—J. P. Morgan, Citicorp, and Bankers Trust—to underwrite commercial paper, mortgage-backed securities, and municipal revenue bonds. It broadened its underwriting authorization still further by next allowing bank holding companies to underwrite corporate stocks and bonds, as long as the revenue the subsidiary derived from that activity was no more than 10 percent of its total revenue. The authorizations were challenged in the U.S. Supreme Court by the Securities Industry Association, while Congress continued to actively deliberate whether the crumbling 50-year-old wall separating banking and the securities business should be rebuilt or totally removed. By 1992, however, the Court had not yet ruled and no congressional consensus on the future of the Glass-Stegal Act had emerged. In the following chapter, we will explore in greater detail the arguments for and against repeal of the Glass-Steagall Act.

Banking Regulations

Most federal banking law is implemented by Federal Reserve regulations. Congress invariably assigns to the Federal Reserve the responsibility for developing the rules, procedures, and requirements to implement new federal banking laws. Thus, the Federal Reserve, through its regulations, acts as an administrative arm of Congress.

In 1992, there were 30 Federal Reserve regulations, each carrying a different letter designation—A through Z, AA, BB, CC, and DD. For ease of analysis, the 30 regulations are grouped into five categories—regulations on monetary policy, on bank safety and soundness, on allowable activities of Edge Act corporations and bank holding companies, on the activities of Federal Reserve banks and Federal Reserve membership, and on consumer protection—as shown in exhibit 9.7. Extended Study 12, "Current Banking Regulations," briefly describes the nature and intent of each regulation.

History of Consumer Credit Legislation

The greatest number of banking regulations today deal with consumer protection issues including unfair and deceptive bank practices, equal credit opportunity, community reinvestment, availability of deposited check funds, truth-in-lending requirements for consumer credit, and truth in savings requirements for consumer deposits. Before 1968, however, the regulation of consumer credit was limited, and was primarily the responsibility of the states. Most states, for example, prohibited usurious interest rates and set ceiling rates on loans to consumers.

EXHIBIT 9.7   Categories of Federal Reserve Regulations

1. Regulations on monetary policy

A	Loans to depositories
D	Reserve requirements
G, T,U, and X	Credit by banks, by brokers and dealers, and by others; rules for margin borrowers
Q	Interest on deposits

2. Regulations on bank safety and soundness

F	Financial disclosure to stockholders and others
L	Interlocking directorates in banking
O	Loans to officers, directors, and stockholders
P	Security devices and procedures
R	Interlocking relationships between banks and the securities industry

3. Regulations on Edge Act corporations and bank holding companies

K	Activities of Edge Act corporations
Y	Activities of bank holding companies

4. Regulations on Federal Reserve membership and Reserve banks' procedures

H	Membership requirements
I	Stock ownership requirements
J	Check-processing and EFT procedures
N	Reserve banks' relations with foreign banks and governments
V	Loan guarantees for defense contractors

5. Regulations on consumer protection

AA	Unfair and deceptive practices
B	Equal credit opportunity
BB	Community Reinvestment CRA ob 1977
C	Home mortgage disclosure
CC	Availability of deposited check funds
DD	Truth in savings
E	Electronic funds transfers
M	Consumer leasing
H	Flood insurance
S	Financial privacy
Z	Truth in lending

The 1968 Consumer Credit Protection Act (widely known as the Truth in Lending Act) was the federal watershed. This legislation was designed to require lenders to make meaningful disclosure of their credit and leasing terms so that consumers could compare the various terms available. Lenders were required to provide consumer borrowers with specific written information on the cost of credit, especially the finance charge (the amount of money paid to obtain credit) and the annual percentage rate (the finance charge expressed as an annual percentage of the funds borrowed). The annual percentage rate allows a comparison of credit costs regardless of the dollar amount of the costs or the length of time over which payments are made.

Congress significantly expanded the Truth in Lending Act after 1968 and enacted other statutes to require disclosure of still more information to borrowers and to curb various unfair and deceptive practices of lenders. Virtually all these laws required the Federal Reserve to implement regulations. More than a dozen major consumer credit protection laws were passed during the 1970s.

Consumer Credit Protection Regulations During the 1970s

Following passage of the Consumer Credit Protection (Truth in Lending) Act of 1968, numerous other consumer credit protection laws were enacted throughout the 1970s:

- ☐ Fair Credit Reporting Act (1970)
- ☐ Credit card amendments to the Truth in Lending Act (1970)
- ☐ Fair Credit Billing Act, amending the Truth in Lending Act (1974)
- ☐ Equal Credit Opportunity Act (1974)
- ☐ Real Estate Settlement Procedures Act (1974)
- ☐ Federal Trade Commission Improvement Act (1975)
- ☐ Home Mortgage Disclosure Act (1976)
- ☐ Consumer Leasing Act (1976)
- ☐ Amendments to the Equal Credit Opportunity Act (1976)
- ☐ Fair Debt Collection Practices Act (1977)
- ☐ Community Reinvestment Act (1977)
- ☐ Electronic Funds Transfer Act (1978)
- ☐ Right to Financial Privacy (1978)

Throughout the 1970s, the staff of the Federal Reserve Board answered inquiries from banks and other creditors on the applicability and interpretation of the Truth in Lending Act. A 1976 amendment to the act provided that creditors could not be sued for engaging in any practice that followed an official interpretation of the Truth in Lending Act by staff of the Federal Reserve Board.

Although these staff interpretations did not have the force of law, most creditors followed them as if they did. In addition, the courts offered further interpretations of the act's regulations. By the end of the decade, there were several hundred reported court decisions on the Truth in Lending Act, about 150 official staff interpretations, and almost 1,300 unofficial staff interpretations.

SIMPLIFIED COMPLIANCE PROCEDURES

The federal bank regulatory agencies use special examinations to determine bank compliance with the consumer protection regulations. Those examinations showed that in the late 1970s, despite a high level of compliance with the intent of the consumer credit laws, many banks were in technical violation of the laws because of misunderstanding, oversight, and clerical error. Those technical violations in some cases led to consumer litigation.

Many banks were not sufficiently familiar with the consumer credit regulations and found compliance difficult. Smaller banks, in particular, possessed neither the personnel nor the resources to study the regulations in depth and to develop procedures for full compliance. Some banks also had difficulty adapting their credit application forms to the various technical restrictions imposed by the laws. In the late 1970s, consumer groups, financial regulators, and Congress gave considerable attention to simplifying the Truth in Lending Act and its implementing regulation, Regulation Z, as a means of easing the compliance burden on banks (particularly since banks passed on to their customers their increased administrative costs), while at the same time providing the public with more meaningful protection.

Consumer groups contended that the disclosure forms given to consumers were too lengthy and difficult to understand. These groups maintained that eliminating unnecessary information from the required disclosure statements would benefit consumers by focusing their attention on more meaningful and useful cost information. Other consumer groups, however, attacked simplification as primarily benefiting creditors. Simplification, they maintained, would reduce the grounds for potential consumer suits under the Truth in Lending Act and destroy creditor innovation in designing and marketing easily understood loan forms and disclosure statements.

After a study of the issue, the Federal Reserve Board in 1977 proposed several amendments to Regulation Z designed to simplify and clarify its disclosure requirements. In 1978, the Senate passed a bill to simplify and reform the truth in lending provisions of the Truth in Lending Act. Most of that bill was incorporated in the Monetary Control Act of 1980 and implemented in 1981 by the Federal Reserve's revision and simplification of Regulation Z. Revised Regulation Z consolidated some 1,500 past interpretations of the Truth in Lending Act, and the Fed announced that it would no longer issue individual interpretations. The new Regulation Z was shortened and simplified because its legal complexity was seen to be a major barrier to bank compliance with the Truth in Lending Act. To make compliance easier, the Federal Reserve also provided standard forms written in simple, nontechnical language for creditors to use in disclosing the credit terms extended.

The Community Reinvestment Act of 1977

The Community Reinvestment Act of 1977 (CRA) was passed by Congress to ensure that banks and other financial institutions serve the mortgage and business credit needs of the communities from which they obtain deposits. Specifically, the act prohibits banks and other financial institutions from engaging in redlining—the practice of excluding certain geographic areas from eligibility for mortgage loans without regard to the creditworthiness of each mortgage applicant and property. Congress also wanted to make banks more responsive to the deterioration of housing in the nation's inner cities and to prevent further deterioration in those areas by ensuring that individuals and small businesses in the inner cities could obtain funds for housing and commercial purposes.

The act requires that bank regulatory examinations include an assessment of the bank's record in meeting the credit needs of its entire community (including low- and moderate-income areas). It also requires federal regulatory agencies to consider a bank's record in this regard when deciding whether to grant approval for new bank branches, mergers, or holding company acquisitions.

Congress left it to the Federal Reserve to define the term *community* as used in the Community Reinvestment Act. It also delegated to the Fed the tasks of setting specific standards for determining whether a depository was serving the credit needs of its community and for determining what evidence the federal regulatory agencies should evaluate in assessing a depository's record.

The Federal Reserve's Regulation BB, which implements the Community Reinvestment Act, uses both geographic and nongeographic factors in defining the term *community*. A simple geographic definition, such as "any city or town where the bank is chartered to do business," was deemed inadequate to reflect significant differences in a bank's size, business orientation, and customer markets. Thus, under Regulation BB, a bank's lending policies are evaluated in the context of its business orientation, its past performance, and its perception of its role and function in local, regional, or national deposit and credit markets.

In the late 1970s, many community groups in major cities, particularly New York, interpreted the Community Reinvestment Act to mean that banks must allocate a portion of their locally obtained funds to local mortgage lending. In the early 1980s, they challenged branch applications of some of the major money market banks on the grounds that the banks' mortgage lending in certain areas of the city was inadequate. Those challenges were unsuccessful because the banks in question were found to be in compliance with Regulation BB's criteria for meeting community credit needs.

By the late 1980s, bank regulators, through their compliance examiners, began to increase their emphasis on bank compliance with all aspects of the consumer protection regulations, especially Regulation BB. That increased attention from examiners, and concerns over possible adverse action by the regulators (such as refused branch applications), prompted many banks to expand their lending to low- and moderate-income segments of their communities.

In 1989's Financial Institutions Reform, Recovery and Enforcement Act, Congress required that banks' compliance examination ratings be made public. Congress reasoned that disclosure of noncompliant banks would be publically embarrassing and would prompt corrective actions. Through 1992, however, few banks and thrifts have been embarrassed; most disclosed ratings have been highly favorable.

Two sources of contention emerged in the 1990s between banks and regulators over Community Reinvestment Act compliance. They involve the applicability of the act to U.S. operation of foreign banks and highly specialized domestic banks, and the criteria regulators use for evaluating compliance.

The Community Reinvestment Act covers all banks and thrifts, including highly specialized banks that provide only a limited range of products and services to particular types of customers, and foreign banks operating in the United States that are principally engaged in corporate and international banking. Such limited-service institutions are as obligated to meet the credit needs of people and business firms in the low- and moderate-income neighborhoods of their communities as are full service, retail-oriented banks.

Regulation BB allows limited-service banks to meet their Community Reinvestment Act obligations in ways other than making appropriate mortgage and small business loans. In 1992 the Federal Reserve established the following acceptable alternatives:

- ❏ purchasing mortgage-backed securities from lending institutions that primarily serve low- and moderate-income areas;
- ❏ purchasing housing, community, and economic development loans from other banks, or from state and local government agencies;
- ❏ purchasing low- and moderate-income government guaranteed loans (or participation in pools representing such loans) from the Small Business Administration (SBA), the Federal Housing Administration (FHA), and the Economic Development Administration (EDA);
- ❏ purchasing state and local government agency residential mortgage or industrial revenue bonds;
- ❏ purchasing limited partnership shares to provide equity financing for public projects, such as construction of low-income housing or providing new small businesses with start-up capital;
- ❏ providing technical assistance to small businesses on financial matters;
- ❏ providing technical assistance to community-based nonprofit self-help organizations in obtaining credit, promoting their activities, maintaining their financial records, training their staffs, or educating community residents in how to use bank credit and deposit services;
- ❏ providing letters of credit or credit lines to community-based organizations or private developers involved in low- and moderate-income housing or small business development;

- ❏ contributing to the financial support of nonprofit neighborhood development corporations, community credit-counseling organizations, and community foundations and loan funds;
- ❏ making a substantial deposit in a community development credit union to help fund the credit union's lending.

Many banks have complained that the criteria that regulators use for evaluating bank compliance with the Community Reinvestment Act are vague and subjective and generate uncertainty, even when a bank has received favorable examination ratings. Some bankers contend that objective, quantifiable standards would be more appropriate than the criteria currently used. For most full-service retail-oriented banks these criteria include the scope of the bank's involvement in community-based low- and moderate-income housing and credit programs, analysis of the bank's mortgage lending (including accepted and rejected applications), and the bank's housing-related investments. Factors such as these are further assessed against each bank's size, business strategy, and financial health.

In 1992, the New York State Banking Department proposed a quantitative system for evaluating banks' compliance with the Community Reinvestment Act. Under the New York system, a bank would receive a numerical grade based on the ratio of its community investments to its insured deposits, with certain investments carrying extra weight in the calculation.

Some bankers contend that using one or two ratios to determine a bank's compliance could be unfair and could force many banks to allocate loans and investments into business areas in which they have no expertise. Other bankers contend that a quantitative evaluation system, despite its flaws, would be better than the current subjective system. New York State regulators see their quantitative approach as a model for other state and federal regulators in the 1990s.

Compliance Examinations

Compliance examinations are generally conducted by bank examiners who are trained to review consumer protection law and regulatory compliance. All federal bank regulatory agencies operate under a common set of guidelines to ensure uniform enforcement of consumer regulations.

Bank examiners use a special instructional manual for each regulation and follow an examination checklist. Each consumer law and regulation is covered by a special report complete with procedures for detecting and correcting violations. A compliance examination typically involves the following steps:

- ❏ a review of the agency's complaint file to note any areas of the bank's operations that may present a problem;
- ❏ an on-site review of the bank's lending forms, credit applications, and disclosure statements;

☐ a review of a statistical sample of the bank's installment loan files for compliance with Regulation Z (including a calculation of annual percentage rates and a determination of whether credit costs have been properly disclosed);

☐ a review of a sample of the bank's mortgage files for compliance with Regulation Z, the Real Estate Settlement Procedures Act, and Regulation H (national flood insurance);

☐ a review of a sample of the bank's accepted and rejected credit applications for compliance with Regulation BB, to determine whether they show any pattern of discrimination or deviation from the bank's established lending policy;

☐ a discussion with bank management that includes any area of concern noted by the examiner; and

☐ a written report of the examination sent to the bank with a request that management respond to the report and comment on how any violations noted will be corrected.

If a violation is discovered through investigation of a specific consumer complaint, the bank not only must take corrective action on the complainant's behalf, but also is required to establish policies to prevent future violations.

Summary

The bank regulatory structure that has evolved in the United States over the years has as its principal goal the safety and soundness of banks. This goal has been pursued over the decades by bank regulation and bank supervision, and has led to the development of three unique features in America's banking and regulatory structure: a dual banking system—in which virtually all banks are regulated and examined by both federal and state authorities; unit banking—in which thousands of small, single-office banks are bound by restrictions on branching and geographic expansion; and extensive correspondent relationships—in which larger banks hold account balances and provide check collection and other services to their respondent banks. The U.S. bank regulatory structure consists of state banking authorities, which examine state-chartered banks; the Federal Reserve, which examines state-chartered member banks; the Comptroller of the Currency, which examines federally chartered (national) banks; and the FDIC, which examines state-chartered banks that are insured by the FDIC, but are not members of the Federal Reserve.

The structure of the U.S. banking industry underwent dramatic change during the 1980s and is likely to continue to change in the 1990s. Major banking laws provided much of the impetus for this change. The Monetary Control Act of 1980 modified the banking regulatory structure by subjecting all depositories to the Federal Reserve's reserve requirements. It also authorized all depository institutions to offer interest-earning checking accounts. The Garn-St Germain Act of 1982 authorized banks to offer money market deposit accounts in competition with money market funds, and broadened the powers of the bank regulatory agencies to assist failing depositories. The Competitive Equality Banking Act of 1987 established maximum check-hold periods for banks, and gave increased authority to the FDIC.

The Financial Institutions Reform, Recovery and Enforcement Act of 1989 restructured the deposit insurance system, established a new Office of Thrift Supervision (OTS), and created the Resolution Trust Corporation (RTC) to manage the closing of insolvent S&Ls. The Federal Deposit Insurance Corporation Improvement Act of 1991 provided new funding for the FDIC, gave the Federal Reserve new regulatory authority over foreign banks operating in the U.S., and instituted new rules to reduce banking risks.

Federal Reserve regulations are the principal body of banking regulations that govern virtually every aspect of a bank's activities. During the 1970s, a wide range of consumer credit protection laws were enacted by Congress and implemented by the Federal Reserve. The bulk of these were incorporated into a simplified version of Regulation Z in the 1980s. Special regulatory compliance examinations help ensure that consumers obtain truth in lending and equal credit opportunity in their dealings with banks.

Questions

1. In what way does the regulation of banks differ from the regulation of other business firms (for example, automobile manufacturing companies)?

2. Does it make a difference whether a new bank obtains a national or a state charter?

3. Explain the terms *dual banking* and *unit banking*.

4. Bankers, regulators, and economists have debated the public benefits and costs of a dual banking system since it became a reality in 1863. What are the arguments for and against dual banking?

5. Who regulates commercial banks in the United States today?

6. Cite three major changes in banking brought about by the Monetary Control Act of 1980. What are the major provisions of the Federal Deposit Insurance Corporation Improvement Act of 1991?

10

Trends and Issues in Banking

Objectives

After successfully completing this chapter, you will be able to

☐ describe the regulatory, competitive, technological, and labor market changes likely to shape banking in the next two decades,

☐ identify the public policy issues in the debate on broadening bank product and service powers and repealing the Glass-Steagall Act of 1933,

☐ summarize the major strategies that banks are implementing to improve profitability, and

☐ cite major personnel trends in the banking industry.

Introduction

Banking is undergoing profound changes that will reshape the products, services, and geographic markets of most banks, as well as the basic structure of the industry itself.

In the 1980s, interest rate ceilings on time and savings deposits were removed, money market deposit accounts became the dominant bank product, and most states removed restrictions on statewide branching and interstate banking. New nonbank competitors took advantage of legal loopholes to begin offering banking services, and banks in turn pressed the regulatory agencies for expanded service powers.

In the early 1990s, the federal deposit insurance system for banks and thrifts was restructured, the pace and size of bank mergers increased, and new capital requirements went into effect that were designed to weed out weak banks. Congress also began considering bills that would permit banks to engage in underwriting, insurance, and real estate brokerage activities, although, through 1992, no bill had been enacted.

Whether or not banks and the public would be well served if banks were permitted to expand their products and services in an interstate banking environment was a key public policy issue in 1992 that remained an unanswered question. Bankers were pressing to know how far Congress was prepared to go in authorizing new powers and at the same time were seeking effective strategies to cope with expected changes.

In this chapter, we will examine some of the major trends and issues in banking today and consider the projections of economists, bankers, and industry consultants for banking through the year 2010.

Predicting the Future of U.S. Banking

Studies of banking trends over the past two decades and examinations of emerging developments offer some insight into how banking might develop in the next two decades.

This method of prediction, called extrapolation, is not foolproof. Sometimes, simple mathematical projections of trends can be misleading because it is hard to judge how long trends will continue. For example, if the rate of bank mergers from 1981 to 1991 continued until the year 2011, only 200 banks would remain. While virtually all banking industry analysts project continued bank mergers and a sharp decline in the number of banks over the next two decades, few see the 1980s pace of mergers continuing unabated over the next 20 years.

Extrapolation of trends also cannot predict banking innovations, new payment practices, or specific banking laws or regulations that will alter the course of banking's development. Nor can extrapolation predict the course of banking developments. For example, bankers were told in the early 1960s that the banking environment of the 1980s would be checkless or even cashless, based on expectations that newly emerging electronic payments technology would transform banking over the next 20 years. Thus, extrapolation could not foresee the public resistance to change and the regulatory constraints that prevented the transformation.

Similarly, few bankers, even those who expected significant regulatory and legal change in the 1970s and 1980s, could have anticipated the fundamental restructuring of banking and banking regulation that Congress advanced in the 1980 Monetary Control Act and the 1989 Financial Institutions Reform, Recovery and Enforcement Act.

Nonetheless, projecting the future on the basis of current trends is an important exercise for banks. It provides a basis for them to initiate programs and strategies for successfully dealing with the future. By identifying trends that may be harmful to their long-term interests, banks can act to forestall the projected effects. They can begin to adapt their operations, technology, business strategies, personnel practices, and interbank relationships to position themselves so that they can garner increased profits and bigger market shares.

Banking Trends

Three major trends over the past two decades are particularly noteworthy:

- ☐ The dominant position of commercial banks in the United States and world financial markets has declined. In the 1970s banks held more than 55 percent of the nation's financial assets. Today, they hold less than 35 percent. In the 1970s, U.S. banks held 30 percent of the world's banking assets; today they hold less than 10 percent. Twenty years ago, 6 of the 10 largest banks in the world were U.S. banks; today no U.S. bank ranks among the world's 10 largest and only 2 U.S. banks rank among the world's 50 largest. In 1992, Japanese banks held about 40 percent of the world's banking assets and Japanese and other foreign banks accounted for more than one-third of all business loans made in the United States.

- ☐ Banks have become less profitable. In the 1970s, banks had stable sources of low-cost funds; interest on checkable funds was prohibited and time and savings accounts were subject to low interest rate ceilings. Today, banks must rely on deposits with interest rates tied to money market rates. On balance, interest expenses rose faster than interest earnings since the deregulation of interest rates in 1980, which narrowed interest spreads and eroded banks' profitability. The profitability of the banking industry steadily declined in the 1980s and from 1983 to year-end 1992, more than 1,300 banks (with assets totaling $200 billion) failed. In 1991, about 1 in 10 U.S. banks registered a loss and 10 of the nation's 48 banks with assets of $10 billion or more were unprofitable.

❏ Banks have become more efficient in their internal operations and more innovative in providing consumers with new banking services and profits. Over the past twenty years, banks have introduced electronic technology to their internal operations and to the delivery of payment services. Virtually all banks today rely on computers and computer-related equipment for check processing, internal recordkeeping, accounting, and interbank transfers of funds. Most banks also have built ATMs and other electronic services into their retail operations. Modifications in banking law and regulations have accelerated these changes and have sparked innovations in banking services and products. In the 1970s, commercial banks had a virtual monopoly in providing checking account and credit services to businesses. Today, banking has become more competitive and more consumer-oriented.

Anticipated Developments

This background of major trends can be used to assess some of the current issues facing banking and to evaluate their likely effect on the future of the banking industry. By the year 2010, significant changes in banking will have occurred. Over the next two decades, economists, bankers, and industry analysts anticipate major developments in the following areas:

❏ new product and service powers

❏ interstate banking

❏ banking industry consolidation

❏ electronic banking services

❏ bank regulatory structure

❏ strategies to maintain banks' profit margins

❏ personnel and labor market trends

New Product and Service Powers

In the 1980s and early 1990s banks have increasingly sought new product and service powers. Bankers have argued that the entry of insurance companies, brokerage firms, finance companies, and retail chains into banking in the 1980s removed the traditional wall of separation that had long existed in the United States between banking and commerce and opened banks to a new source of unfair competition. Banks have been unable to compete effectively for the customers and markets of these new competitors and have lost a substantial share of their own business to these firms. This has happened because banking rules prohibit banks from offering a full range of brokerage, insurance, and investment services and because banks lack the nationwide offices and access to customers enjoyed by most nonbank competitor firms.

In 1992, Congress remained divided on whether to authorize an expansion of bank powers into real estate brokerage, insurance, securities underwriting, and mutual fund investment services (an action favored by most banks); to limit new bank powers to underwriting activities only; or to authorize no new powers. Congressional concern centered on the likely effects of an expansion of powers on bank safety. Three public policy issues in particular were being debated.

First, what financial services are appropriate for bank holding companies to provide, and what services are appropriate for a bank itself to provide? Some members of Congress favored giving banks full-service powers while others wanted to limit new powers or grant no new powers in order to insulate banks from the risks associated with offering additional nonbank services.

Second, if bank holding companies are given new service powers, how can their bank affiliates be insulated from the risks involved in providing these services? In general, Congress favored requiring bank holding companies to establish new subsidiaries to provide all brokerage, underwriting, or insurance services.

Several proposals have called for the authorization of new corporate organizations— financial services holding companies—that could be owned by banks or industrial firms. These new holding companies would be allowed to operate separate banking, brokerage, mutual fund, underwriting, and insurance subsidiaries, each of which would be regulated by the banking, securities, or insurance agency with primary regulatory responsibility for the subsidiary's activity.

Finally, if banking institutions are given expanded powers, how should they be regulated and supervised? Congress generally favored retaining the Federal Reserve as the primary regulator of bank holding companies.

Underwriting

Of all the areas that banks are striving to expand into, underwriting seems to engender the least controversy. Most banking industry analysts expect that, at a minimum, Congress will repeal the Glass-Steagall Act (a section of the Federal Banking Act of 1933) and allow banks and bank holding companies to underwrite stocks and bonds without restrictions.

THE GLASS-STEAGALL ACT

The Glass-Steagall Act of 1933 separates commercial banking from most kinds of investment banking by prohibiting deposit-taking institutions from holding or dealing in stocks and securities (with the exception of U.S. government obligations and the general obligation bonds of states and municipalities). The act also prohibits banks from underwriting revenue bonds issued by state and local governments. This feature of the act became a particular irritant to the nation's large banks in the 1980s. In 1933, revenue bonds accounted for less than 2 percent of all outstanding municipal debt. By the end of the 1980s, however, those bonds constituted more than 70 percent of all securities issued by municipalities.

The Glass-Steagall Act was enacted in response to a view widely held in the 1930s that the practice of allowing a single firm to engage in both securities activities and commercial banking was potentially dangerous. This combination had led, many people thought, to unsound banking practices that contributed to the stock market crash of 1929 and subsequent bank failures during the Great Depression. To prevent a recurrence of this dark episode, Congress in 1933 prohibited commercial banks from underwriting securities. The prohibition was also designed to prevent banks from underwriting the long-term securities of uncreditworthy corporations and then selling the securities to an unsuspecting public to avoid any credit risks to the bank.

Under the Glass-Steagall Act, brokerage firms and investment banks that engaged in underwriting were not permitted to accept deposits. The businesses of commercial banking and investment banking were not allowed to be related even through affiliated companies. Firms that had previously provided both services were forced to split their commercial and investment banking operations into independent businesses. Since 1933, investment banking and commercial banking in the United States have been separate lines of business and have been subject to separate regulation and supervision.

In the 1980s, the sharp line between commercial banks and brokerage firms began to blur as both types of firms increasingly tested the traditional separation between banking and securities activities. The 1980s saw growing affiliations between banks and securities firms, as well as acquisitions of both banks and nonbank banks by securities firms wishing to compete directly in banking activities.

At the same time, commercial banks began to move into the field of discount brokerage. In 1982, the nation's leading money center banks began to acquire or affiliate with established discount brokerage firms. Thereafter, other banks set up their own brokerage operations, clearing trades through conventional securities firms. In some instances, commercial banks and thrifts allowed brokerage firms to establish booths on their banking floors. Today, more than 1,500 commercial banks and thrifts offer brokerage services. Brokerage houses, in turn, offer money market funds and cash management accounts that pay market interest rates and permit overdraft check-writing privileges using a customer's stock portfolio as collateral. In addition to meeting their customers' needs for transaction accounts (liquidity), securities firms offer investment services that are prohibited to commercial banks by Glass-Steagall.

Bankers argue that so long as customers find it convenient to obtain both banking and securities services from one firm, brokerage houses have a competitive edge over commercial banks. In addition, brokerage houses are free from numerous restrictions affecting the competitiveness of commercial banks, such as reserve requirements, capital adequacy requirements, and limitations on loans and investments. This absence of regulation gives brokerage houses significant advantages in competing for banking business.

For these reasons, most bankers argue for repeal of the Glass-Steagall Act, which they contend is no longer necessary. Since the 1930s an elaborate regulatory structure has been put in place to deal with the problems and concerns that the act was intended to address. The securities industry, on the other hand, has lined up against repeal of Glass-Steagall and the entry of banks into underwriting. They contend that the involvement of commercial banks in private securities placement would represent unfair competition. They worry that commercial banks would be in a privileged position to obtain the underwriting business of corporate customers when they seek longer-term financing.

PUBLIC POLICY DEBATE OVER GLASS-STEAGALL

Several public policy issues confront Congress in considering repeal of Glass-Steagall. Most important is whether repeal of the act would increase bank risk and thus threaten the safety and soundness of banking.

Banks already are major underwriters and dealers in U.S. government securities, the general obligation bonds of municipalities, and certain revenue issues. Commercial banks argue that there is no additional risk in underwriting revenue bonds issued by state or local governments, and no fundamental difference in the credit and market risks involved in lending to corporations or underwriting corporate stocks and bonds. They contend that underwriting may actually be less risky to banks than lending funds since, in underwriting, a bank generally holds a security for a few days at most whereas, in lending funds, a bank usually retains the loan asset on its books for a long time. Changes in interest rates and the business condition of the borrower during the period that a loan is outstanding can turn a good loan asset into a poor one, thereby generating more risk to a bank than underwriting a corporate stock or bond.

Moreover, bankers argue, banks already participate in corporate securities markets overseas. Through merchant banking subsidiaries in Europe, U.S. banks freely underwrite and deal in corporate securities, and have done so for decades without impairing the safety and soundness of Europe's banking system.

A second major issue is whether repeal of Glass-Steagall, by allowing commercial banks to underwrite stocks and bonds, would result in a significant potential for conflict of interest or abuse. Again, proponents of repeal point out that the disclosure requirements of the Securities Act of 1933 and the Securities Exchange Act of 1934 effectively curbed speculative abuses and conflicts of interest in securities markets by investment bankers and brokers. They suggest that comparable regulations could be imposed on the underwriting activities of commercial banks.

Many observers fear that repeal of Glass-Steagall would result in widescale merging of banks and brokerage firms, resulting in the formation of huge financial conglomerates that would limit competition. Proponents of repeal, however, note that the 10 largest securities firms already account for nearly 85 percent of the nation's underwriting business. By permitting banks to underwrite securities, they argue, competition might actually be increased. Moreover, legal barriers to concentration can be established by stipulating in any act to repeal, for example, that large banks would be prohibited from merging with large securities firms.

Other Areas of Product and Service Expansion

In the 1980s, state governments were in the forefront of legislative change to allow banks to offer expanded services and products. State-chartered banks in half the states were authorized to provide insurance, real estate brokerage, mutual fund, stock broker-age, and securities underwriting services and to invest in corporate stock and real estate development projects.

Those state legislative changes, coupled with actions by the OCC and the Federal Reserve—and favorable rulings by the courts—have basically made stock brokerage and mutual fund sales permissible activities for almost every bank in the country.

Technically, banks cannot sponsor, distribute, or underwrite mutual funds. Thus, they cannot place their names on the mutual funds they sell to customers. However, banks can broker mutual funds managed by other companies or the securities subsidiaries of their parent holding companies. In 1992, almost all the nation's large commercial banks were offering mutual funds, primarily through securities subsidiaries. Industry analysts estimated that banks held about 10 percent of the mutual funds market.

By 1992, 17 states had authorized state chartered banks to provide general insurance brokerage activities and four of these states (New Jersey, North Carolina, South Dakota, Delaware) had permitted banks to engage in insurance underwriting. (Every state permits banks to sell credit insurance.)

Nationally chartered banks have long been authorized by the OCC to engage in a broad range of insurance and insurance-related activities. These include the underwriting and sale of credit and title insurance and the sale of fixed-and variable-rate annuities. National banks also are allowed to lease branch office space to an insurance agency for a percentage of the agency's sales revenues.

Since 1916, national banks have been permitted to sell all types of insurance from offices located in towns with populations of fewer than 5,000 residents. Purchasers need not be local or even state residents. In 1992, however, a federal court ruled that this authority was actually repealed by the government in 1918. The OCC has appealed this ruling and while the appeal is in process existing insurance activities of national banks with offices in small towns are not affected. The federal appeals process may last until 1994 and the U.S. Supreme Court may ultimately have to resolve this issue. Industry analysts expect, however, that Congress will clarify the government's intent with regard to banks and insurance activities with new federal legislation before then.

Bank holding companies, like national banks, can underwrite and sell credit insurance and sell insurance from offices in small towns. Small bank holding companies also can engage in general insurance agency activities, but cannot sell life insurance or annuities. However, before 1971, bank holding companies had broader insurance authority and several still do.

When the 1956 Bank Holding Company Act was amended in 1971 to cover single-bank holding companies, insurance powers for both multi-bank and single-bank holding companies were restricted, but those companies that had been providing full insurance services were *grandfathered*. Today, about 20 bank holding companies are allowed to provide unlimited insurance agency activities under the 1971 grandfather clause.

The Bank Holding Company Act was amended again in 1982 and still further insurance activity restrictions were placed on bank holding companies. A similar grandfather clause in 1982 permits hundreds of other bank holding companies to continue to provide in the 1990s the more limited range of insurance agency services that they provided between 1971 and 1982.

In 1992, banks received about $300 million in revenues from insurance sales. Industry analysts estimate that if current trends continue, revenues from insurance will continue to increase steadily, with banks selling about $40 billion in annuities by 1995.

The insurance industry contends that state laws authorizing insurance activities for banks and the insurance authority given national banks and bank holding companies by the federal regulators will open the way for the nation's largest banks and bank holding companies to buy existing insurance companies in the 1990s. These acquisitions will reduce the number of insurance industry competitors and thus reduce competition and drive up prices in the insurance industry.

THE LONGER-TERM OUTLOOK

Within the next two decades, all banks will likely be allowed to provide numerous loan and deposit products, underwrite insurance policies and stocks and bonds, and offer brokerage and trading services. Tomorrow's banks also will sell information and advisory services, such as forecasting the outlook for the economy or for specific financial markets; assessing insurance and credit risks and risks in the nation's stock and bond markets. Banks of the future also are likely to offer a range of administrative and custodial services, such as loan administration, insurance policy administration, management of customer accounts, trust administration, stockholder accounting, and safekeeping. Banks also can be expected to provide portfolio management services for pension funds and trust portfolios.

Interstate Banking

As we saw in the previous chapter, interstate banking and branching is another area undergoing considerable change. In the 1980s most of the state reciprocal banking agreements that limited reciprocity to the states in the region will allow entry to banks from all states beginning in 1993. As can be seen in exhibit 10.1, the majority of the West, Southwest, and Great Lakes states will permit interstate banking on either an open entry or national reciprocal basis. The Southeast and New England states will still be limiting interstate banking to banks in their respective regions only. As these laws go into effect, complementary federal legislation to allow banks to branch on an interstate basis is likely.

Interstate banking in the 1990s is not likely, however, to result in the nation's money center banks physically establishing branches in small towns across the country. Rather, interstate banking will probably entail large banks affiliating with smaller banks outside their regions through mergers, holding company acquisitions, and shared participation in financial service delivery systems.

Factors Influencing Interstate Banking

Interstate banking has become a reality mainly because market developments and competitive factors in the 1980s induced a fundamental change in attitude among the states. States increasingly recognized that despite their restrictions and prohibitions interstate banking in various guises already existed. Rulings by the U.S. Supreme Court in the late 1980s upholding states' regional reciprocal banking agreements and interstate linkages of ATMs were also a factor. A number of developments and considerations motivated the states to liberalize their statewide branching and interstate banking restrictions.

GRANDFATHERED INTERSTATE BANKS

One factor was the existence of interstate banks that had been created by bank holding companies before they were prohibited by federal law. In 1956, the Douglas Amendment to the Bank Holding Company Act prohibited bank holding companies from acquiring banks outside their home state unless authorized by state law. However, bank holding companies that already had interstate branches were grandfathered. Thus, 12 bank holding companies—5 of them foreign owned—were permitted to continue to operate outside their home states because they had formed multistate networks before 1956. These holding companies had established a total of 130 out-of-state banks through the 1980s.

EXHIBIT 10.1   **Interstate Banking Regulation in 1993**

	Regional Reciprocal
	National Reciprocal
	Open-Entry
	None

Source: Federal Reserve Bank of Dallas, *Economic Review*, November 1989.

NONBANK SUBSIDIARIES OF BANK HOLDING COMPANIES

Another factor influencing the liberalization of state laws was the fact that nonbank subsidiaries of bank holding companies had never been subject to interstate banking restrictions. In the 1980s, large bank holding companies established extensive multistate financial service organizations, with hundreds of offices throughout the country. In addition, a number of brokerage firms, retail firms, and other nonbank companies found they could enter the banking business by establishing *nonbank banks*. Several bank holding companies also used this legal loophole to establish out-of-state nonbank banks in the 1980s (until Congress prohibited the practice in 1987). Today, 55 multistate bank holding companies operate 7,500 offices, including 1,500 banking offices, outside their home states.

TAKEOVERS OF FAILING DEPOSITORIES

In the 1980s, more than 20 banks gained entry into other states by acquiring a failing savings bank or savings and loan association across state lines. This served to further dissolve the prohibition against interstate branching.

LOAN PRODUCTION OFFICES AND EDGE ACT CORPORATIONS

In recent years, a number of major banks established loan production offices in commercial centers outside their states to service customers with large business loans. A loan production office does not accept deposits, but simply serves as a sales and customer-service center. Thus, these offices are not subject to interstate branching restrictions. Edge Act subsidiaries of banks, which engage exclusively in international banking and investment business, also are permitted to open branches in other states to meet the foreign trade financing needs of bank customers. Again, the existence of these interstate organizations offering banking-type services helped move states to relax their anti-branching position.

EXPANDED BANKING BY PHONE, MAIL, AND LINKED ATMS

The U.S. banking industry became increasingly national in scope in the 1980s as correspondent banks moved interbank funds between different regions of the country, and as banks sold loans from region to region and solicited deposits and loans by mail nationwide. Increasing numbers of banks also began linking their ATMs into vast networks, permitting customers to use ATMs owned by other banks in the network, some of which were out-of-state. In effect, customers who used these ATM networks could withdraw funds from out-of-state locations. States recognized that the coming nationwide expansion of these linked ATM systems (an expectation for the 1990s) would move retail banking significantly closer to full interstate banking.

Banking Industry Consolidation

Another major trend in the years ahead—largely reflecting the increased competition that will come with nationwide banking—is expected to be increased consolidation within the banking industry. As operating costs, loan loss reserves, and capital pressures continue to strain bank profitability, banks can be expected to seek to strengthen their positions through consolidation—by merging with one another, by affiliating with financial service conglomerates, or by purchasing smaller banks.

Thus a period of substantial consolidation is expected in the banking industry during the next two decades. Industry analysts predict that thousands of existing banks and thrifts will go out of business, many of them being absorbed into the nationwide organizations of large financial institutions. However, thousands of strong, community-based banks will survive and profit as independent institutions by serving their local markets through affiliations with national payments networks, such as Visa, MasterCard and interstate ATM systems.

By the year 2010, the number of banks in the United States is likely to decline from today's 12,000 to about 6,000 to 8,000 as banks continue to merge in an effort to reduce operating costs, increase capital and retain competitive market shares of key banking products. However, bank customers are not likely to notice much difference. While merged banks will combine management and back-office operations, relatively few branches are likely to be closed. As exhibit 10.2 shows, the trends of the 1980s suggest that as the number of banks decline in the 1990s, the number of bank branches will continue to increase, perhaps to 60,000. Trends also suggest that a large share of new bank branches in the 1990s will be housed in supermarkets.

Branch offices in supermarkets increased from 200 in 1985 to 1,200 in 1991. Most of these branches were established by banks in the nation's southern and southwestern states. Industry analysts project that by 1994, 300 to 600 additional branches will be housed in supermarkets, most of them established by banks in the northeastern states. Many bankers see in these branches a way to reach and serve, at low cost, a broader base of customers in the 1990s. Supermarket branches are typically staffed by two to five people, equipped with one or more ATMs, and cost about one-third less to build and maintain than conventional stand-alone offices.

Exhibit 10.2   **Number of U.S. Banks and Branches**

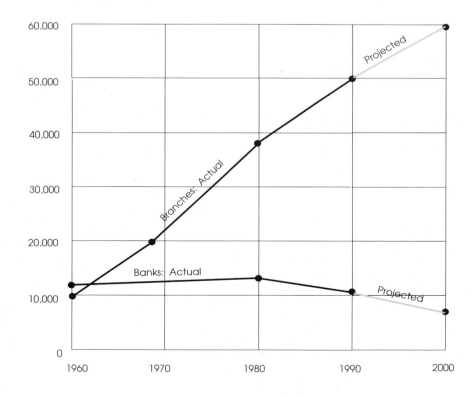

Source: American Banker, April 16, 1991

Projections differ regarding the precise degree of consolidation that will take place over the next 20 years. Some economists project that if all federal and state branching restrictions are removed, the number of banks will decline substantially by the year 2010. They make these predictions by examining the ratio of number of banks to number of people in countries (and states) that have no restrictions on branching, and then applying the same ratio to the United States. For example, Canada has eight large banks that serve 26 million Canadians. Six of those banks operate nationwide. If the United States had the same ratio of banks to people as Canada, America would have only 75 banks, of which about 55 would operate nationwide. The state of California provides another example. California, the most populous state, has permitted state-wide branching since 1909. It has 430 banks that serve 29 million Californians. If the entire country had the same ratio of banks to people as California, there would be only 3,700 banks in the United States.

Most economists contend that such factors as the long-standing profitability and market strength of local banks and the extensive development of bank holding companies and subsidiaries (as opposed to branches), will lead to less dramatic declines. Based on consolidation patterns in other industries, many analysts project that by the year 2010 the structure of the U.S. banking industry will consist of the following four tiers:

Global Banks. The first tier will comprise a select group of full-service financial institutions that operate in both U.S. and overseas banking markets. Not all these banks are expected to be the same as the dominant commercial banks of the 1990s. It is likely that several foreign-owned banks and several nonbanking institutions will be in this tier. The global banks—about 20 to 30—will offer a full range of domestic financial services while playing a major role in international trade and finance. Several Japanese conglomerates will probably dominate this tier with assets approaching $500 billion each; most global banks, however, will probably have assets in the $100 billion range.

Superregional Banks. The second tier will consist of 40 to 60 major regional banks that will provide consumer and business banking products and services—and such specialized international products as foreign exchange and letters of credit—over much larger geographic markets than most regional banks now have. They will each hold assets of $30 billion to $50 billion and will dominate their regions' midsize business and consumer markets.

Specialized Banks. Several thousand banks probably will occupy the third banking tier. These banks will be distinguished by their commitment to a single product line, a specific group of customers, or a select segment of the banking market. The specialized banks will provide customized service in, for example, mortgage lending, short-term business financing, brokerage, or insurance. Residential mortgages probably will be arranged by specialized mortgage banks operating through real estate brokers with funds supplied in the nation's bond markets. Most personal loans probably will be made on credit cards through banks that specialize in installment credit, and small businesses will likely do most of their borrowing from specialized finance companies.

A significant portion of these banks' retail transactions probably will be through electronic terminals linked to stores. The specialized banks will remain competitive with the total service global and superregional banks by offering customized services.

Community-Based Banks. Most of the banking industry will comprise the fourth tier. These banks will provide a broad range of financial services, but will focus only on local markets and customers. The competitive environment in 2010 for third- and fourth-tier banks will be much more intense than it is today, with department store chains, brokerage houses, and finance companies firmly entrenched as active bank competitors.

Franchise Agreements

Many smaller banks are positioning themselves for the competitive environment of the 1990s by entering into franchise arrangements with regional banks. Under a franchise arrangement, a regional bank sells its name and its products to a smaller bank. The smaller bank maintains its own corporate identity and continues to determine its own loan and deposit rates and its own personnel policies. However, the franchise arrangement links the name of the regional bank with the smaller bank through combined advertising, referral cards for check cashing that list both banks, and ATMs that serve both banks. Typically, the regional bank gives its participating franchise banks exclusive contracts that prevent other banks in a franchisee's immediate area or state from joining the franchise network.

Franchising is most frequently used by banks that are too large to focus their business on a particular product or market, but too small to compete directly with the largest banks in their markets. By sharing expenses, franchising also enables some smaller banks to obtain technology, supplies, services, and national advertising that otherwise would be too costly. Franchising also has allowed some regional banks to quicken the pace of interstate branching by acquiring de facto branches outside their home states.

Electronic Banking Services

Over the next two decades, banks are expected to apply electronic technology to more aspects of their internal operations and to the delivery of payments and services. Already, virtually all banks rely on computers and computer-related equipment for check processing, internal recordkeeping, accounting, and interbank transfers of funds. Banks also are increasingly using electronic funds transfer systems in their retail operations.

Coin and currency will continue to play a small but important role in the day-to-day convenience transactions of consumers and retailers. Checks also will continue to be the primary consumer and business payment method. And banks will continue to devote considerable resources and management attention to check processing and collection. What is likely to change by the year 2010, however, is the proportion of paper payments relative to electronic payments. The next two decades will see a much greater proportion of consumer, business, and government payments made electronically. Other likely changes will be improvements in EFT systems, further automation of retail banking services, extension of electronic payments systems to retail outlets, and continued development of network payments systems.

Electronic Funds Transfer Systems

The EFT systems that banks and the Federal Reserve installed in the 1960s and 1970s to move interbank balances increased the speed and efficiency of moving money and made it possible for a broad range of banks to offer electronic transfer services to corporate and individual customers. These EFT systems, primarily FedWire and CHIPS, also allowed banks to increase their volume of payments and make transactions flow through a narrower base of demand deposits and reserves. However, those two factors substantially increased banks' risks in using the electronic transfer systems.

Over the next two decades, improvements in technology will allow banks to manage payments risk while handling a greater volume of electronic information related to payment transactions. Broad use of payment netting arrangements will blunt the accelerating growth of interbank electronic transfers, while new technology will encourage banks to develop specialized electronic payment services for corporate and individual accounts, supported by smaller, more powerful, and less expensive computers. Virtually all depositories will have direct computer-to-computer or terminal-to-computer links to national EFT transfer systems.

Retail Banking Services

Retail banking services as well as internal bank operations will become increasingly more automated. New technology will allow high-volume banks to provide more sophisticated payment services to consumer and corporate customers at lower unit costs. The costs of new technology in the 1980s were more than most small and mid-sized banks could afford. As a result, those banks were unable to provide electronic payment services equal to those of the nation's big banks. However, over the next two decades, the availability of less expensive computers will enable small community-based depositories to match the electronic services of the big banks. Also, many small and mid-sized banks will merge, seek holding company affiliations, or establish service companies under cooperative arrangements, which will enable them to broaden their services.

Service Delivery

Providers of banking services already include nontraditional participants such as department stores, brokerage firms, and telephone companies. The options for delivering banking services to consumer and corporate customers by these nontraditional sources will be greater in 10 years than they are now. More business will be transacted between terminals in retail stores and phones in homes, and cable television and telephone links will allow virtually all banking to be conducted in homes and offices.

However, Americans will still prefer to visit banks to conduct most of their banking business.

NETWORK PAYMENT SYSTEMS

Banks will increasingly rely on networks of ATMs and POS terminals to deliver nationwide retail banking services. Consumers will perform more retail banking activities with credit and debit cards and will increase their use of ATMs, POS terminals, and television and telephone transactions. However, the volume of personal cash and check transactions involving banks will likely be no lower in the year 2010 than it is today.

Bank Regulatory Structure

The U.S. banking industry is likely to remain highly regulated in the 1990s and beyond. The system of regulation and examination that has, for the most part, resulted in a safe and sound banking system is likely to remain unchanged for the foreseeable future.

The nation's dual banking system (in which chartering and regulation are responsibilities shared by the states and the federal government) is likely to continue. However, key functions of the federal bank and thrift regulatory agencies—the FDIC, the OCC, the Federal Reserve Board, the OTS, and the National Credit Union Administration—may be restructured or consolidated within the next two decades.

The current bank regulatory structure is the product of responses to specific problems and needs that have arisen over the last 80 years. Economists, bankers, and government commissions have contended over the years that this structure has led to a duplication of authority, regulatory laxity among agencies wishing to attract constituents, and conflicting and inequitable treatment of similar institutions by different regulators.

A key issue, in the view of many bankers, is whether the existing regulatory structure is adequate for the changing banking environment of the 1990s. They question whether banks should continue to be regulated by laws and agencies created a half century ago to supervise and regulate a banking industry that was very different from the industry that exists today. Many bankers, for example, cite the need for a comprehensive revision of the nation's bank regulatory structure and banking laws so that banks can compete on even terms with nonbank financial institutions.

They further contend that increasing banks' financial services would not establish competitive equality for banks unless the finance companies, brokerage firms, and retail chains that provide banking services are regulated like banks.

In 1992, Congress considered a number of proposals to revise bank service regulations and streamline the federal regulatory structure, in part to address the problem of banks' competitiveness. However, no consensus was reached. Under most of the proposals considered, banks would have been authorized to establish branches in any state. Banks also would have been allowed, through their holding companies, to offer brokerage, insurance, securities underwriting, and mutual fund investment services. The Treasury had further proposed that federal regulation be consolidated to strengthen banking by ending the fragmentation of federal oversight.

For decades, banker and congressional sentiment has been divided on whether concentrating regulatory power in one or two agencies would benefit banks or the public. The appropriate division of responsibilities among the federal regulatory agencies charged with examining banks and supervising their holding companies has also been a highly contentious issue.

Numerous far-reaching, but widely divergent, proposals have been made to change the bank regulatory structure. For example, in 1949 and again in 1961, presidential commissions recommended that all federal supervisory and regulatory functions with respect to banks be consolidated into the Federal Reserve. The 1961 Commission on Money and Credit also recommended that a separate agency be established to supervise federally chartered thrift institutions. In 1962, another presidential commission on banking took the opposite tack and recommended that the Federal Reserve be divested of all its bank supervisory and regulatory responsibilities except those pertaining to monetary policy.

Most recently, in 1984, a Presidential Task Force on Regulation of Financial Services, chaired by Vice President George Bush, proposed to redistribute the responsibilities of the various bank regulatory agencies in a more functional way without fundamentally changing the structure of the agencies themselves.

Under the recommendations of the Bush Task Force, none of the federal regulatory agencies would be eliminated; instead, a new Federal Banking Agency (FBA) would be created within the Treasury Department to assume the regulatory (but not the chartering) responsibilities of the Comptroller of the Currency. The new FBA would supervise, examine, and regulate all federally chartered banks and all but 50 of the largest bank holding companies. The FBA also would take over from the Federal Reserve Board the role of defining which nonbank activities are permissible for bank holding companies.

The FDIC's day-to-day supervisory activities over state-chartered banks would be sharply curtailed, enabling it to concentrate on its deposit insurance function. The FDIC would retain its authority to examine banks for insurance purposes, to deny or revoke insurance, and to set premiums in relation to the stability or lack of stability of a bank's assets. Its examination activities, however, would cover only troubled banks.

Under the Bush Task Force proposals, the Federal Reserve would be responsible for supervising, examining, and regulating the nation's 50 largest international-class bank holding companies. Initially, the Federal Reserve would also assume responsibility (from the FDIC) for the supervision, examination, and regulation of the nation's 7,000 state-chartered banks that are not members of the Federal Reserve. The states, however, would eventually assume this responsibility.

Prospects for Regulatory Consolidation

The legal and regulatory differences among savings banks, savings and loan associations, and commercial banks have all but disappeared. Over the next 20 years, other financial institutions, such as credit unions, finance companies, insurance companies, pension funds, money market funds, and brokerage firms will be offering banking and payment services similar to those offered by banks. In fact, it is likely that the financial services that can be provided by bank holding companies will be broadened and that large companies, such as IBM and General Motors, will be allowed to provide banking services through subsidiaries. Those changes will lead Congress to restructure the powers and responsibilities of the federal bank regulatory agencies.

In the early 1990s, Congress was considering a functional approach to regulating financial service holding companies. Under functional regulation, each agency responsible for a specific financial activity, such as insurance, brokerage, or banking, would be responsible for regulating the subsidiary engaged in that activity regardless of the origin of the holding company. However, some analysts forecast that by the year 2000, the bank supervisory and regulatory functions of the Federal Deposit Insurance Corporation, Comptroller of the Currency, and Federal Reserve Board will be combined into a single agency.

In 1991, Congress restructured the federal deposit insurance system to strengthen the depleted deposit insurance fund and to reduce banks' risk taking. The way banks' insurance premiums are assessed was also changed, from the total amount of the bank's insured deposits to the risk rating of the insured bank. However, as 1993 began, bankers, government officials, and Congress were divided in their views of whether the public, as well as banks, would be best served by 1991's solution to the FDIC's funding needs. At issue was whether structural changes in banking should be made that could help the insurance fund by increasing banks' profitability. Possible changes include authorizing interstate branching and allowing banks to affiliate with insurance companies and securities firms or to offer insurance and investment products.

Although the bank regulatory structure is likely to change over the next two decades, chartering, insurance, and examinations will remain the primary focus of the federal regulatory oversight of banks. Increased regulation may even emerge in the area of bank management controls on information, privacy, and communications security in

EFT systems. The prevailing viewpoint, however, is that regulatory responsibilities will be reallocated among the federal agencies as banks expand more extensively outside their home states and begin providing insurance, real estate, and mutual fund investment services.

Strategies to Maintain Banks' Profit Margins

As fees for banking services exceed interest income as the primary source of bank earnings, the provision of bank services to individual and corporate customers will become increasingly more important. The traditional business of banking—taking in demand deposits and making loans—will shrink in importance during the 1990s as competition increasingly cuts profit margins in those activities.

Lending funds to major corporations will continue to decline as the primary use of banks' funds, although lending to small and midsize companies will continue to be lucrative. As commercial lending becomes progressively less profitable for banks, insurance, mutual funds, and other consumer investment products are likely to become increasingly more profitable. To meet the challenge of that changed environment, banks will have to become expert at selling mutual fund and annuity products together with traditional banking products. The task will be difficult and costly because bank personnel will have to be trained to sell the broad range of savings and investment products that banks may have available in the 1990s.

Reducing Operating Costs

Reducing operating costs became a popular bank management practice in the 1980s; this practice is seen by most industry analysts as continuing well into the 1990s as banks institute strategies to restore profitability.

Most banks focused their cost reduction strategies on the noninterest expense category that increased the fastest in the 1980s—employee benefits costs—and salaries, the core component of bank operating costs. For example, most banks changed their health insurance programs to require employees to pay a share of the costs of medical insurance coverage for dependents and tightened other fringe benefits. Nonetheless, today, employee health insurance coverage, pension benefits, and other salary-related costs still add 25 to 40 percent for every salary dollar spent by a bank. Many banks also instituted one or more of the following staff reduction measures, all of which are likely to be applied periodically in the 1990s.

Layoffs. Many of the nation's largest banks resorted to layoffs in the 1980s and early 1990s in an effort to prune their size and reduce operating costs. However, analysts see a potential danger in the broad application of this expense reduction tactic. They contend that bankwide layoffs often spread uncertainty and lower morale among surviving staff on whom the bank must depend for higher productivity. Unless layoffs are targeted to specific areas in which the bank is reducing its involvement—closing branches or phasing out services—some work processes may be impaired, reducing the bank's efficiency and, ultimately, increasing its operating costs.

Early Retirement. In the 1980s, most large banks offered employees nearing retirement age financial inducements to retire early. Banks generated savings by replacing older workers who were earning high salaries with younger workers at lower salaries and not replacing every retiree. This strategy partially succeeded because the nation's labor force was growing rapidly in the 1980s and young workers were readily available. However, projections show that fewer workers will be entering the labor force in the 1990s than in the 1980s and by the year 2000, one-third of the labor force will be over age 45. Thus, banks' reliance on early retirement programs as a cost reduction strategy may not be effective in the 1990s. Some industry analysts project that banks may have to pay increasingly higher wages in the 1990s to attract and retain essential personnel. As banks recognize this trend, industry analysts forecast that banks will increasingly invest in labor-saving technology and intensify efforts to institute more productivity-generating management and work practices.

Reorganization and Consolidation. Many banks have reorganized their internal management structures to parallel changes in business strategies, have regrouped various line and staff departments to match market conditions and service offerings, and consolidated branch offices to reduce costs. For example, by combining related departments and broadening managers' spans of control over employees, large banks have found that fewer managers, supervisory, and secretarial staff are needed. Also, banks with branch operations have found that a small staff can turn out the same volume of work as a large one by consolidating certain back office operations, such as data processing, accounting, and funds transfer.

In the 1980s, the focus of most bank reorganizations and consolidations was on back-office and operating departments where, despite automation, staff growth had increased steadily since the 1960s. Many banks that automated in the 1960s and 1970s found that automation did not bring lower operating costs along with smaller staffs. In many instances, reductions in low-salaried clerical personnel were more than offset by increases in high-salaried data processing and other computer-related technical personnel. Banks' efforts in the 1980s to reduce operating costs sought to solve this problem.

Over the next decade, it is likely that fewer back-office staff will be needed by banks of all sizes. Many banks will reduce their need for operating staff by buying their data processing, check processing, and accounting services from nonbank companies. Other banks are likely to reduce operating staffs by consolidating more of their branch operations and computer systems at central sites, which will provide all offices with access to computer services through terminals and leased telephone lines.

Hiring Workers over 65 as Part-time Tellers and Clerical Workers. Today, most banks rely on part-time staff for covering peak periods in branches and in back office operations. Many banks have found that they can reduce salary and benefits costs by hiring senior citizens, especially their own retirees, as part-time workers. As hourly wage employees, these workers are paid no fringe benefits, and in the case of retirees, there are no agency fees. Agency fees can raise the hourly cost of a temporary employee about 50 percent above that of a regular employee in the same job. Banks also avoid extensive training costs with retirees who bring their knowledge of the bank and bank operations to their part-time job.

Hiring Contract Personnel. Some banks have reduced costs by hiring personnel on contract as consultants, rather than as employees, in areas where discrete projects or tasks are involved. For example, some banks have disbanded their marketing or data processing units and contracted their former employees, as individuals or as a group, to perform specific tasks, such as conducting a market survey or installing and testing new computer software. The contract guarantees the former employees a certain amount of business (and income) but gives them the freedom to work at other jobs. Banks save because they do not have to pay Social Security taxes or fringe benefits for consultants on contract.

Repricing Services

Another strategy banks are using to protect their profit margins is to reprice services to raise more revenue or offset rising operating costs. Many banks also have reduced the costs associated with small deposits by imposing higher minimum-balance requirements on accounts and by imposing service charges on services previously provided without charge.

Based on current trends, U.S. bank customers two decades from today are likely to be older, more affluent, and better educated—reflecting the increasing longevity of the American population, the increasing number of two-wage-earner households, and the rising level of education and pay of the U.S. work force. Bank customers in 2010 are likely to want more sophisticated financial products and services, such as mobile mortgages (which travel with the mortgagee who moves or relocates), estate planning, and tax advisory services; they are likely to favor convenience and time saving in conventional deposit and payment transactions; and they are likely to be willing to pay a premium for expert and customized services.

Most bank analysts contend that banks need to begin now to adapt today's service offerings and delivery systems to position themselves to meet the banking needs of tomorrow's customers. For some banks, this may mean the establishment of highly automated branches where routine transactions can be completed by computers without bank personnel on the premises. For other banks, a redirection of marketing focus to specialized high-quality financial products and services may be the appropriate positioning strategy. In the broader competitive environment projected over the next 20 years, all banks will probably have to sharpen their marketing skills and their ability to differentiate their products and services from those of other providers of financial services.

Personnel and Labor Market Trends

Bank employment is projected to decline in the 1990s from 1.5 million in 1990 to about 1.3 million by the year 2000, with the bulk of the reduction coming from the nation's larger banks. Industry analysts base this projection on three expectations for the 1990s:

❏ Banks will continue to use strategies designed to reduce operating costs.

❏ The number and size of bank mergers will continue to grow.

❏ Banks will continue to automate.

Few analysts see bank employment declining by more than 20 percent (200,000 jobs) over the next 10 years because increasing growth in the volume of deposits, check processing, and other payments-related work done by banks' back-office personnel will prevent large staff reductions. Some analysts suggest that the decline in bank employment in the 1990s could be as few as 100,000 jobs, noting that, despite massive layoffs at the nation's leading money center banks, total employment at other banks (those with less than $1 billion in assets) actually increased by 6 percent from 1988 to 1992, to 625,000.

In 1960, commercial banks employed about 650,000 people. By 1985, the total banking workforce had grown to more than 1.5 million; then bank employment levels began to decline as banks began to retrench in response to escalating operating costs and declining profits. However, automation played a major role. By the mid-1980s, the productivity-generating effects of increased automation in such areas as check processing, funds transfer, and cash management operations made large-scale clerical and operating staff reductions possible. Most of the banking jobs eliminated in the 1980s were in back-office clerical and data processing areas.

As exhibit 10.3 shows, banking employment is highly concentrated, with the nation's 25 largest bank holding companies accounting for more than 40 percent of all bank employees. Bank employment also is heavily weighted toward teller and clerical jobs.

EXHIBIT 10.3   **Employment at the 25 Largest Banking Companies**
(Adjusted for mergers; companies ranked by total assets on
December 31, 1991.)

Rank	Name of Banking Company	Total Employment 1991	Percentage Change in Employment 1987-1991
1	Citicorp, NY	86,000	-4.4
2	Chemical Banking Corp, NY	43,169	-28.7
3	Bank America Corp., SF	54,400	-8.6
4	Nationbank Corp., Charlotte, NC	57,177	+1.0
5	J. P. Morgan & Co., Inc. NY	13,323	-11.2
6	Chase Manhattan Corp., NY	36,210	-16.9
7	Security Pacific Corp., LA	37,300	-17.0
8	Bankers Trust New York Corp.	12,088	-1.7
9	Wells Fargo & Co., SF	18,830	-14.2
10	First Chicago Corp.	17,014	+11.7
11	First Interstate Bankcorp, LA	30,281	-23.8
12	Banc One Corp, Columbus, Ohio	30,000	+13.1
13	First Union Corp., Charlotte, NC	24,203	-27.4
14	Fleet/Norstar Fin. Group, RI	26,000	-30.5
15	PNC Financial Corp, Pittsburgh	16,908	+6.6
16	Bank of New York Co., Inc.	13,226	-35.9
17	Norwest Corp, Minneapolis	25,500	+23.9
18	Sun Trust Banks, Inc., Atlanta	19,109	-4.7
19	Wachovia Corp, Winston Salem, NC	17,643	+2.7
20	Barnett Banks, Inc., Fla.	17,555	-4.7
21	Bank of Boston Corp	16,100	-21.8
22	Republic New York Corp	4,549	+24.2
23	First Fidelity Bancorp, NJ	11,504	-29.9
24	NBD Bancorp, Inc., Detroit	13,185	+10.5
25	Mellon Bank Corp, Pittsburgh	16,300	-6.1
	Total for 25 Largest Banks	657,574	-11.1
	Total Bank Employment	1,486,159	-3.5

Source: "Ranking the Banks," *American Banker,* 1992.

Exhibit 10.4 shows that the top 17 job categories in banking (out of 258 occupation categories) account for nearly 80 percent of all banking jobs; and that most are bank teller or clerical positions, such as typists, secretaries, and clerks. A profile of banking employment is shown in exhibit 10.5.

EXHIBIT 10.4   **Bank Employment in the 1980s by Major Job Category**

Job Category	Average Number of Jobs
Bank tellers	343,000
Bank managers	280,000
General office clerks	110,000
Secretaries	74,000
Bookkeeping and billing operators	61,000
Clerical supervisors	59,000
Proofreading machine operators	46,000
Computer operators	35,000
Bank statement clerks	29,000
Building custodians	22,000
Typists	20,000
Loan closing clerks	19,000
Banking and insurance credit clerks	19,000
File clerks	18,000
Bill collectors	17,000
Accountants and auditors	16,000
Messengers	14,000
Top 17 Job Categories	1,182,000
Total Banking Employment	1,500,000

Source: Bureau of Labor Statistics; New York Stock Exchange; *American Banker*, April 16, 1991.

Industry analysts forecast that banks will continue to rely on computer technology in the 1990s to reduce their overall employment needs. Many bankers expect that continuing automation over the next two decades will significantly reduce the need for tellers, the largest job category of bank personnel. However, there is no evidence to date that increased automation or ATM deployment has displaced tellers. Automation often requires more bank personnel to maintain computers and software, to supply ATMs with cash, to prepare and tally ATM tapes, and to address consumer inquiries and complaints.

EXHIBIT 10.5   Profile of Banking Employment

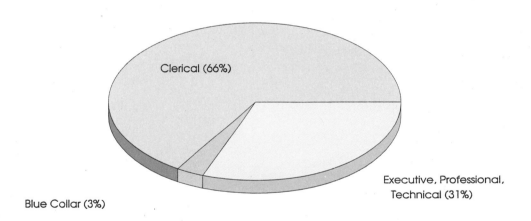

Most banking analysts believe that the application of computer technology in the next 20 years will lead to staff reductions in back-office operations. For example, the use of image-processing systems, which send digitized images of checks and other documents electronically, eliminates the need for many key-punch operations. Analysts also project that many banks will reduce back-office employment needs by ending their in-house processing of checks and accounts-related data. Those banks will purchase necessary computer, accounting, and data processing services from other companies.

The national trend toward applying computer technology to office activities such as secretarial operations will be particularly strong in banking, but this application is not likely to generate substantial staffing reductions. Instead, the nature of clerical, secretarial, and professional functions in banking will change. Personal computers and desktop terminals will give bankers instant access to files and data, and teletype-telephones and interactive television will increase the efficiency of conference calls and meetings. A considerable share of work also will be performed at operations centers remote from banks' head offices, or at home via terminal access to bank computers.

A Changing Labor Force

Banks will face new challenges in recruiting, training, managing, and motivating employees over the next two decades because of profound changes in the workforce. Demographic trends in the 1990s suggest that by the year 2000 the workforce will be older and will comprise more women and minorities than it does today.

These trends suggest that over the next 10 years there will be a disproportionate increase in the number of women and minorities employed in banks and in the number of bank employees in the 30-50 age group. There also will be a shift from the employment of primarily clerical and technical personnel toward the employment of more professional and customer-contact personnel.

Those changes will have a major impact on the personnel policies and practices of banks. Many banks have already modified personnel policies to accommodate the needs and concerns of the changing workforce. These modifications, which are likely to become pervasive in banking in the 1990s, include:

- ❑ health benefits that cover employees' parents as well as dependent children;

- ❑ both paid and unpaid leave for employees to care for a newborn;

- ❑ job sharing, in which two employees share one full-time position;

- ❑ work-at-home arrangements, in which part of the work is done at home;

- ❑ flextime opportunities that allow employees to work 35 to 40 hours in less than 5 days;

- ❑ flexible benefit programs that allow employees to select the benefits that best meet their personal and family needs.

The introduction of new products and services by banks, and banks' continuing adoption of new technology to process data and information also will require bank management to devote increased resources to employee education and training in the 1990s.

Summary

The banking industry is expected to undergo continuing transformation in the 1990s. Bank profits will remain under pressure as banks seek to contain operating costs, while market developments, competitive factors, and state reciprocal banking agreements will make banking more national in scope. The 1990s also may see some restructuring or consolidation of the federal bank regulatory agencies and the repeal or modification of the Glass-Steagall Act of 1933, which prohibits banks from underwriting stocks and bonds.

Mergers and consolidations are expected to reduce the number of depositories, while legal and regulatory differences among most financial service institutions will all but disappear. The business of banking will likely encompass broader financial services, such as mutual funds and insurance. Many of these services will be delivered electronically through home and business terminals linked to banks.

Bank employees in the 1990s will be better trained and more technically oriented, as more bank tasks move increasingly from clerical activities and processing transactions to selling, analysis, and funds management. A key concern of bank management will be employee training and the development of personnel programs and practices that foster job satisfaction while increasing productivity.

Questions

1. Why do most bank analysts anticipate a continuing squeeze on bank profits in the 1990s? What strategies are banks employing to protect their profit margins?

2. What are the major public policy issues in the debate over repeal of the 1933 Glass-Steagall Act?

3. Some bankers contend that federal legislation authorizing interstate banking is unnecessary because changes in technology, competitive relationships, and state laws have made federal interstate banking prohibitions irrelevant. Discuss this position.

4. Based on consensus projections for the 1990s, what impact will electronic and computer technology likely have on bank markets and products, branch banking, check collection and check processing, and bank employment? Do you agree with these projections? If not, why?

5. In light of the likelihood of significant consolidation in banking in the years ahead, what is the likely future of the nation's small community-based banks?

6. In the year 2010, the banking workforce will be better trained, more technically oriented, and more productive than in the 1990s. If you were hired as a management consultant, what suggestions would you make for new training programs and initiatives to ensure adequate preparation of your bank's personnel in the anticipated banking environment of the future?

PART IV *Applications of the Policy Process*

11

Commercial Banks and Monetary Policy

Objectives

After successfully completing this chapter, you will be able to

- ❑ describe how the Federal Reserve determines monetary policy objectives,

- ❑ cite the key measures that are used as operational targets in monetary policy strategy,

- ❑ define defensive open-market operations, and explain how and why the Federal Reserve "plays defense,"

- ❑ cite the major factors other than monetary policy that affect reserves in the banking system,

- ❑ explain how Treasury tax and loan accounts work, and

- ❑ identify ways that the asset/liability management strategies adopted by banks affect monetary policy control.

Introduction

The Federal Reserve's ultimate monetary policy goal is to create monetary conditions conducive to a smoothly functioning, noninflationary economy. To accomplish that, the Federal Reserve sets long-term objectives for employment, price stability, and growth. It attempts to achieve those objectives by influencing money supply and interest rates. The immediate focus, however, is on short-term operational targets (generally bank reserves and the federal funds rate). The Fed tries to hit its operational targets in order to achieve its intermediate objectives, which in turn enable the Fed to meet its long-term goals.

As discussed in previous chapters, the Federal Reserve's primary monetary policy tool is its open-market operations. Its strategy for implementing monetary policy involves both *dynamic* and *defensive* open-market operations. The Federal Reserve buys and sells government securities to counter recession, to contain inflation, or to promote balanced economic growth. This activity is characterized as dynamic open-market operations. In this chapter, we will look at the Federal Reserve's defensive open-market operations—that is, its buying and selling of government securities to offset or nullify undesired day-to-day changes in bank reserves and money supply. We will look at the major nonpolicy factors that cause such changes—namely, the public's handling of cash versus deposit funds, the level of Federal Reserve float, and the actions of the U.S. Treasury.

The chapter concludes with an examination of the interrelationship between the asset/liability management decisions of banks and the Federal Reserve's monetary policy control.

To better understand the nature and purpose of the Federal Reserve's open-market operations from the 1950s to the 1990s, read Extended Study 13, "Evolution of the Federal Reserve's Operating Strategy." You will also find more information on factors that affect reserves in the banking system in Extended Study 14, "Factors Absorbing and Supplying Bank Reserves."

The Monetary Policy Decision-Making Process

The Federal Open Market Committee (FOMC) meets in Washington, D.C. every six weeks or so to set monetary policy. At these meetings, fundamental decisions are made regarding whether monetary policy should be structured to stimulate, restrain, or maintain the status quo of the economy during the upcoming months. Those decisions are embodied in a policy directive sent to the trading desk of the Federal Reserve Bank of New York. That directive specifies not only the ultimate goals of monetary policy but also the precise interest rate, reserve, and money supply growth targets that the trading desk should meet to achieve these goals.

At each FOMC meeting, the seven members of the Federal Reserve Board of Governors and the five Reserve bank presidents that make up the committee review the current status of the economy, examine a range of economic forecasts and projections, and discuss which of the following three policy alternatives to implement:

- ❑ easier monetary policy—characterized by a speedup in reserve and money supply growth and by declining interest rates,

- ❑ tighter monetary policy—characterized by a slowdown in reserve and money supply growth and by rising interest rates, or

- ❑ stable monetary policy—characterized by no change in the pace of reserve and money supply growth and no change in the level of interest rates.

Each policy alternative is examined in the context of the precise interest rate, reserve, and money supply growth targets associated with that approach. The FOMC also reviews the economic implications and GDP forecasts linked to each alternative.

Most FOMC directives call for a stable monetary policy. One reason for this is the complexity of the economy. Monetary policy changes do not begin to affect the economy until months after they are implemented. Therefore, a policy change requires some time to generate the desired results. Another reason for a generally stable monetary policy is the nature of the business cycle. Business activity tends to expand and contract over long cycles. Changing the nation's monetary policy each month—first tightening it and then easing it—would not only be destabilizing to the nation's banking system and credit markets, but also would be inconsistent with those cyclical business patterns.

FOMC policy directives and meeting summaries are made public about six weeks after each FOMC meeting. Each directive includes a general statement of the FOMC's ultimate goals. For example, the May 1992 directive stated, "The Federal Open Market Committee seeks monetary and financial conditions that will foster price stability and promote sustainable growth in output." The arrangement of the goals within the statement usually indicates the FOMC's current sense of priority with respect to each economic objective.

The FOMC directive does not tell the New York trading desk what to buy or sell or precisely when to do so. Those operational details are left to the discretion of the System Open Market Account manager in New York. Once each day, however, at about 11:00 a.m., a conference call is held among the account manager in New York, Federal Reserve staff economists in New York and at the Federal Reserve Board in Washington, D.C., and at least one member of the FOMC; the purpose of the call is to discuss the day's open-market operations strategy and to review updated projections for the policy targets. Under FOMC rules, any three members or the chairman can call an interim telephone meeting if unexpected events affect open-market operations or push interest rates, reserves, or money supply growth off target. Such telephone meetings often are used to modify the policy directive and adjust the policy targets to reflect new economic conditions.

National Economic Objectives

The Federal Reserve's monetary policy strategy is designed to achieve broad national economic objectives, but the emphasis of these objectives has changed somewhat over the years. The 1946 Employment Act established full employment, price stability, and economic growth as the nation's post-World War II economic objectives. Those goals reflected strong national concern regarding the vulnerability of the U.S. economy to high unemployment as it converted from wartime to peacetime production. They also reflected the national consensus that fiscal and monetary policy must prevent the U.S. economy from experiencing another depression.

Wartime factory employee
Photo courtesy of the
Library of Congress.

In the 1950s and 1960s, both the federal government and the Federal Reserve structured their fiscal and monetary policies to promote full employment of the nation's resources. Those policies were reasonably successful in fostering economic growth with price stability. In the 1970s, however, the economy experienced persistent and spiraling inflation, and national concerns changed.

The Full Employment and Balanced Growth Act of 1978 (also known as the Humphrey-Hawkins Act) placed a sharper focus on price stability as a national economic goal and provided the Federal Reserve with a new legislative framework for its monetary policy strategy. Under the Humphrey-Hawkins Act, the Federal Reserve must develop annual objectives for money supply and credit growth that support an expanded—and partially conflicting—list of objectives, as shown in exhibit 11.1.

The Federal Reserve also is required to report periodically to the House and Senate on its performance against these objectives. The Federal Reserve establishes the year's annual money supply and credit growth targets at the February FOMC meeting. Each July, the chairman must report on any revisions to the year's objectives and provide preliminary goals for the next year. Because the Federal Reserve sets its annual targets to cover periods of four successive quarters, midyear revisions are common.

Intermediate and Short-Term Target Strategies

The Federal Reserve implements its monetary policy with an intermediate target (quarter-to-quarter) strategy that focuses on money supply. Under this strategy, the Federal Reserve does not set specific numerical objectives for the ultimate goals of its policy, such as prices, the unemployment rate, and real GDP growth. Instead, targets are set for economic measures (primarily money supply) that fall between the Fed's ultimate policy goals (which the Federal Reserve cannot directly control) and the week-to-week policy operating goals (which the Federal Reserve can directly control).

Thus, the Federal Reserve's open-market operations (its primary monetary tool) focus on short-term operational goals such as bank reserves, interest rates, and money supply, which in turn, and in time, affect the pace and direction of economic activity. By focusing its open-market operations on short-term (week-to-week) targets, such as a selected range for the federal funds rate or a given growth rate for bank reserves, the Federal Reserve attempts to position itself to meet its intermediate (quarter-to-quarter) targets, such as money supply growth. This in turn enables the Fed to reach its long-range economic goals. Exhibit 11.2 illustrates the Federal Reserve's sequential target strategy.

The Federal Reserve's most important intermediate targets are the key measures of money supply—M1, M2, and M3. As is discussed in more detail in Extended Study 1, "The Money Supply," a number of measures are used to track the total amount of money available for spending by the public. The narrowest measure of the money supply is M1, which includes all currency and coin in circulation plus all transaction accounts (both interest-earning and non-interest-earning) at both commercial banks and

EXHIBIT 11.1   **Changing National Economic Objectives**

The Employment Act of 1946	The Full Employment and Balanced Growth Act of 1978 (Humphrey-Hawkins Act)
1. It is the continuing policy and responsibility of the Federal Government to ☐ promote maximum employment, production, and purchasing power.	1. It is the policy of the United States to ☐ promote full employment, increased real income, balanced growth, a balanced federal budget, growth in productivity, an improved balance of trade, and price stability. ☐ place primary reliance on the private sector for accomplishing these goals.
2. The president should submit to the Congress a program for achieving the national economic goals.	2. The president should set budgetary goals to ☐ achieve an unemployment rate of not more than 3 percent for persons aged 20 and over; 4 percent for persons 16 and over. ☐ reduce the inflation rate to 0 percent. ☐ reduce federal spending as a percentage of GDP.
	3. The Federal Reserve Board must report to the Congress twice a year on its monetary policies and their relationship to the national economic goals.

thrifts. M2 is a broader measure of the money the public has immediately available for domestic spending. M2 includes M1 plus all savings and time deposits at banks and thrifts except large certificates of deposit. The M3 measure includes M2 plus certificates of deposit over $100,000 and other highly liquid assets held mainly by big business firms.

Although the Federal Reserve cannot control the growth of the money supply precisely or directly, economists believe that there is a cause-and-effect relationship between the rate of money supply growth and the rate of inflation and output over time. To maintain

EXHIBIT 11.2   **The Federal Reserve's Sequential Target Strategy**

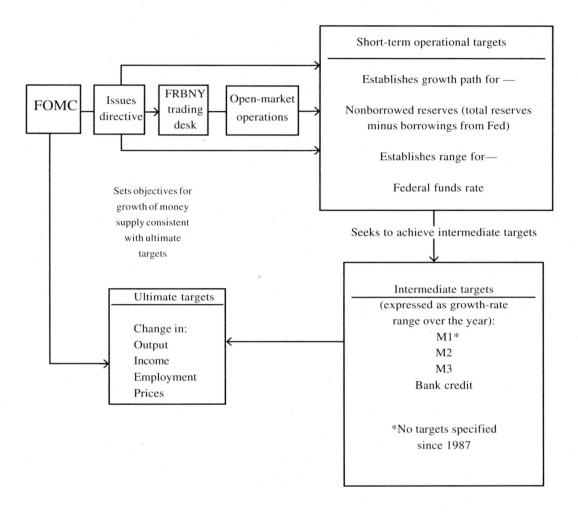

control over these intermediate targets, the Federal Reserve selects short-term operating targets that are closely linked to the intermediate targets and that the Federal Reserve can control tightly on a day-to-day basis. These short-term targets include key measures of reserves, such as nonborrowed reserves (total reserves minus borrowed reserves), and short-term interest rates, such as the federal funds rate.

Other reserve measures that the Federal Reserve uses in evaluating and assessing short-term operating strategy include the following:

☐ total reserves—all banking system assets eligible for meeting reserve requirements (reserve account balances plus currency held in bank vaults)

☐ borrowed reserves—reserves borrowed by depositories from the Federal Reserve's discount window

❏ required reserves—reserves that banks must keep in compliance with reserve requirements

❏ excess reserves—total reserves minus required reserves

❏ net free reserves—excess reserves in the banking system minus borrowings from the Federal Reserve (When borrowings are larger than excess reserves, this measure is referred to as net borrowed reserves.)

❏ basic reserve position—excess reserves minus discount window borrowings and federal funds borrowings

Setting the Targets

At each monthly meeting, the FOMC sets a target for the rate of money supply growth for the next three months. That decision is the first step in the policy implementation process. Next, the FOMC determines the growth of total reserves required to allow for the targeted money supply growth. Specific total reserve growth over the coming three months is estimated for such measures as total reserves and nonborrowed reserves. The FOMC then determines the reserve growth that would be needed each month to achieve the three-month reserve target.

Total reserves are considered to be the primary reserve target objective because additions to total reserves provide banks with a base for creating new deposits and are more closely related to money supply than nonborrowed reserves. Nonborrowed reserves, however, are more directly controllable by the Federal Reserve through its open-market operations. For that reason, open-market operations aim first at the nonborrowed reserve target established to guide policy until the next FOMC meeting. The most important operating target, therefore, is nonborrowed reserves.

The FOMC targets discount window borrowing from one reserve maintenance period to the next in accordance with the targeted growth rate for nonborrowed reserves. At each meeting, the FOMC sets a discount window borrowing level for the banking system. That level of borrowing is then deducted from the estimated level of reserves that banks would have to hold to achieve the money supply growth target. An initial growth path for nonborrowed reserves is then determined using this adjusted total as a base. If market demand for money and reserves deviates from the set trend lines between FOMC meetings, the New York trading desk tries to make the banking system adhere to the intended level of discount window borrowing by adding or draining reserves.

The FOMC uses the federal funds rate as one of its operational targets for gauging the degree of reserve pressure in the banking system. The targeting works as follows: Assume the FOMC believes that a federal funds rate range of 3 percent to 4 percent would be most appropriate on a day-to-day basis for generating the FOMC's longer-term targeted growth in money supply. The FOMC will ask the manager of the New York trading desk to monitor the federal funds rate against this target range. (The target range itself is reviewed and changed, if appropriate, at each FOMC meeting.) If the lower or upper limit of the federal funds range is reached, reserves may need to be drained or added to keep the federal funds rate within the FOMC-specified range. Draining or adding reserves, however, may cause reserves to grow at a rate inconsistent with targeted money supply growth. The chairman of the FOMC will typically call a special meeting or hold a conference call with FOMC members to discuss what policy option to take if it appears that reserve conditions are inconsistent with the federal funds rate target range.

As long as interbank transactions (the buying and selling of reserves) result in changes in the federal funds rate within the targeted range (3 percent to 4 percent in our example), the trading desk will not alter the prevailing balance between the supply of and the demand for bank reserves. Assume, however, that banks' demand for reserves builds and that their competitive bidding for reserve funds drives up the federal funds rate to 4 percent, the upper limit of the target range. If the FOMC concludes that the 4 percent rate reflects too much reserve pressure in the banking system, it would then instruct the New York trading desk to add reserves to the market by purchasing government securities from open-market dealer firms in sufficient quantities to drive down the federal funds rate into the target range. (An open-market purchase by the Federal Reserve adds to reserves and drives interest rates down; an open-market sale by the Federal Reserve takes reserves out of the banking system and drives interest rates up.)

The Federal Reserve's open-market operations are not directed at achieving a specific federal funds rate. They reflect the assessments of the FOMC and the New York trading desk that the supply of reserves needs to be expanded or reduced. The trading desk's open-market actions do, of course, change the federal funds rate, but bringing about a specific interest rate change is not the Fed's primary operational consideration in implementing monetary policy.

As data on the intermediate and short-term target measures become available to the Federal Reserve on a daily, weekly, and monthly basis, decisions are continually made as to whether any changes in open-market operating tactics or policy approach are warranted. Assume again that increased demand for money, and for the bank reserves necessary to support money growth, is driving up the federal funds rate. Also assume that discount window borrowings also increase as banks seek to obtain additional reserves to meet loan demand. If discount window borrowings increase too rapidly, total reserves will likely grow more quickly than targeted. To blunt that growth, the Federal Reserve may decide to lower its nonborrowed reserve target (to offset the increase in discount window borrowings). The Federal Reserve might also raise the discount rate to keep discount window borrowings under tighter control. Even if reserves are held on target, however, money growth could be driven significantly off target on a month-to-month basis because of the broad range of nonpolicy factors that affect the money supply measures.

The intermediate target strategy used by the Federal Reserve today is much different from the strategy the Federal Reserve relied on during the 1950s, when open-market operations became the primary tool for implementing monetary policy, or from the strategies used in the 1960s and 1970s, when containing inflation emerged as the primary focus of monetary policy. To learn more about the Federal Reserve's operating strategy from the 1950s to the 1990s, read Extended Study 13, "Evolution of the Federal Reserve's Operating Strategy."

TARGETING IN THE 1980S AND 1990S

Monetary policymakers experienced technical problems in targeting the monetary aggregates in the 1980s; those problems have continued into the 1990s. The policy of controlling money supply growth to contain inflation or to generate balanced economic growth is based on the premise that the statistical relationship between money growth, GDP growth, and the inflation rate is stable and predictable.

During the 1980s, the *velocity* of money—the turnover rate at which money is used— began to behave unpredictably, as exhibit 11.3 shows. As a result, money supply growth did not track with expected changes in GDP growth or inflation. Because changes in M1 velocity were particularly erratic, the Federal Reserve stopped targeting M1 growth in 1987. Since then, velocity changes in M2 and M3 also have proven difficult to predict.

EXHIBIT 11.3   **Velocity of Money: GDP/M1**
Annual Data

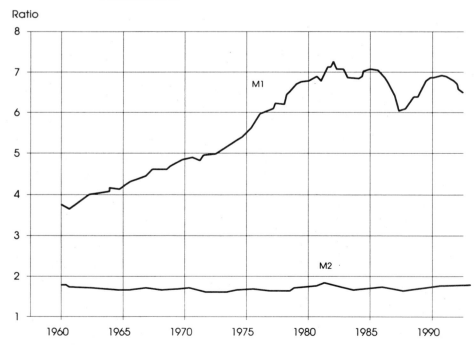

Source: Federal Reserve Bank of Cleveland, *Economic Commentary*, September 1992.

Economists are unsure why the velocity of money, which increased slowly and predictably before 1980, began to behave erratically in the 1980s. Three theories are offered: The removal of interest rate ceilings on bank deposits (from 1980 to 1986) made the public more aware of, and responsive to, changes in interest rates. The public is now more willing to quickly move money balances between accounts and between financial institutions when interest rates change. A second theory holds that the public's preferences for holding discrete "spending" money and "savings" money changed with the advent of interest-bearing transaction accounts in the 1980s. A third theory maintains that the sharp and unanticipated decline in the inflation rate—from more than 10 percent in the early 1980s to 3.5 percent by the mid-1980s—increased the public's willingness to hold money balances relative to other financial assets (since a low rate of inflation leads to only a small erosion in the purchasing power value of money).

Since 1987, the Federal Reserve's money supply targeting has focused on M2 and M3 growth. However, as seen in exhibit 11.4, changes in M2 velocity in the 1990s have been inconsistent with past trends. Exhibit 11.4 shows the close relationship between the velocity (turnover rate) of M2 and the opportunity cost of holding M2 balances in the 1970s and 1980s. (Opportunity cost is the extra earnings that people give up by holding lower-yielding time and savings deposits rather than higher-yielding financial assets, such as stocks and bonds.) When market interest rates rise relative to the interest rates banks pay on deposits, depositors typically withdraw funds from banks to buy financial assets. As a result, M2 velocity increases.

EXHIBIT 11.4 **Velocity of Money and Opportunity Cost**

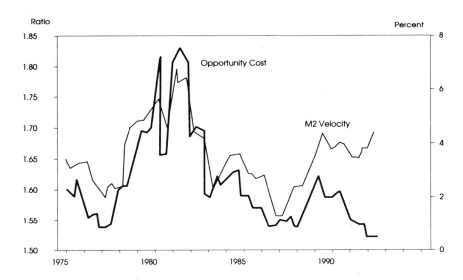

Note: Opportunity cost is defined as the difference between the three-month Treasury bill rate and the average rate available on time and saving deposits.

Sources: Board of Governors of the Federal Reserve System and U.S. Department of Commerce, Bureau of Economic Analysis.

Economists theorize that banks' substantial reductions in interest rates on small denomination time and savings deposits in the 1990s sharply increased the opportunity cost associated with holding M2 balances and generated unanticipated increases in M2 velocity. The increases were unanticipated because conventional measures of opportunity cost, which declined in the 1990s as seen in exhibit 11.4, failed to take into account the large differences in yields available on long-term securities and short-term time and savings deposits on the one hand and the public's willingness to transfer funds between those two categories on the other. Thus, the conventional measures understated opportunity cost.

Forecasting with New Money Supply Measures

Concern over the continued effectiveness of the traditional money supply measures as monetary policy targets has led economists and monetary policymakers to examine the possibility of relying on other monetary aggregates as substitute or supplementary policy guides. Two measures that economists feel may offer better predictive results are *monetary base* and *M1A*.

Monetary base is a money measure that represents the sum of currency and coin outside depository institutions plus total reserves. This measure is considered to be the foundation of all money growth in the banking system.

M1A is a measure of the money supply that includes non-interest-earning demand deposits held by the public plus currency and coin outside depository institutions. M1A corresponds closely to the pre-1980 definition of M1, which did not include interest-earning transaction accounts.

Defensive Open-Market Operations

Bank reserves can be affected by many factors not related to monetary policy, which is a major problem in maintaining monetary policy control. The Federal Reserve tries to take these factors into account when establishing its reserve targets, but their impact is not entirely predictable. As a result, the Federal Reserve must employ a defensive strategy to counter unexpected changes in reserves. *Defensive* open-market operations are those that the Federal Reserve uses to offset or nullify undesired day-to-day changes in bank reserves and money supply.

Factors That Change Bank Reserves

There are numerous factors unrelated to monetary policy that cause changes in the level of bank reserves, often increasing or decreasing reserves from one day to the next in unpredictable ways. The major nonpolicy factors include

❑ the public's handling of cash and deposit funds,

❑ the daily level of Federal Reserve float,

❐ the actions of the U.S. Treasury, and

❐ banks' asset/liability management strategies.

The public's changing preferences for holding currency is the most significant non-policy factor affecting reserves. If people withdraw more cash from banks than they deposit, the banking system loses reserves. Depositors who move funds between types of accounts or between small and large banks also change the amount of required and excess reserves in the banking system because reserve requirements apply only to transaction accounts and reserve requirements differ for large and small banks.

Bank reserves also are affected by the public's movement of funds into and out of institutions not subject to the Federal Reserve's reserve requirements, such as money market funds and brokerage firms. Movement of funds from banks into these institutions reduces bank reserves. An outflow of funds from brokerage accounts and money market funds into bank deposit accounts increases reserves.

Changes in the daily level of Federal Reserve float, which often result from uncontrollable delays in the check collection process, also change reserve levels. An increase in float adds reserves to the banking system; a decrease reduces bank reserves.

The actions of the U.S. Treasury in managing the government's tax receipts and expenditures, in issuing new securities to finance spending or to repay maturing debt, and in monetizing gold or special drawing rights can either increase or decrease reserves as well.

Finally, reserve levels can be affected by the asset/liability management strategies adopted by banks. In addition, it takes time for banks and the public to alter their lending and borrowing behavior when reserves are changed through open-market operations. For example, an increase in total reserves designed to stimulate economic activity will have little effect on money supply growth if banks are not making loans.

Exhibit 11.5 illustrates the major factors that affect bank reserves (including actions that are the direct result of monetary policy). For a more complete look at the factors leading to changes in bank reserves, read Extended Study 14, "Factors Absorbing and Supplying Bank Reserves."

Defensive Open-Market Techniques

The Federal Reserve relies on repurchase agreements (repos) and matched sale-purchase transactions (reverse repos) as its two primary defensive open-market techniques. Both repos and reverse repos involve the temporary purchase or sale of either Treasury securities or federal agency obligations by the Federal Reserve. These transactions have a short-term, self-reversing effect on bank reserves—that is, they first supply reserves and then absorb them, or vice versa. Largely for this reason, repos and reverse repos are widely used by the New York trading desk to offset temporary swings in the level of bank reserves caused by volatile day-to-day factors such as float, currency held by the public, and Treasury deposits at Federal Reserve banks.

EXHIBIT 11.5   **Major Factors Affecting Bank Reserves**

Source of Change	Change in Banking System's Total Reserves		
	Increase	Decrease	No Effect
Public Actions			
Withdrawing cash from banks		X	
Depositing cash for credit to demand and time accounts	X		
Transfering funds from demand deposits to time deposit accounts			X[1]
Treasury Actions			
Transfering Treasury tax and loan (TT&L) funds into Federal Reserve disbursement accounts		X	
Monetizing gold bullion or SDR certificates (and spending monetized funds)	X		
Borrowing money by selling new Treasury bills to dealer firms			X[2]
Other Actions			
A decrease in Federal Reserve float		X	
A decrease in foreign balances at Federal Reserve banks	X		
Monetary Policy Actions			
Purchasing open-market securities	X		
Selling open-market securities		X	
Lending through the discount window to depositories	X		
Increasing reserve requirements			X[3]
Reducing reserve requirements			X[3]

[1]   Increases excess reserves because there are no reserve requirements against time deposits.

[2]   Does not change reserves because the funds used to buy the Treasury securities are deposited in TT&L accounts. However, there is an "economic" effect in that the Treasury now has money to spend that dealers were previously holding out of the spending stream.

[3]   Changes excess reserves but does not change total reserves.

In a repo agreement, the New York trading desk buys a government security from a dealer firm, which agrees to repurchase the security for its original price plus an agreed-upon return within a specified period (up to 15 days, but usually 1 to 7 days). When buying a security under a repo agreement, the payment by the trading desk to the dealer firm results in a credit to the reserve account of the bank in which the dealer firm has its account. As a result, bank reserves are increased. When the dealer firm repurchases the security, the dealer firm's bank experiences a reduction in reserves.

Seasonal use of currency affects bank reserves.
Photo courtesy of AP/Wide World.

Matched sale-purchase transactions, or reverse repos, have the opposite effect on bank reserves. They first withdraw and then return reserves to the banking system. In a matched transaction, the New York trading desk executes two transactions simultaneously for different delivery dates. The trading desk sells securities to open-market dealers, while buying the same obligations for delivery within a few days (usually one to seven days later). The buying dealers pay for their purchases immediately, thereby reducing bank reserves. When the Federal Reserve pays for its repurchase of the securities on the agreed delivery date, reserves are injected back into the banking system.

Applications of Defensive Strategy

The three most significant nonpolicy factors to which the Fed responds are currency, float, and Treasury activities. These factors and the Federal Reserve's defensive strategy responses bear closer examination.

CURRENCY

Because cash held by banks is part of total reserves, every time a depositor withdraws cash, bank reserves are decreased. Conversely, cash deposits increase bank reserves.

As noted previously, the public's behavior with respect to cash is far from random. Cash tends to flow out of banks, draining reserves, on Thursdays and Fridays, particularly before three-day holiday weekends, as depositors increase their holdings of convenience money. Cash tends to flow back to banks, increasing reserves, on Mondays and Tuesdays as merchants deposit cash receipts from weekend sales. Currency also tends to flow out of banks during the first half of every month as paychecks and Social Security checks are cashed.

The Federal Reserve uses defensive open-market operations to offset the impact of cash on bank reserves on a day-to-day basis. However, the Federal Reserve's cash defense is most intense between late November and early January. Early in this six- to eight-week holiday season, the public withdraws $5 billion to $6 billion in cash from the banking system. Later, as money is spent or given as gifts and gratuities, this cash flows back to the banking system. Without open-market operations (and assuming no offsetting reserve inflows from nonpolicy sources), the banking system would lose $5 billion to $6 billion in reserves in late November and early December. Such a reserve drain would not only drive up the cost of reserves and short-term interest rates, but also could make credit unavailable for many businesses needing short-term bank loans to finance inventories during the holiday season. Likewise, the infusion of $5 billion to $6 billion in reserves in late December and early January would likely drive down interest rates and could lead to an inflationary overexpansion of bank lending.

The Federal Reserve uses defensive open-market operations in an attempt to prevent that seasonal fluctuation in reserves. During late November and early December, when banks are losing reserves, the Federal Reserve buys securities to provide new reserves as an offset. In late December and early January, when banks are gaining reserves because of cash deposits, the Federal Reserve sells securities to drain off reserves. The net effect of both the public's cash behavior and the Federal Reserve's defensive open-market operations is to stabilize bank reserves.

The Federal Reserve must, of course, conduct its defensive open-market operations within the broad context of its monetary policy. Thus the net effect of the Federal Reserve's cash defense at the end of the year is not necessarily neutral. For example, assume that the Federal Reserve is pursuing a policy that calls for more monetary restraint in the last quarter of the year. If the Federal Reserve projects that the banking system will lose $5 billion in reserves in late November and early December, it may defend the banking system against this reserve drain by buying only $4.5 billion in securities (thereby adding $4.5 billion in reserves to the banking system). Thus, the banking system experiences a net reserve drain of $500 million, an amount compatible with the Fed's policy calling for end-of-year monetary restraint.

If the Federal Reserve projects that the banking system will gain back $4.5 billion in reserves in late December and early January due to currency deposits, its defensive strategy might be to sell $5 billion in securities. The net effect of this action would also be a reserve drain of $500 million.

If the Federal Reserve's defensive open-market operations were played out within a context of monetary ease, an opposite scenario would develop. The New York trading desk would buy a greater dollar volume of government securities than the amount of the projected reserve drain in late November and sell a smaller dollar volume of securities than the amount of the cash deposit reserve gain projected for late December.

To the extent that consumers' cash behavior on a day-to-day basis and around holiday periods is predictable, the Federal Reserve's defense is easier. Repetitive behavior can be anticipated with reasonable accuracy based on statistical data and factored into each day's defensive strategy. However, the public's short-term cash behavior has become less predictable in recent years. The amount of currency in circulation more than doubled from the early 1970s to the early 1990s, and there was a commensurate increase in the weekly variability of the public's cash holdings from $500 million to about $1 billion. Currency is now the largest single nonpolicy factor affecting bank reserves.

To the extent that any public actions affecting reserves are unpredictable, they can present problems for the Federal Reserve in structuring its day-to-day defensive policy. For example, when the public withdraws funds from demand accounts and places them in interest-earning time accounts and certificates of deposit, excess reserves expand (because demand accounts are reservable liabilities whereas time deposits are not). A shift of funds from small banks to big banks, on the other hand, increases required reserves because reserve requirements for large banks are higher than for small banks. Public actions such as these, as well as unanticipated shifts in the public's cash holdings, can have a profound effect on bank reserves.

FEDERAL RESERVE FLOAT

Another nonpolicy factor for which the Federal Reserve must compensate is the daily level of Federal Reserve float (the extra reserves that exist in the banking system because the Federal Reserve credits banks for deposited checks before the checks are collected). As we saw in chapter 7, changes in the daily level of float cause bank reserves to increase or decrease. Because these changes can be both substantial and unpredictable, the Federal Reserve factors float changes into its defensive open-market operations strategy. An increase in float is counteracted with an equivalent dollar value sale of open-market securities; a reduction in float is countered with an equivalent purchase of securities.

Before 1980, Federal Reserve float was the single greatest factor causing unplanned day-to-day changes in bank reserves. Float averaged about $6.5 billion a day in 1979 and varied from week to week by as much as $1.2 billion. By the mid-1980s, however, the level of float had been reduced to about $500 million a day, with weekly variations down to about $400 million.

Offsetting the level of float in the banking system is not a problem. However, it is difficult to predict the level of daily float since it often rises and falls in response to uncontrollable factors. In the winter months, for example, bad weather may delay interregional check couriers from presenting checks to banks on which they are drawn. A computer breakdown, a flu outbreak among check-processing personnel, or ground transportation delays at a key Federal Reserve check-processing facility also can lead to a sharp increase in float.

The New York trading desk attempts to estimate each day's float change just as it does all other factors affecting reserves. But float estimates, particularly during the winter months, are often off the mark. An estimating error may mean that too many or too few reserves are provided defensively on a given day to offset the impact of the actual change in float on bank reserves. These effects then have to be offset through defensive open-market operations on subsequent days.

TREASURY ACTIVITIES

The third principal nonpolicy factor affecting the level of bank reserves to which the Federal Reserve responds with defensive open-market operations involves activities of the U.S. Treasury. The tax collection, borrowing, and spending activities of the Treasury, and the Treasury's decisions concerning where to deposit and withdraw the government's funds—at the central bank or in private banks—can profoundly affect bank reserves. If Treasury balances at Federal Reserve banks increase (from tax receipts or borrowings), bank reserves decline. If Treasury balances at Federal Reserve banks decrease (because of government spending), bank reserves expand. In the 1980s, weekly swings in reserves caused by Treasury activities averaged more than $800 million.

Treasury Tax and Loan Accounts. To minimize the impact of Treasury actions on bank reserves and monetary policy control, the Treasury uses a special system of deposits called Treasury tax and loan (TT&L) accounts at most commercial banks in the country. All federal tax receipts (mainly payroll tax withholdings) and funds received from the sale of bonds are deposited in these accounts. (Banks that hold TT&L accounts must post collateral, in the form of various government securities, to cover funds in the accounts.) The Treasury also maintains accounts at every Federal Reserve bank. All government disbursements, such as Social Security payments and the civil service payroll, are made from those accounts. As funds are needed to cover disbursements, the Treasury transfers its deposits from the TT&L accounts at commercial banks to the disbursement accounts at Federal Reserve banks. The transfers are made through a series of TT&L calls—notifications to banks of the amount of Treasury funds they must transfer to their district Reserve bank on a specific day.

In 1978, the Treasury modified the TT&L system to require banks holding these funds to pay the Treasury an investment return. At the same time, the Treasury began paying fees to banks that were providing the Treasury with TT&L account-related services.

The Treasury now has two types of TT&L accounts—the remittance option account and the note option account—and offers banks a choice of account relationships. Under the remittance option account, banks can hold TT&L funds for only one day before transferring the funds to the Treasury's disbursement account at the district Reserve bank. Banks choosing this option do not have to pay for the TT&L funds. Although the funds are not of great value to a bank when held for such a short time, they do build up a bank's deposit base and provide for new loans and investments.

Under the note option account, banks can hold TT&L funds for extended periods of time, but they must buy or borrow the funds from the Treasury under an open-ended note arrangement. The interest rate payable to the Treasury under the note arrangement is one-quarter of a percentage point below the average federal funds rate for the period during which the TT&L funds are held.

Corporate Tax Payments. Corporate tax payments also affect bank reserve and money supply growth, and thus are another factor the Federal Reserve must take into account in its defensive open-market operations. Assume that U.S. corporations pay their quarterly taxes to the Internal Revenue Service with $5 billion in checks written on their demand deposit accounts at the nation's banks. Because the Treasury deposits these checks in TT&L accounts at commercial banks rather than in the Treasury's disbursement accounts at the Federal Reserve, bank reserves remain unchanged, even though the money supply declines by $5 billion. This is shown by the following T-account:

Commercial Banking System

Assets	Liabilities
	Demand deposits of corporations -$5 billion
	TT&L accounts +$5 billion

Now assume that the Treasury needs the $5 billion in tax receipts to cover checks that are about to be issued to Social Security recipients. (In reality, about half of all Social Security payments are made by direct deposit in which transfers are made electronically or by magnetic tape. The result, however, is the same as that illustrated here.) Since all Treasury disbursements are made from the Treasury's accounts at the Federal Reserve, the $5 billion on account at commercial banks must be transferred into Federal Reserve banks, which the Treasury does by issuing calls. As a result of that transfer process, the banking system's reserves temporarily decline by $5 billion.

Federal Reserve Banks		Commercial Banking System	
Assets	Liabilities	Assets	Liabilities
	Reserve accounts of banks -$5 billion	Reserve accounts Federal Reserve -$5 billion	TT&L accounts -$5 billion
	Disbursement accounts of Treasury +$5 billion		

The reserve decline is likely to be short-lived, however, because as soon as the Treasury checks are deposited by Social Security recipients, bank reserves will increase to their pre-call level. The money supply also will return to its original level because the $5 billion in corporate tax payments is no longer being held by the government.

Federal Reserve Banks		Commercial Banking System	
Assets	Liabilities	Assets	Liabilities
	Reserve accounts of banks + $5 billion	Reserve accounts at Federal Reserve + $5 billion	Demand deposits of individuals + $5 billion
	Disbursement accounts of Treasury - $5 billion		

In some cases, the decrease in reserves caused by the Treasury's TT&L call may threaten to cause a significant deviation in the Federal Reserve's nonborrowed reserves growth target trend. Usually, the Federal Reserve will not wait for the expected rebound in reserves due several days later when the Social Security recipients deposit their checks. Instead, it will use defensive open-market operations to offset the deviation and keep nonborrowed reserves on track.

By buying $5 billion in government securities on the day of the Treasury call, the Federal Reserve can maintain bank reserves at a constant level. However, the banking system eventually will gain back most of the $5 billion in reserves following the deposit of the Social Security checks. Knowing this, the Federal Reserve may use a repurchase agreement rather than purchase securities outright. In this way, the Federal Reserve can add $5 billion in reserves on the day of the call and automatically take

$5 billion in reserves out of the banking system two or three days later when banks receive the deposited Social Security checks. The use of a repurchase agreement in this instance also would assure banks and money market participants that the Federal Reserve's initial stimulative action (reserve expansion) was not intended to change the fundamental direction of monetary policy.

Debt Management. The Treasury's debt management strategy—its actions in changing the structure or composition of the national debt—is another factor that the Federal Reserve must take into account in planning its defensive open-market operations. For example, the Treasury can choose to issue short-term, intermediate, or long-term securities to meet the government's current spending needs or to replace maturing government securities.

Treasury decisions concerning the structure, composition, terms, and frequency of financing new issues of government securities all affect interest rates and financial conditions. Therefore, in implementing monetary policy the Federal Reserve must continually factor the Treasury's debt management actions into its day-to-day defensive open-market operations. Primarily for that reason, Treasury officials participate in an early morning conference call with the New York trading desk each day. The day's defensive strategy and developments are reviewed, and matters related to the timing, size, and composition of new issues of Treasury securities are discussed.

The government could (but does not) use debt management as a fiscal policy tool to counter recession or contain inflation. To do so, the Treasury would issue only short-term debt during recession and only long-term debt during inflation. By replacing maturing short-term securities with long-term securities during inflation, for example, the Treasury could drive down the price of long-term securities (raising yields) and drive up the price of short-term securities (lowering yields). In theory, if total spending were more sensitive to changes in long-term interest rates than to changes in short-term rates, a lengthening of the federal debt could reduce spending by diverting some consumer and business spending funds into high-yielding, long-term government securities. Thus, the issuance of only long-term debt during inflation would act as a restraint on total spending.

Changes in the structure of the federal debt could also be used to affect total spending by changing the liquidity of consumers, businesses, and banks. If the Treasury replaced maturing 3-month Treasury bills with 20-year bonds, for example, highly liquid near-money substitutes would be replaced with less liquid financial assets. Consumers, businesses, and banks seeking to maintain their prior levels of financial liquidity would have to compensate by holding more money and near-money balances, shifting some potential spending funds into financial assets.

By issuing short-term debt during a recession, the Treasury could drive down the price of short-term securities and raise interest rates. However, because the supply of liquid assets (short-term securities) would increase, consumers, businesses, and banks would find themselves in an unbalanced financial asset position. They would try to regain balance by buying long-term bonds, which would result in a decline in long-term interest rates. If the economic effect of the decline in long-term rates more than offsets the effect of the rise in short-term rates, the net effect of those changes on the economy would be expansionary.

Economists are unsure how effective such debt management strategies would be in countering recession or inflation since the Treasury has not used debt management as a fiscal tool. The issue is somewhat academic since the Treasury's primary motivation in debt management is simply to keep the government's interest costs as low as possible. Nevertheless, its decisions are a factor that the Federal Reserve must consider in its defensive open-market operations.

Monetary Policy and Banks' Asset/Liability Management

The funds management strategies adopted by banks are another factor that can have a considerable impact on the effectiveness of monetary policy. In the 1960s and 1970s, the liability management strategy used by most banks made the Federal Reserve's control over bank reserves and money supply growth more difficult. In the 1980s, the Federal Reserve's monetary control was also complicated by funds management strategies and new techniques that many banks employed to protect themselves against interest rate risk, such as buying and selling loans in the futures market and swapping bonds. At the same time, the monetary policy strategy adopted by the Federal Reserve can have a powerful impact on the asset/liability management strategies that banks adopt. A brief review of the key factors that shape banks' funds management strategies (which were covered in some detail in chapter 8) can provide a foundation for understanding this critical interrelationship.

Asset/Liability Management Committees

Most of the nation's larger banks have committees of senior officers that oversee asset/liability management. Typically, a credit committee establishes the bank's loan policies, evaluates credit risks, and reviews and approves all major credit lines. The asset/liability committee coordinates, or directs, changes in the maturities and types of assets and liabilities that the bank holds.

The primary objective of an asset/liability committee is to monitor liquidity and ensure that the bank is able to meet loan demands through appropriate combinations of asset sales and borrowings to obtain funds. However, the asset/liability committee also decides when and whether to adjust the maturity and terms of the bank's loans, investments, and borrowings in response to monetary policy or other external factors. That strategic decision is generally made in the context of the committee's interest-rate forecasting.

A critical objective in adopting any funds management strategy is to maintain—or improve—the bank's spread between interest payments received on loans and investments and interest costs incurred on deposits and borrowed funds. Most banks aim for a target spread of about 4 percent. That range was considered acceptable in the late 1980s, to cover overhead and risk and still produce a profit margin. To achieve that objective, a committee typically will adopt an integrated strategy that focuses on both sides of the balance sheet.

For example, if a committee believes that monetary policy is going to ease up and that interest rates will decline, it might alter the bank's loan and investment portfolios by making more fixed-rate, long-term loans, easing mortgage terms, buying Treasury securities in the secondary market and lending funds in the Eurodollar market. At the same time, it might adjust the bank's liabilities by increasing federal funds purchases, Eurodollar borrowings, and short-term certificates of deposit to obtain the funds necessary to finance the bank's buildup in assets. The committee might also reduce the bank's advertising for long-term savings certificates or even stop offering them. By allowing the average maturity of the bank's liabilities to decline, the committee would be positioning the bank to obtain maximum benefits from the expected decline in short-term interest rates.

If a bank's asset/liability management committee believes that monetary policy will become more restrictive and interest rates will rise, it would likely extend the maturity of the bank's liabilities, reduce long-term assets, and expand the share of variable rate loans in the bank's portfolio.

The theory behind implementing asset/liability management is straightforward—managing the bank's assets and liabilities by taking advantage of changes in interest rates and maximizing the bank's earnings without exposing the bank unduly to risk or liquidity problems. But forecasting interest rates is difficult and became increasingly more so in the 1980s.

Managing the Investment Portfolio

Changes in interest rates put particular pressure on a bank's asset/liability management committee and its funds management strategy, specifically in relationship to management of the bank's investment portfolio. Significant changes in interest rates upset the balance between the factors that generally shape the composition of a bank's investment portfolio—namely, risk, maturity, quality, marketability, and diversification.

RISK

When a bank makes an investment, it assumes both credit risk (the risk that the issuer of the security may default on the obligation) and interest rate risk (the risk that interest rates will increase, causing the market price of investments to decline). The price of any security is determined by the credit standing of the issuer and the level of interest rates in the market.

Where the credit risk is large, the market price of the security will be influenced more by changes in economic conditions—such as the credit position of the issuer and the state of the economy—than by changes in interest rates. If the issuer's credit standing is beyond question (for example, the U.S. government's), price fluctuations will be determined solely by a change in the interest rate—the higher the interest rate, the lower the price of the security; and conversely, the lower the interest rate, the higher the price of the security.

MATURITY

Interest rate changes normally affect the price of long-term securities more than short-term obligations. Banks could limit their interest rate risk by restricting their investments to short-term obligations, but they usually offer lower yields than long-term obligations. Therefore, banks tend to diversify, spacing the maturities of their investments so that a percentage of their investments mature each year. This sometimes proves a difficult task, however, because many banks also have to schedule maturities to match expected deposit drains or to honor loan commitments.

QUALITY

The quality of a bank's investment portfolio is a measure of its degree of susceptibility to risk of default by debt issuers. Portfolio quality generally reflects a bank's attitude toward risk-return trade-offs. Municipal obligations, for example, offer a higher rate of return than U.S. Treasury securities, but they also carry higher, and varying, risks default.

MARKETABILITY

Since most banks view their investment portfolio as subsidiary to the bank's liquidity needs and its needs to meet loan demand, banks can never be sure they will be holding their investments until maturity. For that reason, banks tend to orient the majority of their investments toward obligations that can readily be sold—those that have ready marketability. The most salable securities in the nation's money markets are Treasury securities and federal agency obligations. Because many municipal obligations are not readily marketable, some banks will not invest large amounts in local government issues despite their tax-exempt status.

DIVERSIFICATION

Most banks try to spread risk by diversifying their investment portfolios among U.S. government, federal agency, state, and local obligations. Diversification avoids the implicit risk of concentrating investments in the obligations of one or two issuers and helps small banks to offset any lack of diversification in their loan portfolios.

The Impact of Liability Management on Monetary Policy

In the 1960s and 1970s, banks that practiced liability management focused on obtaining funds by issuing negotiable certificates of deposit, selling commercial paper through their holding company affiliates, engaging in repurchase agreements, buying federal funds, and borrowing Eurodollars. Those strategies had considerable impact on monetary policy. Shifts from demand deposits (which at that time carried a reserve requirement as high as 16.25 percent) to certificates of deposit or repurchase agreements (which carried 3 percent or 0 percent reserve requirements in the 1960s and 1970s) created excess reserves for banks. Required reserves that previously had to be held against the higher reserve requirement liabilities were freed. As banks used those excess reserves to expand their earning assets, the multiple expansion of bank deposits throughout the banking system added to the growth of the nation's money supply.

As banks shifted more deposits into low reserve requirement liabilities, as was the case throughout the 1970s, the multiple expansion potential of bank lending grew. This in turn also made the Federal Reserve's task of predicting the likely growth of bank reserves and money supply more difficult. Because of that, the Federal Reserve had more difficulty carrying out its monetary policy.

The Federal Reserve's approach to the problem of impaired monetary control caused by bank liability management in the 1960s and 1970s was to use its reserve requirement powers for better structural control. That involved changing the reserve requirements applicable to such sources of reserves as Eurodollar borrowings, commercial paper sales, and repurchase agreements. The Fed also used open-market operations more extensively to counterbalance unplanned growth in excess reserves.

EURODOLLAR BORROWINGS

In the late 1960s, the nation's large banks found their ability to use negotiable certificates of deposit as a means of attracting corporate deposits (and obtaining excess reserves) stymied by the Federal Reserve's Regulation Q ceilings. In both 1966 and 1969, banks found that higher interest rates for Treasury bills and commercial paper had not only made the issuance and secondary market trading of certificates of deposit unattractive, but also precipitated massive certificate of deposit runoffs as deposits matured. The certificate of deposit runoffs caused the nation's largest banks to turn to Eurodollar borrowings as another liability management device to obtain reserves.

Because liabilities to overseas branches (Eurodollar borrowings) were not subject to reserve requirements, the banking system as a whole could carry a large amount of liabilities against a given amount of reserves. The acquisition of reserves by head banking offices through the Eurodollar operations of their branches increased the use of the banking system's reserves by turning some required reserves into excess reserves.

In 1969, the Federal Reserve imposed a special reserve requirement on Eurodollar borrowings in an effort to reduce bank reliance on that source of funds and to improve the Federal Reserve's control over monetary policy. When reserve requirements were restructured by the Monetary Control Act of 1980, a 3 percent reserve requirement was retained for Eurodollar borrowings. The Federal Reserve reduced this requirement to zero in 1990 in an effort to increase excess reserves and stimulate bank lending to move the economy out of recession.

COMMERCIAL PAPER SALES

In the 1960s, the nation's large money center banks began to use their holding company structure to obtain funds through the issuance of commercial paper by their affiliates. The Federal Reserve responded by modifying its reserve requirement rules in 1970 to define as deposits the funds a bank receives from an affiliate's sale of commercial paper, thus making that source of funds subject to reserve requirements.

REPURCHASE AGREEMENTS

In 1969, the nation's large commercial banks began using repurchase agreements as a source of funds. In 1979, the Federal Reserve imposed an 8 percent reserve requirement against repos and certain other managed liabilities (above a base amount) to discourage banks from using repos and other nonreservable liabilities as a source of reserves. The objective of the reserve requirement, which was imposed as part of a special credit restraint program implemented in 1979, was to improve the Federal Reserve's ability to control monetary policy. When the program ended in 1980, the reserve requirement against repos was removed.

The Impact of Bank Strategies in the 1980s and 1990s on Monetary Policy

In the early 1980s, the Federal Reserve adopted an open market strategy targeted toward control of nonborrowed reserves, rather than control of the federal funds rate. Congress also restructured, simplified, and lowered reserve requirements. Those actions nullified most of the incentives the nation's large banks had for shifting deposits from high to low reserve requirement liabilities and caused most banks to alter their asset/liability management strategies.

Banks assumed that interest rates would be subject to wider swings and greater unpredictability under the Federal Reserve's new open market strategy, and with new reserve requirements being phased into place, banks sought to develop new strategies for gaining control over interest rate risk. These strategies included making fewer fixed-rate mortgages, increasing the use of variable rate loans, and swapping bonds. In a bond swap transaction, a bank with a variable-rate bond exchanges its schedule of repayments with that of another bank or corporation that has a bond being repaid at a fixed rate. The swap allows the initiating bank to obtain a stable source of funds or to obtain funds at a lower cost than through more conventional means.

By the mid-1980s, interest rate risk had substantially subsided. The Federal Reserve brought inflation under control and restabilized interest rates by resuming its open market strategy of targeting short-term control of the federal funds rate. In this new environment banks shifted their strategies again—from protecting interest rate spreads from the risks of unpredictable interest rate swings to increasing spreads and profits by positioning assets and liabilities into favorable *asset sensitive* or *liability sensitive* pricing gaps, promoting new services to generate fee income, and selling loans. In the 1990s, banks also began to substantially reduce interest rates on deposits to reduce expenses, and began to shift the composition of their earning assets from loans to securities.

Those strategies complicated the Federal Reserve's task of predicting and controlling the money supply and implementing monetary policy. For example, as banks reduced interest rates on deposits, the public increasingly shifted funds from time and savings accounts to investments in stocks and bonds. Those shifts were largely responsible for holding both M2 and M3 growth well below their annual growth targets, despite substantial declines in short-term interest rates. At the same time, the shifts generated unexpected increases in the velocity of M2 and M3.

The uncertain behavior of both money supply growth and velocity in the early 1990s raised policymakers' concerns over the overall performance of monetary policy and the economy in the mid-1990s.

Summary

Monetary policy is implemented primarily through the Federal Reserve's daily buying and selling of government securities. Those open-market operations, which are carried out by the New York trading desk, follow policy directives that are set every six weeks by the FOMC. Those directives establish not only broad economic policy goals, but intermediate and operational (short-term) strategies that target specific ranges of interest rates, reserves, and money supply growth.

Numerous factors other than Federal Reserve monetary policy can change the level and growth of bank reserves. These range from the public's use of cash to changes in the level of Federal Reserve float and the way the Treasury manages the government's tax collections and disbursements. The Federal Reserve uses defensive open-market operations on a daily basis to offset or nullify changes in reserves caused by factors such as these which, if unchecked, would push reserve growth off target.

The asset/liability management strategies of banks also can have a considerable impact on the effectiveness of monetary policy. Monetary policy, however, can have an even more powerful impact on the asset/liability management strategies that banks adopt.

Banks' attempts to control interest rate risk through asset and liability adjustments are complicated by all the same factors that increase or decrease the amount of reserves in the banking system, which the Federal Reserve seeks to offset or nullify through defensive open-market operations. The ability of banks to accurately assess reserve availability, reserve growth changes, and the future course of interest rates depends mainly on a working knowledge of the Federal Reserve's dynamic and defensive open-market strategy and the external factors that change reserves.

Questions

1. The Federal Reserve's monetary policy strategy involves the setting of three different levels of targets—operational (short term), intermediate, and long term. Why does the Federal Reserve do this?

2. How do dynamic and defensive open-market operations differ? How can you tell whether Federal Reserve open-market operations have been dynamic or defensive in any given week?

3. In what ways can the actions of the public affect bank reserves and money supply growth?

4. What is the purpose of TT&L accounts? How do the remittance and note option accounts work, and how do they affect bank reserves?

5. Over the decades, the Federal Reserve has tried to conduct monetary policy by either controlling interest rates or controlling reserves and money supply growth. What approach does the Federal Reserve use today, and why?

6. Assume the Federal Reserve is on its targeted growth path for nonborrowed reserves. What nonpolicy factors could cause nonborrowed reserves to go off target?

12

Monetary Theory

Objectives

After successfully completing this chapter, you will be able to

☐ define the quantity theory of money and the Fisher equation of exchange,

☐ identify the basic elements of Keynesian income-expenditure theory,

☐ enumerate the basic principles of monetarism,

☐ list the key determinants of income, interest rates, investment spending, and output, and the interrelationships among them,

☐ explain the concepts of marginal propensity to consume, marginal efficiency of investment, and liquidity preference, and

☐ summarize how monetary policy is carried out in the economy.

Introduction

Monetary theory seeks to explain the role played by money in determining levels of employment, production, income, and prices. In this chapter, we will examine the structure and precepts of two bodies of monetary theory—Keynesian theory and monetarism. Understanding the differences between these theories is important because adherents of Keynesian theory and monetarism often disagree on how money and monetary policy work in the economy and, in particular, whether monetary policy should be easy or tight at any given time.

In their attempt to explain economic relationships or processes, economists often develop models that focus only on essential cause-and-effect connections. Such models may be expressed in words, through mathematical equations, or through graphs. We will look at some of the key models used by Keynesians and monetarists in this chapter. To obtain a more complete understanding of the relationships between these models and the transmission of monetary policy, you are encouraged to read Extended Study 15, "A General Equilibrium Model: 1S-LM".

Our review of monetary theory purposely accentuates the differences between Keynesian theory and monetarism. The primary disagreement between the two theories centers on the importance of the money supply as a causal element in effecting economic change. In the extreme, monetarism contends that the money supply is the only causal factor that matters in the economy; Keynesian theory, in contrast, contends that the money supply matters very little.

Most economists today do not consider themselves to be either Keynesians or monetarists. The general principles of both bodies of theory, and much of the analysis by the adherents of both theories, have been accepted and synthesized. Most economists today are eclectic in their view of money's role in the economy; they believe that money supply is one of several important elements that effect change in the economy.

The Quantity Theory of Money

The origins of monetary theory can be traced to the economic beliefs of the eighteenth century when it was believed that a direct and proportional relationship existed between the quantity of money and the level of prices in the economy. That is, an increase in the quantity of money causes an increase in the price level, while a decrease in the quantity of money causes a decline in the price level.

This crude quantity theory of money was developed in greater detail in 1911 by the American economist and mathematician Irving Fisher (1867-1947). In examining the causes of business cycles, Fisher hypothesized a more sophisticated link between the quantity of money and prices through an equation of exchange: $MV=PT$.

Irving Fisher, originator of the modern quantity theory of money.

Photo courtesy of Yale University Archives, Yale University Library.

The equation of exchange states that the quantity of money in circulation at any given time (M) multiplied by the velocity of that money, or the average number of times each unit of money is spent (V), equals the average price of all goods and services sold (P) multiplied by the volume of transactions or total quantity of goods sold (T or Q). (The equation may be expressed as $MV=PQ$ or $MV=PT$.)

In essence, the Fisher equation says that the total amount of money spent on goods and services in the economy (MV) must equal the total amount of money received from the sale of those goods and services (PT). We can see the relevance and practical application of the equation if we consider the nature of the assumptions behind each of its components.

Fisher assumed that in the real world, the velocity of money (V) and the volume of transactions (T) were constant. That is, the rate at which the public spent money (V) was relatively stable, and the volume of the economy's transactions (T) was relatively fixed. Fisher assumed that the economy's output (transactions) was fixed because the economy always tended to operate at full employment. Under these assumptions, if the money supply doubled, the level of prices would double; if the money supply was halved, prices would be halved.

Fisher believed that this direct and proportional relationship between the quantity of money and the level of prices in the economy helped explain business cycles. He held that these cycles were caused by imbalances in the quantity of money and by the response of consumers and businesses to an environment of too much or too little money.

Fisher lacked the economic data to substantiate his theory. Moreover, his assumption that the economy always tends to operate at full employment was invalid. Economists have come to recognize that the economy has no automatic gyroscope that maintains equilibrium at full employment. Thus, a fixed level of transactions, or fixed quantity of goods and services, is no longer an accepted assumption. Economists also recognize that the velocity of money is not a constant. However, because velocity fluctuates on a month-to-month and year-to-year basis over a very narrow and statistically predictable range, for analytic and model-building purposes, velocity can still be treated as a constant.

If we modify Fisher's assumptions somewhat, specifying constant velocity but not an economy at full-employment equilibrium, the Fisher equation offers us a policy guide for monetary control. That is, if the economy is experiencing recession and unemployment, an increase in the quantity of money will spark increased production and employment; if the economy is experiencing inflation, a reduction in the quantity of money will stop the rise in prices.

In a recession, an increase in money (M), when multiplied by velocity (V), which is assumed to be constant, will cause an increase in money received (PT). As producers see demand for their goods increase as a result of increased consumer spending, they expand output (T) by recalling laid-off workers and putting machines back on the production line. It is unlikely that producers would immediately increase prices (P) because to do so would be inconsistent with their attempts to make as much profit as possible in the face of expanding demand.

In a period of inflation, a reduction in money (M), when multiplied by a constant velocity (V), causes a reduction in money received (PT). In theory, producers should lower prices in response to falling demand (spending) for their goods and services. In reality, while some producers respond in this way, many respond by simply cutting production and laying off workers. The price of an item reflects the sum of all the costs incurred in producing the item—wages, rents, interest, and profits. Therefore, a reduction in prices can only be sustained if there are corresponding reductions in costs. Since wages, rents, and interest are largely contractual costs, a reduction in prices effectively means a cut in profits, which many firms are loath to accept. In some cases, producers may even raise prices in the face of declining sales in response to contractu- ally incurred costs, such as annual wage increases under union contracts. Nonetheless, over time, a sustained reduction in money will generate a slowing in production and, in some industries, a decline in prices.

Keynesian Theory

Keynesian theory is based on the writings and teachings of the twentieth-century British economist John Maynard Keynes (1883-1946). His 1936 book, *The General Theory of Employment, Interest, and Money*, established the analytic framework upon which most of the governments of the industrial world today structure their monetary and fiscal policies.

British economist
John Maynard Keynes

Before Keynes, economists believed that the economy, if left to itself, without active government or central bank involvement, would always fully employ the nation's labor and capital resources and maintain its own balance (equilibrium). They maintained that any economic condition that threatened to unbalance the economy, such as a shortage or surplus of goods, workers, or money, would quickly be nullified by increases or decreases in wages and interest rates to maintain equilibrium.

Keynes contended that this theory was no longer valid in the depression environment of the 1930s. He maintained that changes in wages and interest rates could not assure full employment. Keynes believed that full employment could only be assured when there was balance between total income in the economy and total spending—consumption, C, plus investment, I, plus government spending, G—or aggregate demand.

Keynes reasoned that wage reductions, even if they were possible in a highly unionized economy, might not increase employment. Workers might simply spend less, driving down sales and production even more. Moreover, he maintained that interest rates did not reflect the price that banks had to pay to entice people to save, but rather the price that people had to receive to make them give up their preference for holding liquid money assets in exchange for the less liquid financial assets that banks offered. Thus, banks would have difficulty attracting funds if interest rates fell below a certain level because at that price people would prefer to keep their assets liquid. Accordingly, if people began to save more, this would not necessarily lead to lower interest rates and more investment spending. Instead, total demand (spending) for goods might fall, along with employment and investment, until the volume of savings balanced with the volume of investment spending. The economy would be in equilibrium, but not at full employment. Instead, the economy would be in a state of balanced stagnation with a high level of unemployment.

Keynes's solution, based on his theoretical analysis, was to drive total spending (aggregate demand) back up to the level at which all workers would be employed. To accomplish that, the government would make up the shortfall in consumer spending and business investment by increasing its own spending. The government would have to do that whenever the public tended to save more (consume less) than the amount being invested by business. However, the government could not play this compensating or offsetting role if its spending had to be financed with increased taxes (since that would effectively increase consumer savings and reduce spending). Instead, the government's spending would have to be financed by borrowing (running a budgetary deficit).

The Keynesian Relationships

Keynesian theory (known today as income-expenditure theory) is premised on three fundamental economic relationships:

- ❏ $Y = C + I + G$
- ❏ $Y = C + S$
- ❏ $S = I + G$

The first relationship holds that total production, or total income in the economy (Y), must always equal total spending ($C + I + G$). That is, the sum of all consumption, investment, and government spending (aggregate demand) must always equal total production (aggregate supply) because everything produced in the economy is always bought. (Unsold merchandise becomes part of business inventories and as such is counted as part of investment.) Total production and total income (Y) are considered synonymous for ease of analysis. This simplification in Keynesian theory compresses the elements that relate GDP to PI (personal income) in the national income accounts.

An additional simplification assumes no foreign spending in the United States and no U.S. sales abroad.

The second relationship holds that all income (Y) is either spent on goods and services (C) or saved (S). Again, for ease of analysis, it is assumed that no income is paid in taxes to the government.

In theory, the economy will attain equilibrium, which is a state of balance between aggregate demand and aggregate supply, when the third relationship becomes self-sustaining, or when $S = I + G$. That is, the economy will be in equilibrium when the level of investment (I) and government spending (G) being added to the economy's level of consumption exactly offsets the level of savings (S), which is the income consumers are not using to buy goods and services.

These three relationships hold true for an economy at any point. They are axioms that establish a foundation for understanding how changes in income, spending, and savings affect economic relationships. Equilibrium connotes a state of temporary balance that has already occurred. In Keynesian models, the economy may be operating well below its full employment capacity (recession) or well beyond its capacity (inflation) and still be in equilibrium. However, the ideal economic condition—and the one to which monetary and fiscal policy is directed—is to achieve and sustain equilibrium at full employment.

The essence of Keynesian income-expenditure theory is that the interaction of aggregate supply and aggregate demand determines the level of economic activity. When aggregate demand is less than aggregate supply, unsold goods accumulate and businesses are forced to reduce output. If prices do not subsequently decline, then all the decrease in GDP is in real output (recession). When aggregate demand exceeds aggregate supply, goods become increasingly scarce, business profit expectations improve, and businesses increase production. As a result, GDP increases. If, however, the economy is already operating at full employment capacity, all the increase in GDP will be in prices (inflation), not real output. That is, the dollar value of GDP will grow, but not the physical amount of goods and services.

Equilibrium exists when there is no longer a shortage or an excess of spending relative to output; aggregate demand then equals aggregate supply. The challenge for monetary and fiscal policymakers, therefore, is to generate economic conditions in which supply and demand balance at the same time as the economy is fully using all of its productive resources. Keynesian analysis puts its emphasis on determinants of total income—how and why C, I, and G respond to change—as the key to effective policy control. Exhibit 12.1 illustrates the key determinants of income and output, many of which we will explore in the course of this discussion.

EXHIBIT 12.1   Key Determinants of Income and Output

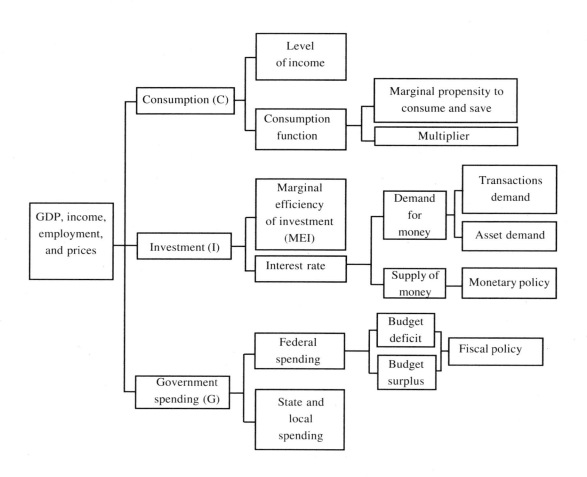

Consumption and Savings

The level of disposable personal income is the key determinant of consumer spending (consumption) and personal savings. Increased income leads to increased spending as we seek to improve our living standards, and to increased savings as we seek to build financial wealth. Statistical evidence provides strong support for a direct relationship between income level and consumption, but economists have come to recognize that other factors can have a major impact on consumer spending behavior as well. These include expectations about future income and prices, the value of our financial assets, and the availability of goods and services for spending.

Assuming these factors remain stable, however, the relationship between income and consumption can be expressed as follows: as our incomes increase, we spend more, but our consumption expenditures represent proportionally less of our total income.

For the purposes of analysis and model building, consumption behavior is expressed as a consumption function, or consumption schedule, as shown by exhibit 12.2. This basic Keynesian model illustrates how much consumers will spend at every level of income, other factors remaining stable. The 45-degree line bisecting the model is a visual guidepost that shows all the points of equality, or equilibrium (*E*), between spending and income. The consumption function is the base upon which all further Keynesian analysis builds.

EXHIBIT 12.2   **The Consumption Function**

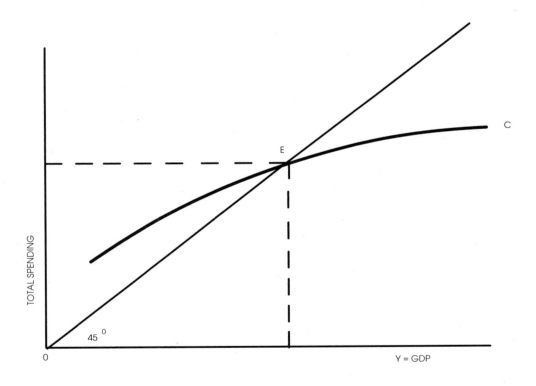

The slope, or curvature, of the consumption function (*C*) reflects the premise that as income initially increases, most of the increase will be consumed while some will be saved. However, as income continues to increase, a smaller and smaller proportion of the increase goes to consumption, while most goes to savings.

The mathematical measure of the slope of the consumption function—the change in consumption per unit of income change—is called the *marginal propensity to consume* (*MPC*). In the consumption schedule shown in exhibit 12.3, the MPC between points *A* and *B* is 0.80; this means that 80 percent of the increase in income between points *A* and *B* is being consumed. The other 20 percent is being saved.

EXHIBIT 12.3   **Measuring the Slope of the Consumption Function**

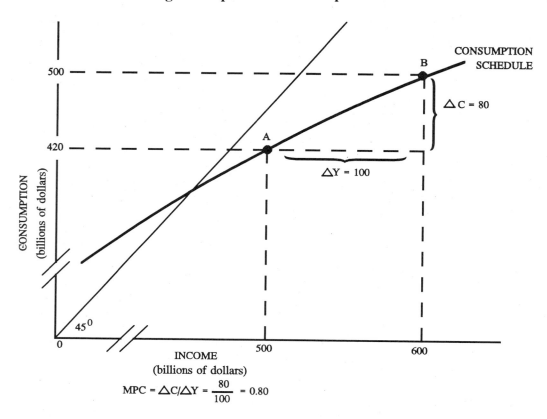

$$\text{MPC} = \Delta C / \Delta Y = \frac{80}{100} = 0.80$$

The MPC of 0.80 is derived by dividing the change in income—$100 billion—into the change in consumption—$80 billion (*MPC* = $\Delta C / \Delta Y$). A change in income to the right of point B will produce a smaller MPC and a larger marginal propensity to save (*MPS*). A change in income to the left of point B will result in a larger *MPC* (more consumption) and a smaller *MPS* (less saving).

The consumption function in exhibit 12.4 that is labeled *C′* shows the impact of an increase in the economy's preference for spending. It shows what would happen if, for example, all consumers were to become wealthier, or expected their future incomes to increase sharply, or expected a surge in inflation. Note that at this higher level of consumption, the marginal propensities to consume and to save—the spending or saving of incremental income—remain the same. Similarly, if all consumers were to become poorer, or expected their future incomes to decline, or expected a decline in prices—all of which occurred during the Depression of the 1930s—the consumption function would shift down below *C*.

EXHIBIT 12.4 **Increase in Consumption**

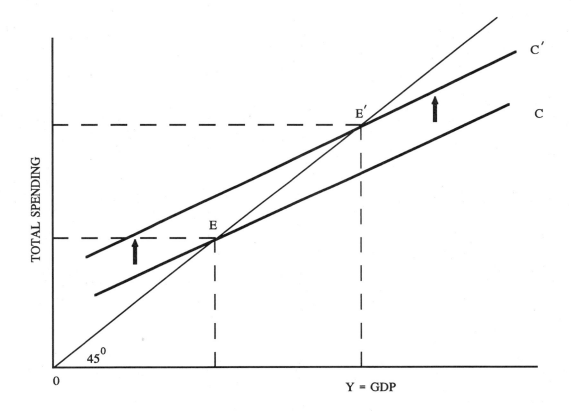

Investment Spending

The primary determinant of the level of investment spending in the economy is the interest rate. Businesses compare the expected rate of return on a prospective investment against the cost of obtaining funds to make the investment or against the opportunity cost of using internal funds for the investment. They invest as long as the return exceeds the rate of interest they must pay, and they continue to invest until the expected return on the last investment dollar equals the interest rate. If the interest rate declines, investment projects with lower expected returns become profitable and investment will increase. If the interest rate rises, investment projects must offer still higher returns to make continued investment profitable.

Because investment spending is not related primarily to the level of income, its introduction to the Keynesian model is treated as an autonomous or separate add-on level of
spending. Assuming a given interest rate, the amount of investment spending that
would be generated at that interest rate will prevail at all levels of income. Thus the *C
+ I* schedule, which is the sum of consumption and investment spending, retains the
same curvature as the *C* schedule, as exhibit 12.5 shows.

EXHIBIT 12.5   **Total Private Spending**

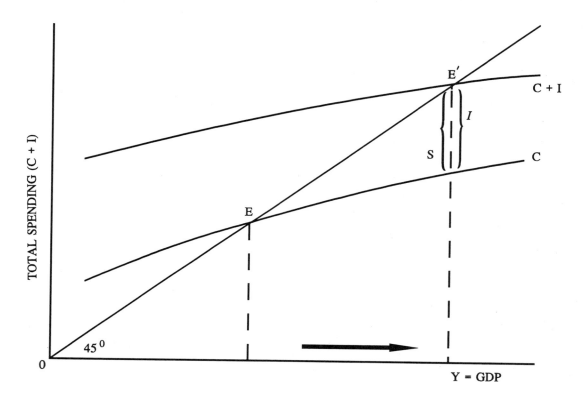

With the introduction of investment spending, equilibrium income and output have
been increased from *E* to *E'*. Note, too, that at *E'* the economy generates a level of
saving that equals the level of investment spending. Savings is the difference between
income (*Y*) and consumption (*C*); on the model, it is the difference between the consumption schedule and the 45-degree line. At *E'*, the level of savings (money not being
used to buy output) is offset by the level of investment spending (money entering the
production and income stream from an outside source).

Assume, however, that the economy, although in equilibrium, is not at full employment. That is, the sum of actual consumption and investment spending (and saving) is

less than what is necessary to sustain full use of the economy's capital and labor resources. This situation is shown in exhibit 12.6.

EXHIBIT 12.6 **Total Private Spending and Full Employment**

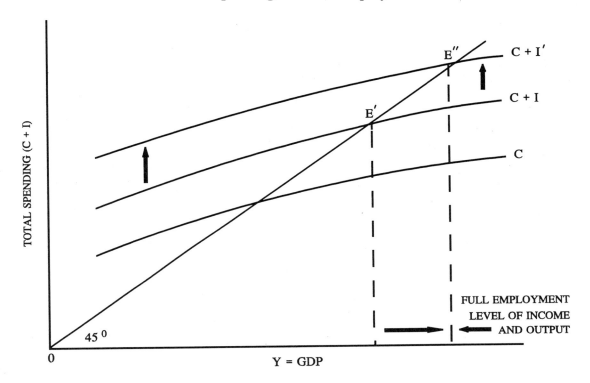

The ideal economic environment, in terms of the Keynesian model, would be one in which $C + I$ intersects the 45-degree line at E'', the economy's full-employment capacity point. For that to occur, however, either the consumption function (C), the investment function (I), or both, would have to increase (shift upward).

When Keynes developed his theories in the 1930s, he saw a depression-era economy in which there were few prospects that consumption or investment spending could be increased to move the economy to full employment. With rising unemployment, falling current income, and bleak expectations for future income, consumption spending was seen as locked in place. With falling sales and stockpiles of unsold merchandise, businesses saw little profitability in increasing investment spending, even though interest rates were low. Thus, investment spending was also seen as locked in place.

To Keynes, the answer lay in a second source of autonomous spending—government spending. The government could move the economy to full employment by increasing its spending sufficiently to compensate for the shortfall in both consumption and investment spending. Exhibit 12.7 shows the introduction of government spending to the model.

EXHIBIT 12.7   **The Introduction of Government Spending**

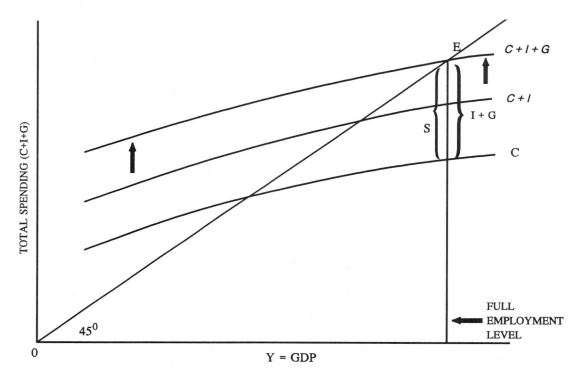

By introducing government spending (G) to the model, the level of $C + I$ is raised to $C + I + G$. The economy is now at equilibrium and at full employment. Note that at E, the level of saving is equal to the level of investment spending and government spending. In effect, autonomous spending offsets the drain on the economy's income and consumption caused by savings.

The Marginal Efficiency of Investment

A key premise of Keynesian theory is that a change in interest rates will change the level of investment spending in the economy. In any economy, at any time, there is usually a range of investment opportunities. There are always a few opportunities that generate inordinately high returns and are profitable under almost any circumstances. However, the profitability of most investment opportunities is uncertain, depending on the costs of making the investment relative to the expected return. The marginal efficiency of investment (*MEI*) curve is an attempt to demonstrate the relationship between the costs of making investments and their expected returns.

On the vertical axis of the model in exhibit 12.8, the range of the economy's investment opportunities is structured in terms of expected investment returns. On the horizontal axis are the corresponding levels of investment spending that would generate returns at least equal to those cited on the vertical axis.

EXHIBIT 12.8 Determinants of Investment Spending

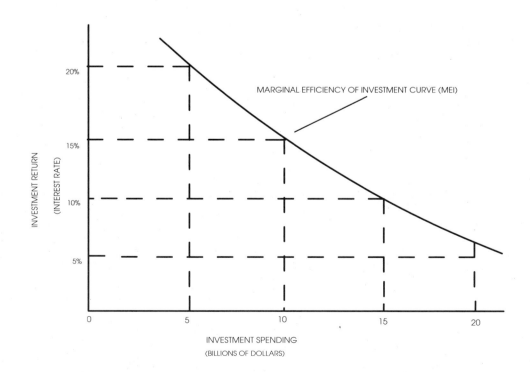

In this model, business firms would obtain at least a 20 percent return on the first $5 billion invested in the economy. If an additional $5 billion were invested, raising the total amount of investment to $10 billion, lower returns (ranging from 15 percent to 19 percent) would be obtained on the additional investment dollars. If business firms continued to invest to the $20 billion level, returns as low as 5 percent could be expected on the last dollars invested. Obviously, businesses would prefer to obtain a 20 percent return on every dollar invested, but the high-return investment opportunities are limited and are chosen first; they are exhausted at the $5 billion investment level. The next best opportunities are then sought. As these opportunities become exhausted, lesser opportunities present themselves until, in descending order, opportunities paying only 5 percent are available at the $20 billion investment level.

How much actually is invested, however, is determined not by the dollar amount or rate of return of the investment but by its profitability. If the market interest rate is 10 percent, for example, any investment return paying at least 10 percent would be profitable. An investment opportunity paying 9 percent, however, would be unprofitable because it would earn less than the cost of the investment.

In exhibit 12.8, $15 billion would be invested at a return of 10 percent. However, if interest rates were to rise to 15 percent, many opportunities that had been profitable (those paying returns of more than 10 percent but less than 15 percent) suddenly would become unprofitable. While the opportunities themselves would not change, the cost of making the investment would change. If a business firm has to pay 15 percent on a loan to obtain a 12 percent return on its use of the loan proceeds, the 12 percent *opportunity* is not profitable. Even if the firm has the money in hand, it would not want to forego the opportunity to earn a 15 percent return by placing the funds in a relatively safe certificate of deposit or money market instrument.

FACTORS INFLUENCING THE MEI CURVE

The MEI (marginal efficiency of investment) curve represents the investment preferences of the business community. While changes in interest rates cause increases or decreases in the level of investment spending (movements up or down the MEI curve), there are some key determinants that affect the preference curve itself (the position of the MEI). These determinants can cause the curve to shift to the right (increase) or to the left (decrease). In so doing, they can affect investment spending independently. We can see this shift of the MEI curve in exhibit 12.9.

Business preferences for investment spending are likely to change whenever there is a change in the business community's expectations about investment income or a basic change in investment costs. Any factor that raises investment revenues or increases the prospects of generating additional investment revenues, such as the development of new technology, will shift the MEI curve to the right (as shown by MEI_1 in exhibit 12.9). At this new MEI curve, businesses are willing to invest more at any given interest rate. Any factor other than the interest rate that increases investment costs or the prospects of generating additional costs—for example, a sharp increase in utility costs—will shift the MEI curve to the left (as shown by MEI$_2$ in exhibit 12.9). At this new MEI curve, businesses will invest less at any given interest rate. Changes in expectations about the future price of capital goods and future sales of goods produced by machines to be purchased, if sufficiently broad based, also will shift the MEI curve to the right or to the left.

EXHIBIT 12.9   A Change in the MEI Curve

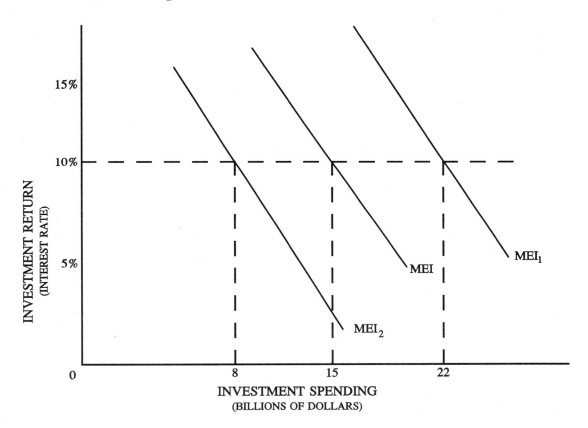

MONETARY AND FISCAL POLICY IMPLICATIONS OF THE MEI CURVE

The monetary policy implications of a shift in the MEI curve are profound. For example, an increase in interest rates designed to blunt inflation by reducing investment spending can easily be nullified if inflationary expectations cause the MEI curve to shift to the right. A decrease in interest rates designed to move the economy out of recession by generating more investment spending may have little effect if business expectations about future sales are so bleak that the MEI curve shifts to the left.

Monetary policy also can be affected substantially by the slope (elasticity) of the MEI curve, as shown by exhibit 12.10. The elasticity of the MEI curve reflects the degree of responsiveness of investment spending to a change in interest rates. A very steep, almost vertical MEI curve, indicates very little responsiveness, or inelasticity. A broad, almost flat MEI curve, indicates substantial responsiveness, or elasticity.

EXHIBIT 12.10　**Response of Investment Spending to Interest Rate Change**

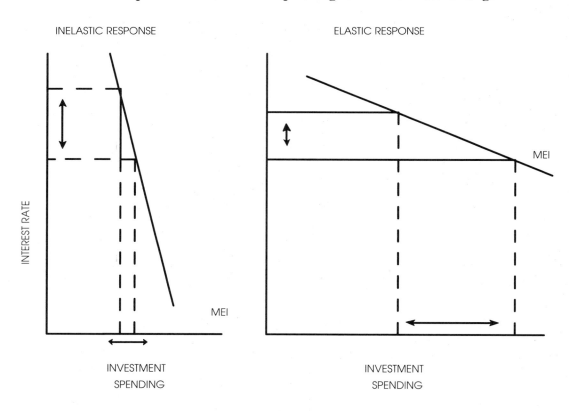

If the economy's MEI curve is highly inelastic, monetary policy must bring about a large change in interest rates to generate even a small change in investment spending. If the MEI curve is highly elastic, even a small change in interest rates will generate enormous changes in the level of investment spending. Unfortunately, economists are unsure whether the U.S. economy's MEI curve is elastic or inelastic; they also do not know exactly what factors affect the responsiveness of MEI. Thus, at any given time, the Federal Reserve's monetary policy may change interest rates too unsubstantially to have an effect or may change interest rates in a small way yet generate too large an effect on investment spending.

The MEI curve also is responsive to fiscal policy. A change in the business investment tax credit affects the basic cost of making all investments and causes the MEI curve to shift. By raising the tax credit—thereby allowing businesses to write off more of their investment costs against taxes owed—the MEI curve is shifted to the right. By reducing the tax credit, the MEI curve is shifted to the left. In theory, the coordinated use of monetary policy and fiscal policy (business tax credit) could offset a miscalculation over the degree of elasticity of the MEI curve and could bring about desired changes in investment spending with smaller changes in interest rates. This coordinated use of monetary and fiscal policy to shift the MEI curve is shown in exhibit 12.11.

EXHIBIT 12.11 **Coordinated Use of Monetary and Fiscal Policies**

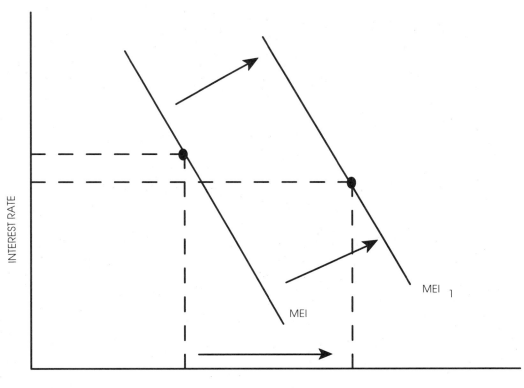

Note: A small reduction in interest rates coupled with an increase in the business investment tax credit, which shifts the MEI to the right, would bring about a larger increase in investment spending than if either monetary policy or fiscal policy were used alone.

Interest Rate Theory

The interest rate is a key element in Keynesian theory. It not only determines investment spending, but is the primary channel through which changes in monetary policy affect income and output. According to Keynes, the rate of interest is the price that brings about balance between the amount of money the public wants to hold in purely liquid form and the amount of money actually available.

THE DEMAND FOR MONEY

Keynes's theory of interest, known as the *liquidity preference theory*, is predicated on the assumption that people prefer to hold money rather than less liquid assets. Interest then is the price that banks and others must pay to get people to give up this preference. The concept of liquidity preference is based on three separate money demand motives: transactions demand, precautionary demand, and speculative demand. The total demand for money in the economy is the sum of these demands.

Transactions Demand. The transactions motive simply means that most people prefer to hold some liquid balances as convenience money to meet day-to-day and week-to-week spending needs. The amount of money that people hold for transactions purposes is directly related to their income level, which is the key determinant of consumer spending. The higher the level of income, the more transactions balances people will hold for convenience spending and other purposes. This relationship is demonstrated in exhibit 12.12.

EXHIBIT 12.12 **Transactions Demand for Money**

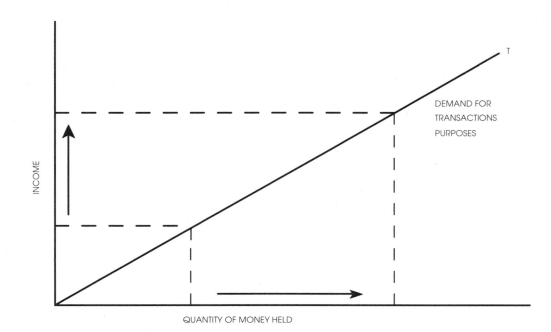

Precautionary Demand. Many people prefer to hold some additional money as a precautionary motive, to cover unforeseen contingencies. This money acts as an emergency liquidity reserve to meet unexpected spending needs or to withstand an unanticipated decline or delay in expected income. For ease of analysis, we shall assume here that precautionary balances are included as part of transactions demand in exhibit 12.12.

Speculative Demand. Some people hold additional money balances because they prefer to speculate about future interest rates and the value of interest-earning assets (securities). Because the price and investment yield (interest return) of securities are inversely related, a purchase of securities followed by a rise in interest rates would generate a capital loss upon sale of the securities. A purchase followed by a fall in interest rates would generate capital gains upon sale of the securities. However, it is exceedingly difficult to know exactly when interest rates will rise or fall. Thus, the speculative motive represents the demand for money balances by those who remain uncertain about the future course of interest rates. They are speculating that by waiting with cash balances they will be in a better position to gain when they ultimately purchase financial assets. In effect, the speculative motive can be thought of as an asset demand for money—a demand for money balances for the purpose of accumulating future financial assets.

The demand for money for speculative purposes is inversely related to the rate of interest. The higher the interest rate, the smaller the amount of speculative balances held. The lower the interest rate, the larger the amount of speculative balances held.

This inverse relationship is rooted in the impact that interest rate changes have on the prices of most of the financial assets on which the public speculates. People hold speculative balances for the purpose of buying financial assets such as bonds. As the interest rate rises, bond prices fall—and the timing is ideal for making bond purchases. When the interest rate is high, the amount of speculative balances being held is low because most investors will have already used their speculative balances to acquire financial assets.

As the interest rate falls, the prices of financial assets rise. Because people are reluctant to buy financial assets when prices are high, they continue to speculate and hold their money balances. The lower the interest rate falls, the greater the amount of money held as speculative balances, as exhibit 12.13 shows.

Total Demand for Money. The total demand for money is determined by both the level of income (transactions and precautionary demand) and the interest rate (speculative demand). If a given level of income is assumed, the total demand for money, known as the *liquidity preference curve*, can be represented as the downward sloping curve seen in exhibit 12.14.

EXHIBIT 12.13 **Speculative Demand for Money**

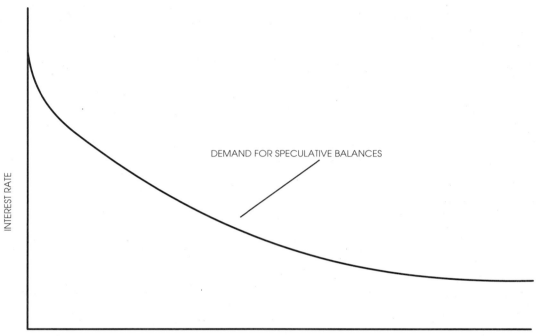

EXHIBIT 12.14 **Total Demand for Money**

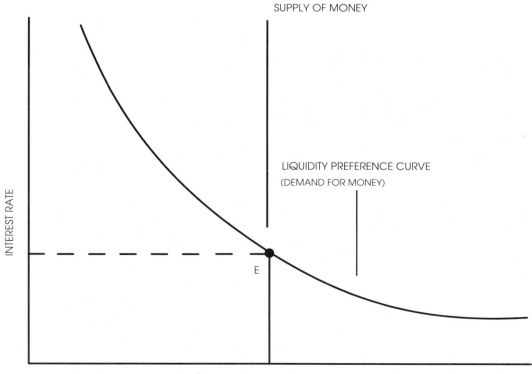

For analytic purposes, the supply of money is assumed to be fixed at any given time, as determined by monetary policy, and can be represented by a straight vertical line. The interaction (intersection) of the supply of money and the demand for money determines the equilibrium interest rate (*E*). This model suggests that at the level of income assumed, the public is willing to hold the quantity of money available only at the equilibrium interest rate.

THE IMPACT OF A CHANGE IN LIQUIDITY PREFERENCE

Exhibit 12.15 demonstrates what happens if the public's demand for money changes. If the public increases its demand for money (shifting the liquidity preference curve to the right), the interest rate will rise (arrow 1). A decrease in the demand for money will likewise cause the interest rate to fall. If the Federal Reserve increases the supply of money (shifting the money supply line to the right, as indicated by arrow 2), the interest rate will fall (arrow 3). Likewise, a decrease in the money supply will cause the interest rate to rise.

EXHIBIT 12.15 **Impact of a Change in Liquidity Preference**

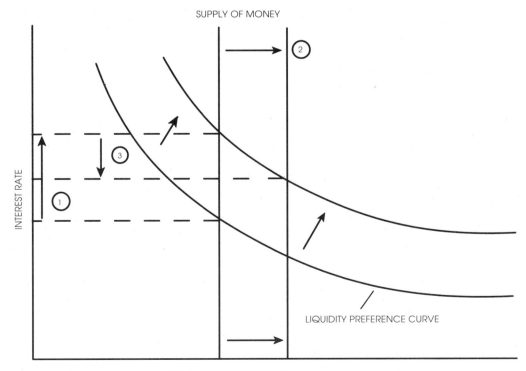

The models in exhibit 12.16 illustrate how a change in the quantity of money affects the economy's income and output level. A reduction in the money supply (a shift of the money supply line to the left in model I) drives up interest rates. At higher interest rates, there is less investment spending (a decline from I_1 to I_2 in model II) because businesses invest only to the point where the MEI equals the interest rate. The reduced investment level (I_2) and the consumption function ($C + I_2$ in model III) together determine a new intersection point with the 45-degree line and establish a new, lower equilibrium level of income and output for the economy (E' in model III). Thus a reduction in the money supply is shown to lead to a reduction in total income (Y) and GDP. An increase in the quantity of money would lower the interest rate, increase investment spending, and drive up $C + I$ to a new, higher equilibrium level of income and output.

EXHIBIT 12.16 **Impact of a Change in Money Supply on Income and Output**

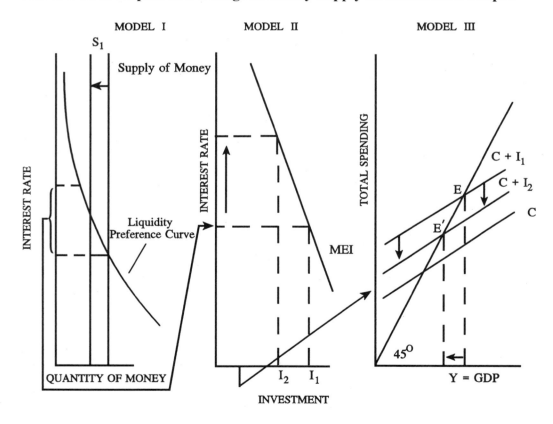

Monetarism

In the 1950s and 1960s, the American economist Milton Friedman, through his writings and his teaching at the University of Chicago, produced the body of economic theory known today as *monetarism*. Friedman not only adapted the quantity theory of money and the Fisher equation of exchange to the modern economy, but also provided considerable statistical support for the theory that money is the most important determinant of economic activity. He did this by using national income accounts data that had not been developed when Fisher postulated his equation of exchange.

Milton Friedman, advocate of monetarism.

Photo courtesy of the University of Chicago.

Friedman maintains that the key relationship in the economy is not the relationship between total income and total spending, as maintained by Keynesian theory, but the relationship between total income and the quantity of money that the public prefers to hold. Friedman contends that the public's preference (demand) for money is relatively stable and predictable. Thus, if the actual amount of money available in the economy differs from what the public wants to hold, consumers and businesses will adjust their spending until they hold money balances in accordance with their preferences.

If the economy has too much money, people and businesses seek to adjust their portfolios by converting excess money holdings into goods and financial assets until they have the balance of money, goods, and financial assets they prefer. If the economy has too little money, people and businesses seek to adjust their portfolios by holding down spending on goods, selling financial assets, and otherwise building up money balances to match their preferences. These portfolio adjustments continue until the public's preferences for money match the actual amount of money available.

To illustrate this adjustment process, imagine that you receive a $1 million check as the winner of a state lottery. You would probably have too much money—that is, an excess of liquid funds relative to your holdings of goods and financial assets. Even if you planned to spend your entire winnings on houses, cars, clothes, and vacation trips, you would likely put the unspent portion of the $1 million in an interest-earning account at a bank, in Treasury bills, or in some other financial asset. You would rebalance your personal portfolio to obtain a better mix of money, goods, and financial assets.

As you spent this money, it would represent income—additional money—to the sellers of the goods and financial assets you bought. These sellers would then face the same problem of excess liquidity that you faced earlier. They too would adjust their money holdings by buying additional goods and financial assets. But again, the money they spent would result in excess liquidity for others.

If people all over the country suddenly received checks for $1 million, they would all be simultaneously adjusting their personal portfolios to reduce their excess liquidity. Intense competition for available goods and financial assets would result, which would soon begin to drive up prices. In time, as prices rose, you might find that you had to hold more money balances simply to match the purchasing power that you had before your $1 million windfall. Inflation would effectively end the adjustment process by forcing people to hold the actual amount of money that now existed, an amount that was substantially increased when everyone received $1 million.

Now assume that, instead of winning the lottery, your work week and your paycheck are halved; you would now have too little money. You would likely respond by stretching every available dollar (slowing down your rate of spending) and perhaps by selling some financial assets to increase your money balances. Assume, however, that everyone else in the economy is in the same predicament. Their responses, like yours, would mean less income for producers and sellers of goods, who in turn, would respond by stretching every available profit, interest, and rent dollar. As a result of those adjustments, the economy would spiral into recession.

At this lower level of economic activity, fewer goods and services would be bought and sold and income levels would be lower. Smaller money balances would be maintained in conformity with the actual amount of money available, which would be less than the amount people previously preferred to hold as money balances.

The Basic Tenets of Monetarism

Over the last two decades, Milton Friedman and other monetarists have developed a broad body of economic theory that has tended to refute Keynesian contentions about how the economy works. Although monetarists themselves disagree about some of the principles and precepts of monetarism, they tend to share certain general views about the workings of the economy and the effects of monetary and fiscal policy on the economy. The basic tenets of monetarism are these:

❒ *The money supply is the single most important determinant of the level of GDP.*

Although many factors affect production, employment, and prices, monetarists believe that a change in the growth of the money supply is the principal determinant of the economy's current level of production and employment and the major determinant of both the current and future level of prices.

Monetarists acknowledge that the economy's GDP growth over very long periods of time will be determined by technology, productivity, and the quantity and quality of the nation's productive resources. However, monetarists maintain that money supply growth must be properly controlled to assure reasonable stability in employment and prices in the present.

Friedman and other monetarists have collected a considerable body of data that they contend is empirical evidence for this fundamental monetarist tenet. These data show the relationship over time between money and income in the United States since the late 1860s, as illustrated in exhibit 12.17. Much of these data are included in Friedman's *A Monetary History of the United States, 1867-1960* (coauthored by Anna Schwartz). Monetarists contend that these data demonstrate that a close relationship exists between money supply and GDP and that changes in money supply tend to cause changes in GDP.

EXHIBIT 12.17 **Money and Business Cycles**

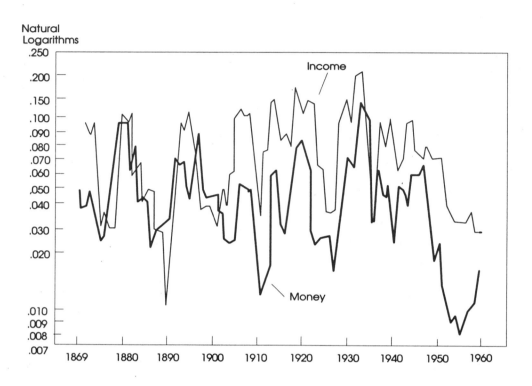

Note: This figure shows the moving standard deviation of annual rates of change in money, 1969-1958, and in income, 1871-1958, four-term series.

Source: M. Friedman and A. Schwartz, "Money and Business Cycles," *Review of Economics and Statistics*, February 1963.

❏ *There is a causal relationship between changes in money supply and changes in income and output. Over long periods of time, however, most changes in money supply cause changes in the price level. These causal relationships are based on the stability (and predictability) of the velocity of money.*

An examination of M1 velocity from 1910 to 1992, as illustrated in exhibit 12.18, shows four different velocity trends. From 1910 to 1930, velocity was relatively stable; it then declined steadily from 1930 to 1945, began to rise sharply and steadily from 1945 to 1980 (increasing at an average rate of about 3 percent annually), and then declined steadily from 1980 to 1992.

EXHIBIT 12.18 **Velocity of Money, 1910-1992**

Note: There is a break in the series in 1960 because the definition of money differed after 1960.

Source: Board of Governors of the Federal Reserve System.

Monetarists point to the reasonable predictability of velocity on a year-to-year basis within each of these periods to support their contentions. They also note the fairly stable cyclical pattern of velocity, which rises during business cycle expansions and falls during contractions. Other economists, however, point to the sharp changes in the velocity trend in 1930, 1945, and 1980 to support their contention that velocity cannot be assumed to be relatively constant.

Moreover, the behavior of both M1 and the velocity of money since 1980 has complicated the debate over velocity and has dealt a severe blow to the monetarist policy contention that Federal Reserve targeting for specific money supply growth rates will produce predictable levels of future output and prices. From 1980 to 1984, the inflation rate declined from 9.7 percent to less than 4 percent. Yet money supply growth did not slow. Indeed, it accelerated from 5 percent growth in 1981 to 9.2 percent growth in 1983. Monetarists presumed that inflation would sharply re-accelerate in the mid-1980s. Instead, the inflation rate continued to track at under 4 percent through 1987, while money supply grew at a rate of 10 percent per year from 1983 to 1987.

Those economic results caught monetarists by surprise because they had not expected the velocity of money to decline after 1980. (From 1982 to 1987, velocity fell at an annual rate of 4 percent.) In effect, the inflationary potential of the sharp growth in money supply in the 1980s was largely offset by declining money velocity. In the absence of such sharp money growth, many economists contend, the economy would probably have fallen into deep recession.

❑ *Changes in the money supply change the level of total spending in the economy through the adjustments that consumers and businesses make in their holdings of financial and nonfinancial assets.*

Monetarists believe that holders of excess money balances attempt to adjust their personal portfolios (through spending on goods and financial assets) to retain a preferred balance among money, financial assets, and goods. As a result, money supply changes affect a broader range of financial assets and interest rates than Keynesian theory suggests. Under Keynesian theory, increases in money supply lead to lower interest rates, which reduce borrowing costs and increase bank lending and business investment spending.

❑ *Fiscal policy will have little effect on total spending or the level of GDP unless the money supply changes.*

Monetarists contend that a fiscal policy calling for an increase in government spending will not move the economy out of recession as long as the government finances its spending increase through increased taxes or borrowings from the public. Both of those financing measures simply reallocate existing money from the private sector to the public sector and thus offer little, net stimulation to the economy.

Likewise, monetarists believe that a tax reduction designed to raise total spending in the context of a balanced federal budget would be ineffective without a change in money supply. Such a tax cut would mean less government revenue and government spending, but increased consumer spending.

According to Keynesian theory, a tax cut increases consumer spending and increases total income. An increase in total income increases the demand for money which, in turn, drives up the interest rate. A higher interest rate pulls some of the public's asset money balances into transactions balances where it is spent. A higher interest rate also results in less investment spending, which blunts some of the stimulus caused by the initial tax cut.

Monetarists believe that the increase in the interest rate that would result in a static money supply environment would likely offset the positive stimulus of the tax cut. Thus, in order for fiscal policy to work as an effective economic control device, it must be complemented with appropriate money supply changes.

❑ *Increases in money supply can lead to increases in interest rates and thus interest rates should not be used as operating targets for monetary policy.*

Monetarists contend that increases in the money supply initially cause interest rates to decline. However, as consumers and businesses begin to spend their excess liquidity and new income is generated, the demand for money is forced up and interest rates begin to rise. Moreover, an increase in money supply fuels market expectations of continued inflation. Lenders add an inflationary premium to real interest rates to protect themselves against the anticipated loss of purchasing power of the money they will receive as repayments over time. Monetarists contend that when money supply is increased, the upward pressure on interest rates tends to exceed the downward pressure, resulting in a net increase in interest rates.

Monetarists further contend that the Federal Reserve's failure to recognize this response of interest rates to increases in the money supply causes the central bank to structure inappropriate monetary policy. The Federal Reserve relies on a short-term interest rate—the federal funds rate—as an operating target. When that interest rate and other short-term interest rates increase, the central bank perceives it as an indicator of the effect of its tight monetary policies and structures policy accordingly. Monetarists, on the other hand, interpret rising interest rates fueled by money supply growth as an indication of an easy monetary policy that suggests further inflation and a lack of Federal Reserve policy control. Thus, monetarists argue that the Federal Reserve should not rely on any interest rate as an operating target but should concentrate instead on controlling the money supply.

> ❏ *Monetary policy should be structured to generate a constant 3 percent to 5 percent annual rate of money supply growth.*

Monetarists contend that changes in money supply cause changes in income and output, but they are unsure precisely how long it takes for those changes to affect the economy. Indeed, monetarists themselves are divided in their assessment of the time lags between money supply changes (cause) and changes in income and output (effect). Milton Friedman maintains that the lag between money supply cause and economic effect may be 18 months or longer, but most monetarists believe the lag time is shorter (about 6 months). This discrepancy reflects the wide time variations found in the data linking money supply changes to GDP changes.

Because the time lags are variable and seemingly unpredictable, monetarists contend that monetary policy should be structured to generate a constant 3 percent to 5 percent annual rate of money supply growth. They would have the Federal Reserve end its attempts at structuring an easy or tight monetary policy to counter recession or inflation, respectively.

A constant rate of money supply growth of 3 percent to 5 percent per year would match the long-term annual growth rate of the U.S. economy. By providing the economy with 3 percent to 5 percent more money each year, monetarists argue that just enough new money would be assured for balanced, sustainable real growth. Although a constant rate of money growth would not rid the economy of business cycles, monetarists believe that in time the economy would rid itself of the more volatile inflationary and recessionary swings in these cycles and would establish a more stable operating environment.

Monetarists contend that the Federal Reserve's discretionary, or counter-cyclical, approach to monetary policy tends to destabilize the economy. They maintain that the Federal Reserve worsens the economy's inflations and recessions by failing to appreciate the long and unpredictable time lag between money supply changes and economic change. As a result, the Federal Reserve tends to overreact when the economy fails to respond to tighter or easier monetary policy. That overreaction invariably provides the economy with too much easing or too much restraint at the wrong time, thereby exacerbating inflation or recession.

PROS AND CONS OF A NONDISCRETIONARY MONETARY POLICY

To prevent the Federal Reserve from using its discretionary judgment in implementing monetary policy, which monetarists claim only makes conditions worse, monetarists have supported federal legislation that would require the Federal Reserve to increase the money supply by a constant rate each year.

Monetarists do not see the imposition of a 3 percent to 5 percent money growth requirement as the ideal policy for all circumstances. If the economy is experiencing inflation, for example, they would prescribe a sharp reduction in money supply growth. Then, as inflation and interest rates decline, recession begins to emerge, and velocity begins to fall, monetarists would sharply increase money growth. Only when velocity finally adjusted to the lower level of inflation and recession would money supply growth be held to the long-term 3 percent to 5 percent rate. However, monetarists contend that there is no way that the Federal Reserve can accurately fine-tune money growth and the economy in this way. Thus, as the next best prescription, they advocate immediate adoption of a constant money growth policy.

In the 1970s, as inflation worsened, monetarism gained many new adherents among economists, the press, and Congress. Several bills were introduced in Congress to require the Federal Reserve to provide a constant rate of money growth. In 1975, Congress passed a joint resolution calling on the Federal Reserve to adhere to a 2 percent to 6 percent annual growth target for the money supply and to report on its performance in achieving targeted growth rates. The Federal Reserve itself moved toward a more monetarist approach to implementing monetary policy from 1979 to 1982 when it shifted its key operational target from the federal funds rate to reserve growth (as discussed in Extended Study 13, "Evolution of the Federal Reserve's Operating Strategy").

Monetarists were put on the defensive, however, in the 1980s. Interest rate volatility generated under the Federal Reserve's more monetarist policy approach caused the central bank to return to tighter control of interest rates after 1982. The validity of the money supply measures as policy targets became increasingly suspect with the introduction of additional interest-earning transaction accounts. Moreover, the velocity of money continued to register sharp annual declines well into the early 1990s. All of those factors raised new questions and renewed skepticism about the validity of monetarist assumptions and contentions.

The monetarists' prescription of an end to Federal Reserve policy discretion and the introduction of a constant money growth rule is based on the implicit assumption that the Federal Reserve completely controls money supply growth. Monetarists believe that if the Federal Reserve were required by law to provide the economy with 3 percent to 5 percent more money each year, the stability of money supply growth and the economy would be assured.

However, as we saw in chapter 11, numerous nonpolicy factors affect bank reserves and money supply growth on a day-to-day and week-to-week basis. Some of these factors are changes in banks' asset/liability management strategies, shifts in the public's relative holdings of cash and time deposits, and flows of funds between the public and the Treasury and between banks and financial institutions that are not subject to reserve requirements. Those nonpolicy factors change money supply and cause deviations in growth from the Federal Reserve's target, irrespective of Federal Reserve intentions or monetary theory. At present, the Federal Reserve cannot assure that its own money growth targets can be attained because it does not have total control over the nation's money supply. The imposition of a 3 percent to 5 percent money growth rule would not ensure any greater control.

Let us assume, however, that the Federal Reserve could provide a constant 3 percent to 5 percent annual increase in the money supply. With the supply of money tightly controlled, the cost of money—the interest rate—would be determined solely by changes in the demand for money. The nation's experience between 1979 and 1982, when interest rates exhibited wide volatility as the Federal Reserve moved toward tighter control of reserves and money growth, supports this contention.

Moreover, in an environment of constant money supply growth, money market conditions would be subject to the broad range of short-term aberrations that the Federal Reserve currently offsets through its defensive open-market operations. Since defensive open-market operations are inconsistent with constant money supply growth, the nation's credit markets and the Treasury's weekly borrowings would be subject to greater uncertainty and would be susceptible to greater jeopardy. If interest rates were volatile and a high degree of market uncertainty and instability existed, consumers, businesses, and banks probably would readjust their portfolios of money and financial assets. This readjustment could make the maintenance of constant money growth still more difficult, if not impossible.

Fiscal Stimulus in the 1990s

In the early 1990s, economists were divided in their views of whether *fiscal stimulus*—an increase in government spending and a reduction in taxes—was an appropriate policy prescription for the sluggish U.S. economy.

Opponents of fiscal stimulus contended that the use of such economic stimulation would re-ignite inflation, deepen the government's budget deficit, and add substantially to the burgeoning level of federal debt. They further maintained that new government spending programs, such as those proposed to rebuild the nation's infrastructure of roads, harbors, and public transportation systems, would take months to plan and enact into law. Enacting tax reduction legislation would also take too long. That is, by the time new government spending programs or reduced taxes were in place, the economy would not need the stimulation.

Proponents of fiscal stimulus contended that without such stimulation the economy of the 1990s would be totally dependant on monetary policy to provide needed push. However, substantially lower interest rates, reduced reserve requirements, and expansive open market operations in the early 1990s had not stimulated sufficient bank lending and business borrowing to trigger stronger economic growth. They contended that any further reduction in interest rates would lead to massive outflows of bank deposits from the United States to other countries as consumers and business firms searched for higher investment returns. Under such circumstances, bank lending and business borrowing would not expand.

Proponents of fiscal stimulus maintained that fiscal stimulation would provide needed policy balance and could be implemented relatively quickly. Moreover, they argued that a program of increased government spending and reduced taxes could be designed to automatically stop when unemployment falls or the economy grows at a predetermined rate or to a predetermined level, thus minimizing the impact of fiscal stimulation on the federal deficit and the level of federal debt.

Summary

Monetary theory serves as an essential foundation for monetary and fiscal policy even though economists do not agree on all the cause-and-effect relationships among the economic variables on which monetary theory is built.

Monetarists maintain that the quantity theory of money is an applicable guide for structuring monetary policy because there is a direct (and causal) relationship between money and GDP, and because changes in the velocity of money are relatively stable and predictable. On the basis of these two premises, monetarists contend that the Federal Reserve can best control the economy by setting and adhering to a constant 3 percent to 5 percent annual money growth target.

Nonmonetarists argue that the velocity of money is not stable and that the Federal Reserve's money growth targets must be flexible. Moreover, Keynesian theory maintains that monetary policy works by affecting the cost as well as the quantity (supply) of money. Interest rate changes affect borrowers, lenders, and the public's financial wealth, generating changes in business investment and public consumption levels which, in turn, alter the economy's level of income and output.

Most economists and policymakers are eclectic in their approach to monetary theory. The difficulty in achieving and maintaining full employment, price stability, and economic growth in recent decades has led to an ongoing reevaluation of the theoretical underpinnings of monetary and fiscal policy and modifications in policy strategies.

Questions

1. Briefly explain the quantity theory of money and the Fisher equation of exchange.

2. A key condition for Keynesian equilibrium is $S = I + G$. Why is this so?

3. What are the determinants of the total demand for money? What would happen to demand if there were a massive increase in banks' issuance, and the public's use, of credit cards?

4. In implementing monetary policy, why does it matter whether the MEI curve or the liquidity preference curve is highly elastic or highly inelastic?

5. What are the major differences between monetarism and Keynesian theory?

6. Why do monetarists contend that the only appropriate monetary policy is a constant 3 percent to 5 percent annual growth in the money supply? Do you agree or disagree with this contention? Why?

13

Policy Goals and the Banking System

Objectives

After successfully completing this chapter, you will be able to

- ☐ define full employment, the unemployment rate, cyclical unemployment, and structural unemployment,

- ☐ differentiate among demand-pull, cost-push, and scarcity-induced inflation, and explain how the wage-price spiral works,

- ☐ explain how consumers, businesses, and financial institutions respond differently to anticipated and unanticipated inflation,

- ☐ describe the trade-off dilemma confronting fiscal and monetary policymakers and explain the relevance of trade-off (Phillips curve) analysis,

- ☐ list the key factors that determine U.S. productivity growth, and

- ☐ cite various approaches being taken by bank management to improve productivity in the 1990s.

Introduction

The goals of the Federal Reserve have changed significantly since it was established in 1913. The original goals were money and banking goals: to meet the public's need for an elastic currency and an efficient national payments mechanism and to meet the banking system's need for a guaranteed source of liquidity and a degree of national supervision. Today the Federal Reserve's focus is on economic goals: namely, to move the economy to a state of full employment, price stability, economic growth, and balance in international trade and payments.

These four economic goals are the broad standards against which modern monetary and fiscal policy performance is evaluated. In this chapter, we will examine the three domestic goals and the problems policymakers face in reducing the unemployment rate, fighting inflation, and increasing U.S. productivity. The nation's goal with respect to international trade and payments is discussed in the following two chapters, which focus on international banking.

The United States has never achieved full employment, price stability, and economic growth simultaneously. Some economists believe that the attainment of these three goals may be mutually exclusive; that is, the attainment of any one or two of the goals may only be possible at the expense of one or more of the others. We will examine that trade-off in this chapter.

To learn about some alternative ways that have been suggested for achieving the nation's economic goals, you are encouraged to read Extended Study 16, "Wage-Price Controls and Indexation."

Full Employment

A primary goal of U.S. economic policy is full employment. Full employment is reached when all of a nation's productive resources—both capital and labor—are fully utilized. In practical terms, full employment is associated mainly with labor, rather than capital, and has come to mean a condition in which all but a reasonable percentage of the nation's labor force is employed.

Exhibit 13.1 shows the nation's unemployment performance from 1910 to 1992. In 1933, with the U.S. economy in the depths of depression, the U.S. unemployment rate reached a record high of 24.9 percent. Just 11 years later, in 1944, with the U.S. economy operating at full wartime productive capacity, the United States registered its lowest unemployment rate ever—1.2 percent. Those unemployment rates represent the extremes of unemployment to date.

EXHIBIT 13.1 **Unemployment Rate, 1910-1992**

Percent

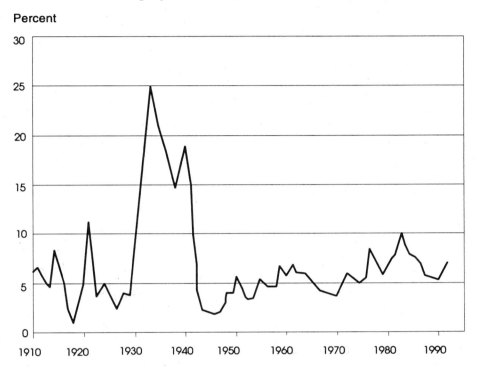

Source: The New York Times, *October 16, 1992.*

There is no absolute measure of what constitutes full employment, or conversely a reasonable percentage of unemployment. Indeed, concepts of reasonable joblessness in the U.S. economy have changed over time. In the 1950s and 1960s, when unemployment stood at 5 percent to 6 percent of the labor force, a 4 percent unemployment rate was considered the short-term full employment goal. In the 1980s and early 1990s, with unemployment at 7 percent to 8 percent for most of the period, a 5 percent to 6 percent unemployment rate was seen as the reasonable short-term goal. Since 1946, when full employment was established as a national goal, the United States has been able to attain its short-term goal only for brief periods—in the early 1950s and in the late 1960s, as exhibit 13.2 shows. (The U.S. briefly touched its upward-revised goal in the late 1980s.)

To understand why the nation's concept of reasonable unemployment has changed over the last three decades and why sustaining full employment has been so difficult, we must first understand how the national unemployment rate is derived.

EXHIBIT 13.2   **Unemployment Rate, 1950-1985**

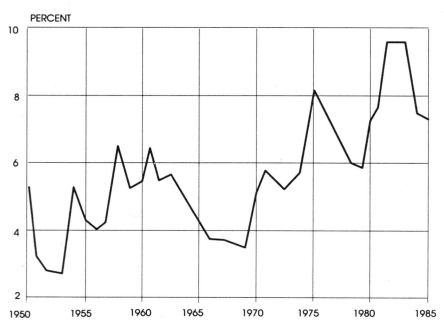

Source: Federal Reserve Bank of St. Louis, *Economic Review,* November 1986.

The Unemployment Rate

The U.S. unemployment rate, the key measure of American joblessness, represents the percentage of the nation's labor force who are currently not working but are seeking a job. The labor force consists of everyone age 16 or older who is either employed or without a job but seeking one. In 1992, the nation's labor force (including 2.0 million members of the armed forces) totaled 129.5 million people. About 64 million other adults are not counted as part of the labor force because they are either full-time students, housewives, retired persons, or are unemployed but not looking for work. The unemployment rate is determined by taking the number of unemployed people in the labor force (about 9 million people in late 1992) as a percentage of the entire labor force. Thus, the unemployment rate in late 1992 was approximately 7 percent.

Increases in the unemployment rate reflect one or both of the following situations: 1) people who were previously employed have lost their jobs, or 2) people who were not previously in the labor force have begun to seek work but cannot find a job. In the early 1990s, more than half the nation's unemployed were people who had lost their jobs during or after the 1990-1991 recession. However, in the early 1980s, about two-thirds of the unemployed were new entrants to the labor force (primarily teenagers who had never worked before) or reentrants to the labor force (primarily women seeking to return to work after many years outside the labor force).

Thus a rising unemployment rate does not necessarily indicate that workers are being laid off, and a falling unemployment rate does not necessarily indicate that laid-off workers are being recalled. For example, in 1992, the unemployment rate declined from a mid-year peak of 7.8 percent to 7.2 percent by year's end, even though total employment remained largely unchanged. The decline in the unemployment rate was due to a decline in the number of people seeking work. About 1.1 million people dropped out of the labor force in 1992 because they became discouraged about the prospects of finding work. Thus the unemployment rate can rise or fall because of an expansion or contraction in the size of the labor force or an increase or decrease in the number of new entrants or reentrants to the labor force. Typically, all these factors affect the unemployment rate.

The Changing U.S. Labor Force

Since the 1970s, the U.S. labor force has expanded steadily. In the 1980s the U.S. economy not only created enough new jobs to sharply expand employment, but also to reduce the unemployment rate. Between 1980 and 1988, more than 14 million new jobs were created, and the unemployment rate fell from 8.2 percent to 5.5 percent, the lowest rate in nine years. From 1989 to 1993, however, virtually no new jobs were created. As seen in exhibit 13.3, the 1990-1991 recession cost the American economy more than 1.5 million jobs, wiping out the previous year's employment gains. There was little job growth in 1992.

The U.S. labor force grew by nearly 30 percent from the early 1970s to the late 1980s, with women constituting two-thirds of the nation's 35 million new workers during that period. The U.S. economy's staggering record of job creation in the 1970s and 1980s, unmatched by that of other industrial countries, generated unprecedented employment, but also masked structural changes in America's work force and the nature of unemployment. A large percentage of new entrants to the labor force in the last two decades were teenagers who had never worked before and women who were reentering the work force without salable job skills. Thus many job seekers found that only low-paying, unskilled jobs were available or they found themselves unemployed for a long time or unable to find work at all.

From the 1930s to the 1970s, the federal government and the nation's large corporations were the primary sources of new jobs in the U.S. economy. In the 1980s, by contrast, virtually all new jobs in the American economy—more than 20 million— came from small and medium-sized businesses, primarily service firms such as restaurants and fast-food chains, hospitals and other medical care facilities, retail stores, regional airlines, management consultant firms, banks, and public utilities.

In the 1980s, the nation's large corporations, primarily those in manufacturing, lost nearly 3.5 million jobs. Federal government employment levels meanwhile remained essentially flat, with only 200,000 or so new jobs added, while service-sector employment continued to expand. Moreover, most of the phased-out manufacturing jobs were low-paying, while many of the newly created service sector jobs—in computer programming and finance, for example—were high-paying. While service sector employment declined during the 1990-1991 recession, jobs in the service sector steadily increased after the recession, in sharp contrast to the declining trend in manufacturing and construction. These trends can be seen in exhibits 13.4, 13.5, and 13.6.

EXHIBIT 13.3   **Private Non-Farm Payroll Employment**

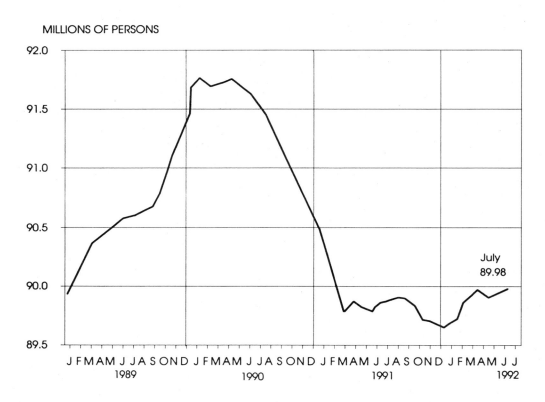

MILLIONS OF PERSONS

July
89.98

J FMAM J JA S OND J FMAM J JA S OND J FMAM J JA S OND J FMAM J J
1989   1990   1991   1992

Source: Federal Reserve Bank of New York

EXHIBIT 13.4   **Service Sector Employment**

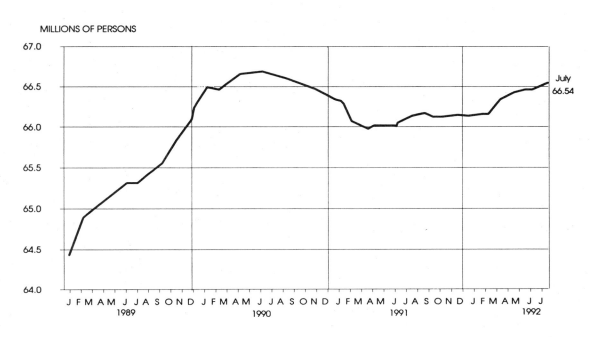

MILLIONS OF PERSONS

Source: Federal Reserve Bank of New York

EXHIBIT 13.5   **Manufacturing Employment**

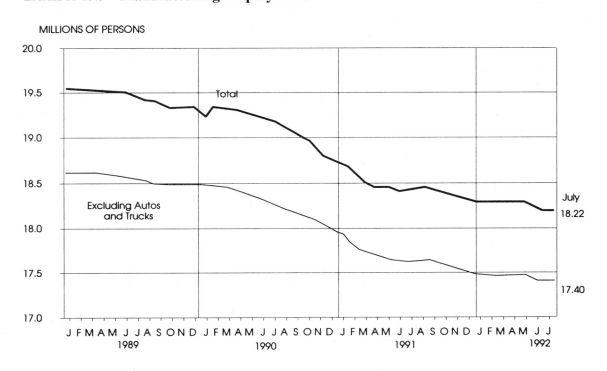

MILLIONS OF PERSONS

Source: Federal Reserve Bank of New York

EXHIBIT 13.6   **Construction Employment**

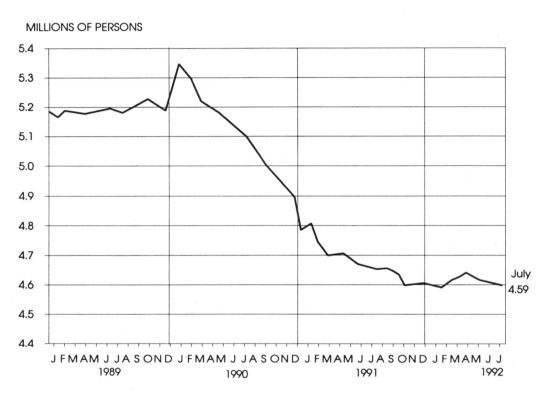

MILLIONS OF PERSONS

Source: Federal Reserve Bank of New York

Theories of Unemployment

In an effort to understand why unemployment exists, economists have identified several different kinds of unemployment: frictional unemployment, seasonal unemployment, cyclical unemployment, and structural unemployment.

FRICTIONAL UNEMPLOYMENT

In a market economy such as ours, where workers are free to change jobs and move from one part of the country to another, some segment of the labor force will at any given time be in the process of voluntarily changing jobs. Typically, these workers will be seeking higher wages, better working conditions, or better advancement opportunities. Such joblessness, which is both temporary and voluntary, is referred to as frictional unemployment and is considered to be an inherent characteristic of a market economy.

SEASONAL UNEMPLOYMENT

Some industries typically experience pronounced swings in business activity and employment during the course of a year because of changes in weather, consumer demand, or production style. Unemployment in retailing, clothing and auto manufacturing, farming, and construction, for example, normally expands at particular times during the year as workers are temporarily laid off in response to seasonal changes in production and demand. Their joblessness is referred to as seasonal unemployment.

CYCLICAL UNEMPLOYMENT

A decline in GDP—a recession—usually is accompanied by an increase in cyclical unemployment. Workers who are laid off because of the economic downturn are normally called back when the economy begins to move into the recovery phase of the business cycle. Economists believe cyclical unemployment can be treated by stimulative monetary and fiscal policy designed to boost aggregate demand, speed up the economy's recovery phase, and drive down unemployment.

STRUCTURAL UNEMPLOYMENT

Many of the nation's unemployed lack the education and skills to fill available jobs (mainly teenagers) or they have been replaced by new technology or foreign competition. Such unemployment is seen as being directly related to the structure of the U.S. economy and therefore is referred to as structural unemployment.

Structural unemployment typically varies greatly among regions of the country and among major ethnic groups, occupations, and industries. In 1992, for example, California and New Jersey had unemployment rates in the 9 percent to 10 percent range while Iowa, Nebraska, and Kansas had unemployment rates of less than 5 percent. Unemployment was particularly high among blue-collar workers and virtually nonexistent among professionals, technical workers, managers, and administrators.

Since 1941, when the government began compiling monthly unemployment data, the unemployment rate for blacks has remained about double the unemployment rate for whites, rising and falling in tandem but rarely if ever tracking below this 2-to-1 ratio. In late 1992, for example, the unemployment rate for blacks stood at 13.8 percent compared with the 6.3 percent average for whites. Unemployment among teenagers was the highest of any group in the economy—about 20.2 percent in late 1992.

Many economists contend that structural unemployment results mainly from a mismatch between the labor skills required by American employers and the labor skills (or lack thereof) of the unemployed. Such a mismatch arises from changes in technology, in international competitive relationships, in the demand for certain products, or in the proportion of different skill groups in the population (for example, an influx of unskilled teenagers into the labor force in the 1980s). Economists further contend that monetary and fiscal policy directed at stimulating aggregate demand will not reduce structural unemployment. Only a policy aimed at preparing the unemployed to fill available job openings will substantially reduce the unemployment rate.

The increasingly structural nature of U.S. unemployment and the high unemployment rates of the 1990s have caused economists to increasingly reexamine traditional theories of unemployment and propose alternatives to conventional monetary and fiscal policies to reduce joblessness.

Proposals to Reduce Structural Unemployment. Proposals to reduce structural unemployment have been directed at a broad range of sources, or causes, of structural joblessness, including the following:

- ☐ technological and competitive displacement
- ☐ teenage job needs
- ☐ reentry into the work force
- ☐ lack of skills and education

The problems of displaced workers have led economists and others to call for government protection against foreign competition through such measures as import quotas, which limit the amount or value of foreign goods that can be brought into this country; local content laws, which require a fixed percentage of the components of U.S.-manufactured items to be made in the United States; and federal subsidies to high-unemployment industries.

To give teenagers more work opportunities, some economists contend that the federal minimum wage should be suspended or substantially reduced for teenagers. However, other economists and union leaders have argued that this would undermine adult minimum wage rates while failing to address the underlying problem—teenagers' lack of skills and education to meet current job demands.

Many potential workers looking for jobs lack relevant information about the wages, working conditions, and job opportunities that are realistically available to them. Obtaining this information takes time, as job seekers search out job prospects and in some cases wait for better job offers. Thus, some unemployment may represent an investment in time made by workers seeking the right job. Any measures or programs that speed the job-finding process by providing accurate information and quickly matching potential workers and job vacancies would reduce unemployment. Among the government programs that have been proposed to accomplish this are expanded federal and state employment agency services, vocational counseling, and the provision of cash subsidies as incentives for job seekers to move to areas where jobs exist.

Some structural unemployment persists because the supply of workers with limited skills and education exceeds the demand for such workers at prevailing wage rates. To reduce this unemployment, the government needs to focus on extensive manpower training and skills-upgrading programs. In the 1960s the federal government initiated a major national retraining program. Initially, it was directed toward regions of the country that had been experiencing high unemployment, but it later was directed toward specific groups of disadvantaged workers. In the late 1960s, however, despite substantial labor shortages and numerous low-paying job vacancies, disadvantaged workers continued to experience high unemployment. Many workers who found jobs through the federal manpower and retraining programs failed to retain them.

Some economists contend that structural unemployment is not rooted in individual behavior and response, but in institutional and social patterns that perpetuate joblessness. Because most jobs available to blacks, teenagers, and women reentering the work force offer little training, limited chance for advancement, and low wages, workers find little incentive to stay in these jobs or perform well. They often develop poor work habits, such as reporting for work late or quitting without good reason within days or weeks after obtaining employment. Workers' poor performance and work habits generate a vicious cycle as employers respond with an unwillingness to train, promote, counsel, or raise the salaries of entry-level employees. Moreover, some employers adopt stereotypical attitudes toward employing teenagers, older women, and blacks, which prevent such workers from being judged on their individual merits. Some economists suggest that measures to expand employment opportunities and attack discrimination in hiring are necessary to break this cycle.

Price Stability

Another primary economic goal of the United States today is price stability. This goal has been broadly defined as attaining an economic environment without inflation or more specifically, an economic environment in which consumers and businesses do not base their financial decisions on expectations of continued inflation. During inflation, the prices of all goods and services increase; and as prices increase, the value of money declines. Improvements in the quality of U.S. goods and services add, on average, about 1 percent to 2 percent to the nation's price structure each year. These increases do not reduce the purchasing power of money because consumers obtain equivalent value for their somewhat more expensive purchases in terms of better or more useful goods. Thus economists do not count those productive increases as inflation.

From 1950 to 1965, the nation achieved its goal of price stability. Consumer prices in the United States increased by only 1.5 percent each year (although unemployment remained in an unresponsive 5 percent to 6 percent range—substantially above the nation's full employment goal, which was then 4 percent). From 1966 through 1980, prices increased at an accelerating rate, averaging about 6 percent each year but reaching double digits at the beginning of the decade. As exhibit 13.7 shows, since the early 1980s, price increases have slowed, averaging about 3 percent to 4 percent per year through 1992. Over the entire quarter century period, however, price increases were well in excess of the nation's price stability goal. The nation's monetary and fiscal policy gave priority throughout most of this period to stopping inflation, yet failed to accomplish that goal.

EXHIBIT 13.7　**Consumer Price Trends**

Percent change from 12 months earlier

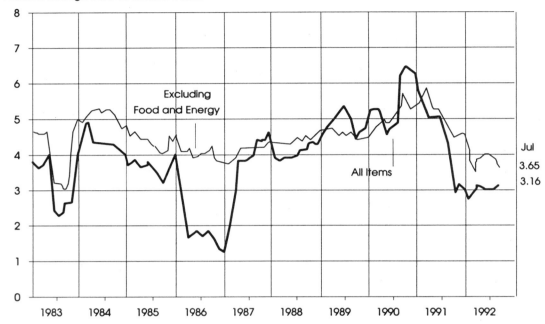

Source: Federal Reserve Bank of New York

Sources of Inflation

Economists classify inflation according to its source, as demand-pull inflation, cost-push inflation, or scarcity-induced inflation.

DEMAND-PULL INFLATION

In demand-pull inflation, prices begin to rise because of excess demand. When total demand (spending) of consumers, businesses, and government exceeds the supply of goods and services available, prices are pulled up by the competitive pressures generated by that spending. Typically, total demand increases faster than the supply of goods available when there is a rapid growth in the nation's money supply. As a result, some economists characterize demand-pull inflation as a condition in which "too much money chases too few goods."

COST-PUSH INFLATION

In cost-push inflation, prices are pushed up by producers who offset increases in their production costs by marking up prices and passing costs on to consumers. As demand-pull pressures drive up prices, workers press for higher wages to compensate for their loss of purchasing power. To the extent that they succeed in obtaining higher wages, they drive up production costs. Producers push up prices to offset these cost increases and to protect their profit margins. As prices increase, workers again see a loss in the purchasing power value of their incomes and press for still higher wages. If obtained, these higher wages again drive up production costs. Prices are ratcheted up in a wage-price spiral, leading to increasingly higher rates of inflation.

SCARCITY-INDUCED INFLATION

With scarcity-induced inflation, prices rise as a result of either a natural or governmentally induced shortage of key commodities or goods. In the 1970s, U.S. inflation was aggravated by a worldwide drought that created a scarcity of wheat and grain (which drove up food prices) and by OPEC's control of world oil supplies—and the consequent fivefold increase in the price of oil.

Gas Station, Virginia, 1979.

Photo © Washington Post. Reprinted by permission of the D.C. Public Library.

Profile of Inflation

The inflation that ravaged the U.S. economy from the late 1960s to the early 1980s—the longest and most severe inflation in the nation's history—originated in the demand-pull pressures of the mid-1960s. The government increased its social service spending to fight a war on poverty in the United States and increased its military spending to fight a war in Vietnam at a time of strong consumer and business spending and a near-capacity economy. Cost-push pressures in the late 1960s carried inflation into the 1970s. The government's attempt to control inflation with wage-price controls in the early 1970s bottled up inflationary pressures temporarily, but when the controls were lifted in 1973, prices began to soar. Prices were propelled upward in part by workers and producers seeking catch-up increases and in part by scarcity-induced inflation (caused by the oil embargo and OPEC's staggering increase in oil prices, coupled with world food shortages).

A severe recession in 1975 had little effect on halting inflation. Indeed, both prices and unemployment increased. A second oil price shock in 1978 added further to inflation, which by 1980 was running at an 18 percent annual rate.

Highly restrictive monetary policy, a severe recession from 1981 to 1982, and a world oil glut, which caused oil prices to decline, broke the nation's inflationary spiral in the early 1980s. By 1983-1984, inflation had sharply decelerated to a 4 percent rate. From 1984 to 1992, inflation stabilized, with consumer price increases averaging only about 3.5 percent per year.

Anticipated and Unanticipated Inflation

The nation's experience with inflation in the 1970s caused economists to modify some of their theories about consumer and business responses to rising prices. Because inflation reduces the value (purchasing power) of money, the longer money is held (not spent), the less valuable it becomes to both consumers and businesses. Thus, one theory maintained that consumers speed up their spending and reduce their savings during an inflation in order to obtain the maximum value (purchasing power) for their income. Similarly, businesses were expected to speed up investment spending.

In the 1970s, however, as inflation soared—increasing from a 3 percent or 4 percent rate early in the decade to double-digit rates late in the decade—businesses steadily slowed their investment spending while consumers spent less and saved more.

Economists now recognize that consumers and businesses react differently to *unanticipated* inflation than they do to *anticipated* inflation. When consumers and businesses correctly anticipate price changes, they behave according to conventional theory—they increase their spending and investment. However, when consumers and businesses must cope with greater inflation than they anticipated, as in 1973 and in 1978 when the U.S. economy was hit with unexpected increases in energy prices, they respond more defensively.

unanticipated
Cut Back

For example, assume that current consumer spending and business investment plans are based on an expected 6 percent increase in prices over the next year. If actual prices begin to increase at a 12 percent annual rate early in the year, consumers and businesses will immediately retrench and cut back on spending. Moreover, the 12 percent inflation rate erodes the purchasing power of savings. Thus additional savings are required to offset the unexpected drain in purchasing power and to maintain savings goals. Again, the appropriate defensive response is to cut back on spending to increase savings.

Effects of Inflation

Inflation reduces the purchasing power of all money, but its effects on consumers, businesses, and governments are borne unevenly. This unevenness adds an important social and political dimension to the problem of inflation. Some of the ways that inflation affects different groups differently have been identified as the income effect, the wealth effect, the tax effect, the profits illusion effect, the international competitiveness effect, and the winners and losers effect.

INCOME EFFECT

Inflation tends to redistribute income from persons with fixed incomes or incomes that are slow to rise, such as retired pensioners, Social Security recipients, and government employees, to those whose incomes rise rapidly, such as self-employed professionals and union workers covered by contracts with built-in cost-of-living adjustments. This is referred to as the income effect of inflation.

WEALTH EFFECT

Rising prices also redistribute wealth from creditors (and savers) to debtors. Banks and other financial institutions that lend long-term money at a fixed interest rate lose money because they are repaid in cheaper dollars than those they originally loaned. Debtors, on the other hand, gain money because they repay borrowed funds with money that is worth less than the money they originally borrowed.

Savers who receive a fixed interest rate of return on their funds, such as persons with traditional passbook savings accounts, lose money if the interest they receive is lower than the inflation rate. In a year of 9 percent inflation, for example, the funds in a 5.5 percent savings account would lose 3.5 percent in terms of purchasing power in the course of the year. Small savers were particularly disadvantaged in the 1970s because, under Regulation Q ceilings, banks were not permitted to pay market interest rates.

As noted previously, the redistribution of wealth generated by inflation occurs mainly when inflation is unanticipated. Many banks were particularly hard hit by the rapid unanticipated acceleration of inflation in the late 1970s and early 1980s. If inflation is fully and correctly anticipated, banks and other lenders typically add an inflation premium to the interest rate they charge to compensate for purchasing power losses over the length of the loan. Correctly forecasting the inflation rate over long periods, however, is not easy. Thus, many banks now seek to protect themselves against unexpected inflation by no longer lending money long term at a fixed rate, but rather at a rate that changes monthly or quarterly. However, in the real world, interest rate ceilings on consumer loans and mortgages sometimes limit the ability of lenders to factor in inflation premiums on these types of loans.

TAX EFFECT

Under the modified proportional structure of the federal income tax and the progressive structure of many state income taxes, inflation acts as a de facto tax increase for wage earners. This reflects the fact that rising prices typically are accompanied by rising wages. But an increase in wages pushes income earners into higher tax brackets, which requires that a larger proportion of the wage gain be paid in taxes.

PROFITS ILLUSION EFFECT

Inflation creates an illusion of profit gains for businesses by driving up the value of inventories and capital and by generating bookkeeping profits on inventory valuation and on capital depreciation. But because inventory and depreciation profits do not take into account replacement costs, bookkeeping profits can grossly exaggerate a company's real earnings and can lead to faulty planning and decision making.

Assume, for example, that an auto producer manufactures a $20,000 car in January. The $20,000 price reflects the cost of materials, labor, and all other costs of producing the car. By December, the car is still at the plant waiting to be shipped to a dealer. However, during the intervening 12 months, prices of materials and auto workers' wages have increased by 10 percent. Thus, cars are now selling for $22,000. Since the car cost only $20,000 to produce earlier in the year, the auto company's books now show $2,000 in added inventory profit. This profit is an illusion, however, because the replacement cost of the car—that is, the cost of producing a similar car—is now $22,000.

INTERNATIONAL COMPETITIVENESS EFFECT

Inflation in the United States also drives up the price of domestic goods relative to goods made in other countries. As U.S. goods become more expensive, foreigners reduce their orders and buy equivalent goods made elsewhere. At the same time, American producers and consumers step up their own purchases of lower-priced foreign goods. The result of this inflation-induced surge in imports and slowing of exports is an erosion of the U.S. trade position. In the 1970s and 1980s, the nation's balance of trade increasingly shifted toward inflation-induced trade deficits.

WINNERS AND LOSERS EFFECT

National statistics mask the most insidious of inflation's effects on the economy—
the fact that it creates specific winners and losers. Because wages increased roughly in
tandem with rising prices in the 1970s and 1980s, real wages in the United States in
the 1980s remained about what they were in the late 1960s. This does not mean,
however, that numerous wage earners and others did not suffer in the last two decades.
The specific impact of inflation on any individual is a function of that person's age, job,
family status, region, buying and investment habits, and other factors. For that reason,
and because inflation redistributes income and wealth in an uneven way, inflation tends
to generate both winners and losers. Exhibit 13.8 identifies some key categories of
winners and losers from the inflation experienced from the mid-1960s to the early
1980s.

EXHIBIT 13.8   **Uneven Effects of Inflation: Mid-1960s to Early-1980s**

Winners	*Losers*
Middle-class and affluent people	Poor people
City dwellers	Suburbanites
People in their 50s and 60s	People in their 20s, 30s, and 40s
Farmers	White-collar workers and professionals
Homeowners in the southern and western states	Homeowners in the northern states
Members of the armed services	Apartment renters
Retired military and civil servants	Corporate employees
Social Security recipients	Holders of passbook savings accounts
Investors in exotic assets such as gold, jewelry, and diamonds	Holders of U.S. savings bonds

The fact that inflation creates winner and loser groups tends to aggravate social and
political tensions and erode social values. Many workers see their hard work rewarded
with wage increases that barely match price increases. Savers see the value of their
savings eroded and perhaps fall below their projected future needs. The history of
inflation's impact on the social and political systems of nations—from Germany in the
1920s to Argentina in the 1940s and 1950s—is fraught with episodes of upheaval that
have led to authoritarian and totalitarian political controls designed to stop inflation.

The Trade-Off Dilemma

Many economists contend that there is an inverse relationship between inflation
and unemployment. That is, the inflation rate can be reduced only at the expense of a

higher rate of unemployment, and unemployment can be reduced only at the expense of a higher rate of inflation.

The trade-off relationship between inflation and unemployment was first proposed in the 1950s by the British economist A.W. Phillips. He formulated the trade-off contention based on studies he did of wages, prices, and unemployment in England. This inverse relationship between inflation and unemployment, which is illustrated in exhibit 13.9, is referred to as the Phillips curve.

EXHIBIT 13.9   **Derivation of Phillips Curves**

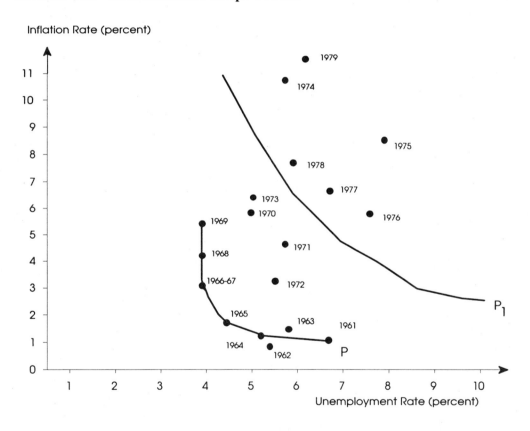

Source: Edmond Seifried, *Economics for Bankers* (Washington, D.C.: American Bankers Association, 1987).

Exhibit 13.10 shows five Phillips curves that depict the changing relationship between inflation and unemployment in the United States from the 1960s through the 1980s. Each curve reflects the various combinations of inflation and unemployment that coexisted during a given period of time. For example, Phillips curve P reflects the relationship between inflation and unemployment during the 1960s.

A shifting of the Phillips curve to the right represents a worsening or deterioration in the economy's trade-off relationship. Thus Phillips curves P1 and P2 reflect increased trade-off costs for both inflation and unemployment, rightward shifts of the curve that most economists believe occurred in the 1970s. Curves P1, P2, and P3 indicate that higher levels of unemployment came to be associated with higher rates of inflation; or conversely, higher inflation rates were associated with any given level of unemployment. In effect, Phillips curves P1, P2, and P3 each represent a progressively poorer trade-off than curve P.

The rightward migration of the curves suggests an overall pattern of rising inflation and rising unemployment. Since 1982, however, unemployment and inflation have both declined substantially, generating a significant leftward shift in the Pillips curve in the late 1980s and early 1990s, as seen in curves P4 and P1.

CAUSES OF THE INFLATION-UNEMPLOYMENT TRADE-OFF

Most economists attribute the behavior of the U.S. economy's inflation-unemployment relationship in the 1970s and early 1980s to price and wage rigidity, a changing labor force, and government policies.

Price Rigidity. In theory, the prices of all goods and services reflect market supply and demand for those goods or services. Indeed, in highly competitive markets, prices do rise or fall as supply and demand conditions change. Most American markets, however, are not highly competitive. In key manufacturing industries, such as the automobile, steel, and appliance industries, two or three large firms dominate the entire market. Their size and market share give them the power to set prices in accordance with profit targets and to raise prices when costs increase even when market demand for their goods is weak. As a result, the prices of some U.S. goods and services tend to rise even when the economy is experiencing recession, while the prices of other goods tend not to fall even when demand slows. Inflation tends to continue when prices fail to respond to market conditions.

Wage Rigidity. Just as a large share of the nation's market for goods is dominated by a few industries that do not respond to downward price pressures, so is a large segment of the nation's labor market dominated by labor unions that do not respond to downward wage pressures.

Most major union contracts are negotiated to cover a three-year period. Thus, unions seek to obtain wage-increase agreements that not only cover current productivity gains and offset current purchasing power losses to inflation, but also seek to cover expected productivity gains and anticipated purchasing power losses due to projected inflation. Some unions include in their wage proposals a margin to cover any unanticipated inflationary losses that workers have experienced during the preceding three years. Other unions structure their proposals to include automatic cost-of-living adjustments that assure union members that their wages will increase proportionally to any cost-of-living increases. Because wage increases called for under union contracts are legally binding for three years, most businesses cannot unilaterally reduce wages when demand for their goods falls.

EXHIBIT 13.10   **Phillips Curves for the United States, 1960s-Early 1990s**

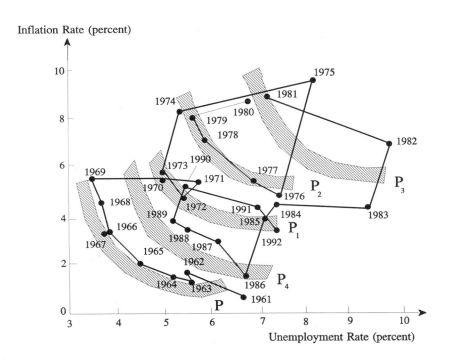

Source: Seifried, *Economics for Bankers*

Changes in the U.S. Labor Force. As noted previously, the proportion of inexperienced and unskilled workers in the U.S. labor force—particularly teenagers—increased significantly in the late 1970s. This increase occurred at the same time as the competitive relationships of U.S. industries with those of other countries changed, displacing many workers. Thus, the existing structural unemployment at that time was further aggravated by changing technology, which reduced the demand for unskilled labor.

The profusion of teenagers in the labor force in the 1970s was a result of high birth rates in the 1950s—the post-World War II baby boom. The increasing participation of women in the labor force—another factor that exacerbated the unemployment situation—has been attributed to the country's changing attitude toward the role of women in society and the impact of almost two decades of inflation that increasingly required two sources of family income to sustain a reasonable standard of living.

The changing labor force; increasingly, the two-income family is becoming an economic necessity.

Government Policies. Many of the federal government's regulations contribute to price and wage rigidity. The minimum-wage law, import quotas on cars, tariffs, and price supports all put a floor under prices and wages.

CHANGES IN WAGES, PRICES, AND UNEMPLOYMENT SINCE 1982

Economists contend that the substantial decline in both unemployment and prices since 1982 reflects profound changes in government policies, composition of the labor force, and competitive relationships that have softened wage and price rigidity. Among these changes have been the deregulation of many industries; union give-backs; declines in union power; reductions in unemployment benefits and teenage job seekers; and changes in foreign competition.

Deregulation. The government's deregulation of numerous industries—from trucking and airlines to communications and securities—put pressure on businesses in the 1980s to rein in operating costs. This led firms to make fewer concessions to union demands and to hire more nonunion workers than they did in the 1970s. The competition spurred by deregulation was also a key motivating factor behind many of the wage concessions granted by both union and nonunion workers to producers in the 1980s.

Union Give-backs. American unions have traditionally shown a strong reluctance to accept reduced wages or benefits when the firms or industries they deal with are in business slumps or are facing strong competitive challenges. Instead, unions have been more willing to accept layoffs and unemployment for some of their members. In the 1980s, however, in the face of growing foreign competition, increased plant closings, and domestic deregulation, many unions accepted reduced wages and benefits to protect jobs and to try to ensure the continued profitability of their employers.

Decline in Union Power. The share of the American work force represented by unions fell from 25 percent in 1981 to about 15 percent in 1992. While this decline primarily reflected plant closings in the heavily unionized manufacturing sector of the economy, unionization rates within manufacturing also declined during this period.

Decline in Jobless Benefits. A dramatic decline occurred in the 1980s in the availability of jobless benefits. In the 1970s, jobless benefits in the form of unemployment insurance payments from state and federal governments were liberally granted to laid-off workers. Some benefits were provided even to workers who had voluntarily left their jobs. In the 1980s, revenue-strained states and the federal government tightened eligibility rules for these unemployment insurance benefits. The ensuing decline in payments induced many laid-off workers to accept an alternative, lower-paying job more quickly or to negotiate a lower wage with their previous employer in order to be rehired.

Decline in Teenage Job Seekers. The number of teenage job seekers began to decline in the mid-1980s in direct, but lagged, response to the low birth rates of American families in the 1960s and 1970s. The result was that the labor force had relatively fewer inexperienced (and hard-to-employ) teenagers in the late 1980s and early 1990s than it did in the 1970s and early 1980s.

Foreign Competition. A high price for the dollar in foreign exchange markets throughout most of the 1980s made U.S. goods expensive to foreigners while making foreign goods highly attractive to U.S. consumers. Concerns over the loss of business to foreign competition motivated many American producers to keep domestic price increases small.

REDUCING INFLATION AND UNEMPLOYMENT TO THE BASE RATE

Some economists contend that the reductions in inflation and unemployment in the 1990s have brought the economy close to its base inflation and unemployment rate.

The concept of a base inflation rate implies that price increases cannot be reduced beyond a certain point because of contractual costs that producers and sellers incur in providing consumers with goods and services. The concept of a base unemployment rate implies that there is a point beyond which the economy cannot absorb any additional unemployed workers. Workers who are unemployed when the base unemployment level is reached are either frictionally unemployed (in the process of voluntarily changing jobs) or structurally unemployed (lacking the skills, training, or education necessary to meet current job demands). Their joblessness cannot be addressed in the short run through stimulative monetary and fiscal policies because their joblessness is not cyclical in nature. Such unemployment is not related to sluggish business or consumer demand for goods and services, as would be the case for laid-off production workers.

Economists who believe that the problem of base unemployment cannot be addressed through stimulative monetary and fiscal policies also contend that any attempt to do so would immediately stimulate inflation. Conversely, they say, the problem of base inflation cannot be solved through restrictive monetary and fiscal policies—and any such attempt would immediately plunge the economy into recession and drive up unemployment.

Some economists, mindful of the trade-off dilemma facing policymakers and the uneven impact of inflation and unemployment on different groups, have advocated the use of wage-price controls as a less socially harmful and more effective alternative than monetary or fiscal policy for dealing with inflation and unemployment. This policy option is discussed in more detail in Extended Study 16, "Wage-Price Controls and Indexation."

Economic Growth

Economic growth, along with full employment and price stability, is another key economic goal of U.S. policymakers. Exhibit 13.11 shows the growth of the U.S. economy during this century, as measured by annual increases in real GDP. However, a more accurate reflection of economic growth is the ability of an economy to increase, over time, its per capita real GDP (output per person). By dividing a nation's real output by its population, economists obtain a per capita measure of goods and services produced. This measure serves as a yardstick of material well-being for comparing a nation's economic growth against its past growth or against the growth performance of other countries.

EXHIBIT 13.11 **Real Gross Domestic Product**

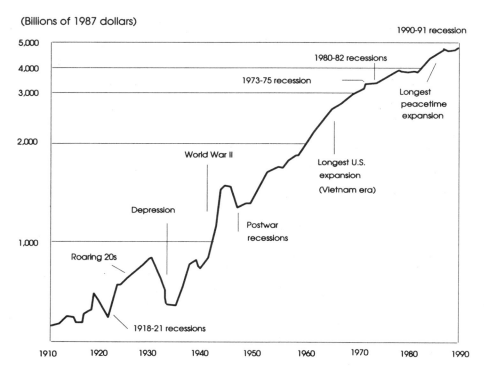

Source: The New York Times, October 16, 1992.

U.S. growth goals in the 1950s and 1960s focused on bettering our economic rivals—the Soviet Union, West Germany, and Japan. Our goals in the 1970s and 1980s focused on reversing a slowdown in growth that, continuing into the 1990s, threatens to reduce U.S. living standards.

Per capita real GDP in the United States increased by 2.5 percent per year from 1960 to 1970. From 1970 to 1992, however, annual per capita GDP growth averaged only about 1 percent. Since the early 1970s, the U.S. economy has grown at a slower rate than that of most other industrial countries, including Germany and Japan. However, because the U.S. has had such a commanding lead in economic growth over other countries, per capita real GDP is about one-third higher in the U.S. today than in Germany and Japan.

Productivity as an Indicator of Economic Growth

Economists have focused increasingly on the slowdown in American productivity—output per hour worked—as the key to the deterioration in the economy's growth performance. From 1937 through 1973, U.S. productivity grew, on average, by

3 percent per year. Since 1973, however, the average annual rate of productivity growth has been 0.9 percent. During the 1980s, U.S. productivity increased by 0.5 percent per year, while Japan's annual productivity grew by 3 percent and Germany's grew by 1.6 percent. As seen in exhibit 13.12, U.S. productivity remains the highest in the world. However, the more rapid gains in productivity registered in other countries in recent decades have resulted in intense competition from foreign producers. The Japanese, in particular, have been able to out-compete U.S. producers in terms of the price and quality of many manufactured goods, including electronic equipment and cars, and have managed to narrow America's international competitive lead. This narrowing trend is illustrated by exhibit 13.13.

EXHIBIT 13.12 Value of Goods and Services Produced by Average Worker in 1990

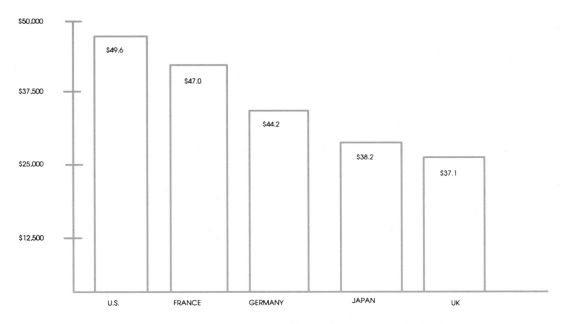

Source: The New York Times, October 13, 1992; Mckinsey Global Institute.

Productivity is more than a key to economic growth. Some economists contend that generating increased productivity is the only long-range solution to controlling inflation and improving national living standards. Without productivity gains, any increase in wages tends to lead to cost-push inflation. However, annual productivity growth of just 2 percent per year would lead to a doubling of U.S. living standards in only 35 years.

From 1973 to 1981, U.S. productivity grew at an average rate of 0.6 percent per year. Productivity growth surged, however, to a 1.7 percent annual rate between 1981 and 1986, but then virtually stopped, growing at a mere 0.1 percent rate each year from 1986 to 1991. Productivity began to increase again in 1992, by about 2.5 percent. Over the last 20 years, the U.S. economy registered smaller yearly increases in productivity than it had, on average, over the prior 100 years.

EXHIBIT 13.13 **U.S. Manufacturing Productivity Compared to Japan and Germany**

Factory productivity for major industries in 1989, United States = 100.

Source: The New York Times, October 13, 1992; McKinsey Global Institute.

REASONS FOR SLOWED PRODUCTIVITY GROWTH

Economists do not know exactly why U.S. productivity slowed in the 1970s or why productivity growth was so anemic in the late 1980s. Nor are they certain that any one reason can explain this performance. However, the erosion in U.S. productivity is generally attributed to a number of changes in the economy that began in the 1970s.

Soaring Energy Prices. In the early 1970s, the economy was jolted by soaring energy price increases and accelerating inflation. A quadrupling of OPEC oil prices in 1974 and a further OPEC oil price shock in 1978 hurt productivity because U.S. industry was forced to conserve energy and adapt to newer, more costly, energy technology. Some studies suggest that the energy price explosion in the 1970s explains more than half of the productivity decline in that decade.

Slowing of Investment Spending. The general uncertainty generated by unexpected inflation also led to a slowing of investment spending and a declining capital-to-labor ratio. As a result, U.S. workers, on average, had fewer machines and tools to work with at the end of the decade than when the 1970s began. Moreover, the machines and tools at U.S. plants were older and less efficient in the 1980s. Because U.S. producers held back on spending to replace machinery, the average age of U.S. manufacturing plants grew by about 10 percent during the decade. Today, the average age of America's machines is 8.5 years—the highest since 1965—and two-thirds of all machine tools used in U.S. factories are more than 10 years old.

Slowdown in Innovation. Contributing to the deterioration in U.S. productivity was a slowdown in innovation and technological change. Studies of U.S. productivity indicate that advances in knowledge account for more than 40 percent of U.S. long-term productivity growth. Although most economists do not attribute the decline in U.S. productivity primarily to changes in American inventiveness, there is some evidence to support this contention. For example, in the 1960s, research and development expenditures of U.S. businesses accounted for about 3 percent of the GDP; in the 1980s, this ratio steadily declined to less than 2 percent. Economists estimate that funds invested by business in research and development yield increases in productivity that, on average, are about 8 times greater than increases generated from equivalent amounts invested in plants and equipment.

New Government Regulations and Tax Laws. Productivity in the 1970s was affected by costly new government regulations covering occupational safety, health, and the environment. Those regulations caused businesses to divert large sums intended for improving the capacity or quality of production to environmental and safety controls. In the early 1980s, however, foreign competition forced many businesses to modernize their plants, to scrap obsolete equipment and close old factories and to cut production costs by permanently laying off workers. As a result, productivity in manufacturing, which had declined in the 1970s, began to grow at rates more consistent with U.S. historic trends—on average, about 3 percent per year through 1986.

However, after 1986 productivity growth essentially stopped and remained stagnant until 1992. Most economists attribute this poor productivity performance to the response of business firms to the Tax Reform Act of 1986. The act ended the government's long-standing investment tax credit, which had effectively provided businesses with a partial government subsidy for continued investment in plants and equipment. It also lengthened depreciation schedules and raised the capital gains tax rate. Those changes all had the effect of raising plant and equipment costs.

Businesses responded by reducing their capital investments. In so doing they impaired the efficient mix of capital and labor they had established earlier in the decade. Many economists see the increase in productivity in 1992 as marking the end of the business adjustment to the 1986 Tax Reform Act and a return to the more efficient mix of capital and labor in use before the act.

Entry of Women and Teenagers into the Work Force. The increasing entry of teenagers and women into the labor force also profoundly influenced productivity in the 1970s and 1980s. The Congressional Budget Office estimated in 1981 that the disproportionate number of women and teenagers who entered the labor force in the 1970s cost the U.S. economy about one-half of a percentage point in annual productivity by reducing the overall level of experience and skill of the labor force. Moreover, the sharp expansion in the labor force in the 1970s, in excess of the nation's capital growth, added to the decline in the capital-to-labor ratio.

Falling Demand for Energy. Some of the slowdown in U.S. productivity can be traced to falling productivity in the nation's electrical and gas utilities. In utilities, most work hours are devoted to maintaining the distribution system. When demand for energy increases and more kilowatts or cubic yards of energy are delivered through the system, productivity increases because the number of hours needed for maintenance remains the same. Conversely, when demand for energy declines, as was the case after 1973 when energy prices soared, the smaller volume of energy being processed through the nation's utilities causes productivity to fall. Economists attribute almost 20 percent of the slowdown in U.S. productivity in the 1970s to the reduced volume of fixed-capacity and fixed-staff operations.

Movement toward a Welfare State. Some economists blame the nation's slowed productivity growth on the U.S. economy's movement away from a free enterprise or market system to that of a welfare state. On the other hand, some industrial countries that have experienced higher rates of productivity growth than the United States have more extensive social welfare systems than the United States. Moreover, the largest growth in per capita GDP in any decade of U.S. history (35 percent) occurred in the 1940s when the economy was almost totally managed by the government for wartime production. The second largest growth (30 percent) occurred in the 1960s when federal social welfare programs were proliferating.

Shift from Manufacturing to Services. Another major reason cited for the erosion of U.S. productivity is the increasing shift of the U.S. economy from manufacturing to services and, particularly, the sharp increase in unskilled service-sector jobs in the 1970s and 1980s. Economic theory has long maintained that productivity gains are harder to generate in service industries than in manufacturing. Productivity gains in manufacturing are generally believed to result mainly from the use of increasingly more efficient machines and technology and not from harder working employees. Because production plants and assembly lines are more readily adaptable to technological improvements than are service activities (for example, jobs at banks, doctors' offices, and barber shops), many economists believe that service-sector productivity will inevitably lag. Support for this theory can be found in the nation's productivity statistics, which show that in the 1980s output per hour worked in the economy's service sector increased by less than one-half of a percentage point per year, while annual productivity in manufacturing grew by 3 percent.

Some economists contend, however, that difficulties in evaluating and measuring service productivity may lead to substantial understatements of productivity growth in the service industries. They suggest that productivity gains in service jobs are not difficult to achieve—for example, through increased reliance on self-service and computerized services, such as the use of ATMs by banks. They also note that productivity in some service industries—communications and rail transportation, in particular—has outperformed the overall trend and registered sharp gains in the 1980s.

Inadequate Investment. Studies of productivity have attributed much of the nation's poor productivity performance to inadequate investment. The reality, however, is not that U.S. businesses invested that much less in the 1970s and 1980s, but that the labor force grew proportionally faster than investment spending. As a result, the amount of capital invested for each worker declined. In effect, the United States was able to stop the decline in productivity and generate small productivity gains by employing more people. The number of people employed in the United States increased from 40 percent of the population in 1970 to 61 percent of the population in 1992.

Many economists contend that increasing productivity is the only way that the United States can assure the economic growth necessary for achieving full employment and price stability and that, in the final analysis, economic growth must be the paramount objective of monetary and fiscal policy.

Productivity in Banking

In an industry in which productivity does not increase, rising production costs invariably lead to higher prices or lower profits. Static productivity poses a particular problem for banks. Rising production costs cannot easily be passed on to consumer and corporate depositors in the form of higher prices. Banks are limited by law and regulation to maximum charges they can impose on a considerable portion of their earning assets, particularly consumer loans and real estate loans. In addition, because the market for banking products and services is highly competitive, loan or service charges that rise too rapidly in relation to charges imposed by competitors can cause a bank to lose depositors and borrowers.

Much of the focus of banks' operating management in the 1980s was on reducing labor costs and improving worker productivity. However, improving productivity in any service industry is difficult. As noted previously, service industries do not readily lend themselves to the operating efficiencies that can be generated through automated production processes. Also, productivity in service industries is not subject to ready measurement.

MEASURING PRODUCTIVITY IN BANKING

Many banking jobs involve analytical, administrative, and managerial work for which quality or productivity improvements cannot easily be evaluated. Thus economists rely on productivity proxies to measure banks' output.

Economists measure banks' deposit activities by counting the number of checks banks handle and the number of deposits and withdrawals banks post. Banks' trust activities are measured by counting the number of accounts being managed; loan activities by the number of new loans made. However, no weight is given to the dollar value of the transactions and accounts banks handle. Most economists maintain that if this factor were included in bank productivity, the measures would show strong steady increases. Nonetheless, they note that the numbers would still not adequately measure the efficiency of bank employees or the quality of their work.

Many banks use various internal efficiency measures as a guide in employee performance evaluations. They assess aspects of employee activities that are readily quantifiable, such as the number of hourly transactions handled by a teller or the number of checking account statements reconciled each day by a clerk. Measures like these indicate productivity for some bank activities, but they do not adequately factor in improvements or deterioration in workmanship over time. Also, measures such as these have limited applicability to the professional, technical, and managerial activities of bank employees where the quality of the work is especially important; these measures focus only on the amount or quantity of work performed rather than its quality.

Most banks have significantly increased productivity in their back offices and data processing centers in recent years. Bank operating officers have employed increasingly more efficient technology to handle a larger volume of paper checks and larger and more complex databases with less human intervention. Some banks now use formulas to measure the productivity of ATMs as an offset to increased teller staffing to handle routine transactions. On balance, technology has improved the speed and accuracy with which money and data are transferred between banks and, more important, between different units within a bank.

Yet for some banks, technology and data processing have not resulted in increased productivity. While automation has enabled them to process a greater number and variety of transactions in less time, the overall quality of their deposit-related services has declined. At some banks, the costs of increased technical staff and computer consultants have outweighed savings resulting from automation. Moreover, not all banks have been able to effectively adapt their organizational and management structures to automated processes to obtain maximum productivity benefits.

PRODUCTIVITY PROGRAMS

Traditional productivity theory attributes gains in output per hour worked to factors that assist workers in producing more. These factors include the amount of capital (machines) available to aid workers, the technology of the machines, the organization of the workers, and inventions and innovations that increase efficiency. Modern productivity theory, however, has focused increasingly on worker attitudes and quality of work life as factors that stimulate or constrain worker output. Thus, many banks are moving to increase productivity by raising the level of their employees' job satisfaction. They are involving employees in management decisions that affect their jobs, providing challenging work that allows for development of skills and abilities, linking compensation more closely to accomplishment, and giving due recognition for work that is done well.

Quality Circle Programs. One innovation that has improved the quality of work life in a number of major banks and industrial organizations is the quality circle, a highly structured program in which management uses employees' expertise to solve problems and improve the company's performance.

The Japanese developed the quality circle concept in the early 1960s using the theories of American behavioral scientists Abraham Maslow, Frederick Hertzberg, and Thomas McGregor. Since the late 1970s, many of the nation's large banks have sought to use quality circles to improve their productivity.

A quality circle program uses a structured process to identify specific problems within the employees' area of responsibility. The employees then discuss the problem, and offer proposals and recommendations to solve the problem. After the quality circle participants agree on a solution to the problem, they take their recommendations to senior bank management. Management not only provides training for the sessions and actively participates in the sessions, but must agree to accept recommendations from these employee groups.

Production-oriented line departments in bank operations areas—electronic funds transfer and check-processing departments, for example—have served as the starting point for most banks' quality circle programs. These programs have resulted in improved routine operations and increased productivity at many banks. In the 1980s, quality circle programs in many banks were expanded to front-office operations, professional departments, and staff departments. Here the results have been less dramatic. Banks have found that productivity improvements in these areas are often small and take longer to develop. They also have found that a quality circle program at the front-office level does not prove effective in the absence of a bankwide management commitment to quality control efforts.

Other Approaches to Productivity. Some banks have sought to develop criteria for measuring the productivity of staff operations and units. In the 1970s, many banks vastly expanded their staff operations, adding to existing staff departments and creating new ones in such areas as marketing, planning, systems development, and employee training. These departments, which are highly labor-intensive and costly, typically do not lend themselves to easy productivity measurement and evaluation.

Banks with a heavy retail and consumer business orientation have sought to reduce the labor-intensive costs of providing services directly to customers. They have developed new ways to accomplish more with fewer tellers and clerks by getting bank customers to do more for themselves—for example, to bank by phone and to use automated teller machines and point-of-sale terminals.

Increased Productivity through Self-Service Banking

Some bankers contend that if bank customers (and bank management) are willing to give up relationship banking, which depends on costly labor-intensive service, banks eventually may be able to reduce the ratio of costs to each unit of service provided. This approach to productivity is similar to that taken by the nation's telephone companies in the 1970s. By sharing technology and systems and persuading customers to accept direct dialing, telephone companies reduced labor-intensive costs (long-line operators) and met growing service demands. The grocery industry met a similar challenge in the 1940s when it successfully introduced the self-service supermarket.

Summary

The three primary goals of U.S. monetary policy today are full employment, price stability, and economic growth. Full employment has proved an elusive goal because many of America's unemployed either lack the education and skills to fill available jobs or have been displaced from jobs by new technology or foreign competition.

Maintaining an economy without inflation has also proved difficult, particularly when inflation is generated by cost-push pressures or scarcity-induced factors. Moreover, because inflation's effects are borne unevenly, the harm that inflation inflicts adds a social and political dimension to the problem. Inflation redistributes income and wealth, creates illusory inventory profits for businesses, and reduces international competitiveness.

Many economists contend that there is a trade-off relationship between inflation and unemployment. That relationship, which can be illustrated using a Phillips curve, provides policymakers with a dilemma.

America's ability to achieve its economic growth goal is directly related to its ability to increase productivity. Without increased productivity, rising production costs invariably lead to rising prices. The need to increase productivity has also become a major goal of most banks in the 1990s.

Questions

1. How can unemployment and employment increase concurrently? How is the unemployment rate determined?

2. Economists attribute inflation to three primary sources. What are they? Why is the wage-price spiral often referred to as the glue that binds the sources of inflation together?

3. What effect does inflation have on the redistribution of income and wealth?

4. Why would an unanticipated inflation rate of 5 percent be more harmful to banks than a correctly anticipated inflation rate of 10 percent?

5. Explain why a tight monetary policy designed to reduce inflation might increase unemployment.

6. What factors determine national productivity? What measures have banks employed to increase productivity?

PART V International Banking

14

The Balance of Payments and Foreign Exchange

Objectives

After successfully completing this chapter, you will be able to

- ☐ define balance of trade and other key balance-of-payments measures,

- ☐ explain the concepts of international reserve assets, the dollar as vehicle money, and the settling of U.S. balance-of-payments deficits,

- ☐ cite factors that contributed to the deterioration of U.S. international trade and investment performance in the 1980s,

- ☐ discuss the merits of current proposals to improve the U.S. trade position, and

- ☐ explain how foreign exchange rates are determined and why they change.

Introduction

The volume of world trade, international investment, and the flow of money between countries has soared in recent decades. As a result, the economic and banking systems of individual countries have become increasingly interdependent. This growing interdependency has required U.S. policymakers to assign a higher priority to the national economic goal of balance in international trade and payments.

In this chapter we will first examine the components of the U.S. balance-of-payments measure in order to understand the nature and scope of the economic and financial interaction between the United States and other countries. We will then look at the importance of the U.S. dollar and the workings of the foreign exchange markets, including how foreign exchange rates are determined. These discussions provide a foundation for understanding the important role of U.S. and foreign banks in facilitating trade and international investment—the subject of the final chapter.

The Balance of Payments

A nation's balance of payments is a statistical record of the money value of all transactions that have occurred between that nation and the rest of the world during a given year. The U.S. balance of payments serves then both as a measure of our performance in the world economy and as a register, over time, of our strengths and weaknesses in the area of international commerce and finance.

In calculating the balance of payments, all outflows of money—including all funds paid for imports of goods and services, foreign investments, loans, or aid to other countries—are recorded as payments. All inflows of money—including all funds taken in from exports to other countries, sales of financial assets or property to overseas purchasers, and repayments of foreign loans—are recorded as receipts. The difference between a nation's total international payments and its total international receipts is its balance of payments.

Balance Measures

A nation's balance of payments is composed of five *balance* measures, each of which focuses analytical attention on a different aspect of the nation's international activity and its international economic position. The measures comprising the U.S. balance of payments, as shown in exhibit 14.1, are balance of trade, balance on goods and services, balance on current account, and two measures of capital flows—basic balance and official settlements balance.

Recept

EXHIBIT 14.1 Components of U.S. Balance of Payments

	Receipts (Inflows)	Payments (Outflows)
Balance of Trade	Exports	Imports
Balance on Goods and Services	-Travel and transportation -Military sales -Fees and royalties from abroad -Earnings from direct U.S. investment abroad -Earnings from portfolio investment abroad -Other receipts	-Travel and transportation -Military outlays abroad -Fees and royalties to foreigners -Payments on direct foreign investment in U.S. -Payments on portfolio investment to foreigners -Other payments
		-Remittances, pensions, and other transfers -U.S. government grants (gifts)
Basic Balance	-Private direct investment in the United States -Private portfolio investment in the United States -Foreign aid repayments	-Private direct investment abroad -Private portfolio investment abroad -U.S. government aid (loans)
Official Settlements Balance	-Foreign government acquisitions of U.S. official reserve assets (mostly government securities) -Statistical discrepancy	-U.S. government acquisitions of official U.S. reserve assets
	Total receipts	Total payments

Left side vertical labels: Balance on Current Account; Capital Flows

BALANCE OF TRADE

The balance of trade is the difference between a nation's exports and imports of goods. A nation that exports more merchandise than it imports is said to have a balance of trade surplus, or a favorable balance of trade. A nation that imports more goods than it exports has a balance of trade deficit, or an unfavorable balance of trade.

In many countries, trade in merchandise is the primary component of their balance of payments; in the United States, merchandise trade represents only about half of the nation's total balance of payments. Merchandise trade also accounts for a larger share of most nations' GDP than it does for the U.S. GDP, although the importance of trade in U.S. economic activity has been increasing. As exhibit 14.2 shows, since 1970, U.S. dependence on foreign imports has more than doubled. Imported capital goods (machines), automobiles, and consumer goods account for most U.S. merchandise imports. Exported capital goods (machines) and industrial supplies account for most of America's merchandise exports.

EXHIBIT 14.2   **U.S. Imports as a Percentage of U.S. GDP**

1960	5.0%
1965	5.0%
1970	6.0%
1975	8.0%
1980	12.0%
1985	11.0%
1990	13.3%

Source: U.S. Department of Commerce

From 1870 to 1970, the United States almost always exported more than it imported. However, as exhibit 14.3 shows, from the mid-1970s to the mid-1980s the United States registered increasingly larger annual trade deficits; since the 1987 deficit, however, America's balance of trade has steadily improved. The 1991 deficit—$73.4 billion—was the smallest in seven years.

The North American Free-Trade Agreement (NAFTA)

In 1992, the United States, Canada, and Mexico agreed, in principle, to establish a free trade area for North America by eliminating all restrictions on imports and exports between their respective countries.

If NAFTA becomes law (the agreement must be ratified by the legislatures of all three countries), the economic implications for the United States could be profound. As exhibit 14.4 shows, Canada and Mexico are already the United States' first and second largest individual country trading partners—Japan is third. Total North American trade is about $200 billion per year. One quarter of this trade is in automobiles and auto parts, with U.S.-Mexico trade in automobile products exceeding $8 billion per year. The United States is also Mexico's largest trading partner; nearly 70 percent of Mexico's imports come from the U.S. and three quarters of Mexico's automobile exports go to the United States.

Most economists believe that a North American free trade zone—which would be the world's largest—will stimulate even greater U.S.-Mexico trade in the 1990s (particularly in automboiles and auto components) and create additional U.S. jobs. U.S. exports to Mexico have more than doubled since 1987 and economists estimate that about 650,000 U.S. jobs are currently related to this growing trade. Estimates of new export-related jobs range up to 130,000 by 1995. However, some economists contend that if Congress ratifies NAFTA, the United States will lose jobs as U.S. industries transfer production to Mexico where wages and other production costs are substantially lower.

EXHIBIT 14.3   **U.S. Balance of Trade, 1971-1991**
(billions of dollars; negative reflects deficit)

1971	-2.3
1972	-6.4
1973	0.9
1974	-5.3
1975	9.0
1976	-9.3
1977	-30.9
1978	-33.8
1979	-27.3
1980	-25.3
1981	-28.0
1982	-36.5
1983	-67.1
1984	-112.5
1985	-124.4
1986	-147.7
1987	-160.3
1988	-127.0
1989	-115.7
1990	-108.8
1991	-73.4

BALANCE ON GOODS AND SERVICES

A broader measure of a nation's balance of payments is its balance on goods and services. This measure includes both the merchandise trade balance plus net export or import of services. As shown in exhibit 14.1, internationally traded services include transportation and tourism, military purchases and sales, receipts of earnings on investments abroad, and payments of earnings on foreign investments. Banking and insurance firms' international transactions are also included.

In the United States, exports of services have traditionally exceeded imports of services. For decades, U.S. earnings abroad from direct investment (Americans' holdings in foreign factories and property) and portfolio investment (Americans' holdings of foreign stocks and bonds) more than offset persistent deficits in the U.S. tourism balance (amounts spent by Americans abroad compared to what foreigners spent here) and net military expenditures abroad. That service surplus helped to partially offset the trade deficit experienced in recent years. In 1987, however, payments to foreigners on their investments here began to exceed earnings on U.S. investments overseas, thus exacerbating the imbalance between America's international receipts and payments. Most economists feared that this reversal in the flow of net investment earnings fore- shadowed a significant deterioration in the nation's current account balance in the late

1980s and early 1990s. However, as exhibit 14.5 shows, since 1987 the U.S. current account deficit has steadily diminished.

EXHIBIT 14.4   **U.S. Exports in 1991**
(billions of dollars)

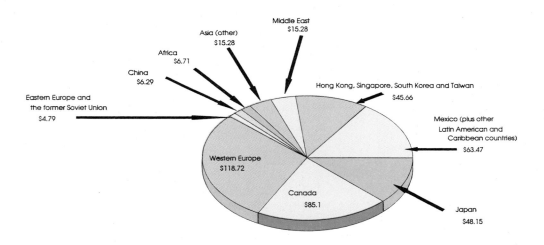

Source: U.S. Department of Commerce, *The Washington Post,* November 16, 1992.

BALANCE ON CURRENT ACCOUNT

   A nation's current account is the value of all its visible and invisible trade with other nations. As such, the balance on current account includes both the goods and services balance plus unilateral transfers (which include private gifts to foreigners and grants-in-aid to foreign governments, other than military grants). In the 1980s, unilateral transfers from private U.S. citizens and the U.S. government to foreigners averaged between $5 billion and $10 billion each year. Exhibit 14.6 shows the trend—adjusted for inflation—of U.S. exports and imports of goods and services, the major component of the current account balance.

The trend shows that in the late 1980s, U.S. exports began to grow faster than U.S. imports, which led to a progressive narrowing of the current account balance. U.S. manufacturing firms that had restructured in the 1980s to reduce production costs and improve the quality of their goods began to regain their international competitiveness.

EXHIBIT 14.5   **U.S. Current Account Deficit**

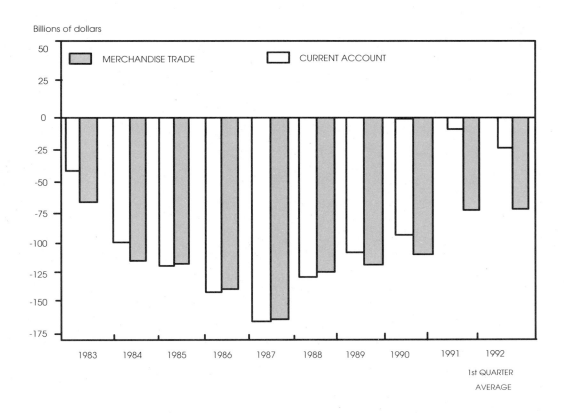

A decline in the value of the dollar relative to other currencies also helped reduce the cost of U.S. goods and services to foreigners.

When the U.S. economy went into recession in 1990, U.S. demand for imported capital goods, automobiles, and consumer goods declined. However, overall foreign demand for U.S. goods and services remained strong. In the early 1990s, increases in U.S. exports to the Asian industrialized countries—Hong Kong, Korea, Singapore, and Taiwan—more than offset declines in exports to key U.S. trading partners—Japan and Germany—whose economies, like that of the U.S., had slowed in the aftermath of recession.

The current account balance measures all the ongoing transactions between the United States and other countries that result in an international transfer of money; it does not, however, reflect inflows or outflows of capital. A current account in surplus reflects a situation in which the United States is able to more than pay for external purchases out of current income. A current account in deficit reflects a situation in which the United

EXHIBIT 14.6   **U.S. Exports and Imports of Goods and Services**
Seasonally Adjusted at Annual Rates

Source: Federal Reserve Bank of Richmond, *Cross Sections*, Volume 9, No. 2, Summer 1992.

States must finance external purchases from borrowings. Long-term trends in the current account balance, as seen in exhibit 14.7 indicate that in the 1980s the United States became a net borrower from, rather than a net lender to, foreign countries.

Current account deficits or surpluses capture the positive or negative contribution of foreigners to domestic aggregate demand. However, the current account measure provides only a partial picture of the U.S. economy's international performance because it fails to take into account capital flowing into or out of the United States. Inflows and outflows of capital can completely offset a current account deficit or surplus and can profoundly affect the domestic economy.

EXHIBIT 14.7   **U.S. International Trade Performance, 1950-1990**
(billions of dollars; negative reflects deficit)

Year	Balance of Trade	Balance on Goods and Services	Balance on Current Account
1950	1.1	2.2	-1.8
1955	2.9	2.9	0.4
1960	4.9	5.1	2.8
1965	5.0	8.3	5.4
1970	2.6	5.6	2.3
1975	9.0	22.9	18.2
1980	-25.3	8.3	1.5
1985	-124.4	-102.7	-117.7
1990	-108.7	-78.2	-99.3

Source: U.S. Department of Commerce

CAPITAL FLOWS, BASIC BALANCE

Capital flows complete the picture with respect to a nation's balance of payments. Again, as seen in exhibit 14.1, capital flows can be further categorized as inflows and outflows of capital comprising the basic balance and those comprising the official settlements balance.

The basic balance isolates long-term capital transactions (those involving investments of one year or more) to focus on any long-term or potentially persistent forces at work in the balance of payments. This measure, which suggests the future course of the country's international performance, also is known as the balance on the current and long-term capital account.

The capital account registers changes in U.S. investment abroad and changes in foreign investment in the United States during the year. An increase in U.S. investment abroad represents a capital outflow, while an increase in foreign investment in the United States represents a capital inflow. On the inflow side, the predominant type of foreign investment in the United States has traditionally been foreign purchases of U.S. government securities and corporate bonds and stocks. This reflects the size and liquidity of U.S. capital markets and the numerous opportunities the United States offers foreign investors. In the 1980s, however, foreign direct investments in U.S. real estate and manufacturing firms increased significantly. On the outflow side, Americans' purchases of foreign manufacturing firms (direct investment) and foreign stocks and bonds (portfolio investment) have typified U.S. investment abroad in recent decades. Most U.S. portfolio investment abroad consists of Americans' purchases of foreign bonds floated in the U.S. capital market. U.S. bank loans to foreigners, a staple of U.S. investment abroad through the 1970s, declined substantially in the 1980s.

CAPITAL FLOWS, OFFICIAL SETTLEMENTS BALANCE

The official settlements balance measures the change in holdings of international reserve assets of the United States and foreign governments during the year. This measure is a gauge of any foreign exchange rate pressure that might be brought to bear on the dollar in foreign exchange markets.

A country generates a balance-of-payments deficit when it spends more abroad than it takes in from abroad. To finance a deficit, a nation, like an individual or business, must draw on its accumulated wealth or it must borrow. When a nation with a balance-of-payments deficit chooses not to (or cannot) borrow, the wealth that it draws on is its international reserves.

International reserves consist of four types of financial assets that governments throughout the world have agreed to accept from each other in payment or settlement of debt. These assets are gold, special drawing rights (SDRs), foreign exchange, and gold tranche—the borrowing privilege of member nations at the International Monetary Fund (IMF).

As exhibit 14.8 shows, the international reserve assets held by the United States consist primarily of foreign exchange and SDRs. This is also true of most other countries. Gold and the borrowing privilege at the IMF (gold tranche) are lesser components of the world's international reserve assets.

Gold. Gold bullion (gold in the form of ingots) held by the governments of the world is one kind of international reserve asset. By international agreement in the 1970s, gold dealings among governments are transacted at the official U.S. government gold price of $42.22 an ounce, rather than at market prices. Because market prices for gold in the 1970s, 1980s, and 1990s have ranged well above this official gold price, countries do not normally settle balance-of-payments deficits by payment in gold.

Special Drawing Rights (SDRs). Special drawing rights, another category of international reserve assets, are created by the International Monetary Fund (IMF) and allocated to participating member countries. IMF members may use SDRs in settlement of financial claims of other member nations.

Foreign Exchange. Foreign exchange is the supply of the world's major trading currencies. These are primarily U.S. dollars and, to a lesser extent, British pounds, German marks, Japanese yen, and French francs. Nations with a balance of payments deficit can pay off the deficit with foreign currencies they hold.

Gold Tranche. IMF member nations have automatic borrowing privileges, or a credit line, at the IMF. Each nation's borrowing privilege, known as gold tranche, is equal to the dollar amount of gold it is required to pay into the IMF as a condition of membership. By international agreement, nations may count these automatic credit lines as part of their international reserve assets.

EXHIBIT 14.8 **U.S. Reserve Assets**
(June 1992)

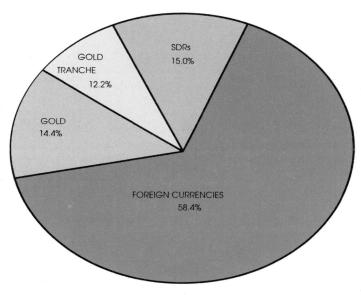

TOTAL: $77.1 BILLION

U.S. Balance-of-Payments Performance

From the 1950s to the late 1970s, the U.S. balance on current account consistently registered small annual surpluses. Since then (see exhibit 14.7), the U.S. balance of trade and balance on current account have registered large deficits that reflect a fundamental change in America's international trade and investment performance.

The deterioration in the U.S. balance of payments in the 1980s was due to huge increases in imports to the United States coupled with weak demand for U.S. exports. Contributing to the slowdown in export growth was the loss of competitiveness of key U.S. industries, such as the steel and auto industries, as well as the external debt problems of such countries as Mexico and Brazil, which are major purchasers of U.S. goods. However, the primary factor causing the deterioration in the U.S. export-import position in the 1980s was the increased price of the dollar in foreign exchange markets. In real terms (that is, adjusting for domestic and foreign inflation), the price of the dollar increased 50 percent against the price of other major trading monies from 1980 to 1984.

As the price of the dollar rises in foreign exchange markets, U.S. goods become increasingly unattractive to foreigners while foreign goods become increasingly enticing to Americans. In essence, an increase in the price of the dollar means that foreigners wishing to purchase U.S. goods and services have to pay more of their currency to buy dollars in the foreign exchange market. Thus a 50 percent increase in the price of the dollar in foreign exchange markets represents to potential foreign buyers a 50 percent markup in the price of all U.S. products. At the same time, the increase in the price of the dollar represents a 50 percent markdown to U.S. buyers in the price of all goods made abroad.

Gold bullion held by the Federal Reserve.

Photo courtesy of the Federal Reserve Bank of New York.

The price of the dollar soared in the early 1980s, mainly because U.S. interest rates remained high while inflation slowed markedly. Because U.S. capital markets offer a broad range of investment opportunities and because the dollar is free from exchange controls, foreigners' demand for dollars for investment purposes typically surges when real U.S. interest rates rise in relation to rates available in their domestic markets.

The dollar reached its peak value against other world currencies in early 1985. From then through 1992, as seen in exhibit 14.9, the dollar's real price fell by 50 percent against the yen, the mark and other currencies. However, this drop in the value of the dollar did not lead to an improvement in the nation's trade and current account performance until late in the 1980s, partly because the dollar's real price did not depreciate relative to the currencies of important U.S. trade partners, notably Canada, Mexico, Taiwan, and Korea. About 20 percent of U.S. exports go to Japan and Europe, where the dollar's falling price in relation to their own currencies made U.S. goods more competitive; but more than one-third of U.S. exports go to Canada, Mexico, Taiwan, and Korea, where the dollar's high price in relation to those currencies initially hurt sales of U.S. goods.

Some economists contend that the dollar's performance in the world's foreign exchange markets in the 1980s benefitted the U.S. economy. The rapid rise in imports to the United States helped economic recovery abroad and enhanced the export earnings of developing countries. The availability of imports at relatively low prices also was a key factor in holding down U.S. inflation. And countering the nation's large current account deficits were sizable inflows of foreign capital that enabled the United States to finance large federal budget deficits at lower interest rates than otherwise would have prevailed.

Other economists point out that the United States paid a high price for these benefits. The growth in U.S. imports throughout the 1980s led to a profusion of U.S. dollars in foreign hands. Foreigners used these dollars to acquire vast quantities of U.S. corporate stocks and bonds, Treasury securities, real estate, manufacturing firms, and bank loans.

EXHIBIT 14.9   U.S. Dollar Against Currencies of 13 Industrial Countries
(Adjusted IMF Index, 1985 = 100)

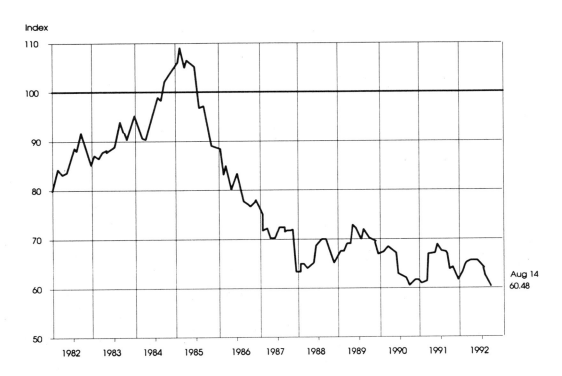

This flood of foreign capital into the United States led to an increase in U.S. earnings outflows to foreigners that, by 1987, exceeded U.S. earnings inflows on American investments overseas. The massive accumulation of U.S. assets by foreigners in the 1980s also shifted the status of the United States from the world's largest creditor nation to the world's largest debtor nation. The net debt of the United States to the rest of the world exceeded $500 billion in 1992. The result of this change in the U.S. balance-of-payments position was that we, as a nation, had to use a growing portion of our domestic income to pay foreigners on their accumulated investments in the United States—a trend that could, in time, reduce U.S. living standards.

Restoring Balance

Reducing the balance-of-payments deficit and restoring the balance between U.S. exports and imports became a higher-priority goal of U.S. monetary and fiscal policy in the late 1980s. Policymakers came to see that a smaller trade deficit was necessary to achieve balanced domestic economic growth. A smaller deficit also would reduce our need to import capital, which adds to the nation's net international indebtedness.

Two key policy approaches have been proposed for dealing with the U.S. balance-of-payments deficit: 1) government intervention in the foreign exchange market to drive down the price of the dollar, and 2) restrictions on imports and capital inflows.

LOWERING THE EXCHANGE RATE

In theory, a government-induced decline in the price of the dollar in the foreign exchange market should improve the nation's trade position by increasing exports from the United States and reducing imports to the United States. A lower price for the dollar makes U.S.-produced goods more attractive to foreigners because they need to exchange less of their own money to buy U.S. goods. At the same time, the lower price of the dollar makes foreign-made goods less attractive to Americans since more dollars are needed to buy the foreign exchange required to purchase imported goods.

Economists have discovered, however, that when a nation lowers its exchange rate, its trade performance does not improve immediately. In fact, trade deficits normally worsen before they begin to narrow. A graph of this trade deficit pattern—characterized by initial deterioration and subsequent improvement—resembles the letter *J*; thus, economists refer to this phenomenon as the *J-curve*.

As noted previously, when the dollar's price declined significantly against the major trading currencies (particularly the yen and the mark) in the mid-1980s, the nation's trade deficit worsened. The volume of U.S. exports expanded, as expected, but the volume of imports continued to soar as well. Some economists contend that the appeal of imports in the mid-1980s did not solely reflect the lagged response associated with the J-curve, but also was related to broad changes in the U.S. economy that have made the United States more dependent on imports.

These changes include the increased reliance of many U.S. companies on foreign sources of supply for their machinery, equipment, and parts. The American automobile industry, for example, imports engines, bearings, tires, and other key components for most U.S.-produced cars. Thus, if domestic auto production increases in relation to foreign car imports, demand for the foreign components needed to produce those domestic cars increases as well. As a result, the importation of components essentially offsets the effect of fewer imports of foreign-made cars.

IMPORT RESTRICTIONS

U.S. restrictions on imports and capital inflows are another method that has been proposed for dealing with the U.S. balance-of-payments deficit. But while import restrictions benefit workers and producers in affected industries, they do so at the expense of consumers who then pay higher prices. Indeed, if import restrictions are sufficiently broad based, subsequent price increases can trigger inflation. Export industries also can be hurt if other countries retaliate against U.S. policy by imposing their own restrictions on imports to their countries from the United States. Moreover, any move to reduce capital inflows to the United States, assuming no expansion in U.S. monetary policy, would likely result in a rise in real interest rates, leading to dislocations in the U.S. credit market. Furthermore, direct controls are inconsistent with free-market precepts and would be administratively difficult to implement and monitor.

Apart from these proposed policy approaches, the U.S. trade position also could improve if the economies of our major trading partners—Japan, Germany, Canada, and Mexico—were to grow at rates considerably faster than that of the United States. This would likely cause demand for U.S. exports to increase at a faster rate than U.S. imports. It is doubtful, however, that foreign governments would agree to overstimulate their economies by implementing easy monetary or fiscal policies since to do so would be inflationary. (Indeed, in 1992, both Germany and Japan resisted strong U.S. pressures to reduce their interest rates on those grounds.)

Conversely, a slowdown in America's economic growth (a recession) would also improve the U.S. trade position by reducing domestic demand for imports. While the 1990-1991 recession helped the U.S. trade position, it is unlikely that U.S. monetary and fiscal policymakers would seek to create a recession as a means to improve trade because a recession also would generate unacceptable rates of unemployment.

The Role of the U.S. Dollar in the World Economy

U.S. policy options for dealing with the nation's balance-of-payments deficits are constrained by the role that the dollar plays in the international economy. Since the 1950s, the U.S. dollar has become the world's predominant *vehicle money*—that is, the money used by the world's traders and investors in international dealings. This transcendent role of the dollar in the world economy results from several characteristics of the U.S. economy and our nation's financial system.

The United States offers other nations the largest supply of goods and services available in the world. We produce more than 50 percent of the gross domestic product of the world's market economies and are the world's largest importer and exporter nation. To obtain U.S. goods and services, foreigners have to accumulate and use U.S. dollars.

Moreover, the political and economic stability of the United States has generated worldwide confidence in the integrity of the dollar as a medium of exchange and store of value. The United States has one of the longest-surviving government structures in the world (only England's is older), and it has never repudiated a debt (including the Revolutionary War debt of the Continental Congress).

The United States also offers international traders, investors, and financial institutions the world's largest investment market and an assortment of credit instruments covering the entire risk and liquidity spectrum. This market is free from exchange controls, which would restrict or limit the movement of money into or out of the United States.

From 1933 to 1971, the U.S. government redeemed dollars held by foreign governments for gold at a fixed price of $35 an ounce. Its gold-redemption pledge made the dollar "as good as gold" in international dealings. The value of the dollar was assured in 1933 when the United States unilaterally raised the world price of gold by 66 percent—from $22 an ounce to $35 an ounce.

Until the late 1960s, the value (price) of the dollar in foreign exchange markets was virtually stable. During the late 1940s and 1950s, there was a worldwide scarcity of dollars and vast demand among the European nations for dollars to rebuild their World War II-shattered industries, as well as strong demand among newly independent developing countries. The international financial system created for the post-World War II world economy was built on the implied premise that U.S. balance-of-payments deficits would meet the world's demand for dollars and that the United States would serve as a kind of global central bank in managing the international financial system.

No other country is big enough, or willing, to have its money serve as a vehicle money in competition with, or as a substitute for, the U.S. dollar. The major reason for that reluctance is that a country must be willing to assume the responsibilities that go along with this designation. This involves maintaining the value and stability of the vehicle money in foreign exchange markets—and giving equal weight to this goal along with domestic economic goals. Even the United States found this responsibility difficult to meet in the 1970s and 1980s.

Balance-of-Payments Settlement

Annual U.S. balance-of-payments deficits mean that in the course of a year, more dollars have flowed out of the United States in payment for foreign goods and services and investments and loans abroad than foreign money has flowed into the country in payment for U.S. goods and services, investments, and loan repayments.

Because U.S. dollars cannot be used in domestic transactions in most foreign countries, foreign holders of excess dollars (representing the U.S. balance-of-payments deficit) typically sell them in the foreign exchange market for domestic money. Those sales, however, invariably drive down the price of the dollar in foreign exchange markets while driving up the price of other monies, often above the level that foreign governments have established as consistent with their domestic and external economic goals. When that occurs, governments intervene in the foreign exchange markets, coming in as sellers of their own money (buyers of dollars) to drive down the price of their own money in exchange markets.

Such intervention does not eliminate the excess dollars generated by the U.S. balance-of-payments deficit. It merely transfers the ownership of the excess dollars from private foreign hands—primarily corporations and banks—to foreign governments and central banks.

Before 1971, foreign governments with unwanted excess dollars could settle with the U.S. government by exchanging the dollars for gold bullion owned by the United States as part of its international reserves. Since 1971, however, dollars held by foreign governments have not been exchangeable for gold. In settling a U.S. balance-of-payments deficit, nations have been left with three options:

- ☐ To hold the excess dollars as part of the nation's international reserve assets— as foreign exchange—for future government intervention in foreign exchange markets. Any attempt to drive up the exchange rate of the nation's own currency requires a sale of dollars (purchase of domestic money).

- ☐ To use the excess dollars to buy U.S. financial assets as an investment vehicle. Dollars that may be needed to intervene in the foreign exchange market can be held in the form of interest-earning U.S. Treasury securities that can be readily sold for dollars.

- ☐ To sell the dollars on the foreign exchange market for some other nation's money. However, any massive selling of dollars will drive the dollar's price down and drive up the price of foreign monies. When the dollar's price falls, U.S. goods become relatively less expensive abroad while the goods of other nations become more expensive to Americans. Moreover, the value of foreign investments in the United States declines while the value of U.S. investments in the selling nation increases.

Given these options, the impact of any U.S. balance-of-payments deficit today increasingly falls on foreign exchange rates.

Foreign Exchange

Foreign exchange consists of foreign currencies, foreign deposit balances in commercial banks, and credit instruments used in trade, such as letters of credit, bankers' acceptances, and bills of exchange (export drafts). To U.S. importers and exporters, all monies other than U.S. dollars are foreign exchange. To Japanese importers and exporters, U.S. dollars and all moneys other than yen are foreign exchange. It should be noted, however, that most of the world's international trade is transacted in U.S. dollars even when U.S. importers or exporters are not involved. Moreover, most of the world's foreign exchange consists only of the monies of the leading industrial nations—U.S. dollars, British pounds, German marks, Japanese yen, Swiss francs, and French francs.

Foreign exchange currencies.

Photo courtesy of the Samuel L. Tillman collection.

Foreign Exchange Rates

A foreign exchange rate is the price of one nation's money in terms of another nation's money. Exchange rates can be expressed in terms of the amount of foreign money for which one unit of domestic money can be exchanged, or in terms of the amount of domestic money for which one unit of foreign money can be exchanged. For example, the exchange rate between the U.S. dollar and the German mark can be expressed either as $1.00 = 1.7 marks, or 1 mark = $0.60. Moreover, by using one nation's money as a common denominator—the U.S. dollar, by international convention—the cross rate of exchange (that is, the price of any two foreign monies in terms of each other) can be obtained. For example, if $1.00 = 1.7 marks and $1.00 = 5 francs, then 1.7 marks = 5 francs; thus the cross rate of exchange will be 1 mark = 2.94 francs, or 1 franc = 0.34 mark.

Exchange rates provide a measure of relative value by indicating how many units of one nation's money must be exchanged for one unit of another. In theory, an exchange rate equates the purchasing power value of two different monies. An exchange rate of $1.00 = 2 pounds sterling and $1.00 = 100 Japanese yen means that 1 pound sterling will command $.50 worth of purchasing power in London while 1 yen will command only $0.01 of purchasing power in Tokyo.

In this example, the pound appears to be expensive and the yen cheap. But this is not the case when prices and costs in England and Japan are matched up. A production worker in Liverpool may receive a weekly wage of 800 pounds, while the same job commands 40,000 yen in Kyoto. Yet both salaries represent $400 in purchasing power in their respective countries. Thus, the exchange rates for British pounds and Japanese yen reflect their relative purchasing power.

Because the U.S. dollar is used commercially as the common standard of value against which all monies are equated, exchange rates also can be viewed as a reciprocal price for the dollar. That is, they not only tell us the value of a foreign money, they also tell us the value of the dollar. A decrease in the price of the mark, for example—from $0.60 to $0.50—means that the value or price of a dollar has increased from 1.7 marks to 2 marks.

In the real world, exchange rates are normally quoted by banks and dealers to the hundredth or thousandth of a U.S. cent because daily exchange rates typically change in these increments. Exhibit 14.10 is a standard listing of foreign exchange rates such as one that might be found in a daily newspaper. For the world's major currencies, up to four different foreign exchange rates typically are quoted: a spot rate, 30-day forward rate, 60-day forward rate, and 90-day forward rate.

The spot rate is the rate you would have to pay for foreign exchange for immediate delivery (two working days in the interbank market; over-the-counter for foreign currency or traveler's checks). The forward rates are what you would have to pay if you signed a contract to buy foreign exchange for a specific future date (30 days, 60 days, or 90 days). In the forward market, you pay for the foreign exchange only when the contract matures and the foreign exchange actually is delivered.

EXHIBIT 14.10 **Foreign Exchange Rates**

FOREIGN EXCHANGE

WEDNESDAY, MARCH 24, 1993

	Fgn. currency in dollars		Dollar in fgn. currency	
	Wed.	Tue.	Wed.	Tue.
f-Argent (Peso)	1.0000	1.0000	1.0000	1.0000
Australia (Dollar)	.7045	.7073	1.4194	1.4138
Austria (Schilling)	.0870	.0871	11.495	11.482
c-Belgium (Franc)	.0297	.0297	33.63	33.63
Brazil (Cruzeiro)	.00004	.00004	22622.39	22395.01
Britain (Pound)	1.4767	1.4832	.6772	.6742
30-day fwd	1.4730	1.4793	.6789	.6760
60-day fwd	1.4693	1.4758	.6806	.6776
90-day fwd	1.4661	1.4726	.6821	.6791
Canada (Dollar)	.8052	.8013	1.2420	1.2479
30-day fwd	.8039	.8001	1.2440	1.2499
60-day fwd	.8026	.7988	1.2460	1.2519
90-day fwd	.8012	.7974	1.2481	1.2541
y-Chile (Peso)	.002586	.002586	386.65	386.70
China (Yuan)	.1712	.1712	5.8411	5.8411
Colombia (Peso)	.001548	.001536	646.00	651.10
c-Czechosl (Koruna)	.0353	.0352	28.32	28.41
Denmark (Krone)	.1596	.1597	6.2675	6.2600
ECU	1.18880	1.18390	.8412	.8447
z-Ecudr (Sucre)	.000549	.000549	1822.02	1821.49
d-Egypt (Pound)	.2999	.2999	3.3340	3.3340
Finland (Mark)	.1699	.1691	5.8872	5.9120
France (Franc)	.1799	.1801	5.5590	5.5515
Germany (Mark)	.6123	.6127	1.6333	1.6320
30-day fwd	.6094	.6098	1.6409	1.6400
60-day fwd	.6069	.6075	1.6476	1.6461
90-day fwd	.6046	.6052	1.6541	1.6523
Greece (Drachma)	.004498	.004505	222.30	222.00
Hong Kong (Dollar)	.1294	.1294	7.7300	7.7295
Hungary (Forint)	.0118	.0118	84.84	84.75
y-India (Rupee)	.0320	.0320	31.250	31.250
Indnsia (Rupiah)	.000482	.000482	2075.03	2075.03
Ireland (Punt)	1.4870	1.4877	.6725	.6722
Israel (Shekel)	.3675	.3679	2.7211	2.7181
Italy (Lira)	.000630	.000631	1588.00	1584.25
Japan (Yen)	.008511	.008633	117.50	115.84
30-day fwd	.008508	.008630	117.54	115.88
60-day fwd	.008508	.008630	117.54	115.88
90-day fwd	.008508	.008630	117.54	115.87
Jordan (Dinar)	1.4832	1.4832	.67422	.67422
Lebanon (Pound)	.000572	.000572	1747.00	1748.25
Malaysia (Ringgit)	.3849	.3850	2.5980	2.5973
z-Mexico(N.Peso)	.321337	.321130	3.1120	3.1140
N. Zeaiand (Dollar)	.5323	.5343	1.8786	1.8716
Nethrlnds(Guilder)	.5453	.5453	1.8337	1.8339
Norway (Krone)	.1441	.1441	6.9375	-6.9375
Pakistan (Rupee)	.0377	.0377	26.53	26.53
y-Peru (New Sol)	.5650	.5620	1.770	1.779
z-Philpins (Peso)	.0394	.0395	25.35	25.34
Poland (Zloty)	.000063	.000068	15847	14706
Portugal (Escudo)	.006612	.006596	151.25	151.60
a-Russia(Ruble)	.001462	.001462	684.00	684.00
Saudi Arab (Riyal)	.2667	.2667	3.7495	3.7495
Singapore (Dollar)	.6094	.6092	1.6410	1.6415
c-So.Africa(Rand)	.3155	.3147	3.1700	3.1776
f-So.Africa(Rand)	.2183	.2181	4.5800	4.5850
So. Korea (Won)	.001261	.001261	793.00	793.00
Spain (Peseta)	.008580	.008595	116.55	116.35
Sweden (Krona)	.1292	.1293	7.7373	7.7358
Switzerlnd (Franc)	.6612	.6616	1.5125	1.5115
30-day fwd	.6598	.6602	1.5156	1.5146
60-day fwd	.6588	.6593	1.5179	1.5168
90-day fwd	.6578	.6583	1.5202	1.5190
Taiwan (NT $)	.0383	.0382	26.13	26.18
Thailand (Baht)	.03940	.03943	25.38	25.36
Turkey (Lira)	.000107	.00107	9371.01	9371.03
U.A.E. (Dirham)	.2724	.2724	3.6715	3.6715
f-Uruguay (Peso)	.000269	.000269	3720.00	3717.47
z-Venzuel (Bolivar)	.0118	.0118	84.8000	84.8800
Yugoslav (Dinar)	.00133	.00133	750.00	750.00

ECU: European Currency Unit, a basket of European currencies. The Federal Reserve Board's index of the value of the dollar against 10 other currencies weighted on the basis of trade was 93.20 Wednesday, up 0.39 points or 0.42 percent from Tuesday's 92.81. A year ago the index was 90.65

c-commercial rate, d-free market rate, f-financial rate, y-official rate, z-floating rate.

Prices as of 3:00 p.m. Eastern Time from Telerate Systems and other sources.

WORLD GOLD

Source: New York Times, March 24, 1993,; The New York Times Company. Reprinted by permission.

Exchange Rate Determination

Although the purchasing power of money establishes the theoretical basis for determining exchange rates, the interaction of supply and demand for a nation's money in the foreign exchange market is the real determinant.

For example, assume that the price of 1 franc is $0.20 ($1.00 will buy 5 francs) and a U.S. importer wants to buy a shipment of French wine that costs 50,000 francs. In order to pay for the wine, the U.S. importer will have to sell $10,000 to buy 50,000 francs for immediate, or spot, delivery. If U.S. demand for francs equals French demand for dollars, the exchange rate will stay at $1.00 for 5 francs. But if the American demand for French goods increases and American importers need more francs (all other supply and demand factors remaining unchanged), the dollar price of francs may be bid up to $1.20 for 5 francs. U.S. importers would then have to pay $12,000 (rather than $10,000) for 50,000 francs.

Exchange rates are influenced by many short- and long-range factors that affect the supply of, and demand for, a nation's money in foreign exchange markets. The model in exhibit 14.11 provides an analytic framework for understanding how supply and demand influence exchange rates.

In this model, the American demand for francs is downward sloping, indicating that the lower the price of francs in the exchange market, the greater the quantity of francs Americans will buy. The upward-sloping supply curve indicates that, the higher the price of francs, the greater the amount of francs the French will be willing to offer in the foreign exchange market. An increase in demand for francs shifts the demand curve to the right, from D to D_1 in exhibit 14.11, indicating that Americans are willing to pay a higher price for any given quantity of francs.

FACTORS INFLUENCING EXCHANGE RATES

Many short-term factors could lead to a shift in demand for French francs. For example, favorable weather patterns affecting French grape crops may increase U.S. demand for francs to buy French wine from a vintage year. Or a change in American clothing styles may increase U.S. demand for francs to buy the latest Paris fashions.

Long-term factors—such as a nation's domestic inflation rate relative to that of its major trade partners—also affect exchange rates. Technology affects exchange rates as new products and processes generate demand for foreign exchange in countries whose technology is less advanced. Political and economic instability also can cause a flight from domestic money to foreign money, thereby affecting a nation's exchange rate.

EXHIBIT 14.11 **Exchange Rate Determination**

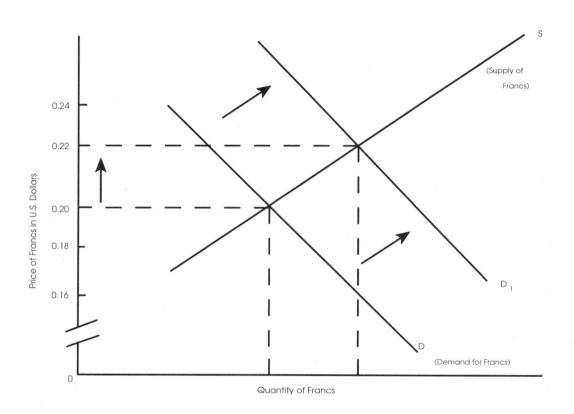

A nation's balance-of-payments position is another major long-term influence. U.S. importers of French goods are not alone in buying francs with dollars; U.S. tourists traveling in France, investors in French markets, borrowers of French money, and speculators who expect to sell francs later at a higher price also engage in foreign exchange. At the same time, the French people, who do their local business in francs, also need dollars to pay for their imports of U.S. goods, to make investments and pay off debts in the United States, and to speculate.

If France has a balance-of-payments deficit, market forces cause its exchange rate to fall because francs pile up in the hands of foreigners. If the supply of francs is greater than the demand for them, the price of the franc falls compared to the price of other currencies. Generally, the opposite occurs when France runs a trade surplus. If demand for francs exceeds supply, the price of francs rises while the price of other currencies falls.

Day-to-day exchange rate fluctuations typically reflect seasonal and temporary factors more than balance-of-payments positions. For example, French exports of certain goods may cluster at certain times of the year. Or France may receive large payments from overseas, perhaps because of a corporation's sending profits back to its home country on a quarterly or annual basis. Such bulges in receipts will typically strengthen the price of the franc if the incoming payments are exchanged for francs. On the other hand, if France experiences a seasonal burst of imports, or outgoing payments to another country, this will tend to weaken the franc.

Governments also influence exchange rates by occasionally intervening in the market, either buying or selling their national money and thereby driving its price up or down.

Because the U.S. dollar is used in the world's foreign exchange markets as the standard of value for defining exchange rates and the vehicle money for international trade and investment, a change in the price of any money means an equal and opposite change in the price of the dollar. As shown in the model in exhibit 14.12, an increase in American demand for francs (a shift from D to D_1) drives up the price of francs in the New York foreign exchange market, from $0.20 a franc to $0.25 a franc; it simultaneously drives down the price of dollars in Paris from 5 francs per dollar to 4 francs per dollar.

EXHIBIT 14.12 **Foreign Exchange Markets**

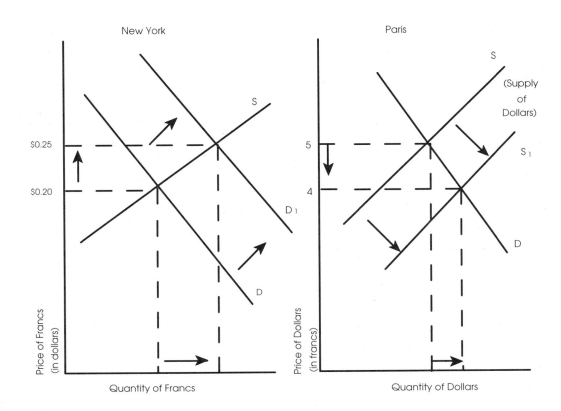

Americans manifest their increased demand for francs (a shift in the demand curve to the right, from D to D_1) by selling dollars to buy francs. The sale of dollars by Americans in the foreign exchange market increases the supply of dollars available to French purchasers of dollars (a shift in the supply curve to the right, from S to S_1) in the Paris foreign exchange market. The increase in supply lowers the price of the dollar in Paris. At the same time, American demand for francs drives up the price of the franc in New York.

Because these price changes can mean the difference between profit and loss on any given international trade or investment transaction, there is an element of risk in international commercial dealings that does not exist in domestic dealings. In the next chapter, we will examine how banks cover the risks inherent in international transactions.

Summary

The U.S. balance of payments is a record of the payments and receipts that have resulted from transactions between the United States and the rest of the world. Inflows and outflows of capital, as well as imports and exports of goods and services, are included. Thus our nation's balance-of-payments performance is a key measure of its performance in the world economy. In the mid-1980s, the U.S. balance of trade and balance on current account, two key components of the total balance of payments, registered progressively larger annual deficits as U.S. imports increased massively. Over this period, the United States moved from its position as the world's largest creditor nation to the world's largest debtor nation. Since the late 1980s, however, America's balance of payments has improved, although annual deficits in key balance of payments measures are still quite large.

 Balance-of-payments deficits are settled by means of international reserve assets. Because of the unique role of the dollar as an international currency, U.S. balance-of-payments deficits may result in other nations holding dollars (or dollar investments) as part of their foreign exchange reserves or selling their unwanted dollars for some other money or financial asset. The impact of such a settlement is reflected in foreign exchange rates.

In theory, foreign exchange rates equate the relative purchasing power of different monies. In reality, the interaction of the supply of, and demand for, currencies in the foreign exchange market is a powerful determinant of exchange rates. The resulting fluctuations in exchange rates can spell the difference between profit and loss for international traders and investors. Ways that exporters and importers can protect themselves from exchange rate losses are discussed in the following chapter.

Questions

1. Explain the relevance of the following balance-of-payments measures: balance of trade, balance on current account, and official settlements balance.

2. Since the United States no longer redeems dollars for gold, how does it settle its payments deficits with other countries?

3. Discuss the merits of current proposals to reduce the U.S. trade deficit. What other course of action would you propose to improve the nation's trade position?

4. How are foreign exchange rates determined? Suggest three factors that would likely cause supply or demand for U.S. dollars in European exchange markets to increase or decrease.

5. "To reduce the U.S. balance-of-payments deficit, the Federal Reserve should drive down the price of the dollar in foreign exchange markets." Discuss the validity of this policy prescription.

6. If prices in Japan increase by 10 percent relative to prices in the United States, what does economic theory predict will happen to the Japanese yen in terms of dollars? Why?

15

The Role of Banks in International Trade and Investment

Objectives

After successfully completing this chapter, you will be able to

- ☐ explain how the foreign exchange market operates,

- ☐ cite ways that market participants can protect themselves against a change in exchange rates through forward purchases and sales,

- ☐ list the key payment and credit instruments used in international trade,

- ☐ identify those nations with the largest banking presence in the United States and explain why foreign banks seek to operate in the U.S. market, and

- ☐ differentiate between the policies of national treatment and reciprocity in regulating foreign banks in the United States.

Introduction

World trade and investment require that banks be able to buy, sell, and transfer foreign currencies internationally on a moment's notice. Banks also provide the short-term financing and long-term loans necessary for effective trade. And they absorb the risk in international financial transactions by offering market participants foreign exchange purchases and sales for future delivery. This chapter explores the key role of banks in international trade and investment and also looks at the principal international payment and credit instruments.

We conclude by focusing on foreign banking in the United States. Key provisions of the International Banking Act of 1978 and the Foreign Bank Supervision Enhancement Act of 1991 are discussed, as are the opposing regulatory principles of national treatment and reciprocity. This discussion highlights the changing competitive and regulatory environment affecting international banking.

The Foreign Exchange Market

The foreign exchange market is the institutional setting in which buyers and sellers of foreign exchange transact business. These buyers and sellers include importers, exporters, tourists, international investors, speculators, and on occasion, governments. The market consists mainly of major banks and foreign exchange dealer firms in key financial centers such as New York, London, Frankfurt, Tokyo, and Hong Kong. Most transactions are conducted via telephone and cable by and through commercial banks.

In New York, the bulk of foreign exchange activity is handled by a few large banks with branches in other countries and a cluster of foreign banks with offices in New York. These banks buy and sell foreign exchange, mainly bank deposits, for corporate and individual customers. The large New York City banks that deal in foreign exchange stand ready to buy or sell any major currency on an ongoing basis, and typically offer more favorable terms on large transactions.

Most of the nation's banks do not deal directly in the foreign exchange market. Rather, they satisfy customer demands for foreign exchange through a credit-line arrangement with a correspondent bank (that is, the respondent bank buys foreign exchange from, or sells it to, the correspondent).

Both banks and corporations routinely use foreign exchange brokers to handle large transactions. Foreign exchange broker-dealer firms act as intermediaries that match up banks holding foreign exchange with those seeking foreign exchange. Even the largest banks often use brokers and dealers, rather than dealing directly with one another, to save time and to remain anonymous until a transaction is arranged. Anonymity prevents competing banks from learning one another's exchange operations and positions.

Foreign exchange brokers do not trade on their own account, but merely arrange transactions for a commission. In the 1980s, more than half the dollar value of foreign exchange transactions involving banks in the United States was channeled through brokers.

The Federal Reserve Bank of New York, acting on behalf of the Federal Reserve System or the U.S. government, is another key participant in the U.S. foreign exchange market. On occasion, its foreign exchange trading room will buy or sell dollars to maintain an orderly foreign exchange market or to increase or decrease the price of the dollar in accordance with national policy. Other central banks do the same in overseas exchange markets.

The primary function of the foreign exchange market is to facilitate the transfer of purchasing power internationally from one national money to another—in 1992, about $1 trillion each day, with transactions in New York accounting for nearly 20 percent of the total.

Another very important function of the market, however, is to provide importers and exporters with short-term credit with which to finance trade. The market also enables traders and investors to minimize the risk that a given foreign trade or investment could be rendered unprofitable because of an unanticipated change in the foreign exchange rate. Traders and investors can protect themselves against that risk through the use of forward purchases and sales.

The Forward Exchange Market

To avoid unexpected cost increases in the event that exchange rates change after a foreign trade has been negotiated but before payment has been made, importers can protect themselves by making a forward purchase transaction. Buying forward is an arrangement whereby foreign exchange is purchased at an agreed-upon price, but payment is not made until the foreign exchange is delivered by the bank at some future date.

Depending on one's expectations about exchange rates, forward purchase transactions may be an attractive option. At any given time, some importers of Japanese products may believe that the spot rate for yen will remain unchanged, while others may think the rate will drop and still others that the rate will increase. Thus, not everyone needing yen will go into the market for forward exchange to cover their transactions. Normally, a U.S. importer of Japanese goods that expects the price of the dollar to increase with respect to the yen will buy forward. If a rate rise is generally expected, buyers of forward exchange will pay slightly more than the spot rate. The size of the premium varies with the outlook and is reflected in the one-month, three-month, and six-month forward rates quoted by banks. The premium is larger when a big rise is expected, and smaller when less of a rise is expected.

Exporters who believe the exchange rate is likely to go down can cover that risk by arranging to sell forward. They do this by contracting to sell the foreign exchange they expect to receive at the same time that they contract with the foreign buyer. In selling forward, the foreign exchange is sold at an agreed-upon price, but delivery is not made until a future date. By selling forward, U.S. exporters can protect themselves against the risk of a decline in the price of the dollar between the time they contract to export and the time they receive a foreign currency in payment. If the market anticipates that the exchange rate will fall, exporters will have to sell forward at a discount—below the spot rate. The forward rate quoted by banks reflects this discount.

Most international trade is not covered by buying-forward or selling-forward arrangements. Most exporters and importers cannot afford, or do not choose, to allocate funds to cover exchange rate risk. Moreover, in some nations, the demand for imports is so strong that a price hike induced by a fluctuation in the exchange rate would have little adverse effect on purchases of foreign goods. Thus, importers can often cover any foreign exchange losses simply by raising their selling prices.

Importers and exporters who buy or sell foreign exchange forward transfer their market risk to banks. The charge for absorbing that risk is included in the price of the forward contract. Some banks try to match forward purchase contracts with forward sales contracts to ensure their market position regardless of the direction of exchange rate changes. Other banks fold customer transactions into their own speculative trading positions. Only about 15 percent of the foreign exchange trading of the nation's largest banks is conducted for customers; the rest is speculative. At most regional and small banks, customer trading accounts for about 40 percent of foreign exchange trading volume.

Forward Exchange Options

In the mid-1980s, many of the nation's large banks began offering corporate customers forward exchange options as an alternative to outright forward purchases and sales as a hedge against exchange rate risk.

A foreign exchange option is a contract, which need not be exercised, to buy or sell foreign exchange at a future date. Banks charge for options whether or not they are executed—at about 1.5 percent to 5 percent of the contract's value, depending on the term of the option. Foreign exchange options allow international traders and investors to protect themselves against unfavorable changes in exchange rates while positioning themselves to benefit from favorable changes.

Assume that a U.S. import firm contracts to buy British goods worth $3 million at a time when the spot exchange rate is 1.5 pounds = $1.00. The import firm will have to pay 4.5 million pounds to the British exporter when payment comes due in three months. To protect itself against exchange rate risk, the import firm may buy a foreign exchange option that gives it the right, but not the obligation, to buy 4.5 million pounds at 1.5 pounds per dollar at a future time. Assume the option costs $100,000.

If over the course of the next three months, the price of the pound fell from 1.5 pounds per dollar to 1.25 pounds per dollar, the dollar would buy fewer pounds. The import firm must now pay $3.6 million (rather than $3 million) to buy 4.5 million pounds. However, it can exercise its option to buy the needed 4.5 million pounds at the agreed price of 1.5 pounds per dollar. In this way the import firm saves $500,000—the savings incurred by the hedging action ($600,000) minus the cost of the option ($100,000).

If the price of the pound remained the same over the three-month period, the import firm could still buy 4.5 million pounds for $3 million without exercising the option. In this case, it would allow the option to expire and would absorb the cost of the option as an additional transactions cost.

If, on the other hand, the price of the pound increased from 1.5 pounds per dollar to 1.75 pounds per dollar over the three-month period, each dollar would buy more pounds. The importer could then buy 4.5 million pounds for about $2.6 million (rather than $3 million). Again, the importer would allow the option to expire and would buy pounds at the more advantageous spot rate. In effect, the change in the foreign exchange rate would result in a $300,000 savings—the $400,000 savings from the lower price of the pounds minus the $100,000 cost of the option.

Under a forward contract, the importer is obligated to buy pounds in the foreign exchange market at the agreed-upon price, regardless of what the market does. In contrast, an option allows the importer to hedge against a possible loss and yet benefit from a possible gain.

Banks that sell foreign exchange options absorb the risk associated with fluctuationss in exchange rates. As with traditional exchange contracts, banks typically either reflect this absorption of risk in their premium charges on options or attempt to balance purchase options against sale options.

Exchange Rate Risk and Government Intervention

A sharp change in exchange rates can spell the difference between profit and loss for international traders and investors. Indeed, the greater the prospect that such changes will occur, the greater the degree of risk. High risk either discourages trade or drives prices higher to finance risk coverage. However, if exchange rates were allowed to fluctuate so widely that market conditions became disorderly, world trade and investment would suffer. Thus nations historically have sought to establish internationally accepted ground rules that allow exchange rates to respond partially to changing supply and demand conditions yet prevent fluctuations that would discourage trade and investment.

(Continued from previous page)

Freely floating exchange rates (rates determined solely by supply and demand) have rarely existed in the real world. In fact, prior to the 1940s, the international financial system operated under a gold standard in which exchange rates were rigidly fixed, varying only within a very narrow range.

From 1944 to 1971, exchange rates were fixed by the Bretton Woods Agreement. Under this international agreement, nations were obligated to maintain the price (par value) of their monies in foreign exchange markets within a range of 1 percent above or below the international price registered with the International Monetary Fund. To maintain par value within this narrow range, nations were required to intervene frequently in the foreign exchange markets against the forces of supply and demand. They bought their national money to drive its price up or sold it to drive its price down.

Early in the 1970s, the fixed exchange rate system based on government intervention in the foreign exchange markets broke down, and nations opted for a looser form of fixed exchange rates known as *managed float*. The major trading nations agreed to move against erratic or excessive fluctuations in exchange rates, but not to intervene against basic market trends. In effect, each nation was free to determine its own exchange rate policies. Under the managed float system, nations intervene only periodically to guide their exchange rate up or down in accordance with their own national economic policies. The United States, for example, generally intervenes only to maintain orderly exchange markets, not to hold the dollar's exchange rate at a particular level.

In 1979, the nations of Europe adopted a system of fixed exchange rates for European currencies. The new European Monetary System (EMS) was formed to accommodate Europe's plan for establishing a single European central bank and single European currency by 1999.

Under the EMS, 11 countries linked their exchange rates together and pledged to maintain the par value of their currencies to the linked rate within a narrow range. Belgium, Luxemburg, Denmark, France, West Germany, Ireland, Italy, and the Netherlands agreed to maintain the par value of their currencies within a range of 2.25 percent above or below the linked rate; Britain, Spain, and Portugal agreed to a somewhat wider 6 percent range.

As was the case under the Bretton Woods Agreement, the EMS requires participating nations to intervene in the foreign exchange market as buyers or sellers of their own currency if supply and demand conditions threaten to push their exchange rate above or below the agreed par value range. Nations that are unwilling (or lack the resources) to do so, are required to change the par value of their currencies relative to the exchange rate link by either *revaluing* (increasing par value) or *devaluing* (reducing par value).

(Continued from previous page)

In 1992, the effectiveness of the EMS as a mechanism for stabilizing European currency values was strongly tested when the value of the German mark began to climb in response to increasing European demand for high-interest-rate German investments and relatively low-priced German goods. (Germany had allowed the exchange rate for the mark—and domestic interest rates—to rise in the 1990s in an effort to attract needed foreign capital to help finance the costs of reunifying West and East Germany.)

As the selling of British pounds, French francs, and Italian lira for marks intensified, the price of the pound and the lira were driven down well below their EMS par value ranges. Italy was forced to devalue the lira by 7 percent and suspend its participation in the EMS, but Britain tried to drive up the pound's value by raising domestic interest rates—an action aimed at stimulating investor demand (and thus the price) for pounds. When that action failed, Britain also suspended its participation in the EMS. By doing so, it effectively devalued the pound.

From 1979 to 1987, various European nations had opted—on 11 different occasions—to revalue or devalue their currencies against the linked EMS exchange rate. The 1992 currency realignments were all the more shocking because they came after five years of relative exchange rate stability in Europe. The realignments raised grave doubts about the future effectiveness of the EMS to stabilize European exchange rates and raised serious questions as to whether Europe's plan for a single European currency by 1999 was realistic.

A major problem with the fixed exchange rate system that nations relied on in the 1950s and 1960s (and the linked European Monetary System) was the conflict governments experienced between the pursuit of domestic economic goals and exchange rate stability—a problem that continues to trouble governments today, even under the managed float system. For example, if the U.S. government does not want the price of the dollar to rise, the Federal Reserve would be instructed to enter the foreign exchange market and buy foreign exchange using dollars as payment. This would increase the market demand for foreign exchange, thereby causing the price of foreign monies to rise and the price (exchange rate) of the dollar to fall, or at least stop rising. This action, however, also would increase the U.S. money supply, which could be inflationary. Every nation faces this trade-off between internal domestic goals and the position of its money in the world's foreign exchange markets.

International Payments

The principal payment devices used in international trade are the *cable transfer* and the *export draft* (bill of exchange).

A cable transfer is an order sent by cable from an importer's bank to a foreign bank directing the foreign bank to pay out a specific sum of foreign money to the exporter. A cable transfer results in an immediate transfer of funds. It differs from a bank draft only in that a written check is not issued or mailed.

Assume that a U.S. importer agrees to purchase British merchandise for 1.5 million pounds at a time when the exchange rate is $1.00 = 1.5 pounds. The import firm could phone its bank to request that 1.5 million pounds be paid directly to the exporter. The bank would then execute the order through a cable transfer, which would entail cabling its branch or correspondent bank in London to pay the U.K. exporter 1.5 million pounds. The import firm could also request that the funds be deposited directly at the exporter's bank in London.

Another way to handle international payments involves an export draft, or bill of exchange. A draft is the basic financial instrument used in international trade to buy goods or services from abroad. It works in somewhat the same way as a check in domestic trade, directing that a specific sum of money be paid. Thus, the importer could buy a pound draft from the bank and mail it to the British exporter directly. A draft is drawn by the importer's bank against foreign exchange balances it holds in a bank abroad, payable at that bank. Payment is made upon receipt of the draft document (sight draft) or within a certain number of days after receipt (time draft).

Whichever method of payment is chosen (cable transfer or export draft), the trade transaction described previously results in the transfer of funds from a U.S. bank's balance at a London bank to the British exporter's account at the London bank or at another bank in England. No currency is shipped. Following is a T-account illustrating the transaction involving $1 million, or 1.5 million pounds.

This T-account shows that, in effect, the U.S. importer purchased part of the New York bank's pound balance at the London bank. For the London bank, the cable transfer or export draft, like an on-us check, simply results in a redistribution of liabilities from one account to another.

New York Bank		London Bank	
Assets	Liabilities	Assets	Liabilities
Balance at London bank -$1 million	Demand deposit of U.S. importer -$1 million		Demand deposit of New York bank -1.5 million pounds
			Demand deposit of U.K. exporter +1.5 million pounds

Most drafts covering exports from the United States are drawn in U.S. dollars, but they may be drawn in other currencies and routed for collection through U.S. banks. Banks act as agents for exporters in dealing with importers' banks because most export drafts specify that the importer's payment should be made directly to the exporter's bank.

Bills of exchange become foreign exchange credit instruments when exporters sell the drafts to local banks for domestic money rather than sending them and waiting for payment in foreign exchange. The purchasing banks either hold the instruments and collect from the importer or sell the instruments to investors to obtain funds immediately.

Bankers' Acceptances

When banks substitute their own credit for that of the importer, the drafts become bankers' acceptances. A bankers' acceptance then is a time draft drawn on and accepted by the bank on which it is drawn. It usually arises in international trade when there is an underlying obligation of a buyer to make payment to a seller at some future time. The bank accepting the draft assumes the obligation of making payment at maturity on behalf of the buyer or the buyer's bank.

Assume again that a British export firm negotiates the sale of $1 million worth of merchandise to a U.S. importer. Under the conditions of the sale, the U.S. importer has until 30 days after delivery to make payment. Yet, the British firm needs the funds immediately to cover its production and payroll costs. A bankers' acceptance might prove useful here.

The British exporter would make an arrangement involving the U.S. importer, the importer's bank, and the exporter's own London bank. The exporter draws up a time draft (order to pay) on the importer's bank stating that certain goods have been shipped to the U.S. company for which $1 million (1.5 million pounds) is payable 30 days after delivery. The exporter can then sell the draft to the London bank for pounds at the spot exchange rate (less a discount for the delay in repayment to the London bank).

The London bank, in turn, sends the draft to the importer's bank in New York where it is accepted by the New York bank. The draft is stamped, appropriately signed, and dated by an officer of the New York bank. In accepting the draft, the importer's bank is effectively substituting its own creditworthiness for that of the importer. Upon acceptance, the draft becomes payable on its due date by the New York bank whether or not the importer pays. Thus, the acceptance is readily salable in the secondary market.

Depending on the London bank's preference, the New York bank either will sell the acceptance, usually at a discount to a dealer in the secondary market, and pay the London bank, or hold the acceptance until it reaches its due date. At that time, the importer pays the New York bank which, in turn, pays the London bank.

In the United States, smaller banks often purchase bankers' acceptances in the secondary market as short-term investment instruments. Acceptances carry reasonably competitive yields in comparison with other money market instruments of comparable maturity. In the 1970s, large banks began to sell participations in bankers' acceptances in $25,000 lots that enabled the smallest banks and even some individuals to invest in them.

More than half of the nearly $40 billion in outstanding bankers' acceptances in the United States in 1992 were third-party acceptances. This means that a foreign bank accepted the draft and sold the acceptance to a U.S. bank to obtain immediate funds. U.S. banks typically rely on the credit standing of the foreign bank in instances of these acceptances. Little, if any, documentation of the underlying trade transaction, such as an invoice or bill of lading, accompanies such an acceptance instrument. However, about 25 percent of the dollar value of U.S. imports are typically financed with documentary acceptances. These acceptances do include documents for each transaction underlying the arrangement. Upon acceptance, the bank detaches the bill of lading from the draft and gives it to the importer so that the shipped goods can be claimed properly.

Dollar Exchange Acceptances

Dollar exchange acceptances are time drafts denominated in U.S. dollars. In the past, they were used by U.S. banks to provide foreign exchange to Latin American countries that had to wait until their single-crop exports could be harvested and sold. Today, these types of acceptances are rarely used, although several U.S. banks still use dollar exchange acceptances to provide the Dominican Republic and Brazil with short-term funds (limited by statute to three months or less).

FINANCING OF EXPORTS AND IMPORTS

International trade in the United States is financed mainly through bankers' acceptances and bank loans. Loans by U.S. banks to foreign importers for the purchase of goods and services from U.S. exporters frequently run as long as 5 years, and in special cases, up to 10 years. Loans to U.S. importers typically are short-term loans and working capital loans. While commercial banks are the main source of credit for both exporters and importers in the United States, some international trade is financed by finance companies and other specialized institutions.

The terms of sale in an international trade transaction usually are a matter of prior arrangement between importer and exporter. The choice of payment and financing method, however, usually depends on such factors as the credit standing of the buyer (importer), exchange controls in the buyer's country, and the seller's competition. Financing methods other than direct bank loans and bankers' acceptances include letters of credit, cash deposits in advance, open-account arrangements, and consignment arrangements.

Letters of Credit

A letter of credit is frequently used by companies ordering goods from foreign suppliers with whom they have no credit relationship. A letter of credit is a declaration by a bank that it will make payments on behalf of a given party under prearranged conditions. Thus, it is a financial instrument that substitutes the bank's credit for the company's credit. It is called a letter because it takes the form of a notification to the party likely to receive the payments.

An export letter of credit allows exporters to receive rapid payment for internationally traded merchandise. For example, assume a German import firm has negotiated a multimillion-dollar series of purchases from a U.S. exporter over the course of the next year and has arranged with its bank for the establishment of a letter of credit. The import firm's bank would instruct its correspondent bank in New York to inform the U.S. exporter that a letter of credit has been established. The letter of credit would authorize the exporter to draw drafts on that bank, by presenting documents that show shipment has been made, to receive funds. (The exporter's bank would act as the collection agent for the draft.)

The import letter of credit is the primary method used to finance commodity imports to the United States. In fact, exchange controls in some countries require that export sales be made on a letter-of-credit basis. Prevailing commercial practices abroad also foster its use. Foreign exporters that lack sufficient information about U.S. importers, or that are unsure of the importer's credit, often specify a letter of credit as a condition of their trade transaction.

In an import letter of credit, the importer's bank establishes the letter of credit and the terms of the arrangement. If the bank requires a guarantee or collateral for the amount it commits to pay under the letter of credit, that is specified in the letter. If funds are to be issued in foreign exchange, that also is specified. Most imports to the United States are settled in dollars, but a growing number of transactions in the 1980s were conducted in the currency of the foreign seller.

Cash in Advance

When the credit of a foreign importer is doubtful or when unstable political or economic conditions might delay payment from abroad, the exporter may prefer not to extend credit terms of any kind and may request payment in cash, in whole, or in part, before shipping the merchandise. Although this payment arrangement affords the exporter the greatest protection, it places the importer at a significant disadvantage. Moreover, in some countries, exchange controls prohibit such prepayment. For these reasons, the volume of international trade conducted on a cash-in-advance basis is small.

Open Account

In an open-account arrangement, the exporter allows the importer to pay for goods at a specified future date, but without any negotiable instrument evidencing the obligation. Exporting on an open-account basis is simple and avoids finance-related charges connected with other payment arrangements. However, legal procedures to enforce payment in cases of dishonored open-account transactions are often complicated. Moreover, in some countries, bankers' acceptances and export draft claims take legal precedence over payment of open-account claims. For these reasons, open-account settlement is used primarily when exporters are dealing with internationally established importers or where legal claims are not likely to arise. Sales of goods by multinational corporations to their own foreign subsidiaries, for example, often are made on open accounts.

Consignment

Under a consignment arrangement, goods are transferred but not sold to an importer. The exporter retains title to the goods until they are sold to a third party. Again, because no tangible obligation exists in this arrangement, problems can arise in trying to obtain payment if the importer defaults. For this reason, most companies make consignment arrangements only with their own subsidiaries abroad.

Foreign Banking in the United States

As we have seen, foreign and domestic banks play a key role in international trade and investment. Partly because of the need to facilitate such transactions, banking has become increasingly international in scope. Exhibit 15.1 shows the assets held by banks in other countries. Japanese banks have the largest international presence, holding close to $2 trillion in assets (mostly loans and securities) in other countries. U.S. banks have the second largest international presence, with more than $700 billion in assets in other countries. Not only do many of the large U.S. banks have foreign branches, but many foreign banks maintain a substantial presence in the United States. Exhibit 15.2 lists the U.S. cities with the highest concentration of foreign banks—led by New York and Los Angeles.

Types of Foreign Banking Offices

In 1992, banks from more than 50 countries had more than 1,000 banking offices in this country; moreover, about 16 percent of all U.S. deposits were held by these foreign-owned banks. These offices take a variety of forms, as exhibit 15.3 shows.

EXHIBIT 15.1   **Assets Held by Banks in Other Countries, 1991**
(billions of dollars)

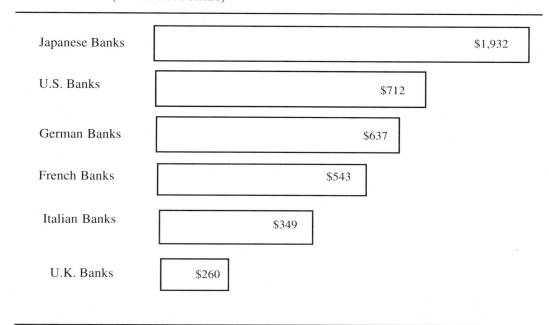

Japanese Banks	$1,932
U.S. Banks	$712
German Banks	$637
French Banks	$543
Italian Banks	$349
U.K. Banks	$260

Source: Bank for International Settlements.

EXHIBIT 15.2   **U.S. Cities with Most Foreign Bank Offices, 1991**

New York	464*
Los Angeles	133
Chicago	80
Miami	65
San Francisco	62
Houston	42
Atlanta	29
Total (for these seven cities)	875
Total for all U.S. (includes three thrift institutions)	1,027

*Includes 249 branches, 127 representative offices, 35 commercial bank subsidiaries, 38 agencies, 10 investment companies, and 5 Edge Act offices.

Source: "Ranking the Banks," *American Banker*, 1992 edition.

EXHIBIT 15.3   **Foreign Banks in the United States, 1991**

Type of Office	Number of Institutions
U.S. branch of foreign bank	386
U.S. agency of foreign bank	223
U.S. commercial bank subsidiary of foreign bank	100
U.S. Edge Act office of foreign bank	18
N.Y. State investment company of foreign bank	11
U.S. representative office of foreign bank	286
Total	1,024

Source: "Ranking the Banks," *American Banker*, 1992 edition.

Most foreign banks that operate in the United States maintain either a branch office or an agency office in the U.S. Any office of a foreign bank in the United States that accepts domestic deposits is considered a branch. An agency is an office of a foreign bank that cannot accept deposits from U.S. citizens or residents, but otherwise operates as a full-service bank. (In New York, many foreign agencies have been granted powers by the state banking department to issue large-denomination certificates of deposit to both domestic and foreign residents. In effect, those agencies function as branches.)

Any bank office in the United States that is owned or controlled by a foreign bank holding company is considered to be a bank subsidiary. U.S. subsidiaries of foreign banks can operate as full-service banks in accordance with the Bank Holding Company Act of 1956.

 Edge Act corporations owned by foreign banks, like those owned by domestic banks, are offices that engage exclusively in international banking and investment business. They can make loans, accept deposits, and provide full banking services, but only if those activities relate to foreign or international transactions. U.S. banks have been permitted to establish such limited-purpose offices in any state since 1919; the International Banking Act of 1978, which effectively ended the ability of foreign banks to branch throughout the United States, authorized foreign banks to establish Edge Act corporations as well. Foreign banks operating in the United States opened more than 40 Edge Act corporations in the late 1970s and early 1980s as a means of extending their operations to other states. By the late 1980s, however, most states had liberalized their branching rules, effectively enabling foreign banks to operate interstate branch offices. As a result, many foreign banks opted to close their Edge Act offices, opening new branches and agencies to establish a nationwide banking presence.

New York State investment companies are similar in form to foreign-owned commercial bank subsidiaries except that they cannot accept deposits unrelated to the conduct of investment business. These investment companies are not subject to banking regulations limiting the amount of money a commercial bank may lend to any one borrower (an amount equal to 15 percent of the bank's capital stock, surplus, and undivided profits). They also face no restrictions on investing in corporate stock.

A representative office of a foreign bank in the United States cannot accept deposits or make loans and investments. However, it enables foreign banks to establish a presence in the United States and to promote their services to U.S. customers. For example, they can provide information and handle administrative matters for U.S. residents who transact business with the foreign bank. Some foreign banks establish representative offices as a means of assessing whether U.S. market conditions warrant their opening a branch or agency in a particular location in the United States.

Why Foreign Banks Maintain U.S. Offices

Both U.S. and foreign banks establish overseas offices in order to provide financial services to domestic customers (multinational corporations) that have foreign operations. However, foreign banks also maintain a substantial U.S. banking presence because of the unique role of the dollar in international finance and the size and prominence of the U.S. economy and its financial markets.

A related reason that foreign banks establish offices in the United States is a desire to acquire a dollar base or to better manage the dollar position of their parent bank. The dollar is the world's principal currency for international transactions, and about 80 percent of international lending is in U.S. dollars. By holding a substantial dollar base in the United States, foreign banks generally can pay less for dollar funds than if they were acquired on an ad hoc basis from abroad. Thus, foreign banks with a presence in the United States have an advantage over other foreign banks in structuring loan charges to their customers.

Foreign banks also establish offices in the United States in order to more effectively finance the exports by their domestic customers of goods to the United States. Foreign banks with a U.S. office can better service their corporate clients in dealing with letters of credit, export drafts, bankers' acceptances, international money transfers, and foreign exchange. Access to the world's largest pool of investment capital and financial instruments also enables foreign banks with U.S. offices to provide better investment services to their corporate clients.

The establishment of a U.S. banking office also enables foreign banks to develop a retail banking business in the world's largest financial market.

The Japanese Presence

The Japanese have established the largest presence insofar as the number of foreign banks in the United States is concerned. That is not surprising given the overwhelming international presence of Japanese banks—as seen in exhibit 15.1—and the large size of Japanese banks. Exhibit 15.4 shows that the seven largest banks in the world (and 12 of the top 20) are Japanese banks. More than 20 percent of the foreign branches and agencies in the United States are those of Japanese banks; they collectively operated more than 100 banking offices (excluding representative offices) in the United States in 1992. In the late 1980s, almost half of the new foreign bank offices established in the United States were opened by Japanese banks.

EXHIBIT 15.4   **The 20 Largest Banks in the World**
(ranked by assets held on December 31, 1991)

Name of Bank	Country	Total Assets (billions of dollars)
1. Dai-Ichi Kangyo Bank, Ltd., Tokyo	Japan	$446
2. Sumitomo Bank Ltd., Osaka	Japan	428
3. Sakura Bank, Ltd., Tokyo	Japan	421
4. Fuji Bank, Ltd., Tokyo	Japan	419
5. Sanwa Bank Ltd., Osaka	Japan	412
6. Mitsubishi Bank Ltd., Tokyo	Japan	391
7. Norinchukin Bank, Tokyo	Japan	308
8. Credit Agricole Mutuel, Paris	France	307
9. Credit Lyonnais, Paris	France	306
10. Industrial Bank of Japan, Ltd., Tokyo	Japan	303
11. Deutsche Bank, AG, Frankfurt	Germany	296
12. Banque Nationale de Paris	France	276
13. Barclays Bank Plc, London	U.K.	258
14. Tokai Bank Ltd., Nagoya	Japan	253
15. Mitsubishi Trust and Banking Corp., Tokyo	Japan	248
16. ABN-AMRO Bank, N.U., Amsterdam	Netherlands	243
17. Sumitomo Trust and Banking Co., Ltd., Osaka	Japan	235
18. National Westminster Bank Plc, London	U.K.	229
19. Mitsui Trust and Banking Co., Ltd., Tokyo	Japan	226
20. Societe Generale, Paris	France	224

The substantial expansion of Japanese banking offices in the United States in the 1980s was motivated by reasons other than the normal ones that cause foreign banks to establish offices in the United States. Other factors included the large accumulation of dollars that Japanese firms acquired from their extensive exports to the United States, the Japanese government's removal of restrictions that had limited the movement of capital funds into and out of Japan, and the opportunity for Japanese banks to expand banking service offerings into areas prohibited by Japanese law, such as trust services.

In the 1990s, Japanese banks began to reduce their holdings of U.S. banking assets. Capital shortages among Japanese banks, an increase in problem business loans both in the U.S. and Japan, and an unwillingness to continue building U.S. market share by making low profit loans were factors that motivated the Japanese banks' retrenchment. However, large, well-capitalized Swiss and German banks offset the Japanese decline by expanding their own holdings of U.S. banking assets. In 1992, Japanese banks still held more than $400 billion in U.S. banking assets, but other foreign banks—mainly European—had increased their holdings to $460 billion. Exhibit 15.5 shows the sharp U.S. asset growth of foreign banks in the late 1980s and the flattening of the growth trend in 1992 caused by the retrenchment of Japanese banks.

Foreign Banks as U.S. Lenders

Foreign banks were major lenders to U.S. business firms in the 1980s, and their share of the U.S. banking market expanded considerably. In 1992, foreign banks held 16 percent of the nation's deposits, 23 percent of the nation's banking assets, and 26 percent of U.S. business loans.

In the late 1980s, large U.S. banks began selling off substantial portions of their business loan portfolios to boost profits. The major buyers of these loans were the U.S. offices of foreign banks. From 1984 to 1992, foreign banks increased their holdings of total U.S. business loans from 9 percent to 26 percent. In 1992, Japanese banks alone held more than 40 percent of all business loans made in California and more than 10 percent of all business loans made in the U.S.

Foreign banks have been avid purchasers of American banks' business loans because those loan acquisitions enable them to quickly build up their loan portfolios with quality assets that they would be unlikely to book on their own. Large Japanese banks in the United States have been the major purchasers. They generally participate (share) in the loans they acquire with other, smaller Japanese banks in the United States.

Foreign banks' increasing market share of U.S. business loans reflects both loan acquisitions and new loans made, but understates the importance of foreign lending to U.S. business firms. If the business loans of offshore *shell* foreign banks, such as those located in the Cayman Islands, are included in the total, foreign banks' share of U.S. business loans would be 45 percent.

EXHIBIT 15.5   **Asset Growth of U.S. Offices of Foreign Banks, 1988-1992**

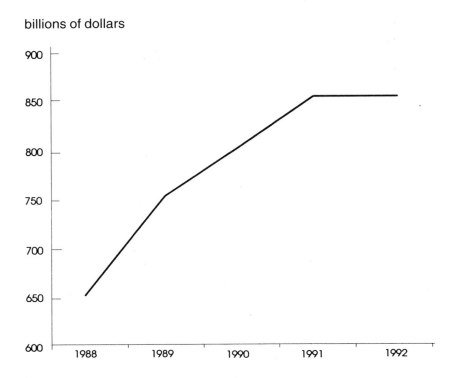

billions of dollars

Source: Federal Reserve Board

International Banking Facilities

To improve the competitiveness of U.S. banks in international banking, the Federal Reserve in 1981 authorized banks operating in the United States to establish international banking facilities (IBFs). These are limited-purpose banking offices that handle offshore loan and deposit business, taking dollar deposits from and extending loans to foreign countries. They are exempt from reserve requirements and state taxation and, from 1981 to 1986, when Regulation Q ceilings on deposits were still in force, were exempt from those ceilings.

IBFs need not be separate physical entities, but can operate as a functional unit within a general-purpose bank. However, IBF accounts must be segregated from domestic accounts.

IBFs can accept deposits only from corporations, banks, and individuals that are outside the United States (nonresidents), and they can make loans that will be used only for foreign purposes. Foreign companies that use IBFs must acknowledge in a signed statement that their IBF activities are not supporting any U.S. transactions.

History of IBFs

In the 1960s, U.S. banks increasingly began to shift their international banking business from their domestic offices to overseas offices. A combination of factors created a strong economic incentive to do so.

The cost of reserve requirements (Regulation D) and FDIC insurance coverage increased the cost of doing banking business in the United States. Because profit margins on international financial transactions are generally fractions of a percentage point, the additional costs imposed by reserve requirements and deposit insurance impaired the competitiveness of U.S. banks relative to banks abroad.

U.S. banks also shifted business to overseas offices because interest rate ceilings (Regulation Q) impaired their competitiveness by limiting the ability of U.S. banks to attract funds. In addition, during the 1960s an interest-equalization tax was assessed on the U.S. borrowings of nonresidents, and a voluntary credit restraint program was implemented to limit lending by U.S. banks to nonresidents.

In response to those factors, American banks not only opened offices in London, Frankfurt, and other financial centers, but also opened so-called offshore facilities in Nassau, in the Bahamas, and the Cayman Islands. Whereas the financial center branches were set up and staffed to do a full-service commercial banking business, the Caribbean branches, with few exceptions, were established as a way to avoid Regulations D and Q and local taxes, and to conduct business that ordinarily would have been done in the United States.

In the mid-1970s, the idea of bringing offshore banking back onshore by allowing IBFs was widely debated in the banking community. A House Banking Committee study on the nation's financial institutions proposed that U.S. banks be allowed to establish such *foreign windows.*

However, three steps were necessary to make the IBF concept work. First, local tax laws had to be changed to exempt IBFs from taxation so that they would be competitive with offshore operations (which are not subject to taxes). Most states enacted such tax exemption legislation in the late 1970s and early 1980s. In addition, Regulation D had to be amended to exempt deposits at IBFs from reserve requirements, and Regulation Q had to be amended to give U.S. banks greater freedom to compete for foreigners' time deposits. The Federal Reserve amended both regulations when it approved the establishment of IBFs in 1981.

From 1981 to 1992, IBF assets grew to more than $400 billion. Of that total, about $300 billion (three-quarters of all IBF assets) was held in New York banks. However, IBFs established by foreign banks in New York held about half the total dollar volume, with Japanese banks holding about half the foreign segment.

A large portion of offshore banking business flowed back to the United States in the 1980s from offshore centers in the Bahamas and Cayman Islands to the newly authorized IBFs. However, IBFs did not eliminate all offshore branches. Some foreign corporations, banks, and individuals still prefer to do their international banking business outside the United States for reasons of secrecy and to put their assets beyond the reach of U.S. courts or the U.S. government.

U.S. Regulation of Foreign Banks

The enactment of the International Banking Act of 1978 brought federal regulation to foreign banks operating in the United States. Prior to that time, the U.S. offices of foreign banks were not subject to the regulations of the Federal Reserve, the FDIC, or the Comptroller of the Currency. The 1978 banking law culminated several years of effort by the Federal Reserve and key members of Congress to impose federal oversight on foreign bank activities in the United States. In so doing, it extended a policy of national treatment to foreign banks operating in the United States, making them competitively equal with U.S. banks. Since 1978, foreign banks have had the same powers and been subject to the same regulations as domestic banks of like size.

International Banking Act of 1978

The International Banking Act made six major changes in U.S. banking law as it affected foreign banks operating in the United States. First, it effectively prohibited any new interstate branching for foreign banks by subjecting them to the 1927 McFadden Act, which requires banks to abide by the branching rules of the states in which they reside. Foreign banks that already had branch offices in more than one state were grandfathered but were required to designate one of those states as the bank's home state. Any additional agencies or branches that the bank might want to establish outside its home state could be established only to take in deposits related to international banking business, not retail deposits. Moreover, within the designated home state, additional deposit-taking branches could be established only if state law allowed.

Second, the International Banking Act gave foreign bank agencies and branches the option of being federally chartered (by the Comptroller of the Currency).

Third, the Federal Reserve's reserve requirements were imposed on foreign agencies and branches whose parent banks held more than $1 billion in total assets. This covered virtually all foreign agencies and branches in the United States. The reserve requirements were imposed to strengthen U.S. monetary policy control and to establish competitive equity between domestic banks and foreign banks of like size. Before 1978, the U.S. offices of foreign banks had a competitive edge over domestic banks because they were not subject to the Federal Reserve's reserve requirements. With the imposition of reserve requirements, foreign branches and agencies were also given access to Federal Reserve payments services and to the Federal Reserve discount window. (Two years later, the Monetary Control Act of 1980 imposed reserve requirements on all agencies and branches of foreign banks not otherwise covered by the International Banking Act and required foreign banks to pay the same prices for Federal Reserve services as domestic banks paid.)

Fourth, foreign bank branches with retail deposit operations were required to obtain federal deposit insurance.

Fifth, foreign banks' nonbanking activities were subject to the 1956 Bank Holding Company Act. In effect, foreign banks operating in the United States were prohibited from owning and operating investment banking and securities affiliates, as are domestic banks under terms of the 1933 Glass-Steagall Act. By effectively prohibiting those activities to foreign banks, the International Banking Act eliminated what many U.S. banks felt was an inequity in their regulatory treatment. However, foreign banks that had established investment and securities affiliates before 1978 were not required to divest them.

Sixth, the International Banking Act divided the general supervision of foreign banks among the federal regulators. The Federal Reserve was given authority to examine any foreign branch or agency. Branches or agencies with a federal charter are supervised by the Comptroller of the Currency; those with FDIC insurance are supervised by the FDIC and the states; and those without FDIC coverage are supervised by the Federal Reserve and the states.

The International Banking Act went a long way toward equalizing the rules under which American banks and the U.S. agencies and branches of foreign banks compete in U.S. banking markets. The act was not solely restrictive, however. In authorizing foreign ownership of Edge Act corporations, Congress also directed the Federal Reserve to liberalize its rules governing those corporations for all banks. Since 1978, Edge Act corporations, which are governed by Regulation K, have been permitted to conduct a broader range of internationally related deposit and loan transactions and are permitted to branch anywhere in the United States. As a result of those changes, both U.S. and foreign banks are able to compete over a broader field of activity and on more equal terms.

Foreign Bank Supervision Enhancement Act of 1991

The Foreign Bank Supervision Enhancement Act imposed new regulations on foreign banks that want to establish banking offices in the U.S. or expand their existing U.S. operations. The act also subjected the U.S. operations of foreign banks to new examination requirements.

The act requires all foreign banks that want to establish new branches or agencies to obtain approval from the Federal Reserve. Prior to 1991, foreign banks had only to meet state licensing requirements or obtain approval from the Office of the Comptroller of the Currency (OCC) to establish a branch or agency. The requirement for additional Federal Reserve approval covers foreign banks that are new to the U.S. and foreign banks that already have U.S. branches and agencies.

As a condition of approval, the Federal Reserve must determine whether a foreign bank applying to open a new branch or agency is subject to comprehensive and consolidated (global) regulation by its home country. If the Federal Reserve finds that home country supervision of the foreign bank is not sufficiently broad, the approval must be denied. Foreign banks with existing branches and agencies in the U.S. are also subject to this provision of the act. That is, they too must demonstrate that their home country's regulators provide comprehensive and consolidated supervision. If they cannot do that, the Federal Reserve is required to close all their U.S. offices.

The Enforcement Act further adds to the Federal Reserve's supervisory oversight of foreign banks in the U.S. by designating the Federal Reserve as the primary regulator of both state-chartered and federal-chartered foreign bank branches, agencies, representative offices, and commercial lending subsidiaries operating in the U.S. Except for representative offices, each foreign office must be examined at least annually. The act does not take from the states, the OCC, or the FDIC their examination authority over foreign banks; it does, however, make the Federal Reserve responsible for conducting either coordinated or separate annual examinations of all foreign banking offices in the U.S.

The Foreign Bank Supervision Enhancement Act was a congressional response to the failure of U.S. federal and state regulators, and foreign country regulators, to detect and prevent the illegal lending and money transfer activities of the Bank of Credit and Commerce International (BCCI) and the Atlanta agency of Banca Nazionale del Lavoro in the 1980s that led to their closing in the 1990s. Heightened sensitivity to the problem of dealing with insolvent saving and loan associations and a growing number of U.S. commercial bank failures in the late 1980s added to congressional concerns over the need for stronger regulation of foreign banks operating in the U.S.

Policy of Reciprocity

The policy of national treatment embodied in the International Banking Act muted, but did not end, the controversy over an alternative policy for regulating foreign banks in the United States. This policy, known as reciprocity, advocates that foreign banks receive the same regulatory treatment as foreign countries adopt for treatment of U.S. banks. Thus banks from countries with liberal banking laws would receive liberal treatment in the United States, while banks from countries with restrictive laws would be regulated restrictively.

A policy of reciprocity was rejected by Congress in 1978 because it seemed inconsistent with our government's pro-competitive philosophy as well as impractical to implement. U.S. banks are exposed to such disparate regulatory treatment throughout the world that any reciprocity-based law for foreign banks would lead to a complex body of divergent rules. It could also create competitive inequities between U.S. banks and U.S. offices of foreign banks.

Most countries impose substantial restrictions on the ownership or presence of foreign banks in their domestic markets—either by law, policy, or administrative practice. One or more of the following restrictions may apply:

☐　no foreign presence of any kind

☐　no foreign commercial bank branches

☐　no taking of deposits (representative offices, however, may be allowed)

☐　no equity interest (or limited equity interest) in local banks (to prevent control)

☐　restriction by type of business (for example, no retail banking allowed)

Exhibits 15.6, 15.7, and 15.8 present a breakdown of countries according to their policies on foreign control of indigenous banks.

In addition to those types of legal and policy restrictions, many countries impose exchange controls that limit or restrict the movement of foreign exchange or domestic funds into or out of the country. Exchange controls tend to benefit domestic banks because they do not need to return earnings or profits to a parent bank in another country.

Most countries do not follow a policy of reciprocity in their dealings with U.S. and other foreign banks for a number of reasons. Many developing countries contend that their fledgling banking industries need protection against the more competitive and established banks of the industrial nations in order to develop the necessary operating efficiencies and financial strength to compete. Some countries see any U.S. or foreign banking presence as a political and economic threat to their national sovereignty, while others seek to protect the narrow financial interest of indigenous bankers (who in many countries hold political as well as financial power). Many industrial countries contend that their restrictions on foreign banks strengthen their domestic monetary policy control as well as their control over the nation's foreign exchange market and foreign exchange rate. Other countries see foreign banking restrictions as a means of insulating the domestic financial system from any external risks associated with the operations and activities of foreign banking offices.

National Regulatory Treatment of Foreign Banks

The International Banking Act of 1978 was an important step in the direction of extending national treatment to foreign banks operating in the United States. However, economists contend that there are two major impediments that make it difficult to truly regulate foreign and domestic banks in the United States equally. These impediments involve worldwide differences in banking systems and differences in regulatory approach.

EXHIBIT 15.6   Countries That Prohibit Foreign Bank Ownership of Indigenous Banks

Countries prohibiting all forms of foreign bank presence
   by law:

Afghanistan	Laos
Cuba	Libya
Ethiopia	Madagascar
Guinea	Nepal
Iraq	Somalia

   by current policy or administrative practice:

Benin	Suriname
Guyana	Tanzania
Kuwait	United Arab Emirates
Netherlands Antilles	

Countries permitting foreign bank presence only via representative offices
   by law:

Algeria	Sweden
Burma	Syria
Colombia	Venezuela
Portugal	

   by policy or administrative practice:

China	New Zealand
El Salvador	Norway
Guatemala	Saudi Arabia
India	Trinidad and Tobago
Indonesia	Turkey
Mexico	

Countries prohibiting foreign banks from purchasing any interest in indigenous banks

Bangladesh	Papua New Guinea
Pakistan	

EXHIBIT 15.7   Countries That Limit Foreign Control of Indigenous Banks

Specific maximum foreign participation allowed by law (percent)

Australia	10	Finland	20
Bermuda	40	Gambia	20
Burkina Faso	49	Japan	5
Canada	10	Nigeria	40
Congo	49	Philippines	30
Denmark	30	South Korea	10
Ecuador	20		

Specific maximum foreign participation allowed in practice (percent)

Bahrain	49	Oman	49
Dominican Republic	30	Qatar	49
Greece	49	Singapore	20
Iceland	49	South Africa	50
Morocco	50	United Kingdom	15

No majority control; no specific maximum

Central African Republic	Malaysia
Cyprus	Malta
Egypt	Netherlands
Ireland	Tunisia

First, the banking systems of most other nations differ in the following ways from that of the United States:

☐ The United States separates commercial banking activities from insurance activities and the underwriting of corporate securities; as exhibit 15.9 shows; this distinction is not made in most other countries.

☐ The United States has imposed narrow geographic limits on banking offices; most other countries permit nationwide banking.

☐ The United Sates does not allow banks to be owned by, or to be part of, industrial companies; many other countries require no such separation.

☐ U.S. banking regulations cover only those banks operating in the United States; foreign branches of U.S. banks and the head offices of foreign banks with U.S. branches are not subject to U.S. banking rules.

EXHIBIT 15.8   **Countries That Do Not Limit Foreign Control of Indigenous Banks**

Argentina	France	Mozambique
Austria	Gabon	Niger
Bahamas	Germany	Panama
Barbados	Ghana	Paraguay
Belgium	Honduras	Rwanda
Belize	Hong Kong	Senegal
Bolivia	Israel	Seychelles
Botswana	Italy	Sierra Leone
Burundi	Ivory Coast	Spain
Cameroon	Jamaica	Sri Lanka
Cape Verde	Kenya	Sudan
Cayman Islands	Lebanon	Switzerland
Chile	Luxembourg	Uruguay
Costa Rica	Mali	Zaire
Djibouti	Mauritania	Zambia
Fiji	Mauritius	

Second, the U.S. approach to bank regulation differs from that of most other countries in the following ways:

❑ Regulation of banks in the United States is shared among several agencies and between federal and state authorities; regulation of banks in most other countries is centralized.

❑ U.S. bank regulatory agencies are essentially independent of political officials; regulators in most other countries are subordinate to political officials.

❑ The United States implements bank regulation through specific rules and regulations that apply to all banks; many other countries, such as England, regulate banks through unwritten rules and general understandings that allow for different applications of the rules for different banks.

❑ Banks in the United States are privately owned; major banks of some countries are government owned.

Thus, while the United States aims to apply a national regulatory treatment that makes little or no distinction between domestic and foreign banks operating in the United States, the banking environment in most nations of the world is so different from ours as to make true equality an impossible goal. The practical result in some cases may be that domestic banks are put at a competitive disadvantage vis-a-vis foreign banks with U.S. operations.

EXHIBIT 15.9   Permissible Bank Activities in Selected Countries

Country	Number of Banks	Underwriting Securities	Insurance	Ownership of Nonbank Companies
Canada	65	Yes	Yes	up to 10% of a company
France	406	Yes	Yes	up to 10% of a company
Germany	341	Yes	Yes	Yes
Japan	153	Limited	No	up to 5% of a company
U.K.	559	Yes	Yes	Yes
U.S.	12,000	No[1]	No[1]	No

[1] Several states permit banks to engage in securities underwriting or insurance activities. However, these activities are prohibited for most U.S. banks.

Source: Institute of International Bankers; *Bankers Magazine*, Nov/Dec 1992.

Reciprocity Between the United States and Japan

Many U.S. bankers and policymakers are particularly disgruntled by the equal regulatory treatment granted Japanese banks operating in the United States. They contend that Japanese banks not only have a competitive advantage in pricing loans (because Japanese banks have been able to obtain capital at substantially lower costs than U.S. banks) but that Japanese banks violate U.S. law by favoring Japanese-owned companies in the U.S. in their lending decisions. Popular belief is that Japanese banks do that by basing their loans on the credit rating of the Japanese parent of the U.S. company. That violates U.S. banking law unless the parent guarantees that the loan will be repaid.

It is also believed that Japan unfairly limits U.S. access to Japanese banking markets. Japanese banks hold more than 45 percent ($400 billion) of all U.S. banking assets held by foreign banks. In comparison, foreign banks (including U.S. banks) hold only abut 3 percent of Japan's total banking assets.

In 1992, the House Banking Committee urged Congress to end national treatment for Japanese banks operating in the United States unless they began lending more to American-owned business firms. A particular irritant to the Committee was its sense that Japanese bank loans have largely gone to America's largest, most highly rated corporate borrowers, and not to mid-sized business firms that typically lack the financing options of larger corporate borrowers.

The likelihood that Congress would reverse the nation's policy of equal regulatory treatment for Japanese or other foreign banks in the 1990s was uncertain. Proponents of equal regulatory treatment note that foreign bank lending to U.S. businesses in 1991 and 1992 remained steady while U.S. bank loans to businesses actually declined. They further note that foreign banks in the United States issue more than half of all letters of credit used to finance America's imports and exports.

Summary

Banks are key participants in the world's foreign exchange markets, transferring money internationally, providing importers and exporters with short-term credit, and providing a means for traders and investors to minimize the risk of exchange rate fluctuations through forward purchase and sale contracts and options. Foreign deposit balances in banks, which can be transferred by cable or export drafts, and credit instruments provided by banks, such as letters of credit and bankers' acceptances, are the principal payment items used in international trade.

Foreign banks maintain a substantial presence in the United States and have acquired an increasing share of U.S. deposits and U.S. business loans. By 1992 they held 16 percent of all U.S. deposits and 26 percent of all U.S. business loans. In 1978, the International Banking Act for the first time imposed federal regulation on foreign banks operating in the United States. Those banks were made subject to the same reserve requirements and branching restrictions that apply to U.S. banks. In 1991, the Foreign Bank Supervision Enforcement Act imposed stricter federal oversight on foreign bank activities in the U.S.

The United States follows a policy of equal regulatory treatment for domestic and foreign banks, rather than a policy of reciprocity. Congress authorized the establishment of international banking facilities in 1981 to enable U.S. banks to compete more effectively in the business of international banking.

Questions

1. What are the three primary functions of the foreign exchange market?

2. Why would a U.S. exporter sell foreign exchange forward? Under what conditions would it be advantageous for a U.S. exporter to buy foreign exchange forward?

3. What is a bankers' acceptance? How does a bankers' acceptance differ from a letter of credit?

4. Cite three reasons why foreign banks maintain branches, agencies, and other banking offices in the United States.

5. Why has the United States adopted a policy of national treatment in regulating foreign banks rather than a policy of reciprocity?

PART VI *Extended Study*

Extended Study Units

Extended Study 1
The Money Supply

In the United States, monetary control has been delegated to the Federal Reserve; the Federal Reserve targets its monetary policy, in large part, against the nation's money supply. The Federal Reserve's objective is to ensure that the U.S. economy maintains a rate of money growth neither too rapid (inflationary) nor too slow (recessionary). Recent innovations in bank deposit products and changes in banking law and regulation, however, have made the tasks of defining the money supply and interpreting its growth exceedingly difficult.

Defining the Money Supply

Money supply is an economist's term for the sum of all the funds that individuals and businesses have immediately available for spending in the domestic economy. The Federal Reserve uses a number of different money supply measures to predict and control the pace and direction of U.S. economic activity in order to ensure the purchasing power of money and a growing economy. The best known of these measures—M1, M2, and M3—are discussed here.

The concept of money supply is based on the theory that people and businesses hold and spend money in predictable ways. Individuals hold and spend money primarily to satisfy their wants and needs in accordance with their incomes, while businesses hold and spend money to enhance their profits or prospects for profit. If we know how much money is immediately available for spending by individuals and businesses and we also know what their preferences are for holding, saving, and spending money, we can predict the course and pace of economic activity. More important, the economy can be controlled to some extent by increasing or decreasing the money supply. According to economic theory, the Federal Reserve's success in controlling the nation's money supply over long periods of time ultimately affects production, employment, income, and price levels.

Money supply is not necessarily synonymous with the amount of coin, currency, and checkable deposits in our economy because spending decisions are not based solely on how much of these three money items we hold. That is because most of the public's financial wealth is not held in money, but rather in near monies. Near monies (which are items that may be good standards of value but nevertheless are not generally accepted as money) include U.S. government and corporate bonds, life insurance policies, pension funds, money market shares, and various types of interest-earning time deposits in financial institutions. Near monies are generally highly *liquid*, which means they can be quickly converted into money.

Individuals and businesses held more than $11 trillion in total financial assets in 1992. Of this amount, about $1 trillion (or one-tenth of the total) was in the form of money (cash and checkable deposits). More than $2.5 trillion (or about one-fifth of the total) was held by individuals and businesses in time and savings deposits in the nation's banks and thrift institutions.

As consumers, we take at least some of these near-money financial assets into consideration when facing major spending decisions. We may look to our savings and time accounts to draw on savings, or look to our credit cards as a source for borrowing funds, or convert a near-money asset, such as funds in a money market account, into spendable money. What is not apparent to economists, however, is just which assets consumers prefer for long-term savings and which near-money assets typically enter into spending decisions. That makes the prediction of spending behavior exceedingly difficult.

The same assessment problem applies to business spending because businesses generally evaluate their spending decisions against the broad range of their financial assets rather than solely against their holdings of cash and demand deposits. Businesses frequently use certificates of deposit, U.S. Treasury bills, and other financial instruments to store purchasing power while assessing their spending options.

Problems of Classification

The problem of what near-money assets to count as part of the money supply has become further complicated by two factors. First, banking innovations and changes in banking law in the 1980s allowed banks and thrifts to offer new types of deposit accounts that pay interest yet are checkable (that is, they are subject both to claim on demand and to transfer by check). These new types of accounts—the negotiable order of withdrawal (NOW) account and automatic transfer service (ATS) account, both authorized in 1980, and the money market deposit account (MMDA), authorized in 1982—have blurred the distinction between funds held for spending transactions and funds held for long-term savings.

The classification of savings and spendable funds also has been complicated by the rapid transfer of vast amounts of funds by consumers in search of greater interest earnings. High interest rates on deposits in the early 1980s induced consumers and businesses to transfer non-interest-earning demand deposit money into a broad range of interest-earning near monies and new interest-bearing checkable deposits. Low interest rates on deposits in the early 1990s induced consumers and businesses to transfer low-paying time and savings deposit money into higher earning near monies, such as stocks and bonds.

Between 1978 and 1982, the public placed about $250 billion in nonbank money market funds, which were not constrained by interest rate ceilings and thus could pay higher interest rates on deposits than banks. In 1982, Congress passed the Depository Institutions Act of 1982 (also known as the Garn-St Germain Act), which authorized banks and thrifts to offer money market deposit accounts that were competitive with money market funds; by mid-1988, the public had placed some $525 billion in those accounts in addition to more than $280 billion in other interest-earning checkable deposits. Such movements of funds made the task of classifying *spending* money and *savings* money—and interpreting money growth—exceedingly difficult in the 1980s.

The task did not get easier in the 1990s. From early-1991 to early-1992, the public withdrew more than $175 billion from time and savings deposits in search of higher interest returns. About $135 billion of those funds were invested in stocks and bonds. Consumers and businesses also used some of those funds to pay off outstanding credit card balances and other loans to banks. Economists contend that these movements of funds distorted the money supply measures; as figure 1 shows, in the early 1990s while the growth of the narrowly defined measure (M1) accelerated, the growth of the broadly defined measure of money supply (M2) slowed. Such conflicting trends add to the difficulty of correctly interpreting the true growth of money (and likely future spending) in the economy.

FIGURE 1   **Conflicting Money Supply Growth Trends in the 1990s**

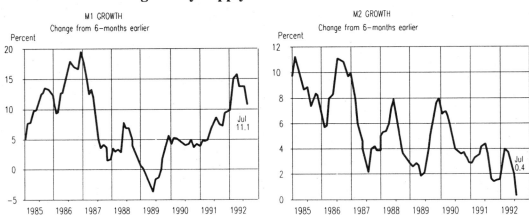

Measuring the Money Supply

The Federal Reserve uses several different measures of money supply (M1, M2, and M3 being the most important), a measure of liquidity (L), and a measure of debt. The relative size of these various measures in 1992—and the components of each—is shown in figure 2.

The most commonly used and narrowest measure of the money the public has immediately available for domestic spending is referred to as M1. This measure counts all mediums of exchange, including interest-earning checkable deposits held by individuals at both banks and thrift institutions. More specifically, M1 consists of the following:

- ❑ currency and coin outside the Treasury, Federal Reserve banks, and commercial banks
- ❑ demand deposits at all commercial banks except
    - ❑ those due to domestic banks, foreign commercial banks, and certain foreign official institutions
    - ❑ those due to the U.S. government

    less

    - ❑ cash items in the process of collection
    - ❑ Federal Reserve float

- ❑ NOW accounts
- ❑ credit union share drafts (interest-earning checking accounts provided by credit unions)
- ❑ savings deposits subject to automatic transfers
- ❑ demand deposits at thrift institutions
- ❑ traveler's checks

FIGURE 2   **Components of the Money Supply, Liquid Assets, and Debt Measures**
(as of July 1992)

		Amount (billions of dollars)
M1:	Currency and coin	$279
	Demand deposits	316
	Other checkable deposits	359
	Traveler's checks	8
	Total	$962
M2:	M1	$962
	Savings deposits and money market deposit accounts	1,134
	Small-denomination time deposits	942
	Overnight RPs	49
	Overnight Eurodollars	19
	Deposits in general-purpose and broker-dealer money market funds	350
	Total	$3,456
M3:	M2	$3,456
	Large-denomination time deposits (over $100,000)	390
	Term RPs	67
	Term Eurodollars	50
	Deposits in institution-only money market funds	202
	Total	$4,165
L:	M3	$4,165
	U.S. savings bonds	145
	Short-term U.S. Treasury bills	327
	Commercial paper	349
	Bankers' acceptances	22
	Total	$5,008
Debt:	Federal debt	$2,912
	Nonfederal debt*	8,518
	Total	$11,430

* Includes state and local government debt and private debt.
Source: Federal Reserve Board, Statistical Release H.6(508)

A broader measure of the money the public has immediately available for domestic spending is known as M2. In addition to the mediums of exchange included in M1, M2 counts near monies that are close substitutes for money, have short maturities (quickly mature into cash), or can be readily sold for cash. M2 consists of the following:

- ❑ M1
- ❑ savings deposits and money market deposit accounts at banks and thrift institutions
- ❑ time deposits with minimum denominations of less than $100,000 (except individual retirement accounts)
- ❑ overnight repurchase agreements issued by commercial banks (A repurchase agreement involves the purchase of a security, usually a three-month Treasury bill, with an agreement that the seller will buy back the security within a specified time—usually a day or two—at an agreed-upon price.)
- ❑ overnight Eurodollar deposits held by U.S. residents at foreign branches of U.S. banks (Eurodollars are broadly defined as any dollar-denominated deposits on the books of banking offices outside the United States, including non-European banks.)
- ❑ shares held in general-purpose and broker-dealer money market mutual funds

A still broader measure of money supply is M3. This measure includes not only the categories of money and near money counted in M1 and M2, but certain highly liquid assets that are used primarily by big business firms. M3 consists of the following:

- ❑ M2
- ❑ time deposits with minimum denominations of $100,000
- ❑ term repurchase agreements and term Eurodollar deposits (those longer than overnight)
- ❑ balances held in institution-only money market mutual funds

The Federal Reserve also uses a broad liquidity measure—L—that recognizes the importance of several key financial instruments in the spending and saving decisions of individuals and business firms. L consists of the following:

- ❑ M3
- ❑ bankers' acceptances (These are promissory note credit instruments that are drawn on and accepted by a bank to finance the export, import, shipment, or storage of goods. To be accepted means that the bank agrees to pay the instrument at its maturity on behalf of its customer, who is obligated to pay the bank the amount being financed.)
- ❑ U.S. savings bonds
- ❑ commercial paper
- ❑ short-term Treasury securities

The Federal Reserve also evaluates the growth of nonfinancial debt in the economy in conjunction with its assessments of the growth of the money supply and liquidity measures. This debt measure consists of the following:

❑ the total of all outstanding debt instruments issued by the U.S. government and the nation's state and local governments

❑ the total of all private debt in the form of outstanding

  ❑ corporate bonds

  ❑ commercial and residential mortgages

  ❑ consumer credit and consumer loans

  ❑ other bank loans

  ❑ commercial paper

  ❑ bankers' acceptances

  ❑ other debt instruments

Each measure of the money supply shares some common characteristics. Each successive (broader) measure of the money supply includes the measure that preceded it—thus M2 includes all of M1 plus near monies, while M3 includes all of M2 plus additional near monies. In addition, no measure of money supply counts the monies or near monies held by banks or the government.

Banks hold money primarily to meet the Federal Reserve's reserve requirements and their own liquidity needs. The government manages the money it holds through two sets of accounts: Treasury tax and loan (TT&L) accounts at thousands of banks and thrifts into which tax receipts and loan proceeds (receipts from the sales of newly issued securities) are deposited, and accounts at the Federal Reserve banks from which disbursements are made. To include monies held by banks and the government in the money supply measures would distort the predictive link between money supply growth and economic activity because the money held by banks and the government is not held primarily for immediate spending on goods and services.

The checking accounts kept in U.S. banks by foreign commercial banks and official institutions are also not included in any of the money supply measures because they are not generally maintained for use in domestic commercial transactions.

Finally, cash items (checks) that are in the process of collection in the banking system and Federal Reserve float (the credit banks receive for checks deposited with Reserve banks before the checks are collected) are subtracted from the total of demand deposits to avoid double counting, and thus overstating the size of the money supply measures.

Collecting Money Supply Data

The collection of money supply data is a burdensome and imprecise task that falls on the nation's 30,000 banks and thrift institutions and the Federal Reserve. About 20,000 banks and thrifts routinely send data to the Federal Reserve through individual Reports of Deposits that cover 13 types of deposits and 3 classes of assets. These reports contain the basic data that comprise all measures of the money supply. Of the data-sending institutions, about 15,000 report weekly; the others provide data to the Federal Reserve quarterly. Small banks, savings and loan associations, and credit unions that are exempt from reserve requirements and data-reporting requirements—about 15,000 depositories—submit deposit data to their chartering agency, which in turn forwards the data to the Federal Reserve. Because of that uneven data flow, the Federal Reserve is constantly revising weekly money supply measures as additional data are received and actual data replace estimated data. The Federal Reserve also adjusts the measures to compensate for seasonal variations in the public's holdings of money balances. Thus the money supply measures are statistical sums, not literal dollars-and-cents counts of the public's monies.

Targeting the Money Supply

Since the 1930s, the success of M1 and M2 growth in predicting the course of the economy has been mixed. Beginning in 1933, the government imposed ceilings on the interest rates that banks could pay on time and savings deposits. These ceilings and the prohibition on the payment of interest on demand deposits tended to distort M1 and M2 trends. During periods when rate ceilings were well above interest rates on U.S. Treasury bills and other money market instruments, funds tended to flow into time and savings deposits at banks, speeding the growth of M2 and slowing the growth of M1. When market interest rates exceeded the rate ceilings, growth of M2 slowed as time deposits were transferred into higher-earning Treasury bills and money market instruments.

In the 1960s, the growth of the narrow M1 measure of the money supply seemed to offer better predictive results for the course of the U.S. economy than the growth of the broader money supply measures. In the 1970s, the M2 measure came closer to the mark. In the early 1980s, the Federal Reserve broadened its monetary policy focus from M1 to the M2 and M3 money supply measures, contending that the growth of the M1 measure was being particularly distorted by changes in bank deposit products and in public money holding and spending practices.

During 1985 and 1986, M1 grew at an average annual rate of 13.5 percent. In prior decades, such sharp growth would have foretold an imminent inflationary outburst. Yet, the nation's inflation rate between 1985 and 1987 averaged under 3.5 percent, a rate more consistent with the slower growth registered by the M2 and M3 measures. In 1987, the Federal Reserve concluded that M1 had lost its predictive link to the economy and abandoned its use as a target for guiding monetary policy; instead, the Federal Reserve began to rely solely on M2 and M3.

Figure 3 illustrates the difficulty that policymakers faced in the 1980s in relying on M1 as a target for guiding monetary policy. It shows that the rate of inflation tracked fairly well with the trend growth of M1 (a two-year earlier moving average) from 1965 to 1981. Beginning in 1982, however, the inflation rate was well below the trend growth of M1. Economists are unsure why. The changing composition of M1 during the 1980s, illustrated in Figure 4, may be one factor.

FIGURE 3   **Inflation and M1-Trend Growth**

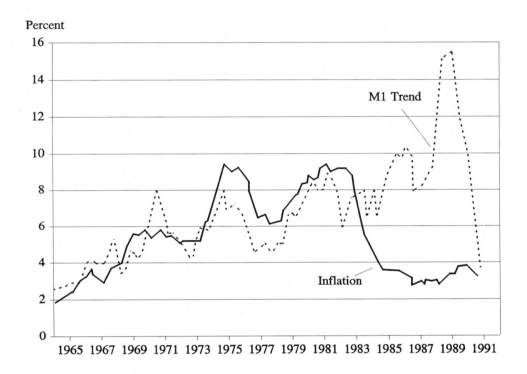

Source: Federal Reserve Bank of St. Louis

In 1993, the Federal Reserve established a target range for annual growth in M2 of 2 percent to 6 percent, and a target range for annual growth in M3 of 0.5 percent to 4.5 percent, as shown in figure 5. This range was considered appropriate for achieving noninflationary growth in the nation's output of goods and services for 1993 and 1994. The Federal Reserve also gives considerable weight to other financial and economic factors, such as interest rates, foreign exchange rates, and the growth of the nation's output (gross domestic product), in implementing monetary policy.

FIGURE 4   **The Changed Composition of M1**

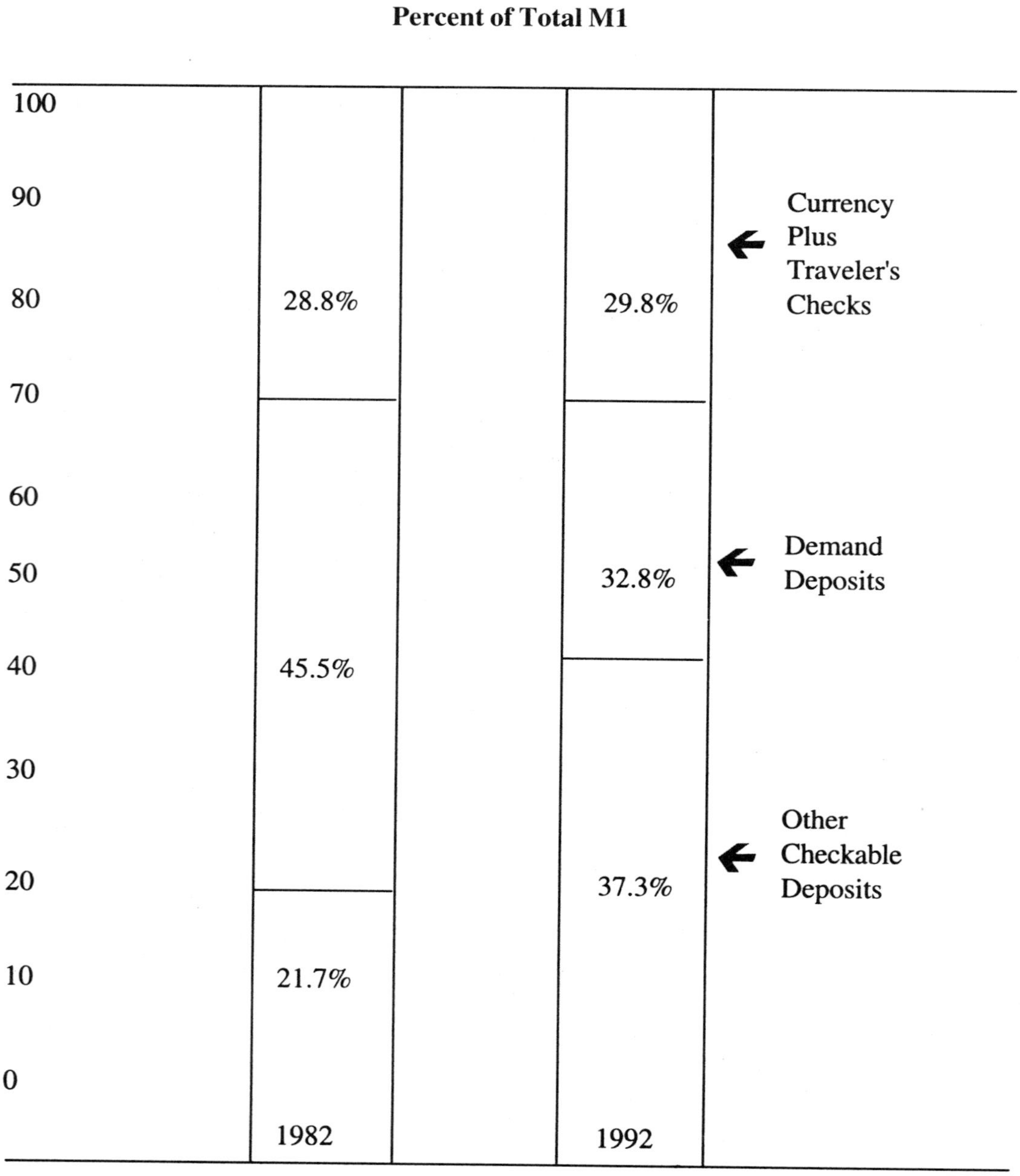

Percent of Total M1

Source: Federal Reserve Bulletin, Table 1.21, August 1992 and August 1982.

FIGURE 5 **Money Supply Growth Targets and Debt Monitoring Range**
(Percentage change from fourth quarter of preceding year to fourth
quarter of year indicated.)

	1991	1992	1993
M2	2.5-6.5	2.5-6.5	2-6
M3	1-5	1-5	0.5-4.5
Nonfederal Debt	4.5-8.5	4.5-8.5	4.5-8.5

Source: Federal Reserve Board, Report submitted to Congress on February 19, 1993.

Extended Study 2
Business Cycles

The U.S. economy is highly susceptible to imbalances in economic activity. These imbalances, known as business cycles, are recurrent, periodic fluctuations in business activity in which stable business conditions decline and then improve again. Business cycles disrupt almost all sectors of the U.S. economy, but never quite in the same way or to the same degree. Over the past century, the U.S. economy has had a growth rate, on average, of about 3 percent to 5 percent of real GDP each year. That growth has been very uneven, however, surging well above the average in some years and declining into recession in others.

Characteristics of Business Cycles

Business cycles are characterized by phases of recession, recovery, and expansion, which occur at irregular intervals and last for indeterminate periods of time. A *recession* is the downward phase of a business cycle; to qualify as a full-fledged recession, a decline in real GDP generally must last for two consecutive quarters (six months). A *depression* is a severe and extended recession during which the decline in real GDP is precipitous. From 1929 to 1933, for example, during the Great Depression, real GDP fell by 50 percent. In contrast, during the 1990-1991 recession, real GDP fell by only about 2 percent. During the recovery phase of the business cycle, the economy regains the level of production that preceded the recession phase. In the expansion phase of the cycle, the GDP surpasses the pre-recession level of production. Since the end of World War II, the U.S. economy has experienced nine recessions and subsequent recoveries and expansions, as shown in figure 1.

FIGURE 1 **Duration and Severity of Post-World War II Recessions**

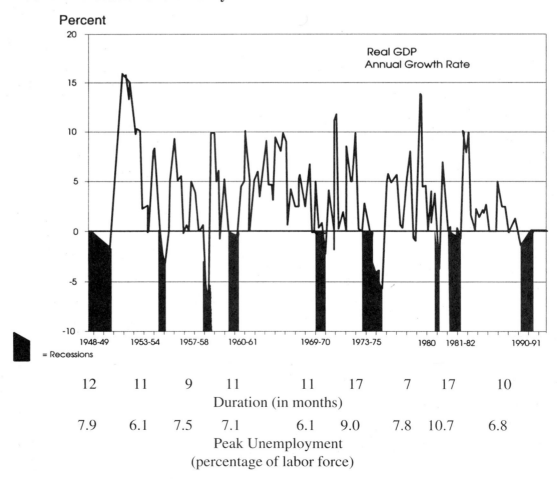

Economists do not understand precisely why business cycles occur, but they can trace these disruptions in economic activity in the United States as far back as the 1790s. Leading analysts of business cycles think that these economic fluctuations are probably related to the following:

- changes in money supply growth
- changes in consumer spending
- changes in business investment spending

If the amount of bank-created money adds too much to the supply of money flowing from income and other borrowing sources, rising prices (inflation) can result. However, if the amount of newly created money adds too little to the existing supply, the economy can begin to contract and move toward recession.

A shift in consumer expectations about the course and direction of the economy, or a change in disposable income levels, can lead to spending changes that catch producers off guard and can help precipitate a business cycle.

The economy responds unevenly to sudden speedups or slowdowns in business firms' accumulation of inventories, replacement of depreciating equipment, or purchases of new capital goods and technology. Such changes in business investment spending can be disruptive to the economy.

Businesses usually try to keep their inventories of unsold merchandise at the lowest level consistent with continued efficient operations. Inventory levels cannot be controlled precisely, however, because in most cases they reflect businesses' expectations of future sales. Thus, if the nation's retailers find they have underestimated consumer demand, they rush to stock up on merchandise to avoid losing sales. That sudden upsurge of orders generates unexpected business for wholesalers and manufacturers and propels the economy ahead. If, on the other hand, retailers overestimate demand and find themselves with several months' supply of unsold inventories, they stop or sharply cut back their purchases from wholesalers and manufacturers. That sudden decline in orders blunts the economy's expansion and slows economic activity.

In a recession, all three factors—changes in money supply growth, consumer spending, and business inventories—may interrelate to slow the economy.

In recent decades, the economy's recessions, recoveries, and expansions have become more readily recognizable and predictable. Recessions have become shorter, averaging about 12 months in duration, while periods of expansion have become longer. Earlier in this century, recessions averaged close to 2 years, and a full business cycle averaged about 4 years. In the 100 years prior to World War II, the U.S. economy was in recession much of the time: for every 48 months of declining production, there were only 52 months of expansion. Since World War II, however, the economy has registered 80 months of expansion for every 20 months of production decline. In fact, the economic expansions of the 1960s (105 months) and the 1980s (90 months) are the two longest periods of expansion on record.

Effects of Business Cycles

Economists recognize that different sectors of the economy experience recession, recovery, and expansion in disproportionate ways.

The nation's heavy manufacturing industries—steel, oil, machine tools, and automobile manufacturing—tend to experience sharp reductions in demand for their products during a recession and sharp increases during a recovery. Those changes in demand are usually accompanied by rapid layoffs of production workers during a recession and almost equally rapid work recalls during a recovery. A particularly deep and long recession also may lead to delays in planned price increases or to selective price cutting in an effort to maintain sales.

The nation's light industries—retailing and manufacturing of consumer household goods—usually experience smaller changes in product demand and resulting employment shifts over the course of a business cycle than do the heavy industries. That is because business purchases of capital goods and consumer purchases of big-ticket items, such as new cars and furniture, are easier to postpone than other purchases when profits and wages begin to decline.

Service industries—which include banking, finance, insurance, and medical care—are usually affected only mildly during a recession. As a result, employment in the service industries tends to be more stable during a recession than employment in other sectors of the economy. Indeed, leading analysts of business cycles contend that the evolution of the U.S. economy from a goods economy to a service economy—and the greater stability of employment that has resulted—has weakened modern recessions.

Sectors of the economy affected indirectly by recession include housing, government, and agriculture. Activity in the housing industry and employment in the construction trades are determined primarily by mortgage interest rates and the availability of funds for mortgages. As such, the housing sector is very vulnerable to the effects of business cycles.

Federal government spending and employment are largely determined by public policy and are generally immune to the effects of a business cycle. However, at the state and local levels, shortfalls of tax receipts during a recession can lead to reduced spending and employment. Tax revenues typically decline during a recession because businesses earn less profit and workers earn less income, resulting in less taxes being paid.

Agricultural production, long considered invulnerable to cyclical swings in economic activity, has become more responsive to changes in investment spending and business cycles in recent decades. That is the result of small farms being replaced by large farming corporations, which rely on mass production methods and extensive investments in capital and technology.

Recession and Expansion in the 1990s

Most economists who have analyzed the nation's business cycles have concluded that no two recessions (and subsequent expansions) are alike. The data suggest that business cycles vary sharply from the average in their duration and severity. Nonetheless, economists use *averages* as a yardstick for comparisons.

The average duration of eight recessions from 1948 to 1982 was about 12 months; during those recessions, real GDP fell, on average, by about 2.5 percent. The 1990-1991 recession could be categorized as milder than average in terms of its length (10 months) and its severity (a real GDP decline of 2 percent). The 1991-1992 expansion could be similarly categorized.

Real GDP grew during the 18 months following recessions from 1948 to 1982 at an average annual rate of about 5 percent. However, from the end of the 1990-1991 recession (April 1991) to October 1992—a period of 18 months—the economy's real GDP grew by less than 2 percent. One result of this slow growth was that fewer jobs were created in 1991 and 1992 than the number of new workers seeking jobs. As a consequence, unemployment, which generally declines in an expansion, increased in 1991 and 1992 above the level registered during the 1990-1991 recession. That unusual increase can be seen in figure 2.

FIGURE 2 **Unemployment Rate**
Seasonally Adjusted

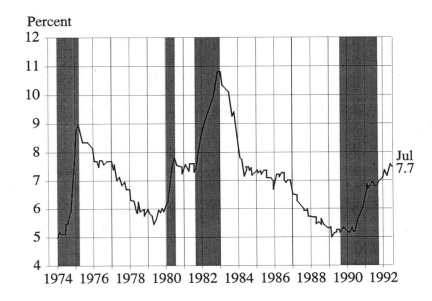

Shaded areas represent periods of recession.

Source: Federal Reserve Bank of New York.

Some economists believe that 1992's slow GDP growth may be part of a long-term sluggish growth trend related to structural changes that businesses began making in their operations in the late 1980s to remain competitive. They note that the 1990-1991 recession occurred during the longest period of slow economic growth since 1945. As seen in figure 3, the annual growth of real GDP has averaged below 2 percent since the second quarter of 1989.

Other economists believe that the high level of consumer and corporate debt accumulated in the 1980s has acted as a drag on economic expansion in the 1990s. They contend that consumers and businesses have been reluctant to borrow additional funds (and step up spending)—even at very low interest rates—because of difficulties in repaying outstanding loans. Still other economists point to the meager growth in disposable personal income in the 1990s, coupled with bleak consumer expectations for the future, as the reason for the economy's malaise.

FIGURE 3 **Changes in Real GDP**

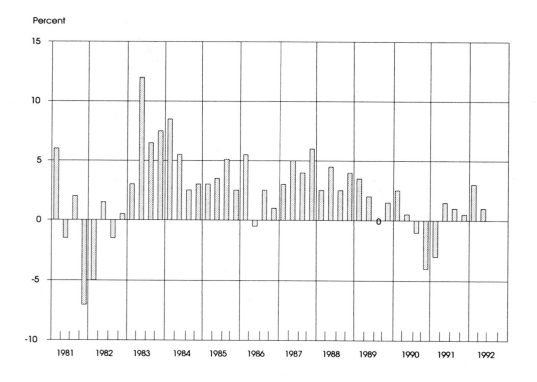

Extended Study 3
Interest Rate Regulation

From 1933 until the 1980s, Congress regulated the interest rates that banks and thrift institutions could pay on deposits by prohibiting the payment of interest on demand deposits and by establishing ceilings on the interest rates that could be paid on time and savings deposits. In the 1960s and 1970s, as market interest rates began to rise above the rate ceilings imposed by Regulation Q (the Federal Reserve's regulation on interest rates), the economy began to experience periodic episodes of disintermediation. Disintermediation occurs when depositors withdraw their funds from a financial intermediary in order to obtain a higher rate on their savings elsewhere. Increasingly, depositors were purchasing U.S. Treasury bills, placing their deposits in money market funds, or otherwise moving their funds to institutions or instruments that were not subject to Regulation Q ceilings.

The disintermediation in the 1960s and 1970s had a devastating effect on the nation's housing industry. Thrift institutions, which are a primary source of mortgage credit, were unable at that time to create demand deposit money when they made loans. Their loans came directly from funds received in the form of time and savings deposits. Thus, when thrifts lost deposits, they lost their ability to make new mortgage loans. As a result, many potential home buyers could not get mortgages and so could not buy existing homes or contract for new ones to be built. The result was a sharp decline in the number of new houses built and an increase in unemployment in the construction trades.

Origins of Regulation

It is not entirely clear why Congress chose to regulate interest rates in the 1930s; there was little congressional discussion of the proposed interest rate ceilings when the Banking Act of 1933 was enacted. There are, however, three likely motivating factors:

☐ bank liquidity problems during the Depression
☐ excessive rate competition among banks
☐ added bank costs of FDIC subscription fees

Congress believed that the payment of interest on demand deposits had contributed to the liquidity problems that banks experienced during the early years of the Depression, particularly because the nation's big banks used the payment of interest on demand deposits to attract the deposits of smaller banks. Many large money market banks used interbank deposit money to make loans to stockbrokers; thus when the stock market collapsed and the broker loans could not be repaid, those banks were unable to meet the demands of their respondent banks for the deposited interbank funds.

Congress also believed that interest rate ceilings and the prohibition of interest on demand deposits would prevent excessive rate competition among banks. That view was based on the belief that many of the bank failures of the 1930s were related to intense rate competition for deposits in the 1920s, a contention that today's economic historians dispute.

Congress further believed that the regulation of interest rates would reduce bank expenses. The Banking Act of 1933 required banks to pay a subscription fee to the newly established Federal Deposit Insurance Corporation to insure deposits. The reduction in bank costs resulting from the interest rate regulations was expected to offset bank payments to the FDIC.

Whatever their underlying premise, the interest rate regulations of the 1930s had little impact on banking or the economy until the 1960s because, until then, market interest rates stayed well below the rate ceilings. It was only as interest rates began to rise in the late 1960s, and as banks and thrifts began to offer inducements to attract deposits, that competition for funds between banks and thrifts began to take its toll.

Consequences of Regulation

In 1966, in an attempt to prevent further disintermediation, the FDIC, the Federal Home Loan Bank Board (the agency that regulated S&Ls in the 1960s), and the Federal Reserve established an interest rate differential between the maximum rates that thrifts and commercial banks could pay on time and savings deposits; thrifts were given a ceiling that was fixed one percentage point higher than banks.

The interest rate differential was imposed as a temporary measure to protect thrifts from competition that might erode their deposits and reduce the supply of mortgage funds. In effect, the regulation gave broad support to the housing industry by trying to guarantee mortgage availability.

The rationale seemed valid. The income of thrifts is linked in a static way to the returns that thrifts receive on long-term fixed-rate mortgages, some made 15 to 30 years earlier. However, the business costs of thrifts increase in direct proportion to the rate of interest they have to pay today to attract and maintain deposits. Without deposit rate ceilings, thrifts would face a profit squeeze during periods of rising interest rates and active competition for deposits.

The interest rate ceilings, however, did not prevent disintermediation. In the late 1960s and early 1970s, banks and thrifts alike lost massive amounts of funds to the money and capital markets where interest rates were not regulated. When the Federal Reserve eliminated the Regulation Q ceiling for large short-term negotiable certificates of deposit in 1970, bank and thrift deposits still flowed to higher-yielding Treasury bills.

In the mid-1970s, the economy experienced another period of disintermediation. That episode was not as severe because in 1973 the Federal Reserve eliminated the Regulation Q ceilings on large, longer-term negotiable certificates of deposit offered by thrifts. In addition, the ceilings on other time deposits were raised to near market rates. Moreover, financial innovation and the growing competitiveness of thrifts led to a progressive narrowing of the interest rate differential between banks and thrifts from one percentage point in 1966 to one-quarter of a point in 1973.

Throughout the 1960s and 1970s, the banking community and Congress debated whether the Regulation Q ceilings and the interest rate prohibition on demand deposits should be eliminated. Despite recommendations to do that by several presidential and congressional commissions during this period, the interest regulations were not ended. Policymakers' opinions began to change, however, with the escalating interest rates of the late 1970s, and yet another episode of disintermediation.

It had become apparent by 1980 that Regulation Q had created a market anomaly. In an environment of rapidly rising interest rates, thrift deposits invariably flowed into other forms of near money that were not subject to ceilings (particularly Treasury bills), leading to a shrinkage of mortgage credit. Because Regulation Q ceilings had already been eliminated for large certificates of deposit, the regulation also generated a market inequity—consumers with limited funds could not obtain a market rate on their savings, whereas large depositors and corporations could. Perhaps most telling, however, was the recognition that banks and thrifts, through their own ingenuity and innovation, had begun to develop new services and new near-money instruments (such as NOW accounts) that effectively circumvented Regulation Q.

Congress finally changed the direction of public policy on interest rate regulation when it enacted the Monetary Control Act of 1980, which mandated a gradual phase-out of Regulation Q (by 1986). Congress also established the Depository Institutions Deregulation Committee—composed of representatives of the major bank and thrift regulatory agencies and the secretary of the treasury—to implement the phaseout in a manner that would avoid market disruptions. In 1982, Congress voted to speed up the phase-out by requiring that the interest rate differential favoring thrifts be ended in 1984. This change was incorporated in a broad package of banking and thrift reform measures contained in the Garn-St Germain Act of 1982.

Extended Study 4

Overview of the Financial Institutions Reform, Recovery and Enforcement Act (FIRREA) of 1989

FIRREA was a legislative attempt to end the S&L crisis that confronted the United States in the late 1980s. This legislation profoundly changed the legal and regulatory environment of both banks and thrifts in the 1990s by:

- [ ] providing funds for closing hundreds of insolvent savings and loan associations and giving new powers to thrift regulators to restrict risky S&L activities
- [ ] changing the laws governing federal deposit insurance to protect the government's insurance funds from the escalating claims of insolvent thrift institutions
- [ ] restricting some thrift powers while expanding others
- [ ] imposing new stringent capital requirements on S&Ls and strengthening regulators' powers to oversee thrift activities

Closing Failing S&Ls

FIRREA established a federal agency to manage the assets of insolvent thrifts—the Resolution Trust Corporation (RTC). In 1989,Congress gave the RTC $20 billion to begin operations. Its initial holdings of failed S&L assets exceeded $100 billion. However, by late 1991, the RTC had exhausted all its funds. In November 1991, Congress gave the RTC an additional $25 billion as a stopgap measure to enable the RTC to continue asset liquidation activities into 1992 while attempts to find a long-term solution to the RTC's funding needs continued.

The act also eased the rules that regulators must follow when closing a failing S&L by authorizing the FDIC to assume the role of conservator or receiver for any failing S&L, whether federal or state chartered. As a conservator, the FDIC can operate a failing S&L until it is sold. As a receiver, the FDIC is required to close the S&L, pay off insured depositors, and liquidate the S&L's remaining assets. The FDIC was further authorized to end deposit insurance coverage for insolvent S&Ls. Before FIRREA, two years was the minimum legal period required before deposit insurance coverage could be removed from a failing bank or thrift.

Bolstering S&L Deposit Insurance

The act established two new government deposit insurance funds under the administration of the FDIC: a Bank Insurance Fund (BIF), which had been administered by the FDIC; and a Savings Association Insurance Fund (SAIF), which replaced the fund formerly administered by the Federal Savings and Loan Insurance Corporation (FSLIC). The FSLIC and the Federal Home Loan Bank Board, the federal regulator of S&Ls, were disbanded. In place of these agencies, FIRREA created a new thrift regulatory agency, the Office of Thrift Supervision (OTS). Both the FDIC and the OTS were given stronger powers to enforce bank and thrift regulations.

The FDIC was required to eliminate any differences that existed in deposit insurance coverage at banks and S&Ls. Today, both insurance funds offer the same protection to depositors. However, BIF and SAIF have different ratios of insurance fund reserves to insured deposits and assess different premiums on their member institutions.

Under FIRREA, both BIF and SAIF must maintain reserve funds equal to 1.25 percent of the total deposits they insure. In 1990, commercial banks paid 12 cents to the FDIC for every $100 in deposits they held in their domestic offices, while S&Ls paid 20.8 cents. The FIRREA premium schedule stipulated that between August 1994 and January 1999 the insurance premium differential between banks and S&Ls would be narrowed and after January 1999, the differential would end entirely, with deposit insurance premiums set at 15 cents per $100 of deposits.

FIRREA gave the FDIC authority, beginning in January 1995, to raise insurance premiums if either the BIF or SAIF ratio of reserve funds to insured deposits threatened to fall below the 1.25 percent standard. However, a spate of bank closings and

FDIC payouts in 1989 and 1990 so depleted BIF revenues that the FDIC was forced to increase banks' premiums to 23 cents per $100 of deposits in 1991. Congress also authorized the FDIC to borrow $30 billion from the U.S. Treasury to replenish its depleted reserve funds. The 1991 FDIC borrowing authorization law requires the FDIC to establish premiums sufficient not only to repay any borrowed funds within 15 years, but to meet FIRREA's 1.25 percent ratio of reserves-to-insured deposits standard.

Restricting Risky S&L Activities

FIRREA changed the mix of activities and investments permissible for thrifts. S&Ls were required to hold 70 percent of their assets in *qualified* thrift investments—essentially housing-related loans and securities. Before FIRREA, S&Ls needed to hold only 60 percent of their assets in qualified thrift investments. FIRREA also narrowed the list of loans and securities considered to be qualified. (In 1991, Congress reduced the 70 percent requirement to 65 percent.)

The OTS was empowered to prohibit undercapitalized S&Ls from soliciting brokered deposits and to impose restrictions on the asset growth of S&Ls that did not meet capital standards. (In 1991, Congress ended deposit insurance coverage for brokered deposits offered by undercapitalized banks and thrifts).

Thrifts also were prohibited from investing in junk bonds (bonds that carry less than investment-grade credit ratings) and from investing in real estate. Real estate appraisal rules for loans also were tightened. S&Ls were additionally subjected to legal limits on the amount of loans they could make to any one borrower. However, FIRREA gave thrifts new power to offer checking accounts to business firms, whether related to a loan or not. Prior to FIRREA, thrifts could establish checking accounts only for firms that borrowed funds from them.

New Capital Requirements

To bolster the capacity of S&Ls to suffer losses without becoming insolvent (a situation that creates a potential drain on federal deposit insurance fund reserves), S&Ls were subjected to three new capital requirements:

☐ FIRREA imposed a new minimum capital requirement of 3 percent on S&Ls. Under this requirement, an S&L must maintain capital (owner's equity) equal to no less than 3 percent of its total assets. Thrifts were prohibited from including most types of goodwill in their measure of capital. Goodwill is the difference between the worth of a company's assets and the market value of the company itself. In essence, goodwill reflects the value of a company's name, reputation, and customer base.

❏ S&Ls also are required to hold an amount of tangible capital equal to no less than 1.5 percent of their assets. An S&L cannot count the value of supervisory goodwill as part of its capital. Supervisory goodwill is the estimated value above a troubled S&L's net worth that a potential buyer might be willing to pay—presumably to obtain the S&L's deposit insurance coverage.

❏ FIRREA further mandated that S&Ls must meet a minimum risk-based capital requirement. Under this requirement, numerical weights (multiples) are applied to S&L assets according to the perceived risk of the assets. The sum of these weighted assets determines the risk-adjusted asset base against which a minimum amount of capital must be held.

Most S&L industry analysts contend that the exclusion of goodwill from capital and FIRREA's stringent capital requirements will cause some solvent thrifts to close in the 1990s if they cannot raise additional capital. Many other thrifts will be able to raise necessary capital only by selling off assets or by sharply curtailing their growth. In either case, analysts project that FIRREA's capital provisions will likely cause the S&L industry to shrink considerably in the 1990s.

Other Reforms and Open Issues

FIRREA, which encompassed nearly 1,000 pages of provisions, covered more than the S&L bailout.

The act expanded the powers of bank holding companies by amending the 1956 Bank Holding Company Act to allow the Federal Reserve to authorize bank holding companies to buy healthy thrifts. Before FIRREA, bank holding companies were prohibited from purchasing thrifts unless the thrifts were insolvent.

In an effort to combat discrimination in housing lending in key urban areas, FIRREA authorized the regulatory agencies to make public, beginning in 1991, previously confidential ratings of bank and thrift compliance with the Community Reinvestment Act of 1977. That act requires banks and thrifts to meet the credit needs of the communities from which they accept deposits.

A number of issues emerged in the legislative debate over FIRREA that could not be resolved in the framework of the act. Instead, Congress stipulated that studies on these issues be undertaken. The Treasury was instructed to study the feasibility of changing the federal deposit insurance programs so that banks' and thrifts' deposit insurance premiums would be assessed on risk rather than on deposit size.

A feasibility study of market value accounting for banks and thrifts also was ordered. Under current bank accounting rules, banks and thrifts carry the value of investments on their books at purchase price. Changes in the market value of those investments are not reflected on the balance sheet unless they are sold or mature. Advocates of market value accounting contend that by requiring banks and thrifts to reflect the market value of their assets on their balance sheets, depositors, stockholders, and regulators could get a more timely and accurate measure of a bank's financial condition. Opponents contend that market value accounting would provide a distorted measure of the financial condition of banks and thrifts that could prove more confusing than current balance sheets.

Congress also instructed the Treasury to study the adequacy of credit unions' capital and instructed the Federal Reserve to examine bank costs and banks' use of service charges and transaction fees with a view toward addressing public perceptions that bank service charges had become excessive. The findings of all these studies are expected to provide the foundation for more fundamental reform of banking rules and practices in the 1990s.

Extended Study 5
Bank Holding Companies

In the 1950s, concern over the potential for concentration in banking posed by bank holding companies (BHCs), and concern that the activities of BHCs could lead to unsound banking practices, moved Congress to legislate federal control over bank holding companies. The Bank Holding Company Act of 1956 applied federal antitrust laws to the activities of multibank holding companies. It also gave the Federal Reserve the power to approve or deny applications from multibank holding companies wanting to acquire additional banks or engage in new business activities. The act limited the nonbanking activities of multibank holding companies to those directly related to banking. Twelve bank holding companies that had formed multistate networks prior to 1956 were permitted to continue providing banking services outside their home states.

Companies that controlled only one bank (one-bank holding companies) were not covered by the 1956 act, primarily because very few such companies existed then. However, in the mid-1960s, many banks began to adopt the one-bank holding company structure as a means to move into broader markets, new activities, and new locations. In 1970, Congress amended the Bank Holding Company Act to cover one-bank holding companies.

Activities of BHCs

Since the 1960s, the Federal Reserve has approved a broad range of separate activities for bank holding companies, allowing them to provide the following banking-related services:

- issuing credit cards
- providing trust services
- selling general and portfolio investment advice, general economic information, and bookkeeping and data processing services
- providing courier services
- providing management consulting services
- issuing traveler's checks and money orders
- dealing in bankers' acceptances and brokering gold bullion
- providing services associated with mortgage banking, finance companies, factoring companies, trust companies, collection agencies, and credit bureaus
- servicing loans
- acting as insurance agents or brokers for credit extensions and underwriting credit-related life, accident, and health insurance
- leasing personal and real property and providing land escrow services
- sponsoring, organizing, or controlling a closed-end investment company
- acting as a general insurance agent in towns with populations of less than 5,000
- providing investment services that promote the welfare of the community
- providing securities brokerage services
- selling property insurance of $10,000 or less through finance company subsidiaries
- providing advisory services for those seeking to buy commodities or foreign exchange
- acting as futures commission merchants
- selling financial counseling, tax planning, and tax preparation services to consumers
- underwriting and dealing in revenue bonds, commercial paper, mortgage-backed securities, and consumer-related receivables
- underwriting and dealing in corporate bonds and corporate stock as long as the revenue from these activities does not exceed 10 percent of the subsidiary's total revenue
- providing financial advisory services to institutions and high net worth individuals
- offering combined investment advisory and securities brokerage services

The Federal Reserve's Criteria

Activities and acquisitions of bank holding companies must be "closely and properly related to banking," according to the Bank Holding Company Act. The Federal Reserve Board uses this criteria to evaluate applications from bank holding companies to engage in new activities.

In determining whether a proposed activity is closely related to banking, the Federal Reserve must examine whether the activity is:

- ❏ one in which banks have traditionally engaged
- ❏ so closely related to traditional banking activities that banks would be well equipped to engage in the activity
- ❏ integrally related to permissible banking activities

If any of these criteria apply, the proposed activity is deemed closely related to banking.

The Federal Reserve must then determine whether the proposed activity is properly related to banking by evaluating the public benefits and costs likely to be associated with the activity.

If, in the Fed's judgment, the holding company's activity would clearly lead to substantial market concentration, decreased or unfair competition, conflicts of interest, or unsound banking practices, it denies the request.

To approve an activity, the Board must be convinced that the activity meets a public need or provides a clear social benefit. In effect, the holding company must present a strong, documented case that shows the Board how the holding company's provision of the new service would generate benefits to the public—such as greater convenience, greater service selection, lower price or more efficiency.

In many applications, the Federal Reserve finds evidence that the proposed activity works both for and against the public good. In those cases, the Federal Reserve Board decides on the basis of net public benefits—that is, it weighs the benefits that would likely accrue against the potential social costs. Land development and commodity trading are two activities that bank holding companies have been prohibited from engaging in because the Board decided that these activities were not closely or properly related to banking—in effect, they failed the net public benefits test.

Under the complex U.S. bank regulatory and supervisory structure, national banks are subject to the rulings of the Office of the Comptroller of the Currency (OCC), their prime regulator. Over the past three decades, the OCC has authorized national banks to provide the same services granted by the Federal Reserve to bank holding companies. However, there have been some anomalies.

In the 1970s, the Federal Reserve Board would not allow bank holding companies to operate travel agencies, a service that about 150 banks—some state chartered, some nationally chartered—were providing at that time. The OCC ruled that this activity was permissible for nationally chartered banks. That gave rise to a situation in which a bank holding company could not operate a travel agency directly, but could provide the service through its nationally chartered bank subsidiary. In a similar anomaly, the Federal Reserve denied real estate brokerage to bank holding companies, but the OCC granted it to nationally chartered banks.

In the 1980s, the Federal Reserve reassessed some it its net public benefits criteria. For example, bank holding companies were allowed to acquire thrift institutions if the thrift could not otherwise remain in business. The severe deposit losses thrift institutions experienced in the 1980s and the Fed's concern for the future viability of the thrift industry prompted this policy change. However, the Federal Reserve deliberately slowed its granting of new powers to holding companies, contending that the banking system and bank regulators needed time to evaluate the changes bank holding companies were bringing to the nation's financial system and the competitive and public benefit effects these changes might have. But bankers contended that this policy slowdown impaired banks' ability to compete with brokerage firms, life insurance companies, and other nonbank institutions that had begun to offer banking services.

In the mid-1980s, the banking industry sought to convince Congress that federal legislation allowing banks to provide insurance, underwriting, and brokerage services was needed to maintain competitive equality among financial institutions. By the late 1980s, however, Congress had not acted and the banking industry shifted its efforts to state legislatures, the courts, and the regulatory agencies. Those efforts helped banks achieve limited underwriting powers for their holding company affiliates in many states and expanded powers in others. Almost half the states authorized state-chartered banks to provide insurance, real estate, brokerage or underwriting services in the 1980s. Some states also permitted banks to invest in corporate stock and real estate development projects.

In 1992, Congress was considering several bills that would permit banks in all states to affiliate with brokerage and dealer firms, to underwrite and sell corporate stocks and bonds without limitations, to permit bank holding company affiliates to sell insurance and mutual funds, and to allow commercial and industrial companies to own bank holding companies.

Source of Strength Doctrine

In regulating bank holding companies, the Federal Reserve has long relied on the source-of-strength doctrine that says that bank holding companies must serve as a source of strength for their subsidiary banks, providing them with capital and other assistance if they run into difficulties. The policy was established to ensure that bank holding companies would support weak subsidiary banks rather than letting them become insolvent, thereby shifting the cost of their failures from their parent holding companies to the FDIC.

The source-of-strength doctrine was not at issue in the 1960s and 1970s because bank holding companies were not pervasive and only 120 banks had failed during both decades. In the 1980s, however, the doctrine became a point of contention between bankers and the Federal Reserve—two-thirds of all banks had become subsidiaries of holding companies and close to 1,000 banks had failed. In 1989, the Federal Reserve initiated a civil suit against Mcorp, which was the second largest bank holding company in Texas before it declared bankruptcy that year. The Federal Reserve maintained that Mcorp had failed to act as a source of strength for its subsidiary banks. Before Mcorp filed for bankruptcy, the OCC had declared 20 of its 25 subsidiary banks insolvent. Closing those banks and paying off depositors cost the FDIC about $2 billion.

Mcorp challenged the Federal Reserve's suit, arguing that the Fed had no legal basis for imposing the source-of-strength doctrine on bank holding companies. The Federal court agreed and noted that if holding companies were required to provide funds to troubled subsidiary banks, they would be wasting their assets, impairing their creditworthiness, and violating their duties to their stockholders. However, the Federal Reserve appealed the ruling to the U.S. Supreme Court, maintaining that nullification of the doctrine would create a regulatory vacuum that could pose substantial risks to the banking system.

In 1991, the Supreme Court ruled in favor of the Federal Reserve, although it did not directly address the legality of the source-of-strength doctrine. That issue, however, is no longer in dispute. Congress enacted legislation authorizing the Federal Reserve to impose the source of strength doctrine on bank holding companies. The 1991 law that bolstered the deposit insurance fund (the Federal Deposit Insurance Corporation Improvement Act) also requires undercapitalized banks to provide regulators with a plan for selling stock, reducing assets, or borrowing funds to rebuild capital. Bank holding companies not only have to guarantee that undercapitalized bank subsidiaries follow their plans but can be required by the Federal Reserve to provide needed capital that is not otherwise obtained. A holding company's maximum capital contribution would be limited, however, to an amount equal to 5 percent of the holding company's total assets.

The Bank Merger Acts of 1960 and 1966

In the 1950s, before banks began using holding companies as a means to expand their size and markets, bank mergers were the primary method of expansion. Bank mergers always required approval of the bank regulatory authorities, and until 1960 approval was usually granted. Little consideration was given to the potential effects of mergers on competition. However, a wave of bank mergers in the 1950s, many of them involving large city banks, prompted Congress to enact the Bank Merger Act of 1960. This act established jurisdiction of the various bank regulatory agencies over bank mergers and made federal antitrust laws applicable to bank mergers. It also established public-interest evaluation criteria to assess the acceptability of proposed mergers, particularly in relation to their effects on competition. Other criteria for bank mergers addressed capital adequacy, future earnings prospects, and management capability.

The Supreme Court handed down decisions on several proposed mergers that were contested by the Justice Department in the early 1960s. In so doing it established some key principles for determining whether a bank merger conformed to the Bank Merger Act. For example, the Court held that commercial banks were subject to provisions of the Clayton Antitrust Act, which makes illegal all combinations (mergers) that are in restraint of trade. In addition, the Court ruled that commercial banking was a separate line of commerce, thus requiring a narrow definition of the relevant market for a bank's business. Those principles blunted the pace of bank mergers by precluding mergers of banks that were significant competitors in the same market (since that would constitute an unreasonable or illegal restraint of trade).

In 1966, Congress enacted a second Bank Merger Act in an attempt to clarify the 1960 law. The 1966 law established that mergers that would substantially lessen competition could not be approved unless there were substantial, overriding public interest benefits. Moreover, it required the bank regulatory agencies to consider whether a proposed merger would lessen potential competition between the merged banks.

The passage of the Bank Merger Act of 1966 eliminated some of the controversy surrounding bank mergers and further slowed their pace until the 1980s.

Bank Mergers in the 1980s

The 1980s saw a strong resurgence in bank merger activity. This, in part, reflected the banking industry's response to the removal of longstanding state restrictions on interstate banking and anticipation that Congress might soon allow interstate branching. (By 1992, all but eight states had ended prohibitions against statewide branching and all but two states had ended entry prohibitions against out-of-state banks.) Some banks merged to protect themselves against eventual out-of-state takeovers. Other banks merged to expand their banking markets into other states. The expansion of intrastate branching in many states also served as a stimulus for some multibank holding companies to consolidate their bank affiliates into larger units.

Another factor was the increase in competition brought about by deregulation of interest rate ceilings on deposits (Regulation Q). Some smaller banks and less profitable banks found it difficult to survive. Mergers allowed those banks to become bigger or to join with stronger banks.

A change in antitrust standards applicable to banks also helped propel the bank merger movement of the 1980s. The change originated in two banking laws—the Monetary Control Act of 1980 and the Garn-St Germain Act of 1982. By giving substantial commercial banking powers to thrift institutions, both laws weakened the principle that commercial banking was a separate line of commerce—the principle that had long served as a basis for preventing bank competitors in the same banking market from merging.

In reaction to this, bank regulators and the Justice Department broadened their measures of banking markets to include thrifts. By counting thrifts as competitors of banks, bank mergers that would have been denied before 1980 were readily approved. In 1985, the FDIC adopted an even broader standard for determining market concentration by including the competition banks face from nonbank financial intermediaries.

Bank regulators also softened their application of merger guidelines that disallow bank mergers that reduce competition. They did that by allowing merged banks to sell off branches or deposits to promote competition and thereby meet regulatory standards. Prior to 1980, bank regulators rarely allowed such divestitures.

Bank Mergers in the 1990s

The 1990s saw the beginnings of the mergers of very large banks in the same geographic area—not to expand their markets, but to improve their profits, strengthen the efficiency of their operations and reduce their operating costs. For example, in California, Bank of America merged with Security Pacific in 1992 to form the second largest bank in the U.S. ($153 billion in assets). In New York, Chemical Bank merged with Manufacturers Hanover Bank to form the third largest U.S. bank ($109 billion in assets).

For large banks, mergers tend to reduce costs in back-office operations, such as those related to check collection, accounting and electronic funds transfer. Costs are reduced because the merged bank can usually absorb the combined back-office workload of both banks without having to retain all the buildings and equipment, operating systems, and technical personnel of both banks. Cost reductions are also generated from the closing of duplicate branches and the release of redundant front-office personnel.

Consumer Banks

In the 1980s, brokerage firms, mutual funds, retail stores, and other nonbank companies seeking to enter the banking business, as well as bank holding companies eager to operate banks outside their home states, found a loophole in the Bank Holding Company Act that enabled them to achieve their objectives. The Bank Holding Company Act narrowly defined a commercial bank as an institution that offers demand deposits and makes business loans. Business firms discovered that they could escape federal regulation under the act by purchasing a bank and then divesting it of either its demand deposits or its business loans. A bank that lacked one of these characteristics became, in effect, a *nonbank bank*, or a *consumer bank*.

That loophole meant that such companies as Sears and J.C. Penney could provide banking services through a consumer bank subsidiary without having to divest themselves of activities not permitted to bank holding companies. It also meant that bank holding companies owning consumer banks could provide banking services outside their home states without having to obtain the permission of those states, as was required by the Bank Holding Company Act.

In 1987, Congress amended the Bank Holding Company Act to close the loophole. It redefined a commercial bank as any institution insured by the FDIC, thus effectively precluding brokerage firms, insurance companies, retail stores, and other nonbank companies from establishing new consumer bank subsidiaries. However, Congress included a grandfather clause exempting the nearly 200 consumer banks that had been established before 1987.

Exhibit 3.5 in chapter 3 lists some of the major nonbank corporations that operate consumer banks under the grandfather clause.

In the 1990s, Congress has sought to address competitive and regulatory issues raised by the existence of consumer banks. These issues have included who should be allowed to own banks, whether banking should be regulated as a separate line of commerce, and whether bank holding companies should be allowed to underwrite stocks and bonds without restrictions and provide brokerage, insurance, and real estate services. However, through mid-1992, Congress and the administration have been unable to reach a consensus on these issues.

Extended Study 6
The Federal Reserve's Statement of Condition

The Federal Reserve issues a weekly financial profile, or consolidated statement of condition, of the 12 Federal Reserve banks. This statement of condition reflects all of the central bank's activities, as well as its special role in the banking system and the economy as the ultimate source of all money.

Figure 1 shows the Federal Reserve's statement of condition, or balance sheet, as of September 1992. As you examine it, you will see that the Federal Reserve has some assets and liabilities similar to those of large correspondent banks, while others are clearly unique to the central bank. By far the principal asset category for Reserve banks is U.S. government securities, while Federal Reserve notes constitute their principal category of liability.

The key difference between the Federal Reserve's books and those of large commercial banks is the way in which the Federal Reserve acquires assets and liabilities. Each time it obtains an asset (and a corresponding liability), it either creates reserves for banks, which adds to their ability to make loans (and create money), or it creates deposits for the Treasury, which adds to the government's ability to spend money.

FIGURE 1   **Federal Reserve Banks' Consolidated Statement of Condition, September 1992**
(billions of dollars)

Assets		Liabilities and Capital Accounts	
Gold certificate account	$11.1	Federal Reserve notes	$300.1
Special drawing rights		Reserve deposits	32.2
certificate account	10.0	U.S. Treasury account	4.0
Coin	0.5	Foreign government accounts	0.2
Loans	0.2	Other accounts	0.3
U.S. government securities	286.2	Deferred availability cash items	7.7
Federal agency securities	5.5	Other liabilities and	
		accrued dividends	1.8
Cash items in process of			
collection	7.9	Total liabilities	346.3
Bank premises	1.0	Capital Accounts	
Foreign currency assets	25.0	Capital paid in	3.0
Other assets	5.2	Surplus	2.6
		Other capital	0.7
		Total capital accounts	6.3
		Total liabilities and	
Total assets	$352.6	capital accounts	$352.6

Assets

As seen in figure 1, the combined assets of the Federal Reserve banks in September 1992 totaled $352.6 billion. Many of the assets listed in the balance sheet of the Federal Reserve are the same as those of large correspondent banks. For example, both the Federal Reserve and large commercial banks hold substantial portfolios of government securities. On the other hand, only the Federal Reserve can hold assets in the form of gold certificates and special drawing rights credits. We will look at each asset account in turn.

Gold Certificate Account

The Gold Certificate Account, the first asset category on the Federal Reserve banks' consolidated balance sheet, is a remnant from earlier decades when Federal Reserve notes issued by the Reserve banks and Federal Reserve deposit liabilities had to be backed by gold. Statutory minimum gold-backing requirements against those Federal Reserve liabilities were abolished in 1965 for deposits and in 1968 for notes. However, each Reserve bank must still maintain collateral equal to the amount of its Federal Reserve notes outstanding. Although the collateral can be virtually any Reserve bank asset, the Reserve banks continue to pledge their gold certificate credits as collateral against issued notes.

The Reserve banks acquired gold certificates (now bookkeeping credits) over the years from the Treasury. When the Treasury bought gold, it would monetize the gold by issuing gold certificates to the Federal Reserve for an equal amount of dollars credited to its demand deposit account at the Reserve banks. Monetization enabled the Treasury to replenish its checking account without having to borrow or draw on tax receipts. It received dollars created for it by the Federal Reserve. The Federal Reserve, in turn, received gold certificates it needed as backing for its note issues and deposit liabilities.

Today, those gold certificate credits serve primarily as an internal medium of exchange among the Reserve banks. Reserve banks settle daily amounts due each other by transferring gold certificate credits to each other's books through the Interdistrict Settlement Account, an account maintained in Washington, D.C. Because amounts due are settled by increasing or decreasing the gold certificate balances held by each Reserve bank, the gold certificates held by the Federal Reserve are continually being redistributed within the system. However, the total remains the same; in recent years, this asset entry on the consolidated statement has rarely changed.

Special Drawing Rights Certificate Account

The Special Drawing Rights Certificate Account represents the U.S. allocation from the International Monetary Fund (IMF) of special drawing rights, an internationally accepted medium of exchange that was created by international treaty in 1969. The Federal Reserve banks acquired special drawing rights (SDR) certificate credits from the Treasury after it monetized the SDRs received from the IMF. As with gold monetization, when the Treasury monetizes SDRs, it issues certificates (credits) to the Federal Reserve. In return, it receives an equivalent amount of dollars posted to its checking account at the Reserve banks.

Coin

The next asset category shows the amount of coin currently on hand in Federal Reserve bank vaults (about $500 million in 1992). Coin held by the Reserve banks is a Federal Reserve asset because all U.S. coinage is issued by the Treasury, and thus is a direct liability of the government, not of the Federal Reserve. The Federal Reserve distributes coin to the nation's banking system in its operational role as the central bank, and it receives excess coin from banks for credit to their accounts at the Federal Reserve.

Loans

The entry under loans represents outstanding credit extended by Federal Reserve banks to depository institutions at the discount window. About $200 million in loans was outstanding in September 1992.

Virtually all discount window loans today are advances. An advance is a loan made on the borrowing bank's own promissory note secured by government securities, paper eligible for discounting, or other collateral acceptable to the Federal Reserve. In the past, most discount window loans were made against the short-term commercial, industrial, or agricultural paper of a bank's customers; this paper was then rediscounted by the Reserve banks. That practice was so closely identified with the Federal Reserve that most of the financial press and the academic community still refer to Reserve bank loans as *discount window loans*, and the Federal Reserve still refers to its interest rate charge for those loans as the *discount rate*.

Under the Monetary Control Act of 1980, all depository institutions, including thrifts, were granted the same access to Federal Reserve loans as member banks. The Federal Reserve Act also gives the Reserve banks power to lend money to foreign governments and central banks (which the Federal Reserve has done), as well as to individuals, partnerships, and corporations under conditions of national economic emergency (which the Federal Reserve has never done). The Federal Reserve has in recent years administered government loans to major American companies in dire financial distress—Lockheed Aircraft and the Chrysler Corporation, for example—on behalf of the U.S. Treasury, but the Federal Reserve has never used its own power to lend funds directly to entities other than depositories.

The System Open Market Account Portfolio

The U.S. government securities and federal agency securities that appear on the consolidated statement are the securities that are purchased by the Federal Reserve Bank of New York for the System Open Market Account. These purchases are made through open-market operations in accordance with the directives of the Federal Open Market Committee. Ownership of the System Open Market Account portfolio, like ownership of the Gold Certificate Account, is proportionally divided among all the

Reserve banks. The exception is securities held under repurchase agreements, which are carried only on the books of the Federal Reserve Bank of New York.

U.S. GOVERNMENT SECURITIES

The category of U.S. government securities represents the total amount of Treasury bills, certificates, notes, and bonds that the Federal Reserve has bought in the open market from dealers in government securities. It is by far the largest asset category, accounting for more than 80 percent of the Reserve banks' assets in September 1992.

On occasion, the Federal Reserve buys government securities from dealers under repurchase agreements; the dealers agree to repurchase the securities within a short, specified period of time. These agreements are used when the Federal Reserve wants to provide a temporary and self-reversing injection of reserves into the banking system. They would be recorded as a separate asset entry on the Federal Reserve's balance sheet.

FEDERAL AGENCY SECURITIES

Federal agency securities represent the securities issued by agencies of the federal government (excluding the Treasury). Federal agencies that have been established to implement the government's farm and home lending programs generally issue securities to finance their activities. Most of these securities are guaranteed, not by the U.S. government, but by the agencies themselves. In 1966, Congress authorized the Federal Reserve to buy or sell federal agency securities in its open-market operations to support the fledgling agency securities market. Again, any Federal Reserve purchases of federal agency securities under repurchase agreements are recorded as a separate asset entry on the consolidated statement.

Cash Items in Process of Collection

The Federal Reserve banks, like all other banks, show cash items in process of collection—that is, checks and other items payable on demand that are in the process of being cleared—as a separate asset account. The amount in this category represents the value of all the checks deposited with the Federal Reserve banks for collection and which, on the date of the statement, are still in the process of being collected.

Bank Premises

This balance sheet entry reflects the value of the land, buildings, and equipment of the 12 Federal Reserve banks and their 25 branches.

Foreign Currency Assets

Foreign currency assets are assets denominated in foreign money. Most are acquired by the Federal Reserve through *swap* drawings in its international role as the U.S. central bank. In a swap drawing, the Federal Reserve and a foreign central bank exchange, or swap, a predetermined amount of each other's currencies for several months. The exchanged currency is then used in the foreign exchange markets to stabilize exchange rates.

Other Assets

The Federal Reserve accrues interest on the government securities it owns or is holding under repurchase agreements. It also earns interest on loans made to depository institutions and foreign central banks, and on foreign currency investments that may have been made in support of its role in stabilizing the value of the dollar in foreign exchange markets. Those accumulated interest earnings are recorded as *other assets*.

Liabilities and Capital Accounts

As with any balance sheet, the left side (assets) of the Federal Reserve banks' consolidated statement of condition must equal the right side (liabilities plus capital accounts). Again, many of the liabilities listed on the balance sheet of the Federal Reserve are the same as those of large commercial banks. For example, both show the demand deposit liabilities of other banks. On the other hand, only the Federal Reserve records currency as a liability.

Federal Reserve Notes

Today, virtually all the nation's paper currency consists of Federal Reserve notes issued by the 12 Reserve banks. This entry on the liability side of the statement represents all Federal Reserve notes in circulation—including what is held by the public, by banks, and by the Treasury. This entry, which came to just more than $300 billion in 1992, is not the same as the currency component of any measure of the money supply. It does, however, serve as a broad gauge on a week-to-week and year-to-year basis of the economy's preference for cash.

Reserve Deposits

The entry for reserve deposits represents the total amount of reserves that depository institutions maintain at the Reserve banks. All depositories are required to meet the Federal Reserve's reserve requirements under the Monetary Control Act of 1980. Those reserve requirements can be satisfied either with vault cash or with demand balances at the Federal Reserve. Most of the nation's small depository institutions can meet their reserve requirements with the vault cash they keep in the normal course of business.

U.S. Treasury Account

The U.S. Treasury account is the balance in the general checking account of the Treasury from which virtually all government checks are drawn. This is by no means a measure of the government's entire money holdings. The Treasury maintains the bulk of the government's money in thousands of Treasury tax and loan (TT&L) accounts at commercial banks and thrifts throughout the country. Most tax receipts and funds received from the Treasury's sale of new government securities are deposited into TT&L accounts to minimize the impact of tax collections and Treasury borrowings on bank reserves.

If the Treasury maintained only one account at the Federal Reserve, tax payments and public purchases of Treasury securities would result in a transfer of reserves from banks to the Federal Reserve, reducing the ability of banks to make loans. That would be the case because checks that were written to pay taxes and buy new Treasury securities would be deposited at the Federal Reserve for collection and credited to the Treasury's general account. Instead, when the government needs money to cover anticipated checks, the Treasury transfers funds from its TT&L accounts to its account at the Federal Reserve.

Foreign Government Accounts

Foreign government accounts represent the demand deposit balances of foreign governments and their central banks held at the Federal Reserve. Transactions for these accounts are handled by the Federal Reserve Bank of New York in its role as operating arm for the Federal Reserve System and the government in international economic matters. However, the deposit liabilities are allocated among all the Reserve banks.

Other Accounts

The entry for *other accounts* includes several deposit categories. The most important of these are the demand balances of international financial organizations, the special checking accounts of the Treasury used in foreign exchange dealings, and the demand accounts of certain U.S. government agencies.

Deferred Availability Cash Items

This entry represents the amount of checks and other cash items that have been received by the Federal Reserve banks for collection, but which will not be credited to the depositing banks' accounts for another one to two days. Reserve banks defer credit according to a time schedule that, in theory, allows time for out-of-town checks to be mailed or transported to the banks on which they are drawn. However, after a maximum of two business days, reserve accounts are credited whether or not the item has actually been collected from the bank on which it was drawn.

Other Liabilities and Accrued Dividends

This category reflects liabilities that the Federal Reserve is accumulating to pay its statutory dividend on Federal Reserve bank stock owned by member banks.

Capital Accounts

The Federal Reserve's capital accounts include capital paid in, surplus, and other capital. In September 1992, the Federal Reserve held $6.3 billion in its capital accounts.

CAPITAL PAID IN

This shows the amount that member banks have paid for Federal Reserve banks' capital stock.

SURPLUS

Surplus reflects the earnings that the Federal Reserve is required by law to retain as a reserve against unforeseen losses.

OTHER CAPITAL

Other capital is the amount of earnings of the Federal Reserve since its last payment of dividends to member bank stockholders and its last payment of interest to the Treasury on Federal Reserve notes (the accounting method used to transfer earnings to the Treasury).

Extended Study 7
Evolution of the Discount Window and the Discount Rate

When the Federal Reserve was established in 1913, the discount rate was the only monetary policy tool authorized by Congress. The economy of 1913 was much different than today's economy, as was the understanding of economists and bankers of how the economy worked and what role the central bank should play in it. Until the 1930s, the Federal Reserve operated passively, responding to changes in the economy's monetary needs but not actively promoting such changes. Its role in the economy was guided by the automatic, self-regulating principles of a doctrine known as the *real bills* or *commercial loan* theory. This doctrine maintained that the economy would balance itself automatically if the nation's supply of money was pegged to the short-term (90-day), self-liquidating inventory loans (commercial loans) made by banks to business and agriculture.

The Commercial Loan Theory

While the commercial loan theory held sway, member banks deposited their reserves with the Federal Reserve banks and in turn, obtained access to credit from the Reserve banks through discount window loans. The Reserve banks' exclusive power to issue paper currency was limited by collateral (backing) requirements tied to the Reserve banks' discount window loans.

When banks reached their lending capacity and had no excess reserves against which new loans could be made, they could obtain additional reserves from Reserve banks by borrowing at the discount window. To obtain credit from the Reserve banks, however, member commercial banks had to present eligible paper for rediscounting. Eligible paper consisted only of the short-term loans (IOUs) that banks had made to businesses and farmers to enable them to buy or manufacture inventories. That narrow definition of eligible paper was based on the belief that only short-term inventory loans were truly supportive of economic growth, and that only a growing economy needed additional money.

The Federal Reserve banks, by making loans to member banks through the discount window, obtained the private IOUs of bank customers—the banks' short-term loan paper. That paper was essential for the issuance of Federal Reserve notes because, under the Federal Reserve Act, Federal Reserve notes had to be backed (collateralized) by 40 percent gold and 100 percent eligible paper. Thus, the supply of paper currency also was linked to the growth of the economy.

According to the commercial loan theory, in a growing economy, demand for short-term inventory loans would be strong and banks would be active lenders. As banks rediscounted their customers' commercial paper at the Federal Reserve's discount window, they would receive additional reserves against which they could expand loans (create demand deposits). Meanwhile, the Federal Reserve would receive additional collateral against which it could issue currency. A growing economy called for more money, and the commercial loan theory seemed to provide the mechanism for supplying it.

The Effects of Recession and Inflation

The commercial loan theory, however, was based on the false premise that short-term commercial loans or *real bills* were always self-liquidating. A business that borrowed from a bank for 90 days to build up its inventories was expected always to be in a position to repay the bank as soon as it sold the inventories. Indeed, the inventories themselves were collateral for the original loan. However, things did not always work as expected. When the economy moved into recession and demand for goods and services slumped, so did demand for loans. Corporations that had borrowed often found themselves unable to sell enough of their inventories to repay earlier loans. Defaulted loans resulted in liquidity problems for banks, but banks that lacked additional eligible paper could not obtain funds from the Federal Reserve. Thus, in times of recession, the commercial loan theory led to further economic contraction and illiquidity for banks.

In periods of inflation, the commercial loan theory also failed. Businesses found that with rising prices, the money value of their inventories rose too, enabling them to borrow more from banks. Rising inventory values allowed banks to obtain more reserves from the Federal Reserve against their inflated loans and in turn gave the Federal Reserve more collateral for expanded currency issuance. Thus, when prices were rising rapidly, the Federal Reserve's adherence to the commercial loan theory added to inflation. In fact, its adherence to the strictures of this theory helps explain why the Federal Reserve could not cope with the collapse of the economy and the banking system in the early 1930s.

Regional Discount Rates

As envisioned in 1913, the commercial loan theory was to be complemented by different discount rates in each of the 12 Federal Reserve districts. Thus, each Reserve bank could pursue a separate monetary policy to accommodate its own region's economic needs. In theory, if developing industry in the South needed easier credit, the Federal Reserve banks of Atlanta and Richmond could set a low discount rate, which, in turn, would keep other lending rates in the region low. At the same time, if business expansion in the North threatened to generate inflation, the Federal Reserve banks of New York, Philadelphia, and Boston could set a high discount rate, which would keep loan rates high in the North and blunt excess lending and subsequent business spending pressure.

This theory quickly gave way to the reality that money and credit do not respect district boundaries—only interest rate differentials and profit incentives. With no impediments to the flow of money among districts, borrowers in the North where interest rates were high would shift loan demand to correspondents in the South where interest rates were low. In time, as money shifted from the South to the North, interest rates would rise in the money supply-depleted South and fall in the money supply-expanded North until a national equilibrium interest rate was reached. The power of the Reserve banks' directors to set the discount rate in their districts is the only vestige of this early approach to regional monetary policy.

Extended Study 8
Uniform Reserve Requirements

In the 1970s, as interest rates and inflation began to soar, banks became increasingly conscious of their profit margins and increasingly aware of the cost burden of the Federal Reserve's reserve requirements. An increasing number of banks withdrew from membership in the Federal Reserve, and few new banks opted for membership. Between 1970 and 1979, the Federal Reserve lost 550 member banks, about one bank per week. Moreover, toward the end of that decade, increasingly larger banks were withdrawing from membership. As a result, the percentage of the nation's banking deposits subject to direct Federal Reserve control declined, from about 80 percent in 1970 to 70 percent in 1979.

That decline in the Federal Reserve's control of the nation's banking deposits was exacerbated by the comparatively faster deposit growth of both nonmember banks and thrifts. In 1950, about 70 percent of all funds in depository institutions was in member banks; by the end of the 1970s, member banks accounted for only 45 percent of all funds.

The Federal Reserve saw the accelerating erosion of its membership base and its control over the banking system's deposits as a threat to its ability to control the nation's money supply and a threat to its broad role as the nation's central bank.

The Uniform Reserve Requirement Proposal

To solve those problems, the Federal Reserve in the mid-1970s asked Congress to amend the Federal Reserve Act to make both state-chartered and national banks subject to the same reserve requirements.

The Federal Reserve's proposal for uniform reserve requirements was not new. For decades it had been seen as a solution to the reserve requirement inequity between state-chartered and nationally chartered banks that had been generated by Congress in 1913. In fact, it almost had become law in the 1930s.

The Banking Act of 1933, which established federal deposit insurance and the FDIC, required state-chartered banks to join the Federal Reserve System by a specified date in order to qualify for insurance. If that provision had remained in force, it would have effectively created uniform reserve requirements through universal membership in the Federal Reserve. However, the Banking Act of 1935 extended the deadline, and before that date was reached, Congress repealed the membership requirement for state-chartered banks.

Uniform reserve requirements were again recommended by two congressional committees in 1950 and 1952, and were endorsed by the Commission on Money and Credit in 1961. They were reaffirmed by the President's Committee on Financial Institutions in 1963 and by the Hunt Commission in 1971—groups established expressly to study the nation's money and banking system and to recommend improvements. Still Congress failed to institute uniform reserve requirements.

Support and Opposition

The Federal Reserve's proposal for uniform reserve requirements became the centerpiece of banking and academic controversy and heated congressional debate throughout the 1970s. The Federal Reserve viewed universal reserve requirements as a more equitable arrangement and as a way to facilitate better management of the nation's money and credit.

Opponents of the Federal Reserve's proposal were primarily state-chartered banks, state banking regulators (specifically, the Conference of State Bank Supervisors), and some members of Congress. They viewed universal reserve requirements as an attack on the dual banking system, an unfair intrusion of the Federal Reserve into state banking regulation, and a bureaucratic grab for power. Some monetary economists also opposed the proposal on the grounds that it would not guarantee the Federal Reserve any greater degree of policy effectiveness and would be costly to large correspondent banks and small nonmember banks.

None of the opponents of the universal reserve requirement proposal, however, addressed the fundamental unfairness of the reserve requirement system that had prevailed in the United States since 1913, in which some commercial banks were "taxed" solely because they were members of the Federal Reserve.

Passage of the Monetary Control Act

The Federal Reserve argued that its reserve requirements served as a fulcrum for monetary policy. The reserve requirements provided a known and controllable base of reserves through which its monetary policy tools (primarily open-market operations) could affect the growth of the money supply in a reasonably predictable way. The varying reserve requirements set by the individual states did not, and could not, do this.

Under the Federal Reserve's rules, reserves had to be held either as vault cash or as funds deposited at a Federal Reserve bank, the only two assets whose supply is totally controllable by the Federal Reserve. Under the state rules, reserves could be satisfied not only with vault cash, but also with deposits at other banks or with interest-earning government securities. But reserves held in this way did not contribute to the leverage of monetary policy because they fell outside the central bank's control.

As noted previously, the growth of deposits outside the Federal Reserve's control in the 1970s weakened the relationship between reserves and money supply. Indeed, as the percentage of deposits held outside the Federal Reserve's control increased, so seemingly did the short-run variability in the growth of the money supply and the Federal Reserve's inability to control that growth. Movements of deposits between member and nonmember institutions (particularly thrifts) seemed to have altered the relationship between the Federal Reserve's control of bank reserves and the nation's total deposits.

In its attempts to restrain money supply growth during periods of inflationary excess in the 1970s, the Federal Reserve tended to increase bank reserves slowly. But the public was shifting deposits to nonmember banks and thrifts at the same time that the Federal Reserve was supplying reserves to member banks. As a result, money supply growth continued unchecked—in part because nonmembers' deposits required smaller, or different, reserves than those at member banks.

From 1960 through 1975, the demand deposit component of the nation's money supply held at nonmember banks grew by about 165 percent while such deposits held at member banks grew by only 60 percent. By the mid-1970s, about 25 percent of the nation's demand deposits were held at nonmember banks, compared with about 15 percent in 1960. Not only were demand deposits at nonmember banks growing faster than at member banks, but the deposit growth of nonmember banks experienced wider year-to-year variations than that of member banks. Those erratic growth rates compounded the Federal Reserve's monetary control problems.

The Monetary Control Act of 1980 sought to address a cluster of problems that had emerged in the U.S. banking system in the 1970s. The Federal Reserve's membership problem and need for stronger policy control were the foremost of these problems, which were addressed by subjecting all depository institutions to the same reserve requirements.

Extended Study 9
Capital Adequacy Standards

In 1988, the bank regulatory authorities of the major industrial nations—the United States, Great Britain and the other the Western European countries, and Japan—established common *risk-based* capital adequacy standards (capital funds as a percentage of a bank's total assets) for large banks involved in international banking. The standard was set at 7.25 percent for 1990 and 8 percent for 1992.

The new standards took into account not only the traditional loan and investment risks that banks incur, but the risks associated with business activities not recorded on the balance sheet. Major off-balance-sheet activities for which banks receive fee income involve loan commitments (binding agreements to lend funds to corporations at a future date) and standby letters of credit (which guarantee specific lending, investment, or business transactions of corporations). As large banks have increased their reliance on off-balance-sheet activities to generate income, bank regulators have become increasingly concerned over the size of the *contingent liabilities* that support those activities—that is, the liabilities (and risks) that the bank must assume if corporations exercise loan commitments and standby letters of credit.

In 1991, the U.S. bank regulatory authorities imposed risk-based capital standards on all American banks. The regulators had become concerned with the capital adequacy of all sizes of banks in response to the increased number of banks that had failed in the 1980s.

Under the capital adequacy standards, banks must meet two *risk-based* capital-to-asset ratio requirements. Under the first requirement, banks must hold an amount of common and preferred stock (called Tier 1 capital) equal to at least 4 percent of their risk-weighted assets. Under the second requirement, banks must hold Tier 1 capital plus other types of stock, subordinated debt, loan loss reserves (up to 1.25 percent of risk-based assets), and debt convertible into stock (called Tier 2 capital) equal to at least 8 percent of their risk-weighted assets. In addition, banks must hold Tier 1 capital equal to at least 3 percent of their total unweighted assets. In practice, however, regulators require a higher percentage for all but the most well-managed banks. Figure 1 shows how banks matched up against risk-based capital standards in 1991.

Banks calculate these risk-based capital requirements by multiplying the amount of assets they have in different asset categories by a factor (weight) keyed to the credit risk (risk of default) of the category. Riskier assets have higher weights and require more capital. For example, a 100 percent weight is assigned to the most risky asset category—business and consumer loans and commercial real estate loans; a 50 percent weight is assigned to residential mortgages and state and local government bonds; a 20 percent weight to federal agency securities; and a zero percent weight to the least risky asset category—U.S. Treasury securities, government-backed mortgages, and mortgage-backed securities guaranteed by the Government National Mortgage Association.

FIGURE 1 **Risk-Based Capital Ratios, by Asset Size of Bank, Year-End 1991**

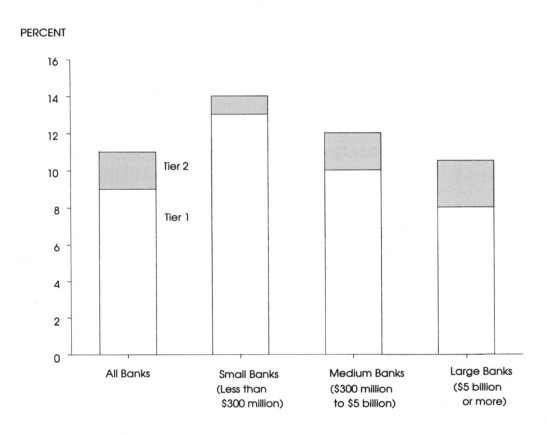

In 1991, Congress also enacted legislation that requires bank regulators to impose progressively stricter restrictions against banks or thrifts whose capital declines. Under the sanctions in effect in late 1992, banks are first placed into one of five categories, based on their capital-to-asset ratios. The categories range from *critically undercapitalized* to *well capitalized*. Then, specific restrictions are applied to banks in the three most undercapitalized categories, as described below.

1. *Critically undercapitalized.* Any bank that has an unweighted Tier 1 capital-to-asset ratio of 2 percent or less will be taken over by the regulators within 90 days. In mid-1992, about 50 banks with more than $20 billion in assets were in this most deficient category.

2. *Significantly undercapitalized.* Banks with risk-based capital-to-asset ratios of less than 6 percent and unweighted Tier 1 capital ratios under 3 percent will not be able to accept brokered CDs, raise their officers' salaries, or pay out bonuses.

Regulators can also limit the interest these banks pay on deposits and can fire senior management. About 50 banks were in this second most deficient capital category in 1992.

3. *Undercapitalized.* Any bank with a risk-based Tier 1 plus Tier 2 capital ratio of less than 8 percent and a unweighted Tier 1 capital ratio of less than 4 percent will not be allowed to increase its assets, expand into new markets, or accept brokered CDs. Moreover, such banks will have to submit a capital restoration plan to the regulators within 45 days. About 150 banks were in this third weakest category in 1992; together with the 50 banks in category two, they held more than $60 billion in assets.

4. *Adequately capitalized.* Banks with risk-based capital-to-asset ratios of at least 8 percent and unweighted Tier 1 capital ratios of 4 percent will not be subject to any regulatory restrictions, although they will need prior FDIC permission to accept brokered CDs. In mid-1992, some 550 banks with $1.2 trillion in assets were deemed to be adequately capitalized.

5. *Well capitalized.* About 11,100 banks with more than $1.7 trillion in assets were categorized as well-capitalized in 1992. This strongest designation is given to any bank that has a risk-based capital-to-asset ratio of 10 percent or more, and an unweighted Tier 1 capital ratio of at least 5 percent. Banks in this category can continue to attract brokered CDs without prior FDIC permission.

Figure 1 shows that larger banks have risk-based capital-to-asset ratios that are considerably lower than small banks. Larger banks have not only had to face new requirements to come up with additional capital in the late 1980s and early 1990s, but were also faced with erosions to capital caused by regulators' demands for additional loan loss reserves. Larger banks have had to set aside substantial additional reserves against anticipated losses on troubled LDC debt and commercial real estate loans made in the 1980s. On the balance sheet, when a bank has to add to its loan loss reserves, the additional reserves are subtracted from the bank's capital (and are subtracted from the value of the bank's loans), thus reducing the bank's capital base. Funds routinely set aside to cover losses are included as *other liabilities*. In mid-1992, the vast majority of banks were meeting the 1992 *risk-based* capital-to-asset ratio requirements.

LDC Debt and Loan Loss Reserves

In 1987, most of the nation's large money center banks and dozens of major regional banks substantially increased their loss reserves against loans made in the 1970s and early 1980s to less-developed countries (LDCs) in Latin America and Asia—primarily Brazil, Mexico, Argentina, Venezuela, and the Philippines. Setting aside funds for LDC loan loss reserves meant substantial reductions in profits for those banks because most of their outstanding LDC loans were large and because loss reserve funds are taken from current earnings.

The movement among banks to increase loss reserves against LDC loans was regarded favorably by most bank analysts and investors in bank stock. They reasoned that because bankers were making more realistic assessments of the risk posed by loans outstanding to LDCs (thereby in effect absorbing future losses in the present), banks would be less vulnerable to future deterioration in prospects for repayment of LDC loans.

In 1987, 15 U.S. banks had debt exposures on LDC loans of more than $1 billion each, for a total of $63 billion in outstanding LDC debt. Those banks had set aside close to $18 billion in loan loss reserves covering, on average, about 28 percent of their risk exposure.

Some bank analysts contended that reserves closer to 50 percent of the loan totals (the margin maintained by most major regional banks against their LDC debt) would more accurately reflect near-term LDC loan repayment prospects. Other observers maintained, however, that a move by the large banks to match the LDC loan reserve margins of the regional banks would not necessarily bolster the financial strength of the large banks or benefit the banking system. A bank's financial strength does not change when it shifts funds to loan loss reserves. The shift is simply a bookkeeping transfer of funds from one account (shareholders' equity) to another account (loan loss reserves). Some analysts warned that if weaker banks increased their loan loss reserves to match the regional average, it could lead to substantial bookkeeping earnings "losses" and erode depositors' and investors' confidence in the soundness of these banks.

Extended Study 10
New Strategies for the 1990s

Most bankers have come to realize that there is no perfect way to manage assets and liabilities so that a bank can be assured that the interest it pays on deposits and borrowed funds will always be less than the interest it receives on earning assets. Working within this realization, however, many bankers have sought to gain greater control over interest rate spread in the 1990s by adopting some new strategies to supplement their management of assets and liabilities. These include the securitization of assets (banks issue securities backed by expected income from such assets as mortgages and credit card loans) and hedging in the futures market. A discussion of these and other strategies follows.

Securitization

Banks that practice securitization package their loans into securities and sell the securities to institutional investors. This strategy enables banks to obtain a new source of funds and to keep some revenue, in the form of servicing fees, from the packaged loans. At the same time, securitization can reduce banks' credit risk if the packaged loans are sold without recourse (a legal claim on the selling banks in the event of default). Loan assets securitized without recourse are no longer carried on the selling bank's balance sheet. Thus, the selling bank is not at risk if borrowers default and it does not have to include the loans as assets when it calculates how much capital it must maintain for regulatory purposes.

Hedging in the Futures Market

Banks that hedge in the futures market seek to reduce the exposure of their securities investments to rising interest rates by selling some of their securities in the futures market. A futures contract for securities is a commitment to buy or sell securities at a future date at an agreed price.

If a bank that engages in hedging expects interest rates to increase, it sells securities in the futures market, locking in a current price for the securities it will deliver at a future date. When interest rates rise, securities prices fall. However, the hedged bank does not sustain a capital loss on the securities it delivers under the futures contract because it locked in the current (higher) price before interest rates rose.

A bank that expects interest rates to fall (and securities prices to increase) can hedge by buying in the futures market. Thus, when rates fall, the hedged bank receives its securities at the lower price agreed to before interest rates fell.

Other Strategies

Banks are seeking to increase their fee income—from selling mutual funds, processing transactions, and charging borrowers higher fees for committing to loans in advance. By imposing high loan commitment fees on borrowers, banks cover the opportunity cost incurred in committing to loans in advance. In the 1980s, banks' noninterest income grew faster than banks' assets, primarily because of loan commitment fees and standby letters of credit fees. The growing importance of fee income to banks can be seen in figure 1, which shows noninterest income accounting for 17 percent of revenues in 1991, compared with 7.5 percent in 1981.

FIGURE 1   **Growth of Noninterest Income as a Source of Commercial Bank Earnings**[1]

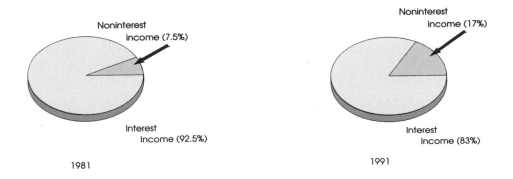

1981

1991

[1]Earnings exclude capital gains on securities sold from investment accounts.

Source: American Banker, September 4, 1992.

Banks are reducing the cost of their liabilities by lowering deposit rates. In fact, banks have been gradually reducing their deposit rates since 1989. For example, the interest rate paid on one-year savings certificates was cut repeatedly from 1989 to 1992 by more than six percentage points. In 1992, most banks also reduced the interest rate paid on passbook savings accounts to 2.75 percent, the lowest rate paid on those accounts since 1936.

Most banks reduced their loan charges in the late 1980s and early 1990s as well, but only about half as much as their reduction in deposit rates. The result of that strategy in 1992 was record growth in profits as banks sharply increased their interest rate spreads.

Some bankers contend that this strategy is unworkable over a long period because banks that cut deposit rates will lose deposits to competitors. However, industry analysts note that banks located in the same region frequently maintain deposit-rate differences on similar accounts of as much as one to two percentage points. Analysts also cite the quality of a bank's service and the convenience of its offices or ATMs as factors that tend to offset lower deposit rates in the view of many depositors.

Banks are seeking to reduce operating expenses and overhead costs by closing marginally profitable branches, selling product lines, cutting back on personalized customer services, restructuring operating departments, and downsizing their back-office staffs. Indeed, in 1991, the nation's 10 largest banks reduced their back-office staffs by more than 12,000 employees. Figure 2 shows the sharp growth in noninterest expense that the nation's largest banks experienced in the 1980s; that growth served as a principal motivation for the strong cost-reduction measures these banks took in the late 1980s and early 1990s.

Charging for services previously provided free and raising both basic and exception-item service charges is another strategy employed by banks to offset costs. Most banks incurred increased noninterest expenses in the 1980s to service a growing volume of new accounts. These banks tended to keep noninterest income and expenses in tandem by raising service fees and charges on transaction accounts to match higher operating costs. In 1992, charges on consumer accounts contributed about 10 percent to banks' noninterest revenues.

Banks have sought to reduce dependence on purchased funds and borrowings as sources of funds. Since the mid-1980s, the nation's money center banks have built increasingly larger bases of stable consumer time and savings deposits. This shift in funding emphasis from reliance on managed liabilities is a result of a shift in money center banks' marketing focus from corporate banking to consumer banking. In the 1990s, consumer services have become more profitable to big banks than corporate lending and reflect the movement of consumer accounts from savings and loan associations to commercial banks.

FIGURE 2   **Noninterest Expense Growth at the 10 Largest U.S. Banking Companies**

	Gross Expenses (Average Annual Growth Rate)	Overhead Costs (Noninterest expense as a Percentage of Interest income)		
	1981-86	1984	1985	1986
Citicorp	19%	49%	46%	45%
Chase Manhattan Corp.	15	54	52	55
BankAmerica Corp.*	11	63	66	66
Chemical New York Corp.*	13	50	49	47
J. P. Morgan & Co.	18	17	10	11
Manufacturers Hanover*	15	50	46	46
Security Pacific Corp.*	18	52	49	51
Bankers Trust N.Y. Corp.	11	27	23	8
First Interstate Bancorp.	13	59	57	54
Wells Fargo & Co.	12	55	50	52
Average	15%	48%	45%	44%

*The 1992 mergers of BankAmerica-Security Pacific, and Chemical Bank-Manufacturers Hanover were motivated, in part, by the prospects of increased profitability from substantial reductions in operating expenses.

Extended Study 11
The Evolution of Bank Regulation

The course of bank regulation in U.S. history has long been shaped by political issues. At the outset, in fact, early Americans even disagreed about the need for banks in their developing economy. The Jeffersonians envisioned the future United States as an agrarian society with little if any need for banks, whereas the Hamiltonians envisioned an industrial society that would need banks to meet burgeoning business credit demands. Because that issue was never resolved, early banking was left to develop along private and state-regulated lines; federal government involvement in banking was an ongoing source of controversy. Most citizens believed that the new federal government should not participate in banking activities; others saw banks as providing a means for the new government to finance itself.

The Nation's First Central Banks

The nation's early experiences with banking reflect these political crosscurrents. In 1781, a reluctant Continental Congress chartered the Bank of North America to finance the military operations of the newly formed federal government. Since it was not clear whether the federal government had the legal authority to charter a bank, the Bank of North America obtained a second charter from the Commonwealth of Pennsylvania.

In 1791, Congress again used its still-questionable authority to charter a bank. It granted a 20-year charter to the First Bank of the United States, largely in response to Alexander Hamilton's urging that a national bank should be established to meet the growing credit demands of our increasingly industrialized economy. Although the bank was successful as a business and also fostered economic growth, its charter was not renewed in 1811. The public felt that a central bank gave the federal government too much power.

Congress chartered the Second Bank of the United States in 1816. It served as both a private and a government bank. As a private bank, the Second Bank made loans and investments, accepted deposits, issued bank notes, and maintained 25 branches across the country. As a government institution, it promoted the safety and soundness of banking by regularly presenting for redemption into gold and silver specie the bank notes of state-chartered banks that were suspected of overissuing. This forced state banks to keep an adequate supply of specie on hand and limited the amount of notes they could issue.

The Supreme Court ruled in 1819 that the national bank was constitutional, but many opponents—including state-chartered banks, merchants, farmers, and politicians— viewed it as too-powerful an institution for a market economy and a political democracy. Thus the charter of the Second Bank of the United States was allowed to expire in 1836.

The Free Banking Era

From 1837 (when the Second Bank of the United States closed) to 1863, banking in the United States was largely free from any federal regulation. This 26-year period is known as the Free Banking Era.

The banking services provided by the Second Bank were so extensive that most states recognized the need to establish new banking offices to fill the void created by its closing. However, most states had complex, time-consuming procedures that required an act of the state legislature to grant a bank charter. Many states chartered banks only for specific purposes, referred to as the *public good*, such as helping to finance a railroad or a bridge. In other states, chartering decisions often were politically motivated.

After the Second Bank of the United States closed, most states began to reform their bank-chartering systems so that new banks could be established quickly and the public could be assured of a stable banking environment and a safe currency. Most states attempted to achieve those goals by enacting free banking laws. These laws allowed anyone to operate a bank provided all notes issued by the bank were collateralized by state bonds deposited at the state auditor's office. In addition, all notes had to be redeemable on demand, at face value, in gold or silver specie. The failure of a bank to redeem a note presented for payment would result in the closing of the bank and the liquidation of the bank's assets to pay off all noteholders.

The absence of ongoing federal government regulation during the Free Banking Era led to a spate of bank closings in state after state. Many bank failures grew out of the fraudulent overissue of paper currency. Dishonest bankers formed *wildcat banks*, named for their remote geographic locations. The banks overissued currency in communities far from their head offices, expecting that because of their remote locations few notes would be presented for redemption. These wildcat bankers profited by quickly closing the banks after all notes were circulated and absconding with the banks' gold and silver coin.

Most bank failures during the Free Banking Era, however, were due to substantial declines in the prices of state bonds rather than to banker fraud. State bonds comprised the bulk of most banks' investment portfolios. Thus when bond prices fell, the state banks faced severe capital losses. Those bookkeeping losses made depositors anxious and led to runs on banks. During these runs, if all depositors' demands for specie redemption could not be honored, the banks were forced to close.

The National Banking System

The federal government, faced with the pressing demands of financing the Civil War, passed the National Currency Act in 1863. The National Banking Act was passed in the following year. These two acts created a system of nationally chartered banks, a national currency, and the Office of the Comptroller of the Currency.

National banking grew out of an ingenious plan developed by Salmon Chase, who served as secretary of the Treasury under Abraham Lincoln, to raise money to finance the union army. Chase faced a depleted treasury and a reluctance to raise taxes on Northern industry. He devised a plan in which the federal government would offer a new type of banking license known as a federal, or national, charter. A bank with a national charter could issue a new form of currency—national bank notes. However, for each note issued, the bank would be required to hold a slightly larger dollar value of government securities as collateral. The banks would purchase the securities directly from the Treasury in exchange for gold and silver specie. In effect, then, the government would receive money assets (gold and silver) in return for its liabilities (government securities).

To enhance the prospects of success for the new national banks, Chase instituted a tax on state bank notes designed to eliminate the competition between state bank notes and national bank notes. Congress gradually increased the tax until state-chartered banks ended the practice of issuing currency. State-chartered banks remained viable, however, because demand deposits rather than bank notes rapidly became the dominant form of money in the U.S. economy and the major source of all banks' funds.

During the decades of dual banking between the Civil War and the start of World War I, there was no uniform code of bank regulations to assure protection of the public's money. Only nationally chartered banks were subject to the stiff capital requirements and lending limits of the National Banking Act and to examinations by the Comptroller of the Currency. Moreover, only national banks were required to maintain reserves against the currency they issued and the deposits they maintained on their books. State-chartered banks were subject to differing state rules and regulations and, in many states, inadequate bank capital, risky bank loans, and insufficient reserves against notes and deposits were common. Without central regulatory oversight, banking practices involving such operational activities as check collection and correspondent accounts developed privately and beyond the scope of national regulation.

The Establishment of Federal Regulatory Oversight

In response to the serious money and banking problems that arose under the fledgling dual banking system, Congress in 1913 established the Federal Reserve as the nation's central bank. One of the Federal Reserve's basic missions was to provide more effective supervision of banking in the United States.

The Federal Reserve has sought to fulfill its mandate in various ways. It issues regulations that outline the boundaries and procedures of acceptable banking practice. It also monitors the safety and soundness of banks by analyzing data and information submitted by banks directly or indirectly through other government agencies. Banks are also routinely examined for compliance with banking laws, regulations, and procedures.

Since the late 1950s, the Federal Reserve has also decided which nonbank activities bank holding companies can engage in. In the late 1960s and 1970s, it issued rules for most federal consumer credit regulations.

The Great Depression of the 1930s, when nearly one-third of the nation's banks failed, prompted congressional recognition of the need for additional banking regulation. In 1933, Congress created the Federal Deposit Insurance Corporation to help stabilize the banking system and protect depositors against loss. Shortly thereafter, the FDIC became the federal supervisory authority over state-chartered banks that are not members of the Federal Reserve System. Since then, the FDIC has become closely associated with the chartering process because the granting of deposit insurance has become a necessary requirement for most banks.

In the 1960s and 1970s, public pressure grew for the government to provide bank depositors and customers with protection from discriminatory and deceptive banking practices. This led to the enactment of numerous federal consumer protection laws and the development of banking regulations to implement them.

The Examinations Process and Rating System

The object of examining and rating banks is to ensure that banks are complying with law and regulation and to assess each bank's financial health on a regular basis.

Rating a bank's financial health enables the regulatory agencies to identify (and monitor) banks whose poor financial condition could threaten the integrity of the banking system and erode public confidence in banks. Poorly rated banks are typically required by the regulators to take corrective actions based on recommendations and instructions from the examiners. By trying to prevent bank problems from deteriorating to the point where FDIC payouts to depositors are unavoidable, the examinations process and rating system also serve as a way for the government to protect the reserves of the federal deposit insurance fund.

Bank examiners rely on the CAMEL rating system for assessing a bank's condition. CAMEL is an acronym for five key criteria—capital, assets, management, earnings, and liquidity—that must be evaluated and scored before an overall rating can be made of a bank's financial health. Examiners rank a bank's performance against each criterion on a scale of 1 to 5, with 1 as the highest rating and 5 as the lowest. A composite rating is then derived for the bank.

A bank's *capital* represents the funds invested in the bank by its owners. Those funds are intended to provide a buffer from any losses a bank might incur on its loans or investments. All banks must satisfy certain minimum capital requirements, generally expressed as a fixed percentage of capital to total assets of the bank. In the 1990s, capital adequacy requirements have been tightened with the introduction of multiple-tiered risk-based capital-to-asset ratios and mandatory sanctions for banks whose capital ratios decline.

In evaluating the quality of a bank's loan and investment **assets**, bank examiners must determine the expected ability of borrowers to make scheduled interest payments and repay principal. If this ability is found wanting, the examiners may categorize the loans as substandard or doubtful. They may even require a bank to charge off loans that are unlikely to be repaid. In all cases, banks are required to set aside funds as loan loss reserves to cover potential losses. Bankers generally take those funds from their current earnings. However, if earnings are insufficient, the funds must be transferred from the bank's capital.

A bank's *management* is rated on its technical competence, leadership, and administrative ability. However, in evaluating management, examiners also take into account the quality of the bank's internal controls, operating procedures, and lending and investing policies. *Earnings* are generally rated against the bank's capacity to cover potential losses and meet its capital requirement. A bank's *liquidity* refers to its ability to readily convert assets into cash to meet depositors' claims. Examiners rate this ability primarily in relation to the volatility of a bank's deposits and the bank's reliance on borrowings.

The regulatory agencies consider banks with composite CAMEL ratings of 1 or 2 to be sound banks in strong condition that are generally permitted to operate without any restrictions. A bank that receives a 3 rating is considered weaker than desired (below average) because it has been found to be deficient in at least some areas covered by the examination. Those banks typically are given specific instructions on how to address their deficiencies. In some cases, however, the regulators may impose restrictions on the practices of a 3-rated bank to prevent a deterioration in its financial condition.

Banks that receive CAMEL ratings of 4 or 5 are considered to be problem banks with severe general weaknesses that could readily bring them to insolvency. They are placed under close surveillance, usually issued directives restricting their activities, and generally required to take immediate corrective actions to shore up their deficiencies.

Restrictions include:

- ❐ more frequent examinations and requirements that bank management provide frequent reports on specific problem areas. The steady flow of information enables regulatory agencies to intervene quickly if conditions worsen.
- ❐ a capital call requiring an undercapitalized bank to raise new funds to meet capital standards within a prescribed time period.
- ❐ directives restricting the bank's activities, such as limiting the amount of dividends the bank can pay to its stockholders and requiring the bank to tighten its lending standards. Directives such as these are legally binding and usually

are issued to a bank's management in the form of a memorandum of under-standing, a written agreement, or a cease and desist order. These official directives are designed to prevent a bank from taking any actions that might further jeopardize its precarious financial health and to protect the deposit insurance fund from potential losses.

If a bank's financial condition deteriorates to the point where it is in imminent danger of becoming insolvent, regulators can invoke harsher restrictions. The FDIC is em-powered to replace a bank's management and assume control over the daily operations of a potentially failing bank.

In 1991, Congress imposed several new requirements on the regulatory agencies designed to strengthen the importance of capital in evaluating banks' safety and to quicken regulators' response to poor banking performance.

Under one of these requirements, the federal regulators will be utilizing a 5-level classification system for evaluating a bank's capital position as a supplement to the CAMEL rating system. A level 1 designation is assigned to the most strongly capital-ized banks; a level 5 to the most weakly capitalized. Progressively more restrictive regulatory actions are triggered automatically if, from one examination to the next, a bank's capital designation falls by one or more levels. By 1994, the regulators must establish additional CAMEL criteria for evaluating bank safety.

A bank's CAMEL rating is confidential and is provided to the bank's senior manage-ment only. However, in its periodic reports to Congress on the health of the U.S. banking system, the FDIC usually discloses the total number of problem banks that it is actively monitoring. In 1992, about 1,000 banks—with about $600 billion in combined assets—had been so identified.

Extended Study 12
Current Banking Regulations

Federal Reserve regulations govern most aspects of bank operations and business activities. Currently, banks are subject to 30 regulations covering five major categories:

- ☐ monetary policy
- ☐ bank safety and soundness
- ☐ activities of Edge Act corporations and bank holding companies
- ☐ activities of Federal Reserve banks and Federal Reserve membership
- ☐ consumer protection

Regulations on Monetary Policy

Monetary policy regulations enable the Federal Reserve to manage the country's money supply so that sufficient money and credit are available at interest rates in line with the nation's economic objectives. Regulations that relate to monetary policy include those governing loans to depositories, reserve requirements, margin credit, and interest on deposits.

Loans to Depositories

Regulation A establishes the conditions and terms under which Federal Reserve banks lend funds to depositories at the discount window. It was the first regulation issued by the Federal Reserve (1914).

Reserve Requirements

Regulation D establishes reserve requirements for all depository institutions. The regulation defines the liabilities that are subject to reserve requirements and specifies the percentages of required reserves that must be applied to reservable liabilities. It also defines the three types of assets that depositories can use to meet reserve requirements: vault cash, balances maintained directly on the books of a Federal Reserve bank, and balances maintained at another institution in a pass-through reserve account. The regulation explains how depositories are to compute and maintain their required reserves and prescribes the penalties for reserve deficiencies. It also establishes procedures and rules for depositories that want to maintain pass-through reserve accounts.

Margin Credit

There are four regulations covering margin credit extended to finance securities transactions. Regulation G covers loans by parties other than banks, brokers, or dealers that are secured by margin securities. Regulation T governs credit extensions made by securities brokers and dealers. Regulation U limits the amount of credit a bank can extend for purchasing and carrying margin securities if the credit is secured directly or indirectly by stock. Regulation X sets out rules for extending credit to those purchasing or carrying securities.

Interest on Deposits

For more than 50 years (from 1933 to 1986), Regulation Q delineated the maximum interest rates that banks could pay on time and savings deposits. Today, Regulation Q prohibits the payment of interest on demand deposits only and sets forth the procedures that banks must follow in paying out time deposits before maturity (the assessment of penalties) and in allowing the withdrawal of savings deposits. The regulation also defines demand, time, and savings deposits.

Regulations on Bank Safety and Soundness

A number of banking regulations are designed to ensure the financial well-being and security of banks. These regulations involve issues of financial disclosure, conflicts of interest, and bank safety and security.

Financial Disclosure

Regulation F covers financial disclosure to stockholders and others. It requires certain state-chartered member banks to register and file financial statements with the Federal Reserve Board.

Conflicts of Interest

Regulation L prevents conflicts of interest or collusion between banks by prohibiting interlocking directorates (a board member serving on the board of more than one bank at the same time). Officers and employees of member banks also are prohibited from simultaneous involvement with other banks. Similarly, Regulation R prohibits directors, officers, and employees of banks from simultaneous involvement in a securities dealer firm. Regulation O prohibits member banks from extending credit to their own officers, directors, and stockholders.

Security Devices and Procedures

Regulation P sets minimum standards for security devices and procedures used by state-chartered member banks.

Regulations on Edge Act Corporations and Bank Holding Companies

Regulation K defines the allowable activities and operations of Edge Act corporations (bank subsidiaries set up to engage in international banking). Regulation Y specifies procedures and criteria the Federal Reserve Board uses to determine permissible activities for bank holding companies.

Regulations on Activities of Reserve Banks and Federal Reserve Membership

Regulations pertaining to the activities of Federal Reserve banks include membership requirements, rules for check processing and electronic funds transfers, specifications on relationships with foreign banks and governments, and procedures for certain loan guarantees by federal agencies.

Federal Reserve Membership

Regulation H is an omnibus regulation that defines membership requirements for state-chartered banks opting to join the Federal Reserve System. (It also prohibits state-chartered member banks from making mortgages in flood-hazard areas unless the mortgages are covered by national flood insurance.) Regulation I details the stock subscription requirements for banks joining the Federal Reserve System.

Federal Reserve Check-Processing Practices

Regulation J establishes the procedures and rules under which the Federal Reserve banks process checks and transfer funds electronically.

The Federal Reserve banks are authorized to issue operating circulars governing the specific procedures and practices that depository institutions must follow if they use the Federal Reserve's check collection service. These circulars cover such operational details as sorting requirements and closing times for the receipt of different classes or types of checks at Reserve banks. One key circular issued by each Federal Reserve bank is a time schedule specifying when checks received by that bank can be counted by the sending bank as part of its reserves (at what point they become available for use by the sender). Federal Reserve banks give either immediate or deferred credit in accordance with the Federal Reserve's deferred availability schedule.

Regulation J also establishes that Federal Reserve banks will receive cash items (checks) only at par (face) value; it also explains the procedures banks must follow for the return of checks and describes general chargeback procedures.

Regulation J also provides rules for funds transfers. Because Fedwire transfers involve the near-instantaneous transfer and settlement of debit and credit balances on the books of Federal Reserve banks, they are more like cash transactions than check transactions. Thus, the rules and procedures governing electronic funds transfers reflect that difference.

Under Regulation J, a Federal Reserve bank may refuse to act on a funds transfer request of a sending (or paying) bank if it believes that the bank has insufficient funds in its account at the Reserve bank to cover the transfer. The regulation stipulates that a sending bank must have on the books of the Reserve bank at the end of the day a balance in fully collected funds sufficient to cover the amount of all transfer items debited against the account during the day.

Relations with Foreign Banks and Governments

Regulation N specifies the relationships and transactions that Reserve banks can have with foreign banks and governments.

Loan Guarantees for Defense Contractors

Regulation V establishes procedures to assist federal agencies in making and administering loan guarantees to contractors involved in national defense work.

Regulations on Consumer Protection

The greatest number of banking regulations deal with consumer protection issues. These regulations cover numerous areas of concern: unfair and deceptive bank practices, equal credit opportunity, community reinvestment, home mortgage disclosures, availability of deposited check funds, truth-in-savings requirements for consumer deposits, electronic funds transfers, consumer leasing, flood insurance, financial privacy, and truth-in-lending requirements for consumer credit. These complex consumer protection regulations are described here only briefly.

Unfair and Deceptive Practices

Regulation AA establishes complaint procedures for consumers who believe a state-chartered member bank has engaged in unfair or deceptive practices.

Equal Credit Opportunity

Regulation B prohibits lenders from discriminating against credit applicants on the basis of age, race, color, religion, national origin, sex, marital status, or receipt of income from public assistance programs. It also establishes guidelines for banks to use in evaluating credit information.

Community Reinvestment

Regulation BB, which implements the Community Reinvestment Act of 1977, specifies the procedures banks must follow to ensure they are meeting the credit needs of their communities. Under Regulation BB, a bank's lending policies are evaluated in the context of its own business orientation, its past performance, and its own perception of its role and function in the community.

Home Mortgage Disclosures

Regulation C requires that depositories making mortgage loans disclose annually the locations of their mortgage loans both inside and outside certain relevant geographical areas.

Availability of Deposited Check Funds

Regulation CC was implemented in 1988 to carry out provisions of the 1987 Expedited Funds Availability Act. It places specific limits on the length of time that banks may place holds on checks deposited by customers before funds can be withdrawn. The regulation also contains rules governing the return of uncollected checks, and establishes endorsement standards for banks when they process checks for collection or return.

Truth in Savings

Regulation DD was issued in 1992 to implement the 1991 Truth in Savings Act. The act requires banks and thrifts to disclose in a uniform manner the deposit interest rates, fees, and other conditions that apply to their time and savings accounts so that consumers can more easily shop for the best selections.

Regulation DD requires that depositories must:

❏ give customers detailed disclosure statements that specify the interest return (yield), fees, and penalties on all of the bank's interest-bearing accounts,

❏ pay interest on entire account balances, not just on *investible* balances (the amount remaining after banks subtract for reserve requirements),

❏ give customers a 30-day notice of any interest rate change the bank plans to make on its deposits. However, to ease the burden on banks and thrifts in implementing this advance notification requirement, the Federal Reserve exempted from the requirement variable rate accounts and time deposits that mature in less than one month. The Federal Reserve also established a less burdensome alternative requirement. Banks and thrifts can provide advance notice on a 20-day sliding scale basis if customers are given a grace period for redepositing maturing CDs. For example, if a bank routinely gives customers a 10-day grace period, it would have to notify customers holding CDs of planned interest rate changes 10 days in advance of maturity,

❏ use *annual percentage yield* as the common standard when advertising deposit interest rates. Banks and thrifts, however, will be allowed a margin of error of

0.5 of 1 percent to protect them from class action lawsuits over small, unintentional mistakes.

Regulation DD was reluctantly adopted by the Federal Reserve. Indeed, several members of the Board of Governors voted against its adoption. They maintained that the regulation was too long (267 pages) and complex, and that banks would incur substantial costs in implementing its provisions. Moreover, all members of the Board expressed concerns that the open disclosure intent of the regulation could backfire by turning banks away from advertising or offering new deposit products. Nonetheless, the Board had to adopt the regulation under provisions of the Truth in Savings Act. However, the Board attempted to soften the cost impact on banks by using every exemption allowed in the act.

To determine whether all of its concerns were valid, the Federal Reserve Board authorized that two surveys be taken—one to determine the costs banks incur in complying with regulation DD and the other to determine if consumers see any improvements in deposit account information disclosure as a result of the truth in savings regulation. The Federal Reserve had never before sought to measure the costs banks incur in complying with regulations or the effectiveness of a new regulation. The results of the Federal Reserve's 1992 surveys are expected to serve as a benchmark for Congress and the Federal Reserve in evaluating the costs and benefits of proposed new regulations.

Electronic Funds Transfers

Regulation E was issued in 1980 to implement the Electronic Funds Transfer Act of 1978. It establishes the rights, liabilities, and responsibilities of consumers and financial institutions using electronic funds transfer services. For example, it limits a consumer's liability for unauthorized use of his or her electronic transfer service or access device to $50 or less. It also requires that consumers be given a written, easily understood statement of the terms and conditions of the electronic funds transfer service that is contracted for, including information on any service charges, rights to stop payment, and the circumstances under which the financial institution would disclose to a third party information about a consumer's EFT account activity.

The regulation also specifies a procedure by which consumers can seek to rectify apparent billing errors in bank statements showing EFT activity. It requires that while a complaint is being investigated, a bank must recredit the consumer's account for the amount in question within 10 days of receiving a written notice of possible error.

Consumer Leasing

Regulation M (a part of Regulation Z until 1981) implements the consumer leasing portions of the Truth in Lending Act, specifying disclosure terms in leasing arrangements.

Flood Insurance

Regulation H prohibits state-chartered member banks from making or renewing loans in flood hazard areas not covered by the National Flood Insurance Program. As noted previously, Regulation H also defines the conditions and membership requirements for state-chartered banks that opt to join the Federal Reserve System.

Financial Privacy

Regulation S establishes procedures and conditions under which financial institutions can be reimbursed for providing financial records to a federal agency.

Truth in Lending

Regulation Z establishes minimum disclosure requirements for banks and others that extend consumer credit, and establishes procedures for resolving billing errors. In passing the Truth in Lending Act in 1968, Congress required the Federal Reserve to write implementing regulations, which became Regulation Z. Since that time, the Federal Reserve has been the principal agency charged with writing regulations to implement other federal consumer credit legislation. Regulation Z was extensively revised, shortened, and simplified in 1981 to make compliance easier.

Extended Study 13
Evolution of the Federal Reserve's Operating Strategy

The evolution of the Federal Reserve's open-market operating strategy can be traced from its attempts to control money market conditions in the 1950s to its concentration on nonborrowed reserves and money supply growth in the 1990s. In the intervening years, the Federal Reserve employed an *even keel* policy and a policy of targeting the federal funds rate and monetary aggregates. From 1979 to 1982, the Federal Reserve temporarily shifted its emphasis from control of the federal funds rate to control of bank reserves. Since 1982, the Federal Reserve has modified its strategy in an attempt to reduce interest rate volatility and strengthen its control over reserve and money supply growth.

Money Market Strategy

In the 1950s and early 1960s, the Federal Reserve relied on a money market strategy in applying open-market operations. Under that strategy, the Federal Reserve's open-market purchases and sales of securities were directed at maintaining stability in financial markets by ensuring that interest rates changed in a gradual and stable manner. Interest rates were edged up gradually if there was a need to slow the economy's rate of expansion and eased gradually if there was a need for economic stimulation.

That money market strategy stemmed in part from concern over the large amount of government securities accumulated in World War II and held by financial institutions. It also stemmed from concern that rapid increases in interest rates would depress securities prices and impair the functioning of the nation's financial institutions and markets.

The Federal Reserve's primary operating target during that period was net free reserves—defined as excess reserves minus reserves borrowed from the Federal Reserve. It used open-market operations and changes in the discount rate to maintain a predetermined level of net free reserves which, in turn, stabilized interest rates. An increase in free reserves reflected an easing of policy, while a decrease (or movement into net borrowed reserves) reflected a tightening of policy.

A major shortcoming of the money market strategy was that the Federal Reserve had few, if any, quantitative targets against which it could assess the effectiveness of its monetary policy over time. Moreover, many monetary economists argued that the Federal Reserve's attempts to control money market conditions were ineffective in achieving economic goals because interest rates and free reserves were not significantly related to employment, output, or price levels.

Even-Keel Policy

In the 1960s and early 1970s, the Federal Reserve's trading desk applied an *even-keel* policy in the days immediately before, during, and after the Treasury borrowed in the open market by selling its new notes, bills, and bonds. During those periods, the Federal Reserve simply attempted to steer the ship of monetary policy on a straight course.

The Federal Reserve's even-keel policy was designed to ensure that the Treasury would have a stable market in which to sell the government's new debt instruments. To accomplish that, the Federal Reserve had to ensure that the amount of reserves in the banking system was sufficient to enable banks to lend to dealers, which in turn would enable the dealer firms to buy the Treasury issues. The Federal Reserve also had to ensure the stability of interest rates during the financing period so that Treasury issues would be attractive. The Federal Reserve did not peg interest rates or drive rates down so that the Treasury would get a favorable rate, but simply sought to ensure that interest rates would remain stable during the period, subject only to shifts caused by market forces and not by changes in Federal Reserve policy.

In tight money periods, the even-keel policy meant a temporary pause in restraint to pump up reserves and to keep interest rates from rising. The Federal Reserve's primary objective was to ensure that there would be sufficient reserves to support loans to dealer firms (for the purchase of new government debt) and that the Treasury would not have to pay excessive interest rates.

In maintaining an even-keel posture, the Federal Reserve also was protecting dealer firms during the few days of the Treasury financing period when dealer firms were most susceptible to losses caused by rising interest rates. Since dealer firms typically borrow funds on a daily basis to carry their inventories, a sharp increase in interest rates on the day after they borrowed funds but before their securities could be sold on the secondary market could cut into their profit margins or even turn an expected profit into a loss.

As the government's debt began to grow during the 1960s and Treasury borrowing began to accelerate, the Federal Reserve used the even-keel policy more and more frequently. The policy began to impair the Federal Reserve's ability to control bank reserves. Thus the Federal Reserve abandoned the policy when it changed its open-market operating strategy in the 1970s in an attempt to achieve better control of reserve and money supply growth.

Reliance on the Federal Funds Rate and the Monetary Aggregates

In the late 1960s and early 1970s, the Federal Reserve adopted a more comprehensive and quantitative strategy, linking short-term targets to intermediate targets and long-term objectives. It dropped net free reserves as an operating target, designating instead the federal funds rate as the key operating target for open-market operations; it also began to set intermediate target ranges for key money supply measures.

This change in operating strategy was motivated by the Federal Reserve's growing concern over rising inflation rates and money supply growth in the late 1960s. Many economists attributed those conditions to the Federal Reserve's failure to control money supply and bank reserves more directly. The Federal Reserve did not, however, change its strategy suddenly.

The Federal Open Market Committee (FOMC) first used a noninterest-rate target in 1966 when it added a proviso clause to its policy directives. This clause established bank credit (total loans and investments in the banking system) as the principal operating target. It authorized the New York trading desk to modify open-market operations as needed to maintain bank credit growth within targeted norms even if it caused the federal funds rate to deviate from its operating target range. In 1970, the FOMC replaced bank credit with M1 in the proviso clause and began to routinely specify numerical target growth rates for various *monetary aggregates* (measures of the money supply) in its monthly policy instructions to the New York trading desk. It also began to assess the effectiveness of monetary policy by how close the New York trading desk came to these numerical targets.

Open-market operating strategy gradually changed in the 1970s; during that time, monetary aggregates came to be viewed as intermediate targets while interest rates came to be used as operating targets. For day-to-day operating purposes, the Federal Reserve established a target range for the federal funds rate. Within that given range of tolerance, the federal funds rate was allowed to respond to market forces of supply and demand. Only if market forces threatened to push the federal funds rate above (or below) the target range ceiling (or floor) would the Federal Reserve intervene by buying or selling securities in the open market.

Open-market operations were directed at keeping the federal funds rate within the target range on a weekly average basis and, at times, on a daily basis. The target range set by the FOMC, sometimes as narrow as one-half of a percentage point and rarely more than one percentage point, was based on the Federal Reserve's judgment of the short-term interest rate level that would be most appropriate for generating its targeted growth in money supply.

The federal funds rate targeting strategy had a shortcoming in that the Federal Reserve would invariably add reserves if strong demand threatened to drive the federal funds rate above the target range ceiling. Those additional reserves in turn provided fuel for new money creation and money supply growth in excess of targeted rates.

A Shift to Reserves (1979-1982)

In 1979, the Federal Reserve again changed its open-market operating strategy. The daily emphasis of open-market operations shifted from stabilizing the federal funds rate to controlling the supply of bank reserves. This change in approach was made to give the Federal Reserve better control over money supply and reserve growth, which had exceeded targeted ranges in the late 1970s. It was also an attempt to reduce inflationary expectations on the part of businesses and the public, which had been fueled, in part, by the Federal Reserve's inability to control money growth. In addition, the Federal Reserve wanted to change the perception of banks and other lenders that credit could be aggressively marketed under any circumstance because the federal funds rate and other money market rates would always be stabilized by the Federal Reserve within a narrow range.

The new operating strategy emphasized reserve paths and targeting to help the Federal Reserve avoid persistent overshooting of its money and reserve growth targets. Under the new strategy, purchases and sales of securities by the New York trading desk were directed not at stabilizing the federal funds rate but at providing a volume of nonborrowed reserves consistent with the FOMC's targeted growth for money supply.

By expanding or contracting the supply of nonborrowed reserves, the Federal Reserve was able to more effectively control money supply growth. The result, however, was substantially greater volatility in the federal funds rate and other short-term interest rates.

Strategy Modifications Since 1982

In 1982, the Federal Reserve changed its reserve path and targeting approach; reserve and money supply growth had been successfully held to target and inflation and inflationary expectations had been reduced. Short-term interest rates, however, had become highly volatile and unpredictable in the early 1980s as a result of the nonborrowed reserves targeting strategy.

The Federal Reserve reinstated the federal funds rate as a key operational target, although it was not given the same exclusive priority it had before 1979. The target ranges established were initially broadened from about one percentage point to four percentage points, then subsequently narrowed in the late 1980s and early 1990s. Nonborrowed reserves remained the primary operating target. However, the automatic response to off-target growth that the Federal Reserve had relied on before 1979 was modified. In the 1970s, when the monetary aggregates deviated from their targets, the New York trading desk's buying or selling response was automatic. Since 1982, the FOMC must decide whether or not to increase or decrease bank reserves to bring the aggregates back on track. Factors that are taken into consideration when there are deviations include the level of long-term interest rates, foreign exchange rates, labor market conditions, and general business expectations about the economy's future.

Extended Study 14
Factors Absorbing and Supplying Bank Reserves

Each week the Federal Reserve issues a statement of factors that have supplied and absorbed bank reserves during the preceding week, including comparisons of changes that have occurred over the previous 52 weeks. This statement is, in effect, a balance sheet of the Federal Reserve's assets and liabilities consolidated with the monetary liabilities of the Treasury. As such, it is a prime source of information and data for tracking inflows and outflows of bank reserves.

Factors Supplying Reserves

Factors that traditionally supply reserves to the banking system include Reserve bank credit, gold stock, special drawing rights certificates, and Treasury currency outstanding. We will examine each in turn.

Reserve Bank Credit

Reserve bank credit consists of reserves supplied to the banking system through open-market operations, loans to depository institutions, float, and Federal Reserve purchases of foreign currency. The Federal Reserve's open-market operations and its discount window loans provide about 85 percent of total reserves in the banking system, and are used as monetary policy tools.

Although Federal Reserve float creates some reserves as well, the Federal Reserve does not use float as a policy device for supplying reserves to banks. Rather, float is treated as an unpredictable and volatile by-product of the check-clearing process that impairs the Federal Reserve's ability to predict and control the growth of bank reserves.

The Federal Reserve's purchases of foreign currency also supply reserves to the banking system. Foreign currency is acquired as part of the Federal Reserve's role in keeping trading in dollars orderly in the foreign exchange market (in accordance with the Federal Reserve's international responsibilities as the U.S. central bank). However, like float, the purchasing of foreign currency is not used as a policy device for supplying the banking system with reserves. To the extent that reserves supplied through the Federal Reserve's foreign exchange intervention are inconsistent with targeted growth for nonborrowed reserves, defensive open-market operations are used to provide an offsetting drain of reserves.

Gold Stock

Prior to 1971, when the U.S. government ended dollar-gold convertibility for foreign governments, Treasury purchases of gold generated increases in bank reserves and the money supply, as shown by the following T-account:

Federal Reserve Bank		First Commercial Bank	
Assets	Liabilities	Assets	Liabilities
	Reserve account of First Commercial bank + $1 million	Reserve account + $1 million	Demand deposit of foreign government + $1 million
	U.S. Treasury account - $1 million		

U.S. Treasury

Assets	Liabilities
Account at Federal Reserve - $1 million	
Gold bullion + $1 million	

In this example, a foreign government exchanged $1 million in gold bullion for $1 million in deposit balances at a U.S. bank. (The foreign government would need the deposit balance to buy U.S. merchandise because gold bullion is not used as a medium of exchange in the United States.) The Treasury bought the gold for $1 million with a check drawn on its disbursement account at the Federal Reserve. When the check was collected, First Commercial's reserve account increased, as did the foreign government's deposit balance. Since the foreign government intended to spend the $1 million on U.S. merchandise, it probably would deposit the Treasury's check in its commercial bank account rather than in its official account at the Federal Reserve. In either case, as soon as the money was spent on U.S. merchandise, the domestic money supply was increased.

The acquisition of gold bullion by the Treasury did more than satisfy America's gold redemption pledge to foreign governments from 1933 to 1971. It gave the Treasury the means to create new money for itself through the act of gold monetization.

TREASURY MONETIZATION OF GOLD BULLION

The Treasury monetized gold by selling it to the Federal Reserve through the issuance of gold certificates for the amount of gold bullion it held. The gold certificates were a legal claim on this gold, which remained in the government's possession in its gold vault at Fort Knox, Kentucky, or in vaults in the Treasury's New York or San Francisco assay offices.

Let us look now at what happens when the Treasury monetizes the $1 million in bullion it purchased from the foreign government:

Federal Reserve Bank

Assets	Liabilities
Gold certificates + $1 million	U.S. Treasury account + $1 million

U.S. Treasury

Assets	Liabilities
Account at Federal Reserve + $1 million	Monetized gold + $1 million

As shown here, gold monetization resulted in an increase in the Treasury's disbursement account at the Federal Reserve; thus it was a means of obtaining new money without borrowing or resorting to taxation. Gold monetization also increased the Federal Reserve's holdings of gold certificates, which the Federal Reserve needed (until 1968) as legal backing for Federal Reserve notes issued and reserve deposits held. Over the decades, the Treasury monetized more than $11 billion in gold bullion, virtually all the gold held by the U.S. government.

Today, the gold certificates held by the Federal Reserve (actually bookkeeping credits) are used as money for transactions between Federal Reserve banks. That is, when one Reserve bank owes funds to another Reserve bank because of interregional check collection, payment is made in gold certificate credits. Each year, the total pool of gold certificate credits is proportionally reallocated among the 12 Reserve banks so that interregional check collection can continue to be efficiently settled among the Reserve banks.

A Treasury sale of gold would generate an initial decline in bank reserves if the foreign government's check were collected through the Treasury's disbursement account at the Federal Reserve. However, the Treasury cannot sell monetized gold because it no longer owns any gold. In the preceding example, the Treasury monetized the $1 million in bullion it had purchased. To sell that gold, the Treasury would first have to buy back the gold certificates it issued to the Federal Reserve. This buy-back would result in a $1 million reduction in the Treasury's disbursement account at the Federal Reserve and a $1 million reduction in Federal Reserve assets. The Treasury's sale of that de-monetized gold would bring in $1 million to offset the Treasury's $1 million reduction caused by the gold certificate buy-back. Although the Treasury's disbursement account would register no net change as a result of these transactions, the Treasury no longer would have $1 million in gold bullion assets.

An examination of gold monetization offers some historical insight into how the Treasury's gold transactions affected bank reserves in earlier decades. It also serves as a frame of reference for understanding issues related to the Treasury's gold transactions today.

If the Treasury were to monetize gold today, it would do so on the basis of the official U.S. government gold price—$42.22 an ounce. The price of gold in the world's private markets, however, is more than eight times this price (abut $350 an ounce in late 1992). Thus, in theory, the market value of the Treasury's gold is more than eight times greater than the $11 billion carried by the Treasury on its books. In theory, the Treasury could monetize more gold by marking up the book value (U.S. government price) of the gold bullion currently in the government's possession and by issuing gold certificates to the Federal Reserve in the amount of the markup. Some economists claim that the government could easily obtain new money in this way for social programs without having to borrow or resort to new taxes.

The basic problem with this policy approach is not technical or procedural, but economic. Monetization gives the Treasury new money to spend with no offset from other spending sectors of the economy. Massive Treasury spending would generate huge amounts of new bank reserves and additions to the money supply. The multiplier impact of these additional reserves on the banking system would, in turn, generate further massive increases in money supply. Unless the Federal Reserve engaged in enormous defensive open-market operations (sales of securities) to reduce bank reserves, and thus bank lending and money creation, the economy would find itself in an inflationary whirlwind. Even if the Federal Reserve succeeded in its defense, the likely impact of massive open-market sales of securities would be skyrocketing interest rates and depressed securities prices that could plunge the economy into deep recession.

Special Drawing Rights Certificate Account

Another way that reserves are supplied to the banking system is through the monetization of special drawing rights (the bookkeeping money balances used by governments in their international monetary dealings with each other). The monetizing of special drawing rights (SDRs) by the U.S. Treasury, like the monetization of gold, supplies reserves to the banking system. When the Treasury monetizes SDRs, it issues certificates to the Federal Reserve banks and receives an equivalent amount of dollars credited to its account at the Federal Reserve. When those funds are spent or transferred to the Treasury's tax and loan (TT&L) accounts at commercial banks, bank reserves increase. Since the 1970s, allocations to the U.S. government's Special Drawing Rights Certificate Account from the International Monetary Fund, which is the central issuing authority for SDRs, have provided about $12 billion in reserves.

Treasury Currency Outstanding

Treasury currency outstanding, essentially coin, is another source of reserves for the banking system. When the Treasury issues coin to the Federal Reserve banks for distribution to depositories, it receives an equivalent dollar value credit to its demand deposit account at the Federal Reserve. When banks acquire coin from the Federal Reserve, they pay with their reserve account deposits. Total reserves do not change, since both vault cash and deposits at the Federal Reserve are part of bank reserves. However, when the Treasury spends its newly created deposit dollars, new reserves are created for those banks in which Treasury checks are deposited.

Factors Absorbing Reserves

At the same time that the banking system is being supplied with bank reserves, other factors absorb bank reserves. Factors that traditionally absorb reserves from the banking system include currency in circulation, Treasury cash holdings and Treasury deposits at Federal Reserve banks, foreign deposits with Federal Reserve banks, and other factors.

Currency in Circulation

Currency in circulation accounts for about 90 percent of all reserves that flow out of banks. When banks receive deposits of currency from the public, their reserves increase. When they pay out currency to the public, their reserves decline.

Treasury Cash Holdings and Treasury Deposits at Federal Reserve Banks

Banking system reserves decline whenever the Treasury builds up its deposits at Federal Reserve banks and whenever the Treasury increases its cash holdings. The Treasury attempts to minimize the effect of its actions on bank reserves by maintaining TT&L accounts at most commercial banks in the nation. In that way, tax receipts and funds received from the sale of government securities to the public do not siphon reserves from the banking system as they would if the funds were deposited in the Treasury's account at the Federal Reserve. However, when the Treasury has to cover checks for Social Security and other government payments that are drawn against its account at the Federal Reserve, TT&L funds held by commercial banks are transferred into the Federal Reserve banks, temporarily reducing banking system reserves.

Foreign Deposits with Federal Reserve Banks and Other Factors

Other factors that lead to a reduction (absorption) in reserves include deposits held at the Federal Reserve by foreign central banks and other official institutions, clearing balances held at the Federal Reserve by nonmember depositories that use Reserve bank payment services, and other Federal Reserve liabilities and capital. When foreign central banks and other financial institutions or nonmember service users increase their deposits at the Federal Reserve, bank reserves are reduced. These deposit increases are normally very small, however, and have little impact on bank reserves.

Principal Factors Affecting Bank Reserves

Three basic factors have caused commercial banks to gain or lose reserves in significant amounts over the years. The first factor is the Treasury's dealings in gold and SDRs. Since the establishment of the Federal Reserve in 1913, banks have gained more than $20 billion as a result of additions to the nation's monetary gold stock and the Special Drawing Rights Certificate Account.

A change in circulating currency is the second major factor affecting reserves. When banks pay out currency to the public, their reserves decline. To obtain currency to satisfy their depositors' demands for cash, banks pay by exchanging reserves on deposit at Reserve banks for the cash. Since 1913, banks have had to pay for some $300 billion of Federal Reserve currency. If no other source of reserves had been open to them, they would, by 1992, have exhausted their $20 billion in reserve deposits and would have been overdrawn by about $280 billion.

Banks still have reserve balances because of the third factor influencing reserves—open-market operations. Over the decades, the Federal Reserve has expanded its investments by nearly $300 billion. Every time the New York trading desk buys securities for the System Open Market Account, it provides banks with new reserves.

Extended Study 15
A General Equilibrium Model: IS-LM

A model that integrates the key relationships that determine interest rates and income levels into one framework has been developed so that the impact of monetary and fiscal policy on the economy can be more readily analyzed and understood. This general equilibrium model incorporates the LM (liquidity preference-money supply) curve and the IS (investment-savings) curve.

The LM curve connects all of the income level and interest rate combinations under which the supply and demand for money would be in equilibrium when the money supply is held constant. The LM curve is shown in figure 1.

FIGURE 1   **The LM (Liquidity Preference-Money Supply) Curve**

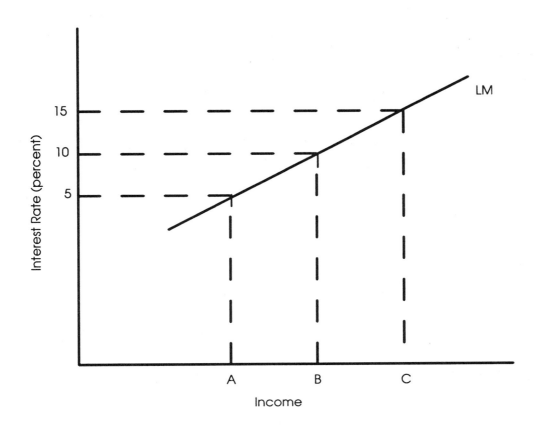

The LM curve indicates the income levels that the economy must generate to make the demand for money equal to the supply of money at different interest rates. For example, if the interest rate is 15 percent, then income level C must be generated to maintain equilibrium. The LM curve also shows the interest rate that must prevail in the economy for money supply and demand to be in equilibrium at different income levels. For example, at income level B, an interest rate of 10 percent will generate equilibrium.

Total economic equilibrium, however, depends on more than balance between money supply and money demand. The level of saving and the level of investment also must balance. The IS curve connects all of the income level and interest rate combinations under which the level of investment spending equals the level of saving. The IS curve is shown in figure 2.

FIGURE 2   **The IS (Investment-Savings) Curve**

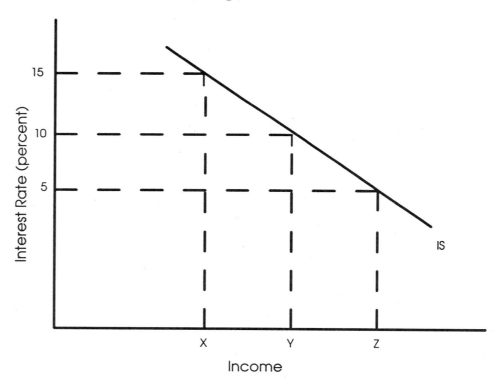

The IS curve shows the level of income that the economy must generate in order for savings to equal investment at different interest rates. The curve also indicates the interest rate that must prevail for savings to equal investment at different income levels.

By consolidating the LM and IS curves into one model—using a single interest rate-income grid, as demonstrated in Figure 3—economists can quickly analyze the bottom-line effects of changes in monetary and fiscal policy and the impact of nonpolicy factors that upset the economy's equilibrium.

FIGURE 3   **The IS-LM Model**

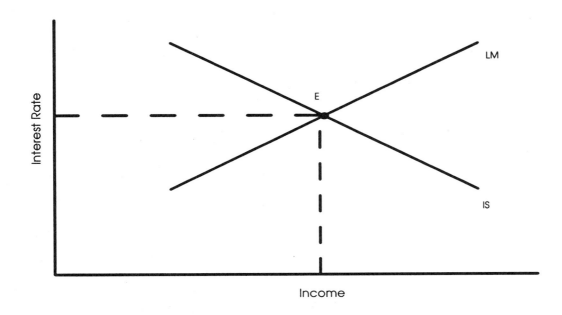

THE IMPACT OF MONETARY POLICY ON THE IS-LM MODEL

The consolidated IS-LM model shows the economy in full equilibrium (E). Balance exists between money supply and demand and between investment and savings flows. Assume, however, that the economy is not at full employment at this level of equilibrium. Appropriate monetary policy under the circumstances of the model in figure 3 would be to increase the money supply. Such an increase would shift the LM curve to the right, as demonstrated in figure 4.

FIGURE 4   **Impact of an Increase in Money Supply on the IS-LM Model**

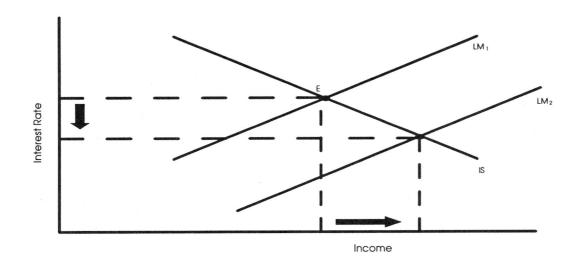

At every combination of equilibrium between money supply and money demand (LM₁), the new, larger money supply now exceeds demand. As the public adjusts its money balances and spending to the increased supply of money, additional income is generated in the economy. With additional income, a greater level of transactions balances is required. As a result, all previous LM equilibrium combinations shift to the right (to LM₂).

The shift in the LM curve to the right reduces interest rates and increases income and output, which are consistent and desired effects of a stimulative monetary policy. A more sophisticated application of the IS-LM analysis would also factor in the slope (elasticity) of both the LM and IS curves (the responsiveness of investment and money demand to the change in money supply). By substituting simultaneous algebraic equations for the geometric relationships represented in the model, quantitative measures of the changes can be established.

THE IMPACT OF FISCAL POLICY ON THE IS-LM MODEL

Now assume that fiscal policy rather than monetary policy is used to stimulate the economy toward full employment. Appropriate fiscal policy would be to increase government spending. The effect of such an increase is demonstrated in the IS-LM model in figure 5.

FIGURE 5   **Impact of an Increase in Government Spending on the IS-LM Model**

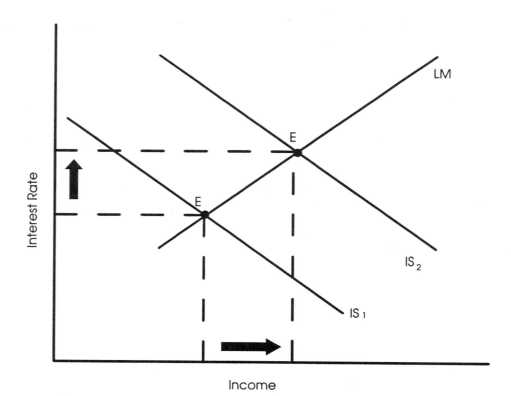

The increase in government spending shifts the IS curve to the right, from IS_1 to IS_2. This shift occurs because at every combination of equilibrium between interest rate and income, the increase in government spending generates a higher level of total spending, total output, and total income. Now a higher level of income is associated with every possible interest rate. However, the interest rate is also driven up because at a higher level of income there is a larger transactions demand for money. Since the IS-LM model assumes a fixed supply of money, the interest rate must increase to maintain equilibrium between money supply and money demand.

The Transmission of Monetary Policy

Most economists believe that monetary policy affects the economy by changing the cost of capital, the availability of credit, and the public's perception of its financial wealth. Economists call this latter phenomenon the *wealth effect*. We can better understand all three effects by considering the impact of a tightening of monetary policy.

The Cost of Capital

Tighter money leads to a smaller supply of bank reserves relative to bank demand for those reserves. Reserves cost more (that is, the federal funds rate is higher) and, in turn, banks charge higher interest rates on loans. As interest rates rise, some potential business borrowers cannot afford the extra interest cost. In effect, the higher interest rates raise the cost of capital (investments) and, for some firms, erase the profit return they would obtain on investments if they could borrow funds at lower interest rates.

As these firms cut back on investment, their lack of spending has a ripple effect on the economy. Reduced business investment means reduced income and spending by other business firms and workers that would otherwise be the beneficiaries of the capital orders and purchases of the companies that deferred their borrowing.

The impact of the rising cost of capital is believed to be responsible for about 50 percent of the effect of tight money on the economy. However, economists are puzzled as to why the steady decline in interest rates in the early 1990s did not have an equally strong effect in stimulating the economy and have questioned whether the cost of capital is as effective in transmitting easy money to the economy as is the case with tight money. One theory is that exceedingly high levels of corporate borrowings in the 1980s found most businesses unable to carry much additional debt in the 1990s, despite low interest rates.

The Availability of Credit

Tighter money affects lenders as well as borrowers, and some of the impact of monetary restraint is believed to be transmitted through the behavior of lenders.

Banks generally seek to meet all customer demands for credit, particularly when interest rates are high. During a period of tight money, however, some banks are unable to obtain the reserves they need to fund all loan requests. Thus, banks may seek to ration customer credit. Typically, they make funds available first to their most valued customers (those with long-standing relationships and good loan repayment histories) and then to customers with relatively weaker credit standings, collateral, and credit repayment histories. Rationing credit often involves imposing more stringent collateral requirements and higher compensating balances on loans, and denying new credit requests. The impact of those rationing actions, like the cost-of-capital effect, is that some business borrowers obtain less credit than they expected or perhaps no credit at all. As a result, the level of investment spending in the economy declines.

The impact of monetary ease is also thought to be partially transmitted through the more liberal and expansive lending behavior of banks. However, in the early 1990s this was not so. Banks effectively rationed credit even though reserves were plentiful and interest rates were declining. Banks responded to new risk-based capital requirements, rising loan loss reserves, and regulatory pressures to reduce lending risk by using available funds to invest in government securities rather than to make loans. One result of that credit rationing was that bank loans to businesses declined in the early 1990s.

In the past, the impact of credit availability was believed to account for about 10 percent of the effect of monetary restraint on the economy. Most of this effect, however, was thought to be related to the availability of mortgage credit and its effect on the housing industry. The impact of disintermediation (the movement of deposits out of intermediaries and into the nation's money markets by persons seeking a higher interest rate) on thrift institutions, which were the main sources of residential mortgage credit, and the mortgage rate ceilings imposed by the states, acted as de facto rationing devices by reducing the supply of available mortgage credit. With less mortgage credit available, fewer houses were sold and fewer new housing units were built. With the elimination of interest rate ceilings in 1987, the growing use of variable rate mortgages in the 1980s, and the expansion of commercial banks' residential mortgage lending in the 1990s, mortgage credit and housing no longer bear the exclusive brunt of monetary policy's availability of credit effect.

The Wealth Effect

Monetary restraint affects spending by upsetting the balance between the amount of liquid money and financial assets the public wants to hold. To implement a tighter monetary policy, the Federal Reserve sells securities from the System Open Market Account portfolio. That action reduces bank reserves and money supply, but also adds additional financial assets to the public's portfolio. In effect, the Federal Reserve creates a temporary imbalance in public preferences by taking away money and substituting financial assets in its place.

The public, however, seeks to regain its preferred balance by selling financial assets (securities) to achieve greater liquidity. As securities are sold, increasing the supply of these financial assets relative to the public's demand for them, securities prices fall and investment yields (interest rates) increase. Because lower securities prices reduce the value of the public's portfolio, balance is obtained with a smaller supply of available money. However, the public perceives that it has lost wealth. Even though actual losses are not incurred until financial assets are sold, the paper loss of financial wealth causes consumers and businesses to alter their spending behavior. On balance, they begin to spend less and save more to compensate for the reduced value of their financial assets. This wealth effect of monetary restraint is believed to account for about 40 percent of the impact of monetary policy on the economy.

Monetary ease increases the value of financial assets by driving down interest rates. As financial asset values increase, the public perceives that it has become wealthier. As a result, people and businesses save less and spend more. In the early 1990s, the Federal Reserve implemented a policy of monetary ease. However, people and businesses did not respond by altering their saving and spending patterns. Economists contend that the public was still adjusting to the more powerful wealth effect caused by the collapse of real estate and housing values in the 1980s.

Some economists maintain that the elimination of Regulation Q ceilings in the 1980s, coupled with broader powers for thrifts and other financial intermediaries, has lessened the impact of interest rate changes on economic activity. Before the 1980s, interest rate ceilings prevented banks and thrifts from attracting sufficient funds to meet all short-term loan and mortgage requests when money became tight. As a result, monetary restraint made its impact on the economy well before interest rates reached double-digit levels. With the removal of Regulation Q ceilings in the 1980s, and the increased reliance of banks and thrifts on variable rate loans and mortgages, some economists contend that monetary restraint must now drive up interest rates substantially and must maintain these rates over a longer period of time to have any effect on dampening demand for credit through the cost of capital or credit availability.

Extended Study 16
Wage-Price Controls and Indexation

Wage-price controls are government-imposed regulations that attempt to limit wage and price increases. Some economists advocate their use as a less socially costly and more effective means of curbing inflation than monetary and fiscal restraint. Other economists believe that indexation—automatically adjusting all income and payments to changes in the cost of living—would lead to a more equitable economy.

Wage-Price Controls

Wage-price controls have been instituted several times in the United States. During World War II (1941-1945), the United States adopted mandatory wage-price controls coupled with coupon rationing of scarce consumer goods. During the Korean War (1951-1952), the United States again resorted to a controls program. Voluntary controls in the form of wage-price guidelines were established in the early 1960s. The United States last used wage-price controls from 1971 to 1973.

Adherents of wage-price controls believe that structural changes in the U.S. economy in the last three decades have made wages and prices increasingly unresponsive to monetary and fiscal restraint. They cite the power of the nation's large unions and large industrial firms to set wages (costs) and prices as much as three years in advance as a key reason for the inability of monetary and fiscal policy to control cost-push inflation in today's economy. They see wage-price controls as possibly the only effective way to stop cost-push inflation.

A second argument in favor of wage-price controls is that the longer inflation continues, the more entrenched it becomes (in other words, inflation feeds on itself). As prices and wages rise, these increases become an expected and accepted foundation for the nation's basic production costs. Consumers and businesses develop an inflationary psychology toward spending, saving, borrowing, and investing. The expectation that prices will be higher in the future leads to an increase in the velocity of spending and borrowing and to other actions that generate the expected inflation. Proponents of wage-price controls believe that such controls can brake these inflationary expectations and prevent spiraling inflation.

Wage-price control advocates also contend that anti-inflationary monetary and fiscal restraint invariably plunges the economy into severe recession. The trade-off for such restraint in terms of unemployment costs has become increasingly high. Proponents of wage-price controls believe such controls would enable the Federal Reserve and the government to implement anti-inflation monetary and fiscal measures in a milder and more evenhanded way without generating severe recession.

Opponents of wage-price controls contend that the use of such controls contradicts the concept of freedom of choice that is held as a basic tenet of American society. They claim that the imposition of government regulation over wages and prices distorts private decisions as to allocation of resources and leads to economic inefficiency and market dislocations by not allowing the pricing mechanism and the profit motive to effect the natural balance between supply and demand.

Opponents of wage-price controls also claim that such controls are inherently unfair, particularly if they are administered in a way that allows for exemptions and exceptions. If some producers or workers are placed partially or wholly outside the program, not only are other producers and workers likely to resist compliance with the controls, but market shortages and surpluses also are likely to develop. Both of those results occurred when such controls were in effect from 1971 to 1973.

Opponents further argue that given the nation's political and governmental structure, it would be impossible to impose a comprehensive wage-price controls program without some information about the proposed program being leaked prematurely to the press and the public. Anticipatory price and wage increases made before the onset of controls could easily negate the anti-inflation impact of the controls.

Finally, opponents of wage-price controls contend that such controls are largely unenforceable. They note that, apart from the highly visible prices of large firms and the wages negotiated by major unions, it would be exceedingly difficult to monitor compliance. They question whether the nation's 10 million small businesses and self-employed workers would adhere to such controls. In addition, they note, myriad personal transactions, ranging from doctors' fees to tips on restaurant meals, would largely fall beyond the scope of even the most comprehensive controls program. Moreover, to administer a fair and equitable national controls program, a vast and costly bureaucracy of government examiners, monitors, administrators, and analysts would be required to oversee the program.

World War II Controls

During World War II, the federal government imposed mandatory wage-price controls to prevent inflation from engulfing an economy whose full productive resources were being almost totally devoted to war production. Wages were frozen, job changes were regulated, labor agreed not to strike, and prices were fixed by the government. To ensure the equitable distribution of consumer goods and commodities in a market environment where prices could not increase to balance supply and demand, a system of coupon rationing was adopted. Under the rationing program, purchasers of scarce goods (such as sugar and meat) had to present government-issued ration coupons.

Although most Americans initially supported the mandatory wage-price controls as a necessary wartime sacrifice, the program ran into problems toward the end of the war. Labor costs rose as workers successfully negotiated new job titles and job upgrades, which carried higher salaries, and negotiated for guaranteed overtime. Some producers reduced the quality of goods in order to expand profits in the fixed-price environment. Black markets also developed where rationed goods could be bought for higher prices, but without coupons. When the wage-price controls were removed in 1945, both consumer prices and wages soared.

Wage-Price Guidelines of the 1960s

In 1962, the government initiated a program of voluntary wage-price guidelines. Labor unions were urged to limit demands for annual wage increases to increases in productivity because such increases were not inflationary. Producers were exhorted not to raise prices. The Kennedy administration successfully browbeat some of the nation's largest unions into abiding by the wage guidelines and convinced some of the nation's largest corporations to hold down prices.

Many economists cite these guidelines as an example of a successful wage-price controls program. Other economists contend that the guidelines worked only because there was no inflationary pressure in the economy at that time. It is doubtful that the guidelines would have held prices and wages down after 1965, when both fiscal and monetary policy became expansionary.

The Phase-Control Program of the Early 1970s

In August 1971, during a period of international monetary crisis, President Nixon introduced a multifaceted wage-price controls program that began with a 90-day freeze on wages and prices. The freeze was designed to shock consumers, businesses, and financial institutions out of the growing inflationary psychology that had developed in the late 1960s. This first phase of the wage-price program was followed by a mixture of voluntary and mandatory regulations in the second phase, which continued through 1972. At the beginning of 1973, as inflation slowed, phase two controls were relaxed and a third phase of the program was introduced. This third phase, however, proved short-lived as inflation began to reaccelerate to new highs. A 60-day price freeze was imposed in June 1973, and a restructured and restrictive fourth phase of the wage-price program followed. The phased control program succeeded in holding inflation to 3.5 percent in 1972 and 1973, but after the program ended, inflation soared.

Proposals to Control Wages and Prices in the 1990s

Some economists argue that wage-price controls were ineffective in the past only because they were short-lived. They contend that permanent wage-price controls would eliminate the nation's inflation psychology and dissipate wage-price pressures by guaranteeing to consumers and businesses that inflation would not occur. That view, however, has never been widely shared. Nonetheless, concerns over strong inflation psychology in the 1990s have sparked renewed interest in possible methods for controlling wages and prices.

One specific proposal made in the 1990s calls for all annual wage increases and cost-of-living wage and payment adjustments to be pegged not to the prior year's inflation rate, but to an inflation projection made by the government for the coming year. Under this proposal, all unions would be required to negotiate wages at the time the projection is made. All government cost-of-living adjustments, such as those made for Social Security payments, also would be made at the time of the projection.

Another long-standing proposal calls for the government to implement a *tax-based incomes policy* as a means to enforce wage-price moderation. Under such a policy, corporate taxes would automatically increase for companies whose annual wage or price increases exceeded the year's inflation rate. Taxes would automatically decline for companies whose annual wage or price increases were less than the year's inflation rate.

Indexation

Some economists see indexation as the preferred long-term answer to dealing with inflation in the U.S. economy. Indexation entails the systematic use of cost-of-living escalator clauses in all money payment contracts.

Under a national program of indexation, all wages, rents, interest payments, profits, taxes, and transfer payments would be tied to cost-of-living escalators so that all monies paid and received would increase proportionally with increases in prices. A 10 percent increase in the price index during the year, for example, would result in a 10 percent increase in wages, rents, interest, profits, taxes, and transfer payments. Indexation would offset any loss in the purchasing power of money with an equivalent increase in the amount of money. Thus, inflation would not result in a redistribution of income or wealth and would not lead to dislocations in consumer and business spending, saving, and investment patterns. Moreover, because inflation in an indexed economy would produce neither winners nor losers, the government could employ stringent anti-inflationary monetary and fiscal policies with broader political and social support than in a nonindexed economy.

A substantial degree of indexation already exists in the U.S. economy. More than 70 million Americans receive at least part of their income in indexed form. Persons receiving income subject to indexation include the following:

- ❑ about one-third of all unionized workers (six million workers covered by contracts containing cost-of-living adjustments that automatically raise wages when prices increase)

- ❑ Social Security recipients

- ❑ retired military and federal civil service employees and their survivors

- ❑ postal workers

- ❑ recipients of food stamps and school lunches

- ❑ most state and local government employees and retirees

- ❑ most recipients of alimony and child care payments

- ❑ private homebuilders whose construction contracts contain escalator provisions

- ❑ many beneficiaries of insurance and annuity policies

Adherents contend that the nationwide application of indexation would bring about a more equitable economy because the benefits and burdens of inflation would be borne evenly by everyone. They also claim that indexation would eliminate any business and union incentives to foster inflationary price and wage actions. In addition, it would eliminate consumer and business *inflation-hedging*—the practice of buying up such nonproductive assets as gold and art objects—which distorts the economy's investment and savings flows.

Opponents of indexation maintain that such a system would institutionalize rather than eliminate inflation. They contend that in an indexed economy, because there are no inflation losers, no social or political pressures would emanate from business or consumer groups for the government to stop inflation. Thus, the government probably would pursue expansionary and stimulative economic objectives. Opponents point to the experience of other countries that employ indexation to illustrate this point.

Opponents further contend that a system of national indexation would nullify the benefits of the indexation that is now in place in the U.S. economy (for Social Security recipients and for other groups that have traditionally lost income and wealth during inflation). Since all income earners would receive the same cost-of-living adjustment, everyone's relative economic position in the economy would remain frozen. Thus, Social Security recipients would fare as poorly as they had before indexation of benefits, which Congress enacted in the 1970s as a means of improving their relative position in an inflationary economy.

The major technical problems with any national indexation program would be the choice of an appropriate index measure and the treatment of existing payment contracts. The use of any broad national measure of inflation, such as the consumer price index (CPI), as the basis for adjusting incomes would likely generate inequities because such measures are averages. Inequities also would be inevitable under any solution to the problem of payment contracts made prior to indexation. For example, long-term corporate and government bondholders would clearly be disadvantaged if they were locked into nonindexed contractual obligations in an indexed economy. On the other hand, holders of fixed-rate mortgages clearly would be disadvantaged if their contracts were converted into indexed obligations in a fully indexed economy.

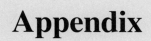

Appendix

Chapter 1
Answers to Discussion Questions

1. *Briefly describe the three functions of money and explain which function, if any, holds the greatest importance.*

Money's basic function is to serve as a medium of exchange—an item that is generally accepted in exchange for goods and services or in the settlement of debt. Money's second function is to serve as a unit of account—a standard of measurement for determining the value of goods and services. Money's third function is to serve as a store of value—a means of holding and accumulating the power to purchase goods and services. To qualify as money, an item must be generally accepted as a nation's medium of exchange; however, all three functions of money must be satisfied if a chosen form of money is to succeed.

2. *Why is fiat money a preferable alternative to commodity money?*

Fiat money is preferable to commodity money because it is usually a better standard of account and store of value. Commodity monies generally lack the physical characteristics of an efficient, practical standard or store of value, namely divisibility, portability, and durability. Fiat money, because of its backing by the law and power of the state, need not have a commodity value equal to its face value. Thus, fiat money such as coin and currency can be designed for durability, divisibility, portability, and protection from counterfeiting.

3. *What is the difference between barter and the use of commodity money?*

In a barter transaction, certain goods and services are accepted in exchange for others based on the mutual needs of the participants. In a commodity money transaction, goods and services can be bought without exchanging other goods and services. Commodity money is similar to barter, however, in that the use of commodity money as an exchange medium is based on its inherent value rather than its representational value or national backing.

4. *"Gold as a commodity money would be a poor medium of exchange in today's American economy." Do you agree or disagree? Explain.*

Gold would be an inefficient and impractical medium of exchange for the millions of transactions involved in today's American economy because it is not readily divisible, portable, nor easy to protect.

5.   *Must fiat money be designated as legal tender by a government in order for it to be generally accepted as a nation's money? Does legal tender status ensure the general acceptability of money? Does government insurance for deposit money affect its acceptability as money? Explain your answers.*

No. In the United States, only coin and currency have legal tender status, but checkable deposits are the preferred means of payment. While legal tender status is usually necessary for fiat money to be generally accepted by a nation, legal tender status does not guarantee national acceptance; the society must first be assured that the designated money will be a good standard and store of value. Government insurance for deposit money increases its acceptability because it protects individual deposits up to a certain limit. Deposit insurance, together with government supervision, has supplanted the public's reliance on legal tender status with confidence in the safety and soundness of the American banking system.

Chapter 2
Answers to Discussion Questions

1. *How does the economy benefit when consumers place their savings in banks and other financial intermediaries instead of holding savings as cash?*

Savings represent a leakage from the economy's circular flow of income and spending. If all savings were held as cash, the economic system might spiral down into a recession; without an infusion of new money, sales would decline, production would be cut, workers would be laid off and, in turn, would spend less. When consumers hold their savings in depositories and investments, commercial banks and other financial intermediaries are able to inject this money back into the economy through loans that enable individuals, businesses, and governments to spend more than they currently have. This keeps the economy in balance.

2. *What functions do financial intermediaries, brokers, and dealers perform that lenders and borrowers could not perform for themselves?*

Financial intermediaries, brokers, and dealers act as middlemen in transactions between lenders and borrowers. By providing established active markets for such transactions, they ensure the rapid and efficient flow of credit throughout the economic sectors of the country.

3. *What would be the economic and financial consequences if the U.S. government announced it was nullifying the federal debt and that in the future the government would spend only the taxes that it collected?*

If the U.S. government nullified its debt, the economic and financial consequences would be devastating. In effect, such action would nullify $4 trillion in wealth shared by consumer, business, and government sectors, both here and abroad, that own the federal debt. If the federal government attempted to limit its spending to collected taxes, it would lose the use of a fiscal policy tool and would be unable to conduct effective fiscal policy.

4. *Why does the Federal Reserve focus primarily on controlling commercial bank lending as opposed to other financial intermediary lending?*

The Federal Reserve focuses primarily on the control of commercial bank lending because commercial banks traditionally were the only intermediaries that could create new demand deposit money. The lending process of commercial banks creates an increasing number of demand deposits throughout the economy. By controlling the amount of money that banks create, the Federal Reserve is able to implement its monetary policy, ensuring against the creation of too much money in the economy, which could lead to inflation, or too little, which could lead to recession.

5.   *Why do rising interest rates affect consumer, business, and government borrowers differently?*

Rising interest rates affect various levels of government differently because state and local governments, unlike the federal government, are often bound by maximum interest rates or limits to their tax base; therefore, they frequently stay out of the credit markets when money is tight.

Large corporations may be less concerned with rising interest rates than small businesses because they can finance their capital spending through bond sales or retained earnings, thereby bypassing the banking system. Small or new businesses, however, have to pay higher rates for funds and they may also find that banks do not have enough available funds to satisfy their credit needs.

For consumers, rising interest rates mean higher rates on variable-rate mortgages and new mortgages. As savers shift their funds from low-paying thrift deposits to other higher-paying savings and investment vehicles, thrifts find it more difficult to make new mortgages. Consumers also may find it harder to obtain automobile loans and other installment credit because state laws limit maximum rates on consumer loans, making it more profitable for lenders to offer business loans that are not subject to usury limits. Faced with higher rates and greater difficulty in obtaining installment credit, consumer purchases of big-ticket items decline.

Chapter 3
Answers to Discussion Questions

1.   *What are the major differences between a commercial bank, a
      savings and loan association, a credit union, and a money market fund?*

Commercial banks, savings and loans, and credit unions are all depository intermediaries, unlike money market funds, which, although similar to depositories,
are technically open-end investment companies that purchase securities for individual or institutional investors. Most legal differences between banks and thrifts
have been eliminated and today the business activities and products of banks and
S&Ls overlap significantly. The primary activities of commercial banks have
traditionally been accepting demand deposits and making loans to businesses,
thereby creating demand deposit dollars. Savings and loans have traditionally
held most of their assets in residential mortgage loans.

Credit unions are cooperatives whose members purchase savings shares, which
allow them to borrow from the pooled savings of members. Credit unions are
considered nonprofit and are not subject to most taxes. They have a competitive
advantage over banks in lending rates because of this status as well as their low
overhead and labor costs.

Money market funds, although fewer in number than banks and thrifts, hold a
large percentage of the funds that flow from consumers and businesses into the
financial markets. Money market funds generally offer higher interest rates than
banks and thrifts because they are willing to invest in more diversified and higher-
risk investment instruments. As a result, money market funds have attracted and
retained deposits, showing phenomenal growth since their inception.

2.   *What competitive advantages, if any, do nonfinancial intermediaries such
      as Merrill Lynch and Sears have over commercial banks?*

Nonfinancial intermediaries (those whose primary business is not lending or
deposit taking) are able to provide financial services that are currently restricted
for most banks, such as insurance, real estate, and brokerage services.
Nonfinancial intermediaries also are not subject to branching restrictions that limit
their marketing efforts and other regulations that banks and bank holding companies are subject to.

3.   *What are the major types of time deposits offered by commercial banks?*

The major time deposits offered by commercial banks include: small denomination certificates of deposit (such as six-month CDs), money market deposits, large denomination time deposits ($100,000 or more), passbook savings deposits, and IRAs and other retirement accounts.

4.   *Explain how a money market deposit account works.*

MMDAs are time deposits on which depositors can write three checks or make three preauthorized transfers each month, while permiting unlimited cash withdrawals or transfers to another account within the same bank. The accounts carry no minimum maturity, but banks may require seven days' notice of withdrawal. MMDAs are not subject to minimum balance requirements but most require balances of $1,000 to $2,500. Most banks also pay split rates on MMDA funds, a lower rate applying if account balances drop below a stated minimum. Unlike accounts held with money market funds, MMDAs are government insured.

5.   *Cite three changes in the deposit structure or operations of financial intermediaries that were brought about by the Monetary Control Act of 1980.*

Changes resulting from the Monetary Control Act of 1980 include the following: The act mandated that all depositories maintain reserves against all transaction accounts and it exempted personal time and savings deposits from reserve requirements. The act also removed restrictions on the geographic expansion and maximum loan values of S&Ls and authorized them to make acquisition, development, and construction loans. The act also gave S&Ls the same powers as commercial banks to issue credit cards, to offer NOW accounts, and to engage in trust and fiduciary activities. The act gave mutual savings banks the option of federal charters, the option of changing from a mutual to a stock-issuing corporate structure to raise needed capital, and the authorization to offer demand deposit accounts to business loan customers as well as to consumers. The act authorized credit unions to make overdraft loans on share draft accounts and to make real estate cooperative loans as well. It also subjected credit unions to the same reserve requirements as banks and other thrifts.

Chapter 4
Answers to Discussion Questions

1. *Explain the use of T-accounts in analyzing the lending process of banks.*

A T-account shows how a single transaction changes a bank's balance sheet without the need to construct a full balance sheet. A T-account shows only the asset or liability account affected by a transaction. Plus or minus signs are used to indicate account increases or decreases. A T-account must balance, with equal pluses (or minuses) on opposite sides, or with offsetting pluses and minuses on the same side. In analyzing commercial bank lending, the T-account shows how cash assets, demand deposits, and required and excess reserves are affected by a loan transaction.

2. *Evaluate this statement: "As my bank's commercial loan officer, I do not create money; I simply lend out the money that depositors have placed in the bank."*

This statement is inaccurate. Commercial loan officers do not lend out depositors' funds; they use depositors' funds as a base on which to create money in the form of a new demand deposit balance for the receiver (business borrower) of the loan. Whenever a bank takes in cash deposits, it must set aside an amount to meet reserve requirements, and can then make loans equal to the remainder. The bank accepts the borrower's debt obligation as an asset and creates a demand deposit balance in the amount of the loan as a liability. Thus, a new loan increases both the bank's assets and its liabilities.

3. *If there were no reserve requirements, could banks create an infinite amount of demand deposits? Would they?*

Theoretically, if a bank were not subject to reserve requirements, it could make new loans (creating new demand deposits) for every dollar it held as cash assets. However, when the proceeds of these new loans were disbursed and the loan funds were transferred through the check collection process, the bank would lose a dollar in cash assets for every dollar it had created. The bank would then find itself without the reserves and the necessary liquidity to operate as a depository institution.

No, because a bank would need to hold a percentage of its assets as cash or on deposit with other banks in order to maintain the liquidity necessary to pay the claims of other banks presenting depositors' checks for collection and to meet cash withdrawals.

4.　*How can a bank that finds itself with a reserve deficiency obtain new reserves? Would these options work if the entire banking system needed additional reserves? Explain.*

A bank with a reserve deficiency has several options in obtaining new reserves: borrowing federal funds from other banks, borrowing from the central bank, selling the government securities it holds as secondary reserve assets in its investment portfolio, calling in loans, or making some other adjustment in its assets and liabilities.

No. With the exception of borrowing from the central bank, these reserve adjustments only redistribute the reserve deficiency throughout the banking system. In such a redistribution, the repayment of bank loans would not result in the making of new loans (and the creation of new demand deposits) because the system would have no excess reserves. Thus, the money supply would contract. The entire banking system can meet a reserve deficiency only with an infusion of reserves from outside the system (i.e., from the Federal Reserve).

5.　*How are federal funds transactions used by banks to adjust their reserves?*

Federal funds are reserves that banks buy from or sell to one another on a daily basis. These transactions are the most popular method used by large banks to obtain needed reserves to fund loans or meet reserve requirements, or to sell reserves in excess of current needs. As banks compete for reserves to expand their own loan and investment portfolios, the cost of federal funds increases. In order to pay the increased cost of borrowing reserves, a bank that wants to expand its earning assets must charge more on loans and earn more on its investments.

EXERCISE:　　**Multiple Expansion of Bank Deposits**

This exercise deals with the multiple expansion of bank deposits under the following simplified assumptions:

- ❏　all bank-created deposits stay in the banking system
- ❏　all newly created funds are held as demand deposits
- ❏　all banks create loans equal to every available (excess) reserve dollar
- ❏　reserve requirements for all deposits = 8%

1.　*What is the multiple expansion equation?*

2.　*What is the multiplier, or expansion coefficient?*

3.   *Complete this chart based on the assumptions above.*

Multiple Expansion of Bank Deposits

Bank Position	New Deposits	New Loans and Investments	Required Reserves
Bank One	$100,000	$_____	$_____
Bank Two	$_____	$_____	$_____
Bank Three	$_____	$_____	$_____
Sum of first 3 banks' deposit expansion:	$_____	$_____	$_____
Sum of remaining banks' deposit expansion	:$_____	$_____	$_____
Total for banking system:	$_____	$_____	$_____

ANSWERS:

1.
$$\frac{1}{\text{Reserve requirement}} \times \text{Initial deposit} = \text{Total deposits}$$

2.   12.5

3.   Multiple Expansion of Bank Deposits

Bank Position	New Deposits	New Loans and Investments	Required Reserves
Bank One	$ 100,000	$ 92,000	$ 8,000
Bank Two	$ 92,000	$ 84,640	$ 7,360
Bank Three	$ 84,640	$ 77,869	$ 6,771
Sum of first 3 banks' deposit expansion:	$ 276,640	$ 254,509	$ 22,131
Sum of remaining banks' deposit expansion:	$ 973,360	$ 895,491	$ 77,869
Total for banking system:	$1,250,000	$ 1,150,000	$100,000

Chapter 5
Answers to Discussion Questions

1. *Why was the nation's check collection system in the nineteenth century inefficient?*

In the 1800s, there was no nationwide system for clearing and collecting checks, direct cross-country relationships were few, and the transfer of money from one part of the country to another was slow and difficult. Inter-regional check clearing and collection involved some inefficiencies: the lengthy and risky circuitous routing of checks across the country; the imposition of exchange charges on checks presented by out-of-town banks; non-par checking that resulted in business firms requiring payment in currency or with a local check; the practice of maintaining compensating balances at numerous banks to collect checks at par; and correspondent banks' practice of using uncollected check funds as reserves.

2. *What four major problems did the Federal Reserve Act of 1913 try to solve?*

The act attempted to correct structural defects in the U.S. banking system, including an inelastic currency, the pyramiding of bank reserves, a lack of central supervision, and an inefficient national payments mechanism.

3. *Based on the structure of the Federal Reserve, what objectives do you think Congress had when it created the central bank?*

The Fed's quasi-governmental, decentralized structure includes government, private, mandatory, and voluntary features in an integrated three-tier pyramid. The Fed's structure reflects a desire for a central bank that would be able to make independent policy decisions and a structure that reflects compromises between competing political and economic interests of the time.

The seven-member Board of Governors is a federal government entity with responsibilities for monetary policy, bank supervision and regulation, and broad oversight of Reserve banks. The nature of board appointments was designed to insulate the board from political pressure, enabling the board to make decisions in the national rather than partisan interest.

The 12 regional district Federal Reserve banks are private and autonomous corporate entities that together make up the central bank. This district structure had two purposes: to decentralize power so that a single central bank would not dominate the nation's economic affairs, and to address the more disparate regional development needs and economic interests of the time.

The 12-member Federal Open Market Committee sets the nation's monetary policy. Its members are drawn from the Federal Reserve Board of Governors and Reserve bank presidents to ensure that the decision-making power of the central bank is shared between private and government sectors and between regional and national interests.

Banks that were members of the Federal Reserve were seen as channels for monetary policy. In a political compromise, state-chartered banks had the option of Federal Reserve membership because Congress was reluctant to impose federal law over state banks, an action that some thought would destroy the dual banking system. Today, monetary policy is channeled through all depository institutions.

4.   *How independent is the Federal Reserve? Would the country be better served if both monetary and fiscal policy were responsibilities of the administration? Why or why not?*

The Federal Reserve is fairly independent because of its quasi-governmental status and decentralized structure. Although the Board of Governors operates as a federal government entity, the 12 Federal Reserve banks are private and largely autonomous. In order to insulate the board from political pressure, presidential appointments to the seven-member Board of Governors are for 14-year terms. And although the Federal Reserve Board must report to Congress twice a year, Congress or the president cannot change board decisions short of legislation. Also, because six of the nine directors of each Reserve bank's board must be nonbankers, the central bank's power does not rest completely with bankers. Finally, the Federal Reserve, through its considerable earnings, has the capacity to fund itself, freeing it from the congressional appropriations process.

The Fed's pivotal function is setting the nation's monetary policy (interest rates and money supply), while the president and Congress are responsible for the nation's fiscal policy (taxation and government spending). Congress established the Federal Reserve to be "independent" so that monetary policy issues would be resolved in the national rather than partisan interest. The separation of monetary policy and fiscal policy decision-making is consistent with the checks and balances that are built into the nation's governmental structure.

5.   *What characteristics do the 12 Federal Reserve district banks and the Federal Reserve member banks have in common? How do they differ?*

The 12 Federal Reserve district banks, like member banks, are private corporate entities that function as autonomous institutions. Unlike member banks, the district Reserve banks hold the banking system's reserves, lend funds to depositories, issue the nation's currency and coin, clear and collect the nation's checks, and provide banking services to the government and to depository institutions.

District Reserve bank boards indirectly influence the monetary policy-making process, and consequently the director selection process and board structure of the district Reserve banks are much more complex than those of member banks. Although district Reserve banks are profit-making entities, a sizable portion of their profits are returned to the Treasury, unlike those of member banks. Other differences are that member banks must subscribe to stock in their district Reserve banks, and member banks may hold national or state charters.

Chapter 6
Answers to Discussion Questions

1. *Discuss the validity of this statement: "The 1980 Monetary Control Act's imposition of universal reserve requirements strengthened the Federal Reserve's ability to conduct monetary policy."*

The Monetary Control Act's imposition of uniform reserve requirements on all depositories undoubtedly strengthened the Federal Reserve's ability to conduct monetary policy because it brought the reserves of nonmember banks under the Fed's control. Prior to the act, nonmember banks were subject only to state reserve requirements, which were based on concerns of liquidity and safety but not of monetary policy. The act broadened the Fed's power to influence the cost and availability of money (through open-market operations that affect reserve levels) because it subjected a greater number of financial institutions to reserve requirements.

2. *How is the discount rate (and discount window lending) used today as a monetary policy tool?*

Today, changes in the discount rate generally support monetary policy changes made weeks or months earlier and already implemented through open-market operations.

Today, discount window lending is primarily a safety valve for individual banks that need to borrow reserves for a day or two until they can make other adjustments in their assets and liabilities. Discount window loans are mainly used by smaller banks under reserve stress due to short-term liquidity drains.

3. *Whenever the Federal Reserve buys or sells anything, bank reserves and the money supply change. Why, then, does the Federal Reserve limit its buying and selling to government securities in the open market?*

The Fed uses the open-market purchase and sale of government securities, in particular, because the active dealer market in government securities ensures the prompt and efficient implementation of open-market operations. A bank might be reluctant to alter its reserves through a purchase or sale of government securities in accordance with the Fed's monetary policy strategy; but a bank has no control over the deposits it holds for dealer firms. Dealer firms are not motivated by concerns of reserves, but by profit concerns of price and marketability; thus, dealers can always be induced to accept a transaction if the Fed offers to sell securities at a low enough price (to reduce bank reserves) or offers to buy securities at a high enough price (to increase bank reserves).

4.   *Changing reserve requirement percentages is one way that reserve require-ments can be used as a monetary policy tool. What are the two other ways?*

The Federal Reserve can reclassify (include or exclude) the kinds of eligible assets that depository institutions can use to meet reserve requirements, and it can reclassify the kinds of liabilities that are subject to reserve requirements.

5.   *Outline an appropriate anti-inflationary economic policy that uses the three monetary and two fiscal policy tools in a complementary way.*

The monetary policy tools to fight inflation include increasing the discount rate, raising reserve requirements, and selling government securities from the open-market portfo-lio; the anti-inflationary fiscal policy tools include increasing taxes and reducing government spending.

6.   *Why is an anti-inflationary fiscal policy more difficult to implement than an anti-inflationary monetary policy?*

An anti-inflationary fiscal policy is difficult to implement for several reasons. The president and Congress have always been reluctant to use the unpopular tool of raising taxes. Cutting government spending is also difficult because much of it is nondiscretionary and thus beyond the short-term control of Congress and the administration.

Fiscal policy tools and monetary policy tools also work in different ways: fiscal policy tools affect income, spending, and savings; monetary policy tools affect interest rates, bank reserves, and money supply growth. Monetary and fiscal policy must work together in the same direction to contain inflation or to counter recession.

EXERCISE: **Economic Policy Problem**

Write *inflation* next to the options that are appropriate for curbing inflation, and write *recession* next to those options that are appropriate for stopping recession.

1.   _____   increasing reserve requirements

2.   _____   decreasing reserve requirements

3.   _____   buying government securities

4.   _____   selling government securities

5.   _____   lowering the discount rate

6.   _____   raising the discount rate

7.   _____   raising taxes

8.   _____   lowering taxes

9. _____ increasing government spending

10. _____ reducing government spending

Indicate whether total spending would increase, decrease, or remain the same, by writing *I*, *D*, or *S* next to the statement.

11. _____ increased government spending is financed by increased taxation

12. _____ increased government spending is financed by increased borrowing

13. _____ government spending and taxation are reduced

ANSWERS: **Economic Policy Problem**

1. inflation
2. recession
3. recession
4. inflation
5. recession
6. inflation
7. inflation
8. recession
9. recession
10. inflation
11. S
12. I
13. S

Chapter 7
Answers to Discussion Questions

1.   *Inasmuch as cash can be counted toward meeting reserve requirements, is it advantageous for a bank to have cash on hand in excess of its daily needs?*

No. Although a primary responsibility of banks is satisfying the public's need for cash, a bank that holds excess cash misses revenue opportunities because idle cash earns nothing. Excess cash on hand also presents storage and security problems.

2.   *What are the three basic ways that interbank checks are collected in the United States? What factors determine a bank's choice?*

U.S. banks collect interbank checks through local clearing houses, correspondent banks, and the Federal Reserve. Clearing houses are used by banks in a given area that regularly receive checks drawn on each other. The clearing house arrangement cuts the cost of transporting and presenting checks to numerous other banks. Correspondent banks are used for check collection by smaller banks that do not own reader-sorters or that do not have direct account relationships with the Federal Reserve. Larger banks clear checks directly through Federal Reserve banks. This is particularly true of correspondent banks that require interregional collection.

3,   *Explain how a local clearing house operates and the advantages it offers for clearing checks.*

In a clearing house arrangement, representatives from banks in a given area that regularly receive large numbers of checks drawn on each other meet at a central site. There they exchange and collect payment for local checks. Collection is made by netting the amounts presented by each bank against the others. At major regional clearing houses settlement for the transactions is made against the Federal Reserve accounts of participating banks. The advantage of the clearing house arrangement is that banks need not transport and present checks individually to numerous other banks. This and the fact that a bank need only maintain one low-balance clearing account for check settlement, as opposed to numerous accounts at several banks, make the check collection process more efficient and cost-effective.

4.   What are MICR instructions, what is their significance, and how do banks manage MICR data flow?

MICR instructions are magnetic ink character recognition symbols that appear on the bottom of checks, allowing reader-sorter machines to process checks at high speed. MICR encoding shows the check writer's account number, the check number, and the dollar amount of the check; the check routing procedure (including the Federal Reserve district, clearance through a head office, branch office, or special arrangement, and immediate or deferred credit); the bank's identifying number; and a number to verify routing accuracy.

The use of MICR instructions allows banks with computerized systems to record data and post credits and debits to individual accounts quickly and efficiently. Magnetic tapes are made of all MICR data at the end of the day— or more frequently, depending on a bank's size and its volume of check transactions. After the day's final tape is made, the bank enters the data into its master files, updating each account's debits and credits for the day and computing a new closing balance. The sum of these account balances is the demand deposit total in the bank's daily statement.

5.   What is Federal Reserve float, how does it occur, and how does it differ from bank float? In your answer, explain how uncollected funds differ from available funds.

Federal Reserve float represents the extra reserves that exist in the banking system when the Fed credits banks for checks presented but not yet collected. Depending on the paying bank's proximity to a Federal Reserve bank, the account of the depositing bank is credited on the day of presentation or within a maximum of two business days, whether or not the Fed has processed the checks or has shipped them to the paying bank. The depositing bank can use the funds for reserves or other purposes as soon as its account is credited. Federal Reserve float exists until the paying bank's Reserve account is debited.

Bank float represents the funds available to a bank that result from the time lag after a check deposit is credited and the time the depositor is able to use the funds. Uncollected funds are those that have been credited to a depositor's account but are not collected and not available for withdrawal by the depositor. Available funds are those that a depositor can withdraw.

6.   Why have retail electronic funds transfer systems and services been slow to develop in the United States? Is the electronic payments revolution in U.S. banking inevitable? Justify your answer.

Retail EFT services have been slow to develop in the United States because customers are reluctant to accept new technologies; because customers like the service and the price of the paper-based products that banks offer; and because commercial laws and regulations have been slow to adapt to the use of EFTs. Today, automated teller machines are widely used. Point-of-sale terminals are not yet widely used because of several drawbacks: they eliminate the float available to consumers through check or credit card payments; they tie retailers to one bank; and they can be used only by customers of participating banks. Telephone bill-paying services have not had widespread consumer appeal, nor have home banking (personal computer) services, which most consumers find too complicated and too costly.

Banks and banking industry analysts disagree on the future general acceptance and widespread use of EFTs. Some banks feel that technology will speed the change, while others point out that significant changes in public attitudes and banking law are necessary before technological advancements will take hold.

Chapter 8
Answers to Discussion Questions

1.   *Discuss the constraints commercial banks face in their pursuit of profits.*

One major constraint is the increased cost to banks of deposits and other sources of funds. Another is the losses incurred by banks on problem loans. Banks have to pay interest on an increasingly larger share of their total deposits. At most banks, depositors have shifted their funds from demand deposit accounts to interest-paying transaction accounts and have demonstrated a willingness to withdraw funds to obtain higher-yielding returns elsewhere. The impact of these shifts in deposits has been particularly strong on smaller banks.

Losses on loans have cut into bank profitability in recent years, especially losses on agricultural loans (particularly for small banks in agricultural states), energy loans, commercial real estate loans, and loans to less-developed countries (particularly by the largest banks). Profitability has been further constrained by the setting aside of increased amounts of loan loss reserves against the prospect of future loan losses.

2.   *Cite the three largest loan categories on commercial banks' books and two characteristics that differentiate each loan category.*

The three largest loan categories are business loans, real estate loans, and consumer loans. Business loans are typically short-term loans that carry low processing costs and relatively low risk. They can be single-payment or installment loans, secured by collateral or unsecured. Not subject to usury limits in most states, they offer considerable pricing flexibility but generally low yields. They may involve loan commitment fees or require compensating balances.

Real estate loans are classified by type of collateral rather than according to intended purpose. Because they are fully collateralized, they are among the lowest-risk loans. They are, however, subject to usury ceilings in most states.

Consumer loans are subject to usury ceilings in many states, carry relatively greater credit risk than other loans, are subject to numerous consumer protection regulations, and carry relatively high processing costs. Some banks book consumer loans as discount loans.

3.   Why would a business firm pay a loan commitment fee? Why would a bank impose a compensating balance on a loan? Why would a bank participate in a loan with another bank?

Business firms pay loan commitment fees in exchange for the preauthorization of a loan to be made weeks or months ahead, which ensures that credit will be available when they need it.

Banks impose compensating balances on loans to increase their profitability; by investing the compensating balances, banks increase their return on the loans. Compensating balances also give banks extra protection in the case of default because existing deposit balances can be used to offset outstanding loan balances.

Loan participations enable smaller banks to undertake loans that otherwise would be too large to absorb individually. Participating banks commit fewer reserves and take on less risk. Also, banks participate in large loans that would be legally prohibited otherwise. Correspondent banks participate in large business loans as part of their respondent relationships and to diversify their own portfolios.

4.   Why do banks buy securities? Explain the difference between U.S. Treasury securities, federal agency securities, and municipal obligations.

Banks buy securities to provide a secondary source of liquidity, to earn interest income as well as capital gains, and to counterbalance risks taken in bank lending. Bank purchases of local government securities also help to promote account and deposit relationships. Banks also can use securities to meet pledging requirements against trust operations and as collateral for government deposits.

U.S. Treasury securities include Treasury bills, notes, and bonds. They are free of credit risk, traded in a large secondary market, and their income is exempt from state and local taxes. Banks use Treasury securities as short-term investments and as a secondary source of liquidity for expected and unexpected demands for funds. The Federal Reserve implements its monetary policy by buying and selling Treasury securities in open-market operations.

Federal agency obligations are issues of federally owned or sponsored agencies and corporations. They are second only to Treasury securities in safety and marketability, and offer somewhat higher yields. Some provide income free from state and local taxes.

State and local obligations (municipal securities) include short-term tax anticipation notes and tax warrants and long-term bonds issued by state and local governments and their agencies. These obligations are higher in credit risk than Treasury or federal agency securities. Municipal securities pay lower interest returns than other securities, but income earned on these issues is exempt from federal income tax.

5.   *What are the objectives of an asset allocation strategy?*

The overall objective of an asset allocation strategy is to expand bank earnings by continually reallocating bank assets. After meeting the bank's operating and fixed-asset expenses, bankers using the asset allocation strategy allocate funds in four ways to achieve various objectives: first to primary reserves in order to meet reserve requirements and daily liquidity needs; next to secondary reserves to cover deposit outflows; then to the bank's income account (loan portfolio) to meet all loan demand; and finally to the bank's residual account to make investments in securities.

6.   *What is liability management? If you were in charge of liability management at your bank, what sources of managed liabilities would you rely on and why?*

Liability management involves the use of borrowed or purchased money to fund loan and investment growth. Banks using this approach try to fund a desired increase in their assets by increasing their liabilities using controllable financial instruments and market practices. These instruments and practices may include borrowing federal funds, issuing negotiable certificates of deposit, borrowing Eurodollars, using the proceeds of commercial paper sold by affiliates, engaging in repurchase agreements, and selling loans under repurchase agreements.

7.   *What tactics can be used to implement a spread management strategy?*

Maturity matching, duration matching, and variable rate pricing of all loans and deposits are three tactical approaches that a bank can use to match its assets and liabilities for the purpose of maintaining a constant interest rate spread. In maturity matching, bankers attempt to match the maturities of specific loans and investments with the maturities of specific deposit liabilities. In duration matching, bankers attempt to match their assets and liabilities based on the average length of time that these are expected to remain on the balance sheet. In imposing variable rates on both loans and deposits, bankers seek to protect the bank's spread from unexpected interest rate changes. Since both deposit rates and loan charges are increased or decreased in tandem, a bank's interest spread remains constant whether interest rates go up or down.

EXERCISE 1: **Balance Sheet Problems**

Problem 1

Assume

❑   Required reserves against transaction deposits = 10%

❑   Required reserves against time deposits = 5%

The First Commercial Bank

Assets		Liabilities and Capital	
Cash	500	Transaction deposits	40,000
Reserve account	7,500	Savings deposits	10,000
Correspondent		Time deposit (CDs)	30,000
deposits	2,000	Borrowing from FRB	1,000
Securities	30,000	Total Liabilities	81,000
Loans	40,000	Capital	9,000
Building	10,000	Total Liabilities	
Total Assets	$90,000	and Capital	$90,000

Based on this balance sheet, First Commercial Bank's

1.   primary reserves are

2.   secondary reserves are

3.   total reserves are

4.   required reserves are

5.   earning assets are

6.   First Commercial could create _____ of new money.

Problem 2

Assume

Required reserves against transaction deposits = 10%

Required reserves against time deposits = 5%

Commercial Banking System
(millions of dollars)

Assets		Liabilities and Capital	
Vault cash	5,000	Transaction deposits	
Cash items in process		(private)	140,000
of collection	20,000	(bank)	10,000
Federal Reserve		(U.S. govt.)	2,600
balances	29,000	Time deposits	280,000
Balance at banks	10,000	Federal Reserve	
Securities	100,000	borrowings	1,400
Loans	270,000		
Total Assets	$434,000	Total Liabilities	$434,000

Based on this balance sheet (in millions of dollars), the banking system's

1.   excess reserves are

2.   secondary reserves are

3.   required reserves are

4.   total reserves are

5.   earning assets are

6.   net free reserves are

EXERCISE 2:   **Performance Ratio Problem**

Balance Sheet of Second Community Bank

<u>Assets</u>

Cash and due from banks	$105,216,000
Federal funds sold/Securities purchased under agreements to resell	157,998,000
Securities	247,254,000
Loans	340,104,000
Property and other assets	39,798,000
Total assets	$890,370,000

<u>Liabilities and Capital</u>

Transaction deposits	$257,403,000
Time and savings deposits	441,810,000
Federal funds purchased/ Securities sold under agreements to repurchase	103,201,000
Other liabilities	24,698,000
Total liabilities	$827,112,000
Capital	63,258,000
Total liabilities and Capital	$890,370,000

Income Statement of Second Community Bank

<u>Interest Income</u>

Interest on loans	$48,204,195
Interest on securities	18,522,125
<u>Noninterest Income</u>	21,708,078
Total Operating Income	$83,434,398
<u>Interest Expense</u>	
Interest on deposits	$56,867,695
<u>Noninterest Expense</u>	
Salaries and benefits	9,382,920
Loan loss provisions	810,204
Other operating expenses	2,044,837
Total Operating Expenses	$69,105,656
<u>Income Before Taxes</u>	$14,328,742
Less taxes	5,294,229
<u>Net Income</u>	$ 9,034,513

Based on the balance sheet and the income statement, what is Second Community Bank's

1.   return on assets (net income/assets)

2.   return on equity (net income/equity)

3.   ratio of capital to assets (equity/assets)

4.   ratio of loans to deposits (loans/deposits)

5.   Interest expenses represent ——————— % of Second Community Bank's total operating expenses.

6.   Salaries and benefits represent ——————— % of Second Community Bank's total operating expenses.

7.   What other information is needed to assess Second Community Bank's performance?

ANSWERS: Balance Sheet Problems

Problem 1

1. $10,000
2. $30,000
3. $8,000
4. $5,500
5. $70,000
6. $2,500

Problem 2

1. $4,740
2. $100,000
3. $29,260
4. $34,000
5. $370,000
6. $3,340

ANSWERS: **Performance Ratio Problems**

1.   1.01%
2.   14.28%
3.   7.10%
4.   48.64%
5.   '82.29%
6.   13.58%
7.   a qualitative evaluation of management performance

Chapter 9
Answers to Discussion Questions

1.   In what way does the regulation of banks differ from the regulation of other business firms (for example, automobile manufacturing companies)?

The regulation of banks is shaped by certain public policy goals that do not apply to other business firms, specifically: to maintain public confidence in the safety and soundness of the banking system; to protect banks, their depositors, and their communities from bank failures; to foster healthy competition in banking; to protect bank owners from fraud and mismanagement; and to protect bank customers against discrimination or other abuses. Because banks have the power to create money, they are more closely regulated than other private companies and, in terms of regulatory supervision, bear a closer relation to public utilities than to private businesses.

2.   Does it make a difference whether a new bank obtains a national or a state charter?

Yes. A bank's choice of charter will determine to what degree federal or state government will share in the bank's regulatory control and examination, that is, whether a bank's primary regulator will be a state or a federal agency. Federally (nationally) chartered banks must be Federal Reserve members and must be FDIC-insured, but state-chartered banks have the option of joining the FDIC and/or the Federal Reserve. The Comptroller of the Currency oversees nationally chartered banks; the Federal Reserve focuses on state-chartered member banks; and the FDIC examines state-chartered banks that are FDIC-insured but not members of the Federal Reserve. The choice of a state or federal charter is also important because state laws often differ from federal laws in their restrictions on bank branching and product powers.

3.   Explain the terms <u>dual banking</u> and <u>unit banking</u>.

Dual banking refers to the dual regulation of U.S. banks that allows a bank to be chartered by either the federal government, through the Comptroller of the Currency, or by the state in which the bank is located and through a series of membership options that subject banks to the regulation of both the federal government and the state. Unit banking refers to the single bank office structure of the U.S. banking industry that has been shaped by federal and state laws that have severely limited branching, merging, and interstate expansion.

4.   Bankers, regulators, and economists have debated the public benefits and costs of a dual banking system since it became a reality in 1863. What are the arguments for and against dual banking?

The arguments for dual banking are that it reflects the system of checks and balances on which our government is based, allowing banks to counter abusive or inadequate regulatory control by changing their type of charter at any time. Proponents of dual banking also feel that it allows state governments to regulate banks in ways that more closely reflect the needs and concerns of the banks' local communities and depositors. It is also felt that dual banking promotes innovation and experimentation at the state level without a national disruption of the banking system.

The arguments against dual banking are that it works counter to the public good because much of the nation's rural and suburban population does not benefit from the services and products of large money center banks due to prohibitions against bank branching. The lack of uniformity among state banking laws is seen by some as disruptive to the banking environment. Also, because banks can shop for a charter from state to state, decisions on state chartering may hold the potential for pressure and political favor. Finally, some bankers feel that state governments do not have adequate resources to ensure highly paid and well-trained bank examiners, that dual examinations are a waste of time and money, and that dual regulation enables banks to play off federal and state regulators against each other.

5.   *Who regulates commercial banks in the United States today?*

Depending on type of charter, banks are regulated by a state agency, a federal agency, or a combination of both. The current bank regulatory structure includes state banking departments, the Comptroller of the Currency, the Federal Reserve, and the Federal Deposit Insurance Corporation.

6.   *Cite three major changes in bank regulation brought about by the Monetary Control Act of 1980. What are the major provisions of the Federal Deposit Insurance Corporation Improvement Act of 1991?*

The Monetary Control Act of 1980 phased out interest rate ceilings on time and savings deposits at banks and thrifts; increased FDIC insurance coverage on all deposit accounts to $100,000; gave broader powers to savings banks, S&Ls, and credit unions, thereby altering the competitive relationship between banks and thrifts; extended the Federal Reserve's reserve requirements to all depository institutions; authorized the use of transaction accounts on a national basis; gave all depositories equal access to the Federal Reserve's discount window; and required the explicit and uniform pricing of Federal Reserve services under uniform terms for all depository institutions.

The Federal Deposit Insurance Corporation Improvement Act of 1991 provided new funding for the depleted federal deposit insurance fund; limited the FDIC's use of the *too big to fail* policy and poorly capitalized banks' use of brokered CDs; gave the Federal Reserve new authority to examine the branches, agencies, and nonbank operations of foreign banks in the United States; required the federal bank regulators to build into the bank examination rating specific regulatory sanctions for banks with capital deficiencies; and mandated uniform disclosure of banks' deposit rates and fees (Truth in Savings Act).

Chapter 10
Answers to Discussion Questions

1.   *Why do most bank analysts anticipate a continuing squeeze on bank profits in the 1990s? What strategies are banks employing to protect their profit margins?*

Banks are expected to feel continuing constraints on profitability due to growing operating expenses, increasing interest costs on deposit funds, and rising marketing and advertising costs.

In order to protect bank profit margins, bankers will have to reassess the appeal and effectiveness of their bank products and services. A bank's marketing activities and products may have to focus on one or two market groups that can be served most effectively and most profitably, a trend that may lead to the segmentation of banking into separate product and service markets. Banks undoubtedly also will strive to contain their operating costs by charging specific fees for their various services and by instituting cost containment strategies directed at such fast-rising operating cost components as health insurance benefits and automation costs.

2.   *What are the major public policy issues in the debate over repeal of the 1933 Glass-Steagall Act?*

One major public policy issue in the debate is whether or not repeal of the act would increase bank risk, thereby threatening the safety and soundness of banking. Many commercial bankers argue that they already underwrite and deal in numerous securities. They point out that lending to corporations is as risky, if not more risky, than underwriting corporate stocks and bonds, and that banks already participate in securities markets overseas.

A second issue involves the potential for conflict of interest if banks are allowed to underwrite stocks and bonds. Bankers in favor of repeal argue that regulations to limit this possibility could be enacted for commercial banks as they have been for investment bankers and brokers.

A third issue is whether or not repeal of the act would lead to widescale mergers of banks and brokerage firms, thereby limiting competition and creating financial conglomerates. Bankers in favor of repeal argue that competition would increase because a small number of large securities firms already handle the greatest percentage of the U.S. underwriting business.

3.   *Some bankers contend that federal legislation authorizing interstate banking is unnecessary because changes in technology, competitive relationships, and state laws have made federal interstate banking prohibitions irrelevant. Discuss this position.*

This position can be supported by the following: most of the states now permit both <u>interstate</u> branching and <u>interstate</u> banking through reciprocal agreements. In addition, numerous states have extensive interstate linkages of ATMs; many interstate banks were created by bank holding companies and were grandfathered; and many bank holding companies and nonbank businesses established interstate financial service networks by acquiring consumer banks. Banks and bank depositors also can freely move funds to different regions by phone and computer terminal. However, it can be argued that federal legislation would provide necessary uniformity between states so that fair competition would be assured.

4.   *Based on consensus projections for the 1990s, what impact will electronic and computer technology likely have on bank markets and products, branch banking, check collection and check processing, and bank employment? Do you agree with these projections? If not, why?*

Electronic and computer technology is expected to have a marked impact in the following ways: more banking transactions will be handled at terminals in retail stores and at home through cable television and by phone; most banks will be linked by computer to national funds transfer systems; the current volume of check transactions will not subside, but a greater number of transactions will be made electronically; check truncation will become more commonplace; banks of all sizes will be able to increase the speed and broaden the application of data and money transfers; because of the ready availability of inexpensive computers, all banks will be able to provide sophisticated cash management services to customers at lower costs; and nonbank competitors also will strive to make the best use of the new technology.

5.   *In light of the likelihood of significant consolidation in banking in the years ahead, what is the likely future of the nation's small community-based banks?*

Small community-based banks will continue to constitute the bulk of the banking industry. These banks will continue to provide a broad range of services, but to a more narrowly defined market. Such banks will face increasingly intense competition and greater business risks.

6.   *In the year 2010, the banking workforce will be better trained, more technically oriented, and more productive than in the 1990s. If you were hired as a management consultant, what suggestions would you make for new training programs and initiatives to assure adequate preparation of your bank's personnel in the anticipated banking environment of the future?*

New training programs and initiatives should take into account the changing nature of the banking workforce and the rapidly changing banking environment. Clerical, professional, and executive functions all will require greater training in computer technology and automation; banks will need fewer clerical workers (although this work category will remain significant) and more technical, professional, and managerial workers. More women are likely to be employed by banks and more people aged 30 to 50. Future bank employees are likely to be more concerned with job satisfaction and job security than salaries and a major emphasis of bank management will have to be on improving the quality of worklife. Such an emphasis will likely generate increased productivity.

Chapter 11
Answers to Discussion Questions

1.   The Federal Reserve's monetary policy strategy involves the setting of three different levels of targets—operational (short-term), intermediate, and long-term. Why does the Federal Reserve do this?

In order to reach its long-term (year-to-year) targets for employment, price stability, and economic growth (over which the Federal Reserve has no direct control), the Federal Reserve tries to reach intermediate targets for the money supply (over which the Fed has some control). The Fed tries to achieve these intermediate (quarter-to-quarter) targets, in turn, by focusing on short-term (week-to-week) operational objectives for the growth rate of bank reserves and the federal funds rate, which it can control directly. Thus, the Fed focuses its open-market operations on short-term targets that it can directly control in order to meet intermediate targets, which eventually influence the long-term targets that are beyond the Fed's direct control.

2.   How do dynamic and defensive open-market operations differ? How can you tell whether Federal Reserve open-market operations have been dynamic or defensive in any given week?

Dynamic open-market operations involve the Fed's buying and selling of government securities to counter recession, to contain inflation, or to promote balanced economic growth. Defensive open-market operations are made to offset or nullify undesired day-to-day changes in bank reserves and money supply—changes unrelated to monetary policy, such as the public's handling of cash and deposit funds, the daily level of Federal Reserve float, the actions of the U.S. Treasury, and the asset-liability management strategies of banks.

 The Fed's defensive open-market techniques include repurchase agreements and reverse repos, which are temporary purchases or sales of Treasury or agency obligations. These instruments are short-term and self-reversing; they first supply and then absorb reserves, or vice versa. Defensive operations are characterized by the Fed's use of these techniques.

3.   In what ways can the actions of the public affect bank reserves and money supply growth?

Whenever the public withdraws cash from the banking system it decreases total bank reserves (of which cash is a part). Similarly, whenever the public deposits cash it increases bank reserves. If the Fed did not take defensive action to ensure its short-term objectives regarding reserves, it would not be able to achieve its intermediate money supply targets. Many actions of the public are predictable, such as seasonal cash needs or weekend withdrawals. Other public actions can be more problematic. A shift of funds from demand accounts to high interest-earning time accounts and certificates of deposit increases banks' excess reserves because these deposit instruments do not require reserves. A shift of funds from small to big banks increases required reserves because large banks have higher reserve requirements than small banks.

4. *What is the purpose of TT&L accounts? How do the remittance and note option accounts work, and how do they affect bank reserves?*

As Treasury balances at Federal Reserve banks increase (from tax receipts or borrowings), bank reserves decline; as Treasury balances at Reserve banks decrease (due to government spending), bank reserves increase. The purpose of TT&Ls is to minimize the impact of Treasury actions on bank reserves and monetary policy control.

TT&L accounts are accounts maintained at commercial banks for the U.S. Treasury. Federal tax receipts and funds received from bond sales are deposited in TT&Ls. When the Treasury needs funds to meet Social Security payments, civil service payroll, and other government disbursements, it transfers its deposits from TT&Ls at commercial banks to its disbursement accounts at Federal Reserve banks.

Under the remittance option, banks are not required to pay for TT&L deposits (which build up a bank's deposit base and provide for new loans and investments), but they may hold the funds for only one day. Under the note option, banks may hold the funds for extended periods, but they must pay interest on the funds.

5. *Over the decades, the Federal Reserve has tried to conduct monetary policy by either controlling interest rates or controlling reserves and money supply growth. What approach does the Federal Reserve use today, and why?*

Today, the Federal Reserve emphasizes the control of nonborrowed reserves and money supply growth through open-market operations. In the 1970s, the Fed concentrated on a target range for the federal funds rate, but whenever strong demand drove the federal funds rate above the targeted range ceiling, the Fed invariably added reserves, which in turn caused new money creation and money supply growth beyond the Fed's targets. This difficulty in controlling money supply growth led the Fed to focus in the 1980s on controlling levels of nonborrowed reserves through open-market operations in order to better control money supply growth.

6. *Assume the Federal Reserve is on its targeted growth path for nonborrowed reserves. What nonpolicy factors could cause nonborrowed reserves to go off target?*

The targeted growth of nonborrowed reserves could be driven off target by numerous factors: by bank depositors who increase their cash deposits or cash withdrawals, and who move funds between types of accounts, between small and large banks, or into institutions not controlled by the Federal Reserve; by an increase or decrease in the daily level of Federal Reserve float; by the U.S. Treasury's management of its tax receipts and spending; by banks' asset/liability management strategies; and by the time lag between the implementation of a money policy strategy and the public's awareness of it and consequent changes in lending and borrowing patterns.

Chapter 12
Answers to Discussion Questions

1.   Briefly explain the quantity theory of money and the Fisher equation of exchange.

The quantity theory of money holds that there is a direct and proportional relationship between the quantity of money and prices: an increase in the quantity of money causes an increase in prices; a decrease in the quantity of money causes a decrease in prices.

The Fisher equation of exchange ($\underline{MV}=\underline{PT}$ or $\underline{MV}=\underline{PQ}$) states that the quantity of money in circulation at any given time ($\underline{M}$) multiplied by the velocity of that money ($\underline{V}$) equals the average price of all goods and services sold ($\underline{P}$) multiplied by the volume of transactions or total quantity of goods sold ($\underline{T}$ or $\underline{Q}$). In other words, the total amount of money spent on goods and services must equal the total amount of money received from the sale of those goods and services.

2.   A key condition for Keynesian "equilibrium" is $\underline{S}=\underline{I}+\underline{G}$. Why is this so?

When the level of savings in the economy is offset exactly by the level of investment and government spending (that is, when $\underline{S}=\underline{I}+\underline{G}$), the economy will attain equilibrium (balance between aggregate demand and aggregate supply). If aggregate demand exceeds aggregate supply, goods become scarce, businesses expect higher profits and increase their production, and the GDP increases (producing inflation if the economy is already at full employment); if aggregate supply exceeds aggregate demand, goods remain unsold, businesses reduce output, and GDP declines (producing recession if prices do not decline).

3.   What are the determinants of the total demand for money? What would happen to demand if there were á massive increase in banks' issuance, and the public's use, of credit cards?

The total demand for money is determined by the level of income (which affects transactions demand and precautionary demand) and the interest rate (which affects speculative demand). The higher the level of income, the more money people will hold for transactions purposes and precautionary motives. Speculative demand for money is inversely related to interest rates: the higher the rates, the lower the prices of bonds and the smaller the amount of speculative balances held (because most speculative funds have already been used to purchase bonds).

A massive increase in bank issuance and public use of credit cards would indicate a change in the public's liquidity preference. Such an increase would presumably lower the transactions and precautionary demands for money, causing interest rates to fall and raising consumption and investment to a higher equilibrium level of income and output.

4. *In implementing monetary policy, why does it matter whether the MEI curve is highly elastic or highly inelastic?*

If the MEI curve is highly elastic, investment spending is highly responsive to small changes in interest rates; if the curve is inelastic, investment spending is much less responsive to interest rate changes. Thus, in implementing monetary policy, the Federal Reserve would have to bring about a larger change in interest rates to achieve a small change in investment spending if the MEI curve were inelastic; on the other hand, a small change in interest rates brought about by the Fed's monetary policy could lead to very significant changes in the level of investment spending if the MEI curve were highly elastic.

5. *What are the major differences between monetarism and Keynesian theory?*

Keynesian theory maintains that the key relationship in the economy is that between total income and total spending. Monetarism maintains that the key relationship in the economy is that between total income and the quantity of money that the public prefers to hold. Based on this fundamental difference, monetarists believe that changes in the money supply will cause changes in income and output, changes in price levels over time, and changes in total spending in the economy. Monetarists also believe that without money supply changes, fiscal policy changes will have little effect on total spending or GDP.

6. *Why do monetarists contend that the only appropriate monetary policy is a constant 3 percent to 5 percent annual growth in the money supply? Do you agree or disagree with this contention? Why?*

Monetarists contend that a constant 3 percent to 5 percent annual growth in money supply would match the U.S. economy's long-term annual growth rate, and would provide the economy with just enough new money for balanced, sustained growth. They contend that because of the variable and unpredictable time lags between changes in money supply and the consequent changes in income and output, the Fed's countercyclical approach to monetary policy actually destabilizes the economy. They also maintain that the Fed invariably overreacts when the economic response to monetary policy changes is slow. Economists vary in their opinions as to the legitimacy of these contentions.

Chapter 13
Answers to Discussion Questions

1.   How can unemployment and employment increase concurrently? How is the unemployment rate determined?

Unemployment and employment can increase concurrently if new entrants or reentrants to the labor force expand the size of the labor force and some obtain jobs while others do not. Even though no existing workers are being laid off and employment is actually increasing, unemployment is increasing as well.

The unemployment rate is determined by taking the number of unemployed people in the labor force as a percentage of the labor force (everyone over age 16 employed or seeking a job). Thus, the unemployment rate represents the percentage of the U.S. labor force that are not working and are seeking work.

2.   Economists attribute inflation to three primary sources. What are they? Why is the wage-price spiral often referred to as the glue that binds the sources of inflation together?

One source of inflation is demand-pull inflation, in which prices begin to rise because the demand for goods and services exceeds the supply, a typical occurrence when there is rapid growth in the nation's money supply. Another source is cost-push inflation, in which producers pass on their increased production costs to consumers in the form of price markups. A third source is scarcity-induced inflation, in which prices rise as the result of a shortage of key commodities or goods, whether induced by nature or government action.

In a wage-price spiral, demand-pull pressures pull up prices, and workers seek higher wages to counteract their loss of purchasing power. If the higher wages are paid, production costs rise, which in turn pushes up prices due to cost-push inflation. The result is that workers again lose purchasing power and again press for higher wages, which, if obtained, again push up production costs and eventually prices.

3.   What effect does inflation have on the redistribution of income and wealth?

Inflation redistributes income from those with fixed or slow-rising incomes (such as pensioners, Social Security recipients, and government workers) to those whose incomes rise rapidly or contain cost-of-living adjustments (such as self-employed professionals and union workers).

Inflation redistributes wealth from creditors and savers to debtors, particularly when the inflation is unanticipated. In inflation, creditors who make longer-term, fixed-rate loans lose money because they are repaid in dollars that have less value than those originally lent. Savers who use fixed-rate savings instruments lose money if the interest rate they receive on their funds is lower than the inflation rate.

4. *Why would an unanticipated inflation rate of 5 percent be more harmful to banks than a correctly anticipated inflation rate of 10 percent?*

With an anticipated inflation, banks and other lenders can compensate for expected purchasing power losses over the life of their loans by adding an inflation premium to the interest rates they charge on loans. If the inflation is unanticipated and if banks hold substantial amounts of fixed-rate loans, they will be repaid in inflated dollars that have less purchasing power than those originally loaned.

5. *Explain why a tight monetary policy designed to reduce inflation might increase unemployment.*

There is an inverse relationship between inflation and unemployment. Some economists believe that when the economy is close to its base inflation rate (that is, when goods and services cannot bear any further price reductions because of producers' contractual costs), tight monetary policy designed to reduce inflation might push the economy into recession and drive up unemployment.

6. *What factors determine national productivity? What measures have banks employed to increase productivity?*

National productivity (output per hour worked) is determined by such factors as the amount of capital invested per worker, the age of a country's plants and equipment, innovation and technological change, and the level of education of the work force.

Banks have attempted to increase their productivity by improving the quality of work life at their banks; by increasing their investments in automation and electronic processing technology; and by reducing labor costs. Most large banks have established specialized data processing centers with more efficient and highly automated technology to handle greater volumes of data with fewer personnel. Some banks have instituted quality circle programs in which employees' experiences are used to improve efficiency and performance. Other banks have used incentive-based salary systems, flexible salary structures, bonuses and recognition programs, broader career paths, and job enrichment programs to improve employee job satisfaction, which is an essential element in generating productivity in service-based industries, such as banking. Banks with heavy retail and consumer business have tried to increase productivity through greater emphasis on self-service banking.

Chapter 14
Answers to Discussion Questions

1. *Explain the relevance of the following balance-of-payments measures: balance of trade, balance on current account, and official settlements balance.*

Balance of trade is the difference between a nation's exports and imports of goods. A trade deficit is said to result if a nation imports more goods than it exports; a trade surplus, if it exports more than it imports.

Balance on current account measures all ongoing transactions between the United States and other countries resulting in international transfers of money, including the balance on goods and services plus unilateral transfers. It is only a partial measure of U.S. international performance because it does not reflect capital inflows and outflows, which can completely offset account deficits or surpluses.

Official settlements balance is part of the capital flows measure (together with basic balance). Official settlements balance measures the change in holdings of international reserve assets of U.S. and foreign governments during the year. It indicates foreign exchange rate pressure on the dollar in foreign markets.

2. *Since the United States no longer redeems dollars for gold, how does it settle its payments deficits with other countries?*

Because the U.S. dollar has become a world money, the United States settles its payments deficits with other countries primarily by having these other countries hold their excess dollars or use their excess dollars to buy or hold U.S. Treasury notes or bonds. To a lesser extent, the United States settles through its international reserve assets of foreign exchange and gold tranche (borrowing privilege at the International Monetary Fund equal to the dollar amount of gold paid in as a condition of membership).

3. *Discuss the merits of current proposals to reduce the U.S. trade deficit. What other course of action would you propose to improve America's trade position?*

Current proposals to reduce the U.S. trade deficit include government intervention in the foreign exchange market to drive down the price of the dollar, and restrictions on imports and capital inflows. Lowering the exchange rate might eventually increase U.S. exports and reduce imports, but the U.S. trade position would likely worsen before it improved because of the historical economic pattern of time-lag in import reduction known as the J-curve; because U.S. manufacturers cannot fully meet domestic product demand; and because many U.S. companies rely on foreign sources of production for equipment and parts.

Restrictions on imports and capital inflows benefit workers and producers in affected industries, but force consumers to pay higher prices. Broad restrictions would cause price hikes that might result in inflation. Foreign industry retaliation also might hurt U.S. production and exports. A reduction in capital inflows without an expansion in U.S. monetary policy would likely raise interest rates. Basically, such restrictions and controls are inconsistent with free-market concepts and are difficult to implement.

4.   *How are foreign exchange rates determined? Suggest three factors that would likely cause supply or demand for U.S. dollars in European exchange markets to increase or decrease.*

Exchange rates express how much foreign money will exchange for one unit of domestic money, or how much domestic money will exchange for one unit of foreign money. By international convention, the U.S. dollar is used as a common denominator for determining the cross-rate of exchange between two foreign monies; as such, exchange rates also indicate a reciprocal price for the dollar. Exchange rates are quoted by banks and dealers. A variety of exchange rates are quoted for the world's major currencies, depending on whether transactions are spot or forward purchases. The final determination of exchange rates results from the influence of many factors that affect supply and demand for a nation's money in the foreign exchange market.

Factors that might cause the supply or demand for U.S. dollars to increase or decrease in European exchange markets include seasonal and temporary factors, favorable or unfavorable conditions for production, the intensity of foreign interest in U.S. products and services, domestic inflation rates, technological advances, political and economic stability or the lack of it, national balance-of-payments positions, and government intervention in the market.

5.   *"To reduce the U.S. balance-of-payments deficit, the Federal Reserve should drive down the price of the dollar in foreign exchange markets." Discuss the validity of this policy prescription.*

Driving down the price of the dollar will drive up the prices of other foreign monies, causing foreign governments to sell their own monies, and effectively transferring ownership of excess dollars from private foreigners to foreign governments and central banks. While this policy may ultimately reduce the U.S. balance-of-payments deficit by making American goods and services more attractive to foreigners pricewise, while reducing domestic demand for imports, it also may impair the special role that the U.S. dollar plays in the world economy. The United States must maintain the value and stability of the dollar as a vehicle money in foreign exchange markets, even while trying to meet its domestic economic goals.

6.   *If prices in Japan increase by 10% relative to prices in the United States, what does economic theory predict will happen to the Japanese yen in terms of dollars? Why?*

If prices in Japan increase by 10 percent relative to U.S. prices, the Japanese yen will be worth 10 percent less in terms of local purchasing power, and U.S. dollars will be worth more. For example, assume that 100 yen = $1.00. After a 10 percent increase in prices in Japan, it will take 110 yen to buy Japanese goods or services that previously cost 100 yen. Assuming no rise in prices in the United States, $1.00 will now be worth 110 yen in purchasing power, while 100 yen will now be worth $0.90 in exchange value.

Chapter 15
Answers to Discussion Questions

1.   What are the three primary functions of the foreign exchange market?

The three primary functions of the foreign exchange market are the international transfer of purchasing power from one national money to another; the provision of short-term credit to importers and exporters for the purpose of financing trade; and the provision of forward purchase and sale contracts and options to enable traders and investors to minimize the risk of exchange rate changes in their transactions.

2.   Why would a U.S. exporter sell foreign exchange forward? Under what conditions would it be advantageous for a U.S. importer to buy foreign exchange forward?

A U.S. exporter might sell foreign exchange forward believing that the exchange rate is likely to go down. By selling forward, the U.S. exporter protects against a possible decline in the dollar's price between the time it ships the exported goods and the time it receives payment for the goods in a foreign currency. A U.S. importer might buy foreign exchange forward if it anticipated that the dollar's price would increase with respect to foreign monies.

3.   What is a bankers' acceptance? How does a bankers' acceptance differ from a letter of credit?

A bankers' acceptance is a time draft instrument accepted by and drawn on a bank that substitutes its own credit for that of an importer or buyer; the draft is payable on the due date by the accepting bank whether or not the importer or buyer pays, and thus is readily salable in the secondary market.

A bankers' acceptance is similar to a letter of credit; in fact, many bankers' acceptances are created when payment is made by letter of credit.

4.   Cite three reasons why foreign banks maintain branches, agencies, and other banking offices in the United States.

Foreign banks maintain U.S. branches, agencies, and other banking offices to provide financial services to their domestic customers (mostly multinational corporations) that have foreign operations; to acquire a dollar base or better manage the dollar position of their parent banks; to aid their domestic customers in more effective financing of exports of goods to the United States; to provide better investment services to their corporate clients; and to develop a retail banking business in the world's largest financial market.

5.   *Why has the United States adopted a policy of national treatment in regulating foreign banks rather than a policy of reciprocity?*

Foreign banks in the United States are subject to federal oversight and national treatment, making them competitively equal with U.S. banks and subjecting them to the same regulations as domestic banks. A policy of reciprocity (the same treatment for foreign banks that their individual governments give U.S. banks) would be inconsistent with the U.S. philosophy of competitive equality; a policy of reciprocity also would be impractical to implement because of the diversity of rules that would be needed to reflect the treatment of U.S. banks and bank offices in the foreign countries of the world.

Index

Thank you for using this American Bankers Association/American Institute of Banking textbook. Your responses on the following evaluation will help shape the structure and content of future editions. <u>Return your completed form to your instructor or fold in three and mail to</u>: American Institute of Banking, Attn: Manager, Product Development, 1120 Connecticut Avenue, N.W., Washington, D.C. 20036.

Name of Chapter _____

Name of Bank _____

TEXTBOOK/COURSE ATTRIBUTES

Importance Factor   **Satisfaction Level**

Very Important			Not Important		Completely Satisfied			Not Satisfied

1	2	3	4	**Textbook covered all important topics**	1	2	3	4
1	2	3	4	**Content was easy to read and understand**	1	2	3	4
1	2	3	4	**The graphics and examples were helpful**	1	2	3	4
1	2	3	4	**I can use what I've learned in this course in my work**	1	2	3	4

	Excellent			Poor
What was your overall opinion of the textbook?	1	2	3	4

Did your instructor use any additional materials to teach this course?
( ) Yes   ( ) No

If Yes, please check all that apply
( ) Transparencies/Overheads   ( ) Handouts
( ) Other textbook (please specify)_____

Number of AIB courses you have taken in past three years:
( ) 0   ( ) 1-2   ( ) 3-5
( ) More than 5

AIB course taken through:(Please check all that apply)
( ) AIB Chapter/Study Group
( ) AIB Correspondence Study Program
( ) Other (please specify)_____

Currently working toward an AIB Diploma/Certificate?
( ) Yes   ( ) No

If yes, please specify:
( ) Bank Operations   ( ) Consumer Credit
( ) Commercial Lending   ( ) General Banking
( ) Mortgage Lending   ( ) Accelerated Banking
( ) Customer Service   ( ) Securities Services
( ) Supervisory

Asset size of your bank:
( ) 0-$75m   ( ) $76-$250m   ( ) $251-$500m
( ) $501-$1b   ( ) over $1b

Number of employees in your bank:
( ) 1-10   ( ) 11-20   ( ) 21-40
( ) 41-90   ( ) 91-200   ( ) 201-350
( ) 351-2,000   ( ) over 2,000

Job Title:_____

Major Job Responsibility:
( ) Lending   ( ) Marketing   ( ) Operations
( ) Compliance   ( ) Auditing   ( ) Human Resources
( ) Trust   ( ) Customer Svc.   ( ) Branch Admin.
( ) Securities Processing   ( ) Security/Risk
                                            Management
( ) Other (Please specify)_____

Years in Banking:
( ) 0-2   ( ) 3-5   ( ) 6-10
( ) Over 10

Highest Education Level:
( ) High School   ( ) Some College   ( ) BA/BS Degree
( ) Advanced Degree

Age:
( ) under 25   ( ) 25-35   ( ) 36-45
( ) over 45

Name_____
Bank_____
Address _____
City _____ State _____ Zip _____
Telephone (____) _____

( ) Please send me more information on AIB's Diploma/Certificate Program.

( ) Please send me more information on AIB's Correspondence Study Program.

Comments (please identify any specific suggestions you have that may improve the overall effectiveness of this publication):

_____
_____
_____
_____
_____
_____
_____
_____
_____
_____
_____
_____

NO POSTAGE
NECESSARY
IF MAILED
IN THE
UNITED STATES

BUSINESS REPLY MAIL
FIRST CLASS MAIL PERMIT NO. 10579   WASHINGTON, DC

POSTAGE WILL BE PAID BY ADDRESSEE

American Bankers Association
Attn: Manager, Product Development, AIB
1120 Connecticut Avenue, N.W.
Washington, DC 20077-5760